Enterprise Information Systems IV

Enterprise Information Systems IV

edited by

Mario Piattini

Universidade de Castilla-La Mancha,
Ciudad Real, Spain

Joaquim Filipe

Escola Superior de Tecnologia de Setúbal,
Setúbal, Portugal

and

José Braz

Escola Superior de Tecnologia de Setúbal,
Setúbal, Portugal

KLUWER ACADEMIC PUBLISHERS

DORDRECHT / BOSTON / LONDON

Library of Congress Cataloging-in-Publication Data

ISBN 1-4020-1086-9

Published by Kluwer Academic Publishers,
P.O. Box 17, 3300 AA Dordrecht, The Netherlands.

Sold and distributed in North, Central and South America
by Kluwer Academic Publishers,
101 Philip Drive, Norwell, MA 02061, U.S.A.

In all other countries, sold and distributed
by Kluwer Academic Publishers,
P.O. Box 322, 3300 AH Dordrecht, The Netherlands.

Printed on acid-free paper

Printed in the Netherlands.

TABLE OF CONTENTS

PREFACE

This book includes a set of selected papers from the fourth "International Conference on Enterprise Information Systems" (ICEIS 2002), held in Ciudad Real, Spain, 2 to 6 April 2002.

Following the line started in 1999, ICEIS has become a major point of contact between research scientists, engineers and practitioners on the area of business applications of information systems.

The conference included four simultaneous tracks: "*Databases and Information Systems Integration*", "*Artificial Intelligence and Decision Support Systems*", "*Information Systems Analysis and Specification*", and "*Internet Computing and Electronic Commerce*". Although ICEIS 2002 received 220 paper submissions from 30 different countries, only 89 papers were accepted as full papers. From these 89 papers, the Program Committee selected only 30 for inclusion in this book. These figures demonstrate the strict quality criteria and the intention of maintaining a high quality level for future editions of the conference and this book series.

A number of additional keynote lectures, workshops, case studies and tutorials were also held. We would like to thank in particular the collaboration of the following invited speakers: Ilia Bider (IbisSoft), Masao J. Matsumoto (University of Tsukuba), Ned Chapin (InfoSci Inc.) and Oleg Gusikhin (Ford Motor Company).

Many people contributed to the success of ICEIS 2002. We would like to thank all the authors who have submitted their papers to this conference, and all the members of the Program Committee for their diligent and expert reviewing. Special thanks to the steering committee and to Vitor Pedrosa for their help and encouragement. The conference also acknowledges the hard work of the organizing committee in Ciudad Real and the sponsorship of the University of Castilla-La Mancha, Fundación Cintel, Gesein, Getronics, Intersystems and Oracle.

Mario Piattini
Joaquim Filipe
José Braz

CONFERENCE COMMITTEE

Conference Chair:

Joaquim Filipe, Escola Superior de Tecnologia of Setúbal, Portugal

Programme Co-Chairs:

Mario Piattini, Escuela Superior de Informática, Universidad of Castilla-La Mancha, Spain
Bernadette Sharp, Staffordshire University, School of Computing, Beaconside, Stafford, UK
Slimane Hammoudi, École Superieur de l' Ouest, France

Organising Committee:

Mario Piattini, Marcela Genero, Ismael Caballero, Coral Calero, María del Pilar Castellanos, José Jesús Castro, José Antonio Cruz, Eduardo Fernández-Medina, Félix Oscar García, Mª Teresa García-Madrid, Luis Jiménez, Joaqui Martín-Albo, Alfonso Martinez, María Dolores Mateos, Carlos Medina, David Miranda, José Angel Olivas, Macario Polo, Manuel Prieto, Francisco Ruiz, Manuel Angel Serrano and Aurora Vizcaino, Universidad de Castilla-La Mancha, Spain.
Artemio Franco Sánchez, Universidad Autónoma de Tamaulipas, Mexico.

Senior Programme Committee:

Amaral, L. (PORTUGAL)
Baeza-Yates, R. (CHILE)
Bézivin, J. (FRANCE)
Bonsón, E. (SPAIN)
Carvalho, J. (PORTUGAL)
Cheng, A. (USA)
Coelho, H. (PORTUGAL)
Delgado, M. (SPAIN)
Dietz, J. (NETHERLANDS)
Dignum, F. (NETHERLANDS)
Figueiredo, A. (PORTUGAL)
Greene, T. (UK)
Guimarães, N. (PORTUGAL)
Gupta, J. (USA)
Liu, K. (UK)
Luker, P. (UK)
Lyytinen, K. (FINLAND)
Manolopoulos, Y. (GREECE)
Martins, J. (PORTUGAL)
Matsumoto, M. (JAPAN)
Odell, J. (USA)
Smirnov, A. (RUSSIA)
Stamper, R. (NETHERLANDS)
Tari, Z. (AUSTRALIA)
Toro, M. (SPAIN)
Warkentin, M. (USA)
Weigand, H. (NETHERLANDS)
Welty, C. (USA)

Programme Committee:

Aguilar, J. (SPAIN)
Albers, P. (FRANCE)
Alderson, A. (UK)
Al-Jadir, L. (LEBANON)
Antunes, P. (PORTUGAL)
Aparício, J. (PORTUGAL)
Barro, S. (SPAIN)
Belo, C. (PORTUGAL)
Bernus, P. (AUSTRALIA)
Bittel, O. (GERMANY)
Boavida, F. (PORTUGAL)
Brisaboa, N. (SPAIN)
Calero, C. (SPAIN)
Camp, O. (FRANCE)
Canós, J. (SPAIN)
Castillo, E. (SPAIN)

Castro, J. (SPAIN)
Castro-Schez, J. (SPAIN)
Cernuzzi, L. (PARAGUAY)
Cesare, S. (UK)
Chu, W. (TAIWAN)
Clarke, R. (AUSTRALIA)
Claude, C. (FRANCE)
Corchuelo, R. (SPAIN)
Costa, E. (PORTUGAL)
Coulette, B. (FRANCE)
Cox, S. (UK)
Dolado, J. (SPAIN)
Eardley, A. (UK)
Emery, D. (UK)
Favela, J. (USA)
Ferreira, P. (PORTUGAL)
Flory, A. (FRANCE)
Fred, A. (PORTUGAL)
Garbajosa, J. (SPAIN)
González, P. (SPAIN)
Gough, T. (UK)
Govaere, V. (FRANCE)
Grönlund, Å. (SWEDEN)
Gustavsson, R. (SWEDEN)
Heng, M. (AUSTRALIA)
Herrera, F. (SPAIN)
Huang, K. (NETHERLANDS)
Jaime, A. (SPAIN)
JiménezLinares, L. (SPAIN)
Joyanes, L. (SPAIN)
Karacapilidis, N. (GREECE)
Labidi, S. (BRAZIL)
LeóndeMora, C. (SPAIN)
Libourel, T. (FRANCE)
Linna, M. (FINLAND)
Lopes, G. (PORTUGAL)
Lopes, J. (PORTUGAL)
Madeira, E. (BRAZIL)
Malekovic, M. (CROATIA)
Mamede, N. (PORTUGAL)
Marcos, E. (SPAIN)
Martins, M. (PORTUGAL)
Moghadampour, G. (FINLAND)
Olivas, J. (SPAIN)
OlsinaSantos, L. (ARGENTINA)
Parets-llorca, J. (SPAIN)
Pastor, Ó. (SPAIN)
Penzel, T. (GERMANY)
Peters, S. (NETHERLANDS)
Pimentel, E. (SPAIN)
Pires, F. (PORTUGAL)
Pirotte, A. (BELGIUM)
Plodzien, J. (POLAND)
Poels, G. (BELGIUM)
Polo, M. (SPAIN)
Ramos, P. (PORTUGAL)
Revenu, M. (FRANCE)
Riquelme, J. (SPAIN)
Rodriguez, P. (SPAIN)
Rosa, A. (PORUTGAL)
Sahraoui, H. (CANADA)
Salem, A. (EGYPT)
Schoop, M. (GERMANY)
Shankararaman, V. (UK)
Shao, J. (UK)
Shi, Z. (CHINA)
Silva, A. (PORTUGAL)
Silva, A. (PORTUGAL)
Silva, M. (PORTUGAL)
Soule-Dupuy, C. (FRANCE)
Sun, L. (UK)
Taniar, D. (AUSTRALIA)
Toval, A. (SPAIN)
Ultsch, A. (GERMANY)
Vasiu, L. (UK)
Verdier, C. (FRANCE)
Vernadat, F. (EU)
Vila, M. (SPAIN)
Wilson, D. (UK)
Yang, H. (UK)
ZongKai, L. (CHINA)

Invited Speakers:

Ilia Bider, IbisSoft, Sweden

Giovanni Cantone, Università degli Studi di Roma "Tor Vergata", Italy

Ned Chapin, InfoSci Inc., USA

Thomas Greene, MIT Laboratory for Computer Science, USA

Oleg Gusikhin, Ford Motor Company, USA

Qusay H. Mahmoud, University of Guelph, Canada

Masao J. Matsumoto, University of Tsukuba, Japan

Antoni Olivé, Universitat Politècnica de Catalunya, Spain

Raghavan "Rags" Srinivas, Sun Microsystems, USA

E-COMMERCE CONCERNS: DO WE NEED TO CHANGE SOME SYSTEMS?

Contribution to Closing Panel

Ned Chapin
Information Systems Consultant, InfoSci Inc., Box 7117, Menlo Park CA 94026–7117, USA
Email: NedChapin@acm.org

Key words: Navigation, Currency, Confidence, Scent, Supply chain, Customer, Denial of service, Accuracy, User

Abstract: For e-commerce to become successful, web sites must become easy for even first-time users to navigate through, and what is presented on the site must be both current and accurate. The customer or supplier (user) must have confidence that interactions and transactions are secure, and are neither more or less than intended by the user. The organization must have confidence that it can still know its users and be immune from denial of service attacks. To make these situations come to fruition, we will need to enhance our enterprise systems and many of the supporting systems.

1 PANEL TOPIC

The topic for this panel, "E-commerce, the next step: promises and problems" is my take-off point. My focus on this panel topic involves five points: navigation and scent, currency and accuracy, security and confidence, customer and supply chain, and denial of service and knowing the user. My ending discussion asks about the action needed.

2 NAVIGATION AND SCENT

Who is to be the user of the web site intended for e-commerce? For e-commerce, an organization's web site may be accessible by users generally, such as customers and by suppliers and by other persons or organizations. Or the organization can restrict it, as by requiring returning customers or suppliers to have and use passwords, and as by having different sites for customers and potential customers, and for its current and potential supply chain participants.

How easily and how quickly can the user find what the user wants on an e-commerce web site? As a general rule, even for a novice to the site, it should rarely take from the home page more than three clicks of the mouse. The casual site visitor will rarely do more than one click. Only the very motivated or very persistent user will invest more than a dozen clicks to find what that user is looking for on an e-commerce site. The user who gives up on a site without finding what was sought, is unlikely to return to try again, is likely to bad-mouth the site, and has made a negative contribution to the organization's bottom line [1].

The research on site visitors underlines the major significance of the convenience of site navigation. The model, it turns out, is almost identical to the model that describes how nearly all wild animals find food in their native habitats [2]. Superficially, it looks much like an optimized trial and error process. Consider a deer, or a squirrel, or a tiger, for example. The ones that die of malnutrition or starvation are the ones that are less successful on their many tries during a month to find wanted food. They typically have a higher proportion of tries that did not yield the desired results. By contrast, the successful ones "get the scent" and follow it to the food sought.

On e-commerce web sites, one powerful aid helping the user follow the scent is an on-site search capability. With such a capability available, even the novice user can reduce the number of clicks required to find what the user is looking for. The returning user who is not following bookmarks, can usually find something within three clicks, when the search capability is a good one. A good search capability does not just report a failure and then quit; instead, when it does not find an exact match, is reports the best alternatives and offers suggestions.

Some users who either have had no good experiences or suffered experiences with poor search capabilities, decline to use on-site searches. They put their effort into navigating from the site's home page. To serve them, home pages and gone-to pages must be made easy to navigate from, with comprehensive clearly defined relevant choices.

3 CURRENCY AND ACCURACY

An e-commerce site that has out-of-date product descriptions or non-current prices or availability data does not serve the user well. Yet many organizations have designed and implemented their e-commerce sites to require skilled labor, and sometimes a lot of it, in order to update the pages [1]. A design that gives a reasonable cost of updating depends upon how much will likely have to be updated and how often.

To help build user credulity in dealing with an organization via an e-commerce site, organizations have found it worthwhile to state clearly and in more than one place on the site, what the update policy is for a page (such as "Every specification and every price for the items you have selected will be honored as shown if you place your order now by clicking here."). Showing on a page when the most recent change was made can also strengthen user credulity (such as "Updated at 13:41 hours on 6 April.").

Finding out only at check-out time that stock on hand is not enough to satisfy an order, destroys user credulity. Having orders rejected that were placed via an e-commerce site for such reasons as "Stock number not valid" or "Back ordered: cannot be shipped at this time" or "Not sold for shipment to France and Switzerland." impairs an organizations's bottom line and builds business for competitors.

4 SECURITY AND CONFIDENCE

Intelligent business practices protect business intelligence [3]. When a user contacts an e-commerce site, does the site contacted provide to the user confidence that everything is private? For example, if the user is asked for a password, are the request and the user's response both encrypted? How are cookies transmitted and stored? What control over the data does the user have? What data does the organization collect about the user and the transaction or inquiry while the user is online, and how are they communicated and in what protected form are they held by the organization? And how are they used, passed on, given out or sold by the organization? The interaction via a e-commerce site should be no more than and no less than what it appears to the user.

What data are communicated to the user to build user confidence in the security and privacy of the user's contact? How are the organization's data and systems, including an enterprise system, protected and managed to ensure data integrity and data safety? How does the site show concern for the user, as by providing access to a "help" service or technical support, showing that the organization and its products or services are trustworthy and reliable, etc.?

5 CUSTOMER AND SUPPLY CHAIN

An organization's first attention to an e-commerce site nearly always goes to one intended for a customer to use and is "push" oriented [3]. The common initial typical site orientation is to provide the equivalent of a product display case, so that the user can click to get more detail. Depending upon the product or service, this initial emphasis usually soon gets augmented with "Let us close a sale!" online. For B2C (business to consumer) or retail sites, the "shopping cart" model is common. For B2B (business to business) or wholesale sites, the picture is more varied. With some trepidation, still more may be added, usually FAQ data (frequently asked questions) and user support or some form of making help available to the user.

Potential or existing supply chain participants are also targets for e-commerce sites, and are rarely "push" oriented [4]. Instead, they provide a self-screening for potential supply chain participants, and data about how the organization manages and uses its supply chain. Soliciting better quality, price or responsiveness in the supply chain can result in improvements in the bottom line for the organization. Some of the more advanced e-commerce sites that are supply chain oriented use the sites to facilitate communication along the supply chain, and hence are significantly contributed to by the supply chain participants.

6 DoS AND KNOWING THE USER

DoS (denial of service) occurs when erstwhile users so flood a site with attempts to access its content that the servers supporting the site are either so slowed down that users give up waiting for responses, or are so overloaded that they fail (crash). The denial comes in that wanted and intended users are unable to get through the clutter created by the erstwhile users, so that the wanted users are adversely affected [5]. The organization is also adversely affected, because the e-commerce site is unable to perform as intended.

DoS can be self-caused (but rarely is) by the organization for its customer-oriented site as when a promotion (such as a special sale or big price reduction or new product promotion) is exceptionally successful in attracting a great sudden surge of site visits.

Commonly DoS episodes are attacks by competitors or hackers or "enemies" (such as a disgruntled customer or former employee) with the intention of doing harm to the organization's bottom line. To help forestall and to help combat DoS attacks, knowing who are the customers, supply chain participants, site visitors and competitors can lead to early warnings about possible impending attacks, and to the accurate identification of the perpetrators [6]. General site security is also vital in preventing DoS attempts from being seriously damaging to the organization.

7 ACTION NEEDED?

What is it going to take for e-commerce sites to achieve the significant potential they offer to an organization? Or put another way, how are we going to get there from here? Two answers are obvious, and they in turn involve still other questions and answers.

One common proposed answer is only partly true, so let us take it up first. That proposed answer is to replace the organization's existing systems with new systems, specifically designed and implemented for doing e-commerce successfully. The track record for such major jumps is very sobering, and the sides of the track are littered with expensive failures, and not all of them are "dot com" cases [7]. An alternative and successful track record has been laid down by building upon successful "brick and mortar" activities. This usually keeps costs down while the benefits are slowly building up from the e-commerce site, thus providing some protection for the organization's bottom line.

One of the obvious answers is to enhance the existing enterprise system with e-commerce site capabilities. Without the direct and enthusiastic support of the supplier of the enterprise system, this answer is very difficult to achieve in practice at a reasonable cost. The supplier of the enterprise system wants a generic version that an organization can customize. Typically this results in doing business in a way significantly influenced by the enterprise system supplier. To extend the customization to fit fully the way the organization wants to do business typically raises the cost, sometimes past the point of being financially justifiable.

The other obvious answer is to make major enhancements in the systems that interact with the enterprise system. Since putting an enterprise system in a wrapper is almost always uneconomic, the usual action is the middleware route. This can result in higher costs since there is more software to maintain, but it can help preserve and present the "face to the world" that the organization wants by making the way it does business be distinctively its own.

8 CONCLUSION

E-commerce is going to continue to expand and grow in importance for nearly all major organizations. Eventually it will be a central part in enterprise systems. To get there will require not only systems evolution but shouldering major continuing efforts in software maintenance.

REFERENCES

1. Nielsen J. *Designing Web Usability.* New Riders Publishing Co.: New York NY, 1999; 432 pp.
2. Work pending publication from researchers at Xerox Parc: Palo Alto CA, 2002.
3. Bergeron BP. *Essentials of CRM: A Guide to Cus-tomer Relationship Management.* JohnWiley & Sons, Inc.: New York NY, 2002; 220 pp.
4. Chopra S, Meindl P. *Supply Chain Management.* Prentice Hall College Division: Englewood Cliffs NJ, 2000; 544 pp.
5. Meadows C. A formal framework and evaluation method for network denial of service. *Proceedings 1999 IEEE Computer Security Foundations Work-shop.* IEEE Computer Society Press: LosAlamitos CA, 1999; 4–13.
6. Geng X, Whinston AB. Defeating distributed denial of service attacks. *IT Professional* 2000; **2**(4):36–41.
7. Jones TC. Minimizing the risks of software deve-lopment. *Cutter IT Journal: The Journal of Infor-mation Technology Management* 1998; **11**(6):13–21.

E-WORKCELL: A VIRTUAL REALITY WEB-BASED DECISION SUPPORT SYSTEM FOR ASSEMBLY LINE PLANNING

Oleg Gusikhin, Erica Klampfl, Giuseppe Rossi
Celestine Aguwa, Gene Coffman, Terry Martinak
Ford Motor Company
MD 2122 SRL, P.O. Box 2053 Dearborn, MI 48121-2053
ogusikhi@ford.com

Key words: web-based client server, virtual reality, multimedia, automotive assembly.

Abstract: This paper is devoted to an example of the advantages of intranet applications of e-technology. We describe a new multimedia decision support interface that exploits web-enabled database information to provide an interactive planning tool for the automotive assembly line. Specifically, we integrate a web-based client server architecture, a Virtual Reality Modeling Language (VRML) interface, analytical modeling, and simulation. The system is designed to facilitate collaboration between the different functions that participate in the assembly line planning process.

1 INTRODUCTION

The most widely publicized applications of e-Technology are business-to-business and business-to-consumer e-commerce. However, intracompany applications have emerged in the last few years as extremely valuable business tools; for a number of companies the financial benefits from these applications greatly exceed those from the more publicized internet e-commerce. Furthermore, in today's enterprise information environment there is a strong push to use web-based applications as the interface of choice to data stored in corporate databases. The multimedia capability of the web provides efficient and effective ways to develop web-based interfaces that are equivalent to stand alone systems in terms of functionality and performance (Huang and Mak, 2001). This paper describes a new multimedia database interface, which takes advantage of Virtual Reality Modeling Language (VRML) to provide an intuitive representation of relevant data combined with analytical modeling and simulation functionalities. This development specifically addresses the problem of planning and optimizing the layout of a workstation (workcell) in automotive assembly lines.

In an automotive assembly line, the vehicle to be built moves through hundreds of workcells. In each workcell, certain components get installed or other operations are performed. The efficiency of the assembly process depends crucially on the layout of the individual workcells. Until now, workcell layout design has been a cumbersome, semi-manual process. The approach described here represents a quantum leap in the level of efficiency, data accuracy, ease of use, and capabilities for collaboration between different groups who have a stake in the process. Rather than concentrating on the details that one could get with any CAD system, we focus on the work cell layout process at a macro level. Thus, we address the core of the work cell layout and task allocation process.

The thousands of elementary tasks required to build each vehicle model typically are listed and described in central corporate databases (Rychtyckyj, 1999). Starting from this information, industrial engineers at the assembly plants where a given vehicle has to be built, allocate the elementary tasks pertaining to the construction of that vehicle to different workstations along the assembly line and thus, to different operators. Furthermore, industrial engineers at the assembly plants determine the layout of each workstation and the specific order (sequence) in which the elementary tasks within each workstation have to be performed.

The allocation and workstation design process often reflects information that is specific to each assembly plant (such as the physical layout of the assembly line environment). As a result, when the same vehicle is built at different assembly plants there may be significant differences between the plants in the way tasks are allocated and workcells are configured. In recent years there has been a move towards allowing the line operators to have greater say on the task allocation and workcell layout planning process. It is believed that greater line operator involvement may serve to correct awkward tasks distributions and increase the operators' job satisfaction: this should ultimately translate into improved product quality.

Until now, the arrangement of a worker's area and the determination of his/her walking path has been performed manually with paper and pencil, or at some plants with the aid of a two-dimensional non-interactive computer program. For certain operations requiring ergonomic assessment, planning engineers use detailed, three-dimensional computer aided design (CAD) representations of an operator's workcell. This state of affairs is unsatisfactory for at least three reasons. First, when performed in this way, the planning process is cumbersome and time consuming. Second, the tools that have been used until now are static and suitable only for engineering planning: they do not support real-time line operator interaction. Third, since the process is largely manual, it is not easy for industrial engineers to uncover the layout that will produce the shortest operator walking path. In other words, inefficient choices (i.e., choices forcing the operator to needlessly spend time walking) may be made. In this regard, it should be kept in mind that there are many factors that complicate the choice of the best arrangement. Just to cite a few: for each workcell there are several bins of parts and tools that need to be positioned; there may be external constraints (e.g., fixed obstacles, such as pillars located within the workcell); the operator moves at a speed that changes depending on the weight of the part he/she is carrying; the assembly line may be building a certain vehicle mix (e.g., two or three different vehicle models on the same line: then, at each workstation, different tasks may have to be performed depending on which vehicle is moving through).

In spite of extensive research in the area of moving assembly line design and of line balancing (Ghosh and Gagnon, 1989), the practical application of published algorithms is limited. This is because of two main reasons. First, the published algorithms are not sufficiently flexible to model the actual conditions of assembly line workstations. Second, accurate data is difficult to obtain and maintain: often, there is no current record of a workcell layout; that is, when a workcell layout is modified the corresponding central records are not updated.

Our approach addresses these flexibility and data propagation issues, as well as many more. It speeds up and improves the workcell layout process and integrates, within a web based Virtual Reality Modeling Language (VRML) interface, mathematical algorithms that compute the operator walking time for a given cell layout (location of part bins and of tools). Specifically, the tool provides the following:

- It is intuitive and easy to use; therefore, line operators with minimal training should be able to input data and obtain solutions for their cell layouts.
- It allows for real-time scenario planning since, given a workcell layout, it provides instantaneous calculations of the total time required to perform the tasks assigned to that workcell, and of the total walking time. This feature allows the user to study a large variety of possibilities, a process that is very difficult using the paper and pencil method.
- It is web-based so that it is not tied to any specific piece of hardware, and as a result, it is universally accessible.
- Any changes made by the user can be stored in a central database so that updated information is not lost. This feature allows for propagation of best part allocations and of optimal walking paths from worker to worker.
- It supports simulation of the operator walk through the VRML interface: thus, it allows users to see how their work-plans affect neighboring operator workcells.
- It can provide advice on walk path optimization with respect to given layout/process constraints. This feature should greatly cut down the inefficiencies arising from the current process.

The rest of this paper is organized as follows. In the next section we provide background information on existing methods. In Section 3 we briefly describe VRML capabilities relevant to our development. To be complete, we discuss the calculations of walking time in Section 4 . In Section 5 we discuss the system architecture and the functionality of our tool. The final section summarizes our results and discusses future enhancements of the tool.

2 EXISTING METHODS

Traditionally, there are two main approaches to the arrangement of an operator's workcell: the first is usually referred to as the "pencil and paper approach," and the second uses a two-dimensional computer representation of the vehicle moving within a workcell. Both systems require a large amount of industrial engineering time and do not directly address the issues of task sequence and path optimization in a moving assembly line. As noted in the introduction, there are also tools, such as those produced by Tecnomatix (http: //www.tecnomatix.com) and Delmia (http: //www.delmia.com), that give detailed, three-dimensional representations of an operator's workcell. Ordinarily, these tools are used only if there is a need to address ergonomic issues: this is because they are cumbersome and extensive training is required in order to use these tools proficiently. All of these approaches require a great deal of data transfer between systems, which is a time consuming and error prone process.

In the manual "pencil and paper approach," the workcell is divided into squares, and time is divided into discrete time steps: a certain number of time steps (dependent on the operator velocity) is required for the operator to move across a square. On the paper, a transparent vehicle is moved in discrete steps to determine the intersections between the moving car (on a moving assembly line) and the operator's walk path. This manual approach can be very tedious because of the large amount of manual calculations required for each path and workcell. When any of the part bins are rearranged or the line speed is changed, the calculation must be repeated to obtain the new total time. It should not be surprising if this method often fails to produce the optimal workcell arrangement (the one that leads to the shortest walking time). The fact that the method is used for each workcell in the assembly line compounds the inefficiencies.

The two-dimensional computer-based approach uses an animation of the actual sequence of work elements in an operation: input information includes rack layouts, vehicle speed and configurations, task description and times (including walk times) associated to a task. Based on this input information the two dimensional computer based tool allows the user to see where an operator would perform a given task. While this approach represents an improvement over the paper and pencil method, there is no attempt to compute walking time based on workcell layout and no attempt to systematically optimize workcell configuration.

3 VRML

Virtual Reality Modeling Language (VRML) is an open standard to design virtual reality worlds accessible through the world wide web (WWW). As the term virtual reality implies, VRML provides an immersive, three-dimensional environment, which allows navigation within and interaction with objects in the environment. Viewing the virtual reality world requires a VRML plug-in to a web browser. The most commonly used VRML plug-ins freely available for download are Cosmo Player (http://www.cai.com/cosmo), Blaxxun (http://www.blaxxun.com), and Cortona (http://www.parallelgraphics.com).

VRML is stored in a text file, which can be created with any text editor or word processor. There are also a number of specialized authoring tools in the market that facilitate editing VRML worlds in 3D. Another approach is to automatically generate a VRML file from the application program. In the WWW environment, VRML, similar to HTML, can be generated dynamically using any server scripting technique, such as CGI, ASP, Java Servlet. Finally, most of the commonly used CAD or mark-up systems (ProE, ROBCAD) allow exporting to a VRML file format. This provides an efficient way to incorporate already existing 3D images in the application.

The virtual reality world is described by a hierarchy of nodes, which are the main building blocks of VRML. Each node is characterized by its type and a specific set of fields associated with it. There are different types of nodes serving different functions in the virtual world. For example, the 3-D scene is described by the set of nodes representing geometrical shapes and their spatial positions. The dynamic behavior of the model is realized through the mechanism called *routes*, which connects the fields of a pair of nodes in such a way that the change of the field value in one node triggers changes in the other node. Using multiple routes, a single event can be propagated through the entire model, dynamically changing properties of the objects. A special type of node called *sensors* initiates events in the model. Sensors are associated with events that are external to the model, such as user action or time change. For example, the user interaction with the model is typically implemented through the sensors, which react to viewer actions, such as move, click, and drag over the given shape. When the corresponding action is performed, the sensor generates an output event that can be routed to other nodes to change their properties. The animation is typically implemented using *TimeSensor* and *Interpolator* nodes. A TimeSensor node implements the clock that controls the playback of animation, while the Interpolator nodes describe the sequence of positions or orientations associated with different instances of the clock time.

Overall, VRML contains more than fifty different nodes to represent complex, 3-D graphical scenes, enhance user navigation, and implement special effects and features. In addition, when an application requires a custom behavior, VRML offers a *Script* node to implement domain-specific algorithms using Java, JavaScript or VrmlScript (a subset of JavaScript). For a detailed exposition on VRML, refer to Ames et al. (Ames et al., 1996) or to Roehl et al. (Roehl et al., 1997).

In many instances it is desirable to combine a VRML interface with a traditional 2-D layout of data and controls. It can be done by combining VRML with a Java applet in the same HTML page. The Java applet can communicate with VRML through an External Authoring Interface (EAI), which allows the Java applet to access and change the properties of VRML objects, as well as receive notifications of events.

VRML 2.0 is a readily available and cost effective tool (VRML requires minimal capital, development, training and maintenance costs) that can be integrated into an existing web-based client/server architecture to implement a comprehensive graphical user interface. The advantages of such an interface are especially apparent when the application domain is essentially three-dimensional. There are a number of reports on successful applications of VRML in engineering and manufacturing. See (Indrusiak and da Luz Reis, 2001) and (Ressler et al., 1999) for examples.

Of course, VRML does not provide the same geometrical precision and functionality that CAD systems provide. Though, in many cases, the data that we are interested in represents the spatial and possibly temporal relations between individual objects, rather than the geometrical details and accuracy of individual objects, themselves. In this case, the application data, which uses a predefined set of 3-D images representing specific domain objects, generates the scene "on the fly." In many cases the object representation can be simplified or even approximated by the basic geometrical shapes, such as box, sphere, and cylinder.

4 CALCULATIONS OF WALKING TIME

In this section we describe how to calculate the total time needed by the operator to complete all tasks given the position of the part bins and the sequence of tasks. Examples of tasks include walking from a given point to a bin, walking from a bin to a tool location, walking from a bin to a vehicle, picking up a part from a bin, picking up a tool, and installing a part in the vehicle. The total cycle time is the sum of the time the operator needs to walk and the time required to pick up parts, install parts, and perform other non-walking tasks. The walking time calculations belong to either of two types: the calculation of time required to walk between two fixed points and the calculation of time required to walk between a fixed point and a point where the operator moving at a certain velocity reaches a specific point on the vehicle, which is moving at a different velocity. These two types of paths are shown in Figure 1; Path 1 (the path between the two fixed points (x_m, y_m) and (x_k, y_k)) belongs to the first type, and Path 2 (the path between the fixed point (x_k, y_k) and the point at which the operator intersects the vehicle (x_V, y_V)) belongs to the second type. A fixed point can be a part bin location, a tool location, a user defined starting point, or a departure point from the vehicle.

When the operator approaches the vehicle to install a part, he/she is required to install the part in a specific location on the vehicle. Vehicles are typically divided into several zones, and we approximate the install location of the part by the center point of the zone in which that install location resides.

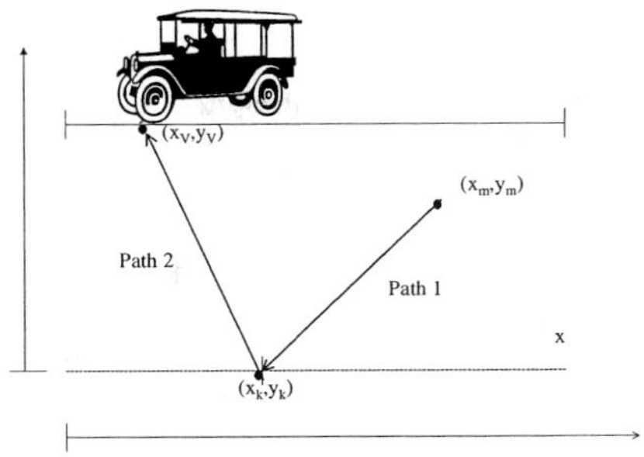

Figure 1: This picture shows the two different types of walking paths considered in our calculations of an operator's walking time.

Prior to describing the walking time calculations, we define the following variables, which represent the values that are used in the calculations. These variables whose values are expected to either be input by the user or read from a database are

x_c = the x-coordinate position of the vehicle at $t = 0$
y_c = the y-coordinate position of the vehicle at $t = 0$
v_c = the velocity of the vehicle
v_o = the velocity of the operator
$z_x(j)$ = the x-coordinate for zone j
$z_y(j)$ = the y-coordinate for zone j
t_n = the time to perform a specific non-walking task

In addition to these, we define the variables whose values are obtained in the course of the calculations

t_p = the time it takes to go between two fixed points (associated with Path 1 in Figure 1)
t_c = the time it takes to go from a fixed point to the vehicle (associated with Path 2 in Figure 1)
$t_I(k)$ = the running time after the kth task of the sequence has been completed. After the last task has been completed, it is the total time associated with the sequence.
t_T = the running time (defined for those tasks which involve walking to the vehicle) at which the operator reaches the vehicle zone to which he/she is directed.

Now that we have defined the input variables, we will describe the calculations associated with Path 1 and Path 2 in Figure 1. Recall that to cover a given distance, an object moving at a constant velocity will need a $time = \frac{distance}{velocity}$. Hence, we obtain the time that the operator needs to walk between any two fixed points (x_m, y_m) and (x_k, y_k) by dividing the distance between the two points by the velocity v. We call this time t_g, and thus,

$$t_g = \frac{1}{v}\sqrt{(x_m - x_k)^2 + (y_m - y_k)^2}. \quad (1)$$

As a result, the time t_p associated with Path 1 is just t_g where the velocity is equivalent to the velocity of the operator. So,

$$t_p = \frac{1}{v_o}\sqrt{(x_m - x_k)^2 + (y_m - y_k)^2}.$$

Therefore, if task k involved walking between two fixed points, then the running time t_I would be updated in the following way:

$$t_I(k) = t_p + t_I(k-1).$$

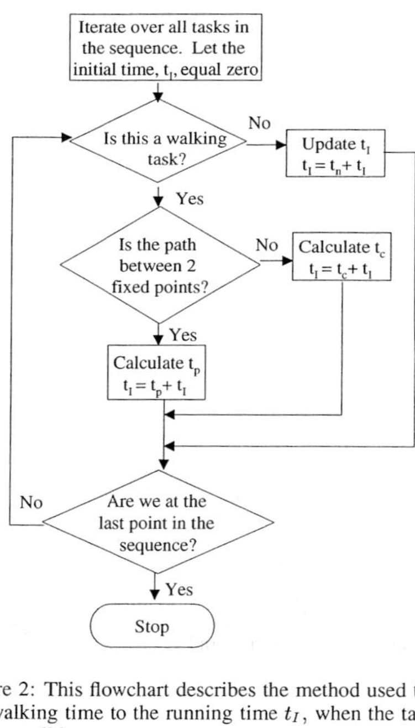

Figure 2: This flowchart describes the method used to add the walking time to the running time t_I, when the task involves walking.

Second, we consider the time t_c associated with Path 2. Recall that t_c is the time that the operator needs to walk from point (x_k, y_k) leaving at time t_I to zone j of the vehicle. We do not know the point x_m where the operator intersects the vehicle, but we do know that this point equals the distance that the vehicle will have traveled to get to this point x_m plus an offset based on the initial position of the vehicle and on the location of the vehicle zone to which the operator is directed. The distance traveled by the vehicle is given by the velocity of the vehicle times the total time t_T that will have elapsed by the time the operator reaches the vehicle zone to which he/she is directed. Since t_T represents the total time required to reach x_m (the unknown point), we can let $x_m = t_T v_c + x_c + z_x(j)$. We can also let y_m be the initial position of the vehicle in the y direction plus the y-coordinate position of the zone to which the operator is directed ($y_m = y_c + z_y(j)$). So, substituting $t_g = t_T - t_I$ and the aforementioned values of (x_m, y_m) into equation 1, we get

$$t_T - t_I = \frac{1}{v_o}\sqrt{(t_T v_c + x_c + z_x(j) - x_k)^2 + (z_y(j) + y_c - y_k)^2}. \quad (2)$$

Since t_T is in both the left and the right side of equation 2, we solve equation 2 for t_T and get

$$t_T = \frac{v_c(a - x_k) + v_o^2 t_I}{v_o^2 - v_c^2} + \frac{\sqrt{v_o^2(v_c t_I + a - x_k)^2 + (z_y(j) + y_c - y_k)^2(v_o^2 - v_c^2)}}{v_o^2 - v_c^2}. \quad (3)$$

(For notation simplification, we let $a = x_c + z_x(j)$). Therefore, the time t_c associated with Path 2 is

$$t_c = t_T - t_I.$$

Therefore, if task k involved walking from a fixed point to the moving vehicle, then the running time t_I would be updated in the following way:

$$t_I(k) = t_c + t_I(k-1) = t_T.$$

The flowchart in Figure 2 describes the method used to calculate the entire time necessary to perform all tasks in a given sequence and for a given cell layout. We iterate over all tasks in a prescribed sequence, calculating the time the operator needs to walk between locations where the known walking tasks must be performed. We use the two types of path calculations:

1. calculation of the time between two fixed locations (t_p represents this time)
2. calculation of the time between a fixed location and a location where the operator intersects the moving vehicle (t_c represents this time). At this intersection the operator will usually begin a part installation or read instructions from the vehicle. The operator and the vehicle will likely move at different velocities.

We keep track of the running time, which is the time required to perform the sequence of all tasks up to the current one (t_I represents this time and is initialized as zero and updated after each path calculation).

5 SYSTEM ARCHITECTURE AND FUNCTIONALITY

This section describes the overall system architecture and the functionality of our workcell layout tool. Figure 3 exhibits the overall system architecture of our workcell planning tool. The architecture is that of a typical Web client/server system. The server script dynamically generates a VRML scene, such as the one in Figure 4, from a set of predefined three-dimensional objects using information about their spatial and temporal relations that is stored in a database. VRML approximates most of the objects, except the operator object, using basic geometrical shapes, such as boxes. However, in some instances it is desirable to use an image that is close to the actual object in order to improve the conceptual understanding of the scene. For example, substituting a geometric shape with a three-dimensional image of the actual vehicle being assembled may help to improve the accuracy of the study. Fortunately, most three-dimensional vehicle images exist in corporate CAD libraries, which can be easily accessed and exported to VRML. When the scene is loaded to the client VRML browser, the operator path is calculated according to algorithm described in Section 4 and superimposed on the workcell image (see Figure 4). This algorithm is implemented in a Java class. The user can then rearrange the locations of the part bins,

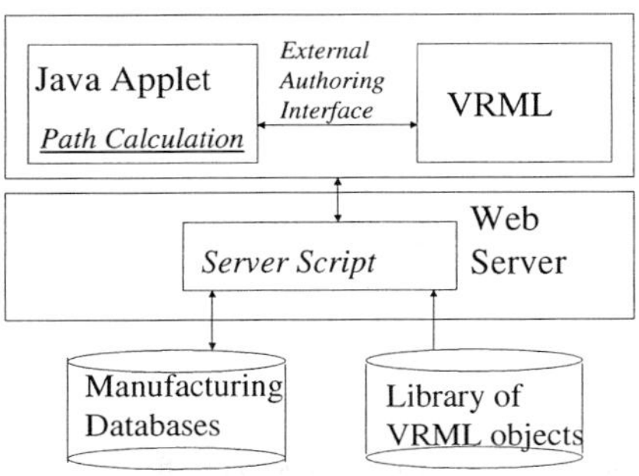

Figure 3: This picture shows the overall system architecture of our workcell planning tool.

tools, initial vehicle, and operator locations by clicking and dragging corresponding objects in the VRML scene. VRML generates an event with *drag*, which triggers recalculation of the operator walk path simultaneously with its visual adjustment. This allows for "what if" analysis to be accomplished in a very rapid manner compared to the other methods discussed in Section 2. By default, the user can drag the object along the horizontal plane, which is the most often used function in the workcell planning what-if analysis. However, when required, the user may switch this default behavior associated with the drag action to movement in the vertical direction or rotation of the object (this vertical movement represents part bins that may be located on a shelf or parts arriving on a conveyor belt). In addition, the user can analyze how the speed of the line affects the operator's walking time (work load) by increasing or decreasing the line speed.

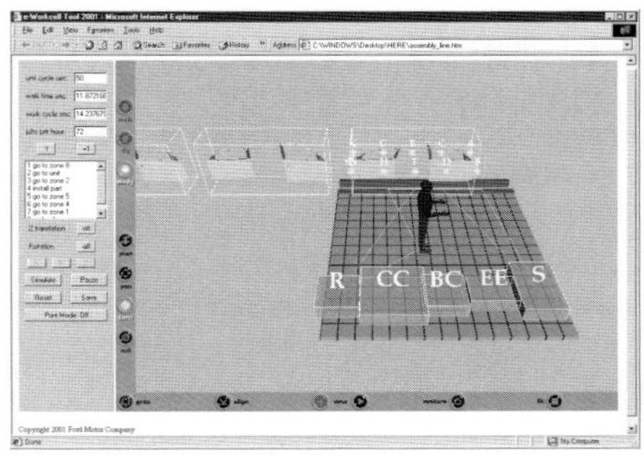

Figure 4: This picture shows a graphical representation of an operator's workcell based on user inputs.

The system also provides the capability to simulate the assembly operation. This capability is implemented using the VRML animation technique. Simulation allows the user to study the details of an operator's moves within the workcell synchronized with the move of the unit. This feature is very useful for validating the input data and feasibility of the given workcell arrangement, especially for complex operator paths. It can also be used to see how the design of a given workcell affects neighboring workcells.

When satisfied with the developed workcell arrangements, the user can save the results back into the database. This is done through a Java applet, which queries VRML to obtain current locations of the cell objects and updates the database. Since all information is maintained in the database, it could be used for future workcell planning, analysis, and improvement. Note that the interface is a three-dimensional visualization tool; hence, several views can be obtained and printed, especially the two-dimensional for a mark-up study or to be posted on the wall for the operator's use.

As shown in Figure 4, the HTML page contains both a VRML and Java Applet, which are linked through EAI. The Java applet shows some aggregate information on the critical parameters of the workcell, such as unit cycle time, operator cycle time, walk time, and line speed. These parameters dynamically change with the changes in workcell arrangement. Furthermore, the Java panel contains a set of control buttons for line speed adjustment, simulation, three-dimensional object manipulations, and communication of the results back to the database.

One of the main advantages of the proposed system is that it integrates a Web-based client server, a Virtual Reality interface, and mathematical models so that workcell arrangement can be designed, analyzed, simulated, documented, and maintained over corporate networks. This allows the workcell planning tool to efficiently interface with and complement other corporate systems involved in workcell studies.

6 SUMMARY

The application described in this paper provides an example of an intracompany use of e-Technology. This application leverages web-based technology (e.g. VRML) that was originally meant to enhance the business-to-consumer e-commerce environment. The VRML interface provides an ideal collaborative setting for planning and optimization of workcell layouts in automotive assembly: it interprets the abstract mathematical models into intuitive three-dimensional scenes. This interface combines mathematical algorithms and visualization capabilities in a novel way. The new system not only greatly simplifies the workcell design process for industrial engineers, but also helps make workcell layout analysis accessible to line operators. Thus, it should help in broadening the range of decision makers involved in the assembly line planning process. By simplifying the workcell configuration process and by providing advice in the form of mathematically optimal solutions to the workcell layout problem, the new interface should facilitate the analysis of how decisions made at the workcell level impact overall assembly line operations and ultimately, lead to greater assembly line efficiency.

Currently, the system is being used by Planning engineers and Product Specialists in a number of automotive assembly plants at Ford Motor Company. Users have reported enormous savings of time and increased efficiency; they have confirmed that usage of the new tool has led to deeper analysis and better planning of operators' workcell layouts. Furthermore, it facilitates collaboration, it simplifies work practices, and it leads to better allocation decisions.

We believe that this project demonstrates the potential of VRML to incorporate sophisticated data analysis and manipulation features into existing web-based data management systems in an efficient and effective way.

Acknowledgments

We acknowledge Jennifer O'Hara and Audrey Bielawa for user input, Serguei Vassiliev and John Dennis for technical support, and Armeka Sullivan for Industrial Engineering input. We also acknowledge Randy Beckner, Nestor Rychtyckyj, Ron Tucker, and Rob Salowitz for invaluable assistance during all phases of the project.

REFERENCES

Ames, A., Nadeau, D., and Moreland, J. (1996). *VRML 2.0 Sourcebook*. John Wiley & Sons, Inc.

Ghosh, S. and Gagnon, R. J. (1989). A comprehensive literature review and analysis of the design, balancing and scheduling of assembly systems. *Int. J. Prod. Res.*, 27(4):637–670.

Huang, G. Q. and Mak, K. (2001). Web-integrated manufacturing: recent developments and emaerging issues. *Int. J. Computer Integrated Manufacturing*, 14(1):3–13.

Indrusiak, L. and da Luz Reis, R. (2001). 3d integrated circuit layout visualization using vrml. *Future Generation Computer Systems*, 17:503–511.

Ressler, S., Godil, A., Wang, Q., and Seidman, G. (1999). A vrml integration methodology for manufacturing applications. In *VRML'99, Fourth Symposium on the Virtual Reality Modeling Language*, Paderborn, Germany.

Roehl, B., Couch, J., Reed-Ballreich, C., Rohaly, T., and Brown, G. (1997). *Late Night VRML 2.0 with Java*. Ziff-Davis Press.

Rychtyckyj, N. (1999). DLMS: Ten years of AI for vehicle assembly process planning. In *AAAI'99/IAAI'99 Proceedings*, pages 821–828, Orlando, Florida. AAAI Press.

NEW TECHNOLOGY - GREAT OPPORTUNITIES
How to exploit them

Ilia Bider
IbisSoft, Box 19567,SE-104 32 Stockholm, Sweden
Email: ilia@ibissoft.se

Maxim Khomyakov
Magnificent Seven,1-st Baltiyskiy per. 6/21-3, 125 315 Moscow, Russia
**Died December, 2000*

Key words: e-business, business communication, object-oriented modeling, business modeling, man-machine interaction

Abstract: Full exploitation of a new computer technology, Internet in particularly, is impossible to achieve without redesigning the business to align it with the new technology. One of the most important tasks of such redesign is reengineering of business processes. Implementation of more effective processes is impossible without a proper computer support. A computer system that is aimed to support business processes, e.g., workflow management system, possesses a number of properties that are different from the properties of traditional business information systems. The modeling techniques widely used for traditional system development might not be appropriate for the development of computerized support for business processes, new modeling techniques should be considered for this end. A possible approach to creating such a technique is presented in the paper. It is based on defining interactions without explicit communication. Interaction is realized via active relationships that can propagate changes from one object to another. Based on this idea, which comes from the previous research work of the authors, the paper discusses the issues of introducing "*harnesses*" on the interactive behavior, finding the right place for the end-users in the model, and modeling distribution of tasks between different users.

1 INTRODUCTION

We start with a story from the book of Douglas Adams "Hitch Hiker's Guide to Galaxy". According to this story, many millions of years ago a race of hyperintelligent pan-dimensional beings built themselves a stupendous super computer to answer "The Ultimate Question of Life, the Universe and Everything". The computer worked for 7.5 millions of years and gave an answer ***forty-two***. To understand the meaning of the answer the pan-dimensional beings asked what the question was. The supercomputer could not tell the question but suggested to design a much more powerful computer that could tell it.

The computer technology is becoming better with each day. But it more and more looks like an answer (forty-two) for real-life questions that are not always trivial to formulate. The new technology, Internet in particularly, creates great opportunities for companies and organisations to access global markets for products, services, skilled labour, and investment capital. This is by providing exceptionally effective and inexpensive channels for communication, payment, and even delivery (at least of some products, e.g., software, information, music).

However, the new technology creates only opportunities; to fully exploit them, it is not enough just to adopt the technology. In addition, a company or organization often needs to change its way of conducting business. For example, employing the Internet for accepting customer orders in combination with e-marketing may result in substantial increase in the amount of incoming orders and requests for information. If the company's internal organisation has not been adjusted to handle the increased number of orders, the result will be frustrated customers who are not receiving their goods in time, receiving the wrong goods, or not receiving them at all.

The most successful examples of employment of the Internet technology come from the companies that were in the mail-order business for some time. This is because their internal organisation has already been adjusted to what is needed for employment of the new technology. More specifically:

- They already had an assortment of products that their customers where used to buying without first seeing.
- They had sales and marketing information in form of catalogues that was relatively easy to convert into the electronic form.
- They were tuned to handle large volumes of incoming orders, and returns (the latter is as important, as handling orders).

The companies and organizations entering the e-business without a relevant prior experience (for example, of mail-order business) need to understand all business consequences of this move before acquiring the new technology. We believe that to fully exploit opportunities of new technology the following steps should be undertaken:

- Redesign the way of running business (to get the most from the modern technology).
- Create computer support for running the redesigned business.
- Introduce electronic channels for communication with the external world.

One of the main tasks when aligning a business according to the above steps is reengineering (or sometimes engineering) of internal business processes and introduction of computerized support for running them. In this paper, we first discuss why greater attention should be given to business processes from organisational perspective. After that, we consider a problem of finding a modelling technique appropriate for the task of developing computerized support for business processes. The latter part of the paper represents a shorten version of our presentation at ICEIS 2002 (Bider & Khomyakov, 2002).

2 WHY BUSINESS PROCESSES?

The greatest advantage of the new technology is inexpensive channels of communication easily available even for small companies and organizations. These channels allow to arrange:

- Peer-to-peer communication between the company or organization and its customers, potential as well as existing, and supplies.
- Mass communication with the external world, which allows to inform large groups of individuals and organizations about products and services delivered by a given company or organization.

Both types of communication are intrinsically linked to the internal business processes of the given company or organization.

Peer-to-peer communication is used for accepting orders, information requests, complaints, etc. Introducing electronic means for pear-to-pear communication, like email, and Web-based systems, can help to reduce the burden on call-centres and departments of technical support, sales, etc. However, a user of the fast communication channels, usually, has a presumption that fast channels ensure prompt responses. If this is not true, the users will be discourage to use the new channels, and the burden on call centres will increase instead of decreasing.
To solve the problem, the business processes that are to be initiated via the new channels should be analysed and optimised in order to fulfil the user's expectations. The incoming message should be promptly redirected to the responsible individual/department and go through all the relevant individuals/departments in a timely manner. It is also desirable to give the channel's users a possibility to follow-up their requests as they go through the organization.
Summarizing the above, there is no use in introduction of fast channels for peer-to-peer communication with the external world, until the company or organization introduces fast channels for internal communication.

Before appearance of the new technology, the channels for ***mass communication*** were affordable only for relatively large companies and organisations. With introduction of the new technology, such channels became available even for small organisations, via for example, email lists and Web sites. However, using such channels presumes understanding of basics of mass communication, which includes such questions as:

- Who your addressees are and what kind of information they might be interested in, and what kind of channels they are able to access?
- What do you want to achieve with each act of communication, e.g. remind of your existence, inform about new products?

- How to pre-process, and package various information messages in one communication sending?
- Where to get the relevant information and how to get it in a timely fashion?

All these questions are of equal importance. However, without solving the last one, the new technology will not work, as we will get Web sites in which the information is never updated. The readers will loose the interest to visit such sites, and thus all investment in the new technology will be lost.
Obtaining the relevant information in timely fashion is not a trivial task as, normally, it is not gathered in one place, but it is evenly spread through the whole organization. Some part of the relevant information might be found in the electronic form in various computer systems that are not connected to each other. Some relevant information may exist in the internal documents in various stages of preparation. The rest of relevant information might be in the heads of individuals participating in the business.
Introducing separate information-gathering procedures can be quite expensive and inefficient. A more efficient way is to direct this information to the information channel as soon as the information is produced in the frame of some business process. To arrange such "in-time" gathering we need:

- Identify all business processes that can serve as sources of information for mass communication.
- Describe and analyse them.
- Reengineer each process by introducing operations of information forwarding in the points of the process where this information is obtain or produced.
- Introduce the redesigned processes in operational practice, which may require acquiring of a proper computerized support.

3 WHY NEW MODELING TECHNIQUES?

It is a well-known fact that introduction of efficient business processes in the organizational practice is impossible without a proper computer system of a workflow or groupware type. Such systems represent a new generation of business applications that we call *human-assisted* to differentiate them from traditional *human-assisting* business applications.
A *human-assisting* system helps a human being only to perform certain activities, e.g. to write a letter, to print an invoice, to complete a transaction, etc. The relations between these activities, and the aim of the whole process are beyond the understanding of the system, but are a prerogative of the human participant. In a *human-assisted* system, the roles are reversed, the system has a complete picture of the process and is involved in all activities. Only when the system cannot perform some activity on its own, it will ask the human participant for assistance.
The difference between the old and new generations is essential, and it can be traced in all aspects of system development, including user-interface, see Fig. 1a,and b.

The "human-assisted" systems possess some unique

Figure 1a: Human-assisting system: a powerful toolkit.

Figure1b: Human-assisted system: an assembly line

properties that should be taken into consideration when choosing modeling techniques suitable for their development:

1. There is no clear separation between the user and the system. Even after the system has been installed, some functions meant for the computer may be handed back to the user. And vice versa, some functions meant for the human being may be handed to the computer.
2. The system has essential knowledge about its users. It should not only restrict access to various functionality and data, but it should also know to which user to turn when requesting assistance of a certain kind.

3. The system is both reactive and proactive. Not only the user can request an action from the system, but also the system can anticipate and request an action from the user.

The properties listed above create a different set of requirements for modeling techniques and languages than the one that can be derived from the properties of the traditional business applications. First of all, the user becomes an integral part of the model. As the distribution of business tasks between the user and the system can change during the system's lifetime, the behavior of the user should be described in the same way as the behavior of other components of the model. Otherwise, redistribution of tasks will require rebuilding the model. Additionally, as the system can request actions from the user, his/her representation cannot differ much from the representation of other components of the system.
Making the user part of the model moves us from the *open system* concept to the *close system* concept (for the difference see (Kurki-Suonio et al., 1999, Wegner, 1997)), and thus from modeling software systems to modeling business reality. To succeed with the latter, we need to "liberate modeling from programming level abstractions", the topic extensively covered in (Kurki-Suonio et al., 1997).
We have doubts that currently widely spread modeling techniques can adequately represent human-assisted systems. For example, the concept of *"use case"* is difficult to apply to the human-assisted systems, as it is not clear who is using whom, the end-user the system or the system the end-user.
The new generation of business applications requires new modeling techniques that could adequately represent a *"flexible symbioses"* between the computer system and its users. In the rest of the paper, we discuss one approach to representing such symbioses based on our previous research work (Bider et al., 2000). We do not insist that that suggested approach is the best way of solving the problems of modeling human-assisted systems. However, we consider it suitable enough to present in a structural way what the problems are and how they can be solved.
The rest of the paper has the following structure. In Section 4, we present the main idea of our modeling technique in very informal way. In section 5, we shortly overview the basic formal notions of our model from (Bider et al., 2000), and in section 6, we illustrate these notions with an example. In section 7, and 8 we discuss the place of the user in the model. In section 9, we list some research areas correlated with our approach. In section 10, we summarize the results of the research presented in the paper.

4 MODELING FLEXIBLE SYMBIOSES

The *"flexible symbioses"* means cooperation between the system and its users where the distribution of responsibilities between them may change in time. It means that the points of interaction between the system and its users may change and we need to have a model in which such changes do not require substantial modifications.
The word "interaction" means that the state and/or behavior of one of the interacting entities (objects, components, etc.) affects the state and/or behavior of other entities that participate in the interaction. The traditional object-oriented approach of modeling exploits explicit communication as a means of interaction (via objects sending messages to each other or themselves). This is not the only way of achieving interactive behavior. An alternative approach can be derived from the well-known saying "If you wish to change the world, start with yourself." This statement presumes that by changing its own state or behavior, the entity may cause changes in other entities. Naturally, this is impossible if this entity is totally isolated from other entities; the saying presumes that:

– each entity has many relationships with other entities,
– these relationships can propagate changes in one entity to the others without explicit communication (be it command-style, or negotiation-style communication).

Let us consider an example from Fig. 2 were two

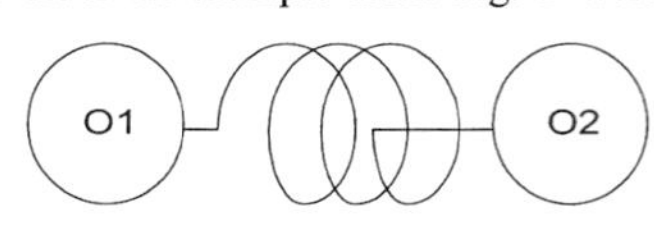

Figure 2: Two balls connected by a spring.

balls are connected by a spring. Suppose the centers of these balls are fixed and cannot be moved. Assume that the balls are made from some elastic material, and each ball can change its shape and degree of elasticity.
Presume that at some moment of time the first ball changed its shape as shown on the left in Fig. 3, and became hard, while the second ball remained to be elastic. Then the spring will force the second ball to change its shape, as shown on the right in Fig. 3.

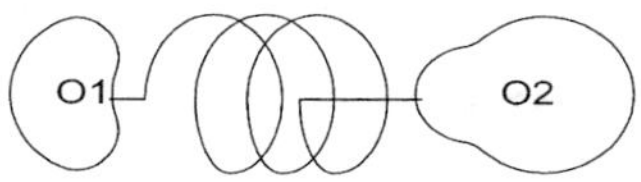

Figure 3: The spring adjusts the shape of the second ball.

The above example can be modeled as two objects connected via a computational device which we call a connector, see Fig. 4. The connector contains the text of a physical law that governs the spring functionality. The connector watches the objects it hangs upon, i.e., their shapes and degrees of elasticity. As soon as it discovers some changes in one or both of the objects it adjusts their shapes according to the spring law. In the real world, the spring and the balls are not floating in an empty space, but are part of some larger entity. The larger entity can also be modeled as an object in whose body the spring connector with its operands (objects the connectors hangs on) is included. The third object, *O*3, in its turn, can have active relationships with other objects. The actions of these relationships can result, for example, in the spring-balls assembly being removed from the body of *O*3.

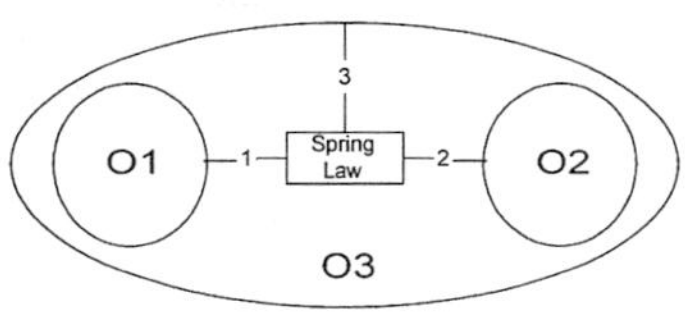

Figure 4: The connector with its operands is part of the object O3.

The connector that guards some law over its operands operates on the principle of localism. Namely, it knows nothing about the objects beyond its operands, and thus, neither can change them nor use them in its work. Consider the fact that the spring can break down as a reaction on the balls becoming too large or too small. To cover this situation, object *O3* is made an operand of the spring connector. This allows the spring connector to remove itself from the body of the object *O*3. If at this moment objects *O*1 and *O*2 have no other connection to object *O*3, or its other sub-objects, they disappear from *O*3 altogether.

We believe that the idea of active relationships and its realization through the concepts of law, object, and connector constitute a promising approach to modeling interactive behavior of human-assisted business applications. The natural question arises: where is the user, is it a connector, or an object? The answer is that he/she *is both*.

5 BASIC NOTIONS

In this section, we give a short overview of the basic notions of the objects-connectors model. These notions formalize the example discussed in the previous section. Additional informal explanation is given in the next section where a more complex example is discussed.

The objects-connectors model describes the world as consisting of:

- a set of *typed atoms A*,
- a set of *objects O*,
- a code of *laws* Λ, and
- a set of *connectors CON*, each connector hanging on a group of objects that must obey a certain law.

Atoms represent the usual notion of elementary data types, like integers, floats, strings, etc. We assume that each atom from *A* is assigned a type τ. By A_τ, we will denote the set of all atoms of the type τ.

Atoms are the only elements of the model that can be described independently of other notions. All other notions are interconnected. The objects are used to represent complexly structured entities. At each moment of time an object can be characterized by its state. The state is not more than a set of connectors from *CON* included in the body of the given object.

Let *P(CON)* be the power set of *CON* (a set of all subsets of connectors), and $\perp$ a special symbol that represents the embryo state of the object. A function

st: O —> P(CON) $\cup$ {$\perp$},

that assigns each object $o \in O$ its state is called a *state function.* A function *w* that maps the time axis *T* into the set of all possible state functions *ST*:

w: T —> ST

is called a *world.* The world determines the state *w(t)(o)* of any object *o* at any point of time *t*. For simplicity, we consider the discrete time axis with starting point, i.e. it consists of all nonnegative integers called *time ticks*.

A *law* λ is defined as a 5-tuple <*name, arity, type, condition, action*>. The *name* assigns a name to the law. The *arity* is a positive integer $n > 0$ which defines the number of objects this particular law concerns. The law can be unary, binary, etc. The type of the form $\tau 1$ x $\tau 2$ x ... x τk, $k \geq 0$, where τi is an atomic type, defines how many atoms and of which types can be taken into consideration by the law.

Let $\lambda = \langle name, n, type, condition, action\rangle$ be a law. Consider a world w at a moment of time t. Let $\boldsymbol{v} = \langle v_1, \ldots, v_k\rangle$ be a k-tuple of atoms of type *type*, and $z = \langle x_1, \ldots, x_n\rangle$ be an n-tuple of objects from O. Then the *condition* is a predicate that given $\boldsymbol{v}$, z, w, and t determines whether the law with parameters $\boldsymbol{v}$ holds for objects from z in world w at time t. The action provides the next state of objects from z for the points for which the law is violated. In other words, the action assigns a punishment for breaking the law. The simplest type of laws is a *trivial* law for which the *condition* is always true, and the *action* is always empty.

Finally, a connector is a triple $c=\langle\lambda,\boldsymbol{v},z\rangle$, where λ is an n-ary law of type $\tau 1 \times \tau 2 \times \ldots \times \tau k$, $\boldsymbol{v} = \langle v_1, \ldots, v_k\rangle$ is a k-tuple of atoms such that $v_i \in A_{\tau i}$, $i = 1, \ldots, k$, and $z = \langle x_1, \ldots, x_n\rangle$ is an n-tuple of objects. If the law is trivial, the connector just represents a passive relationship between its operands, eventually assigning some properties to the relationship with the help of its k atoms (if any). This case corresponds to the usual notion of relationship from the ER model (Chen, 1976). If the law is nontrivial, the connector forces the objects' structure and behavior to be in sync with each other and, possibly, with the properties of the relationship (if there are any atoms). This is the case of active relationship. If a connector's law holds on its operands, we say that the connector is *satisfied*, otherwise we say that it is *unsatisfied*.

The dynamics of the objects-connectors model can be defined by a machine in which a connector is regarded as a processing unit that monitors its operands. A connector

- *awakes* when one of its operands has been changed,
- *checks* whether the law still holds by reading the condition,
- *restores* it when it has been broken,
- *falls asleep*.

The machine has also a central unit that resolves conflicts when several connectors demand access to the same objects.

6 ANALYSIS OF AN EXAMPLE

In this section, we illustrate the basic notions from the previous section by means of an example, and we discuss some important features of the model while referring to this example. The example represents a kind of distributed sort, and it is similar to the distributed exchange sort algorithm from (Aaltonen, 1998) expressed in modeling language *Disco* (Disco).

Consider a simple promotion queue shown in Fig. 5. The queue consists of a number of cells, e.g., in a hospital. The cells are ordered according to the complexity of their equipment. Each cell can have one inmate. Each inmate has a priority assigned to it. Each cell has a special measuring-device to which an inmate is connected. This device evaluates the state of the inmate and sets its priority. A new inmate can be placed in any empty cell. The queue should function in such a way that the inmates with higher priorities are placed in the better-equipped cells.

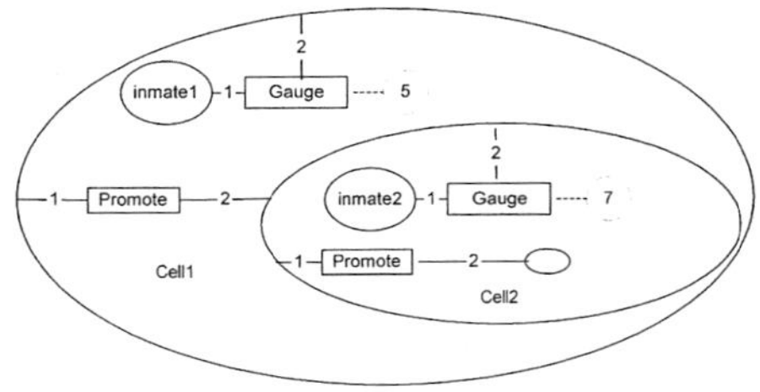

Figure 5: A promotion queue with measuring-devices.

Two laws are used for this model, *priority*, and *gauge*. The *gauge* connector is satisfied if the overall state of the *inmate* is reflected by the atomic value assigned to this connector. If the state of the inmate is not reflected by the atom, the atomic value should be changed. The legal way of changing an atom in the model is by substituting the whole connector. Thus, when the *gauge* connector is not satisfied, it replaces itself with the same gauge connector but with another atomic value assigned to it. This situation corresponds to the pointer changing its position on the dial of a real physical gauge.

The *promote* law has two operands and no atoms. It holds when a connector *priority* in its first operand assigns a lower priority to the inmate than a similar connector in its second operand. Thus, in Fig. 5, the *promote* connector placed in *cell*1 is satisfied. If the connector is not satisfied, it swaps inmates between its first and second operands. If the second cell is empty, it just moves the inmate from *cell*1 to *cell*2. Note that if the first cell is empty, the law is always satisfied.

An example in Fig. 5 illustrates how the decomposition is done in the objects-connectors model. The *gauge* connector is responsible for moving the pointer of the dial. He does it by watching the state of his first operand and evaluating it. The *promote* connector knows nothing about the internal states of the inmates included in its operands. It watches only the gauges' dials, which is enough for this connector to decide on and complete the action. In other words, the *promote* law analyzes its operands only at depth 1. It "sees" what connectors exist in its operands, including the atomic values assigned to these connectors. Actually, the idea of reduced visibility is the reason why the dial of the gauge is modeled by an atom and not by an object.

The law in our model can take into account not only the current state of its operands, but their histories too. The *promote* law does not need any historical information, its *condition* and *action* are based on the current readings of the gauges. The *gauge* itself, however, may take into account historic information. For example, if we evaluate the state of the patient in the hospital, his absolute high temperature may not be enough to assign him a high priority; we need to know whether the temperature was rising, falling, or it remained the same for some time.

The objects-connectors model is state-oriented, i.e. the state is its basic notion. The example in Fig. 5 shows that state-orientation does not necessarily mean the absence of encapsulation. The idea of encapsulation is widely accepted, as it is not always possible or reasonable to know the state of an object in order to interact with it, the knowledge of the object's behavior should be enough. This idea is one of the grounds of the classical object-oriented programming. However, methods of the classical object-oriented programming are not the only approach to defining behavior. Actually, to understand the behavior of an object without looking inside it, one needs to watch some wider area in which this object operates. In our example, the *promote* connector makes its decisions based on watching the interaction between the inmate and the measuring-device inside the cell.

7 WHERE IS THE USER?

The model described in the previous sections looks quite deterministic. The determinism would be justified if when modeling the reality, we could have the exact knowledge of all laws that act in it. This is not true in practice where we always model only a part of the reality. There are two sources of non-determinism when modeling business reality. Firstly, the behavior of some elements of business reality cannot be fully understood or controlled because they are external for the given business, for example, customers or suppliers (see the discussion of this topic in (Wegner, 1997)). Secondly, even the part of business reality that could be understood and controlled might be too complex to be described deterministically from the very beginning. Full understanding, if any, of this part of reality could be reached long after the business application has been designed and introduced in the operational practice. Thus, a strategy of stepwise refinement of the model is required (for more on this topic see (Kurki-Suonio et al., 1999)).

To express the idea of insufficient knowledge of reality, we exploit a notion of non-deterministic law. We differentiate two types of non-determinism: firing non-determinism, and action non-determinism. For a law with *firing non-determinism*, an action can be defined even for the cases where the law holds. A connector that imposes such a law may be awoken even when none of its (visible inside the model) operands has been changed. A law with *action non-determinism* can specify two different actions for the same behavior of its operands. A connector entrusted with such a law appears to be taking different courses of action in the same situation. Of course, a law can have non-determinism of both types, firing, and action.

Connectors with non-deterministic laws, which we call boundary connectors, are our means of modeling interaction with the external world, e.g., people, or electronic devices. As part of the law is known, the external world cannot function arbitrarily. The known part of the non-deterministic laws constitutes a harness (in terminology of (Wegner, 1997)) on the external world behavior.

Now, the user's role becomes clear, he/she is to help the connectors with non-deterministic laws. Such connector may be thought of as having a terminal where a human being can help the connector to do its job, see Fig.6.

Figure 6: Boundary connector.

Let us assume that a connector's law has action non-determinism. Then it is up to the connector in case when its operands have been changed, to request the human assistance via the terminal by beeping, blinking, etc. After providing assistance, the human being may return to his other occupations, drinking coffee, for example, until the connector calls him again. Action non-determinism may vary from allowing any possible structural changes in the connector's operands to a selection from a list of predefined choices (menu).

Now, let a connector's law have firing non-determinism. Such connector can be represented as a big button that the user presses from time to time based on observations that lie beyond the boundaries of the computer system. Then it is up to the connector to do the rest of the job.

Returning to the example from the previous section, suppose the gauge from the promotion queue in Fig. 5 cannot always automatically evaluate the state of the inmate, and requires human assistance from a nurse, or a doctor from time to time. To cover this case, the *gauge* law should be made non-deterministic. It might be enough to have the action non-determinism in this case. The *gauge* connector can ring the bell requesting the doctor to attend the patient and reevaluate his/her state when needed.
Another situation that can require human assistance in the promotion queue in Fig.5 is when the *promote* connector cannot complete the task of switching inmates between the cells. Again, we can solve the problem by making the law of this connector non-deterministic. An alarm would ring requesting the workers to move the inmates around according to the instructions. If both *gauge* and *promote* laws become non-deterministic, the example in Fig.5 will look like Fig. 7.

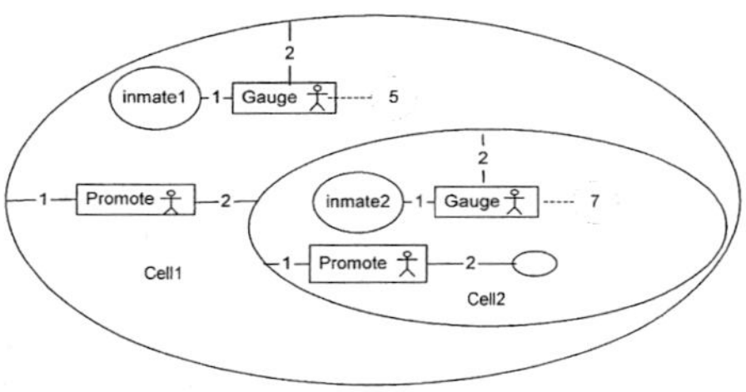

Figure 7: Human-assisted promotion queue.

The above two cases illustrate that representing the user as a boundary connector insures flexibility in distribution of business tasks between the system and the user (see the properties of human-assisted systems in section 3). In the initial introduction of the system, some connectors may be defined as boundary, thus requiring user participation. After acquiring more knowledge on business laws, they may be substituted by fully deterministic laws. Vice versa, some laws that seemed to be fully deterministic may prove to need human assistance after all. Switching between deterministic and non-deterministic laws will require adding/removing a user dialog script, which is a minor problem comparing to changing the model (as normally is required in the traditional approaches).

8 HOW TO DISTRIBUTE THE USER?

As was explained in the previous section, the role of the user is to assist boundary connectors. This idea would be enough for modeling purposes if there were only one user in the system. He/she would be the only person to serve all connectors that require human assistance. In the normal business reality, there are many users, and they can be distributed between various business tasks in many different ways. Let us return to the example when the *gauge* connector in Fig. 5 cannot automatically evaluate the state of an inmate, and requires human assistance. The distribution of human resources between different cells may vary from each cell having its own nurse (doctor) to the only person who serves all cells. The actual scheme, certainly, depends on the level of the gauge's intelligence. The more intelligent is the gauge, the less human resources it requires.
The distribution of users between various boundary connectors is not a simple task because the number of connectors and available users change in time. To cope with this task, we need to augment the objects-connectors model described in the previous sections. First of all, we need to be able to distinguish one user from another. The natural way of doing this is by representing each user as an object. Actually, the users are always part of business reality as they, normally, are employees of the company or organization whose business is to be modeled. And each employee should be represented in the model as he/she has many business processes connected to it. For example, his/her salary should be calculated monthly, his/her professional level should be maintained via various training programs, etc.
Secondly, we need a way of assigning an object that represents the user to the connector he/she is to assist. This can be done by introducing in the model a set of assignment operators *Q*. Different assignment operators serve to name various type of assistance the user can provide when helping a connector to do its job, e.g., a head master, assistant, etc. To each assignment operator *q* from *Q*, we attach a type in the form of $\tau 1 \times \tau 2 \times \ldots \times \tau k$, $k \geq 0$, where τi is an atomic type. The type defines the number and types of atoms that can be used to describe the assignment. The atoms can be used, for example, to define an interval of time when a particular user is to assist a particular connector. This time may be absolute, or repetitive, e.g. each day from 9 a.m. to 12 a.m.
Let *q* be an assignment operator of type $\tau 1 \times \tau 2 \times \ldots \times \tau k$, $k \geq 0$, and let $v = <v_1, \ldots, v_k>$ be a *k*-tuple of atoms, such that $v_i \in A_{\tau i}$, i = 1 ,..., *k*, and *o* an object

from *O*. Then the expression $q_v(o)$ is called a *resource allocation*. By assigning each connector that exists in the world *w* at time *t* a set of resource allocations, we complete our model with the means to express resource assignments. The assigned set can be empty, which is always the case with totally deterministic connectors. But it might be empty for boundary connectors too, which expresses the fact that human resources have not been allocated to this connector yet.

Now, we need to understand *who* will be assigning resources. This, naturally, is a connector, as it is the only element of our model that can perform actions. A new connector appears in our world only when some other connector introduces it in the course of its action. If the new connector has a non-deterministic law, human resources should be assigned to it. This may be done by the connector that introduced the given one into the world. But it might also be done by some other connector that serves as a resource manager. The latter watches the object where new boundary connectors are being introduced, and as soon as it "sees" a connector without resource allocation, it performs resource assignment.

The two situations mentioned above have analogues in the management practice. The first case corresponds to a project manager that both defines a task, and assigns an available resource to it. The second case corresponds to the matrix management, where the project manager just defines a task, and a separate resource manager finds appropriate resources to complete it. Note that both the connector that creates a given boundary connector, and the one that assigns resources (if it is separated from the first one) can be boundary connectors themselves operated by a human project (resource) manager.

And finally, we need to understand how the assignments are done, which is the most difficult task. The simplest case of assigning resources is the assignment to "myself", which means that the creator of a new boundary connector assigns to it the same resource as it has itself.

When a task should be scheduled to somebody else, the assignment job becomes more complicated. So far, we considered any law to be independent of objects it is meant to govern. The text of the law is external to the model, and the law condition and action do not depend on particular objects, only the object's structure and behavior matter. However, when assigning resources, we need to refer to particular objects that represent the users. To cover the new challenge, additional modification of our model is required. At least some laws should become a part of the model. The natural way to do this is by representing a law as an object. An example of such representation is shown in Fig. 8.

A law object in Fig. 8 is built with the help of three trivial laws *LawText*, *LawArity*, and *LawResource*. The unary connector *LawText* attaches the *text of the law* to the law object. The text of the law is expressed by an atom of some special type. This is a program written in some law programming language. The unary connector *LawArity* defines the *arity* of the law represented by the *law* object. The arity is defined by an atom of type *integer*. The *LawResource* connectors attach various resources to the given law, and assign *resource names* with the help of *string* atoms. The text of the law does not refer to the actual objects. It refers only to the resource names. The *LawResource* connectors perform binding of the resource names to the actual resources that exist in the world.

To make the law object work, we need to extend the definition of connector given in section 2. Now, we allow connectors to be defined as pairs $c=<o,z>$, where *o* is an object from *O*, and $z = <x_1, ..., x_n>$ is an *n*-tuple of objects. We refer to this type of connectors as to *compound connectors* to differentiate them from the old-style connectors, which we call *basic connectors*.

As the law of a compound connector is an object, it can be changed by actions of other connectors. A change in the law object will force all connectors that impose this law to wake up, and check whether the changed law still holds for their operands. This check concerns both the states of the connector's operands, and the allocation of resources. Assume, for example, that the resource binding of the law in Fig. 8 has been changed so that some *user*3 now functions as an *Assistant* resource instead of *user*2. Then for all existing connectors that impose this law, resource assignments should be adjusted. This task is entrusted to appropriate "resource managers".

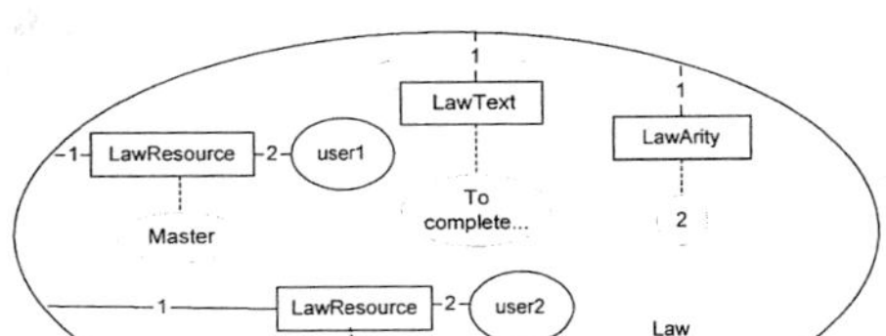

Figure 8: A law represented as an object.

Usually, there are several users that can do a particular type of job. When choosing one of them, the resource manager (i.e. a connector that serve as such) should take into account other assignments of this user. It means that we need to reformulate the principle of localism mentioned in section 3. For resource assignment, a resource manager needs to see all resource allocations made for the resources under his "supervision".

Observe that direct binding of users to a law as in Fig. 8 was used only for demonstration purposes. Actual binding can be done indirectly by referring in law objects only to user roles, and separately assigning the roles to the users.

9 RELATED WORKS

The idea of a device that guards some condition and performs some action when the condition is true is not new in the computer science theory and practice. It is expressed by such well-known metaphors as demons in AI and triggers in databases, and it is used in a number of modeling languages, see, for example, (Disco). More on related works and how approach differs from them see in (Bider & Khomyakov, 2002)

10 CONCLUDING REMARKS

In section 4, we listed and explained three most important properties of human-assisted systems, namely:

1. No clear separation between the user and the system.
2. Substantial knowledge about the end-users.
3. Proactivness of behavior.

Consider how they are covered in our approach. As was shown in section 6, the first and third properties can be expressed in our model via the notion of boundary connector. By changing the law from deterministic to non-deterministic or vice versa, we can move the responsibility for executing a task from the system to the user, or from the user to the system. Laws with action non-determinism cover the situations when the system requests help from the user (proactiveness).

As was shown in section 8, the second property requires a substantial extension of the model from (Bider et al., 2000). Allocation operators should be introduced, and users and laws should be represented as objects. Only the last task, i.e. formal representation of laws as objects is finished at this time. Solving other tasks constitutes our research plans for the future.

As was stated in the introduction, formulating questions may be more important than finding answers. In this paper, we focused more on questions, than answers. Independently of whether our answers will prove to be right or not in the longer run, we feel that the questions we raised in the paper are essential for proper use of modern technology in business.

REFERENCES

Aaltonen, T., 1998. Example: Distributed Exchange Sort. www.cs.tut.fi/laitos/DisCo/examples/sort/sort.html.

Bider, I., Khomyakov, M. and Pushchinsky, E., 2000. Logic of Change: Semantics of Object Systems with Active Relations. In *Automated Software Engineering*, Vol. 7:1, pp. 9-37.

Bider, I., Khomyakov, M. 2002. If you wish to change the world, start with yourself. An alternative metaphor for objects interaction. In: *Proceedings of ICEIS 2002 - the Fourth Conference on Enterprise Information Systems*, Vol 2, ICEIS Press, pp. 732-742.

Chen P. P., 1976. The entity-relationships model: towards a unified view of data. In *ACM Trans. on Database Syst.* 1(1), 9-36.

Disco. http://www.cs.tut.fi/ohj/DisCo/.

Kurki-Suonio, R., and Mikkonen, T., 1997. Liberating Object-Oriented Modeling From Programming-Level Abstractions. In *ECOOP'97 Workshop Reader*, Springer, LNCS 1357, 195-199.

Kurki-Suonio, R. and Mikkonen, T., 1999. Harnessing the power of interaction. In *Information Modelling and Knowledge Bases*. H.Jaakkola, H. Kangassalo, E. Kawaguchi eds., IOS Press,1-11.

Wegner, P. , 1997. Why interaction is more powerful than algorithms. In *Communication of the ACM*, 40(5), 80-91.

HOW INFORMATICS CAN SOLVE METHODOLOGICAL GAP IN E-BUSINESS MODELING

Prof. Dr. Masao J. Matsumoto
Graduate School of Business Sciences
The University of Tsukuba, Tokyo
mjm@gssm.otsuka.tsukuba.ac.jp

Key words: e-business architecture, enterprise modeling method gap, business architecture verification.

Abstract: e-business architecture modeling method is needed in many of industrial sectors either on their stand-alone or interrelated basis. However, most of the methods do not provide seamless support for business and technical aspects of e-business architecture modeling. This paper points out several non-trivial problems that e-business modelers are currently encountering. This also presents some come-up from the Interprise Modeling research project touching on VPI method that is featured as a seamless support for value-centric e-business architecture modeling.

1 INTRODUCTION

What do you mean by the term "***e-business architecture***"? The architecture represents fundamental structure for e-business and comprises of basically two folded disciplines of business and technical. The ***business half*** represents such aspects as business method and process defined on top of business objectives and concept. The ***technical half*** represents Information Technology (IT)-related matters such aspects as data and information modeling and their exchange scheme throughout and among enterprises, transaction process and workflow design, messaging and web service-oriented architecture, backend integrity and so on. The purpose of this technical half is to realize the business scheme defined in business half and to put it into work in an actual e-business environment.

Therefore, e-business architecture dominates a core portion in e-business modeling and must be a key to make e-business happen, so that how soundly you can model the architecture becomes crucial factor. Attentions have been drawn in industry and government looking for any sound and seamless methods that allow you to model business aspects as well as technical aspects as a whole set in a coherent way. One of the most serious issues at which engineering e-business is facing today is that there exists ***un-neglected gap*** between business and technical modeling methods, mainly due to different origins where each of disciplines stem from.

The current situations show that each discipline stays within the domain and only deals with its own, say, business modeling methods only deal with business aspects of e-business, while technical modeling methods only with the technical aspects. Almost no method can be available for use for designing both business and technical aspects of e-business at same time in a single shot. Very few of methods have been developed, deployed and exploited so far as a "***seamless***" method that deals with whole aspects of modeling e-business architecture.

2 PROBLEMS

2.1 Business interpretation

Let's look at the current situations of some industries in terms of e-business evolution. Trade business community is still suffering from drawback problem in exploiting the EDEN/TEDI in Japan and the bolero in EU. The major reason why it isn't exploited as expected is from lack of affordability in software product provisions/buying that allow one to build up good enough solution to large variety of documents forms utilized in trade business.

In Financial institutions, business process integration has been evolved steady like from the intra institute process-base, to the alliance-based external process integration, to electronic clearing for manufacturing supply chain networks. However, we seldom find any standardized reference business model like SCOR. The major problem is from lack of ability of Straight Through Processing, STP in short, for large scaled process integration. Enterprise Application Integration and B2B transaction process capability are not enough to solve this kind of problems. Method is needed to business process modeling and its process automatic translation to execution for put it into practice.

In manufacturing and logistics, IT, especially enterprise information systems, must follow or even lead the leading edge of business competency pursuit. Extensive research has to be made to verification soundness of business process evolution, since the build and implementation of web based information infrastructure will not assure enterprise competency, even you will take supply chain renovation and customer relation-centric strategy. The problem is from lack of methods to make verification which process model is sound, say, stand alone enterprise process model, autonomous distributed process model or the else.

2.2 Technical interpretation

There are a lot of problems that e-business related people are encountering today in their business architecture design and put it into work in actual business setting.

- As of e-business Cycle Support, Lack of whole e-business cycle support method and technology

Any existing methods and technologies are of lack of such support for the cycle of e-business that spans from earlier phase of business planning, modeling, analysis and design to later phase of development and implementation of the corresponding information system.

- As of Business Life Cycle Support, Neither whole nor part of business "life cycle" support method and technology are available for use

Business life cycle represents whole phases of a business from its start-up, growth, peak, going-down and shutdown. Business strategy varies from innovation-oriented to full product line offers and repeated improvements to cost-conscious depending on at which stage the business resides in throughout the life cycle. No modeling method is available for such business life cycle support. However, most of currently available modeling methods only focus on specific life cycle phase.

- As of Verification support for business architecture and model, not yet well verification for each pairs of business architectural components

Business process verification may be somehow supported for itself in terms of cost and time. However, the business process verification cannot be supported to business model, since reasonable verification method for business model's validity is seldom available for use. The

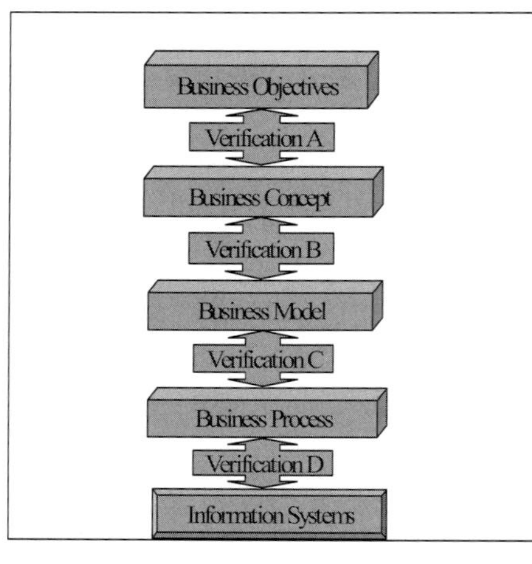

Figure 1 Verifications needed in Business Architecture Modeling

other verification supports for business architecture and model are not yet field proven in a practical sense. Theoretically, business model is usually defined on top of business process, but nevertheless business model could not be always verified to business concept. Likewise, though business concept is usually defined on top of the business model, but nevertheless business concept could not be always verified to business objectives. The verification for upper level of business architecture, including business objectives and concept, could only be possible to do intuitive-basis.

- As of Verification support for value creation, Difficult to field prove in a tangible-basis of value creation verification

Value creation is analyzed by such arbitrary method like **Value Proposition Innovation**, VPI, but the verification of the value proposition innovation is rarely possible to accomplish in its feasibility in either theoretical or practical sense. It is difficult to verify any come-ups from the value proposition innovation in its advantage, particularly in a sense of **tangible** advantages.

- As of Verification support for business model in its competency and competitiveness, Lack of verification method of business model

Business modeling method has neither been so well formed nor exploited so far. More over the verification method for business model feasibility is very rare for use, so that business model competency and competitiveness analysis has to be done without utilizing method.

- As of Seamless support of business architecture to technical architecture, there is Gap between Business and Technical Architecture Design

Very few specialists can perform both Business and Technical Architecture designs. Very few methods can make seamless support for both of them in a convergent way, due to mainly the historical reason of method evolution in diversified fields such as business administration, management science, business engineering, systems engineering, software engineering, solution engineering.

3 SOLUTIONS

Today, there are considerable numbers of methods that are available for use in modeling e-business architecture. However, very few of method could provide extensive solutions for fixing the issues stated in the previous chapter of this paper and for allowing one to model e-business architecture seamlessly. There are un-neglected gap lay down between business and technical architectures to model. Most of the methods serve for exclusively either business architecture modeling or technical, and seldom serve for both of them.

In order to clarify a positioning of several existing e-business modeling frameworks or methods, two-dimensional axis are introduced, let's say, horizontal and vertical seamless modelings. The horizontal seamless modeling represents how several different e-business concerns like communication interface, middleware interface, application processing can be analyzed and seamlessly modeled, while the vertical seamless modeling represents how several different e-business concerns like business objectives, architecture, business model and process, workflow and dataflow, relevant information systems can be analyzed and seamlessly modeled.

Each axis has two major different degrees of the extent that represents how seamless modeling has been and is took place, let's say, state-of-the-practice or state-of-the-art.

SCORE and other reference enterprise models fall into the first category of evolution in which both horizontal and vertical seamless modelings are in state-of-the-practice.

e-marketplace architecture like ***rosetta.net*** and ***bolero.net*** falls into the second category of e-business in which horizontal seamless modeling is in state-of-the-art and provides a way of forming e-business architecture comprising of several business and technical conceptual components, while vertical modeling has nothing to do except limited scale of customization which allows you to do under some constraints set out within each e-business architecture, so that vertical modeling is in the state-of-the-practice.

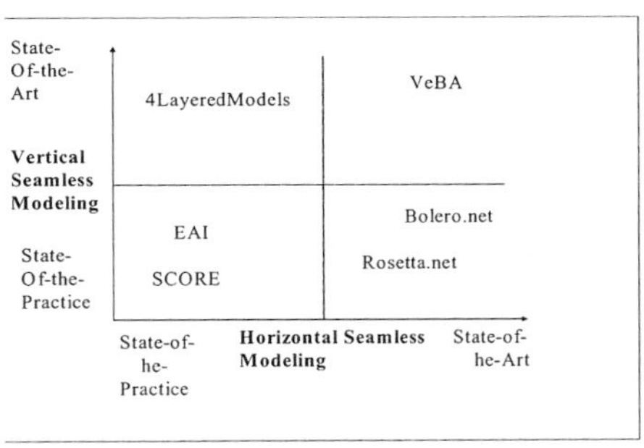

Figure 2 Positioning of outstanding modeling

e-marketplace approach is EDI-conscious and good for data exchange but shows explicitly no way of business architecture innovation except those features already built-in within the framework.
Four layered modeling scheme defined, for example by OMG, provides a mechanism in which you can instantiate meta model from mete-meta model, and then model from meta model, and in turn instance from model and so on. In this sense, the modeling scheme falls into the third category, say, being state-of-the art in vertical modeling, while horizontal modeling is in state-of-the-practice. With respect to horizontal modeling, how to seamlessly modeling the relevant concerns is totally up to your choice.
The ***Value-centric e-Business Architecture*** modeling method, ***VeBA*** in short, falls into the fourth category of the evolution that is in state-of-the-art on both vertical and horizontal axis. The VeBA method has been developed by the author and about to be brought into experimental use by industry and academia organizations from the SWIM community as a launch program.

4 VEBA METHOD

VeBA (Matsumoto, 2002) is one come-up from e-business architecture modeling study project which has been undertaken by the author of this paper with collaborations from The Interprise Modeling Research Group, Graduate School of Business Science, The University of Tsukuba, Tokyo and the IEICE (2002) SWIM community (2002).
VeBA provides a method that allows one to model, analysis and evaluate e-business architecture on the basis of value proposition needed for ***Internet worked enterprises, interprise***. in short.

4.1 Definition of Value

Value is a driver deemed by executives and management for succeeding enterprise and the activities carried out. The management style is often so called Value-based Management (Donovan et al., 1998). Value must be brought into any stakeholders, say, shareholders, customers, and employees. Value could be created by proposition and practice put into the business conducted along with the proposition. Value could be measured in several different ways, however cash flow basis measurement must be of more realistic and appropriately convenient.

Table 1. Comparison

	VeBA	Others
Centric	Value	Operation
Modeling Scheme	Seamless	Fragmented
Innovation	Explicit	Implicit
Business-Technical Gap	Monolithic	Un-neglected
Reliability	Theory accompanied	Belief based

4.2 Value Proposition Innovation

In order to have interprise competitive, value proposition innovation must be a key factor. As competitive situations always change, interprise value proposition must be keep innovating and should not stall all the time at the same proposition level. How to keep innovate value proposition would become crucial for interprise survival. Therefore, value proposition innovation method plays crucial role in e-business architecture modeling. In VeBA project, a method called **Value Proposition Innovation, VPI** in short, has been developed for this purpose. VPI method facilitates diagrammatic representation of whatever innovated and the diagram presents two folded-views, say, descriptive (as is) and normative (to-be), so that architect can make distinction between normative view of value proposition and descriptive and convince those who may concern of the proposition.
The VPI method provides procedural steps for value proposition innovation. As the steps of VPI method are more complicate, only summarized steps are presented in this paper:
1. Describe the existing value proposition and ask reasons about as-is: Evaluation is often made from customer view.
2. Disintermediation of agent: Explore any possibility of disintermediation of existing agents and study any feasibility of disintermediation to see performance and value total increase.
3. Envisage new value proposition: find new value proposition carried out by interprise (Matsumoto, 2000), that is a concatenated word

of Internet worked enterprise.
4. Reintermediation: determine new value proposition in detail including redefinition of agent role.
5. Depict value map: visualize value map in which value contributors can exchange their value each other.

Under the e-business goals and/or objectives, you can explore value proposition innovation as much as you want utilizing method like VPI. Fig. 3 demonstrates some example views of come-up from certain service industry's value proposition innovation.

4.3 Value Proposition Verification

In order to verify come-up from value proposition innovation to e-business goal, you have to check whether or not requirement of expected cash flow could be met by innovation. For accomplishing this verification, you have to decompose value map into value driver relationship model and check it to see whether you can convince to the model through sensitivity and scenario analysis.

5 DISCUSSION

e-business is a kind of business, so that e-business could not be survival without taking into consideration to balance sheet and profit and loss of enterprise. However, you should be aware that you could not find any value proposition even watching out very carefully balance sheet and profit and loss, since the sheet only telling you what enterprise accomplished in a certain fiscal quarter or year through all the activities performed by employees and not telling what you should do next. In this sense, what factors are regarded crucial in e-business design includes such tasks as value proposition innovation, business model forming, business process modeling and restructuring, information systems modeling and implementation. Each of these tasks could be done anyhow, however it is not so easy to do all these tasks as a whole unless any appropriate method is available. Usually it is very difficult for any one to accomplish all these tasks in a single blow spanning modeling, innovate, design, development and implement e-business. A seamless support method like VPI

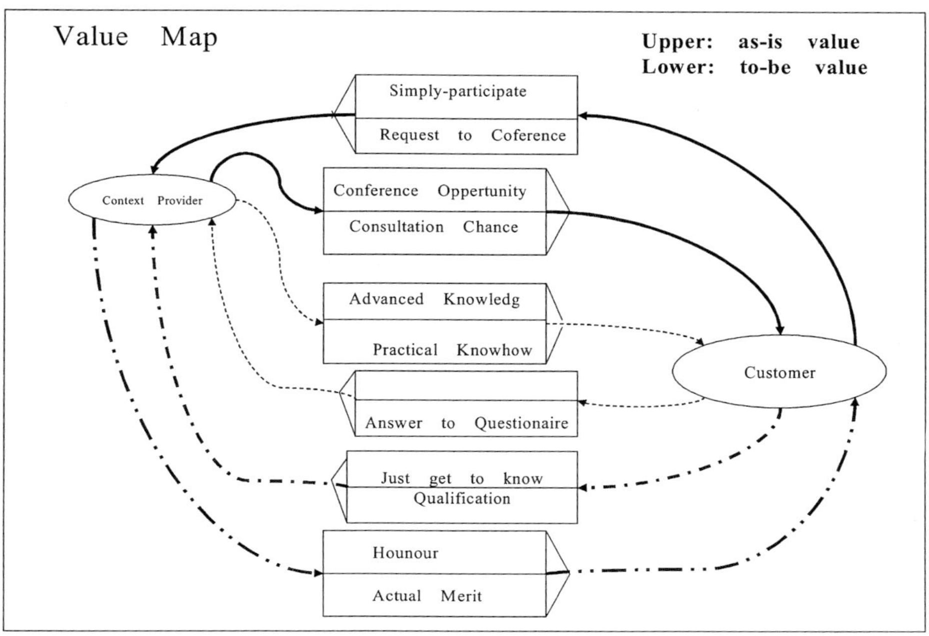

Figure 3 Example of VPI's value map

and others developed in the Interprise Modeling Method is useful for e-business related people including e-business framework designers, architects, modeling experts, information systems solution specialists and e-business consultants and, of course, even enterprise executives and management who are in charge of executing the e-business at interprise.

6 CONCLUSION

e-business will not be dead, as far as it can give people advantages. In order to survive in this sense, e-business has to be repeatedly innovated by it self. The issue is how you can do it. Obviously any suitable method and perhaps relevant technology must help one modeling and implementing e-business.

It is gradually proved that seamless modeling method is definitely needed for carrying out e-business architecture build and implement smoothly. VPI and corresponding methods developed in Interprise Modeling Method research project in Japan would be a candidate for solution to such issues stated earlier.

REFERENCES

Matsumoto,M.J., 2002. *Interprise Modeling* (to be published)

The Institute of Electronics, Information and Communication Engineers (IEICE), 2002. See http://www.ieice.org/eng/index.html

SoftWare Interprise Modeling Research Committee (SWIM-RC), 2002. See http://www.ieice.org/iss/swim/jpn/index.html

Matsumoto,M.J., 2000. A Perspective on Interprise Modeling Research stem in the New Millennium, Proc. IEICE SWIM Workshop, pp.1-13.

Donovan,J., Tully,R., and Worton,B., 1998. The Value Enterprise, McGraw-Hill.

PART 1

Databases and Information Systems Integration

DATA REPRESENTATION IN INDUSTRIAL SYSTEMS

Claudia Raibulet, Claudio Demartini
Dipartimento di Automatica e Informatica, Politecnico di Torino, Cso Duca degli Abruzz,24, Turin, Italy
Email: raibulet@athena.polito.it, demartini@polito.it

Key words: Industrial data models, STEP, industrial-specific language, XML.

Abstract: The specification and implementation of data related to heterogeneous resources are still actual problems in industrial systems in spite of the variety of data storage models and technologies available on the market today. And this is because industrial resources have associated proprietary specifications and implementations for their related data. The paper proposes two possible solutions to these problems. The first specifies a Distributed Repository Model that aims at providing a unified/common view of the heterogeneous resources in an industrial system. This approach makes use of the ISO 10303 standard. The second proposes the definition of an industrial-specific language that provides the syntax and the rules to create logical data models for industrial systems. It is based on the eXtensible Markup Language. Both approaches are independent of any implementation detail and/or storage-model architecture. A comparison of the two solutions is provided at the end of the paper.

1 INTRODUCTION

Nowadays industrial systems are distributed and heterogeneous. They contain resources provided by various manufacturers/vendors that define the resource related data in a proprietary format with a specific description and implementation. Moreover, in an industrial system the resources are spread over various geographical locations, and so is their related data. But, these aspects should be transparent to the user who interacts with the system. He/she should access and manipulate the system's data as if it were stored locally and in a unique format/model of storage.

This paper presents two solutions to the problems presented above. They are based on two different technologies: the ISO 10303 standard [ISO10303-1, STEP Standard] and the eXtensible Markup Language (XML) [Elliote, Goldfarb, XML].

The former defines the specification of a Distributed Repository Model (DRM) that aims to provide a uniform/unified view of the system's heterogeneous resources, independent of their proprietary characteristics and implementation details. The DRM model makes use of the ISO 10303, also known as STEP - STandard for the Exchange of Product Model Data. The conceptual model of DRM has been specified in a formal language named EXPRESS [ISO10303-11], which is one of the description methods [ISO10303-1] defined within STEP. An important characteristic of the DRM conceptual model is that it is independent of any implementation detail. The specification of DRM has been developed as part of the ESPRIT project "Network Oriented Application Harmonization" (NOAH).

Further, the paper proposes an implementation example of the DRM model. The example makes use of two of the implementation forms provided by STEP: the Part 21 file format [ISO10303-21] and the Standard Data Access Interface (SDAI) [ISO10303-22]. Part 21 defines the structure of the physical files where data is effectively stored. SDAI provides the mechanisms to access and manage DRM data. A main feature of SDAI is that it allows data instances to be manipulated as if the conceptual model were identical to the physical one.

The second approach proposes the definition of an industrial-specific language (IndML - Industrial Markup Language) as a solution for the description of heterogeneous resources in industrial systems. The language provides the syntax and the rules to create logical models for industrial systems. It defines the elements that describe an industrial system and its components, as well as the connections among them. Data models based on IndML are independent of any implementation detail and/or storage model architecture. Data instances are accessed and managed according to their description in IndML. The specification of IndML has been developed within the Cofin 2001 Project, which is supported by "Ministero Italiano dell'Istruzione, dell'Universita' e della Ricerca".

If such a language to be accepted in the industrial world, it should be based on a standard/technology available on the market and preferably already tested in other domains. There is a standard that provides powerful mechanisms to define such a language and that fulfills this requirement too: XML. XML is defined as a meta-markup language, which is used to design domain-specific markup languages, called XML applications [Elliote, Goldfarb]. IndML is an XML application.

The remainder of the paper is organized as follows. Section 2 presents an overview of STEP technologies used for the DRM model. Section 3 contains a description of the DRM model together with several aspects related to its implementation. Section 4 presents an overview of XML technology. Section 5 contains a description of the IndML language. A comparison of the two approaches is presented in Section 6. The summary of the paper is described with in Section 7.

2 THE STEP STANDARD

STEP standard aims to provide a neutral mechanism to represent product data throughout its lifecycle, independent of any particular implementation detail or constraint. In order to achieve this scope, STEP separates data models from implementation forms. This means that data models, defined using STEP technology, are independent of the various ways in which they can be implemented.

The standard provides several description methods and implementation forms. Description methods include languages and methods that are used to specify data models. Implementation forms define formats for data instances and values related to STEP-defined models, and mappings between data models and these formats.

2.1 EXPRESS Language

The most important description method defined by STEP is EXPRESS formal language. EXPRESS has been designed to specify conceptual data models. A data model provides the definition, the structure, the format, and the semantic of the data that describes a system. EXPRESS is a formal specification language that is used to describe the structure of data together with the constraints that may apply to it.

The language is based on the entity-attribute-relationship model, but it also embodies object-oriented features such as abstraction, inheritance, and modularisation.

2.2 Part 21 File Format

An EXPRESS specification model represents the formal description of a data model, while Part 21 is the physical format for storing data instances associated to the model. STEP Part 21 describes the structure of an ASCII file that contains values related to the entities and attributes defined in an EXPRESS data model. The file is organized in such a way that both reading and writing of data instances are possible. The content of Part 21 files is created according to EXPRESS data models and is associated to specific examples.

2.3 Standard Data Access Interface

The objective of SDAI is to allow applications to store, access, manipulate, and share data through a standard interface. To achieve this goal it provides mechanisms necessary to access data instances according to a logical model, therefore independently of the internal model of storage. Due to the fact that SDAI is based on a conceptual data model, different implementation approaches can be considered for data storage without any change being made to the interface/application level.

For data models defined in EXPRESS, SDAI provides the specification of a standard Application Program Interface (API) [JavaSDAI, STEP Tools]. Through this API, data is accessed as if the physical model of storage were identical to the logical model.

3 THE DRM MODEL

The primary goal of the DRM is to provide a general information model for data related to industrial systems, independent of any specific implementation aspect. DRM specification aims at unifying the conceptual representation of the devices within complex systems, enabling heterogeneous devices to be accessed and manipulated according to a common approach, regardless of their specific implementations. The advantage of this approach is that the model provides a unified view for the installation, the maintenance, and the management of distributed resources in an industrial system.

```
ENTITY device ABSTRACT SUPERTYPE OF (ONE OF (simple_device, complex_device));
      id                  :STRING;
      name                :STRING;
      model               :STRING;
      version             :STRING;
      parameters          :LIST [0:?] OF parameter;
UNIQUE
      id_rule             :id;
END_ENTITY;

ENTITY complex_device SUBTYPE OF (device);
      devices             :LIST [1:?] OF device;
      connections         :LIST [0:?] OF connection;
      description         :STRING;
END_ENTITY;
```

Figure 1: EXPRESS Definition for the Device Model

3.1 The DRM Conceptual Model

The conceptual model of DRM defines an abstract view of the data related to an industrial system in terms of an object-oriented paradigm: the model describes objects, their attributes, and the relationships among them. The basic abstract objects identified for the description of DRM are:

Function block: it is a software functional unit comprising an individual, named copy of a data structure and associated operations specified by a corresponding function block type. It has associated an algorithm described by an external reference (e.g., a state chart representation). The input of a function block is specified by zero or more input parameters. The output of a function block is specified by zero or more local variables used by its algorithm. It is implemented by one or more physical devices.

Local variables and parameters: they are software entities associated with a function block that keep the values used by the function block's algorithm. Local variables are defined within the scope of a function block. Parameters are input/output events that do not carry associated data (i.e., boolean values) or input/output variables.

Logical structure: it represents the way in which function blocks are connected within the system. The connections are specified in terms of connected parameters. There are two types of connections: one-to-one (a direct connection between an output port and an input port) and one-to-many (a direct connection between an output port and two or more input ports). Connections are implemented by physical networks.

Physical structure: it describes the way in which devices are connected within the system. One-to-one and one-to-many connections are specified in terms of ports.

3.2 The DRM Device Model

Figure 1 presents a simplified version of the device model as defined within DRM. The device entity is defined as a supertype of simple and complex devices. The main difference between a simple and a complex device is that the complex one can be logically and/or physically decomposed in a series of sub-devices. Thus, its definition contains a list of the devices, which compose its structure, and a list of the connections among these devices. Each device, simple or complex is identified by a unique id.

3.3 STEP Standard for DRM

Figure 2 shows a schema that summarizes the implementation process of DRM. The conceptual model has been specified using the EXPRESS formal language. The data instances related to the model are stored in Part 21 files, which have been generated using ECCO Toolkit [ECCO].

An object-oriented approach has been chosen for the implementation of the DRM model. Thus, the EXPRESS model has been translated into an object-oriented language. Java classes and interfaces equivalent to the EXPRESS model have been generated using ST-Developer Tool [ST-Developer]. Data stored in Part 21 files is accessed through the SDAI. A System Management Application [Raibulet], based on mobile agents, has been developed to access and to manage DRM data.

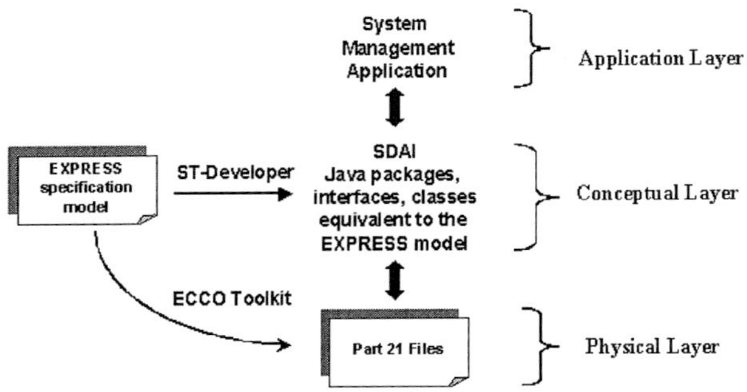

Figure 2: The Development Process of DRM

3.4 The XML Technology

XML is a platform-independent data representation technology that provides flexible and efficient methods for the description of the structure and the meaning of data, as well as for the exchange of data among various applications. Its prime scope has been to address the weaknesses of HTML, which does not support the description of data content and the management of remote information.

An important advantage provided by XML technology is that it defines the mechanisms necessary to share both data and its format among different applications. This fact facilitates the cooperation and the integration of data from different sources and/or applications. XML technology separates the structure and the content of data from its presentation, so that data results obtained from various data models can be presented in a unique/uniform way as if data were stored in the same format; alternatively, the same data can be presented in different formats according to the applications/users requirements. Further, XML is considered self-describing because it gives all the freedom to the application developer to define meaningful tags that describe the data.

3.5 XML Applications

XML is a meta-markup language. It defines the syntax and the rules necessary to define domain-specific markup languages, which are called XML applications. The development of an XML application consists in the definition of a vocabulary and a grammar, which establish the syntax and the semantics of a specific language. Both vocabulary and grammar respect the fundamental rules specified by XML. The vocabulary and the grammar of an XML application are defined within a Document Type Definition (DTD) [Elliote, Goldfarb, XML] or an XML Schema [Elliote, Goldfarb, XML].

4 INDUSTRIAL MARKUP LANGUAGE - INDML

This section proposes the definition of an industrial-specific language as a solution for the representation of heterogeneous data in industrial systems. The language named Industrial Markup Language - IndML is an XML application. There are at least two major reasons why XML has been chosen for the definition of IndML: XML is a non-proprietary format for data representation; and XML is implementation and storage-architecture independent.

Usually, data related to industrial devices is represented in proprietary formats. This aspect makes it difficult to integrate data related to heterogeneous devices in industrial systems. A proprietary format to be adopted by all the device manufacturers/vendors as a de facto standard for data representation in industrial systems is hard to achieve primarily for political reasons. IndML is a non-proprietary and a neutral format for industrial data. It defines a standard format for the representation and exchange of data. The chances of being accepted by the industrial community are high. The effort made by manufacturers/vendors to translate their data into an XML-based format would be the same for all. An alternative approach could be the implementation of mechanisms that translate the data from proprietary formats into IndML, and vice versa.

XML applications define data formats that are independent of any implementation detail and/or storage-architecture model. This gives a high degree of flexibility to the design and to the implementation of applications/systems that deal with XML defined data. XML data may be stored in relational and/or object-oriented databases [Cheng], or in XML files [Java XML]. It can be accessed and managed according to its XML-based representation and independent of the effective model of storage.

The definition of IndML language consists in the definition of a grammar and a vocabulary for the industrial domain. IndML aims to define the elements and the attributes necessary to describe data related to industrial systems from the input and output parameters of a resource to the complex resources and the connections among them. These elements and attributes are used to define logical models for actual industrial systems. They represent the vocabulary of the language. The grammar of IndML is established through the relations specified among the elements and the attributes of the language. The vocabulary and the grammar of IndML are specified in both DTD and XML Schema terms.

4.1 The IndML Device Model

Figure 3 shows a description of a complex device in DTD terms (left) and in XML Schema terms (right). In XML Schema it has been possible to specify that each complex device has associated a unique id. Further, it can be specified that the id field should respect a given regular expression: for instance, an id is composed by two letters and four digits (see Figure 3).

The elements and attributes defined in IndML are the result of a comparison and, in the same time, a joint of the available and already used industrial description languages and standards such as DeviceNet [Fowler], Proficus-DP [Fowler], IEC 61915 [Fowler], EDIF [Fowler], STEP, and so on. And this is because of two important reasons. The first is that IndML should be able to describe any industrial resource, device, parameter, attribute, etc. The second is related to the fact that IndML aims to become a unique and unified standard language for industrial data. Thus, it should be able to provide an equivalent representation for any other existing representation of industrial data.

The development of an industrial-specific language needs to have the cooperation of o large number of industrial manufacturers/vendors. Currently, we are developing a simple prototype of this language, which we intend to propose to the NOAH partners, as a starting point, for the development of an industrial language, which can be considered as an alternative solution to the DRM approach.

IndML.dtd

```
...
<!ELEMENT complex_device (id,
                          name,
                          model,
                          version,
                          parameter*,
                          device+,
                          connection*,
                          description
                          )>

<!ELEMENT id              (#PCDATA)>
<!ELEMENT name            (#PCDATA)>
...
```

IndMl.xsd

```
...
<xsd: element name="complex_device"
              type="complex_device_type"/>

<xsd:complexType name="complex_device_type">
   <xsd:sequence>
      <xsd:element name="id"          type="idType"/>
      <xsd:element name="name"        type="string"/>
      <xsd:element name="model"       type="string"/>
      <xsd:element name="version"     type="string"/>
      <xsd:element name="parameter"   type="parameterType"/>
      <xsd:element name="device"      type="deviceType"/>
      <xsd:element name="connection"  type="connectionType"/>
      <xsd:element name="description" type="string"/>
   </xsd:sequence>
</xsd:complexType>

<xsd:unique name="idUnique">
   <xsd:selector                      xpath="complex_device"/>
   <xsd:field                         xpath="@id"/>
</xsd:unique>

<xsd:simpleType name="idType">
   <xsd:restriction base="xsd:string">
      <xsd:pattern value="[A-Z]{2}d{4}/>
   </xsd:restriction>
</xsd:simpleType>
...
```

Figure 3: A complex_device Definition in DTD terms (left) and in XML Schema terms (right)

5 INDML VS. DRM

This section aims at comparing the two solutions presented above. The comparison focuses on the following aspects: technologies/standards used, model/language specification, interoperability, data exchange mechanisms, reusability, flexibility, and development costs.

5.1 Technologies/Standards

Both DRM and IndML are based on important standards/technologies. DRM makes use of STEP, which is the main international industrial standard for product data representation and exchange available today. IndML makes use of XML, which is an on fashion and more and more frequently used technology in IT today, from data storage and content management to the last trend towards Internet services. One of the most important features provided by XML is an easy-to-parse syntax for data representation in any type of application.

STEP is a well-defined standard, which was published in its initial release in 1994. It is still extending, trying to update its parts and to introduce new parts in order to meet the requirements of the IT market.

XML was published in its initial release in 1998, and it is still under development. It is a new and modern technology, which is "changing the way software is written, sold, and used" [Goldfarb]. The price paid to exploit the advantages of an enhanced technology is related to the fact that changes are occurring at a more rapid pace than they are in a stable standard such as STEP.

5.2 Model/Language Specifications

Both standards/technologies provide methods to specify and to represent data models. STEP EXPRESS is a formal specification language. It is a high level modeling language, which is used to define data models independent of any implementation detail. It is used to describe the structure of data and the constraints that may apply to it.

XML is a meta-markup language, which provides the mechanisms to define domain-specific languages. While EXPRESS defines specific data models, XML defines domain-specific languages, which are further used to define particular data models. The advantages provided by IndML are those provided by a language (a vocabulary and a grammar), while the advantages of DRM are those provided by a specific data model (a fixed set and combination of types and entities).

The EXPRESS language is definitely superior to a DTD, there is no doubt. But the XML Schema is comparable to EXPRESS. Both implement the abstraction, inheritance, and modularization concepts. An example of a difference between the two languages is that EXPRESS defines more aggregate types then XML Schema, while XML Schema provides a better support for the definition and manipulation of regular expressions within the definition of data models/languages. But both provide valid alternatives that can solve such problems.

A main advantage provided by XML technology is that it supports the exchange of both data and its structure, while STEP defines mechanisms to exchange only data. Thus, interoperability among various heterogeneous systems is better achieved using XML.

5.3 Interoperability

Interoperability is an important issue in distributed heterogeneous systems. Interoperability has three levels and all of them should be taken into consideration when developing complex systems. The three levels are: syntactic, semantic, and behavioral.

The syntactical interoperability regards the representation of data and its manipulation by various applications. Both standards/technologies ensure syntactical interoperability.

An elevated level of interoperability is the semantic one, which refers to the understanding of data. The complexity and the cost of achieving semantic interoperability are higher than for achieving syntactical interoperability, and this is because it requires content analysis.

The solution provided by STEP to achieve semantic interoperability is the definition of a set of Application Protocols (AP) [ISO10303-1] within the standard. These APs define and fulfill the requirements of an identified data application related to a specific need. Usually, applications based on STEP are developed on top of the APs and make use of their defined entities and types, which have standard meanings (due to the fact that they are published as parts of STEP standard).

XML attempts to overcome the barrier between the syntactic and the semantic levels of interoperability, in that it defines not only a standard syntax to represent and to exchange data, but also a standard framework to specify the semantic content of data. And semantic interoperability can be achieved by the standardization of the tags' and attributes' meaning especially in the areas that aim to establish automatic interoperability among their-based data/applications. The standardization of domain-specific element types and attributes achieves the semantically meaningful labeling of content in particular domains/industries.

Neither STEP, nor XML do not address the behavioral level of interoperability. However, behavioral interoperability can be implemented using platform-neutral programming languages, such as Java.

5.4 Data Exchange

Both standard/technologies provide a neutral format to exchange data instances. There are two advantages provided by XML in front of STEP. XML allows the exchange of both data and its structure. And XML has been designed to exchange data over the Internet. This does not mean that XML data cannot be exchanged over other types of environments. It means that XML data and structure can be easily exchanged over the Internet and among any type of applications.

5.5 Reusability

STEP standard separates conceptual models from implementation forms. This allows the reusability of various parts of an application and/or of an entire application. Further, the same conceptual model can be implemented in different ways. Suppose that initially, an object-oriented implementation has been chosen for the DRM conceptual model. Data instances are stored in Part 21 files. After a while, the requirements change, and the object-oriented implementation of DRM should be transformed into a relational database. The EXPRESS model and the Part 21 files are saved and transformed into relational terms without any loss of information and with a minimum effort.

XML technology introduces the DTD and the XML Schema concepts that define domain-specific vocabularies. The same DTD/XML Schema can be shared by different applications. XML is implementation and storage architectural independent. Moreover, XML separates the structure and the content from its presentation. This fact allows the integration of data from various sources and its presentation in a uniform way. Or, the same data can be presented in different ways.

5.6 Flexibility

Both technologies support the definition of conceptual/logical models that are independent of any implementation detail. This fact gives a high degree of flexibility to the design and to the implementation of the technologies-based applications.

For STEP-based applications, the link between a physical model and a conceptual model is implemented by the SDAI. Modifications carried out at the application level will not affect the storage model, and vice-versa. Moreover, data is accessed and manipulated as if the conceptual model were identical to the physical one.

XML is flexible and extensible. It provides flexible mechanisms to define meaningful tags for the description of data. XML-defined data is independent of any platform or application. Further, XML allows an incremental development of the technology-based applications.

5.7 Development Costs

STEP is an expensive standard in that documentation and tools are on charge. An immediate consequence of these aspects is that also STEP developers are expensive.

In contrast to STEP, XML is a free technology. In addition, it is very well documented and there are a lot of tools that help developers to implement XML-based applications. An immediate consequence of these aspects is that XML is used in more and more IT areas, such as software engineering, e-commerce, graphics, multimedia, etc., as well as in other domains, such as mathematics, chemistry, music, finance, and many others.

5.8 Instead of Conclusions

From the comparison presented in the previous section, results that both approaches provide advantages and disadvantages. The main advantage offered by DRM model regards the fact that this approach is based on a stable standard, that provides both description methods and implementation forms. Its main disadvantage is that it does not provide support for several main requirements of the IT market today (i.e., it was not designed to exchange data over the Internet, it does not allow the exchange of both data and its structure, etc). However, STEP is working to overcome these problems: for instance it is working on Part 28 "XML representation of EXPRESS schemas and data". Another disadvantage of the first solution proposed by the present paper is that STEP is expensive, and this happens in the era of open standards, free and well-documented specifications, documentations, and technical supports.

The IndML approach is based on a new and modern technology that provides a revolutionary way to represent and to exchange data among various applications, as well as over the Internet. XML has already gained acceptance in various domains, and a lot of standards/applications/tools aim to provide specifications and mechanisms able to integrate their technologies with XML. An example that confirms this fact is STEP and its Part 28. Then, why not developing a new industrial language from scratch that is not constrained by any previous specification and translation/compatibility problems, but which learns and maintains the advantages of the previous standards and, in the same time, uses actual technologies?

The main advantages offered by the IndML approach result from the mechanisms and concepts introduced by XML technology. The enhancement provided by XML and implicitly by IndML regards the possibility to exchange both data and its structure, the possibility to separate data from its presentation, the representation and exchange of data over Internet and among any type of applications, and so on. Moreover, IndML provides a domain-specific language, not just a data model. Using IndML, various industrial data models can be designed. Further, all these advantages are free of charge and also well documented. The most important disadvantage provided by IndML is related to the fact that it is based on a new technology, which is still under development and thus, changes within the standard are occurring frequently enough.

6 SUMMARY

This paper has presented two possible solutions to specify and to implement data related to heterogeneous industrial systems. Both solutions are based on the idea to separate conceptual/logical models from possible implementation forms and/or other implementation details. This approach gives a high degree of flexibility to the design and to the implementation of applications that deal with such data models.

The STEP based approach has been developed within ESPRIT Project NOAH. The DRM model has been validated on an actual example in an IAM-Pilot laboratory at CESI in Milan, Italy. The XML based approach aims to provide an alternative and enhanced solution to the DRM model. It is a prototype that can be used as a starting point to develop an industrial-specific language.

REFERENCES

Cheng, J., Xu, J., 2000, XML and DB2. In *Proceedings of the 16th International Conference on Data Engineering*, pp. 569 – 573

ECCO Toolkit - http://www.pdtec.de/

Elliote, R., H., 1999, XML Bible, IDG Books Worldwide, Inc.

Fowler, J.,1995, STEP for Data Management, Exchange and Sharing, Technology Appraisals Ltd.

Goldfarb, C.F., 2001, Prescod, P, The XML Handbook, Prentice-Hall, Inc.

ISO10303-1, 1994, Industrial automation systems and integration – Product data representation and exchange – Part 1: Overview and fundamental principles

ISO10303-11, 1994, Industrial automation systems and integration – Product data representation and exchange – Part 11: Description methods: The EXPRESS language reference manual, International Organization for Standardization, Switzerland, 1994

ISO10303-21, 1992, Industrial automation systems and integration – Product data representation and exchange – Part 21: Clear text encoding of the exchange structure

DIS/WD10303-22, 1996, Industrial automation systems and integration – Product data representation and exchange – Part 22: Implementation methods: Standard data access interface specification

Java – SDAI binding , http://www.mel.nist.gov/step/stage_0/wg11/javasdai.txt

Java XML, http://java.sun.com/xml/

Raibulet, C., Demartini, C., 2000, Mobile Agent Technology for the Management of Distributed Systems – a Case Study, Computer Networks, Elsevier Science B.V., Vol. 34, Nr. 6, December, pp. 823-830

STEP Tools, Inc., 1996, SDAI Library Reference Manual, New York

STEP Standard - http://www.nist.gov/sc4/www/stepdocs.htm

ST-Developer Tools – http://www.steptools.com

XML Specification – http://www.w3c.org/xml/

AN XML-BASED VIRTUAL PATIENT RECORDS SYSTEM FOR HEALTHCARE ENTERPRISES

Zhang Xiaoou, Pung Hung Keng
School of Computing, National University of Singapore, Singapore 119260
Email: iscp9150@nus.edu.sg, dcsphk@nus.edu.sg

Key words: Virtual patient record system, XML, HL7, XSLT, CDA, healthcare enterprises

Abstract: With the advent of shared care, there is a need to integrate patient records which spread in disparate information systems. In this paper, the design and implementation of an XML-based Virtual Patient Records System, XVPRS, is described. It uses World Wide Web to consolidate patient data across multiple organizations. The system uses XML-encoded HL7 as the application level protocol between legacy systems and XML as the main information format in the system itself. XVPRS also demonstrates how to transmit and process a clinical document using CDA. Our experience in XVPRS shows that using XML as the primary information format not only simplifies the development of single information system but also facilitates information integration among enterprise systems.

1 INTRODUCTION

Healthcare enterprises are undergoing a revolution due to the greater mobility of the population as a whole. This increased mobility results in patient's medical information being accumulated in a variety of locations. Furthermore, these patient records are kept in heterogeneous and yet autonomous Health Information Systems (HISs), which are usually implemented on different platforms and programming languages. The medical information of a patient is therefore scattered. This makes it extremely difficult for a single HIS to provide a seamless, comprehensive and cost-effective patient care. Clearly, there is a need for these HISs to collaborate and share information. One neat solution is based on the "virtual patient record" idea, through which the relevant patient information scattered in various systems are retrieved and composed dynamically, before presenting them to the users with an illusion that they are accessed from their own HIS. In other words, a virtual patient record is a unified set of data that exists in network in its aggregate form simultaneously populated from multiple HISs (David, et al., 1996).

Several systems have already been implemented to generate such virtual patient records. W3-EMRS (Isaac, et al., 1996(a); Isaac, et al., 1996(b); Wingerde, et al., 1996) is a medical record system enabling the share of patient data across multiple institutions. It is built on a three-layer architecture, which includes 1) a common information model, called Common Medical Record (CMR); 2) a visual presentation layer which describes the layout of data elements (e.g. a time-ordered list for patient medications) in the CMR; and 3) a screen rendering layer which implements the visual presentation in a user interface technology. CareWeb (John and Charles, 1997) is another implementation of the W3-EMRS architecture. It used Visual Basic complemented by ActiveX components for HL7 messaging. TeleMed (David, et al., 1998) is a JAVA/CORBA-based virtual patient record system. It dealt with healthcare components as objects and distributed them via the CORBAmed standard.

Although these systems can successfully integrate information, they still have some limitations. The use of COM or CORBA makes the information sender and receiver tightly coupled; consequently, if the implementation at one side changes, the other side will break. The different tiers of the systems are also tightly coupled. Programmers working at any of the tiers often have to write entire application just to test a specific functionality they are developing. The developer of the logic tier, for example, needs to write an application that simulates all the calls that the presentation tier may make. This results in a long development cycle and heavy burden of debugging (Bruce, 1999). Additionally, the text-based HL7 makes translation of HL7 to/from database manipulation language difficult and error-prone.

1.1 XML for Integration of Enterprise Information

XML has now opened a completely new approach and perspective in document storing, processing and message transmission. The separation of document structure (Document Type Definition (DTD) or schema), content and presentation (stylesheet) in XML allows these three entities be independently designed, created and managed (Chronaki, et al., 2000). This will further reduce management overhead and time spent on development. The separation of data from presentation enables us to present multiple views of the same data by using different stylesheets; this will also lead to a seamless integration of data from diverse sources without changing the presentation. The separation of structure from content allows us to exchange information among heterogeneous systems by using a consensus DTD. If the XML message transmitted among organizations conforms to the predefined DTD, the sender does not need to make any assumption about what will happen once the message is received. Instead it only cares about that the message sent out is in conformance to the pre-agreed DTD. Furthermore, the receiver can change or modify its own implementation at any time without breaking the sender, so long as it can still understand the messages to receive. This loosely coupled feature improves the interoperability among organizations. If any organization wishes to join the information exchanging group, the only thing it should ensure is to be able to emit XML messages that can be understood by other group members (Bruce, 1999; Andrew and John). Some leading organizations in standardizing healthcare information and communication have begun their work on using XML as the main encoding syntax, such as Health Level Seven (HL7) (HL7, 1999) and American Society for Testing and Materials (ASTM).

1.2 Overview of XVPRS

XVPRS is a system which can consolidate clinical data across multiple heterogeneous electronic medical records (EMRs). It is designed for use by a Specialist Diabetic Clinic within a loosely coupled healthcare enterprise consisting of several hospitals, polyclinics, and clinics of private practicians in Singapore. Based on the paper-based medical record in the clinic, XVPRS supports the share of patient record data (e.g. test results, patient history) and clinical documents (e.g. visit notes). The data coming from different sources can be integrated and presented as a common document to the physicians. The application level protocol used is the HL7 V2.3. Instead of using its text-based format, we used the XML encoding provided by HL7 as supplementary messaging syntax (HL7 XML Special Interest Group, 2000). The clinical documents for sharing are encoded in XML format based on the HL7 Clinical Document Architecture (CDA) (Health Level Seven, 2000). Not only is XML used in communicating with external healthcare information systems, it is also used throughout the XVPRS as an internal message format. The XVPRS is implemented in Java; it is functional and will soon be deployed for a clinical field trial. The application logics of XVPRS are encapsulated into JavaBean; Serlvet is used to send/receive messages and JSP is used to construct user interface. XML enabled browser is used as the user front end.

2 ARCHITECTURE

XVPRS architecture consists of three layers as shown in Figure 1: the screen rendering layer, the data integration layer and the Common Medical Record (CMR) layer. There are also several gateways mediate transformations of data among these layers (Isaac, et al., 1996(b)). The CMR is a common information model that lets XVPRS be independent of the site database design. The CMR layer specifies what concepts are allowed to show to the user and the relationships among these concepts. It also defines a set of terminologies for all corresponding terms from the legacy EMRs to map to. Our CMR, implemented using HL7, supports patient previous history, current symptoms, drug allergies, laboratory tests, and visit notes.

The second layer in XVPRS is the data integration layer, which is different from the W3-EMRS's visual presentation layer. In W3-EMRS, visual presentation layer does two things: 1) extracting relevant data which may be the same type or may have same semantics from all the result messages coming from legacy EMRs and 2) based on the meaning of these data, deciding which layouts should be used to present them and how to present them. Those layouts will be translated into a specific user interface technology in the screen rendering layer. When a user in W3-EMRS wants to view the data in another layout, or a new layout is introduced to show the data, both the visual presentation layer

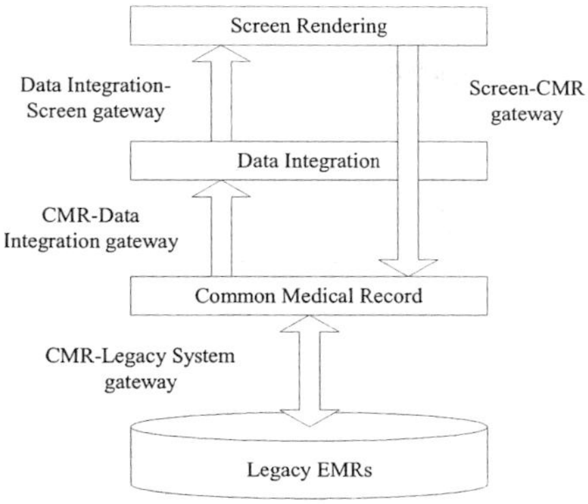

Figure 1: Three layers of XVPRS

and the screen rendering layer need to be changed. In XVPRS, we use XML as the message syntax, which separates data from presentation. Then we can integrate all the data, which is still in XML format, in the data integration layer, while leaving the job of presenting these data to the screen rendering layer. The selection of relevant contents from the integrated XML document and show of these contents in a preferred layout are considered only in the screen rendering layer. The advantage of using XML document here is that once the user interface is required to change, only the screen rendering layer needs to be changed, other layers will not be affected. Hence, in the data integration layer we just create an XML document which integrates all the data in returned messages to be ready for use in the screen rendering layer.

Web is our choice of technology for implementing the screen rendering layer. That means all the patient data is shown in HTML. In healthcare domain, there is also a great demand for presenting and printing clinical document in a 'good manner' due to the large amount of the documents created. To fulfill this requirement, we provide PDF as the alternative choice for users to view and print clinical documents. To present data in various formats, we only need to apply different stylesheets, each of which can generate a specific rendering language, to the same XML data transmitted from data integration layer. However, in W3-EMRS, the screen rendering layer needs to translate visual layouts into different user interface technologies.

Several gateways are used to translate data among these layers. Screen-CMR gateway translates the user inputs, which are in local data format, to CMR. CMR-Legacy system gateway translates HL7 queries that refer to the CMR information model into queries in the local database manipulation language or translates the local data into CMR and creates the required HL7 messages. CMR-Data integration gateway creates an XML document to include all the XML messages received. Data integration-Screen gateway uses stylesheets to render XML message to several kinds of languages such as HTML and PDF. Among all these layers, only CMR-Legacy system gateway needs to be rewritten for each distinct EMR.

In XVPRS, we use XML intensively throughout (Figure 2): data can be stored in XML database, exchanged in XML message, processed in XML format and displayed by rendering XML messages.

The aforementioned layers and gateways divide the operations on XML message into three parts. The CMR layer corresponds to XML generation. No matter where the legacy data is stored, either in object-oriented database or in relational database or in plain text file, the data is encapsulated in XML message after it goes through the CMR layer. At the data integration layer, DOM, XSLT and other technologies are used to transform one XML structure to another. This layer corresponds to XML processing. At the last layer, XSLT is used as main technology to render XML on various types of clients. This layer is responsible for XML presenting.

As we can see in Figure 2, when XML is used within organization, the implementation of each XML layer is independent of others. When XML is used as a protocol among organizations, different kinds of enterprises can easily communicate with each other. Hence, XML offers significant benefits for enterprise systems development and enterprise information integration.

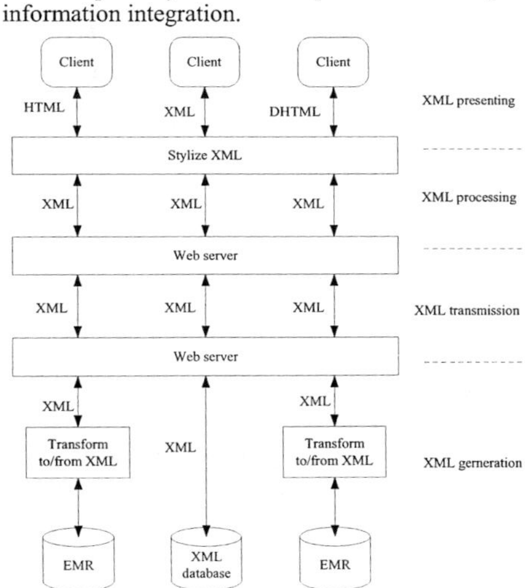

Figure 2: XML in XVPRS

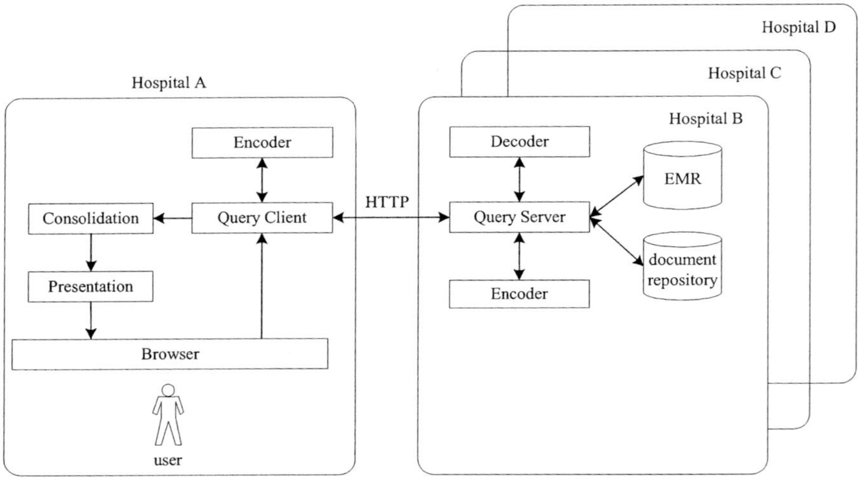

Figure 3: Components of XVPRS

3 IMPLEMENTATION

The XVPRS implemented consists of the following functional components: information query and transmission, consolidation of data and presentation of data (Figure 3).

3.1 Information Query and Transmission

The user chooses from browser the type of information he/she wants to query for a given patient. This user request is then sent to Query Client which is a servlet on the web server waiting for the user's invocation. After receiving the user request, Query Client generates the relevant data required for that query and calls the corresponding template in Encoder to package these data into an HL7 message. Together with the request, Query Client also gets from user a list of hospitals that the user wishes to query. Query Client then sends, using HTTP protocol, the generated HL7 message to these hospitals. Query Client mediates among multiple sites and the end user. It basically implements the functions of the Screen-CMR gateway.

Our implementation corresponding to the CMR-Legacy system gateway is the Query Server, which is also a servlet. After receiving an XML-based HL7 message from Query Client, Query Server calls Decoder to translate the message into the format the local medical system can operate on. The local system then constructs a database manipulation language, in our case, SQL for simple data and XPath for CDA document, to query its own underlying EMR. The results are translated again into XML-based HL7 message through Encoder and are sent back, by Query Server, to Query Client.

The Encoder and the Decoder are two JavaBeans that are responsible for translating local data structure to/from XML encoded HL7 message. These two components are independent of any EMR.

3.2 Consolidation

After the Query Server sends back the EMRs' responses, the XML generation part is complete. Next, the system needs to consolidate the returned results. This part corresponds to the XML processing in Figure 2. Query Client forwards all the response messages returned by the Query Server to a consolidation program. Since HTTP is stateless, to indicate which query these messages refer to, the user query information is also forwarded together with these messages. In the consolidation program, messages are merged in an XML document according to their types and the user query is also inserted into the resultant document. This merged XML document acts as a data warehouse, which contains the query sent out by the user and all the results for his query. The presentation layer can then select any data in this warehouse for display.

3.3 Presentation

The merged XML document mentioned above could contain several HL7 messages, each of which in turn could contain several CDA documents, test results or patient history information, depending on the query type. To present these data, we adopt both DOM and XSLT. DOM is used to generate a table which gives some basic information on the CDA documents returned; XSLT is used to present test results, patient history and CDA document itself.

3.3.1 Render XML Document Using DOM

We use DOM to generate a table that lists all the CDA documents' sources plus their creation dates, and provides buttons to display CDA documents. DOM parses each HL7 message first, and then picks up CDA documents together with their creation dates and sources. This information is used in generating the HTML table. Once a user wishes to view a CDA document, he/she just clicks on the button. Upon which, the CDA document embedded as hidden field in this button is sent to server-side to be processed for displaying. Parsing and extracting information are implemented in JavaBean; JSP is used to generate HTML.

3.3.2 Render XML Document Using XSLT

The transformation of XML document by XSLT can be carried out either on the server-side or on the client-side. Since a CDA document is itself an XML document, we use XSLT to render it. To display CDA document in either HTML format or PDF format, we must have an XML parser, an XSLT processor and an XSL FO engine. Although the XML parser and the XSLT processor are available in IE5.0 or above, the XSL FO engine can only run on server. Thus, we rendered CDA document only on the server-side. We used Cocoon1.8 (Apache Software Foundation Cocoon, 1999) which supports XML parser, XSLT processor and XSL FO, to generate PDF on the server.

Presenting patient history is done on the client-side. In our system, patient history includes three classes of information: previous history, current symptoms and drug allergies. Although they are included in one HL7 message, we do not display them all in one view. Instead we make each class of information one view and display each of these views separately. We could have gone the conventional route and use server-side JSP. In that case, each JSP page is responsible for generating one table for one view. The drawbacks of this approach would be that three pages would need to be maintained and changing views would require a round-trip to the server. In XVPRS, which uses XML and XSLT on client-side, when a user clicks a button to change from one view to another, different stylesheets are applied to different parts of the XML message. In this way, data is sent to the client only once without the need for a round-trip to the server (Richard, et al., 2000).

4 SHARE OF CLINICAL DOCUMENTS

Routine operations in hospitals involve many clinical documents. Different from fragmentary data, such as patient name, age, blood pressure, a clinical document is an assemblage of clinical information and these data should be transmitted and presented as a whole. XVPRS used HL7 CDA to share clinical documents among hospitals. HL7 CDA is a document markup standard that specifies the structure and semantics of clinical documents for the purpose of exchange. A clinical document marked up using CDA standard is called a CDA document.

4.1 Structure and Content of Clinical Documents

So far there is no standard defining the contents of each type of clinical document. What contents can be included in a document is decided by individual hospital. For example, a document named "progress report" may include patient's history in one hospital but may not in another.

Although CDA is a specification that defines the structure and semantics of clinical documents, the latest issued standard, CDA Level One, provides markups only for document structure. Content constraints based on document types will be provided by CDA Level Two and CDA Level Three. Even in CDA Level One, no further restrictions are given about what structure should be used for content. For example, the physical examination can be marked up in either "<section><paragraph><content>" or in "<section><list><item><content>". Therefore when writing the XSLT stylesheet for CDA document, we must guarantee that the XSLT stylesheet has information on how to display every markup that could appear in the document, otherwise some parts of document may not be shown.

4.2 Storage of CDA Documents

Usually each hospital stores clinical documents in a document repository, which is separated from the EMR. Since a CDA document is an XML string, we store CDA documents in an XML database. This type of database uses XML document as its fundamental unit of storage. When saving an XML document, the database will ask for document schema and store the DOM of the document. With the help of DOM and schema, query to a portion of an XML document is very efficient. In XML database, XPath is usually taken as the query language. As the data in and out XML database is in XML format, there is no need to have encoder or decoder to do the transformation job.

4.3 Multimedia in CDA Documents

Sometimes a clinical document may have multimedia data in it, such as an image. When the document is marked up into a CDA document, the image cannot be put into CDA. Instead we added a markup "<observation_media>" under the markup which is associated with the image. The attribute or child node of "<observation_media>" indicates the place to find the image. When the document is required, program will check whether there is any "<observation_media>" markup in the document. If there is, the program will get the image using the indication and send the image with the document. Using this approach, a CDA document can contain more than one multimedia objects, and they may be of any type.

4.4 Sending CDA Documents in an HL7 Message

From the perspective of an HL7 V2.x message, a CDA document is a multimedia object, to be exchanged as a Multipurpose Internet Mail Extensions (MIME) package, encoded as an encapsulated data type (ED). Multimedia objects referenced by the CDA should also be put into the MIME packages (Health Level Seven, 2000).

4.5 Display CDA Documents

To display a CDA document consisting multimedia information, we first parse the HL7 string and use its DOM to find the node which contains the MIME package. Using the boundary in the package and the MIME type, we can separate a CDA document from multimedia objects it references to. For the CDA document, we decode it back to XML string, which can then be used for queries. For the multimedia objects, we store them to memory with their encoded formats intact.

When a user selects a CDA document to view at client-side, the control goes back to the server. The program in the server checks whether the selected document has multimedia objects associated with it. If it has, the objects will be inserted into the document. We directly present GIF images or JPEG images to the user, while provide the URL to other type of objects as hyperlinks. For example, when the object is a DICOM image, the user can view the image by clicking on the link in the document, a DICOM viewer will be invoked to display the image. All the objects referenced are saved on server right before they are inserted into the document. To avoid one document's objects overwriting the other document's objects, we use a timestamp as part of the file name. After saving the objects, we insert the URLs of the objects to the document.

5 SECURITY

Security is crucial for system sending sensitive information over Internet. But as a prototype system, we did not consider security in XVPRS as critically as we should. Currently we just use the simple username-password pair for authentication.

Two primary requirements about security are encryption to keep confidential information private, and digital signatures to provide authenticity, integrity and non-repudiation (Ed, et al., 2001). XML encryption and XML signature are two new security initiatives designed to fulfill these requirements. The beauty of these two standards is that they have the ability to encrypt or sign only specific portions of the XML tree rather than the complete document. This flexibility is critical in situations where it is important to ensure the integrity of certain portions of an XML document, while leaving open the possibility for other portions of the document to change. In the future, we will include these two mechanisms to XVPRS.

6 CONCLUSION

Using XML as the main message syntax in information system brings many benefits. Information in heterogeneous applications, enterprises and databases can be easily exchanged; data from disparate sources can be effectively combined and different styles and presentations of the information can be efficiently generated. All these illustrate that XML is very suitable for use in enterprise information integration and will become a prevalence technology in this area.

REFERENCES

Andrew, L. and John, M. XML, Web Services, and the .NET Framework, http://www.vbxml.com/xml/articles/dotnetintro/.

Apache Software Foundation Cocoon, 1999. Apache Software Foundation. http://xml.apache.org/cocoon1/index.html.

Bruce, K., 1999. XML Makes Object Models More Useful. http://www.informationweek.com/741/41adxml.htm.

C. Chronaki, P. Lelis, M. Tsiknakis and S. C. Orphanoudakis, 2000. XML Technology in support of Clinical Protocols for Teleconsultation. Mednet 2000, 22-24 November 2000, Brussels, Belgium.

David, W. F., James, E. G., Eugene, M. G. and Torsten, A. S., 1998. TeleMed: Development of a Java/CORBA-based Virtual Electronic Medical Record. *RSNA'98.*

David, W. F., Richard, L. P., David, G. K. and James, L. C., 1996. Experiences with a Distributed Virtual Patient Record System. *1996 Fall AMIA.*

Ed, S., Paul, M. and Carlisle, A., 2001. An introduction to XML digital signatures. http://www.xml.com/pub/a/2001/08/08/xmldsig.html.

F.J. van Wingerde, Jiri, S., Peter, K., Peter, S., Charles, S., David, R., Shawn, M., G. Octo Barnett and Isaac S. K., 1996. Using HL7 and the World Wide Web for Unifying Patient Data from Remote Databases. *Proceedings 1996 Fall AMIA 643-647.*

Health Level Seven, 1999. Health Level Seven, Version 2.3. Health Level Seven.

Health Level Seven, 2000. Clinical Document Architecture Framework, Release 1.0. Health Level Seven.

HL7 XML Special Interest Group. HL7 Recommendation: Using XML as a Supplementary Messaging Syntax for HL7 Version 2.3.1. Health Level Seven.

Isaac, S. K., Philip, G., James, F., Christopher, C. and Peter, S., 1996 (a). Building National Electronic Medical Record Systems via the World Wide Web. *JAMIA 1996 May-Jun;3(3):191-207.*

Isaac, S. K., F.J. van Wingerde, James, C. F., Christopher, C., Peter, K., Shawn, M., Henry, C., David, R., Charles, S., Octo, B. and Peter, S., 1996 (b). Sharing Electronic Medical Records Across Multiple Heterogeneous and Competing Institutions. *Proceedings 1996 Fall AMIA 608-612.*

John, D. H. and Charles, S., 1997. Virtual Consolidation of Boston's Beth Israel and New England Deaconess Hospitals via the World Wide Web. *1997 AMIA Fall Symposium*

Richard, A., Mark, B., Michael, K., Steven, L., Brian, L., Didier, M., Stephen, M., Nik, O., Bruce, P., Jonathan, P., Peter, S. and Kevin, W., 2000. *Professional XML.* WROX.

USING FULL MATCH CLASSES FOR SELF-MAINTENANCE OF MEDIATED VIEWS

Valéria Magalhães Pequeno, Vânia Maria Ponte Vidal
Computer Department, Federal University of Ceara
Campus do Pici, Caixa Postal 12166, Fortaleza, Ce, Brasil
Email: vmp@fct.unl.pt, vvidal@lia.ufc.br

Key words: Data Integration, Mediator, Materialized View Maintenance

Abstract: Sharing information among multiple heterogeneous and autonomous data sources has emerged as a new and strategic requirement in modern enterprises. In this paper, we use a mediator-based approach for integrating multiple heterogeneous data sources. The mediator supports materialized views (mediated views) which are stored in a centralized repository. The queries on the view can be processed directly from the integrated view, with no need for accessing the remote sources. The main difficulty with this approach is to maintain the consistency of the materialized view with respect to the source databases updates. Usually, match classes are not self-maintainable. In a prior paper, we presented a technique for self-maintenance of full match classes. In this work, we show how to make other types of match classes self-maintainable by using full match classes as auxiliary classes.

1 INTRODUCTION

Over the last years, the number of applications requiring integrated access to multiple heterogeneous and autonomous data sources has increased immensely. The data integration problem has been strongly studied in the literature (Batini et al., 1986; Zhou et al., 1996).

Several integration system architectures are based on mediators. A mediator is a facility which supports an integrated view over multiple data sources (also called mediated integrated view). A schema for the integrated view is available from the mediator. Thus, queries and updates can be executed using that schema. The mediated integrated view can be either virtual or materialized. In the virtual approach, the data remains in the local sources. For that reason, queries submitted to the mediator are decomposed at run time into sub-queries on the local sources. The results from these sub-queries are translated, filtered and merged, and then, the final answer is returned. In the materialized approach, information from each data source is extracted in advance and then, translated, filtered, merged and stored in a centralized repository. Thus, when a query arrives, it can be evaluated directly from the repository, and no access to the local data sources is required. Therefore, queries can be answered quickly and efficiently since the information is directly available. However, a critical point in the materialized approach is the following: views must be updated in order to reflect changes in the local data sources.

Basically, there are two strategies for materialized view maintenance: re-materialization and incremental maintenance. In the re-materialization strategy, all the view's data are re-computed at pre-established times. On the other hand, in the incremental maintenance strategy (Zhou et al., 1996), a mechanism periodically modifies only part of the view's data to reflect the updates occurred in the local sources. Although incremental maintenance is often significantly more efficient than re-materialization, it still can be expensive, since it may require querying remote source. There are situations where it is necessary to fetch additional data from the local data sources in order to determine what view updates are necessary, to correctly maintain the view, in response to a data source update. In view maintenance, a view is said to be *self-maintainable* (Gupta et al., 1996) when no additional queries over data sources are required to maintain that view. Self-maintainability is an important characteristic for mediated views, because it may be slow to access remote data sources or even impossible to do it, since those sources may be not always available.

Our work use a mediator-based approach for integrating multiple heterogeneous data sources. The mediator supports materialized views. In our integrating strategy, *Correspondence Assertions* (CA) (Vidal and Winslett, 1994) are used to formally specify the relationship between the mediator's schema and the source databases' schemas. In this way, the mediator's correspondence assertions semantically specify how the mediator's objects are materialized from source objects. Our formalism is advantageous in providing a better understanding of the mediator semantics and to automate some aspects of data integration.

In this paper, we focus on the problem of self-maintainability of a special type of classes, the *match classes*. These classes correspond to the relational model's outerjoin view defined by a "natural outer-equijoin in the key attributes" (Gupta et al., 1997). Recently, this type of classes has gained importance because they are common in integrated views. However, in most situations, as we discuss in this paper, match classes are not self-maintainable. In a prior work, we presented a strategy to perform the self-maintenance of a special type of match class, called *full match classes* (FMC), which corresponds to relational views defined by a "natural full outer-equijoin in the keys attributes". In this paper, we show that other types of match classes can easily become self-maintainable using FMCs as auxiliary classes.

The remainder of this paper is organized as follows. In Section 2, we present the basic concepts of the object model used for modelling the view schema and the source DBs schema. In Section 3, we give an informal overview of the idea behind this paper and contrast previous approaches with one presented here. In Section 4, we present the formalism we use to specify the relationship between the mediated view schema and the source databases schemas. In Section 5, we show how any type of match class can easily become self-maintainable using a full match class as auxiliary class. Finally, in Section 6, we present our concluding remarks.

2 TERMINOLOGY

In this section, we present the basic concepts of the object model needed for the remainder of the paper. According to the object model described in ODMG-97 (Cattell et al., 1997), we distinguish objects from literals as follows: objects represent real world entities and have unique identifiers(OID), while literals are special types of objects that have no identifiers.

An object is an instance of a class. Thus, classes serve as templates for their instances. All classes have a extent, which is defined as the set of all instances of a class at a given moment. There are two types of classes: the *object classes*, whose instances are objects; and the *literal classes*, whose instances are literals. A class definition is a tuple <*properties*, *operations*> that specifies the set of properties and the set of operations that are common to all instances of the class.

A property of a given class can be defined as a functional relationship between objects of that class and the objects (or literals) of the property's domain. Depending upon the type of its domain, the properties can be classified into *attributes* and *relationships*. The domain of an attribute is a literal class. For instance, the attribute **employeeName**, whose domain is the class STRING, is an attribute that relates an object of the class EMPLOYEE with an instance of the class STRING, which is a literal. On the other hand, the domain of a relationship is an object class. For example, the property **div** of the class EMPLOYEE, whose domain is the class DIVISION (Dom (**div**)= DIVISION), relates the objects of the class EMPLOYEE with the object of class DIVISION.

Properties also can be classified into *singlevalued* and *multivalued.* A class property is denoted singlevalued when each instance of the class can be related to at most one object of the property's domain. Therefore, the value of this property is an atomic object, which is an instance of the property's domain. A class property is denoted multivalued when each instance of the class can be associated to many instances of the property's domain. Therefore, the value of a multivalued property is a collection of objects, which are instances of the property's domain.

An object-oriented schema is a set of definitions of classes that serve as templates to generate the application domain objects. In the diagram of Figure 1, rectangles represent classes; single arrows represent singlevalued relationships and double arrows represent multivalued relationships.

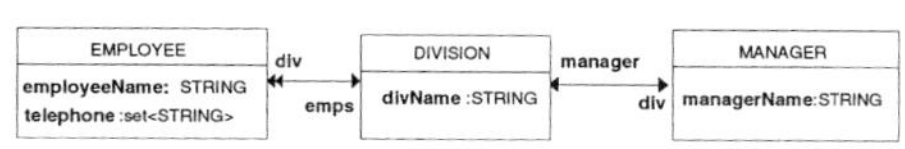

Figure 1: An object oriented schema

Objects also can be related through paths connecting two or more properties. Taking, for instance, the schema of Figure 1, one can observe that an employee is related to his/her division manager through the path **div • manager**. Now, we formally define path as:

Definition 1 (Path) *Let* $\mathbf{C}_1$, $\mathbf{C}_2$, ..., $\mathbf{C}_{n+1}$ *be classes of a schema and* $\boldsymbol{p}_1$, ..., $\boldsymbol{p}_n$ *be properties such that* $\boldsymbol{p}_i \in props(\mathbf{C}_i)$ *and* $Dom(\boldsymbol{p}_i) = \mathbf{C}_{i+1}$, $1 \leq i \leq n$. *Therefore,* $\boldsymbol{p}_1 \bullet \boldsymbol{p}_2 \bullet \ldots \bullet \boldsymbol{p}_n$ *is a path of* $\mathbf{C}_1$. *This means that the instances of* $\mathbf{C}_1$ *are related to the instances of* $\mathbf{C}_{n+1}$ *through the path* $\boldsymbol{p}_1 \bullet \boldsymbol{p}_2 \bullet \ldots \bullet \boldsymbol{p}_n$.

3 MOTIVATING EXAMPLES, PREVIOUS APPROACH AND OUR APPROACH

This section gives an informal overview, based on a simple example, of the idea behind this paper and contrasts previous approaches with ours.

Consider the two database schemas $\mathbf{DB}_1$ and $\mathbf{DB}_2$ and the view schemas $\mathbf{V}_1$ and $\mathbf{V}_2$ shown in Figure 2.

The view class STUDENT_v is object preserving[1] (Guerrini et al., 1997), where each object in STUDENT_v is semantically equivalent to an object of the class STUDENT. If a student is also an employee, then there will be only one corresponding object in the view class STUDENT_v for which the values of the properties $\mathbf{name}_v$ and $\mathbf{telephone}_v$ are defined from the corresponding object in STUDENT, and the values of the properties $\mathbf{wage}_v$ and $\mathbf{divName}_v$ are defined from the corresponding object in EMPLOYEE. If a student is not an employee, then there will be one corresponding object in the view class STUDENT_v, which has null value for the properties $\mathbf{wage}_v$ and $\mathbf{divName}_v$.

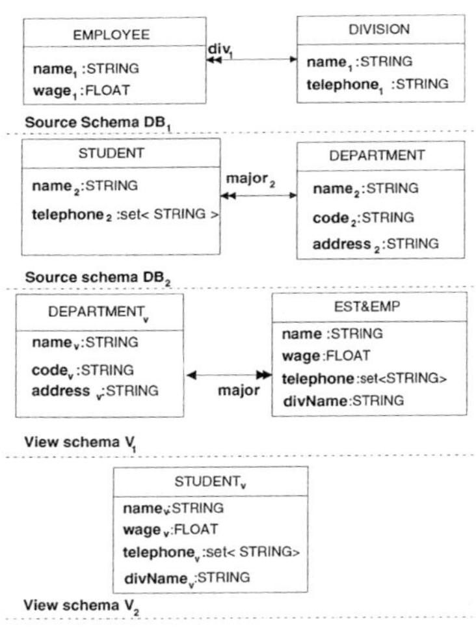

Figure 2: Source databases schemas $\mathbf{DB}_1$ and $\mathbf{DB}_2$ and views schemas $\mathbf{V}_1$ and $\mathbf{V}_2$

[1]A view class is an object preserving when each object in the view is semantically equivalent to an object in a source database. Two objects $\mathbf{e}_1$ and $\mathbf{e}_2$ are semantically equivalent ($\mathbf{e}_1 \equiv \mathbf{e}_2$) if $\mathbf{e}_1$ and $\mathbf{e}_2$ represent the same object in the real world.

3.1 Incremental Maintenance of Materialized View

Now we will discuss the issue of incrementally maintaining the materialized view $\mathbf{V}_2$. Figure 3 shows the basic architecture for incremental view maintenance that has been used in many projects (Zhuge et al., 1996).

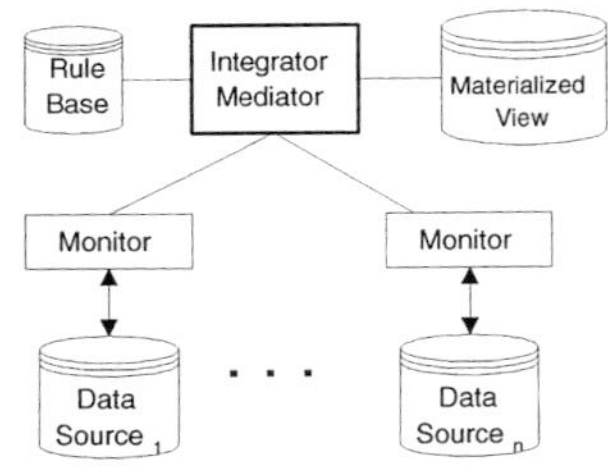

Figure 3: Architecture for incremental view maintenance

At each source, a monitor is responsible for identifying changes in the source data and notifying them to the warehouse. At the warehouse, the integrator mediator receives the source changes and correctly maintains the materialized view to reflect changes to the source DB. Several works present algorithms and formalisms for specifying incremental propagation of updates from source data to views, including (Gupta et al., 1993; Zhou et al., 1996). Reference (Zhou et al., 1996) uses a rule base in the integrated view for supporting the propagation of incremental update at the source DB to the warehouse. The rules allow a relatively declarative style of programming, thus increasing reusability and maintainability.

In our example, to maintain the view class STUDENT_v, we need rules for dealing with insertion, deletion and modifications of objects in the bases classes EMPLOYEE and STUDENT, and also rules for dealing with modifications in the base class DIVISION. Figure 4 informally describes the rule for dealing with insertions in STUDENT. According to this rule, the insertion of an object **s** in STUDENT will require the insertion of a corresponding object in the view class STUDENT_v, (there is a one to one correspondence between the objects in STUDENT_v and the objects in STUDENT). However, before doing that, we should first verify whether already exists an object **e** in EMPLOYEE such that **s** *match* **e** ($\mathbf{s} \equiv \mathbf{e}$). If it does exist, the object resulting from the fusion of **s** and **e** is inserted in STUDENT_v. Otherwise, the object created from **s** is inserted in STUDENT_v.

Using the architecture of figure 3, a view is self-maintainable with respect to an update τ in the source database **D** if the view can be updated using the old

When insert(**s**) in STUDENT
/* **s** is the inserted object in STUDENT*/
Then If there exists **e** in EMPLOYEE such that **s** ≡ **e** then
Insert an object **s'** in STUDENT_v such that **s'** is the fusion of **s** and **e**
Else
Insert an object **s'** in STUDENT_v such that **s'** ≡ **s**

Figure 4: Rule for STUDENT_v maintenance with respect to insertions in STUDENT

view value and the changes τ, without accessing any base relations. Therefore, the view class STUDENT_v is not self-maintainable with respect to insertions in STUDENT, since it involves querying the base class EMPLOYEE for matching objects in EMPLOYEE with the inserted object.

Object matching is an important aspect of data integration and it can be expensive to compute. Most systems (Widjojo et al., 1990) assumes that a universal key is available for performing object matching. References (Zhou et al., 1996; Papakonstantinou et al., 1996; Widjojo et al., 1990) consider the problem of object matching in contexts where universal keys are not available. In this work, we do not address this problem and, as proposed in (Zhou et al., 1996), we assume that match criteria is specified by a high-level mechanisms and that defines 1:1 correspondences between the objects in families of corresponding classes.

3.2 Our Approach

In our integrating strategy, we extend the architecture depicted in Figure 3, in the following way (see Figure 5): At each local data source S, an active module, named local mediator, with local event-condition-action rules (ECA rules), is responsible for identifying changes in the data of S, and for sending to the integrator mediator the sequence of updates to be performed in the materialized view.

In our approach, the maintenance process consists of two steps:

1. When a relevant[2] update τ occurs in a local source **S**, a local rule is fired, sending the integrator mediator the sequence of updates which should be performed in the view to reflect the changes in **S**.
2. Periodically, the integrator mediator processes the requested updates, hence, updating the views classes.

[2]An update in a local source **S** is relevant to a view if the new state of **S** becomes inconsistent with respect to the state of the view.

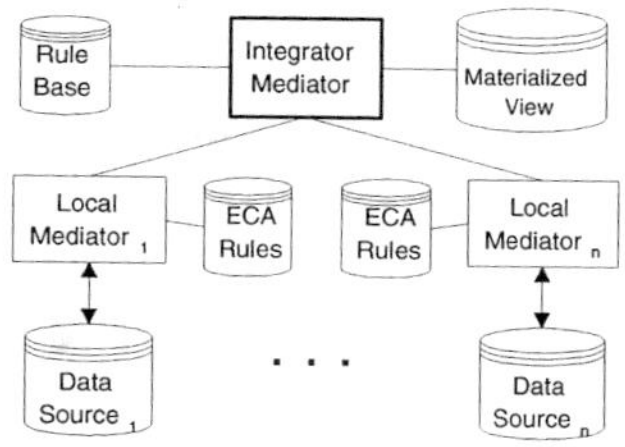

Figure 5: Architecture of the proposed integrating mechanism

In our approach, a class is self-maintainable with respect to an update τ in the local source **S** if, without accessing any base relations, the view can be updated using the old view value, the changes τ, and any information from the local source **S**. The advantage of our approach, is that, when additional information from the local source **S** is needed, it can be locally extracted from **S** and sent to the integrator mediator. Avoiding, in that way, later access to the source DB. As we show in (Vidal and Pequeno, 2000), our approach can manage self-maintenance of Full Match Classes (FMC). In Section 5, we present how other types of math classes can easily become self-maintainable using FMCs as auxiliary classes.

4 USING CORRESPONDENCE ASSERTIONS FOR SPECIFYING THE SEMANTICS OF MEDIATED VIEWS

The Correspondence Assertions (CAs) of a view class formally specify the relationships between the view class and its base classes. Correspondence assertions are special types of integrity constraints that are used to assert the correspondence among schemas components. In this work, we use the view correspondence assertions to specify how the view objects are synthesized from the base class objects. In this way, the mediator's correspondence assertions semantically specify how the integrated view objects are materialized from sources' objects. Our formalism is advantageous in providing a better understanding of the semantics of mediated views, and in helping to automate some aspects of data integration.

In the case of match classes, since they are object-preserving classes, their relationships with the base classes can be specified by the following three types of Correspondence Assertions: Extension Correspondence Assertion, Property Correspondence Assertion and Path Correspondence Assertion.

The Extension Correspondence Assertions (ECA)

are used to specify which objects of the base classes should have a corresponding *semantically equivalent* object in the view. We define the *root classes* of a view class **V** as all the classes that are related to **V** through some ECA, which means that in the root classes there are objects that are *semantically equivalent* to the objects of the view class. Consider, for example, the match class STUDENT_v shown in Figure 2. The STUDENT_v root classes are STUDENT and EMPLOYEE, which are related to STUDENT_v through the following ECAs: Ψ_1: $\text{STUDENT}_v \equiv \text{STUDENT}$ and Ψ_2:$\text{STUDENT}_v \oslash \text{EMPLOYEE}$. Ψ_1 specifies that STUDENT_v and STUDENT are equivalent; i.e., for each STUDENT object there is one semantically equivalent object in STUDENT_v, and vice-versa. Ψ_2 specifies that the classes STUDENT_v and EMPLOYEE can have objects in common. According to the type of ECA relating a view class to its root classes, we distinguish six different types of view classes (Vidal and Winslett, 1994): *equivalence*, *selection*, *union*, *difference*, *intersection* and *overlapping*.

The Properties Correspondence Assertions (PrCAs) and Path Correspondence Assertions (PaCAs) specify how the values of the properties of view class objects are derived from the values of the properties of its base class objects. For example, the property $\mathbf{wage}_v$ of the view class STUDENT_v (Figure 2) is defined by the PrCA: $\text{STUDENT}_v.\mathbf{wage}_v \equiv \text{EMPLOYEE}.\mathbf{wage}_1$, which specifies that given an instance **s** of STUDENT_v, if there is an instance **e** of EMPLOYEE, such that $\mathbf{s} \equiv \mathbf{e}$, then $\mathbf{s}.\mathbf{wage}_v = \mathbf{e}.\mathbf{wage}_1$. Otherwise, $\mathbf{s}.\mathbf{wage}_v$ = nil. A PaCA specifies the derivation path of a derived property. We call a property of *derived property* when one is semantically equivalent to a path with more than one property. For example, the property $\mathbf{divName}_v$ of class STUDENT_v is a derived property with derivation path $\text{STUDENT}_v.\mathbf{divName}_v \equiv \text{EMPLOYEE}.\mathbf{div}_1 \bullet \mathbf{name}_1$, which specifies that given an instance **s** of STUDENT_v, if there is an instance **e** of the EMPLOYEE, such that $\mathbf{s} \equiv \mathbf{e}$, then $\mathbf{s}.\mathbf{divName}_v = \mathbf{e}.\mathbf{div}_1.\mathbf{name}_1$. Otherwise, $\mathbf{s}.\mathbf{divName}_v$ = nil. It is important to notice that a view class property can be associated with more the one PrCA and/or PaCA. For example, the property $\mathbf{name}_v$ of the view class STUDENT_v has the following PrCAs: $\text{STUDENT}_v.\mathbf{name}_v \equiv \text{EMPLOYEE}.\mathbf{name}_1$ and $\text{STUDENT}_v.\mathbf{name}_v \equiv \text{STUDENT}.\mathbf{name}_2$. This means that the values of $\mathbf{name}_v$ can be derived from $\mathbf{name}_1$ and $\mathbf{name}_2$.

5 SELF-MAINTENANCE OF NOT FULL MATCH CLASSES

In (Vidal and Pequeno, 2000), we show that the proposed approach, described in section 3, can manage self-maintenance of Full Match Classes (FMC). In this section we show that other types of math classes can easily become self-maintainable using FMCs as auxiliary classes.

A match class **F** is full when its extent is defined by the union of its root classes' extents; a full match class has similar properties to those of a relational view defined by a "natural full outer-equijoin in the key attributes" (Gupta et al., 1997). Formally, a full match class, **F**, is defined by the following ECA $\mathbf{F} \equiv \mathbf{C}_1 \cup ... \cup \mathbf{C}_m$, where $\mathbf{C}_1, ..., \mathbf{C}_m$ are the root classes of **F**. Note that, since a class cannot have duplicated objects, if $\mathbf{c}_i$ is an instance of $\mathbf{C}_i$ and $\mathbf{c}_j$ is an instance of $\mathbf{C}_j$ such that $\mathbf{c}_i \equiv \mathbf{c}_j$, for $1 \leq i, j \leq m$ and $i \neq j$, then there will exist only one object **f** in the extent of **F** such that $\mathbf{f} \equiv \mathbf{c}_i \equiv \mathbf{c}_j$. The properties of **F** are semantically equivalent to the properties or paths of its root classes; therefore, path and property assertions are used to formally especify how the values of the properties of **F** are derived from the values of the properties of its root classes. In the view schemas of Figure 2, the class EST&EMP is a full match class, while the class STUDENT_v is not.

Match classes that are not full, are not self-maintainable, either. Consider, for example, the match class STUDENT_v in Figure 2. Note that the rule of Figure 4 requires an access to the source $\mathbf{DB}_1$, in order to verify whether already exists an object in EMPLOYEE which is semantically equivalent to the object inserted in STUDENT. This information can be obtained neither locally, in $\mathbf{DB}_2$, nor in the view. Therefore, STUDENT_v is not self-maintainable. However, it can become self-maintainable by using the full match class EST&EMP as an auxiliary class. In this case, STUDENT_v is derived directly from the class EST&EMP and it can be implemented as a virtual class or as a materialized class. If it is implemented as a virtual class, its definition is a mere selection (*select* **e** *from* **e** *in* EST&EMP *where* "STUDENT" *in* **e.classes**). If it is implemented as a materialized class, then it can be directly maintained from the auxiliary class EST&EMP, and there is no need for generating local rules to maintain it.

The idea is that the updates in the source DBs can be propagated (by local rules) to the auxiliary classes and the updates in the auxiliary classes can be then propagated (by global rules) to the original view classes. As we will show next, it is possible to guarantee that once auxiliary classes are consistent with the source databases and the original view classes are consistent with auxiliary classes, then original view classes are consistent with the source DBs. Thus, it is not necessary to create local rules for the maintenance of original view classes.

In the rest o this Section consider **V** a match class such that **V** is not full and inherits properties from root classes $\mathbf{C}_1, ..., \mathbf{C}_m$ and from no other one.

Our approach for making the match class **V** self-maintainable consists of the following steps:

Step 1: *Define the Auxiliary class $\mathcal{A}$.*

In order to make possible the self-maintenance of the view class **V**, the auxiliary class $\mathcal{A}$, which is a full match class, should be defined as follows:

- The extension of $\mathcal{A}$ is defined by CA: $\mathcal{A} \equiv \mathbf{C}_1 \cup ... \cup \mathbf{C}_m$. Thus classes $\mathbf{C}_1, ..., \mathbf{C}_m$ are root classes of $\mathcal{A}$.
- The properties of $\mathcal{A}$ are defined as follows:

1. For each property ***p'*** of **V** is defined a property ***p*** in $\mathcal{A}$, such that $\mathcal{A}.\boldsymbol{p} \equiv \mathbf{V}.\boldsymbol{p}'$ being defined a correspondent CA switching ***p'*** for ***p*** for each PrCA/PaCA involving **p'**.
2. For each ***p'*** of $\mathbf{C}_k$, $1 \leq k \leq m$, which is necessary for determining the semantic equivalence among objects or is used in a predicate for selecting members of view class **V**, it is defined a property ***p*** in $\mathcal{A}$ such that $\mathcal{A}.\boldsymbol{p} \equiv \mathbf{C}_k.\boldsymbol{p}'$ or in case the required value is from classes related to $\mathbf{C}_k$, $\mathcal{A}.\boldsymbol{p} \equiv \mathbf{C}_k.\boldsymbol{p}' \bullet \varrho$, where ϱ is a path.
3. The property **classes**, which has its value as a set of names of root classes of which an object is a member (**classes**: set(STRING)).

Step 2: *Generate the local rules for maintenance of the auxiliary class $\mathcal{A}$.*

In (Vidal and Pequeno, 2000), we show that the local rules for maintenance of full match classes can be defined based on correspondence assertion for the mediated view, which formally specify the relationships among the mediated view and the local data sources' schemas. An advantage of using correspondence assertions is that the rule generation process can be automated.

Step 3:*Define the view class V in terms of the auxiliary class $\mathcal{A}$.*

As we already mentioned, the view class **V** can be implemented as a virtual class as well as a materialized one. If **V** is virtual, then the definition of this class is determined from $\mathcal{A}$. Otherwise it is materialized and an extension to this class is explicitly created.

In Table 1 we define how to map the ECAs between **V** and the local classes in ECAs between **V** and the auxiliary class $\mathcal{A}$. Using the new assertion, we can define the query which derive **V** from the auxiliary class $\mathcal{A}$ (in case **V** is virtual), or generate the rules that maintains V to reflect updates occurred in the auxiliary class $\mathcal{A}$ (in case **V** is materialized).

Step 4:*Generate the global rules for maintenance of V.*

In case **V** is materialized, we have to generate the rules that updates V to reflect the updates occurred in the auxiliary class $\mathcal{A}$. In order to generate rules for maintenance of V, we use V's Correspondence Assertions. We developed in (Pequeno, 2000) some algorithms, which receive as input the CAs from a view

Correspondence Assertions between V and local classes	**Correspondence Assertions between V and class $\mathcal{A}$**
$V \equiv C_1$	$V \equiv \mathcal{A}[\text{"}C_1\text{"} \in \mathit{classes}]$
$V \equiv C_1[\mathsf{p}]$	$V \equiv \mathcal{A}[\mathsf{p} \wedge \text{"}C_1\text{"} \in \mathit{classes}]$
$V \equiv C_1$ - C_2	$V \equiv \mathcal{A}[\text{"}C_1\text{"} \in \mathit{classes} \wedge \text{"}C_2\text{"} \notin \mathit{classes}]$
$V \equiv \cup_{i=1}^{n} C_i$	$V \equiv \mathcal{A}[\text{"}C_1\text{"} \in \mathit{classes} \vee ... \vee \text{"}C_v\text{"} \in \mathit{classes}]$
$V \equiv \cap_{i=1}^{n} C_i$	$V \equiv \mathcal{A}[\text{"}C_1\text{"} \in \mathit{classes} \wedge ... \wedge \text{"}C_v\text{"} \in \mathit{classes}]$

Table 1: Mapping of the ECAs

class and automatically generate the necessary rules for its maintenance. In this paper, we just illustrate this process with an example.

Consider the FMC EST&EMP and the view class STUDENT_v presented in Figure 2. For the maintenance of STUDENT_v some rules must be generated to maintain CA Ψ: STUDENT_v $\equiv$ EST&EMP["STUDENT" $\in$ **classes**]. For the maintenance of Ψ, a rule must be generated for the following relevant operations: (i) insertions in EST&EMP.**classes** and (ii) deletions in EST&EMP.**classes**, which are the update operations in EST&EMP which identify the insertions and deletions of objects in EST&EMP.

The rule generated for the maintenance of Ψ in relation to insertion in EST&EMP.**classes** is shown in the Figure 6. Observe that the event of this rule is parameterised with the object **e** (which was inserted or updated in the EST&EMP class) and with the value v, which corresponds to the name of the origin class of the object inserted in EST&EMP. These parameters can be referenced on the action of the rule. The action of this rule consists in inserting the object **e** in STUDENT_v, if this object is a member of STUDENT_v's root class, that is, STUDENT. The rule generated for the maintenance of Ψ in relation to deletions in EST&EMP.**classes** is similar to the rule in Figure 6; as the reader can check, it is enough reading deletion/delete where is written insertion/insert.

When insertion(v,**e**) in EST&EMP.**classes**
/*v is the name of the class inserted in EST&EMP.**classes***/
Then If v== STUDENT then
Insert **e** in STUDENT_v

Figure 6: Rule for maintenance of Ψ in relation to insertions in EST&EMP.**classes**

6 CONCLUSIONS

In this work we focused the problem of incremental maintenance and self- maintenance of match classes in integration views. When dealing with this problem, we proposed a strategy for self-maintenance of full match classes in an incremental way and we showed how to make other types of match classes self-maintainable by using a full match class as auxiliary class.

The problem about incremental maintenance of materialized views has been quite studied lately (Gupta et al., 1997; Gupta and Mumick, 1999; Griffin and Libkin, 1998). The most part of these works has been provided for relational views. In (Gupta et al., 1997) it was developed an algorithm for the incremental maintenance of outerjoin and match views. They identified in which conditions an outerjoin view is self-maintainable. Therefore their strategy has some restraints, besides it can not be adapted to the objects model, since it is not possible to deal with properties relationship. The value of this kind of property are objects and the source OIDs do not have any meaning in the integrator mediator. As shown in (Pequeno, 2000) our strategy goes beyond the restraints present in (Gupta et al., 1997), once it allows the self-maintenance of FMCs with derived properties and relationships.

The reference (Gupta and Mumick, 1999) expands the work of (Gupta et al., 1997) because it considers other kinds of outerjoin views, although it remains with the same restraints of the latter version. In (Griffin and Libkin, 1998) was developed algebraic chance propagation algorithms for the maintenance of the outerjoin view. According to the authors, the strategy used makes possible an efficient derivation of self-maintainable expressions. Neither one or the other strategy (Griffin and Libkin, 1998; Gupta and Mumick, 1999) can be applied to the objects model, once they work with algebraic expressions and the operator outerjoin is not yet defined in the algebra of objects.

In our approach, FMCs are self-maintenable and are maintained by the sources' rules. Such rules reflect the changes in the source DB and specify the sequence of updates to be performed in the view. The rule generation is obtained with bases in the CAs, which formally specify how source DBs are related to the mediated view. An advantage of using CAs is that they allow us to formally justify that the rules generated by our approach correctly maintain the view.

In this paper we showed how FMCs could be used as auxiliary classes in order to make possible the self-maintenance of any type of match classes. Once auxiliary classes are materialized, generic match classes can be implemented as virtual or as materialized. This is advantageous because a user defining view classes has more flexibility to implement original view classes.

REFERENCES

Batini, C., Lenzerini, M., and Navathe, S. (1986). A comparative analysis of methodologies for database schema integration. *ACM Computing Surveys*, 18(4):323–364.

Cattell, R., Barry, D., Bartels, D., Berler, M., Eastman, J., Gamerman, S., Jordan, D., Spreinger, A., Strickland, H., and Wade, D. (1997). *The Object Database Standard ODMG 2.0*. Morgan Kaufmann Publishers.

Griffin, T. and Libkin, L. (1998). Algebraic change propagation for semijoin and outerjoin queries. In *SIGMOD Record*, volume 27(3).

Guerrini, G., Bertino, E., Catania, B., and Molina, J. (1997). A formal model of views for object-oriented database systems. In *Theory and Practice of Object Systems*, pages 157–183.

Gupta, A., Jagadish, H., and Mumick, I. (1996). Data integration using self-maintainable views. In *Proceedings of the 5th Int'l Conf. on Extending Database Technology*, pages 140–144, France.

Gupta, A., Jagadish, H., and Mumick, I. (1997). Maintenance and self-maintenance of outerjoin views. In *The Third International Workshop on Next Generation Information Technologies and Systems*, Neve Illan, Israel.

Gupta, A., Mumick, I., and Subrahmanian, V. (1993). Maintaining views incrementally. In *Proceedings of the ACM SIGMOD*, pages 157–166.

Gupta, H. and Mumick, I. (1999). Incremental maintenance of aggregate and outerjoin expressions. Stanford University.

Papakonstantinou, Y., Abiteboul, S., and Molina, H. (1996). Object fusion in mediator systems. In *Proceedings of the 22nd VLDB Conf.*, India.

Pequeno, V. (2000). Auto-manutenção de classes de fusão em visões de integração de dados. Master's thesis, Federal University of Ceara, Brazil.

Vidal, V. and Pequeno, V. (2000). Self-maintanance of match classes in integrated views. In *Anais do XV Simpósio Brasileiro de Banco de Dados*, Brasil.

Vidal, V. and Winslett, M. (1994). Preserving update semantics in schema integration. In *Proceedings of the Third Int'l Conf. on Information and Knowledge Management*, pages 263–271, Maryland-USA.

Widjojo, S., Hull, R., and Wile, D. (1990). A specificational approach to merging persistent object bases. In Dearle, A., Sahw, G., and Zdonik, S., editors, *Implementing Persistent Object Bases*. Morgan Kaufmann.

Zhou, G., Hull, R., and King, R. (1996). Generating data integration mediators that use materialization. *Journal of Intelligent Information Systems*, 6(2/3):199–221.

Zhuge, Y., Molina, H., and Wiener, J. (1996). The strobe algorithms for multi-source warehouse consistency. In *PDIS*, pages 146–157, Florida.

A SYSTEM FOR DATA CHANGE PROPAGATION IN HETEROGENEOUS INFORMATION SYSTEMS

Carmen Constantinescu*, Uwe Heinkel*, Ralf Rantzau, Bernhard Mitschang
Institute of Parallel and Distributed High-Performance Systems, University of Stuttgart, Breitwiesenstr. 20-22, D-70565 Stuttgart, Germany
Email: {Carmen.Constantinescu, Uwe.Heinkel, Ralf.Rantzau, Bernhard.Mitschang}@informatik.uni-stuttgart.de

Key words: Information systems, integration of heterogeneous data sources, XML technology

Abstract: Today, it is common that enterprises manage several mostly heterogeneous information systems to supply their production and business processes with data. There is a need to exchange data between the information systems while preserving system autonomy. Hence, an integration approach that relies on a single global enterprise data schema is ruled out. This is also due to the widespread usage of legacy systems. We propose a system, called Propagation Manager, which manages dependencies between data objects stored in different information systems. A script specifying complex data transformations and other sophisticated activities, like the execution of external programs, is associated with each dependency. For example, an object update in a source system can trigger data transformations of the given source data for each destination system that depends on the object. Our system is implemented using current XML technologies. We present the architecture and processing model of our system and demonstrate the benefit of our approach by illustrating an extensive example scenario.

1 INTRODUCTION

Corporate IT infrastructures typically comprise distributed heterogeneous information systems. In this paper, we focus on the management of data stored in these systems. In particular, we present a mechanism to transform and deliver data from one system to the needs of the receiving systems. The mechanism developed generates output data based on a collection of data dependencies between the distributed information systems and the transformation specifications associated with each dependency. This approach increases system autonomy, because specific system features are treated within a dependency only, and the usage of global structures is abandoned.

In this section, we give some background information on data change management for enterprise information systems and the motivation for developing our system. Then, we briefly introduce the main concepts used in our approach, which are further detailed in Section 2.

1.1 The Problem of Data Change Management

Most enterprises are forced to innovate their products and services and to improve their business processes ever more quickly to remain competitive. This is due to the turbulences observed on the markets: the supply of and demand for resources change more radically and abruptly than in the past. The ability to adapt to market changes is a key success factor.

1.1.1 Data Producers and Consumers

An enterprise can be viewed as a set of business units that are connected by information flows and resource flows. A business unit, characterized by the

* This work was partially supported by the German Research Society (DFG/SFB 467)

autonomy to manage its own resources, is responsible to deliver services or goods, which are further processed by other business units. Furthermore, business units frequently run their own information systems to manage the data tailored for the respective business processes.

Business units act as producers and consumers of information. Hence, change propagation between business units means, among other things, the propagation of data between the corresponding information systems. However, due to the autonomy of business units, not all information systems store information using the same data representation. Furthermore, some data is relevant only to a single information system, while other data is relevant to several systems and is stored locally, possibly using different representations. Thus, data changes in one system have different effects on data stored in other systems. Consider, for example, a manufacturing enterprise with several business units. Let us focus on the two service-oriented business units *Order Management* (OM) and *Facility Layout Design* (FLD). Suppose that a customer orders a large number of certain products. The OM business unit is responsible to generate optimal plans using production planning and control methods (Wiendahl & Westkämper, 2001). This may lead to a capacity increase of machines. The FLD business unit is responsible to generate factory plans that are used to adapt the real factory layout (Westkämper & von Briel, 2001).

Because of the need for additional machines, the FLD may have to position them in the factory layout. This causes a change of the material flow, affecting the processing of other orders as well. The information about new transportation times has an effect on OM, thus establishing a mutual information dependency between OM and FLD. Data changes in one of the information systems have to be reflected in the data of the other system. In general, an information system of a business unit produces data which is consumed by one or more other information systems, i.e., there is a 1-to-N data dependency. In our example, the OM business unit changes or creates data describing production plans. The FLD business unit then receives data on new production plans and adapts its data describing the factory layout. This example is further detailed in Section 3, showing technical aspects of the internal processing of our data change management system.

1.1.2 System Heterogeneity

Due to the autonomy of business units and the heterogeneity of their IT infrastructures, it is often infeasible or too expensive to manage a single, integrated enterprise information system that feeds all business units with their data. Hence, enterprise change management should be supported by a generic approach to solve data change management. Such an approach should be able to manage data dependencies and help to transform data stored in a source information system into data stored in the depending information systems.

1.2 A Generic Approach for Data Change Propagation

We first briefly discuss our approach using general terms and concepts that we introduce in this section. In Section 2, we present the architecture and details on the technologies employed in the proposed system.

A *data model* is a description of data structures. For example, in the object-oriented model, data structures are classes, and relations in the relational model. Classes also specify *methods* but we focus on the data aspect, only. Therefore, we are only interested in the *attributes* of the classes.

A *data schema* is an instance of a data model, i.e., the specification of data structures for an application. For example, in the relational model, an employee can be represented by a relation with the attributes (and types) *empno* (integer), *name* (string), *birth* (date), etc.

We define a *system* as an application or an information system. A system can act as a producer and/or consumer of data.

A directed relationship from a single data producer, named *source system*, to a single data consumer, named *destination system*, is called *dependency*. We say that the destination system is *dependent* on the source system.

A data change occurring in one system has an impact on all dependent systems. For example, two systems store data objects that represent the same information but possibly using different data models and data schemas. Thus, a change of such data in one system requires a change in the other, sometimes involving complex adaptations.

In this paper, we merely consider updates of instances of a data schema but we do not consider changes of the schema itself. For example, in the relational data model, our approach manages the update of attribute values in tuples of a relation but not the manipulation of attribute data types, the addition of attributes, etc. The management of schema (meta data) changes remains as our future work.

A *change propagation* is the process of forwarding a data change from a source system to a dependent system. The process of change propagation includes transformations and filtering of the changed data that is delivered to the dependent system.

A *transformation* is an operation that maps given input data into output data according to a specification. The specification defines how the contents and schema of the input data have to be adapted to represent valid target data.

Filtering is an operation that accepts or rejects the execution of a transformation according to a constraint, which is an expression (a set of conditions) over the contents of the input data of a transformation.

1.3 Overview of a Data Change Management System

We develop a data change management system, called Stuttgart Information and Exploration System (SIES) (Constantinescu, Heinkel, Rantzau & Mitschang, 2001), illustrated in Figure 1, which manages the change propagation between several systems. It consists of two main components, called *Propagation Manager* and *Federation Manager*. We use the term *propagation dependency* to describe a dependency as defined in Section 1.2. A propagation dependency specifies a source system, a single dependent system, and a *propagation script*. The propagation script contains information required for transformations (defined by *transformation scripts*), filtering, and routing. The Propagation Manager transforms, filters, and routes changed data using the dependencies that have been created, stored, and updated by the Federation Manager. The *Repository* stores propagation dependencies, schema descriptions of the systems, and propagation and transformation scripts.

We designed our system to have the following features. It must be possible to *add new systems* without much effort, i.e., SIES has to provide software, called wrappers, that is able to track data updates in a system and to map between its own data model and the Propagation Manager data model.

Another requirement is to support the *addition, removal,* and *update* of *dependencies* and *transformation specifications.* SIES needs to provide a user-friendly graphical user interface that allows to manipulate the dependencies and the associated scripts and to register them in a repository. Furthermore, SIES should offer a library of simple and frequently used transformations that can be called within newly created propagation scripts, tailored for a new system. Of course, the user interface should also allow to adapt given transformations, or to create new ones and to add them to the library for future reuse.

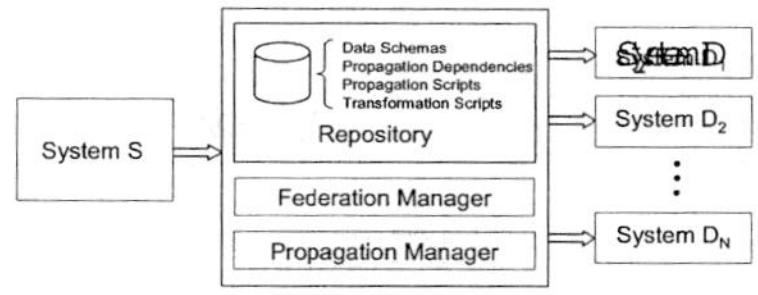

Figure 1: SIES, a data change management system

SIES has to provide a high degree of *reliability* and *availability*. For example, failures in participating systems have to be handled in a way that other systems are unaffected.

Finally, SIES has to be *scalable*, i.e., the resources (time and memory) required to manage dependencies should grow (linearly) in proportion to the number of dependencies and, of course, also in proportion to the amount and size of data to be transformed and propagated.

In this paper, we focus on one component of SIES, the Propagation Manager.

2 THE PROPAGATION MANAGER

The central component of our data change management approach is the Propagation Manager. This section describes this component regarding its functionality, architecture, and processing model.

2.1 Functionalities

The task of the Propagation Manager is to transform a source data object into a destination data object. Such a transformation has to be triggered automatically whenever the value of the source data object changes. Thus, the Propagation Manager combines two functionalities: a) the processing of a transformation and b) the propagation of updated data object values from one system to several dependent systems. The second functionality can be seen as a way to provide (some degree of) consistency between data stored in different systems.

2.2 Architecture

In this section, we describe the architecture of the Propagation Manager, which is responsible for change propagation. The Propagation Manager consists of several sub-components, sketched in Figure 2. One of them is the Transformation Manager, which itself is composed of the Script Engine, the Mapper, and the Filter. The Script Engine interprets a propagation script, associated

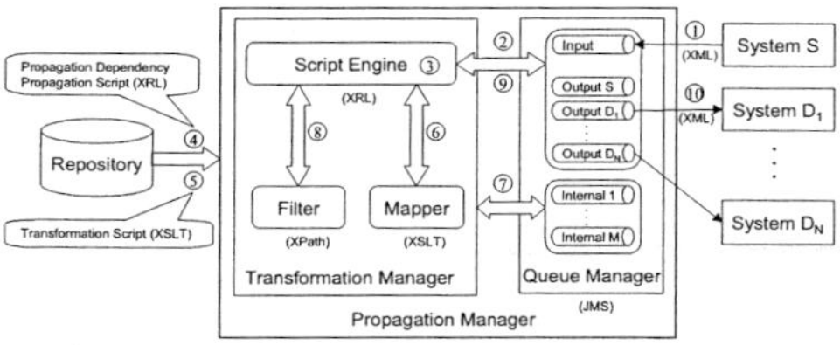

Figure 2: Propagation Manager architecture. The technologies employed are shown in brackets.

with a propagation dependency. The script specifies several operations for transforming, filtering and routing the changed data. The Script Engine calls the Mapper to perform the transformation of a source data object (based on a change) into a destination data object. If the destination system requires special constraints, specified in the propagation script, the Script Engine invokes the Filter. The Filter then informs the Propagation Manager if a data change should be ignored or if the destination system has to be updated. The Queue Manager is used to exchange messages between the involved systems. It manages the Propagation Manager's input queue, the systems' output queues and several internal queues of the Transformation Manager.

2.3 Processing Model

In the following, we describe the internal flow of information needed to propagate a change, illustrated in Figure 2. The figure shows a sequence of processing steps which belong to four main stages:

1. Fetch a new message from the input queue (steps 1 and 2),
2. select applicable propagation dependencies (3, 4, 5),
3. execute corresponding propagation scripts (6, 7, 8), and
4. put processed messages into the output queues (9, 10).

In the following subsections, we explain these stages in detail.

2.3.1 Message In- and Output

The Queue Manager has a single input queue and for each connected system one output queue. It also manages the internal queues of the Transformation Manager to store intermediate transformation results. Whenever a system connects to the Propagation Manager, it is assigned an output queue where it can fetch messages from. We assume that an average system stays connected for a relatively long time.

All systems connected to the Propagation Manager have to be extended by wrappers. The wrapper is responsible to detect a change in the source system, called System *S* in Figure 2, to create a message according to a given format, and to send it to the input queue of the Propagation Manager (step 1 in Figure 2). A dependent system, named System D_i, is responsible for fetching the propagated message from its queue (10).

2.3.2 Dependency Selection

The dependency selection is initiated by the Queue Manager, which notifies the Script Engine about a new message in the input queue (2). Then, the Script Engine fetches the new message and interacts with the Mapper and the Filter components to transform and filter the given source data object according to each propagation script. The repository stores, among other things, propagation dependency specifications. They have the following structure: (SourceSystem, PropagationScript, DestinationSystem). The parameter PropagationScript denotes the name of a propagation script stored in and managed by the repository. The propagation script contains information regarding the transformation scripts and the output queue of the destination. The Script Engine extracts from the message header the name of the source system that has sent the message (3). Based on this information, the Script Engine retrieves all propagation dependencies matching the message's source from the repository (4). A matching dependency contains information about the propagation script and indicates the destination output queue.

A propagation script is a *template*, i.e., it contains the code to be interpreted by the Script Engine and placeholders that are replaced (using a simple parser) by textual values of the current dependency, like the actual names of the source and destination system. The code also specifies the names of one or more transformation scripts, which are stored in the repository. The use of templates allows a propagation script to be employed for various dependencies that require the same transformations. Hence the code of a propagation script does not have to be replicated for each dependency. A transformation script is a piece of code that is interpreted by the Mapper. The Script Engine retrieves the transformation scripts from the repository (5).

2.3.3 Propagation Script Execution

The propagation script execution consists of transforming, filtering and routing steps. It is triggered by the Script Engine which calls the Mapper (6). The Mapper performs the transformations corresponding to the retrieved transformation scripts. All messages exchanged between the Transformation Manager's components are temporarily stored in internal queues (7).

If the Script Engine detects a filter expression (a constraint) in a transformation script, it calls the Filter (8). The Filter decides if the message is routed to the destination system or discarded. A filter expression can appear anywhere in a transformation script because the decision whether to skip a change can be based on results of transformations. If the Filter concludes that there be an output message, the Script Engine puts the message into the output queue of the dependent system (9).

2.4 Implementation

So far, we have introduced the general concepts and the architecture of our approach. In this section, we discuss the implementation of our concepts using various state of the art technologies.

2.4.1 Messages and JMS

The sources and destinations of data dependencies may have different data models and data schemas. We use XML to specify the schemas of the connected systems because of its flexibility to adapt it to ones needs. Suppose that a source system uses the relational data model to manage its data objects. For instance, consider a table (source object) consisting of many rows where only a single row has changed. We suggest using XML Fragment Interchange to send only a fragment of the original XML document, representing the changed row in the source data, together with some context information.

The communication between the Propagation Manager components as well as between the Propagation Manager and the external systems is implemented using the Java Message Service (JMS). The body of a message received from a source system contains the changed data according to the XML format. We employ for communication the message-oriented middleware which provides a means for asynchronous application-to-application communication via message queuing (Leymann, 1999).

2.4.2 Transformation Scripts and XSLT

We use an XML-based language, called eXtensible Stylesheet Language Transformations (XSLT), to transform XML documents in the Mapper component. During a complex propagation, several XSLT files can be involved. For a single transformation, an XSLT processor reads the XML document representing the source data and interprets it according to the specified transformation script. The calls of transformation scripts are embedded in propagation scripts.

2.4.3 Propagation Scripts and XRL

We use the eXchangeable Routing Language (XRL) (van der Aalst & Kumar, 2000; Kumar & Zhao, 1998) for propagating changed data between dependent systems. This is an XML dialect and can thus be processed by any XML parsers, which are widely available. XRL is aimed at asynchronous, flow-type applications and provides a mechanism to describe processes at an instance level.

We extended XRL according to our propagation purposes by three new elements: transform, propagate and message_event. A *transform* element specifies a subject message, transformed using a given transformation script, named *template*, and a *result*. The routing schema manages a processed message using an internal name. The *propagate* element puts a subject message into a specified destination queue. A *message_event* element defines an event. This allows to fire an action if a certain message arrives in an input queue. An example XRL file that contains these new elements is presented in Section 3.2 and illustrated in Figure 4.

2.4.4 Repository and UML

We specify the systems' data schemas using the Unified Modeling Language (UML), which it is becoming a de-facto standard for object-oriented modeling. We use a repository system as a common place to store systems' data schemas and the propagation and transformation scripts because of the following advantages: a) a repository is a shared database with value-added services like versioning, configuration management and context-management, and b) it is a valuable basis for the reuse of the stored objects.

3 EXAMPLE SCENARIO

In the following sections we describe an extensive example that illustrates the usage of our technologies

```
<?xml version="1.0" encoding="ISO8859-2"?>
<production_order>
  <operation>
    <transport start="M002" dest="M001" ual="A12">
      <part no="P001" amount="5000"/>
    </transport>
  </operation>
  <operation>
    <drilling unit="M001" cost_center="DM1">
      <part no="P001" amount="5000"/>
      <manufacturing_lead_time days="0" hours="3"
                                        mins="40"/>
    </drilling>
  </operation>
  <operation>
    <transport start="M001" dest="M003" qual="C13">
      <part no="P001" amount="5000"/>
    </transport>
  </operation>
  <operation>
    <milling unit="M003" cost_center="BM2" >
      <part no="P001" amount="5000"/>
      <manufacturing_lead_time days="0" hours="1"
                                        mins="13"/>
    </milling>
  </operation>
</production_order>
```

Figure 3: Changed production order (om.xml)

introduced before. It highlights our main concepts for data change management: the transformation, filtering and routing of data changes.

3.1 Data Change Management in Manufacturing

Our scenario refers to a manufacturing enterprise that receives a new order. At least two systems of the enterprise are affected by the new order: OM and FLD, which store, among other things, data about the resources needed to manufacture products, like human resources and machines.

As a result of a new order from a customer, the OM System, the source system, creates a new, optimized production order. This describes the manufacturing process plan in terms of transportation and manufacturing operations containing data regarding parts, machines, transportation and manufacturing lead times. The FLD System manages a database of the geometry (width, length, height) of machines as well as the current layout of the factory, i.e., the positions of the facilities. Several dependencies are defined between these systems. In order to create a new facility layout, based on simulation and optimization techniques, the FLD System processes the changed order data, potentially enriched by additional data from other systems. For example, if the changed production order involves a new machine, the FLD System will retrieve from its local data the corresponding geometry/size of the machine and an optimal position has to be computed.

In our scenario, the additional data represents the qualification and the hourly wage of the employee involved in operating a new machine, stored in a third system, the Strategic Management System (SM). In our approach, the additional data is not part of a propagation dependency. As a result, our scenario involves three systems: the OM and FLD Systems are dependent on each other, while the SM System has the role of a supplier of additional data.

```
<?xml version="1.0" encoding="ISO8859-2"?>
<xrl:ROUTE id="ex" created_by="script_designer"
                   creation_date="29-10-2001">
  <xrl:SEQUENCE>
    <xrl:WAIT sync="1">
      <xrl:MESSAGE_EVENT source="OM"
                         type="production_order" name="om"/>
    </xrl:WAIT>
    <xrl:TRANSFORM subject="om" template="om2fld.xslt"
                                name="t1"/>
    <xrl:PROPAGATE subject="t1" destination="FLDQ"/>
  </xrl:SEQUENCE>
</xrl:ROUTE>
```

Figure 4: Propagation script (om2fld.xrl)

We assume that the Federation Manager has already created the schema descriptions of these three systems and the propagation dependencies between them, including the propagation and transformation scripts. All this information is stored in the repository. The source system wrapper has to notify SIES about the change of some source data as well as to provide the changed data itself. The Propagation Manager then triggers the change propagation, based on the stored dependencies among the systems. The propagated change, enriched by the additional data, is then sent to the destination system, FLD, which computes a new facility layout.

3.2 Change Propagation

Based on this overall view of the scenario, we now present details of the scripts used to process our example change propagation.

We assume that the OM System changes data related to production orders. A production order consists of transportation and manufacturing operations applied to a part. A part is specified by its number and the ordered quantity. A manufacturing operation selects the machine corresponding to a specified processing step, i.e., drilling, milling, and the corresponding manufacturing lead time. A transportation operation specifies a start and a destination machine.

A change in the OM System is specified as an XML message that has to be propagated to the dependent system, FLD. Figure 3 presents the XML document (om.xml) representing the changed production order, extended by a drilling and a milling manufacturing process. As a result, two new machines are added, machines M001 and M003, and the associated manufacturing lead times and transportation operations are specified.

This message has to be transformed, filtered and routed. First, the message is put into the input queue of the Queue Manager. The Script Engine fetches the message and retrieves the propagation dependencies that match the specified OM source in the message header. One XRL propagation script (om2fld.xrl), is retrieved from the repository (Figure 4). It consists of the following routing schema:

```
<?xml version="1.0" encoding="ISO8859-2"?>
<xslt:transform version="1.0"
  xmlns:xslt="http://www.w3.org/1999/XSL/Transform">
  <xslt:output method="xml" encoding="ISO8859-2"
                                   indent="yes"/>

  <xslt:template match="/production_order">
    <material_flow>
      <xslt:apply-templates select="."/>
    </material_flow>
  </xslt:template>

  <xslt:template match="//transport">
    <xslt:element name="transport">
      <xslt:attribute name="start">
        <xslt:value-of select="@start"/>
      </xslt:attribute>
      <xslt:attribute name="dest"
        <xslt:value-of select="@dest"/>
      </xslt:attribute>
      <xslt:element name="part">
        <xslt:attribute name="no">
          <xslt:value-of select="part@no"/>
        </xslt:attribute>
        <xslt:attribute name="amount"
          <xslt:value-of select="part@amount"/>
        </xslt:attribute>
      </xslt:element>
      <xsl:variable name="qual" select="@qual"/>
      <xslt:element name="employee">
        <xslt:attribute name="qualification">
          <xslt:value-of select="@qual"/>
        </xslt:attribute>
        <xslt:attribute name="hourly_wage"
          <xslt:value-of select=
          "document('http://www.SM.com/employee.xml')
                //employee[qual@q=$qual]h_wage@h_w"/>
        </xslt:attribute>
      </xslt:element>
    </xslt:element>
  </xslt:template>
</xslt:transform>
```

Figure 5: Transformation script (om2fld.xslt)

```
...
<material_flow>
  <transport start="M002" dest="M001">
    <part no="P001" amount="5000"/>
    <employee qualification="A12" hourly_wage="129"/>
  </transport>
  <transport start="M001" dest="M003">
    <part no="P001" amount="5000"/>
    <employee qualification="C13" hourly_wage="45"/>
  </transport>
</material_flow>
...
```

Figure 6: Propagated production order (fld.xml)

1. Wait for an event representing a message from the OM System. It contains the changed production order (om.xml), managed internally under a specified name, *om*.

2. Transform the received message *om* using the transformation script (om2fld.xslt), specified as a template. The resulting message is assigned an internal name, here *t1*.

3. Propagate the subject *t1* to the specified destination output queue, here FLD queue.

The Script Engine interprets the propagation script and retrieves the specified transformation script (om2fld.xslt) from the repository (Figure 5). This matches the *transport* node of the source document (om.xml) and retrieves its corresponding attributes (start, destination, qualification, part number, and part amount). These are used to define in the result document (fld.xml) (Figure 6) the associated *transport* node with the attributes *start* and *destination*, and the elements *part* and *employee*. The attributes of the *part* element (*number* and *amount*), are selected from the source document. The attributes of the *employee* element (*qualification* and *hourly_wage*) represent the required additional data from the SM System, specified by the URL of the document, http://www.SM.com/employee.xml.

The Mapper performs the transformation, illustrated before, using an XSLT processor, and sends the result to the Script Engine. In our example, no filter expression is involved. The resulting XML file is put into the body of a message that is delivered to the FLD System's output queue. It contains the following data: a) the transportation operations from machine M002 to M001 and from M001 to M003, respectively and b) the employees' qualifications and hourly wages corresponding to the manufacturing operations.

4 RELATED WORK

Our approach is designed to propagate changed data between dependent autonomous and heterogeneous systems. One of the main objectives is to provide support for routing of changed data between dependent systems. We envision two directions that achieve this objective. One is to use a language comprising routing constructs required to design a routing schema. This approach belongs to the field of workflow definition and workflow management systems (van der Aalst & Kumar, 2000; Kumar & Zhao, 1998). Our Propagation Manager implementation is based on XRL, a simple routing language, which is less powerful than a workflow definition language.

The second strategy is to build *(heterogeneous) agent systems* that can communicate intelligently with one another (Nwana, 1996). Heterogeneous agent systems are represented by the integration of two or more agents which belong to two or more different agent classes (collaborative, interface, mobile, information/Internet, reactive, hybrid and smart agents).

Another field related to our approach is *replication*, which is the process of maintaining several copies of the same data in several systems. The objective is to access data locally in order to improve response times and to reduce the communication overhead with other systems.

There are two main techniques to update replicated tables: table snapshots (Adiba & Linfsay, 1980) and triggers (Hanson & Widom, 1993). Table snapshots allow an asynchronous update of replicas, while the processing of triggers is synchronous. The trigger approach is more flexible than table snapshots since it allows defining actions being applied to replicas that are different from the update operations applied to the original copy. Furthermore, other objects/tables besides the replicas can be manipulated as well. The concept of triggers is a characteristic of *active database systems*. Triggers are closer to our approach than table snapshots due to their flexibility for transformations. Furthermore, our approach is designed to preserve the local autonomy of the data sources as much as possible. For example, we require the data sources to provide a mechanism to detect changes. If a data source happens to be a database system then triggers could be used to notify the local wrapper about the data change, which is then responsible to generate an input message for the Propagation Manager.

5 CONCLUSION AND FUTURE WORK

Current IT infrastructures need a flexible, loosely coupled approach to propagate data changes between enterprise information systems while preserving their data management autonomy. We suggest a software component, called Propagation Manager, that manages dependencies between data stored in potentially different schemas and models. The data is not replicated in the Propagation Manager but only the data schemas of the systems connected to the Propagation Manager are stored in a repository. The Propagation Manager transforms an XML input message into an XML output message based on a transformation specification that has been defined for a data dependency. Such a transformation can be composed of several smaller transformation activities (XSLT scripts). By employing script templates, our approach allows for a reuse of transformation code for many dependencies.

In some situations it is useful to prevent data propagation. This can be achieved by applying constraints (XPath expressions) on the message input or on the intermediate results of transformations.

Our current propagation approach and system implementation manages 1-to-1 data dependencies. We currently investigate how to manage 1-to-N and M-to-N dependencies using a single XRL script instead of employing several 1-to-1 XRL scripts. This may have positive performance effects for the Propagation Manager because only one script instead of several would have to be processed. We intend to employ the XQuery language to query the repository. Furthermore, we plan to integrate XQuery statements into the transformation scripts to offer even more flexibility for transformations. This would add another XML technology to our system, thus making it an XML-dominated middleware component.

Meta data changes do not occur as frequently as changes of operational data. However, it is important to support the change of data schemas in our approach. As we have mentioned in Section 1.2, the Propagation Manager does not cover such changes but we intend to extend our system into this direction.

REFERENCES

van der Aalst, W., & Kumar, A. (2000). XML Based Schema Definition for Support of Inter-organizational Workflow. In *Proceedings of 21st International Conference on Application and Theory of Petri Nets* (ICATPN 2000), Aarhus, Denmark.

Adiba, M., & Lindsay, B. (1980). Database Snapshots. In *VLDB*, Montreal, Quebec, Canada, pp. 86-91.

Constantinescu, C., Heinkel, U., Rantzau, R., & Mitschang, B. (2001). SIES – An Approach for a Federated Information System in Manufacturing. In *Proceedings of the International Symposium on Information Systems and Engineering* (ISE 2001), Las Vegas, Nevada, USA, pp. 269-275.

Gray, J., Helland, G., O'Neill, P., & Sasha, D. (1996). The Dangers of Replication and a Solution. In *Proceedings of the 1996 ACM SIGMOD International Conference on Management of Data*, Montreal, Canada, pp. 173-182.

Hanson, E., & Widom, J. (1993). An Overview of Production Rules in Database Systems. In *The Knowledge Engineering Review*, Vol.8, No.2.

Kumar, A., & Zhao, Z. (1998). Workflow Support for Electronic Commerce Applications. In *International Conference on Telecommunications and Electronic Commerce*, Nashville, TN, USA.

Leymann, F. (1999). A Practitioners Approach to Data Federation. In *4. Workshop Föderierte Datenbanken*, Berlin, Germany, CEUR-WS/Vol. 25.

Nwana, H. (1996). Software Agents: An Overview. In *Knowledge Engineering Review,* Vol. 11, No. 3, pp. 205-244.

Westkämper, E., & von Briel, R. (2001). Continuous Improvement and Participative Factory Planning by

Computer Systems. In *CIRP Annals Manufacturing Technology*, Nancy, France, pp. 347-352.

Wiendahl, H.-H., & Westkämper, E. (2001). Situation-Based Selection of PPC Methods: Fundamentals and Approaches. In *CIRP 34th International Seminar on Manufacturing Systems*, Athens, Greece, pp. 241-246.

Wiesmann, M., Pedone, F., Schiper, A., Kemme, B., & Alonso, G. (2000). Understanding Replication in Databases and Distributed Systems. In *Proceedings of 20th International Conference on Distributed Computing Systems* (ICDS 2000), Taipei, Taiwan, Republic of China, pp. 264-274.

SEMI-AUTOMATIC WRAPPER GENERATION AND ADAPTION

Living with heterogeneity in a market environment

Michael Christoffel, Bethina Schmitt, Jürgen Schneider
Institute for Program Structures and Data Organization, Universität Karlsruhe, Karlsruhe, Germany
Email: {christof,schmitt,schneider}@ira.uka.de

Key words: Wrapper generation, Provider integration, Web interfaces, Open markets

Abstract: The success of the Internet as a medium for the supply and commerce of various kinds of goods and services leads to a fast growing number of autonomous and heterogeneous providers that offer and sell goods and services electronically. The new market structures have already entered all kinds of markets. Approaches for market infrastructures usually try to cope with the heterogeneity of the providers by special wrapper components, which translate between the native protocols of the providers and the protocol of the market infrastructure. Enforcing a special interface to the provider limits their independence. Moreover, requirements such as a direct access to the internal business logic and databases of the providers or fix templates for internal data structures are not suitable to establish a real open electronic market. A solution is the limitation of the access to the existing Web interface of the provider. This solution keeps the independence of the providers without burdening them additional work. However, for efficiency reasons, it keeps necessary to tailor a wrapper for each provider. What comes more, each change in the provider or its Web representation forces the modification of the existing wrapper or even the development of a new wrapper. In this paper, we present an approach for a wrapper for complex Web interfaces, which can easily be adapted to any provider just by adding a source description file. A tool allows the construction and modification of source descriptions without expert knowledge. Common changes in the Web representation can be detected and comprehended automatically. The presented approach has been applied to the market of scientific literature.

1 INTRODUCTION

The success of the Internet does not only allow the connection of computers and business partners world-wide. It has also opened the way to completely new business models for electronic business and electronic commerce. Supply and commerce over the Internet have already entered all kinds of markets. The consequence is the development of new market structures, often also the development of completely new electronic markets. Not only traditional vendors and suppliers have used the "electronic chance", also a large number of new providers has appeared, following new innovative business ideas and offering a large range of goods and services. Expectation for the future see a continuos growth of the importance of electronic business and the number of providers.

These new electronic markets lack appropriate market infrastructures. However, approaches for market infrastructures have to face the problem of the heterogeneity and the autonomy of the providers. A common way is the installation of wrapper components that act as representatives of the providers in the market. Since these wrappers can be integrated in the market infrastructure, they can easily be addressed by customers or other market components. However, until now there is no common solution for the way a wrapper accesses to the underlying provider. Trying to enforce standards like ODBC and JDBC for relational databases and Z39.50 for library catalogues or the presence of a special interface only for the wrapper leads to a restriction of the autonomy of the providers and often also to a limitation of the possible capacity. Much more, such approaches limit the development of real open markets, where customers and providers are free to enter and leave in their own decision.

Our approach focuses in the use of already existing interfaces of the provider. Since the presentation of information in the Internet is done by static or dynamic HTML Web pages, the use of this Web interface by a wrapper component to connect the providers to the market infrastructure promises a solution of the problem of heterogeneity and autonomy. A change to XML as language for Web information representation, which can be expected in the future, will even enhance the capacity of the Web interface.

Figure 1 shows a general market infrastructure with components representing customers and providers and additional components for market-internal services.

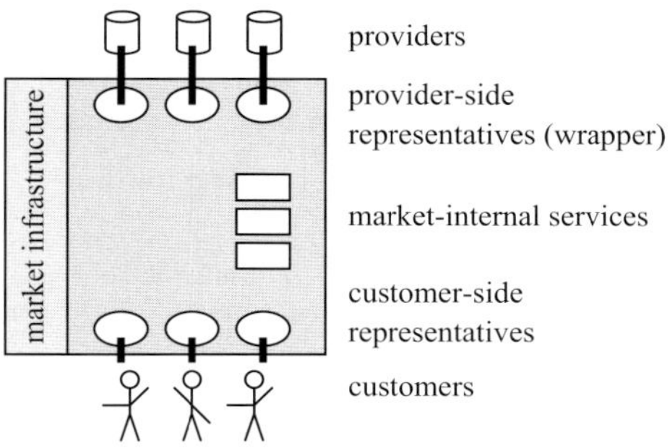

Figure 1: General market infrastructure.

For efficiency reasons, it is necessary to tailor a wrapper for a provider. What comes more, for every change in the provider's offers, conditions, prices, etc., and also for every change in the Web interface, the wrapper has to be re-written or at least adapted. Doing all this manually takes a big amount of time and expenses, and it this is not practicable in a larger dynamic market.

In this paper, we present an approach for a flexible wrapper component for Web interfaces, which can be adapted to the interface of a provider by loading a source description file. We also present a tool for the generation of source description files for a given provider.

The paper is organized as follows. After an overview on related approaches in section 2, we introduce our wrapper component in section 3. The process of the generation of the source description is presented in section 4. In section 5, we discuss how minor changes in the Web representation can be detected without having to edit the source description. Section 6 contains an overview of the implementation and section 7 first experiences of the application of our approach in a special electronic market. We conclude the paper in section 8.

2 RELATED WORK

There are various approaches for wrapping Web data sources. However, approaches like JEDI (Huck, Frankenhauser, et al., 1998), Garlic (Roth und Schwarz, 1997), TSIMMIS (Hammer, Breunig, et al., 1997), or Disco (Tomasic, Raschid et al., 1996) present no capable solution for wrapper generation. Instead of this, manual work is necessary.

UMICAS (Gruser, Raschid, et al., 1998) allows accessing semi-structured data represented in HTML interfaces. The extraction process is oriented on a tree representation of the HTML document. Simple Extractors perform extraction rules written in the Qualified path expression Extractor Language (QEL). Complex extractors use the services of the single extractors and build a higher level of extraction. However, the extraction process is limited to single pages (and this way not appropriate for most Web sites). There are graphical tools for wrapper generation, but their use is limited, because extraction rules have to be set up manually.

W^4F (World Wide Web Wrapper Factory) uses three different rule sets for the wrapper (Sahuguet and Azavanz, 1999). Retrieval Rules define the loading of Web pages from the Internet and their transformation in a tree representation. Extraction Rules define the extraction of values in the tree using the HTML extraction language (HEL). For each extracted argument, an ex expression in the Nested String List (NSL) is created. Navigation over different structured pages is not possible. Mapping Rules describe the creation of Java objects for the extracted data. The creation of these different rule sets is supported by a collection of different tools. However, for the final definition of the wrapper's behavior, the collection of the rule sets used lies in the hands of the user.

XWRAP (Liu, Pu, et al., 2000) provides a graphical tool for the semi-automatic generation of wrappers for Web interfaces, although the use of the wrapper is limited to patterns for the creation of XML documents out of selected Web pages. The wrapper generator allows to download Web pages from the Internet and automatically detects and removes errors in the HTML document. Region Extraction Wizards create extraction rules for values contained in the Web site, using regular expression for paths in a tree representation of the HTML document. However, a navigation over structural different Web pages is not supported.

Lixto (Baumgartner, Flesca, et al., 2001) desribes a similar approach, using different tools. Lixto contains a visual and interactive wrapper generator, which uses the declarative extraction language Elog. The Extractor can use these Elog files to create a Pattern Instance Bases for different attributes contained in the HTML page extraction from HTML page. The XML Generator transforms Pattern Instances to XML documents. Again, the construction of the Pattern Instances is restricted to one Web page.

3 WRAPPER

In this section, we want to discuss the properties and the design of our suggested flexible wrapper for Web interfaces (Pulkowski, 1999). The principle design of our wrapper can be seen in figure 2.

Each wrapper contains at least the following basis modules: coordinator, validation, planner, and converter. The coordinator is the wrapper's interface to the market infrastructure. This means, the design and the functionality of the wrapper is independent from the environment it is to operate. Especially, the coordinator receives and interprets queries from other market components and sends back the results. The validation module checks whether a query is syntactically and semantically correct. If necessary, the query is corrected, or an error message is sent back to the querying party.

A correct query will be handed over to the planner. The planner determines how to perform the query, which pages are needed, which results can be found on each page, and how to navigate between the pages. The central data structure used for the planning process is the navigation graph, which determines the structure of the Web interface. The planner creates a query plan, which is transmitted to the converter. According to the query plan and the navigation graph, the converter sends the query to the provider's Web interface, then extracts the necessary attribute sets out of the resulting HTML pages. Doing this, the converter navigates autonomously between different static and dynamic pages of the Web interface. The coordinator sends the result sets to the querying party.

The following modules are needed only for commercial providers: authorization, cost monitor, and protocol module. The authorization module proofs whether the querying party is allowed to perform queries to the provider, and which rights may be granted. The cost monitor pre-calculates the costs for the performance of the query. It determines whether the query may be performed or not. If necessary, e.g., if a cost limit given by the customer is too low, the customer will be informed about this situation. Additionally, the cost monitor controls the converter and can suspend the query process, if a cost limit is reached. The protocol module protocols

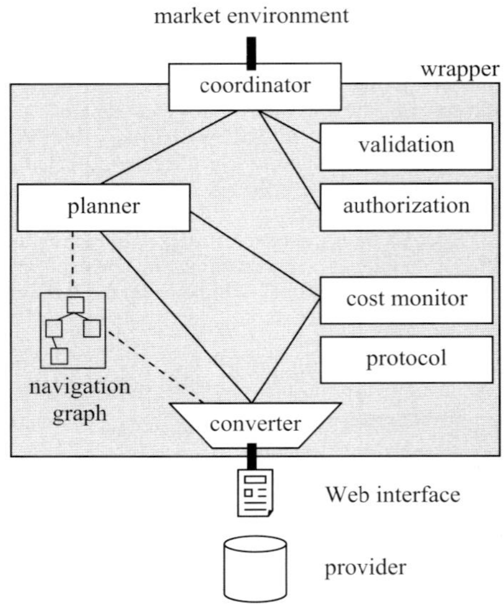

Figure 2: Wrapper design.

all actions of the wrapper. This protocol can be used in case of law-suit.

In this paper, we abstract from metadata management. It is necessary that the wrapper holds (and maintains) much more metadata than needed for query and result translation. These additional metadata are needed by other market components and should be collected in a step additional to the creation of the source description. For more details compare (Christoffel, Pulkowski, et al., 2000).

The design of the wrapper is independent from the provider it is connected. Hence, all information needed to tailor the wrapper for a provider must be contained in the source description file. This file is an XML document containing information about the query format, costs for accessing pages, result types, the structure of the result pages, etc. Also queries and result sets are embedded in XML documents.

Extraction rules needed for the extraction of values from HTML pages are formulized as Extended Hierarchical Path Expressions (EHPE), embedded in XML. Simplified, EHPE follow the following grammar:

expression := (node)+ (op)+.
node := node-name [index].
node-name := tag | **pcdata**.
index := index, index | number
| number - number | number - | - number | * .
op := **att** (identifier) | **txt**() | **split**(regex)
| **match**(regex) | **search**(regex).

An extended hierarchical path expression consists of a sequence of one or more nodes, followed by a sequence of one or more operators. Each node consists of a node name and an index. The sequence of the nodes describes the sequence of nodes visited when following a path from the root of a tree representation of the HTML document to the considered node. The node name can be any legal HTML tag or the keyword pcdata which stands for an arbitrary character sequence. Each tag that can be used to encompass parts of a document can also open a new level of hierarchy. Since each level of the HTML tree can contain several nodes with the same name, the index describes the number of the considered node in the order of appearance in the level (starting with 0). The index can be any sequence or range of nonnegative integers. The symbol * is used as a shortcut for all appearances of the node name in the level.

On the nodes the following operators can be applied: att, txt, split, match, and search. att should only be applied on a node referencing a tag. It returns the value of the attribute given as argument (as character sequence). txt is used for extracting text out of an HTML document. Applied to a pcdata node, it returns the character sequence the node stands for; applied to any other leaf node, it returns an empty list. Applied to an inner node, however, txt is recursively applied to all nodes of the subtree under the node (depth first), returning a nested list of all texts in the subtree in the order of appearance. The last three operators should be applied to a character string and take a regular expression as argument. split should be applied on a character string that contains substrings separated by a delimiter and returns a list of these substrings. match returns the given string if this string matches the regular expression, otherwise it returns an empty string. search extracts a substring that fits the regular expression.

Whenever hierarchical path expression do not describe one single node but a list of nodes, the operators are applied to every node contained in the list. In this case, the result of the EHPE is a list of the results for each node contained in the list.

Examples for these hierarchical expressions are:

- html[0]body[0]table[0]tr[*]th[1]table[0}tr[*]txt()
- html[0]body[0}table[0]att(border)
- html[0]body[0]table[0]tr[*]th[0}pcdata[0]txt() split(" ")

4 WRAPPER GENERATION

Creating the source description file for a provider manually is tricky and time-consuming, especially because the files have to be adapted for nearly every change in the provider or its Web interface. However, a fully automatic generation is not possible, since the semantics of the Web pages are not known in the general case. A human user, in the other hand, often can interpret the content of a Web page very easily. So we created a wrapper generator (which generates only the source description files, despite of the name), which bases on interaction with a user. The wrapper generator should be intuitive in use and ease the work of the human user as far as possible.

The metaphor that underlies the generation process is generation by example. The user has to perform a sample query on the provider and mark the important elements in the pages; the real generation process is done by the generator.

The generation process consists of three steps. First, the user chooses an entry page for the search by either directly giving the URL or by navigation. Second, the user selects one form on the entry page and starts the search by entering arguments. It is not really important, which arguments the customers enters, because the wrapper generator automatically analyzes the form, enabling the wrapper to send queries autonomously, using all available parameters. Third, the user marks relevant attributes contained on the result pages. He/she can select single attributes or use a multi-selection mode, where the wrapper generator automatically tries to find hierarchical path expressions for a larger group of nodes from two selections of the user. The user is free to navigate between Web pages, even if these are structurally completely different. The wrapper generator automatically finds all paths of navigation among the Web pages.

The design of the wrapper generator is presented in figure 3.

The wrapper generator consists of the following modules: user interface, planner, converter, generator, and data module. Among this, planner and converter are already known from the wrapper design. The user interface is essential for the wrapper generator, because each user, who is in most cases not a computer scientist, should be able to work with it without long training. The user interface provides both views on the source and the source description. The generator module creates hierarchical path expressions for selected parts of the HTML tree. The data module is responsible for file operations. For efficiency reasons, the data module supports a cache manager for previously loaded Web pages.

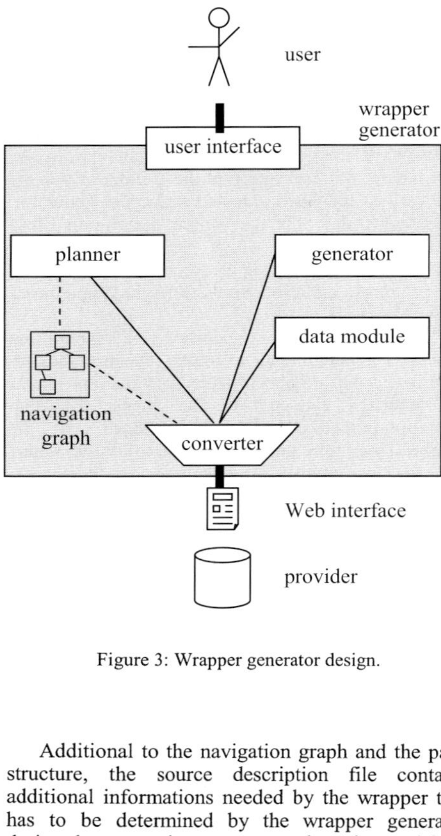

Figure 3: Wrapper generator design.

Additional to the navigation graph and the page structure, the source description file contains additional informations needed by the wrapper that has to be determined by the wrapper generator during the generation process, such as the need for a login or cost factors. The source description file contains also entries that are not needed for the wrapper but for the wrapper generator to repeat the generation process at any time. The wrapper generator can restore the environment of the last use, and the user can instantly do the needed changes.

5 WRAPPER ADAPTION

In many cases, changes in the provider's offers and its Web representations force a modification of the source description file. The wrapper generator opens a comfortable way to do modification without having the need to repeat the entire generation process. As far as possible, however, the detection of smaller changes and the modification of the source description should be done without human help.

An important class of changes are modifications in the Web site. The re-arrangement of the elements in the web page or simply the addition of some tags can make the wrapper useless, if due to the changes the extraction rules are now inconsistent, or, worse, they are still consistent but extract the wrong data.

The detection algorithm also works if changes imply several attributes. For each of these considered attributes, a test data set must be available, together with the queries that are used to generate these data sets. For error detection, the queries are repeated and the results are compared with the test data. Major differences indicate the use of an extraction rule that is no more valid.

The idea behind the detection algorithm is that the test data can be found on the result pages, but maybe at a different position than expected. However, if the attribute can be found on a series of web pages that are identical in their structure, then it can be found on each of these web pages at the same position. So we search the result pages for each appearance of the test data in the document text. Then we count the number of matches for each node of the HTML tree. With a certain probability, the node with the highest number of matches is the node, where the attribute can be extracted. The extraction rule for this node will be the new rule for the attribute. Of course, it is possible that a test string can also be found at any other node by chance. But since this match will not be found in other web pages, the number of matches for this node will be 1.

If the results can be found in a list on one page only, the algorithm has to be modified. The result is a set of nodes that can be described by one expression rule (using the * wildcard).

6 IMPLEMENTATION

Figure 4 shows the user interface of the wrapper generator. The user interface shows three different views of the source: the tree view, the text view, and the browser view. The actions that can be performed by the user always depend on the context.

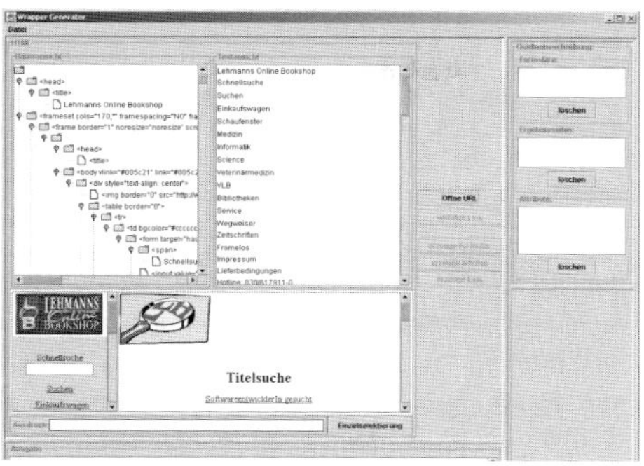

Figure 4: User interface of the wrapper generator.

Figure 5 shows the interface of the wrapper generator during the generation process. The wrapper generator can handle several HTML files at the one, and the user can switch among them freely. By selecting relevant attributes, extraction rules are created and added to the source description.

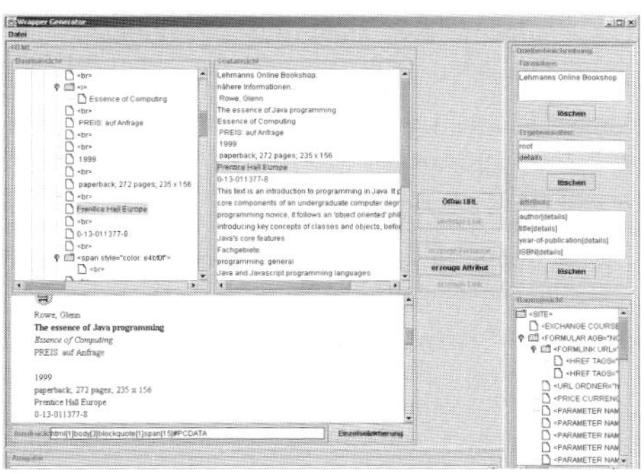

Figure 5: User interface of the wrapper generator.

Both wrapper and wrapper generator have been implemented with Java 2, using the additional packages JavaRegex for the implementation of regular expressions, JTidy for the correction of the loaded HTML pages, and XML4J for the generation and administration of XML data structures.

7 APPLICATION

The wrapper presented in this paper has been used for accessing data sources in a special kind of information market, namely the market of scientific literature. This market shows the importance of a uniform access to the information providers. While the supply on scientific literature worldwide is very rich and still growing, search for literature is a large, time-consuming work, especially if a list of providers has to be accessed sequentially. The trend of the commercialization of the Internet can make literature search also become very expensive.

Within the UniCats project, a market infrastructure is being developed for this special market (Christoffel, Pulkowksi et al., 1998). The project is funded by German Research Foundation (DFG) as a part of the strategic research offensive Distributed Distribution and Processing of Digital Documents (V^3D^2).

Figure 6 shows the architecture of the UniCats system. In addition to the wrappers we have developed two other market components until now: user agents that act as representatives of the customers (Schmitt and Schmidt, 1999), and traders that provide a market-internal service of provider selection (Christoffel, 1999). Technical basis of the infrastructure is the UniCats environment, a framework for independent and communicative UniCats agents (Christoffel. Nimis, et al., 2000).

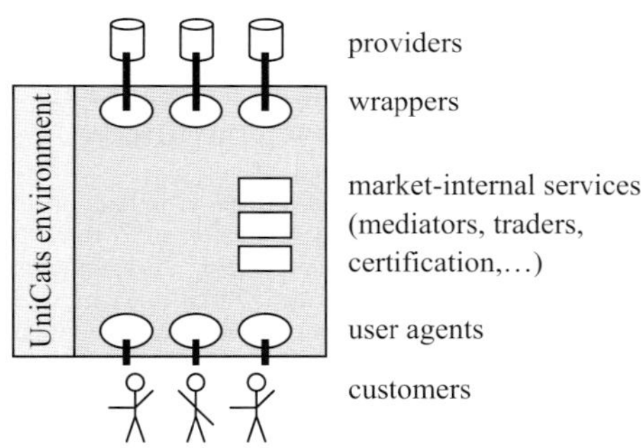

Figure 6: UniCats architecture

We proved the functionality of the wrapper generator in an experiment with 8 human test persons, who had never had worked with the wrapper generator before. After an introduction of 15 minutes, the test persons had to perform three tasks. Each task contained the development of a source description file for one information provider. The difficulty of the task increased, while the degree of details in the instructions decreased. The candidates had no help except a 4-page description of the user interface; question were not allowed. For each task, we assessed the needed time and the quality of the created source description.

For the experiment, we chose three very different sources, which have different requirements, but all are in a sense typical for the selected market: Indiana University Knowledge Base, Lehmann's Online Bookshop, and the catalogue of the university library of Karlsruhe. According to their own statements, the first two sources were not known to the candidates, while the third source was known to all.

The first result was that nearly all constructed wrappers (24 in total) work. Only in two cases a wrapper has been constructed with limited functionality. In one case a wrapper has been constructed with more functionality than demanded in the instruction.

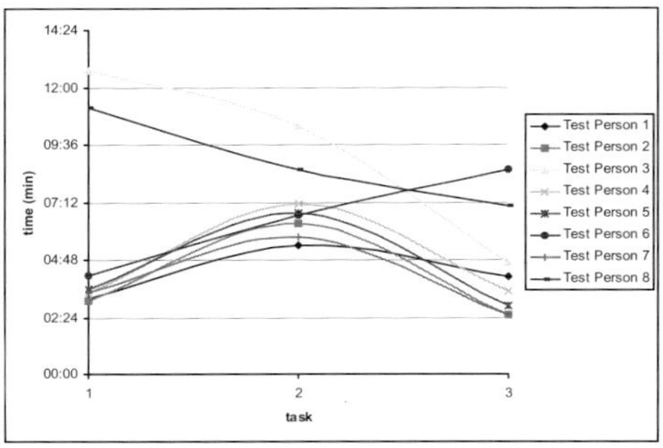

Figure 7: Results of the experiment.

Figure 7 shows a graphical visualization of the measured times needed to perform the three tasks. The average times needed are 5:36 minutes for task 1, 7:07 minutes for task 2, and 4:31 minutes for task 3. Unfortunately, we can not give a comparable value for the time needed for a manual creation of the source descriptions for the three tasks, because we did not want to except this work from a volunteer. According to an expert, a trained computer scientist needs about 2 hours for the creation of a source description for literature sources of a comparable degree of difficulty.

Perhaps the most interesting result of the experiment is that all candidates found the handling of the wrapper generator intuitive and were able to instantly work with the generator. In figure 7, we can also read that a training effect has started very early, since most candidate could increase their speed in task 3, the most difficult task of all.

8 CONCLUSIONS

In this paper, we presented an approach for a wrapper component for the connection of heterogeneous providers in an open market. The wrapper can be adapted to different providers by loading a source description file. The source description file can be created semi-automatically with the help of a wrapper generator.

For this approach, we have shown a range of advantages:

- The wrapper uses no connection to the provider but its Web interface.
- It is possible to install a wrapper for a provider without knowledge about internal data structures and business logic.
- The wrapper can operate on complete Web sites containing many static and dynamic structurally different Web pages. The wrapper can also be used for commercial Web sites.
- The use of the wrapper generator corresponds to the performance of a query. It does not need any expert knowledge.
- An existing source description can easily be modified, and this way the wrapper can comprehend any changes of the provider. Smaller changes can be comprehended automatically.
- The implementation of wrapper and wrapper generator is platform-independent.
- The wrapper has been designed for the use in a market infrastructure. Test applications in a real market scenario have started.

In the future, the challenges will lie in the application of the approach for other domains and markets. Potential application fields include meta search engines and product catalogues for online distributors.

REFERENCES

Baumgartner, R., Flesca, S., Gottlob, G., 2001. Visual Web Information Extraction with Lixto. In *Proceedings of the 27th Conferenc on very Large Data Bases,* Rome, pp. 119-128.

Christoffel, M., Pulkowski, S., Schmitt, B., Lockemann, P., 1998. Electronic Commerce: The Roadmap for University Libraries and their Members to Survive in the Information Jungle. In *ACM Sigmod Record 27 (4)*, pp. 68-73.

Christoffel, M., 1999. A Trader for Services in a Scientific Literature Market. In *Proceedings of the 2nd*

International Workshop on Engineering Federated Information Systems. infix, pp. 123-130.

Christoffel, M., Pulkowski, S., Lockemann P., 2000. Integration and Mediation of Information Sources in an Open Market Environment. In *Proceedings of the 4th International Conference Business Information Systems*, Springer, pp. 82-90.

Christoffel, M., Nimis, J., Pulkowski, S., Schmitt, B., Lockemann, P., 2000. An Infrastructure for an Electronic Market of Scientific Literature. In *Proceedings of the 4th IEEE International Baltic Workshop on Databases and Information Systems*, Kluwer Academic Publishers, pp. 155-166.

Gruser, J.-R., Raschid, L., Vidal, M., Bright, L., 1998. Wrapper Generation for Web Accessible Data Sources. In *Proceedings of the 3rd International Conference on Cooperative Information Systems*, New York City, pp. 14-23.

Hammer, J., Breunig, M., García-Molina, H., Nestorov, S., Vassalos, V., Yerneni, R., 1997. Template-based Wrappers in the TSIMMIS System. In *Proceedings of the 26th International Conference on Management of Data,* Tucson, pp. 532-535.

Huck, G., Frankenhauser, P., Aberer, K., Neuhold, E., 1998. Jedi: Extracting and Synthesizing Information from the Web. In *Proceedings of the 3rd International Conference on Cooperative Information Systems,* New York City, pp. 32-43.

Kushmerick, N., 1999. Regression testing for wrapper maintainance. In *Proceedings of the 16th National Conference on Artificial Intelligence (AAAI-99),* Orlando.

Liu, L., Pu, C., Lee, Y.-S., 2000. An XML-enebled Wrapper Construction System for Web Information Sources. In *Proceedings of the 15th International Confernce on Data Engineering*, San Diego, IEEE, pp. 611-621.

Pulkowski, S., 1999. Making Information Sources Available for a New Market in an Electronic Commerce Environment. In *Proceedings of the International Conference on Management of Information and Communication Technology,* Copenhagen.

Roth, M., Schwarz, P., 1997. Don't Scap It, Wrap It! A Wrapper Architecture for Legacy Systems. I *Proceedings of the 23rd International Conference on Very Large Data Bases,* Athens, pp. 266-275.

Sahuguet, A., Azavant, F. 1999. Building Light-Weight-Wrappers for Legacy Web Data-Sources Using W4F. In *Proceedings of the International Conference on Very Large Data Bases,* pp. 738-741.

Schmitt, B., Schmidt, A., 1999. METALICA: An Enhanced Meta Search Engine for Literature Catalogs. In *Proceedings of the 2nd Asian Digital Libraries Conference*, Taipei.

Tomasic, A., Raschid, L., Valdruriez, P., 1996: Scaling Heterogeneous Databases and the Design of Disco. In *Proceedings of the 16th International Conference on Distributed Computing Systems*, Hong Kong, pp. 449-457.

FSQL: A FLEXIBLE QUERY LANGUAGE FOR DATA MINING

Ramón Alberto Carrasco, María Amparo Vila
Dpto. de Ciencias de la Computación e I.A., Universidad de Granada, Granada, Spain
Email: rcarrasco@caja-granada.es, vila@decsai.ugr.es

José Galindo
Dpto. de Lenguajes y Ciencias de la Computación, Universidad de Málaga, Spain
Email: ppgg@lcc.uma.es

Key words: Flexible Queries, Fuzzy SQL, Data Mining, Fuzzy Databases, Artificial Neural Networks

Abstract: At present we have a FSQL server available for Oracle© Databases, programmed in PL/SQL. This server allows us to query a Fuzzy or Classical Database with the FSQL language (Fuzzy SQL). The FSQL language is an extension of the SQL language, which permits us to write flexible (or fuzzy) conditions in our queries to a fuzzy or traditional database. In this paper we show an extension of FDBR architecture of FSQL for fuzzy handling of different types of data. The main advantage is that any user can to define his own fuzzy comparator for any specific problem. We consider that this model satisfies the requirements of Data Mining systems (handling of different types of data, high-level language, efficiency, certainty, interactivity, etc) and this new level of personal configuration makes the system very useful and flexible.

1 INTRODUCTION

In the last years, the management applications have been popularised and widely extended. In these applications, the database management is very important. Thus, the final users use many times the DBMS (Database Management Systems) directly or through an interface program (front-end).
On the other hand, the fuzzy databases have been developed in the last years, rising up different models [14], among which they highlight the Prade-Testemale model, the Umano-Fukami model, the Buckles-Petry model, the Zemankova-Kaendel model and the GEFRED model by Medina-Pons-Vila [13]. This last model represents an eclectic synthesis of the different models, which have appeared to deal with the problem of the representation and management of fuzzy information in relational databases (FRDB). Besides, for the GEFRED model, the FSQL language [8,9,10], a fuzzy (or flexible) query language based on the SQL language, has been defined. This language allows us to express sentences taking into account the characteristics of imprecise information. Thus, as we will see, the FSQL queries allow expressing fuzzy conditions, to calculate fulfilment degrees, to establish fulfilment thresholds... Some applications for FSQL Server can be found, for example, in [1,2,3,4,10,11].
First, we include a brief explanation of the main advantages of the FSQL `SELECT` sentence, in order to express fuzzy queries. Besides, we explain the FRDB architecture for the FSQL Server (a more detailed description of this can be found in [8,10]). Then, we extend the FRDB architecture for fuzzy handling of different types of data. After, we show some examples using the improved FRDB architecture on different types of data or with different fuzzy comparison functions. Thus, we define a method of ranking fuzzy numbers using Artificial Neural Networks (ANN). Therefore, we use the defined comparison method to compare fuzzy quantities in FSQL, allowing any user to train his own fuzzy ANN comparator. Thus, the trained ANN will be a special comparator for any specific problem. A more extend information on this can be found in [4].
According to [5] Data Mining (DM) is a process of non-trivial extraction of implicit, previously unknown and potentially useful information (for instance knowledge rules, constraints and regularities) from the data in a database. We consider that this model satisfies the requirements of

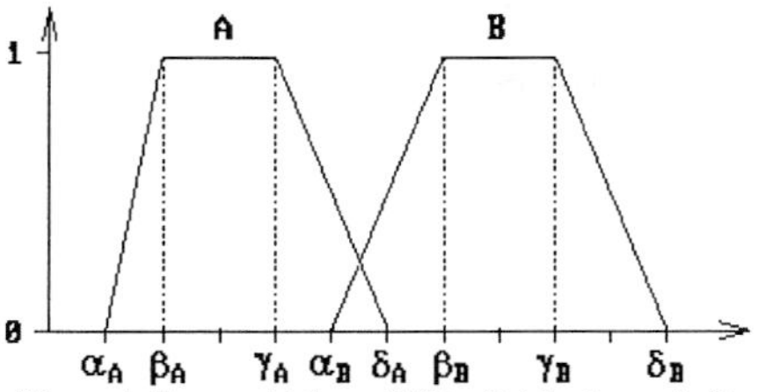

Figure 1. Trapezoidal possibility distributions: A, B.

DM systems [5,6,7] (handling of different types of data, high-level language, efficiency, certainty, interactivity, etc) and this new level of personal configuration makes the system very useful and flexible. Finally, we present an example used in our test, and we suggest some conclusions.
The example is in the context of a bank. This area needs a Data Mining system tailored to its needs, because this area manages very large databases and these data has a very concrete meaning. Thus, data must be treated according to this meaning.

2 FSQL A LANGUAGE FOR FLEXIBLE QUERIES

The FSQL language [8,9,10] extends the SQL language to allow flexible queries. We have extended the `SELECT` command to express flexible queries and, due to its complex format, we only show an abstract with the main extensions added to this command:

- **Linguistic Labels:** If an attribute is capable of undergoing fuzzy treatment then linguistic labels can be defined on it. These labels will be preceded with the symbol $ to distinguish them easily. Every label has an associated trapezoidal possibility (Figure 1) or it is a scalar if there is a similarity relationship defined between each two labels in the same domain.
- **Fuzzy Comparators:** In addition to common comparators (=, >, etc), FSQL includes fuzzy comparators in Table 1. There are some different kinds of fuzzy comparators. The most important is used to compare two trapezoidal possibility distributions A, B with A=$[$\alpha_A,\beta_A,\gamma_A,\delta_A$] B=$[$\alpha_B,\beta_B,\gamma_B,\delta_B$] (see Figure 1). In the same way as in SQL, fuzzy comparators can compare one column with one constant or two columns of the same type. More information can be found in [9,10]. These definitions are based in typical possibility comparators in fuzzy set theory.

Fuzzy Comparator (fcomp) for:		Significance
Possibility	Necessity	
FEQ	NFEQ	Fuzzy EQual
FGT	NFGT	Fuzzy Greater Than
FGEQ	NFGEQ	Fuzzy Greater or Equal
FLT	NFLT	Fuzzy Less Than
FLEQ	NFLEQ	Fuzzy Less or Equal
MGT	NMGT	Much Greater Than
MLT	NMLT	Much Less Than

Table 1. Fuzzy Comparators for FSQL

- **Fulfilment Thresholds γ:** For each simple condition a Fulfilment threshold may be established with the format *<condition> THOLD* γ, indicating that the condition must be satisfied with a minimum degree γ in [0,1] fulfilled.
- **CDEG(<attribute>) function**: This function shows a column with the Fulfilment degree of the condition of the query for a specific attribute, which is expressed in brackets as the argument.
- **Fuzzy Constants**: In FSQL we can use and store all of the fuzzy constants, which appear in Table 2.

F. Constant	Significance
UNKOWN	Unknown value but the attribute is applicable
UNDEFINED	The attribute is not applicable or it is meaningless
NULL	Total ignorance: We know nothing about it
A=$[$\alpha_A,\beta_A,\gamma_A,\delta_A$]	Fuzzy trapezoid ($\alpha_A\leq\beta_A\leq\gamma_A\leq\delta_A$): See Figure 1
$label	Linguistic Label: It may be a trapezoid or a scalar (defined in FMB)
[n, m]	Interval "Between n and m" ($\alpha_A=\beta_A$=n and $\gamma_A=\delta_A$=m)
#n	Fuzzy value "Approximately n" ($\beta_A=\gamma_A$=n and n-$\alpha_A=\delta_A$=margin)

Table 2: Fuzzy Constants of FSQL

2.1 FRDB architecture of FSQL

At present we have a FSQL Server available for Oracle© Databases, programmed in PL/SQL. Basically, the architecture of the FRDB with the FSQL Server is made up by:
1.**Data**: Traditional Database and Fuzzy Meta-knowledge Base (FMB).
2.**FSQL Server**.

2.1.1 Data: Traditional Database and FMB

The data can be classified in two categories:

- **Traditional Database**: They are data from our relations with a special format to store the fuzzy attribute values. The fuzzy attributes are classified by the system in 3 types:
  - Fuzzy Attributes **Type 1**: These attributes are totally crisp (traditional), but they have some linguistic trapezoidal labels defined on them, which allow us to make the query conditions for these attributes more flexible. Besides, we can use all constants in Table 2 in the query conditions with these fuzzy attributes.
  - Fuzzy Attributes **Type 2**: These attributes admit crisp data as well as possibility distributions over an ordered underlying domain. With these attributes we can store and use all the constants we see in Table 2.
  - Fuzzy Attributes **Type 3**: These attributes have not an ordered underlying domain. On these attributes some labels are defined and on these labels a similarity relation has yet to be defined. With these attributes we can only use the fuzzy comparator FEQ, as they have no relation of order. Obviously we cannot store or use the constants fuzzy trapezoid, interval and approximate value of Table 2.

- **Fuzzy Meta-knowledge Base** (FMB): It stores information about the FRDB in a relational format. It stores attributes which admit fuzzy treatment and it will store different information for each one of them, depending on their type:
  - Fuzzy Attributes **Type 1**: In order to use crisp attributes in flexible queries we will only have to declare them as being a fuzzy attribute type 1 and store the following data in the FMB: Trapezoidal linguistic labels: Name of the label and α_A,β_A, γ_A and δ_A values (as in Figure 1). Value for the margin of the approximate values (see Table 1). Minimum distance in order to consider two values very separated (used in comparators MGT/NMGT and MLT/NMLT).
  - Fuzzy Attributes **Type 2:** As well as declare them as being a fuzzy attribute type 2, these attributes have to store the same data in the FMB as the fuzzy attributes Type 1.
  - Fuzzy Attributes **Type 3:** They store in the FMB their linguistic labels, the similarity degree amongst themselves and the compatibility between attributes of this type, i.e., the attributes that use the same labels and that can be compared amongst themselves.

2.1.2 FSQL Server

It has been programmed entirely in PL/SQL and it includes 3 kinds of functions:

- **Translation Function**: It carries out a lexical, syntactic and semantic analysis of the FSQL query. If errors, of any kind whatsoever, are found, it will generate a table with all the found errors. If there are no errors, the FSQL query is translated into a standard SQL sentence. The resulting SQL sentence includes reference to the following kinds of functions.
- **Representation Functions**: These functions are used to show the fuzzy attributes in a comprehensible way for the user and not in the internally used format.
- **Fuzzy Comparison Functions**: They are utilized to compare the fuzzy values and to calculate the compatibility degrees (CDEG function).

3 EXTENDING FRDB ARCHITECTURE OF FSQL

We have already applied FSQL to DM processes [1,2,3,4]. Handling of different types of data is a necessary property for DM systems. Our objective is increasing the potential of FSQL in order to complete this property. Therefore we have extended the FRDB architecture at two levels:

1. **Data**: Traditional Database and FMB.
2. **FSQL Server**.

3.1 Data: Traditional Database and FMB

- **Traditional Database**: There are different kinds of data in a database used in diverse applications (relational data, objects, hypertext, etc.), therefore it would be desirable that a Data Mining system would carry out its work in an effective way. In order to manage these data we defined:
  - Attributes **Type 4**: These attributes are a generic type (fuzzy or crisp), which admit some fuzzy treatment. We permitted this attribute is formed by more than a column of the table. With these attributes we can store and use the constants linguistic label in Table 2.

- **Fuzzy Meta-knowledge Base** (FMB): We have modified the FMB, such it stores information for the fuzzy treatment of the attributes Type 4.
  - **Fuzzy Comparison Functions**: The user can define the functions of comparison (Table 1) for the treatment of each attribute of Type 4. The format is: *CDEG(A fcomp B)->[0,1]* with *CDEG* the compatibility degrees, *A*, *B* two

attributes or linguistic labels Type 4 and *fcomp* any fuzzy comparator in Table 1. The user can associate each attribute functions already defined in the FMB

- **Representation Functions**: The user can optionally define it to show the attributes in a more comprehensible way. Of course the user can associate each attribute functions already defined in the FMB
- **Linguistic labels**: They represent a concrete value of the attribute.
- **Complex attributes**: We permitted this attribute is formed by more than a column of the table. Therefore the FMB stores information on structure of the attributes Type 4.

3.2 FSQL Server

As we have seen, Translation and Representation Functions are now in FMB for the attributes Type 4. Therefore the FSQL Server have been modified only in the next functionality:

- **Translation Function**: The lexical and syntactic analysis of the FSQL query for attributes Type 4 is the same that rest of attributes. We have modified the semantic analysis for such attributes. The FSQL query is translated into a standard SQL sentence using the enhanced FMB above explained. Therefore we can use new type of data only including information about it (functions, labels, etc.) in the FMB.

4 USING THE EXTENSION OF FRDB ARCHITECTURE OF FSQL

Now, we can use FSQL for any data type. We need only to have the comparison functions and to fill the FMB for this attribute (Type 4).

Thus by example, for an attribute Type 4 defined as several numeric columns of a Table we can defined on it FEQ comparators following: Euclidean Distance, Mahalonobi Distance, Sokal&Michener Distance (if all columns of the attribute have only binary values), etc.

Besides non-structured attributes (as strings, documents, graphics, etc.) can be used with FSQL if we can to define the comparison functions on it.

This also allows us have a more subjective vision of original FSQL comparators for possibility distributions. Following we have a new definition of this FSQL comparators for fuzzy attributes Type 2 based on Artificial Neural Networks (ANN). More information can be found in [4].

4.1 Fuzzy Comparator in FSQL using ANN

There are several methods to compare fuzzy attributes because the process of comparison of imprecise data is a diffuse process. Often this problem is not solved satisfactorily because it is difficult for a decision-maker to accept that some of the algorithmic methods in the literature [17] could adequately perform his own way to decide. Hence, the decision-maker would like to have a personal method, which implements his own criteria to compare fuzzy numbers especially in the face of conflictive cases like in Figure 2.

Solving this problem seems a very appropriate field for ANN because for most people it is easy to see that the trained ANN has learnt with examples given by him. That is not so clear with the algorithmic methods. Requena et al. [15] propose a method of ranking fuzzy numbers using ANN. Next we describe such method shortly.

Often trapezoidal possibility distributions are used representing fuzzy attributes in many systems, FSQL included (see section 2). Thus, the problem is to compare two trapezoidal possibility distributions A, B with $A=\$[\alpha_A,\beta_A,\gamma_A,\delta_A]$ $B=\$[\alpha_B,\beta_B,\gamma_B,\delta_B]$. Therefore, the inputs to the network are 8 (4 for each fuzzy number) and 1 output with 3 possible values: A<B, A=B y A>B. The initial objective is to select an ANN structure capable to learn, and therefore to reproduce different comparison fuzzy numbers methods, considering for them the same topology and learning algorithm methods have coherent behaviour which may not be found in the human decision-makers, and because it is a simpler and more direct way of obtaining learning examples. If the learning is good from different comparison methods [12,16] with these characteristics, then we can deduce that this model can be used to learn the behaviour of any human decision-maker with a minimal level of coherence.

With the basic structures of 16 neurons with one hidden layer, 12+6 neurons for 2 hidden layers, initial values of 0.5 and 0.1 for the learning rate, backpropagation algorithm, and considering a basic learning set (with conflictive cases included) the authors obtain a sufficiently good learning of the behaviour of any real decision-maker, when comparing fuzzy numbers.

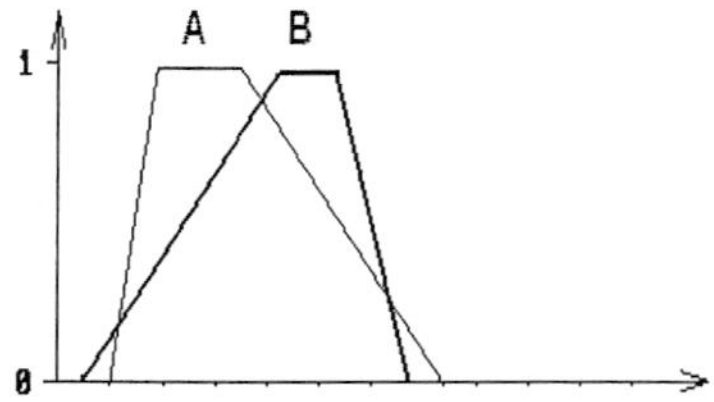

Figure 2: Conflictive case to compare fuzzy numbers.

Now, it is necessary to relate the FSQL environment above explained with this ANN method. To do it, we will introduce a general definition of FSQL operators using ANN. We suppose that we want to comparate two trapezoidal possibility distributions A and B (Figure 1) with $A=\$[\alpha_A,\beta_A,\gamma_A,\delta_A]$ $B=\$[\alpha_B,\beta_B,\gamma_B,\delta_B]$. CDEG is used in FSQL to show a column with the fulfilment degree of the fuzzy condition. Therefore we will proceed to define CDEG for each fuzzy comparator using a procedure based on the ANN above explained.

Previously, we define the function:

fcomp_ann (A, B, fcomp, dpc_fcomp_i)

where:

- **fcomp** is a fuzzy comparator for FSQL (see Table 1)
- **dpc_fcomp_i** is the decision personal criteria of the user *i* for the comparator *fcomp*. This parameter contains all information above the ANN trained by que user *i* (weights matrix) for the comparator *fcomp*.

Thus the user *i* trains a network (based on the ANN above explained) for the comparator *fcomp* thought a set of examples (fuzzy numbers with intersection with conflictive cases includes). For this examples he decides if A *fcomp* B is true except whether the *fcomp* is FEQ then the user must give the degree fulfilment in this set {0.2, 0.4, 0.6, 0.8}. Therefore the possible values of *fcomp_ann* are:

- If fcomp <> {FEQ} then

fcomp_ann (A, B, fcomp, dpc_fcomp_i)=
1, if *A fcomp B* with *dpc_fcomp_i*
0, otherwise

- If fcomp = {FEQ} then

fcomp_ann (A, B, fcomp, dpc_fcomp_i) =
{0.2, 0.4, 0.6, 0.8} degree fulfilment A FEQ B with *dpc_fcomp_i*

How we have seen, CDEG returns the fulfilment degree in [0,1] of the fuzzy condition. But he function *fcomp_ann* defined (for the comparators of inequality) only allows us ranking the possibility distributions A and B. Therefore we needed a method in order to express such fulfilment degree. In order to express the distance between two fuzzy numbers, Requena et al. [15] define the decision personal index DPI as an application from the fuzzy numbers set to raking in $\Re$ (real line). However when FSQL compare A and B it does not have information about the rest of fuzzy numbers which it is a dynamic information (possible values of the fuzzy attributes). In order to solve this problem we have developed the following method.

Firstly we define the function *df_ann (A, fcomp, dpc_fcomp_i)* which returns a value in [0,1] which is the crisp value that represents to *A* with the criteria of the user *i* learnt by the ANN for the *fcomp* comparator:

df_ann (A, fcomp, dpc_fcomp_i) = $(a_1 + a_2) / 2$

where

a_1 = Inf {a ∈ $[\alpha_A, \delta_A]$ / *fcomp_ann* (a, *A*, *fcomp*, *dpc_fcomp_i*) = 1}

a_2 = Sup {a ∈ $[\alpha_A, \delta_A]$ / *fcomp_ann (A*, a, *fcomp*, *dpc_fcomp_i*) = 1}

For the implementation of this function we have used a method of binary search in order to find a_1 and a_2. In practique in order to be more precise than the third decimal (for a_1 and a_2) place does not produce any improvement to represent *A*.

We have that *Ham* $(a,b)_{max,min}$ is a function witch returns the absolute difference between two real numbers *a* y *b* previously convert to [0,1]:

$$Ham\ (a,b)_{max,min} = \\ |\,[(1 - max/(max - min)) + a * (1 / (max - min))] \\ - [(1 - max/(max - min)) + b * (1 / (max - min))]\,|$$

Now we proceed to define each one of the FSQL comparators considering that $max=Max(\delta_A,\delta_B)$ and $min=Min(\alpha_A, \alpha_B)$. The following definition can be incorporate without problems to the enhaced FMB of FSQL above explained:

CDEG (A FGT B) =
- 1, if $\gamma_A >= \delta_B$
- 0, if $\gamma_B >= \delta_A$ or *fcomp_ann (A, B, FGT, dpc_FGT_i)*=0
- $Ham_{max,min}$[(*df_ann(A,FGT,dpc_FGT_i)*, (*df_ann (B, FGT, dpc_FGT_i)*], otherwise

CDEG (A FGEQ B) =
- 1, if $\gamma_A >= \beta_B$
- 0, if $\beta_B >= \delta_A$ or *fcomp_ann (A,B,FGEQ, dpc_FGEQ_i)*=0
- $Ham_{max,min}$ [(*df_ann(A,FGEQ, dpc_FGEQ_i)*, (*df_ann(B,FGEQ,dpc_FGEQ_i)*], otherwise

CDEG (A FEQ B) =
- 1, if $\alpha_A=\alpha_B$ and $\beta_A= \beta_B$ and $\gamma_A=\gamma_B$ and $\delta_A=\delta_B$
- 0, if $\delta_A < \alpha_B$ or $\delta_B < \alpha_A$
- *fcomp_ann (A,B,FEQ,dpc_FEQ_i)*, otherwise

For the next comparator (MGT) we define A_M=\$[α_A-M, β_A-M, γ_A-M, δ_A-M] with M is the minimum distance to consider two attributes as very separate. M is defined in FMB for each attribute.

CDEG (A MGT B) =

$$\begin{cases} 1, \text{ if } \gamma_A >= \delta_B+M \\ 0, \text{ if } \delta_A <= \delta_B+M \\ \quad \text{or } fcomp\_ann\ (A_M, B, FGT, dpc\_FGT_i) = 0 \\ Ham_{max,min}\ [(df\_ann\ (A_M,FGT,dpc\_FGT_i), \\ \quad (df\_ann\ (B, FGT, dpc\_FGT_i)], \text{ otherwise} \end{cases}$$

This system (FSQL and ANN comparators) has been applied in a context of bank customers in a real life situation. The banking expert has identified relevant attributes: payroll, credit card use level and average account balance. Payroll is a binary attribute that indicates if the client receives payroll through the financial company (value Y) or not (value N). The level of use of the credit card is represented by fuzzy values obtained through an analytic study in the company data warehouse system. The average account balance store fuzzy values based on the average of the last 12 months.

In this context, the following kinds of queries are very useful and with a trained ANN for fuzzy comparators, the bank can obtain information from the database that it is not explicitly. Of course, the goodness of the resulting values depending on the training stage.

```
SELECT AccountNumber, CDEG(*)
FROM   Customers
WHERE  Payroll = 'N'
AND    Credit_Card_Use FEQ $Medium
       THOLD 0.7
AND    Balance         FGT #300000
       THOLD 0.7
ORDER BY 2 DESC;
```

5 CONCLUSIONS

FSQL Server is an useful tool for DM process [1,2,3,4] and other applications [10,11]. However, it has a very important limitation, the handling of different types of data. In this paper we have showed an extension of FDBR architecture of FSQL that avoid this problem and make new definitions of operations and data very flexible. Thus, any user can define his own fuzzy comparator for any type of data. As example, we have defined fuzzy ANN comparator for any specific problem.

REFERENCES

[1] R.A. Carrasco, J. Galindo, M.C. Aranda, J.M. Medina, M.A. Vila, "Classification in Databases using a Fuzzy Query Language". 9th International Conference on Management of Data, COMAD'98, Hyderabad (India), December 1998.

[2] R.A. Carrasco, J. Galindo, M.A. Vila, J.M. Medina, "Clustering and Fuzzy Classification in a Financial Data Mining Environment". 3rd International ICSC Symposium on Soft Computing, SOCO'99, pp. 713-720, Genova (Italy), June 1999.

[3] R.A. Carrasco, M.A. Vila, J. Galindo, J.C. Cubero, "FSQL: a Tool for Obtaining Fuzzy Dependencies". 8th International Conference on Information Processing and Management of Uncertainty in Knowledge-Based Systems, IPMU'2000, pp. 1916-1919. Madrid (Spain), July 2000.

[4] R. Carrasco, J. Galindo, A. Vila, "Using Artificial Neural Network to Define Fuzzy Comparators in FSQL with the Criterion of some Decision-Maker". In "Bio-inspired applications of connectionism.-2001", eds. J. Mira and A. Prieto, Lecture Notes in Computer Science (LNCS) 2085, pp. 587-594. Ed. Springer-Verlag, 2001, ISBN: 3-540-42237-4.

[5] M. Chen, J. Han, P.S. Yu, "Data Mining: An overview from a Data Base Perspective". IEEE Transac. On Knowledge and Data Engineering, Vol 8-6 pp. 866-883, 1996.

[6] M.A. Vila, J.C. Cubero, J.M. Medina, O. Pons, "On the use of Soft Computing Techniques in Data Mining Problems". Technical report #DECSAI-96-01-12. Department of Computer Science and Artificial Intelligence. Universidad de Granada. Spain (1997).

[7] W.J. Frawley, G. Piatetsky-Shapiro, C.J. Matheus, "Knowledge Discovery in Databases: An Overview" in G. Piatetsky-Shapiro, W.J. Frawley eds. "Knowledge Discovery in Databases" pp. 1-31, The AAAI Press, 1991.

[8] J. Galindo, J.M. Medina, O. Pons, J.C. Cubero, "A Server for Fuzzy SQL Queries", in "Flexible Query Answering Systems", eds. T. Andreasen, H. Christiansen and H.L. Larsen, Lecture Notes in Artificial Intelligence (LNAI) 1495, pp. 164-174. Ed. Springer, 1998.

[9] J. Galindo, J.M. Medina, A. Vila, O. Pons, "Fuzzy Comparators for Flexible Queries to Databases". Iberoamerican Conference on Artificial Intelligence, IBERAMIA'98, pp. 29-41, Lisbon (Portugal), October 1998.

[10] J. Galindo, "Tratamiento de la Imprecisión en Bases de Datos Relacionales: Extensión del Modelo y Adaptación de los SGBD Actuales". Ph. Doctoral Thesis, University of Granada (Spain), March 1999. www.lcc.uma.es

[11] J. Galindo, J.M. Medina, J.C. Cubero, O. Pons, "Management of an Estate Agency Allowing Fuzzy Data and Flexible Queries". EUSFLAT-ESTYLF

Joint Conference, pp. 485-488, Palma de Mallorca (Spain), September 1999.
[12] R. Jain, "Tolerance Analisys using fuzzy sets". Internat. J. Systems Sci, 7, pp 1393-1401, 1976.
[13] J.M. Medina, O. Pons, M.A. Vila, "GEFRED. A Generalized Model of Fuzzy Relational Data Bases". Information Sciences, 76(1-2), pp. 87-109, 1994.
[14] F.E. Petry, "Fuzzy Databases: Principles and Applications" (with chapter contribution by Patrick Bosc). International Series in Intelligent Technologies. Ed. H.-J. Zimmermann. Kluwer Academic Publishers (KAP), 1996.
[15] I. Requena, M. Delgado, J.L. Verdegay, "Artificial neural networks learn the criteria of a real decision-maker to compare fuzzy numbers". Fuzzy Sets and Systems 64, pp 1-19, 1994.
[16] R.R. Yager, "Ranking fuzzy subsets over the unit interval". Proc. CDC, pp 1435-1437, 1978.
[17] Q. Zhu, E.S. Lee, "Comparison and ranking of fuzzy numbers". Fuzzy Regression Analysis. J. Kacpryk and Fedrizzi, eds. Omnitech Press, Warsaw, Poland, pp 21-44, 1991.

USING DATA MINING TECHNIQUES TO ANALYZE CORRESPONDENCES BETWEEN USER AND SCIENTIFIC KNOWLEDGE IN AN AGRICULTURAL ENVIRONMENT

D. Sánchez, J.M. Serrano, M.A. Vila
Department of Computer Science and A.I. University of Granada
{daniel,jmserrano,vila}@decsai.ugr.es

V. Aranda, J. Calero, G. Delgado
Department of Pedology and Agricultural Chemistry. University of Granada
varanda@ujaen.es, {varanda, gdelgado}@ugr.es

Key words: Information Fusion, Correspondence Analysis, Approximate Dependencies, Association Rules, Soil Classification.

Abstract: The incorporation of technology is recognized as one of the main factors affecting the future evolution of agriculture. In this context, a big effort is being devoted to the development of systems to manage knowledge about the different aspects of cultivation, to be employed for decision-making purposes. An important problem here is that in many occasions, information and knowledge employed to make decisions about a certain topic come from different sources. This is actually the case in the soil setting with scientist and user knowledge. The fusion of information is needed in order to facilitate the analysis, comparison and exploitation of knowledge coming from different sources. One particular case is that of having two different classifications (partitions) of the same set of objects. A first step to integrate them is to study their possible correspondence. In this paper we introduce several kinds of possible correspondences between partitions, and we propose the use of data mining techniques to measure its accuracy. For that purpose, partitions are represented as relational tables, and correspondences are identified with association rules and approximate dependencies. The accuracies of the former are then measured by means of accuracy measures of the latter, and some results relating accuracy values to correspondence cases are shown. Finally, we provide some examples of application of our proposal in a real-world problem, the integration of user and scientific classification of soils, that is of primary interest for decision making in agricultural environments.

1 INTRODUCTION

Nowadays, an usual problem in the real world is the increasing amount of information available in several forms. Related to this, the necessity to represent, manage, and access this information appears. In order to solve these problems, a number of proposals and solutions has been introduced within several research areas.

One of these problems is the fusion of information coming from different sources (Appriou et al., 2001). In this work we are interested in one particular case of information fusion: that of integrating two or more different classifications of a set of objects. Moreover, we provide a group of tools to study possible correspondences between classes.

More concretely, an example of this problem is the integration of scientific and user classification of soil. Scientists and farmers make use of different knowledge and techniques to classify soils, obtaining different classifications. On the basis of their own classifications, both provide knowledge to make decisions in order to improve the final production in farms. Hence, a very interesting task is to study correspondences between classifications of these different sources, in order to contrast information and knowledge coming from these sources.

In general, we deal with two or more partitions of the same set of objects, and we expect to know about all possible and interesting correspondences between them. This information can be represented as a table in a relational database, in the following way: every object o is represented in a tuple (row) t_o, and every partition is an attribute (column). The value of a cell for a given object (row) and partition (column) is the class in the partition where the object is.

According to this formulation, finding correspondences between classes can be seen as a special case of information fusion, normally referenced as merging databases. Specifically, looking for global correspondences between classifications can be seen as an schema integration problem (Cholvy and Moral,

2001) based on identifying attribute correspondences (Li and Clifton, 2000). Here, the idea is to determine if a set of attributes has the same semantics and contain the same information, which may be expressed in a different way.

In other order of things, the analysis of partial correspondences can be seen as a field matching problem (Monge and Elkan, 1996; Cholvy and Moral, 2001). In this case, the idea is to find values of attributes that play the same role in the database. This problem is related to that of finding attribute correspondence, since a correspondence between attributes can be seen as a set of correspondences between values.

In this paper we introduce the use of data mining techniques to analyze correspondences between classifications that are represented in the form of relational tables. Specifically, we use approximate dependencies (Delgado et al., 2000; Blanco et al., 2000) and association rules (Agrawal et al., 1993; Berzal et al., 2001).

The paper is organized as follows: in section 2 we describe the different kinds of correspondences between attributes we are interested in. The first kind, local correspondences, are studied in section 3, while we deal with partial and global correspondences in section 4. In section 5 we briefly introduce the case where more than two partitions can be treated, and give a set of related properties. Section 6 is devoted to show some examples and experiments. Finally, section 7 contains discussions and references to future research.

2 PROBLEM STATEMENT

Let O be a set of objects, that we assume to be finite, and let $A = \{A_1, A_2, \ldots, A_p\}$ and $B = \{B_1, B_2, \ldots, B_q\}$ be two partitions of O, i.e., $A_i, B_j \subseteq O$ and $A_i, B_j \neq \emptyset$, with $A_{i_1} \cap A_{i_2} = \emptyset \quad \forall i_1, i_2 \in \{1, \ldots, p\}$ and $B_{j_1} \cap B_{j_2} = \emptyset\ \forall j_1, j_2 \in \{1, \ldots, q\}$. Also

$$\bigcup_{A_i \in A} A_i = \bigcup_{B_j \in B} B_j = O$$

As indicated in the introduction, we are going to represent partitions A and B by means of a table, and we shall use the notation for relational databases. We call this table r_{AB}. Each row (tuple) and column (attribute) of r_{AB} will be associated to an object and a partition, respectively. This way, we assume $|r_{AB}| = |O|$.

We shall note t_o the tuple associated to object o, and X_P the attribute associated to partition P. The value for tuple t_o and attribute X_P, $t_o[X_P]$, will be the class for o following P, i.e., $t_o[X_P] \in P$. Table 1 shows an example.

The following result is immediate.

Object	**tuple**	X_A	X_B
o_1	t_{o_1}	A_1	B_2
o_2	t_{o_2}	A_2	B_2
o_3	t_{o_3}	A_1	B_1
$\vdots$	$\vdots$	$\vdots$	$\vdots$

Table 1: Table r_{AB}.

Proposition 2.1 *Let $A_i \in A$ and let $o \in A_i$. Then $t_o[A] = A_i$.*

Proof: Trivial. □

2.1 Correspondences

We want to study the following kinds of possible correspondences between A and B:

Definition 2.1 Local correspondence. *Let $A_i \in A$ and $B_j \in B$. There exists a local correspondence from A_i to B_j when $A_i \subseteq B_j$.*

Definition 2.2 Partial correspondence. *There exists a partial correspondence from A to B, noted $A \Rrightarrow B$, when $\forall A_i \in A\ \exists B_j \in B$ such that $A_i \subseteq B_j$.*

Definition 2.3 Global correspondence. *There exists a global correspondence between A and B, noted $A \equiv B$, when $A \Rrightarrow B$ and $B \Rrightarrow A$.*

Partial and global correspondences relate partitions, while local correspondences relate classes. Local correspondences are useful for two reasons:

- If a partial correspondence holds, local correspondences allow us to describe the particular correspondences between classes from A and B. We call this set of correspondences the model of the correspondence.
- If a partial correspondence does not hold, local correspondences can offer some information about less general kinds of relations between partitions.

Let us remark that we are interested not only in perfect correspondences, but also in correspondences with possible exceptions. The idea is that it is very difficult in general to find perfect correspondences between partitions. At the same time, if only a few objects break the correspondence, this keeps being an interesting information for us. Hence, we are concerned with measuring the accuracy of (local, partial, global) correspondences between partitions.

2.2 Properties

Some properties of the just defined correspondences are the following:

Proposition 2.2 *$A \Rrightarrow B$ iff for every object $o \in O$, $t_o[X_A] \subseteq t_o[X_B]$.*

Proof:

- $\Rightarrow$ If $A \Rrightarrow B$ then $\forall A_i \in A\ \exists B_j \in B$ such that $A_i \subseteq B_j$. In particular, $\forall o \in O\ \exists B_j \in B$ such that $t_o[A] \subseteq B_j$. Since $o \in t_o[A]$ and $o \in t_o[B]$ then $t_o[B] = B_j$ and hence $t_o[A] \subseteq t_o[B]$.
- $\Leftarrow$ Let $A_i \in A$. Since $A_i \neq \emptyset$ then $\exists o \in O$ such that $o \in A_i$ and hence $A_i = t_o[A] \subseteq t_o[B] \in B$. Hence, $A \Rrightarrow B$.

□

Following proposition 2.2, we consider that there is a partial correspondence $A \Rrightarrow B$ if, for any $o \in O$, knowing the class to which o belongs following A, we are able to know the class for o following B.

Proposition 2.3 *If $A \Rrightarrow B$ then $\forall B_j \in B\ \exists A' \subseteq A$ such that*

$$\bigcup_{A_i \in A'} A_i = B_j$$

Proof: Let $A \Rrightarrow B$ and let $B_j \in B$. Let $A' = \{t_o[A] \mid o \in B_j\}$. Obviously

$$B_j \subseteq \bigcup_{A_i \in A'} A_i$$

Moreover, $t_o[A] \subseteq t_o[B] = B_j\ \ \forall t_o[A] \in A'$ (prop. 2.2). Hence

$$\bigcup_{A_i \in A'} A_i \subseteq B_j$$

Therefore

$$\bigcup_{A_i \in A'} A_i = B_j$$

□

Corollary 2.3.1 *If $A \equiv B$ then $\forall A_i \in A\ \exists B_j \in B$ such that $A_i = B_j$.*

Corollary 2.3.2 *If $A \equiv B$ then $A = B$.*

3 LOCAL CORRESPONDENCES

In order to analyze the presence of local correspondences, we are going to use association rules (Agrawal et al., 1993), specifically following the model introduced in (Sánchez, 1999; Berzal et al., 2001).

3.1 Association rules

When mining for association rules, we assume that we are dealing with a set of items I, and that data appears in the form (or can be interpreted as) a set of transactions, where each transaction is a subset of I. We call this structure a T-set.

Association rules are "implications" that relate the presence of itemsets (sets of items) in transactions of a certain T-set. We say that the rules hold in the T-set. A classical example consider that items are things we can buy in a market, and transactions are market basket containing several items. A T-set is then a set of market baskets. In this framework, association rules relate the presence of items in the same basket, for example "every basket that contains bread contains butter", usually noted $bread \Rightarrow butter$.

In real world application, however, it is difficult to find rules that hold with total accuracy in a T-set. But rules with high accuracy can be interesting, so we are concerned with measuring the accuracy or rules.

Accuracy is not the only way to assess rules. Even if the accuracy is high, it could happen that the set of transactions where the rule holds is so small that the rule is uninteresting. This leads to the necessity to assess association rules by measuring both their accuracy and their interest, the latter being based on the percentage of transactions where the rule holds.

For this purpose, the ordinary measures proposed in (Agrawal et al., 1993) are *confidence* and *support*, both based on the support of an itemset (a set of items). The support of an itemset is the percentage of transactions where the itemset appears. Given a set of items I and a set of transactions T on I, the support of an itemset $I_0 \subseteq I$ is

$$supp(I_0) = \frac{|\{\tau \in T \mid I_0 \subseteq \tau\}|}{|T|} \quad (1)$$

i.e., the probability that the itemset appears in a transaction of T. The support of the association rule $I_0 \Rightarrow I_1$ in T is

$$Supp(I_0 \Rightarrow I_1) = supp(I_0 \cup I_1) \quad (2)$$

Support of a rule is indeed the percentage of tuples where the rule holds.

The classical accuracy measure is confidence, defined as

$$Conf(I_0 \Rightarrow I_1) = \frac{supp(I_0 \cup I_1)}{supp(I_0)} = \frac{Supp(I_0 \Rightarrow I_1)}{supp(I_0)}. \quad (3)$$

However, several authors have pointed out some drawbacks of the support/confidence framework (see (Sánchez, 1999; Berzal et al., 2001) for a brief review). Hence, other accuracy measures have been employed. Shortliffe and Buchanan's certainty factors (Shortliffe and Buchanan, 1975) have recently been proposed as an alternative to confidence, thereby solving the drawbacks which this has (Berzal et al., 2001). The certainty factor of a rule is defined as

$$CF(I_0 \Rightarrow I_1) = \frac{(Conf(I_0 \Rightarrow I_1)) - S(I_1)}{1 - S(I_1)} \quad (4)$$

if $Conf(I_0 \Rightarrow I_1) > S(I_1)$, and

$$CF(I_0 \Rightarrow I_1) = \frac{(Conf(I_0 \Rightarrow I_1)) - S(I_1)}{S(I_1)} \quad (5)$$

if $Conf(I_0 \Rightarrow I_1) < S(I_1)$, and 0 otherwise.

Certainty factors take values in $[-1, 1]$, indicating the extent to which our belief that the consequent is true varies when the antecedent is also true. It ranges from 1, meaning maximum increment (i.e., when A is true then B is true) to -1, meaning maximum decrement.

3.2 Analyzing local correspondences

The analysis of local correspondences can be performed by looking for association rules in the table r_{AB}, where we represent both partitions A and B.

When mining for association rules in a relational table, it is usual to consider that the table is a T-set, where each tuple is a transaction and every item is a pair ⟨ Attribute, value ⟩ (usually noted [Attribute=value]).

In our case, items take the form $[X_A = A_i]$ and $[X_B = B_j]$. This way, the rules

$$[X_A = A_i] \Rightarrow [X_B = B_j]$$

and

$$[X_B = B_j] \Rightarrow [X_A = A_i]$$

tell us about possible local correspondences between classes A_i and B_j.

Specifically, the certainty factor of rules measure the accuracy of the local correspondences. In particular, let $Supp(A_i, B_j)$, $Conf(A_i, B_j)$ and $CF(A_i, B_j)$ be the support, confidence and certainty factor, respectively, of the rule

$$[X_A = A_i] \Rightarrow [X_B = B_j]$$

The following properties hold:

Proposition 3.1 *The support of the item* $[X_A = A_i]$ *is*

$$Supp([X_A = A_i]) = \frac{|A_i|}{|O|} \quad (6)$$

Proof: Trivial. □

Proposition 3.2 *The support of the rule* $[X_A = A_i] \Rightarrow [X_B = B_j]$ *is*

$$Supp(A_i, B_j) = \frac{|A_i \cap B_j|}{|O|} \quad (7)$$

Proof: Trivial. □

Proposition 3.3 *The confidence of the rule* $[X_A = A_i] \Rightarrow [X_B = B_j]$ *is*

$$Conf(A_i, B_j) = \frac{Supp(A_i, B_j)}{Supp([X_A = A_i])} = \frac{|A_i \cap B_j|}{|A_i|} \quad (8)$$

Proof: Trivial. □

Proposition 3.4 *If* $CF(A_i, B_j) = 1$ *then* $A_i \subseteq B_j$.

Proof: Let $CF(A_i, B_j) = 1$. Then by equation (4) $Conf(A_i, B_j) = 1$, and by equation (8) $|A_i \cap B_j| = |A_i|$. Therefore, $A_i \subseteq B_j$. □

Hence, a rule with maximum accuracy represents a local correspondence from the class in the antecedent to the class in the consequent. The following corollary is immediate

Corollary 3.4.1 *If* $CF(A_i, B_j) = CF(B_j, A_i) = 1$ *then* $A_i = B_j$.

In general, if $CF(A_i, B_j) > 0$, knowing that $o \in A_i$ increases our belief that $o \in B_j$. The value of $CF(A_i, B_j)$ measures the increment.

Proposition 3.5 *If* $CF(A_i, B_j) = 0$ *then*

$$\frac{|A_i \cap B_j|}{|B_j|} = \frac{|A_i|}{|O|}. \quad (9)$$

Proof: Let $CF(A_i, B_j) = 0$. Then $Conf(A_i, B_j) = Supp([X_B = B_j])$, and by equation (8)

$$\frac{Supp(A_i, B_j)}{Supp([X_A = A_i])} = Supp([X_B = B_j])$$

so

$$\frac{Supp(A_i, B_j)}{Supp([X_B = B_j])} = Supp([X_A = A_i])$$

Hence

$$\frac{|A_i \cap B_j|}{|B_j|} = \frac{|A_i|}{|O|}$$

□

This proposition tell us that the proportion of objects in B_j that are in A_i is the same as the proportion of objects in O that are in A_i. This means that when $CF(A_i, B_j) = 0$ there is statistical independence between the facts $o \in A_i$ and $o \in B_j$.

Proposition 3.6 *If* $CF(A_i, B_j) = -1$ *then* $A_i \cap B_j = \emptyset$.

Proof: Let $CF(A_i, B_j) = -1$. Then by equation (5) $Conf(A_i, B_j) = 0$, and by equation (8) $|A_i \cap B_j| = 0$. Therefore, $A_i \cap B_j = \emptyset$. □

In general, if $CF(A_i, B_j) < 0$, knowing that $o \in A_i$ reduces our belief that $o \in B_j$. The value of $CF(A_i, B_j)$ measures the decrement.

4 PARTIAL AND GLOBAL CORRESPONDENCES

By definition, the analysis of partial and global correspondences can be performed on the basis of local correspondences, but we need a way to integrate the information given by the latter. We are going to use another data mining technique, the search for approximate dependencies (Bra and Paredaens, 1983; Ziarko, 1991) to analyze partial correspondences. As we shall see, approximate dependencies integrate the information given by a set of association rules.

4.1 Approximate dependencies

In the following, let $RE = \{At_1, \ldots, At_m\}$ be a relational scheme and let r be an instance of RE such that $|r| = n$. Also, let $V, W \subset RE$ with $V \cap W = \emptyset$, and let $dom(V) = \{v_1, \ldots, v_K\}$ and $dom(W) = \{w_1, \ldots, w_M\}$ be the values of V and W appearing in r.

A functional dependence $V \to W$ holds in ER if and only if for every instance r of ER

$$\forall t, s \in r \;\; if \; t[V] = s[V] \; then \; t[W] = s[W] \quad (10)$$

Approximate dependencies can be roughly defined as functional dependencies with exceptions. The definition of approximate dependence is then a matter of how to define exceptions, and how to measure the accuracy of the dependence (Bosc and Lietard, 1997). We shall follow the approach introduced in (Sánchez, 1999; Delgado et al., 2000; Blanco et al., 2000), where we applied the same methodology employed in mining for AR's to the discovery of AD's.

The idea is that, since a functional dependency "$V \to W$" can be seen as a rule that relates the equality of attribute values in pairs of tuples (see equation (10)), and association rules relate the presence of items in transactions, we can represent approximate dependencies as association rules by using the following interpretations of the concepts of item and transaction:

- An item is an object associated to an attribute of RE. For every attribute $At_k \in RE$ we note it_{At_k} the associated item.
- We introduce the itemset I_V to be

$$I_V = \{it_{At_k} \mid At_k \in V\}$$

- T_r is a T-set that, for each pair of tuples $< t, s > \in r \times r$ contains a transaction $ts \in T_r$ verifying

$$it_{At_k} \in ts \Leftrightarrow t[At_k] = s[At_k]$$

It is obvious that $|T_r| = |r \times r| = n^2$.

Then, an approximate dependence $V \to W$ in the relation r is an association rule $I_V \Rightarrow I_W$ in T_r (Delgado et al., 2000; Blanco et al., 2000). The support and certainty factor of $I_V \Rightarrow I_W$ measure the interest and accuracy of the dependence $V \to W$. In particular, the following property holds:

Proposition 4.1 ((Blanco et al., 2000)) *If $CF(V \to W) = 1$ then $V \to W$ is a functional dependence.*

4.1.1 Model of an approximate dependence

The model (also called "theory" in (Pfahringer and Kramer, 1995; Blanco et al., 2000)) of an approximate dependence is a set of association rules that describe the relations between values of the antecedent and consequent of the dependence.

In previous sections we have related the quality of an AD to the quality of the model describing it. The AR's that form the model of an AD are defined in r. They relate the presence of values of attributes in tuples, i.e. items are pairs <attribute, value> (that we note [attribute=value]) and transactions are tuples. In this subsection we provide an interpretation of the support, confidence and certainty factor of an AD based on the support, confidence and certainty factor of the AR's that form the model of the AD. We consider confidence in this subsection because the certainty factor is based on it, though only support and certainty factor are to be used in finding AD's. First, we formalize the concept of model of an AD.

Definition 4.1 ((Blanco et al., 2000)) *The model of $V \to W$, noted $Th_{[V \to W]}$, is*

$$\{Ru_{ij} \mid \exists t \in r \; with \; t[V] = v_i \wedge t[W] = w_j\}$$

where Ru_{ij} is the association rule $[V = v_i] \Rightarrow [W = w_j]$. We shall note s_{ij}, c_{ij} and cf_{ij} the support, confidence and certainty factor of Ru_{ij}, respectively.

The following properties relate the support and accuracy of a dependence to the support and accuracy of the rules of its model

Proposition 4.2 ((Blanco et al., 2000))

$$Supp(V \to W) = \sum_{Ru_{ij} \in Th_{[V \to W]}} s_{ij}^2$$

Proposition 4.3 ((Blanco et al., 2000))

$$\frac{1}{Conf(V \to W)} =$$

$$= \sum_{Ru_{ij} \in Th_{[V \to W]}} \left(\left(\frac{s_{ij}^2}{Supp(V \to W)} \right) \frac{1}{c_{ij}} \right)$$

By these properties, we can see support and confidence of an approximate dependence as an aggregate or summary of support and confidence of the rules of its model. The same can be claimed of the support of any itemset I_V and I_W with respect to the support of the values of V and W respectively.

Since certainty factors are based on support and confidence, the certainty factor of a dependence can also be seen as an aggregate of support and accuracy of the rules of its model. In particular, the following property holds:

Proposition 4.4 ((Blanco et al., 2000)) *If* $c_{ij} = c_0$ *and* $cf_{ij} = cf_0$ $\forall Ru_{ij} \in Th_{[V \to W]}$ *then* $Conf(V \to W) = c_0$ *and* $CF(V \to W) = cf_0$.

This proposition tell us that when all the rules in $Th_{[V \to W]}$ have the same confidence and certainty factor, those are the confidence and certainty factor of the dependence.

4.2 Analyzing partial correspondences

The analysis of partial correspondences can be performed by looking for approximate dependencies in r_{AB}. If the dependence $X_A \to X_B$ holds, there is a partial correspondence from A to B. The certainty factor of the dependence measures the accuracy of the correspondence.

Let $CF(X_A, X_B)$ be the certainty factor of $X_A \to X_B$.

Proposition 4.5 $CF(X_A, X_B) = 1$ *iff* $A \Rrightarrow B$.

Proof:

$\Rightarrow$ If $CF(X_A, X_B) = 1$ then $X_A \to X_B$ is a functional dependence, i.e., there is a perfect correspondence between values of X_A and X_B. Hence $CF(A_i, B_j) = 1$, so $A_i \subseteq B_j$, and finally $A \Rrightarrow B$.

$\Leftarrow$ If $A \Rrightarrow B$ then $A_i \subseteq B_j$ $\forall A_i \in A, B_j \in B$. Hence $CF(A_i, B_j) = Conf(A_i, B_j) = 1$ $\forall A_i \in A, B_j \in B$ and by prop. (4.4), $CF(X_A, X_B) = 1$.

□

Another property, this time regarding independence, is the following:

Proposition 4.6 ((Blanco et al., 2000)) *If* X_A *and* X_B *are independent then* $CF(X_A, X_B) = 0$.

As we have just seen, we use the accuracy of approximate dependencies and association rules to measure the accuracy of partial and local correspondences respectively. By definition, a partial correspondence consists of a set of local correspondences. In the same way, we have seen how approximate dependencies can be represented by a set of association rules, and the relation between accuracy of dependencies and rules. Therefore, it is inmediate that these relations can be extended to the case of partial and local correspondences.

In (Sánchez, 1999; Blanco et al., 2000) an algorithm to search for approximate dependencies in relational tables is proposed. This algorithm has some interesting features:

- It is efficient since its complexity is linear with respect to the number of tuples in the relation. The complexity in the number of attributes is exponential, but this is unavoidable in the worst case.
- It allows to obtain approximate dependencies and their models at the same time and expending exactly the same time and space.

The algorithm is designed to find approximate dependencies between any pair of attributes (or sets of attributes) in a table. This can be useful for us when we have several partitions. In this case, we can represent each one by a column, so that the algorithm can analyze correspondences between any pair of partitions.

An interesting case is when more than partitions we have hierarchies, i.e., sets of nested partitions. In this case, we can represent each level of each hierarchy (partitions at last) in one column, and the algorithm would analyze correspondences between hierarchies at several levels at the same time. This will be an object of future research.

4.3 From partial to global correspondences

We have measured the accuracy of local and partial dependencies by means of certainty factors, so we are interested in using the same measure to assess global correspondences. This leads to the following definition:

Definition 4.2 *The certainty factor of* $A \equiv B$ *is*

$$\min\{CF(X_A, X_B), CF(X_B, X_A)\}$$

The rationale behind this definition is that a global correspondence $A \equiv B$ hold when the partial dependencies $A \Rrightarrow B$ and $B \Rrightarrow A$ hold, and it is usual to obtain the certainty factor of a conjunction of facts as the minimum of the certainty factors of the facts.

The following property holds:

Proposition 4.7 ((Sánchez, 1999))

- $CF(A_i, B_j) > 0$ *iff* $CF(B_j, A_i) > 0$.
- *If* $CF(A_i, B_j) \leq 0$ *then*

$$CF(A_i, B_j) = CF(B_j, A_i)$$

Corollary 4.7.1 *The certainty factor of* $A \equiv B$ *has always the same sign as the certainty factors of* $A \Rrightarrow B$ *and* $B \Rrightarrow A$.

5 ANALYSIS OF SEVERAL PARTITIONS

One interesting problem is the analysis of correspondences between more than two partitions. Several situations are possible that can be solved in different ways, but an useful case is to obtain two partitions by combining several partitions into a single one.

An usual way to combine partitions is the following: given partitions A and B, we name AB to the partition

$$AB = \{A_i \cap B_j \mid A_i \in A, B_j \in B\} \setminus \{\emptyset\} \quad (11)$$

This way, we obtain a cross-classification of the set of objects on the basis of existing classifications. We shall note A_iB_j to the set of objects $A_i \cap B_j$.

In this paper we shall deal with only three partitions at a time, but the results can be easily generalized. Let A, B and C be three partitions of O.

Proposition 5.1 *A local correspondence* $A_iB_j \subseteq C_k$ *holds iff the association rule* $[X_A = A_i][X_B = B_j] \Rightarrow [X_C = C_k]$ *holds with* $CF = 1$.

Proof: □

The interpretation of this correspondence is that knowing the class for a given object o following A and B, we know the class for o following C.

Proposition 5.2 *A partial correspondence* $AB \Rrightarrow C$ *holds iff the approximate dependence* $X_AX_B \rightarrow X_C$ *holds with* $CF = 1$.

Proof: □

We shall use the CF of rules and dependencies to measure the strength of local and partial correspondences respectively. The following properties hold:

Proposition 5.3 $Conf(A_i, B_jC_k) \leq Conf(A_i, C_k)$.

Proof:

$$Conf(A_i, B_jC_k) = \frac{supp(A_i \cap B_j \cap C_k)}{supp(A_i)} \leq$$

$$\leq \frac{supp(A_i \cap C_k)}{supp(A_i)} = Conf(A_i, C_k)$$

□

Proposition 5.4 *Let* $A_i \subseteq B_j$. *Then*

1. $Conf(A_iB_j, C_k) = Conf(A_i, C_k)$.
2. $Conf(A_i, B_jC_k) = Conf(A_i, C_k)$.

Proof: $A_i \subseteq B_j$ means $o \in A_i$ implies $o \in B_j$. Hence, $supp(A_i \cap B_j) = supp(A_i)$.

1.

$$Conf(A_iB_j, C_k) = \frac{supp(A_i \cap B_j \cap C_k)}{supp(A_i \cap B_j)} =$$

$$= \frac{supp(A_i \cap C_k)}{supp(A_i)} = Conf(A_i, C_k)$$

2.

$$Conf(A_i, B_jC_k) = \frac{supp(A_i \cap B_j \cap C_k)}{supp(A_i)} =$$

$$= \frac{supp(A_i \cap C_k)}{supp(A_i)} = Conf(A_i, C_k)$$

□

Proposition 5.5 *Let* $C_k \subseteq B_j$. *Then* $Conf(A_i, C_kB_j) = Conf(A_i, C_k)$.

Proof: $C_k \subseteq B_j$ means $o \in C_k$ implies $o \in B_j$. Hence, $supp(C_k \cap B_j) = supp(C_k)$ and

$$Conf(A_i, C_kB_j) = \frac{supp(A_i \cap B_j \cap C_k)}{supp(A_i)} =$$

$$= \frac{supp(A_i \cap C_k)}{supp(A_i)} = Conf(A_i, C_k)$$

□

We conjecture $CF(A_i, B_jC_k) \leq CF(A_i, C_k)$.

Proposition 5.6 *Let* $A_i \subseteq B_j$. *Then* $CF(A_iB_j, C_k) = CF(A_i, C_k)$.

Proof: Trivial since by proposition 5.4, confidence does not change, and the consequent is the same. □

Proposition 5.7 *Let* $C_k \subseteq B_j$. *Then* $CF(A_i, C_kB_j) = CF(A_i, C_k)$.

Proof: Trivial since in this case $supp(C_k \cap B_j) = supp(C_k)$ and, by proposition 5.4, confidence does not change. □

Proposition 5.8 *Given attributes* X_A, X_B *and* X_C *corresponding to partitions* A, B *and* C, $Conf(X_A, X_BX_C) \leq Conf(X_A, X_C)$.

Proof: As we show in (Blanco et al., 2000), confidence of an approximate dependence is a weighted sum of confidence of the rules of its model, the weights being all positive. From proposition 5.3 it follows that $Conf(X_A, X_BX_C) \leq Conf(X_A, X_C)$. □

We also conjecture the property $Conf(X_AX_B, X_C) \geq Conf(X_A, X_C)$.

Proposition 5.9 *Let* $A \Rrightarrow B$. *Then*

1. $Conf(X_AX_B, X_C) = Conf(X_A, X_C)$.
2. $Conf(X_A, X_BX_C) = Conf(X_A, X_C)$.

Proof: Similar to proposition 5.8 but making reference to proposition 5.4. □

Proposition 5.10 *Let* $C \Rrightarrow B$. *Then* $Conf(X_A, X_BX_C) = Conf(X_A, X_C)$.

Proof: Similar to proposition 5.8 but making reference to proposition 5.5. □

We also conjecture the properties $CF(X_A X_B, X_C) \leq CF(X_A, X_C)$ and $CF(X_A, X_B X_C) \leq CF(X_A, X_C)$.

Proposition 5.11 *Let* $A \Rrightarrow B$. *Then* $CF(X_A X_B, X_C) = CF(X_A, X_C)$.

Proof: By proposition 5.9 we know confidence remains the same. This occurs also to the support of the consequent, so the certainty factor does not change. □

Proposition 5.12 *Let* $C \Rrightarrow B$. *Then* $CF(X_A, X_B X_C) = CF(X_A, X_C)$.

Proof: Similar to proposition 5.11 but making reference to proposition 5.10 □

5.1 Practical considerations

A simple way to analyze correspondences between several partitions at a time is to obtain AB from A and B, but this is a hard work when the number of objects and partitions is high.

For the particular case of categorical attributes in databases, the problem can be seen as an information fusion problem where we are interested in discovering whether several variables play the role of several others. A clear example in the setting of soil classification is the variable color. For scientific analysis, color is represented by means of three variables, while users employ a single categorial value. Hence, we must perform an analysis of the correspondence of the partitions induced by several variables at a time.

For this purpose, algorithms like the one proposed in (Blanco et al., 2000) are suitable, because they are designed to discover approximate dependencies between several attributes at a time. This algorithm employs the support of an attribute to bound the search for dependencies. This is needed by several reasons. First, the number of potential dependencies is exponential in the number of attributes, so it is important that some mechanism to predict that a dependence is not interesting, avoiding its analysis, is available. Second, when the number of attributes is very high, it is very likely that the corresponding partition is a set of singletons. In this case, we can find a perfect partial correspondence from the aforementioned partition to any other, and that can be misleading. Fortunately, in this case the set of attributes has the minimum support, so we can detect and avoid this problem.

Further details about the role of support and algorithms can be found in (Blanco et al., 2000).

6 EXPERIMENTATION

Our intention in this section is that of, in one hand, make clear the most interesting properties for association rules and approximate dependencies, and in the other hand, discover how far the classification criteria of the three knowledge types used respecting to soil match. This second part is the one with maximum interest for soil scientists and farmers.

Soil is a natural body, obtained from the genesis due to the interaction between different environmental features, like weather, geological material, relief, vegetation, and, in great measure, human activities (FAO, 1998). From user (farmers) perspective, soil is the mean of production in cultivation, olive trees in our case. In this way, the so-called "User knowledge" is essentially based in utilitary criteria. Taxonomic systems, like the one introduced in (FAO, 1968), which is the basis for the 1:200000 Soil Units Maps for the province of Granada (Pérez-Pujalte and Prieto, 1980), try to compensate the existing gap between the views of soil as a natural body and as a mean of production. For this reason, a set of parameters affecting to agriculture, based on utilitary features, is added by FAO Taxonomic system over the existing genetic criteria. This can be called "Taxonomic-cartographic knowledge" or "Soil map knowledge". Finally, we have considered a third type of knowledge, "Expert knowledge", which responds to our research group experience. It has a local character and is essentially based on features relating to soil genesis. Tables 4,7,6 show the three classifications based in user, soil maps, and expert knowledges, respectively.

6.1 Searching for local and partial correspondences

In order to prove the proposed model, we have applied it over a practical example, consisting of a set of results obtained from the first, exploratory analysis in a previous work over olive trees cultivation in the province of Granada, Spain. This project, financed with FEDER funds, covers the main objective of build a decision-making model for agricultural managers. According to this, a number of surveys was collected, relating location, managing, production and soil information about olive farms. A detailed description of the surveys and the followed process can be found in (Serrano et al., 2001)

In (Aranda et al., 2002), a first classification for parcels, involving soil attributes, was presented. It was obtained by means of user knowledge, that is, the collected surveys. The considered parcels were distributed in a total of 19 clusters. Let *grupos* be this classification. A scientific classification was previously presented in (Pérez-Pujalte and Prieto, 1980), based on the keys proposed in (FAO, 1968). Here, a total of 21 land types, called *soil maps units*, are found, but only 19 are suitable for olive trees cultivation. Let *codunida* be this other classification. Finally, in order to complete the knowledge types over soil, we need to consider a third type, previously defined as expert knowledge. Let *exp13* be the partition obtained from this classification, giving a total of 13 soil classes.

Later, the considered classifications were modified in order to reduce the number of classes,

- On one hand, the original 21 classes in the scientific classification were regrouped in 6, attending to resemblances in the land structure (calcic regosols, distric regosols, etc.). Let *grunida* be the associated variable.
- For the user-defined classification, obtained from a hierarchical clustering, we studied the resulting dendogram and reduced to 4 the number of classes. Let *grupos4* represent this new partition.
- And finally, let *exp5* be the reduction from 13 to 5 for the expert knowledge based partition.

As it can be noticed, each classification has two hierarchical levels, one of them with a higher number of classes than the other. Hence, a close relation is expected to be found between the original and the reduced one. For example,

$codunida \Rrightarrow grunida$, CF = 1.0, but
$grunida \Rrightarrow codunida$, CF = 0.199,
$exp13 \Rrightarrow exp5$, CF = 1.0, but
$exp5 \Rrightarrow exp13$, CF = 0.16, and
$grupos \Rrightarrow grupos4$, CF = 1.0, but
$grupos4 \Rrightarrow grupos$, CF = 0.10

Partial correspondences between this hierarchical levels can be found by means of approximate dependencies. As expected, the reciprocal dependencies have nearly null certainty factors. Three functional dependencies, $codunida \rightarrow grunida$, $exp13 \rightarrow exp5$, and $grupos \rightarrow grupos4$, can be inferred from this set of approximate dependencies, (see proposition 4.1).

First, we try to know how significant soil genesis knowledge from experts is over profile classification given by FAO, necessary for the 1:200000 soil map elaboration. As a partial correspondence, we must remark the following,

$grunidad \Rrightarrow exp5$, CF = 0.45

This one let us establish a relatively high correspondence level (certainty factor) between soil maps and expert knowledge. This fact means that soil genesis criteria given in the map partially match with expert criteria, exclusively genetic. It can be observed that this correspondence is established between two partitions at the same hierarchical level, each one with a similar number of classes (see tables 2,3).

The following example shows how the certainty factor increases, by means of ascending in the hierarchical level in the antecedent but leaving constant the consequent, since a functional dependence can be found between partitions with a hierarchical relation,

$codunidad \Rrightarrow exp5$, CF = 0.80

On the opposite, the following approximate dependencies,

$exp5 \Rrightarrow grupos4$, CF = -0.04, and
$exp13 \Rrightarrow grupos4$, CF = -0.05

show that when the certainty factor is very low, this transitive effect can not be almost appreciated.

Unfortunately, nor global or partial correspondences were found between expert and user knowledge nor user and soil maps knowledge. It was predictable, since we are working in a environmentally complex province, with multiple environmental variables and genesis factors possible combinations. This fact may be due to the particularity of the crop, perfectly adapted to the different Mediterranean environments. Therefore, it is difficult to relate soil suitability prediction with cartographic FAO criteria (Sys et al., 1991) or purely genetic ones.

But we can remark some local results. For example,

$[grunida = class_4] \Rightarrow [grupos4 = class_1]$, CF = 1.0,

$[grunida = class_6] \Rightarrow [grupos4 = class_1]$, CF = 1.0

These association rules compound an example of local correspondences between these classes. A strong dependence between *grunida* and *grupos4* is found, but in a few cases, and only in one direction. In *grupos4*, class 1 corresponds to brown-colored and low sloping soils. An interpretation could be that both soil types ($Xerosols$ for class 4, and $Luvisols$ for class 6) are included in the same group (see proposition 3.4).

Despite of the fact that a little number of partial correspondences can be found, in these cases we must remark the related local correspondences between partition values, as the following ones,

$[grunida = class_2] \Rightarrow [exp5 = class_2]$, CF = 0.95,

$[exp5 = class_2] \Rightarrow [grunida = class_2]$, CF = 1.0,

$[codunida = class_3] \Rightarrow [exp5 = class_2]$, CF = 0.95,

$[codunida = class_3] \Rightarrow [grunida = class_2]$, CF = 1.0,

In this example, the fourth association rule is trivial, since the functional dependence $codunida \rightarrow grunida$ holds, as we said before. Moreover, the information fusion between expert and soil maps knowledge is total, due to *Fluvisols* are always located in river floodplains, easily identifiable by means of expert criteria. Hence, this unit diagnosis is very fiable without no necessity of analytic FAO criteria.

Another interesting example which shows how a large soil maps unit implies a expert class is the following,

$[grunida = class_1] \Rightarrow [exp5 = class_3]$, CF = 1.0

This fact is significant since a priori all parcels over *Litosols* would be associated to class 1 in *Exp5* partition by any soil scientist with no local information about the province of Granada and the olive tree cultivation. This looks logical due to the fact that olive crop can not appear over *Litosols* "sensu stricto", as it is a non-suitable soil for tree-based cultivation. However, minority soils called "inclusions" appear in this soil maps unit, possibly corresponding to class 3 in *Exp3*. The cartographic finality of the FAO classification create this kind of events.

The two previous examples let us establish an information flow between both classifications. However, it is more complex in the case of the predominant classes. *Regosols* conform the 52% in the surveys. By its own nature, these are soils hard to classify, more in Mediterranean climate and little compacted and bases-rich geological material. It is showed in the continuous changing in classifications in successive FAO editions (FAO, 1968; FAO, 1998). This imprecision can be inferred from the following association rules,

$[exp5 = class_3] \Rightarrow [grunida = class_3]$, CF = 0.39

$[grunida = class_3] \Rightarrow [exp5 = class_3]$, CF = 0.67

$[exp13 = class_4] \Rightarrow [grunida = class_3]$, CF = 0.87

$[exp13 = class_5] \Rightarrow [grunida = class_3]$, CF = 0.41

$[exp13 = class_6] \Rightarrow [grunida = class_3]$, CF = 0.65

$[exp13 = class_7] \Rightarrow [grunida = class_3]$, CF = -0.31

Soils in class 3 (*Exp5*) relate deficiently to *Regosols*, although the certainty factor is relatively significant. Within the subunits in class 3 (*Exp5*), subunit 4 is the one that better matches to *Regosols* terms here, due to the predominance of this kind of genetic environment in Granada. See table 6 for details.

Associations with subunits 5 and 6 in *Exp13* also appears to be relatively good. We can see that the common feature within the subunits with higher certainty factor is the little compacted rock as marl, even more than evolution degree or slope. It was expected since both subunits have topographical interrelations called "catenales".

Within subunits associated to other geological materials, that with lower evolution degree and higher slope (class 5 in *Exp13*) is the only one that an expert would easily view as *Regosol*. However, that with higher evolution degree and lower slope, class 7, would not be classified as *Regosol*, as showed by a negative certainty factor.

Respecting to *Cambisols*, with a relevance of 29% on the surveys, the following partial correspondences, by means of association rules, are obtained,

$[exp5 = class_4] \Rightarrow [grunida = class_5]$, CF = 0.85

$[exp13 = class_7] \Rightarrow [grunida = class_5]$, CF = 0.34

$[exp13 = class_9] \Rightarrow [grunida = class_5]$, CF = 0.34

It can be proved how soils in class 7 (*Exp13*), not viewed as *Regosols*, can be associated to *Cambisols*. Soils from other classes, as class 4 in *Exp5* and class 9 in *Exp13*, can be ambiguously included in *Cambisols*.

Summarizing, partial correspondences between user and soil maps knowledge can only be found in classes representing non-predominant soils (nearly a 17% in the collected surveys) as *Litosols* and *Fluvisols*. In the remaining cases, the certainty factors show a moderately low partial correspondence. Only at a local level, we can find more information.

When we try to fuse information from soil maps or expert knowledge with user knowledge, the resulting certainty factors are lower, as we expected since classification criteria are very different. The following rules can be found,

$[grunida = class_2] \Rightarrow [grupos4 = class_1]$, CF = 0.40

$[codunida = class_2] \Rightarrow [grupos4 = class_1]$, CF = 0.38

Fluvisols always are soils of this type, very suitable for olive tree cultivation ($grupos4 = class_1$, as we can see in table 5). At this point, both classifications match, showing that FAO classifications include utilitary criteria.

$[grupos4 = class_3] \Rightarrow [grunida = class_3]$, CF = 0.28

$[grupos = class_1 1] \Rightarrow [grunida = class_3]$, CF = 0.23

At the opposite, as it can be seen, *Regosols* conform an heterogeneous soil unit including user groups and subgroups less suitable for olive tree cultivation, as we expected.

Parcels in the survey where *Cambisols* are predominant, matches with soil groups more suitable by means of user knowledge (*Cambisols* are suitable for olive tree cultivation). Hence, a certain level of information fusion is possible.

Finally, information fusion between expert and user knowledge provides very similar results, in example,

$[exp5 = class_2] \Rightarrow [grupos4 = class_1]$, CF = 0.38

$[exp13 = class_2] \Rightarrow [grupos4 = class_1]$, CF = 0.35

Both local correspondences are good, since both antecedent and consequent are soil classes considered very suitable. Moreover, they match in all features excepting in that class 2 in *Exp5* is 'plain' and class 1 in *grupos4* is 'moderately sloping' (see tables 5,3).

$[exp5 = class_3] \Rightarrow [grupos = class_1]$, CF = -0.23

$[grupos = class_3] \Rightarrow [exp5 = class_3]$, CF = 0.24

Both subgroups (classes 1 and 3 in *grupos*) conform suitable soils for cultivation. However, class 1, brown-colored, tends to a non-association with class 3 in *exp5*, as showed by the negative certain factor. Brown color represents a higher evolution degree than the characteristic color in class 3 in *Exp5*. That is why this is a significant feature in information fusion between expert and user knowledge, combining utilitary and genetic aspects.

$[exp13 = class_6] \Rightarrow [grupos4 = class_1]$, CF = 0.41

Again, this association rule shows how soils from class 3 in *Exp5* (class 6 in *Exp13* is included in class 3 in *Exp5*), relatively low evolved, match with the user group with higher suitability.

Hence, we can assess that the user cluster with highest suitability tends to associate with soils considered by the expert as low evolved, carbonated and deep. This is expected according to the studied zone, where low evolved soils are *Fluvisols* or *Regosols* over marls, non-coherent, and with a high water storage (Pérez-Pujalte and Prieto, 1980).

Table 2: Table grunida

Unit	Description
1	Litosols
2	Fluvisols
3	Regosols
4	Xerosols
5	Cambisols
6	Luvisols

6.2 Global correspondences in practice

Finally, we take a look at an example where a nearly global correspondence can be found. Now, the classifications to be considered are the following,

- *kmcluster*. Starting from the original user knowledge classification, *grupos*, the number of classes was reduced using a k-means technique, resulting in a total number of 4 classes.
- *hcluster*. A hierarchical clustering, the nearest neighbor method, with a Euclidean distance and means normalizing with Z scoring, was used for the same original classification. Here, a number of 4 clusters was finally obtained, too.

As we can see, both cases use the same classification but different methods. Here, the following approximate dependencies are obtained,

$kmcluster \Rrightarrow hcluster$, CF = 0.827, and

$hcluster \Rrightarrow kmcluster$, CF = 0.893

In these dependencies, the certainty factor is very near to 1 for both dependencies. If a certain relaxation degree is considered, we can conclude that $kmcluster \equiv hcluster$, that is, we have a global correspondence involving these attributes, with a CF = 0.827, according to definition 4.2.

Looking for local correspondences, we can find the following association rules,

$[hcluster = class_1] \Rightarrow [kmcluster = class_1]$, CF 1.0,

$[kmcluster = class_1] \Rightarrow [hcluster = class_1]$, CF 0.945,

$[hcluster = class_2] \Rightarrow [kmcluster = class_2]$, CF 0.859,

$[kmcluster = class_2] \Rightarrow [hcluster = class_2]$, CF 0.717,

$[hcluster = class_3] \Rightarrow [kmcluster = class_3]$, CF 0.947,

$[kmcluster = class_3] \Rightarrow [hcluster = class_3]$, CF 0.947,

$[hcluster = class_4] \Rightarrow [kmcluster = class_4]$, CF 0.611,

$[kmcluster = class_4] \Rightarrow [hcluster = class_4]$, CF 0.904

We can see the almost perfect fit between these two classifications, due to the similar methods used (k-means and k-nearest neighbors).

6.3 Correspondences between more than two partitions

Counting with more than two partitions, as in our case, let us to look for some of the properties intro-

Table 3: Table exp5

Unit	Description
1	Soils over carbonated compacted rock
2	Soils over recent alluvial deposits
3	Soils over marls, marl-limestones, phyllites, conglomerates and colluvium, carbonated or recarbonated materials, moderately-high sloping, low-medium evolution degree
4	Soils of medium-high evolution degree over colluvium or conglomerate, low-moderately sloping
5	Soils over micaschist and quarcites

duced in section 5. For example, if we take a look to the following approximate dependencies,

$codunida, grunida \Rrightarrow exp5$, CF = 0.80, and
$codunida \Rrightarrow exp5$, CF = 0.80,

Since $codunida \subseteq grunida$, we can conclude that proposition 5.6 holds.

Another example is the resulting of looking at these approximate dependencies,

$exp5 \Rrightarrow codunida, grunida$, CF = 0.10, and
$exp5 \Rrightarrow grunida$, CF = 0.10,

By proposition 5.7, we can prove that $codunida \subseteq grunida$, as we expected.

7 DISCUSSION

The study of local, partial and global correspondences is useful for certain kinds of information fusion tasks. We have proposed to measure the accuracy of these correspondences on the basis of certainty factors of association rules and approximate dependencies, using a representation of partitions in relational tables. Several properties that relate values of certainty to possible situations regarding correspondences are provided.

Using data mining techniques for information fusion in the field of soil science appears to be very promising. This may be due to heterogeneity and imprecision associated to the different soil knowledge sources. The possibilities in translation of user knowledge to scientist terminology in order to later employ it in decision-making would be very interesting, due to the easiness and large extension of this knowledge source.

In this attempt of information fusion, we prove the difficulties of the procedure. Mainly, these are caused by the different classification criteria: from the utilitary to the genetic. In our case, the particularity of olive tree cultivation also takes part, capable of easy adaptability to great part of soils in the province of Granada.

For this kind of studies, it would be desirable to essay and upgrade new techniques in user knowledge extraction, as it is the one with greater imprecision and uncertainty. In (Calero et al., 2002), a first approximation to the problem of comparing classic techniques of multivariate analysis as, for example, correspondence analysis, with our proposal is presented. It can be seen how not only both techniques give similar results, but that in certain cases as ours, data mining techniques are more desirable. This will be studied in more detail in the future.

Moreover, we believe that the algorithm to search for approximate dependencies and their models, proposed in (Blanco et al., 2000) will be very useful when comparing several partitions at a time. The case of hierarchies comparison is particularly interesting for us. This will be the main topic in a future work.

REFERENCES

Agrawal, R., Imielinski, T., and Swami, A. (1993). Mining association rules between sets of items in large databases. In *Proc. Of the 1993 ACM SIGMOD Conference*, pages 207–216.

Appriou, A., Ayoun, A., Benferhat, S., Besnard, P., Cholvy, L., Cooke, R., Cuppens, F., Dubois, D., Fargier, H., Grabisch, M., Kruse, R., Lang, J., Moral, S., Prade, H., Saffiotti, A., Smets, P., and Sossai, C. (2001). Fusion: General concepts and characteristics. *Int. Journal of Intelligent Systems*, 16(10):1107–34.

Aranda, V., Calero, J., Delgado, G., Sánchez, D., Serrano, J., and Vila, M. (2002). Flexible land classification for olive cultivation using user knowledge. In *Proceedings of 1st. Int. ICSC Conf. On Neuro-Fuzzy Technologies (NF'2002)*. To appear.

Berzal, F., Blanco, I., Sánchez, D., and Vila, M. (2001). A new framework to assess association rules. In Hoffmann, F., editor, *Advances in Intelligent Data Analysis. Fourth International Symposium, IDA'01. Lecture Notes in Computer Science 2189*, pages 95–104. Springer-Verlag.

Blanco, I., Martín-Bautista, M., Sánchez, D., and Vila, M. (2000). On the support of dependencies in relational databases: strong approximate dependencies. Data Mining and Knowledge Discovery, Submitted.

Bosc, P. and Lietard, L. (1997). Functional dependencies revisited under graduality and imprecision. In *Annual Meeting of NAFIPS*, pages 57–62.

Bra, P. D. and Paredaens, J. (1983). Horizontal decompositions for handling exceptions to functional dependencies. *Advances in Database Theory*, 2:123–144.

Calero, J.A., Serrano, J.M, Aranda, V., Sánchez, D., Sánchez-Marañón, M., Vila, M.A., Delgado, G. "Evaluacíón del olivar granadino con información del usuario empleando técnicas de análisis multivariante y data mining". Proceedings of the 1st International IFOAM Scientific Conference on Ecological Olive Growing: Production and Culture. Puente Génave (Spain), 24-25 May'2002. To appear.

Cholvy, L. and Moral, S. (2001). Merging databases: Problems and examples. *Int. Journal of Intelligent Systems*, 16(10):1193–1221.

Delgado, M., Martín-Bautista, M., Sánchez, D., and Vila, M. (2000). Mining strong approximate dependencies from relational databases. In *Proceedings of IPMU'2000.*

FAO (1968). Definitions of soil units for the soil maps of the world. Technical report, FAO. World Soil Resources Reports 33.

FAO 1998. The world reference base for soil resources. World Soil Resources Rep. 84. ISSS/AISS/IBG/ISRIC/FAO, Rome.

Li, W. and Clifton, C. (2000). SEMINT: A tool for identifying attribute correspondences in heterogeneous databases using neural networks. *Data Knowledge Engineering*, 33(1):44–84.

Monge, A. and Elkan, C. (1996). The field matching problem: Algorithms and applications. In *Proc. KDD'96*, pages 267–270.

Pérez-Pujalte, A. and Prieto, P. (1980). Mapa de suelos 1:200000 de la provincia de granada y memoria explicativa. Technical report, CSIC.

Pfahringer, B. and Kramer, S. (1995). Compression-based evaluation of partial determinations. In *Proc. First Int'l Conf. Knowledge Discovery and Data Mining (KDD'95)*, pages 234–239.

Sánchez, D. (1999). *Adquisición de Relaciones Entre Atributos En Bases de Datos Relacionales (Translates to: Acquisition of Relationships Between Attributes in Relational Databases) (in Spanish).* PhD thesis, Department of Computer Science and Artificial Intelligence, University of Granada.

Serrano J.M., Vila M.A., Aranda, V., Delgado G.(2001). "Using Fuzzy Relational Databases to represent agricultural and environmental information. An example within the scope of olive cultivation in Granada". Mathware & Soft Computing VIII, n.3, pp. 275-289.

Shortliffe, E. and Buchanan, B. (1975). A model of inexact reasoning in medicine. *Mathematical Biosciences*, 23:351–379.

Sys I.C., Van Ranst E. & Debaveye I.J., 1991. "Land Evaluation. "Agricultural Publications, n. 7. University Ghent.

Ziarko, W. (1991). The discovery, analysis and representation of data dependencies in databases. In Piatetsky-Shapiro, G. and Frawley, W., editors, *Knowledge Discovery in Databases*, pages 195–209. AAAI/MIT Press.

Table 4: Table grupos

Unit	Description
1	Deep, not detected crust, high tractorability, moderately sloping, low rockyness, rills not detected, material losing not detected, clayey, dark brown
2	Deep, not detected crust, high tractorability, flat, low rockyness, rills not detected, material losing not detected, clayey, light brown
3	Deep, not detected crust, high tractorability, moderately sloping, low rockyness, presence of rills, material losing not detected, clayey, dark gray.
4	Deep, not detected crust, high tractorability, moderately sloping, low rockyness, rills not detected, material losing not detected, clayey, dark gray.
5	Deep, not detected crust, low tractorability, moderately sloping, low rockyness, presence of rills, material losing detected, clayey, dark gray
6	Moderately deep, crust moderately deep, medium tractorability, moderately sloping, medium rockyness, rills not detected, material losing not detected, loamy, dark brown
7	Moderately deep, crust moderately deep, medium tractorability, moderately sloping, medium rockyness, rills not detected, material losing not detected, clayey, light brown
8	Moderately deep, deep crust, high tractorability, moderately sloping, low rockyness, rills not detected, material losing not detected, loamy, dark brown
9	Shallow, shallow crust, high tractorability, moderately sloping, high rockyness, rills not detected, material losing not detected, sandy, light gray
10	Deep, not detected crust, medium tractorability, moderately sloping, high rockyness, presence of rills, material losing detected, loamy, dark brown
11	Deep, not detected crust, low tractorability, sloping, medium rockyness, rills not detected, material losing not detected, loamy, light brown
12	Moderately deep, crust moderately deep, low tractorability, moderately sloping, high rockyness, presence of rills, material losing detected, clayey, red
13	Moderately deep, not detected crust, medium tractorability, sloping, high rockyness, presence of rills, material losing detected, sandy, dark brown
14	Deep, not detected crust, low tractorability, very sloping, medium rockyness, presence of rills, material losing detected, loamy, light gray
15	Moderately deep, crust moderately deep, high tractorability, flat, low rockyness, rills not detected, material losing not detected, clayey, light brown
16	Moderately deep, crust moderately deep, low tractorability, sloping, medium rockyness, presence of rills, material losing detected, clayey, dark gray
17	Moderately deep, crust moderately deep, high tractorability, moderately sloping, low rockyness, presence of rills, material losing detected, clayey, dark gray
18	Moderately deep, shallow crust, low tractorability, very sloping, medium rockyness, presence of rills, material losing detected, clayey, light gray
19	Deep, deep crust, low tractorability, very sloping, high rockyness, presence of rills, material losing detected, sandy, dark gray

Table 5: Table grupos4

Unit	Description
1	Deep, crust not detected, high tractorability, moderately sloping, low rockyness, not detected rills, material losing not detected, clayey, light gray
2	Moderately deep, moderately deep crust, low tractorability, sloping, medium rockyness, presence of rills, material losing detected, loamy, dark gray
3	Deep, deep crust, medium tractorability, moderately sloping, medium rockyness, not detected rills, material losing not detected, loamy, light brown
4	Moderately deep, deep crust, high tractorability, moderately sloping, medium rockyness, presence of rills, material losing detected, clayey, light gray

Table 6: Table exp13

Unit	Description
1	Soils over carbonated compacted rock, shallow, variable evolution degree, high sloping
2	Soils over recent calcareous alluvial deposits
3	Soils over recent non-calcareous alluvial deposits
4	Soils over marls, moderately deep-deep, moderately-high sloping, low evolution degree
5	Soils over marl-limestones, phyllites, conglomerates and colluvium, moderately deep, high sloping and low evolution degree
6	Soils over marls, deep, moderately sloping, no calcic horizon, medium evolution degree
7	Soils over marl-limestones, phyllites, conglomerates and colluvium, moderately deep-deep, moderately sloping, calcic horizon, medium evolution degree
8	Soils over gypsic marls, low-medium evolution degree
9	Soils of medium evolution degree over colluvium or conglomerate, low sloping, moderately deep, calcic or petrocalcic horizon
10	Soils of high evolution degree over colluvium or conglomerate, low sloping, moderately deep-deep, calcic or petrocalcic horizon
11	Soils of high evolution degree, deep, no petrocalcic horizon
12	Soils over micaschist and quarcites of low evolution degree, shallow-moderately deep, high sloping
13	Soils over micaschist and quarcites of medium-high volution degree, moderately deep, low-moderately sloping

Table 7: Table codunida

Unit	Description
1	Litosols
2	Calcareous fluvisols
3	Eutric fluvisols
5	Calcareous regosols
6	Calcareous-eutric regosols
8	Calcareous regosols-calcic xerosols
9	Calcareous regosols-calcic cambisols
10	Calcareous regosols-litosols-calcic cambisols
11	Calcareous-eutric regosols-eutric cambisols
12	Calcic-gypsic xerosols-calcic cambisols
14	Calcic cambisols
15	Calcic cambisols-calcareous regosols
16	Calcic cambisols-chromic luvisols
17	Calcic cambisols-calcareous regosols-litosols
19	Eutric cambisols-eutric regosols-chromic luvisols
20	Eutric cambisols-chromic luvisols
21	Chromic luvisols

IMPLEMENTATION OF FUZZY CLASSIFICATION QUERY LANGUAGE IN RELATIONAL DATABASES USING STORED PROCEDURES

Yauheni Veryha
ABB Corporate Research, Wallstadter Str. 59, 68526, Ladenburg, Germany
Email: yauheni.veryha@web.de

Key words: Information systems, data mining, fuzzy classification, relational database.

Abstract: A framework of the fuzzy classification query language (fCQL) for data mining in information systems is presented. The fuzzy classification query language provides easy-to-use functionality for data extraction similar to the conventional non-fuzzy classification and SQL querying. The developed prototype is based on the stored procedures and database extensions of Microsoft SQL Server 2000. It can be used as data mining tool in large information systems and easily integrated with conventional relational databases. The benefits of using the presented approach include high flexibility for data analysis, user-friendly data presentation at the report generation phase and additional data security features due to the introduction of additional view-based data layer.

1 INTRODUCTION

The vast expansion of the Internet gives rise to a significant growth of the number of huge online databases. Therefore, data mining with its goal of reducing the complexity and the number of computations in very large databases attracts more and more attention from the information industry (Abdennadher and Schuetz, 1998; Bellma and Vojdani, 2000; Chen, 1998; Han and Kamber, 2001; Han et al., 1999; Zadrozny and Kacprzyk, 1998). At the stage of the typical data classification in information systems, there appear some types of uncertainty, for instance, when the boundaries of a class of objects are not sharply defined (Bosc, 1998; Kacprzyk and Zadrozny, 2000). In this case, the most common, useful and widely accepted solution is the introduction of fuzzy sets (Bellma and Vojdani, 2000; Blanco et al., 2000; Bosc and Pivert, 2000; Dubois et al., 2000; Schindler, 1998). Fuzzy sets provide mathematical meanings to the natural language statements and become an effective solution for dealing with uncertainty. The approach of fuzzy set theory with its membership functions is widely used to form a realistic description of the evaluation. Different criteria with separate scales and optimization objectives can be combined into a joint response measure - the aggregated value of the membership (Zimmermann, 1992; Zimmermann and Zysno, 1980). A number of different schemes and tools for the implementation of fuzzy sets in database management systems have been proposed in recent years, such as fuzzy querying, fuzzy extension of the SQL (Structured Query Language), fuzzy object oriented database schemes, etc. (Abdennadher and Schuetz, 1998; Bellma and Vojdani, 2000; Bosc, 1998; Bosc and Pivert, 2000; Carrasco et al., 1999; Dubois et al., 2000; Han et al., 1999; Kacprzyk and Zadrozny, 2000; Zadrozny and Kacprzyk, 1998). However, the reality shows that despite of large importance of data mining, fuzzy methods are not widely used in relational database systems in practice. The main reason is that the large majority of the proposed fuzzy methods for data mining requires to change the conventional relational database structure or to add special features to the database management tools, for example, to modify the functionality of the conventional SQL (Bosc and Pivert, 2000; Han et al., 1999; Kacprzyk and Zadrozny, 2000). Most of the database system owners and users do not want to switch to fuzzy database structures and, therefore, cannot apply fuzzy querying in their databases.

Here, it is proposed to use a framework based on the fuzzy classification (Schindler, 1998; Zimmermann and Zysno, 1980) and fuzzy classification query language (fCQL) for data mining and data warehouse management. The main benefit of this framework is that there is no need to modify the functionality of the conventional relational databases. All manipulations can be done as an extension of the database schema by applying fuzzy data classification. Therefore, all benefits of using fuzzy sets and fuzzy classification in data mining, like user-friendly data presentation, precision of the data classification, use of linguistic variables instead of numeric values, easy-to-use facilities for querying the extended database schema, etc., will become available for the users of the conventional relational databases.

2 CONVENTIONAL DATA CLASSIFICATION IN RELATIONAL DATABASES

The most common way of querying relational database tables is through SQL. If one wishes to analyze data in the database tables, one should follow a KDD (Knowledge Discovery in Databases) process (Han and Kamber, 2001). In principle, this process consists of six stages, namely, data selection, cleaning, enrichment, coding, data mining, and reporting. This paper is concentrated on data mining techniques, namely, conventional and fuzzy data classification using atomic values of attributes and their implementation in relational databases.

In order to show the difference in the data presentation before and after use of data classification, the following simple example can be considered. The example database includes OFFERS table that contains the data about suppliers (Supplier column), materials (Material column), material quality (Quality column), and delivery delay (Delay column). The example data relation is presented in Table 1.

Material	Supplier	Quality	Delay
802.025	BAW	sufficient	8
802.025	DG	average	5
802.025	KBA	sufficient	7
802.025	MD	sufficient	9
802.025	MTX	high	2
802.025	MAM	low	7
840.024	KBA	low	9
840.024	ZT	average	2
840.024	MTX	high	4
840.024	MAM	average	6
809.200	MD	average	4
809.200	DG	high	8
809.200	KBA	sufficient	3
809.200	ZT	high	9

Table 1: OFFERS table

In order to query the presented data and produce a list of 'good' suppliers, one can use a typical SQL query, such as, SELECT Supplier, Material, Quality, Delay FROM Offers WHERE (Quality = 'high' or Quality = 'average') and (Delay < 5), assuming that 'good' suppliers are those who provide the material of 'high' or 'average' quality with the delay of less than 5 hours. For small data tables, this approach is acceptable. However, if the number of the attributes is more than 5 and the ranges of data in columns will be significantly larger, the queries become much more complex. In order to simplify data mining in large databases, one may use conventional data classification (Han and Kamber, 2001). Here, for simplicity, we will go on with the introduction of conventional data classification for simple OFFERS table. To define classes, we introduce the atomic values for Delay and Quality attributes (it is especially important for attributes with large intervals of numeric values). We define 'acceptable' and 'not-acceptable' atomic values for Delay attribute. The atomic value of 'acceptable' is assigned for the interval of (1 - 5), and the atomic value of 'not-acceptable' is assigned for the interval of (6 - 10). The atomic value of 'good' is assigned for the 'high' and 'average' Quality attribute values. Similarly, the 'bad' atomic value is assigned for the 'sufficient' and 'low' Quality attribute values. As soon as the definition of the atomic values is done, it is easy to define all classes for the suppliers:

- C1 – Extend Relationship Class with atomic values ('acceptable', 'good').
- C2 – Complain About Delay Class with atomic values ('not-acceptable', 'good').
- C3 – Improve Quality Class with atomic values ('acceptable', 'bad').
- C4 – Evaluate Relationship Class with atomic values ('not-acceptable', 'bad').

The distribution of suppliers from OFFERS table among the introduced classes is graphically presented in Fig. 1.

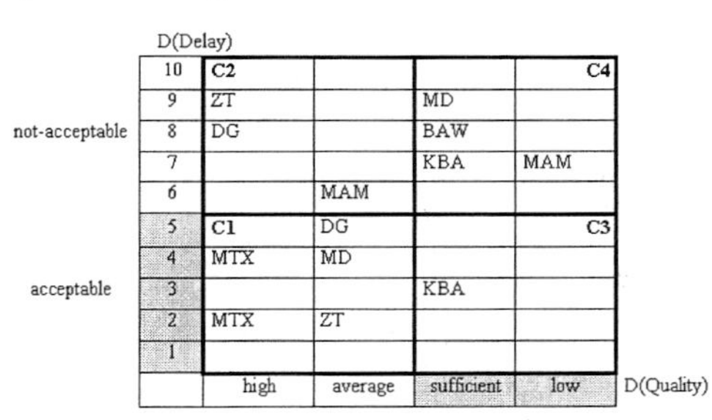

Figure 1: Conventional non-fuzzy classification of suppliers.

In order to find all members of 'Complain About Delay' class C2 (see Fig. 1), one can query the initial OFFERS table with simple SQL query, namely, SELECT Supplier, Material, Quality, Delay FROM Offers WHERE (Quality = 'high' or Quality = 'average') and (Delay > 5). Thus, the conventional non-fuzzy data classification can be easily done using native SQL queries.

The main problem of the presented conventional data classification is that the information about suppliers is not sufficient, for example, some suppliers, like DG and KBA (see Fig. 1), belong to different classes. Here, it is impossible to distinguish to which class the supplier belongs more and to which less due to the precise boundary definition of the atomic values. It is obvious, when using precise boundaries in the data classification, that some information about suppliers gets lost in later data analysis (Han and Kamber, 2001). Thus, the generated reports based on this simple data classification are not precise enough. In order to improve the precision of the data classification, it is proposed to use fuzzy data classification (Schindler, 1998).

3 FUZZY DATA CLASSIFICATION IN RELATIONAL DATABASES

In order to get more detailed information about the suppliers membership in the classes, one can introduce fuzzy classification of data (Schindler, 1998; Zimmermann, 1992) and linguistic variables (Schindler, 1998). As an example, we can consider the Delay attribute as a linguistic variable. The area of definition of the linguistic variable is the domain D(Delay). Similarly to the assignment of the atomic value, Delay linguistic variable possesses the set of terms T(Delay) = {acceptable, not-acceptable} with the verbal terms 'acceptable' and 'not-acceptable' which define appropriate equivalence classes (1 - 5) and (6 - 10). The most important feature of the linguistic variables is that every term of the linguistic variable represents a fuzzy set. The membership function of the fuzzy set is defined over the domain of the corresponding attribute. For instance, in Fig. 2, the delay of 5 days is at the same time acceptable and not acceptable; in both cases the membership function μ has the value 0.5, i.e. $\mu_{acceptable}=0.5$ and $\mu_{not\text{-}acceptable}=0.5$. The membership of an object in a specific class can be calculated by an aggregation over all terms of the linguistic variables which define the class. The terms "acceptable" and "good", for instance, describe the class C1. The membership, therefore, is a conjunction of the corresponding values of the membership functions $\mu_{acceptable}$ and μ_{good}. There exists quite a number of operators which calculate conjunctions of membership function values (Zimmermann, 1992; Zimmermann and Zysno, 1980). For example, one can apply the γ-operator which is used as a "compensatory AND" and was empirically tested in (Zimmermann and Zysno, 1980).

The membership $\mu_{\tilde{A}_i,comp}(x)$ $\mu_{\tilde{A}_i,comp}(x)$ of the x object with m linguistic variables to the given classes can be calculated based on the following equation:

$$\mu_{\tilde{A}_i,comp}(x)=\left(\prod_{i=1}^{m}\mu_i(x)\right)^{(1-\gamma)}\left(1-\prod_{i=1}^{m}(1-\mu_i(x))\right)^{\gamma},$$

$$x\in X,\quad 0\le\gamma\le 1$$

where γ is the control parameter with the default value of 0.5 (Zimmermann and Zysno, 1980), $\mu_i(x)$ is the membership value of x object to a particular linguistic variable, m is the number of linguistic variables. Based on the γ-operator, the values of the supplier's membership are calculated and presented in Fig. 2.

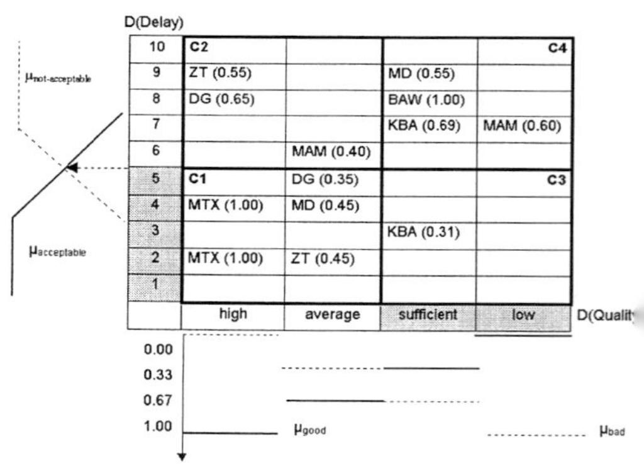

Figure 2: Fuzzy classification of data with appropriate membership functions.

The main benefit of the fuzzy data classification becomes clear if we compare the presentation of classes C1, C2, C2 and C4 in Fig. 1 and Fig. 2. As it is shown in Fig. 2 with fuzzy data classification, one can not only determine the members of the given classes but also compare the level of the membership to the particular classes, that is very important for data analysis. For example, based on the fuzzy classification, one can say that MAM supplier belongs more to the C4 class than to the C2 class (see Fig. 2). Thus, the membership values can be very useful for searching the best suppliers in the given class. They become important criteria for evaluating the suppliers; one only needs to compare the membership values of the suppliers of a particular class. For example, if two suppliers offer the same quality and delivery delay for the given material, we can compare their membership values. The supplier with a higher membership value to C1 class can be considered to be better. In this case, the membership value is similar to the deviation in the statistics and shows the distribution of the supplier membership to different classes. For example, in order to get suppliers that belong to C2 class (see Fig. 2), one could get the data output after fuzzy classification as the database view which is shown in Table 2. Based on the given view one can say that DG supplier belong to this class more than MAM and ZT suppliers due to the higher value of the membership function.

Supp-lier	Class	Qua-lity	Delay	Mem. value
MAM	C2	good	not-acceptable	0.4
ZT	C2	good	not-acceptable	0.55
DG	C2	good	not-acceptable	0.65

Table 2: Database view for C2 class members

The use of the fuzzy classification provides higher accuracy of the data presentation and gives a more precise description of data in generated reports. On the other hand and due to the fact that the membership values of the suppliers have to be calculated with rather complicated mathematical formulas, the SQL querying process becomes complicated. There are different approaches for the implementation of the presented fuzzy classification in practice. One of the direction is the use of the fuzzy querying languages as the extension of the conventional SQL (Chen, 1998; Han et al., 1999; Kacprzyk and Zadrozny, 2000). Here, it is proposed to use the fuzzy Classification Query Language (fCQL) for fuzzy classified data querying .

4 FCQL FOR FUZZY CLASSIFIED DATA QUERYING

The goal of the fCQL is to provide a database view or report, similar to the one presented in Table 2, of the fuzzy classified data using simple and easy-to-use queries. In order to implement the fuzzy Classification Query Language for relational databases, the best solution is to provide an interpreter that translates the easy-to-use fCQL commands into SQL queries. The user can formulate fCQL queries with well-defined terms and has no need to know the definition of the equivalence classes in details. In addition, all complex mathematical formulas for the calculation of the membership functions are hidden from the user.

The simplified syntax of the fCQL is given as:

classify *<Object>*
[**into**] *<View>*
from <Relation>
[**with**] <Classification_condition>

For example, the fCQL query '**classify** Supplier **into** Suppliers **from** Offers'" performs a classification (see Fig. 2) of all suppliers from the OFFERS table (see Table 1) into the SUPPLIERS view. The SUPPLIERS view content is presented in Table 3.

Supp-lier	Class	Qua-lity	Delay	Mem. value
DG	C1	good	acceptable	0.35
MD	C1	good	acceptable	0.45
ZT	C1	good	acceptable	0.45
MTX	C1	good	acceptable	1.00
MAM	C2	good	not-acceptable	0.4
ZT	C2	good	not-acceptable	0.55
DG	C2	good	not-acceptable	0.65
KBA	C3	bad	acceptable	0.31
MD	C4	bad	not-acceptable	0.55
BAW	C4	bad	not-acceptable	1.00
MAM	C4	bad	not-acceptable	0.60
KBA	C4	bad	not-acceptable	0.69

Table 3: SUPPLIERS view

After this step, the data from the SUPPLIERS view can be further queried using conventional SQL for data analysis and report generation. On the other hand, the user can use the fCQL query '**classify** Supplier **from** Offers' without **into** clause in order to output the same results on the screen. The extended fCQL query '**classify** Supplier **into** Report **from** Offers **with class is** "C2" ' will generate the REPORT view with the data presented in Table 2.

The fCQL has been designed in the spirit of the conventional SQL. Instead of specifying the attribute list in the **select** clause, the name of the object column to be classified must be given in the **classify** clause. The **where** clause is changed to a **with** clause in order to distinguish from SQL and give a better meaning of the fCQL functionality. The partial syntax of the fCQL is the following:

<ClassificationQuery>	**classify** <Object> **into** <View > **from** <Relation> [**with** <ClassificationCondition>]
<ClassificationCondition>	<ClassSelection> | <AttributeSelection> [**or** <AttributeSelection>]...

Instead of specifying a class by its name, it is possible to use the linguistic descriptions of the equivalence classes, for instance, '**classify** Supplier **into** Report **from** Offers **with** Delay **is** "Acceptable" **and** Quality **is** "Good" '. Thus, the fCQL provides a very user-friendly solution for the fuzzy classification of data. Much more, the functionality of the fCQL is fully based on the conventional SQL. This simplifies the process of its implementation in the conventional relational databases. However, in order to implement the fCQL, an appropriate software architecture is necessary.

5 FUZZY CLASSIFICATION AND QUERYING IMPLEMENTATION IN RELATIONAL DATABASES

The implementation scheme of the fCQL for fuzzy classified data includes the following steps:
Design of database tables or views for later querying using fCQL for fuzzy classified data.

1. Design of database extensions (additional tables that contain linguistic variables, membership values, descriptions of atomic values, etc.).
2. Design of interpreter for fCQL transformation into native SQL for the given relational database management system using lexical, syntactical and semantic analysis of queries.
3. Generation of database reports and views using fCQL querying of fuzzy classified data, formed on the Steps 1 and 2.

The simplified architecture for the developed framework implementation is presented in Fig. 3.

Processing of the SQL queries by the interpreter includes two main stages:

- Syntactical and semantic analysis of fCQL string clauses.

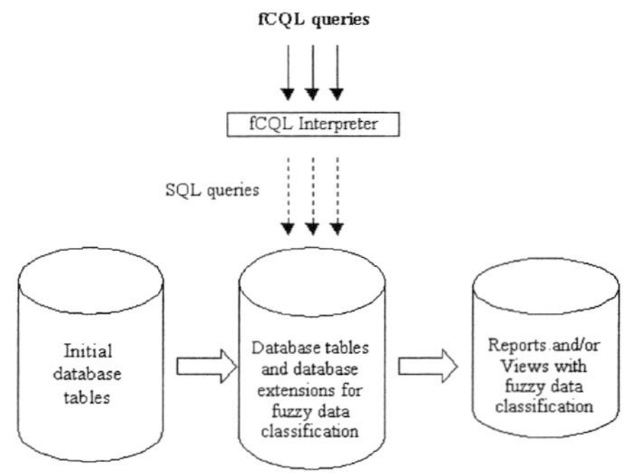

Figure 3: Architecture of fuzzy classification and querying implementation in relational databases.

- Execution of native SQL sub-queries (grouping of objects into classes, calculation of "compensatory AND" membership of objects to the classes, calculation of normalized membership of objects to classes, etc.) with parameters from fCQL clauses.

The developed fuzzy classification and querying framework implementation is illustrated by simple database example that is similar to the one presented in the beginning of the article. Due to the large popularity among database users, the Microsoft SQL Server 2000 database management system was chosen as the basic platform for the fuzzy classification implementation. The embedded Transact-SQL language of the Microsoft SQL Server 2000 provides all required functionality for the interpreter development as the stored procedure. However, the interpreter was developed with the assumption that similar interpreter could be further developed for other platforms, like Oracle or SyBase, using their embedded SQL versions. The interpreter was realized as the stored procedure on the Microsoft SQL Server 2000 that could translate the fCQL queries into the Transact-SQL queries. The lexical and syntactical analysis was done by Transact-SQL using the Transact-SQL functions for strings and embedded Microsoft SQL Server 2000 stored procedures.

The simple database scheme example in the normalized form is presented in Fig. 4. In order to extend the current database scheme for working with the fuzzy classified data, the following database schema extensions, i.e. tables and relationships, were provided for the fuzzy classification, as shown in Fig. 5. In addition to the initial OFFERS, MATERIALS and SUPPLIERS tables (see Fig. 4), the following classifications tables were added (See Fig. 5): fDELAY, fQUALITY, fCLASSES, fCLASSESDEFINITION and fLINGUISTICVARIABLES.

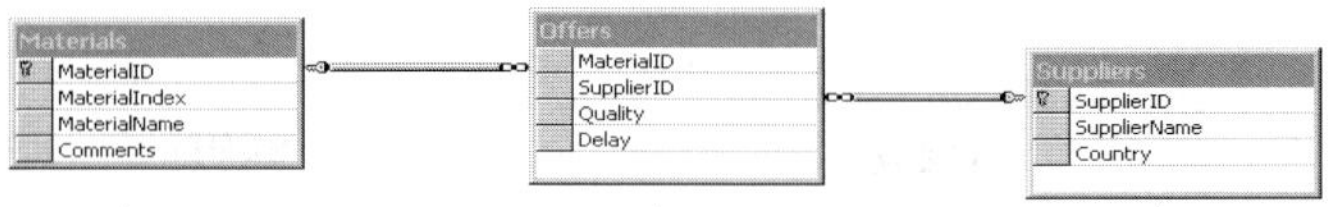

MaterialID	MaterialIndex	MaterialName	Comments
1	802.025	Plastic material	Suitable for in-home use.
2	809.200	Plastic material	Toxic
3	840.024	Plastic material	Suitable only for out-home use.

SupplierID	SupplierName	Country
1	BAW	Germany
2	DG	France
3	KBA	Poland
4	MD	Austria
5	MTX	Germany
6	MAM	Italy
7	ZT	France

MaterialID	SupplierID	Quality	Delay
2	7	high	9
2	2	high	8
2	4	average	4
3	6	average	6
1	4	sufficient	9
1	1	sufficient	8
1	3	sufficient	7
1	6	low	7
2	3	sufficient	3
1	2	average	5
1	5	high	2
3	5	high	4
3	7	average	2
3	3	low	9

Figure 4: Database schema example with content and relationships.

Additional tables include the definition of the classes, linguistic variables and their dependencies. In order to query the given database and receive the fuzzy classified data report similar to the one shown in Table 3, it is required to perform the native Transact-SQL query without interpreter, as shown in Fig. 6. Instead of this, one can use a very simple fCQL query with the help of the fCQL interpreter and receive the same results, as it is shown in Fig. 7.

As it is clear from the presented example, the use of the fCQL is much more easier than the direct use of the native Transact-SQL.

6 CONCLUSIONS

Fuzzy classification framework for relational databases using fCQL querying have been presented. The main benefits of using fuzzy classification and fCQL querying are the following:

1. Good integration with the conventional databases and high flexibility for data analysis.
2. User-friendly data presentation for the report generation phase with linguistic variables and fuzzy values that lead to more descriptive queries for the data analysis phase and, therefore, allow decreasing time spent on extracting required information from the given databases.
3. The user or database administrator does not have to change the underlying databases, which are, in practice, very large. With the developed approach, one operates on the database schema level by defining an appropriate fuzzy classification with linguistic variables.
4. The fuzzy classification architecture provides additional data security features due to the introduction of an additional view-based data layer which hides the numerical values from the users. At the same time, the information is available for querying using linguistic variables.
5. The fuzzy classification framework gives the possibility to compress the data using classes, linguistic variables and atomic values for querying. This feature is particularly important for very large databases.

For the implementation of the fuzzy classification framework, the prototype based on the Microsoft SQL Server 2000 was developed. The interpreter for fCQL querying was developed using Transact-SQL. The use of the interpreter on the server side as the stored procedure gave large benefits due to the simple fCQL querying based on the conventional SQL, close integration with the database and easy distribution due to its availability for all users of the database.

The developed fuzzy classification framework can be recommended to be used as the data mining tool. Future works include testing of the developed framework on the large database from industry.

ACKNOWLEDGEMENTS

This work was funded in part by the Swiss National Science Foundation Grant Nr. 83R-064657.

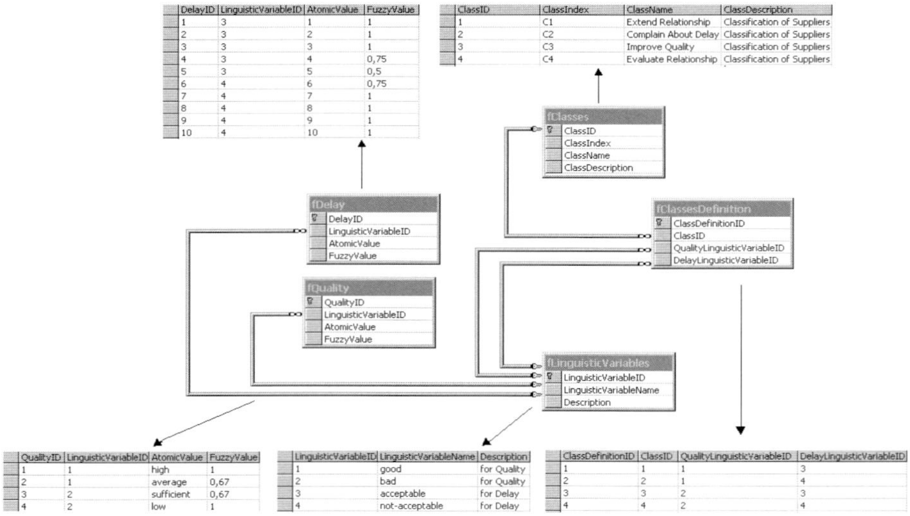

Figure 5: The database extension tables and relationships for fuzzy classification.

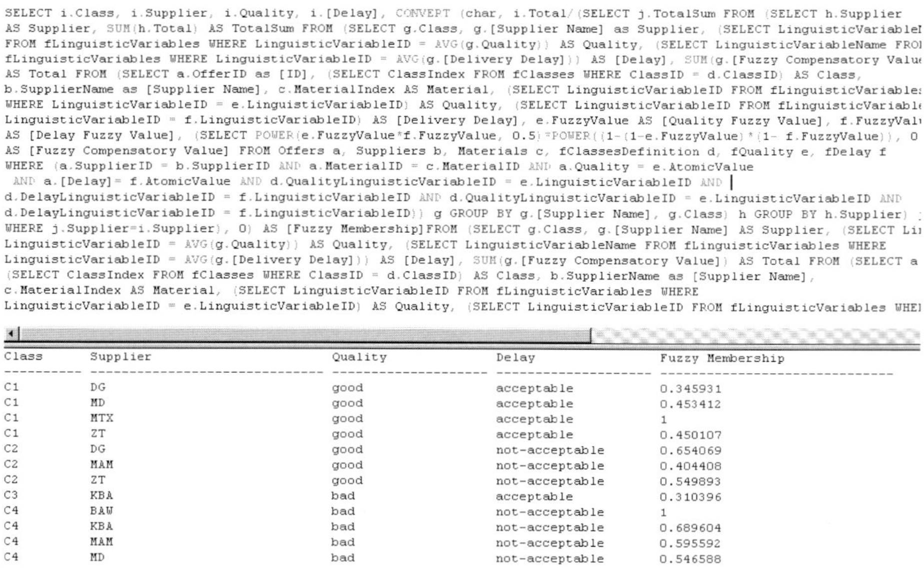

```
SELECT i.Class, i.Supplier, i.Quality, i.[Delay], CONVERT (char, i.Total/(SELECT j.TotalSum FROM (SELECT h.Supplier
AS Supplier, SUM(h.Total) AS TotalSum FROM (SELECT g.Class, g.[Supplier Name] as Supplier, (SELECT LinguisticVariableI
FROM fLinguisticVariables WHERE LinguisticVariableID = AVG(g.Quality)) AS Quality, (SELECT LinguisticVariableName FROI
fLinguisticVariables WHERE LinguisticVariableID = AVG(g.[Delivery Delay])) AS [Delay], SUM(g.[Fuzzy Compensatory Valu
AS Total FROM (SELECT a.OfferID as [ID], (SELECT ClassIndex FROM fClasses WHERE ClassID = d.ClassID) AS Class,
b.SupplierName as [Supplier Name], c.MaterialIndex AS Material, (SELECT LinguisticVariableID FROM fLinguisticVariable
WHERE LinguisticVariableID = e.LinguisticVariableID) AS Quality, (SELECT LinguisticVariableID FROM fLinguisticVariabl
LinguisticVariableID = f.LinguisticVariableID) AS [Delivery Delay], e.FuzzyValue AS [Quality Fuzzy Value], f.FuzzyVal
AS [Delay Fuzzy Value], (SELECT POWER(e.FuzzyValue*f.FuzzyValue, 0.5)*POWER((1-(1-e.FuzzyValue)*(1- f.FuzzyValue)), 0
AS [Fuzzy Compensatory Value] FROM Offers a, Suppliers b, Materials c, fClassesDefinition d, fQuality e, fDelay f
WHERE (a.SupplierID = b.SupplierID AND a.MaterialID = c.MaterialID AND a.Quality = e.AtomicValue
 AND a.[Delay]= f.AtomicValue AND d.QualityLinguisticVariableID = e.LinguisticVariableID AND
d.DelayLinguisticVariableID = f.LinguisticVariableID AND d.QualityLinguisticVariableID = e.LinguisticVariableID AND
d.DelayLinguisticVariableID = f.LinguisticVariableID)) g GROUP BY g.[Supplier Name], g.Class) h GROUP BY h.Supplier)
WHERE j.Supplier=i.Supplier), 0) AS [Fuzzy Membership]FROM (SELECT g.Class, g.[Supplier Name] AS Supplier, (SELECT Li
LinguisticVariableID = AVG(g.Quality)) AS Quality, (SELECT LinguisticVariableName FROM fLinguisticVariables WHERE
LinguisticVariableID = AVG(g.[Delivery Delay])) AS [Delay], SUM(g.[Fuzzy Compensatory Value]) AS Total FROM (SELECT a
(SELECT ClassIndex FROM fClasses WHERE ClassID = d.ClassID) AS Class, b.SupplierName as [Supplier Name],
c.MaterialIndex AS Material, (SELECT LinguisticVariableID FROM fLinguisticVariables WHERE
LinguisticVariableID = e.LinguisticVariableID) AS Quality, (SELECT LinguisticVariableID FROM fLinguisticVariables WHE
```

Class	Supplier	Quality	Delay	Fuzzy Membership
C1	DG	good	acceptable	0.345931
C1	MD	good	acceptable	0.453412
C1	MTX	good	acceptable	1
C1	ZT	good	acceptable	0.450107
C2	DG	good	not-acceptable	0.654069
C2	MAM	good	not-acceptable	0.404408
C2	ZT	good	not-acceptable	0.549893
C3	KBA	bad	acceptable	0.310396
C4	BAW	bad	not-acceptable	1
C4	KBA	bad	not-acceptable	0.689604
C4	MAM	bad	not-acceptable	0.595592
C4	MD	bad	not-acceptable	0.546588

Figure 6: Screen of native Transact-SQL querying of fuzzy classified data.

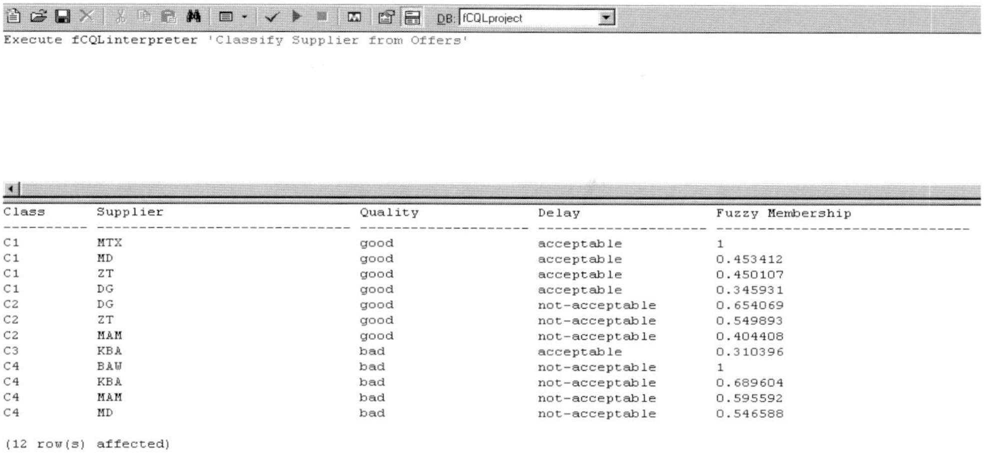

DB: fCQLproject

```
Execute fCQLinterpreter 'Classify Supplier from Offers'
```

Class	Supplier	Quality	Delay	Fuzzy Membership
C1	MTX	good	acceptable	1
C1	MD	good	acceptable	0.453412
C1	ZT	good	acceptable	0.450107
C1	DG	good	acceptable	0.345931
C2	DG	good	not-acceptable	0.654069
C2	ZT	good	not-acceptable	0.549893
C2	MAM	good	not-acceptable	0.404408
C3	KBA	bad	acceptable	0.310396
C4	BAW	bad	not-acceptable	1
C4	KBA	bad	not-acceptable	0.689604
C4	MAM	bad	not-acceptable	0.595592
C4	MD	bad	not-acceptable	0.546588

(12 row(s) affected)

Figure 7: Screen of fCQL query execution using interpreter as the stored procedure.

REFERENCES

Abdennadher, S., Schuetz, H., 1998. Flexible Query Language. In Proc. of *Flexible Query Answering System Conference*, Roskilde, Denmark. Springer, pp. 1-14.

Bellma, M., Vojdani, N., 2000. Fuzzy Prototypes for Fuzzy Data Mining. *Studies in fuzziness and soft computing*. Vol. 39, pp. 175 – 286.

Blanco, I., Cubero, J., Pons, O., Vila, A., 2000. An Implementation for Fuzzy Deductive Relational Databases. *Studies in fuzziness and soft computing*. Vol. 53, pp. 183 – 208.

Bosc, P., 1998. On Diverse Answers Issued from Flexible Queries. In Proc. of *Flexible Query Answering System Conference*, Roskilde. Denmark, Springer, pp. 55 – 67.

Bosc, P., Pivert, O., 2000. SQLf Query Functionality on Top of a Regular Relational Database Management System. *Studies in fuzziness and soft computing*. Vol. 39, pp. 171 – 191.

Carrasco, R. A., Galindo, J., Vila, M. A., and J. M. Medina, 1999. Clustering and Fuzzy Classification in a Financial Data Mining Environment. In Proc. of *3d International ICSC Symposium on Soft Computing SOCO'99*. pp. 713-720.

Chen, G., 1998. *Fuzzy Logic in Data Modeling - Semantics, Constraints and Database Design*, Kluwer. London.

Dubois, D., Nakata, M., Prade, H., 2000. Extended Divisions for Flexible Queries in Relational Databases. *Studies in fuzziness and soft computing*. Vol. 39, pp. 105 – 121.

Han, J., Kamber, M., 2001. *Data Mining: Concepts and Techniques*, Morgan Kaufmann Publishers. New-York.

Han, J., Larshmanan, L., Ng, R., 1999. Constrained – Based, Multidimensional Data Mining. *Studies in fuzziness and soft computing*. Vol. 39, pp. 46 – 50.

Kacprzyk, J., Zadrozny, S., 2000. On Combining Intelligent Querying and Data Mining Using Fuzzy Logic Concepts. *Studies in fuzziness and soft computing*. Vol. 53, pp. 67 – 84.

Schindler, G., 1998. *Fuzzy Datenanalyse durch kontextbasierte Datenbankanfragen*, DUV/Gabler. Wiesbaden, Germany.

Zadrozny, S., Kacprzyk, J., 1998. Implementing Fuzzy Querying via the Internet/WWW: Java Applets, Actve X Controls and Cookies. In Proc. of *Flexible Query Answering System Conference*, Roskilde, Denmark. Springer, pp. 382 – 392.

Zimmermann, H.-J., 1992. *Fuzzy Set Theory - and Its Applications*, Kluwer. London, 2nd edition.

Zimmermann, H.-J., Zysno, P., 1980. Latent Connectives in Human Decision Making. *Fuzzy Sets and Systems*. Vol. 4, No. 1, pp. 37 – 51.

PART 2

Artificial Intelligence and Decision Support Systems

STORAGE OF FUZZY INFORMATION IN CONTINUOUS CLASSIFYING ASSOCIATIVE MEMORIES

Antonio B. Bailón
Dpto. Lenguajes y Computación, Universidad de Almería
La Cañada de San Urbano 04120 Almería (Spain)
Email: bailon@ual.es

Miguel Delgado   Waldo Fajardo
Dpto. Ciencias de la Computación e Inteligencia Artificial, Universidad de Granada
C/Daniel Saucedo Aranda s/n 18071 Granada (Spain)
Email: {mdelgado,aragorn}@decsai.ugr.es

Abstract: In this paper, we analyze the use of the Continuous Classifying Associative Memory (CCLAM) to store imprecise information expressed with linguistic terms. Freedom in the choice of the functions which control the operation of the CCLAM equip this memory with the capacity to adapt to different information storage and recovery needs. We begin with the problem of storing linguistic terms by memorizing the patterns formed by the degrees of compatibility with these terms. This will allow the use of CCLAM to compute the firing strength of rules whose antecedent is expressed in linguistic terms. After that, the problem of storing Mamdani and TSK rules is discussed.

1 INTRODUCTION

There is one serious problem in associative memories: their low storage capacity caused by the appearance of spurious patterns, that is to say patterns which do not correspond to any of the ones stored.

The CLAM [(Bailón et al., 2000)] solves the problem of capacity by avoiding the factors which limit it: spurious states and data dependency. It does so by not limiting the type of data which can be stored and preventing interference between any of the stored patterns which would produce spurious patterns.

If we reflect on the type of information that human beings normally memorize or use in their reasoning, we find that they manage a large quantity of imprecise concepts. Although this might seem like a limitation, it enables them to successfully face up to extremely complicated tasks in which computers, although a lot more precise than humans, fail. This inverse relationship between precision and complexity is expressed in Zadeh's incompatibility principle(Zadeh, 1984).

If we wish to model complex systems, we need to reduce the precision with which they must be dealt. Consequently, memories capable of storing imprecisely expressed information are necessary. The CCLAM [(Bailón et al., 2002)] is an associative memory that stores arbitrary spatial patterns. Its flexible configuration allows its use to store and recover imprecise information in different situations.

Some fuzzy information systems can be modeled as systems based on fuzzy rules. There are two main kinds of fuzzy rules: Mamdani rules and TSK rules.

Mamdani rules [(Mamdani and Assilian, 1975)] are those whose antecedent and consequent are imprecise, normally expressed with linguistic terms. An example of Mamdani rule is "If speed is low positive and position is zero then force is low negative". In this rule "low positive", "zero" and "low positive" are linguistic terms whose meaning is represented with fuzzy sets. For that reason it is necessary to fuzzyfy the actual speed and position to compute the satisfying degree of the rule and afterwards we need to defuzzyfy the imprecise information generated by the rule to get the final result.

TSK rules [(Sugeno and Takagi, 1985)] are those with imprecise antecedent and precise consequent where the antedecent is expressed with linguistic terms and the consequent is a function of the input values. An example of TSK rule is "If weigth is heavy and height is tall then force=100+height+2ůweight". In this rule "heavy" and "tall" are linguistic terms giving an imprecise antecedent but it has a precise consequent expressed as a first order polinomial (then the rule is said to be a first order TSK rule).

Whatever the kind of rule is, the fuzzy antecedent and consequent can be described using labels on which the respective linguistic variables can take a value. The rule is then coded in a vector whose components represent the compatibilities of the antecedent and the consequent with the linguistic labels on which they are evaluated.

This representation of the rules allows them to

be stored and recovered using associative memories. However, we expect the memory to behave in a special way because when a pattern is provided as an antecedent, we hope to obtain a consequent which does not necessarily need to be one of the patterns stored but rather the application of all the rules which are fired.

The use of the CCLAM enables fuzzy rules to be stored and recovered efficiently. It also allows the use of any t-norm and t-conorm to obtain the consequent from the application of the rules which are fired.

First we will introduce the CCLAM, an associative memory model which stores arbitrary spatial patterns. After describing its capabilities we will use it to store labels of linguistic variables. This will allow the storage of imprecise information expressed in linguistic terms and will help to compute the firing strength of the antecedents of imprecise rules. Finally we will use CCLAM's to store Mamdani rules and TSK rules. This work ends with a selected bibliography.

2 CONTINUOUS CLAM

The Continuous Classifying Associative Memory (CCLAM) [(Bailón et al., 2002)], based on the CLAM [(Bailón et al., 2000)], is an associative memory model which stores arbitrary spatial patterns. The topology of the CCLAM (fig. 1) is different from the CLAM in that all the PE are continuous instead of bipolar and binary. The activation signal received by the PE does not need to exceed the threshold for the element to be activated, and its activation function is:

$$f(x) = \begin{cases} 0 & \text{if } x < 0 \\ x & \text{if } 0 \leq x \leq 1 \\ 1 & \text{if } x > 1 \end{cases} \tag{1}$$

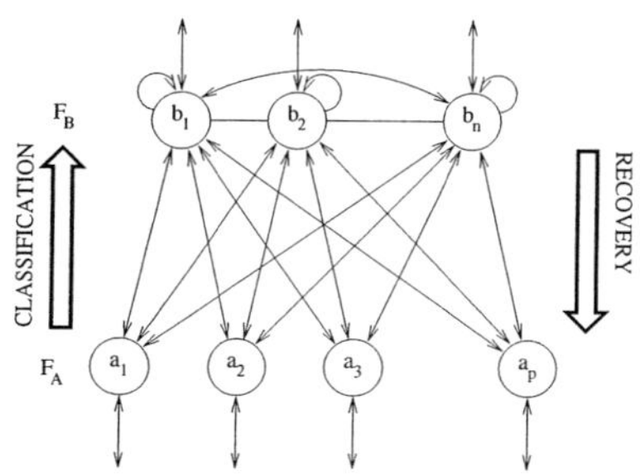

Figure 1: Continuous Classifying Associative Memory (CCLAM)

There are as many PE in the F_A layer as components of the patterns to store. The input patterns will be presented and the stored patterns will be recovered in this layer.

The PE of the F_B layer represent the stored patterns. The number of these is variable and it changes dynamically with the learning, in such a way that, as in the discrete CLAM, there will always be as many PE in the F_B layer as stored patterns. The activation state of these indicates the degree to which the pattern associated to each of them is recognized.

When the CCLAM operates, we can distinguish two processes: classification and recovery. The classification process receives an input pattern in the F_A layer and in each element of F_B it obtains a value which indicates the degree to which the input pattern resembles the stored pattern presented in F_B. The recovery process receives the degrees to which we refer to each of the stored patterns in F_B, and it recovers a combination of these paterns in F_A.

The F_B layer is competitive. The weights of the competition signals between the PE of the F_B layer are represented in a β_{nn} matrix, with n being the number of patterns stored and β_{ij} being the weight of the connection which exists between b_i and b_j. The connection weight indicates the degree of competition so that a connection from the element i to j with zero weight indicates that the element i does not compete with the j; if the weight is one, the element i competes with the j with a maximum degree indicated by its activation state. If all the competition connections have a unitary weight, we obtain a competition in which the same importance is given to all the patterns; if all the weights are zero, we cancel the competition.

For the competition, we must establish whether the winning PE will retain its activation state or take the value 1 as its new state. Let Y_i be the activation state of the elements of B_i. If after competition, the winning element retains its state, the activation value of B_i will be:

$$\begin{cases} Y_i & \text{if } Y_i \geq Y_j \beta_{ji} \quad \forall j \\ 0 & \text{otherwise .} \end{cases} \tag{2}$$

If the winner has the value 1, the new value of B_i will be:

$$\begin{cases} 1 & \text{if } Y_i \geq Y_j \beta_{ji} \quad \forall j \\ 0 & \text{otherwise .} \end{cases} \tag{3}$$

If there is more than one winning element, one of them will be selected following some pre-established selection criterion.

As the competition established in F_B may be different in the classification and recovery phases, we can really consider two weight matrixes where β_{ij}^C is the competition weight of i towards j in the classification process and β_{ij}^R is the competition weight of i towards j in the recovery process.

During the classification process, we present an input pattern in F_A and in the F_B layer we either obtain the degree of compatibility which exists between each of the stored patterns and the input pattern or we find that the only active element is the one representing the pattern which is most compatible with the input pattern. This will depend on the type of competition which is established.

In the recovery process, we present the degrees to which we refer to each of the stored patterns in F_B and we recover a combination of these patterns in F_A.

2.1 Learning

During the learning process, memorization of the pattern involves creating a new PE in F_B and the appropriate adjustment of the weights of the new connections which are made between the elements in F_A and the new PE.

The learning process consists of the following steps:

1. Arrival at F_A of a pattern to be memorized.
2. Verification that the pattern has not been previously memorized.
3. Creation of a new PE in F_B associated to the pattern.
4. Adjustment of the competition weights of the F_B layer.
5. Adjustment of the weights of F_A towards the new PE.

2.1.1 Verification that the pattern has not been previously memorized

In order to check that the pattern has not yet been stored in the memory, the classification process is carried out with this pattern as the input of the memory and the result obtained is checked.

The classification process enables us to specify two functions, Υ^C and Ψ^C, so that the memory behavior can be adapted to our needs. In a further section we will discuss that choice. Here to check prior pattern memorization, the following functions will be used:

$$\begin{array}{l}\Upsilon^C(x,y) = 1 - |x-y| \\ \Psi^C = \text{arithmetic mean.}\end{array} \tag{4}$$

With this configuration, the input pattern is compared with each of those stored, component by component. The signal received by the PE of the F_B layer can only have a value of one if the input pattern and the stored pattern coincide.

In the F_B layer, we ensure that all the weights are equal to one and that the winning element retains its activation state during the competition phase. In this way, if any element with value equal to one remains after the classification process, this implies that the input pattern coincides with one of those stored and the learning of this should not therefore be repeated.

2.1.2 Adjustment of the competition weights of the F_B layer

In the F_B layer, the weight of the (i,j) connection indicates the degree to which the activation signal of the PE associated to the i-th pattern is compared with that of the j-th. If the weight of the connection is one, the two activation states of the connected PE are compared; if the weight is zero, this means that there is no competition between the connected PE; other intermediate values indicate different degrees of influence.

As the F_B layer is dynamic, for each stored pattern, it is necessary to assign the weights of the connections which go to the new PE which represents the pattern.

The weight of the competition connection between two PE can be seen as the relative importance which is given to the two patterns represented by the connected PE. We will generally find that all the competition connections have the weight $\beta_{ij} = 1$ to reflect that the same importance is given to all the patterns.

The weights established for the competition in the classification process can be different from those of the recovery process. β^C_{ij} will be the weight of the competition which exists between the PE i and j during the classification and β^R_{ij} the weight during the recovery.

2.1.3 Adjustment of the weights of F_A towards the new PE

The number of PE in the F_B layer is dynamic, so that when a new pattern is stored, a new PE is created in the F_B layer associated to this pattern.

When the pattern $X = (x_1, \ldots, x_p)$ is stored, the value $m_{pi} = x_i$ is assigned to the weights of the connections of the PE in the F_A layer towards the new b_p PE in the F_B layer.

A CCLAM which has stored p patterns of n components will have an associated weights matrix which represents the weights of the connections between the PE in the F_A and F_B layers.

$$M_{np} = \begin{pmatrix} m_{11} & \cdots & m_{1p} \\ \vdots & \ddots & \vdots \\ m_{n1} & \cdots & m_{np} \end{pmatrix}. \tag{5}$$

Therefore, the storage of the set of patterns $X_1, \ldots, X_n$, with $X_i = (x_{i1}, \ldots, x_{ip})$ will result in the weights matrix:

$$M = \begin{pmatrix} x_{11} & \cdots & x_{1p} \\ \vdots & \ddots & \vdots \\ x_{n1} & \cdots & x_{np} \end{pmatrix}. \tag{6}$$

For each new stored pattern, a row is added to the weights matrix with the weights of the connections of the PE in the F_A layer towards the new PE in F_B which represents the new pattern.

The weights of the connections between the two layers in the classification process may be different to those of the recovery process. In order to differentiate between them, we will call the weights matrix in the classification process M^C, and the weights matrix in the recovery process M^R.

2.2 Classification

In the classification process, the PE send activation signals from the F_A layer towards the F_B layer. When an input pattern is presented in the F_A layer, activation states are obtained in the F_B layer which represent the similarity which exists between the pattern and each of the stored patterns.

The classification process has the following steps:

1. A pattern $X = (x_1, \ldots, x_p)$ arrives at the F_A layer.
2. The signal propagates towards the F_B layer so that the b_i PE receives the activation signal:

$$\begin{aligned} y_i &= \Psi^C \left\{ \Upsilon^C \left(x_i, m_{ij}^C \right) \right\}_{j=1\ldots p} = \\ &= \Psi^C \left(\Upsilon^C \left(x_1, m_{i1}^C \right), \ldots, \Upsilon^C \left(x_p, m_{ip}^C \right) \right). \end{aligned} \tag{7}$$

   where Υ^C and Ψ^C are functions bounded to the interval $[0, 1]$. The choice of these functions depends on the behavior which we would like the memory to present according to our needs.

3. The PE in the F_B layer compete with the intensity reflected in the weights matrix β^C.
4. We obtain the result of the classification process in the F_B layer. The activation state obtained in the PE in the F_B layer indicates the degree to which the input pattern is classified as belonging to each of the classes represented by the stored patterns.

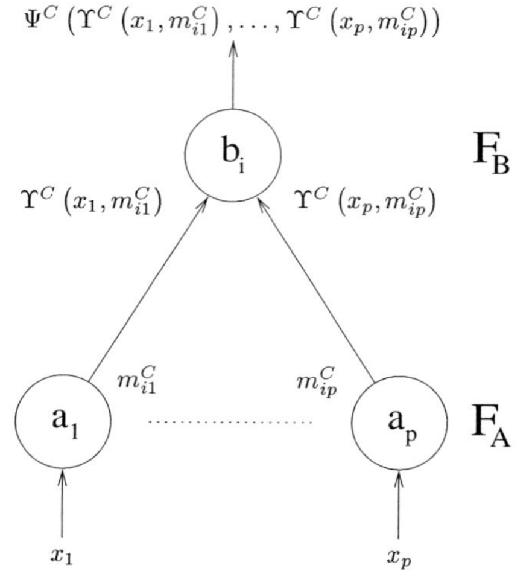

Figure 2: Flow of information in the classification process.

2.3 Recovery

In the recovery process, the information flows in the opposite direction to the classification process. In the F_B layer is presented an input pattern which represents the degree of recovery of each stored pattern. Recovery has the following steps:

1. A pattern $Y = (y_1, \ldots, y_n)$ arrives at the F_B layer.
2. The PE in the F_B layer compete with each other with the β^R weights matrix. The new activation states form the pattern $Y' = (y'_1, \ldots, y'_n)$.
3. The signal propagates from the F_B layer towards the F_A layer so that the a_i PE receives the activation signal:

$$\begin{aligned} x_i &= \Psi^R \left\{ \Upsilon^R \left(y'_j, m_{ji}^R \right) \right\}_{j=1\ldots n} = \\ &= \Psi^R \left(\Upsilon^R \left(y'_1, m_{1i}^R \right), \ldots, \Upsilon^R \left(y'_n, m_{ni}^R \right) \right). \end{aligned} \tag{8}$$

   where Υ^R and Ψ^R are functions bounded to the interval $[0, 1]$. The choice of these functions depends on the behavior which we would like the memory to present.

4. In the F_A layer, we obtain the pattern resulting from the recovery process. This may be one of the stored patterns or a combination of them.

3 STORAGE OF LABELS OF LINGUISTIC VARIABLES

If we want to store patterns which code different characteristics of a set of objects, we need to use several linguistic variables to describe them. In order to store information about several linguistic variables, the continuous classifying associative memory will be used as a structural element so that we will have a CCLAM for each linguistic variable as well as another CCLAM which will unify all the information and will receive (in the layer F_A) the signals obtained in the layers F_B of the CCLAMs associated to the linguistic variables.

Each CCLAM associated to a linguistic variable will have as many PEs in F_A as linguistic variables defined on the variable and as many PEs in F_B as memorized patterns. The unifying CCLAM will have

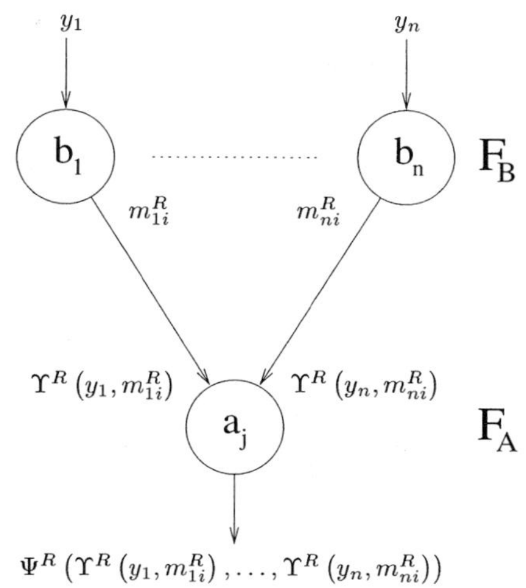

Figure 3: Flow of information in the recovery process.

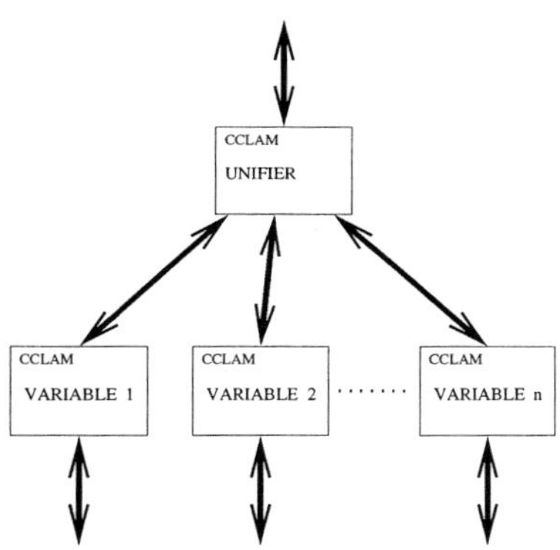

Figure 4: Use of CCLAM's to store linguistic values.

as many PEs in F_B as memorized patterns. For each linguistic variable in F_A, there will be as many PEs as stored patterns.

For each linguistic variable we will compute the similarity which exists between the input coded value and the stored value and the unifying CCLAM will combine all the information in order to determine what pattern will be recovered. The behavior of the system in the classification and recovery phases in the CCLAMs associated to linguistic variables and in the unifying CCLAM will be shown below.

3.1 Classification

In the classification process the pattern with the greatest similarity to the input pattern is determined and recovered. This entire process in divided into two phases.

The first phase occurs in the CCLAMs associated to the linguistic variables. In each, the similarity which exists between the input pattern and each of the stored patterns is determined.

In the second phase, developed in the unifier, from the individual similarities obtained in the first phase, we obtain the overall similarity which exists between the input pattern and the memorized patterns. The pattern with which it shares the greatest similarity will be the one selected.

3.1.1 CCLAM associated to linguistic variables.

The comparison made by using Υ^C and Ψ^C will show us the degree of similarity between the input pattern and the stored patterns.

The Υ^C function indicates the similarity which exists between the individual components. For that reason we propose to use $\Upsilon^C(x, y) = 1 - |x - y|$.

The function Ψ^C is responsible for combining the particular information obtained from the components and that's why we propose the arithmetic mean of their similarities.

The F_B layer receives the mean of the degrees of similarity which exist between the components of the input pattern and those of the stored patterns. The PE with the greatest activation state will be the one which represents the stored pattern closest to the input pattern.

There will be no competition in the layer F_B since the aim of the competition is to select the PE which represents the closest pattern and this task is carried out by the unifier after receiving the information from the rest of the CCLAM.

3.1.2 Unifier

The CCLAM that unifies the information receives in its F_A layer the state of the PEs of the layer F_B of the CCLAM associated to the linguistic variables.

Let X be the PE of the F_A layer which receives its activation state of the element representing the j-th pattern of the CCLAM associated to the i-th linguistic variable. Let Y be the PE of the F_B layer associated to the pattern k-th. The weight of the connection made between X and Y is:

$$w_{ijk} = \begin{cases} 1 & \text{if } j = k \\ 0 & \text{otherwise}. \end{cases} \tag{9}$$

That is to say, the PEs associated to the same pattern have a weight of one whereas the rest have a weight of zero. Consequently, each PE of F_B only receives information from the PEs of F_A associated to the same pattern.

For the propagation of the signals from the layer F_A to the layer F_B we will configure the CCLAM with:

- The function $\Upsilon^C(x, y) = xy$ that ensures that each PE of the F_B layer only receives signals from the elements associated with the same pattern.
- The arithmetic mean used as the Ψ^C function to compute the global similarity which exists between the input pattern and the corresponding stored pattern.
- A competition in which the winning element takes the value of one that ensures that the only active PE of F_B is the one which represents the stored pattern which is most similar to the input pattern. For this, the competition weights are asigned the value 1 so that the same importance is given to all the PE.

3.2 Recovery

The recovery process begins once the stored pattern to be recovered has been determined. The unifier will only transmit the selection to the CCLAMs associated to the variables so that these can recover the information of the pattern selected.

3.2.1 Unifier

During the recovery, the unifier transmits the selection made to the CCLAMs associated to the variables.

The weights of the connections between the layers F_A and F_B are the same as those established in the classification phase, that is to say the PEs associated to the same pattern are linked with a connection with a weight of 1 whereas the others are linked by connections with a weight of 0.

Competition is nullified since the elements have already competed at the end of the classification phase and only one of them is active. The competition weights are therefore set to zero $\beta_{ij}^R = 0 \quad \forall i, j$.

Using $\Upsilon^R(x, y) = xy$, each element of F_A will only receive information from the PEs associated to the same pattern. In this way, the elements of F_A associated to the selected pattern will receive an active signal from F_B. The elements associated to unselected patterns will receive all the signals at zero.

Using $\Psi^R(x_1, \ldots, x_n) = \max\{x_1, \ldots, x_n\}$, only the elements of F_A associated to the pattern to be recovered remain active.

3.2.2 CCLAM associated to linguistic variables.

Each CCLAM associated to a linguistic variable receives a signal from the unifier which leaves a single active PE in its layer F_B. This element, whose state is 1, is the one which represents the pattern to be recovered. It is not therefore necessary to establish a competition between the PEs of F_B so that all the weights will be set at zero $\beta_{ij}^R = 0 \quad \forall i, j$.

The function Υ^R y Ψ^R which will be used are the minimum and the maximum, respectively. This ensures that all the inactive PEs of F_B send zero activation signals and that the final activation state of the elements of F_A is the one received from the element which represents the pattern which will be recovered.

3.3 Example

We are going to store the height, weight and age of a set of individuals. These attributes will be expressed in linguistic terms.

Let us take the linguistic variable HEIGHT. In this linguistic variable we are going to use the linguistic labels VERY SMALL, SMALL NORMAL, TALL AND VERY TALL. The linguistic labels VERY LIGHT, LIGHT, NORMAL, HEAVY AND VERY HEAVY will be used with the linguistic variable WEIGHT. Finally, we will take the linguistic variable AGE with which the linguistic labels CHILDHOOD, PUBERTY, YOUTH, MIDDLE AGE, THIRD AGE AND OLD AGE will be used.

The patterns which we wish to store correspond to three people and are shown in tables 1, 2 and 3.

	HEIGHT				
	VS	S	N	T	VT
Toni	0	0	0	0.5	0.5
David	0	0	0.9	0.1	0
Ana	0	0	0.2	0.8	0

Table 1: Height of three people.

	WEIGHT				
	VL	L	N	H	VH
Toni	0	0	0	0.9	0.1
David	0	0.3	0.7	0	0
Ana	0	0	0.6	0.4	0

Table 2: Weight of three people.

	AGE					
	C	P	Y	MA	TA	OA
Toni	0	0	0.8	0.2	0	0
David	0	0	0	0.4	0.6	0
Ana	0	0.9	0.1	0	0	0

Table 3: Age of three people.

The learning process will produce the following weights matrixes :

$$M_{HEIGHT} = \begin{pmatrix} 0 & 0 & 0 & 0.5 & 0.5 \\ 0 & 0 & 0.9 & 0.1 & 0 \\ 0 & 0 & 0.2 & 0.8 & 0 \end{pmatrix} \quad (10)$$

$$M_{WEIGHT} = \begin{pmatrix} 0 & 0 & 0 & 0.9 & 0.1 \\ 0 & 0.3 & 0.7 & 0 & 0 \\ 0 & 0 & 0.6 & 0.4 & 0 \end{pmatrix} \quad (11)$$

$$M_{AGE} = \begin{pmatrix} 0 & 0 & 0.8 & 0.2 & 0 & 0 \\ 0 & 0 & 0 & 0.4 & 0.6 & 0 \\ 0 & 0.9 & 0.1 & 0 & 0 & 0 \end{pmatrix} \quad (12)$$

$$M_{UNIF.} = \begin{pmatrix} 1 & 0 & 0 & 1 & 0 & 0 & 1 & 0 & 0 \\ 0 & 1 & 0 & 0 & 1 & 0 & 0 & 1 & 0 \\ 0 & 0 & 1 & 0 & 0 & 1 & 0 & 0 & 1 \end{pmatrix} \quad (13)$$

Let us suppose that the pattern (H, W, A) is provided as input where H is the subpattern which expresses the height, W expresses the weight and A expresses the age. The height, weight and age indicated at the input are:

$$H = (h_{VS}, h_S, h_N, h_T, h_{VT}) = (0,0,1,0,0)$$
$$W = (p_{VL}, p_L, p_N, p_H, p_{VH}) = (0,0,0.5,0.5,0)$$
$$A = (e_C, e_P, e_Y, e_{MA}, e_{TA}, e_{OA}) = (0,1,0,0,0,0).$$

The pattern presented at the input is therefore:

$$(0,0,1,0,0,\ 0,0,0.5,0.5,0,\ 0,1,0,0,0,0).$$

The functions used to transmit the information from the layer F_A towards F_B in the CCLAMs associated to the linguistic variables are $\Upsilon^C(x,y) = 1 - |x-y|$ and Ψ^C arithmetic mean.

The classification process which is carried out in the CCLAM associated to the height produces the results shown in Table 4. In the cell corresponding to row S and column T the result of the function $\Upsilon^C(h_T, m^C_{T,S})$ appears. At the end of the row, the value returned by Ψ^S is shown when applied on all the values of this row.

The values received in the F_B layer are $Y_{Toni} = 0.6$, $Y_{David} = 0.96$ and $Y_{Ana} = 0.68$.

Υ^C	VS	S	N	T	VT	Ψ^C
Toni	1	1	0	0.5	0.5	0.6
David	1	1	0.9	0.9	1	0.96
Ana	1	1	0.2	0.2	1	0.68

Table 4: Classification results of the height CCLAM.

All the competition weights have a value of zero so that all the PEs of the F_B layer retain their state.

The classification process which is carried out in the CCLAM associated to the weight produces the results shown in Table 5. In the cell corresponding to row S and column T the result of the function $\Upsilon^C(p_T, m^C_{T,S})$ appears. At the end of the row, the value returned by Ψ^C is shown when applied on all the values of this row.

Υ^C	VL	L	N	H	VH	Ψ^C
Toni	1	1	0.5	0.6	0	0.62
David	1	0.7	0.8	0.5	1	0.8
Ana	1	1	0.9	0.9	1	0.96

Table 5: Classification results of the weigth CCLAM.

The values received in the F_B layer are $Y_{Toni} = 0.62$, $Y_{David} = 0.8$ and $Y_{Ana} = 0.96$.

All the competition weights have a value of zero so that all the PEs of the F_B layer retain their state.

The classification process which is carried out in the CCLAM associated to the age produces the results shown in Table 6. In the cell corresponding to row S and column T the result of the function $\Upsilon^C(e_T, m^C_{T,S})$ appears. At the end of the row, the value returned by Ψ^C is shown when applied on all the values of this row.

Υ^C	C	P	Y	MA	TA	OA	Ψ^C
Toni	1	0	0.2	0.8	1	1	0.67
David	1	0	1	0.6	0.4	1	0.67
Ana	1	0.9	0.9	1	1	1	0.97

Table 6: Classification results of the age CCLAM.

The values received in the F_B layer are $Y_{Toni} = 0.67$, $Y_{David} = 0.67$ and $Y_{Ana} = 0.97$.

All the competition weights have a value of zero so that all the PEs of the F_B layer retain their state.

At the input, the unifying CCLAM receives the signal from the layers F_B of the CCLAMs associated to the height, weight and age. When this signal is propagated towards F_B using the functions Υ^C and Ψ^C, the signals received are $Y_{Toni} = 0.21$, $Y_{David} = 0.27$ and $Y_{Ana} = 0.29$.

All the competition weights have a value of one. The element which wins the competition passes to state one while the others remain deactivated. The state of the elements of F_B after the competition will therefore be $Y_{Toni} = 0$, $Y_{David} = 0$ and $Y_{Ana} = 1$. This means that the stored pattern closest to the input pattern corresponds to Ana.

During the recovery, the unifier transmits the selection carried out to the CCLAMs associated to the variables.

The competition is nullified once $\beta_{ij}^R = 0 \quad \forall i, j$ has been established which is why the PEs of F_B retain their state.

As the weights of the connections which are established between the layers F_A and F_B are the same as those established in the classification phase and the product is used as the Υ^R function, the PEs associated to the same pattern are those which receive non-zero signals. In this way, the signal received in the layer F_B of the CCLAM associated to the height is $Y_{Toni} = 0$, $Y_{David} = 0$ and $Y_{Ana} = 1$, the signal received in the CCLAM associated to the weight is $Y_{Toni}0$, $Y_{David} = 0$ and $Y_{Ana} = 1$ and the signal received in the CCLAM associated to the age is $Y_{Toni} = 0$, $Y_{David} = 0$ and $Y_{Ana} = 1$.

In the recovery process there is no competition in the CCLAMs associated to linguistic variables, that is to say the weights have been adjusted so that the competition does not modify any activation state. Since the weights are $\beta_{ij}^R = 0 \quad \forall i, j$, no element changes state.

The signals propagated from F_B towards F_A in the CCLAMs of the height, weight and age are shown in Table 7

HEIGHT				
VS	S	N	T	VT
0	0	0.2	0.8	0

WEIGHT				
VL	L	N	H	VH
0	0	0.6	0.4	0

AGE					
C	P	Y	MA	TA	OA
0	0.9	0.1	0	0	0

Table 7: Patterns recovered in the F_A layers.

Therefore, the pattern which is most similar to the input pattern which is recovered $(0, 0, 0.2, 0.8, 0,\ 0, 0, 0.6, 0.4, 0,\ 0, 0.9, 0.1, 0, 0, 0)$ is the one corresponding to Ana's stored information.

4 STORAGE OF MAMDANI FUZZY RULES

When the type of information that we need to store is made up of Mamdani fuzzy rules, we can expect a different behavior than that obtained when only object attributes are stored.

The storage of rules entails memorizing the pairs of patterns (antecedent, consequent) whereas the storage of object information entails memorizing individual patterns.

When we store object attributes, we want the system to recover the stored pattern which is closest to the input pattern. When we store rules of the form (antededent, consequent), when a pattern is provided as the antecedent we can expect to obtain a consequent pattern which need not necessarily be one of the stored patterns but rather the result of the application of all the rules which are fired.

In order to store rules for inference purposes, we have a CCLAM for each of the linguistic variables of the antecedent and another CCLAM for the consequent. The memories associated to the antecedent will receive a pattern as the input which will determine the state of the system on which the rules will be applied. Each of these memories will calculate the degree to which the value of the linguistic variable which it represents causes the firing of each of the rules. An additional CCLAM will unify all the information finding the total degree to which each rule is fired. This information is then sent to the memory which stores the consequents so that the appropriate combination of these may be recovered.

We can look at this outline in more detail. Let us suppose the linguistic variables $A_1, A_2, \ldots, A_n$ form the antecedent and the linguistic variable C forms the consequent.

Let assume that the terms sets are $\{t_{i1}, t_{i2}, \ldots, t_{iq_i}\}$ for A_i, $i = 1, \ldots, n$ and $\{c_1, \ldots, c_m\}$ for C.

Then the set of rules to be stored is $\{R_1, R_2, \ldots, R_p\}$, where each rule is of the form *IF* a_1 *AND* a_2 *AND* ... *AND* a_n *THEN* b with:

$$\begin{aligned} a_j &\in \{t_{j1}, \ldots, t_{jq_j}\} \\ b &\in \{c_1, \ldots, c_m\}. \end{aligned} \tag{14}$$

Below we will specify the behavior of the CCLAM associated both to the antecedent as well as to the consequent.

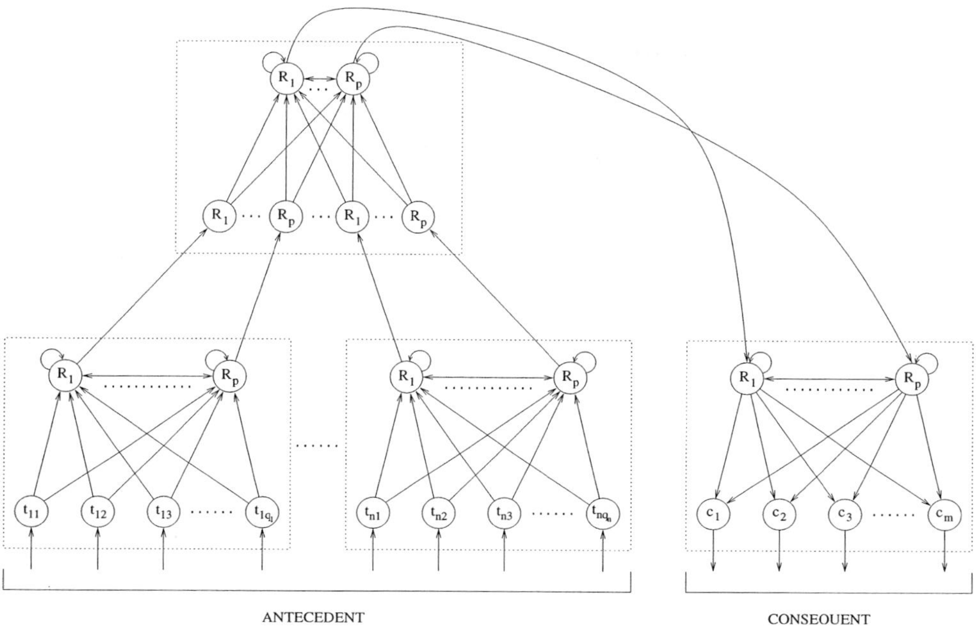

Figure 5: Storage of rules using CCLAM

4.1 Antecedent

The CCLAMs associated to the linguistic variables of the antecedent and of the unifying CCLAM make up the antecedent. In these memories, only the classification process will be used, that is, the information will only flow from the layer F_A towards the layer F_B.

4.1.1 CCLAM associated to a linguistic variable of the antecedent.

In the memories associated to the linguistic variables of the antecedent the degree to which each of the stored rules is applicable will be determined.

Since the rules are encoded in the weights of the connections between the layers F_A y F_B, a t-norm will be used as the Υ^C function. In this way, so that an PE of F_B receives a non-zero signal it is necessary for the input pattern to activate an PE of F_A which is part of the rule represented by the element of F_B.

The function Ψ^C which is used is a t-conorm so that only the elements which received a non-zero signal from F_A remain active in F_B. The activation state which results in the PE of F_B reflects the degree of fulfillment of each of the stored rules.

The competition of F_B will be nullified because we want to know all the rules which will be fired and not only the one which will to the greatest extent. Therefore, the weights of the competition connections will be $\beta_{ij}^C = 0 \quad \forall i, j$.

4.1.2 Unifier

The unifying CCLAM will have as many PEs as memorized rules in F_B and there will be as many PEs as rules for each linguistic variable of the antecedent in F_A. The weights of the connections which are established between the layers F_A and F_B are such that the PEs associated to the same rule are united by connections with a weight of zero whereas the remainder are united by connections with a weight of one. This allocation of weights is due to the fact that the value of one is the neutral element of the t-norms, which will be useful in the spreading of information from F_A to F_B.

The degree with which a rule is fired is calculated by applying a t-norm to the extent to which the antecedent variables are fulfilled. For this, a t-norm will be used, normally the minimum, as the function Ψ^C. This t-norm will be applied to information from the PEs of F_A.

We want that only the activation states of the PEs associated to the same rule are considered. To achieve this, it is necessary to receive the neutral element of the t-norm from the PEs associated to different rules. Given the weights of the connections between the layers F_A and F_B, the selected Υ^C function ought to be a t-conorm, for example the maximum. The PEs associated to the different rules, since they are connected with unitary weights, send the neutral element of the t-norm towards F_B; since the elements associated to the same rules are connected with zero weights and these are the neutral elements of the t-norm, they send their own activation state towards F_B.

We eliminate the competition from F_B since we are not searching for a winning rule but rather the degree to which each of them is fired. The competition weights will therefore be $\beta_{ij}^C = 0 \quad \forall i, j$.

For their activation state, the PEs of F_B finally have the degree to which the rule which represents each of them must be fired.

4.2 Consequent

The CCLAM associated to the consequent receives the activation state of the PEs of the layer F_B from the unifier as the input. That is to say, each PE takes the degree to which the rule to which it is associated as the activation state. The result which we expect to obtain is that obtained from the application of all the rules which must be fired.

We do not want there to be competition between the PEs of F_B because we are not searching for a winning element. All the competition weights are therefore nullified $\beta_{ij}^R = 0 \quad \forall i, j$.

As the Υ^R function, a t-norm will be selected. In this way, the rules which are not fired, that is to say those whose representing elements have a zero activation state, will send the value zero (which is the neutral value of the t-conorms) towards the layer F_A. Selecting one t-conorm as the function Ψ^R, we obtain the result of the application of all the rules which are fired in F_A.

4.3 Example

Let us suppose that using CCLAM we want to store the set of rules of a braking system. The aim of the system is the braking of a moving object by applying a force that depends on the position and speed of it.

Let us suppose that we express the position by means of the linguistic variable POSITION using the linguistic labels HIGH NEGATIVE, LOW NEGATIVE, ZERO, LOW POSITIVE and HIGH POSITIVE for this.

The speed will be expressed by means of the linguistic variable SPEED using the linguistic labels NEGATIVE, ZERO and POSITIVE.

The response offered by the system for the braking of the moving object will correspond to the force which it is necessary to apply to it. This will be represented by the variable FORCE using the linguistic labels HIGH NEGATIVE, LOW NEGATIVE, ZERO, LOW POSITIVE and HIGH POSITIVE.

The set of rules which characterize the system is:

1. If high positive position and zero speed then high negative force.
2. If low positive position and positive speed then low negative force.
3. If low positive position and negative speed then zero force.
4. If high negative position and zero speed then high positive force.
5. If low negative position and negative speed then low positive force.
6. If low negative position and positive speed then zero force.
7. If zero position and zero speed then zero force.

The set of CCLAM which will store the rules will memorize trios of patterns (P, S, F) where P and S are the patterns which represent the position and speed of the moving object respectively and F is the pattern which represents the force which it is necessary to apply to stop it. The coding of the rules will produce the set of patterns shown in Table 8.

	Position					Speed			Force				
Rule	HN	LN	ZE	LP	HP	NE	CE	PO	HN	LN	ZE	LP	HP
1	0	0	0	0	1	0	1	0	1	0	0	0	0
2	0	0	0	1	0	0	0	1	0	1	0	0	0
3	0	0	0	1	0	1	0	0	0	0	1	0	0
4	1	0	0	0	0	0	1	0	0	0	0	0	1
5	0	1	0	0	0	1	0	0	0	0	0	1	0
6	0	1	0	0	0	0	0	1	0	0	1	0	0
7	0	0	1	0	0	0	1	0	0	0	1	0	0

Table 8: Set of encoded rules.

In order to memorize the rules, we will use four CCLAMs. Two of them will be used to store the antecedents of the rules, that is to say the values of position and speed. Another CCLAM will unify the result of these two memories and the information obtained will be sent to a fourth and last CCLAM responsible for recovering the information relating to the force which must be applied.

After the learning process, the CCLAM associated to the position will have the following weights matrix:

$$M = \begin{pmatrix} 0 & 0 & 0 & 0 & 1 \\ 0 & 0 & 0 & 1 & 0 \\ 0 & 0 & 0 & 1 & 0 \\ 1 & 0 & 0 & 0 & 0 \\ 0 & 1 & 0 & 0 & 0 \\ 0 & 1 & 0 & 0 & 0 \\ 0 & 0 & 1 & 0 & 0 \end{pmatrix}. \quad (15)$$

The weights matrix of the CCLAM associated to the speed is:

$$M = \begin{pmatrix} 0 & 1 & 0 \\ 0 & 0 & 1 \\ 1 & 0 & 0 \\ 0 & 1 & 0 \\ 1 & 0 & 0 \\ 0 & 0 & 1 \\ 0 & 1 & 0 \end{pmatrix}. \quad (16)$$

The information from the memories associated to position and speed is propagated towards the unifying CCLAM. This has fourteen PEs in F_A (seen for each of the two linguistic variables of the antecedent) and seven elements in F_B. The weights matrix is:

$$M = \begin{pmatrix} 0\,1\,1\,1\,1\,1\,1\,0\,1\,1\,1\,1\,1\,1 \\ 1\,0\,1\,1\,1\,1\,1\,1\,0\,1\,1\,1\,1\,1 \\ 1\,1\,0\,1\,1\,1\,1\,1\,1\,0\,1\,1\,1\,1 \\ 1\,1\,1\,0\,1\,1\,1\,1\,1\,1\,0\,1\,1\,1 \\ 1\,1\,1\,1\,0\,1\,1\,1\,1\,1\,1\,0\,1\,1 \\ 1\,1\,1\,1\,1\,0\,1\,1\,1\,1\,1\,1\,0\,1 \\ 1\,1\,1\,1\,1\,1\,0\,1\,1\,1\,1\,1\,1\,0 \end{pmatrix}. \quad (17)$$

The CCLAMs associated to position and speed and the unifying CCLAM are those involved in the classification process. From an input pattern specifying the position and speed of the moving object, we obtain the degree to which each of the system rules is fired. This information is sent to a CCLAM which recovers a pattern which represents the force that the system of rules has determined must be applied. The weights matrix of this CCLAM associated to the force is:

$$M = \begin{pmatrix} 1 & 0 & 0 & 0 & 0 \\ 0 & 1 & 0 & 0 & 0 \\ 0 & 0 & 1 & 0 & 0 \\ 0 & 0 & 0 & 0 & 1 \\ 0 & 0 & 0 & 1 & 0 \\ 0 & 0 & 1 & 0 & 0 \\ 0 & 0 & 1 & 0 & 0 \end{pmatrix}. \quad (18)$$

Bearing in mind the above, the set of CCLAMs used to memorize the rules is shown in figure 6 (in order to make the representation easier the CCLAM associated to the force has been rotated so that its F_A layer is above and F_B is below). In the CCLAMs associated to the position, speed and force, the connections with a weight of 0 are represented using broken lines and the connections with a weight of 1 with solid lines. In the case of the unifier, the connections with a weight of 1 are represented using broken lines whereas those with a weight of 0 are shown with solid lines.

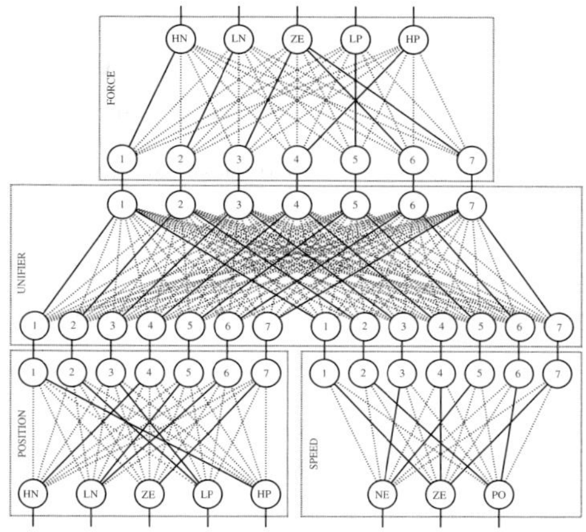

Figure 6: Set of CCLAMs which store the rules of the braking system.

In order to determine the value of the force necessary to stop the moving object we will use the t-norm of the minimum and the t-conorm of the maximum. Therefore, the function Υ of the CCLAMs associated to linguistic variables will be the minimum and the function Ψ will be the maximum.

Let us suppose that we want to stop a moving object which is at a position $\frac{1}{4}$ high negative, $\frac{3}{4}$ low negative and that it moves at a speed $\frac{1}{2}$ negative, $\frac{1}{2}$ zero. The patterns which code the situation are:

$$\begin{aligned} P &= \left(\tfrac{1}{4}, \tfrac{3}{4}, 0, 0, 0\right) \\ S &= \left(\tfrac{1}{2}, \tfrac{1}{2}, 0\right) \end{aligned} \quad (19)$$

As the pattern P is supplied to the input of the CCLAM associated to the position, the signal propagated from F_A to F_B is shown in the Table 9. In the cell corresponding to row S column T the returned result by $\Upsilon^C\left(P_T, m^C_{T,S}\right) = \min\left(P_T, m^C_{T,S}\right)$ appears. At the end of the row is the value provided by Ψ^C since this is applied on the values of this row.

In the same way, since the pattern S is provided to the input of the CCLAM associated to the speed, the signal propagated from F_A towards F_B is shown in the Table 10. In the cell corresponding to row S and column T the result of the function $\Upsilon^C\left(P_T, m^C_{T,S}\right) = \min\left(P_T, m^C_{T,S}\right)$ appears. At the end of the row is the value returned by Ψ^C since this is applied on the values of this row.

Υ^C	HN	LN	ZE	LP	HP	Ψ^C
1	0	0	0	0	0	0
2	0	0	0	0	0	0
3	0	0	0	0	0	0
4	$\frac{1}{4}$	0	0	0	0	$\frac{1}{4}$
5	0	$\frac{3}{4}$	0	0	0	$\frac{3}{4}$
6	0	$\frac{3}{4}$	0	0	0	$\frac{3}{4}$
7	0	0	0	0	0	0

Table 9: Application of Υ^C and Ψ^C in the CCLAM associated to position.

Υ^C	NE	ZE	PO	Ψ^C
1	0	$\frac{1}{2}$	0	$\frac{1}{2}$
2	0	0	0	0
3	$\frac{1}{2}$	0	0	$\frac{1}{2}$
4	0	$\frac{1}{2}$	0	$\frac{1}{2}$
5	$\frac{1}{2}$	0	0	$\frac{1}{2}$
6	0	0	0	0
7	0	$\frac{1}{2}$	0	$\frac{1}{2}$

Table 10: Application of Υ^C and Ψ^C in the CCLAM associated to speed.

The result obtained in the two previous CCLAMs is sent to the unifier. The pattern $\left(0,0,0,\frac{1}{4},\frac{3}{4},\frac{3}{4},0\right)$ is received from the memory associated to position, and the pattern $\left(\frac{1}{2},0,\frac{1}{2},\frac{1}{2},\frac{1}{2},0,\frac{1}{2}\right)$ is received from the memory associated to speed.

The signal propagated from F_A towards F_B is shown in the Table 11. In the cell corresponding to row S and column T appears the result which $\Upsilon^C\left(P_T, m^C_{T,S}\right) = \max\left(P_T, m^C_{T,S}\right)$ provides. At the end of the row is the value returned by $\Psi^C = \min$ since this is applied on the values of this row.

	POSITION							SPEED							
Υ^C	1	2	3	4	5	6	7	1	2	3	4	5	6	7	Ψ^C
1	0	1	1	1	1	1	1	$\frac{1}{2}$	1	1	1	1	1	1	0
2	1	0	1	1	1	1	1	1	0	1	1	1	1	1	0
3	1	1	0	1	1	1	1	1	1	$\frac{1}{2}$	1	1	1	1	0
4	1	1	1	$\frac{1}{4}$	1	1	1	1	1	1	$\frac{1}{2}$	1	1	1	$\frac{1}{4}$
5	1	1	1	1	$\frac{3}{4}$	1	1	1	1	1	1	$\frac{1}{2}$	1	1	$\frac{1}{2}$
6	1	1	1	1	1	$\frac{3}{4}$	1	1	1	1	1	1	0	1	0
7	1	1	1	1	1	1	0	1	1	1	1	1	1	$\frac{1}{2}$	0

Table 11: Application of Υ^C and Ψ^C in the unifier CCLAM.

The result obtained by the unifier indicates that the applicable rules are the fourth and the fifth with degrees $\frac{1}{4}$ and $\frac{1}{2}$, respectively. The pattern obtained $\left(0,0,0,\frac{1}{4},\frac{1}{2},0,0\right)$ is sent to the CCLAM associated to force so as to proceed with the recovery of the information being searched for.

The signal propagated from F_B towards F_A is shown in the Table 12. In the cell correpsonding to row S and column T the result given by the function $\Upsilon^R\left(P_T, m^R_{T,S}\right) = \min\left(P_T, m^R_{T,S}\right)$ appears. At the end of the row is the value returned by $\Psi^R = \max$ since this is applied on the values of this row.

Υ^R	1	2	3	4	5	6	7	Ψ^R
HN	0	0	0	0	0	0	0	0
LN	0	0	0	0	0	0	0	0
ZE	0	0	0	0	0	0	0	0
LP	0	0	0	0	$\frac{1}{2}$	0	0	$\frac{1}{2}$
HP	0	0	0	$\frac{1}{4}$	0	0	0	$\frac{1}{4}$

Table 12: Application of Υ^R and Ψ^R in the CCLAM associated to force.

Therefore, in order to stop a moving object which is at a position $\frac{1}{4}$ high negative, $\frac{3}{4}$ low negative and which moves with a speed $\frac{1}{2}$ negative, $\frac{1}{2}$ zero, it is necessary to apply a force $\frac{1}{2}$ low positive, $\frac{1}{4}$ high positive to it.

5 STORAGE OF TSK RULES

Takagi-Sugeno-Kang rules [(Sugeno and Takagi, 1985)] are those with imprecise antecedent expressed in linguistic terms and precise consequent expressed as a function of the input values. TSK rules are less human readable than Mamdani rules but provide more precise results. Let $R_1, \ldots, R_p$ be the rules of the system and $x_1, \ldots, l_q$ be the input values:

$$
\begin{aligned}
R_1 &: \text{If } x_1 \text{ is } A^1_1 \text{ and } \ldots \text{ and } x_q \text{ is } A^1_q \text{ then} \\
&\qquad y_1 = c^1_0 + c^1_1 x_1 + \ldots + c^1_q x_q \\
R_2 &: \text{If } x_1 \text{ is } A^2_1 \text{ and } \ldots \text{ and } x_q \text{ is } A^2_q \text{ then} \\
&\qquad y_2 = c^2_0 + c^2_1 x_1 + \ldots + c^2_q x_q \\
&\vdots \\
R_p &: \text{If } x_1 \text{ is } A^p_1 \text{ and } \ldots \text{ and } x_q \text{ is } A^p_q \text{ then} \\
&\qquad y_p = c^p_0 + c^p_1 x_1 + \ldots + c^p_q x_q
\end{aligned}
\tag{20}
$$

The firing strength of rule R_i is computed with:

$$\alpha_i = \min_{j=1}^{q} \left\{ A^i_j\left(x_j\right) \right\} \tag{21}$$

where $A^i_j\left(x_j\right)$ is the membership degree of value x_j to the fuzzy set A^i_j. The final output valueof the system is computed as the weighted sum of the y_i values weighted with the strength α_i of the rules:

$$Y = \frac{\sum_{i=1}^{p} \alpha_i y_i}{\sum_{i=1}^{p} \alpha_i} \tag{22}$$

We will use CCLAM's to form a complex system that allows the storage of TSK rules. Additionally this system will provide the appropiate output due to a particular input. This will be achieved in some steps.

5.1 Calculus of the satisfying degree of x_i against each rule

To compute the satisfying degree of the rules when the input pattern $x_1, \ldots, x_q$ is presented, a CCLAM will be used to compute the satisfying degree of the rules for each particular x_i. After that, in the next section the particular degrees will be unified.

For each input value x_i it is necessary to compute its membership degree against every fuzzy set A_i^j to witch it is compared in the rule. We denote the special EPs that compute this membership degree with the label $\mu_{A_i^j}(x_i)$.

Let $A_i^1, \ldots, A_i^p$ be the linguistic terms where the variable x_i take its linguistic values. It isn't necessary the fuzzy sets $A_i^1, \ldots, A_i^p$ to be all different.

Let $B_i^1, \ldots, B_i^{n_i}$ be fuzzy sets that satisfy:

- $B_i^v \neq B_i^w \quad \forall v \neq w$
- $\forall B_i^v \exists A_j^w \quad B_i^v = A_j^w$

The configuration of the CCLAM that computes the satisfying degree of x_i against each rule is:

- The F_A layer has n_i PE's, one for each fuzzy set $B_i^1, \ldots B_i^{n_i}$. These PE's receive the membership degree of input value x_i to each fuzzy set B_i^j.
- The F_B layer has p PE's, one for each rule. In them we obtain the satisfying degree of each rule.
- The association of the fuzzy sets to their corresponding rule are coded in the weights of the conections made between the two layers. The weight of the connection made between B_i^j and R_i^k is:
  - 1 if the rule R_i^k includes "x_i is B_i^j".
  - 0 otherwise.
- The functions Υ^C and Ψ^C are configured to allow the PE's of F_B layer to receive its input from the correct element in F_A
  - $\Upsilon^C(a, b) = \min(a, b)$
  - $\Psi^C(r_1, \ldots, r_p) = \max\{r_1, \ldots, r_p\}$
- There isn't competition in F_B because we don't need a winner but the satisfying degree of each rule.

5.2 Calculus of the satisfying degree of each rule

When we have obtained the satisfying degree of each input value x_i against each rule, we need to aggregate that information to compute the overall satisfying degree of each rule when the input values $x_1, \ldots, x_q$ are presented. To do this we use a CCLAM with the following configuration:

- There are $q \times p$ PE's in F_A layer. The element R_i^j receives the degree in which the input value x_j fires the rule rule R_i.
- In F_B the are p PE's, one for each rule, where the satisfying degree of each rule is obtained.
- The weights of the connections made between the two layers are established so that each PE in layer F_B receives its input from those elements in F_A that represent the partial satisfying degree of the rule that it represents. The weight of the connection made between R_i^j and R_k is:
  - 1, if $i \neq k$.
  - 0, otherwise.
- The Υ^C and Ψ^C functions are the appropiate t-norm and t-conorm used to compute the firing strength of the rule.
  - $\Upsilon^C(a, b) = \bigoplus(a, b)$
  - $\Psi(u_1, \ldots, u_n) = \bigotimes(u_1, \ldots, u_n)$
- There isn't competition in layer F_B because we don't need a winner but the satisfying degree of each rule.

5.3 Computation of the consequents of the rules

First order TSK rule based systems have rules whose consequents are of the form:

$$y_i = c_0^i + c_1^i x_1 + \ldots + c_q^i x_q \tag{23}$$

We can compute the consequents of all the rules with a CCLAM that receives the input values of the system, $x_1, \ldots, x_q$, and returns the consequents $y_1, \ldots, y_p$ of the rules.

To achieve that, the configuration of the CCLAM is:

- There are $q + 1$ PE's in F_A layer, one for each input value $x_1, \ldots, x_q$ (these elements receive their activation from the input values of the system) and an aditional element named x_0 associated with the term c_0^i which input is always one.
- There are p PE's in F_B layer where the consequents of the rules are obtained. These elements are named $y_1, \ldots, y_p$.

- The weight of the conection made from the element x_i to y_j is c_i^j.
- The Υ^C and Ψ^C functions compute the products and sums present in equation (23).
  - $\Upsilon^C(s,t) = s \times t$
  - $\Psi(u_1, \ldots, u_n) = \sum_{i=1}^{n} u_i$
- The isn't competition in F_B layer because we don't want a winning element but the values generated by each consequent of the rules.

5.4 Computation of the output of the system

As seen before, we have obtained the satistaction degrees of the rules and the output generated by them. Now it is necesary to aggregate those results by means of a weighted sum. Let $\alpha_1, \ldots, \alpha_p$ be the satisfying degrees and $y_1, \ldots, y_p$ be the output of the rules. The result of the weighted sum is the output of the whole system:

$$Y = \frac{\sum_{i=1}^{p} \alpha_i y_i}{\sum_{i=1}^{p} \alpha_i} \quad (24)$$

5.5 Whole system

The system that stores the TSK rules is formed by the CCLAM's seen above. It receives its inputs $x_1, \ldots, x_q$ and computes the satisfying degree and the output of each rule. Then combines this information to obtain the output Y (figure 7).

5.6 Example

Let us supose that we want to store a set of rules that computes the power-down supply current in a microcontroller depending on its voltage and temperature.

The set of rules which characterize the system is:

1. If low voltage and low temperature then $I = 0.1 \times voltage + 0.01 \times temperature$
2. If high voltage and low temperature then $I = 0.4 \times voltage + 0.01 \times temperature$
3. If low voltage and high temperature then $I = 0.1 \times voltage + 0.05 \times temperature$
4. If high voltage and high temperature then $I = 1 \times voltage + 0.1 \times temperature$

To compute the firing strength of the rules, the voltage, measured in volts, is fuzzyfied taking values in terms of a linguistic variable VOLTAGE. The CCLAM that computes the satisfying degree of the rules due to a particular voltage has two PE's in the F_A layer representing the terms VLOW and VHIGH and has four PE's in the F_B layer representing the rules of the system. The weights of the connections made between the elements depend on the rules (table 13).

	R_V^1	R_V^2	R_V^3	R_V^4
VLOW	1	0	1	0
VHIGH	0	1	0	1

Table 13: Connection weights in the CCLAM associated to the voltage.

The firing strength of the rules due to a particular temperature is computed with a CCLAM that has two PE's in the F_A layer representing the terms TLOW and THIGH of the linguistic variable TEMPERATURE in wich the crisp value is fuzzyfied. In the F_B layer there are four PE's that represent the rules of the system. The weights of the connections made between the PE's of the two layers are shown in table 14.

	R_T^1	R_T^2	R_T^3	R_T^4
TLOW	1	1	0	0
THIGH	0	0	1	1

Table 14: Connection weights in the CCLAM associated to the temperature.

A CCLAM is used to unify the firing strength obtained in the previous memories. Its inputs come from the F_B layers of the CCLAM's associated to the voltage and temperature. For that reason it has eigth PE's in the F_A layer. There are four PE's in the F_B layer representing the rules. The weights of the connections made between the elements of the two layers are shown in table 15.

	R_V^1	R_V^2	R_V^3	R_V^4	R_T^1	R_T^2	R_T^3	R_T^4
R1	0	1	1	1	0	1	1	1
R2	1	0	1	1	1	0	1	1
R3	1	1	0	1	1	1	0	1
R4	1	1	1	0	1	1	1	0

Table 15: Connection weights in the CCLAM that computes the firing strength of the rules.

These CCLAM's compute the firingth strength of the rules. Now it's necessary a CCLAM that computes the output of each rule. This CCLAM has two inputs that correspond to the crisp values of voltage and temperature. In the F_B layer there are four PE's where the output of each rule is obtained.

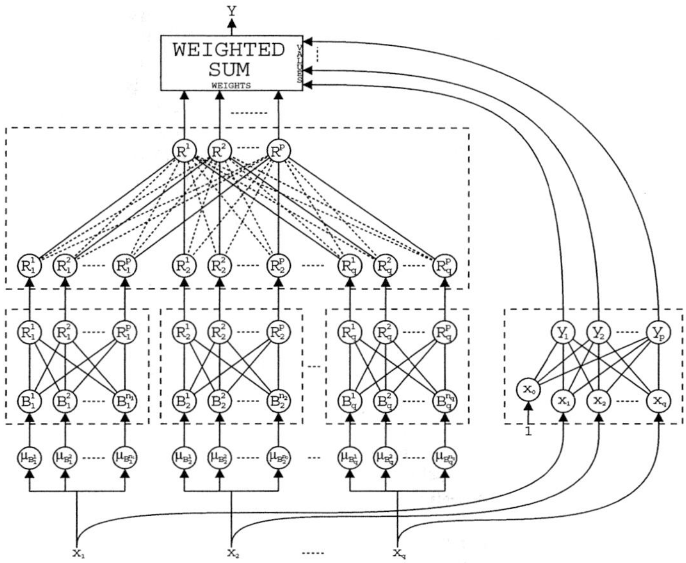

Figure 7: Use of CCLAM's to store TSK rules.

The coeficients of the polynomials that constitute the consequents of the rules are coded in the weigths of the connections made between them PE's of the two layers as shown in table 16.

	y_1	y_2	y_3	y_4
voltage	0.1	0.4	0.1	1
temperature	0.01	0.01	0.05	0.1

Table 16: Connection weights in the CCLAM that computes the output of the rules.

The final output of the system is computed as the sum of the values of the consequents weighted by the firingth strength of each rule.

Let $voltage = 5v$ and $temperature = 70^oC$ be the inputs of the system.

The membership degree of the crisp value $5v$ to the fuzzy sets associated to the terms VLOW and VHIGH are $\mu_{VLOW}(5v) = 0.2$ and $\mu_{VHIGH}(5v) = 0.8$.

The CCLAM associated to the voltage receives as input the values 0.2 and 0.8. The signal propagated from F_A to F_B is shown in the Table 17. In the cell corresponding to row G column H the returned result by $\Upsilon^C\left(R_V^G, m_{H,G}^C\right) = \min\left(R_V^G, m_{H,G}^C\right)$ appears. At the end of the row is the value provided by Ψ^C since this is applied on the values of this row.

Υ^C	VLOW	VHIGH	Ψ^C
R_V^1	0.2	0	0.2
R_V^2	0	0.8	0.8
R_V^3	0.2	0	0.2
R_V^4	0	0.8	0.8

Table 17: Application of Υ^C and Ψ^C in the CCLAM associated to voltage.

The membership degree of the crisp value 70^oC to the fuzzy sets associated to the terms TLOW and THIGH are $\mu_{TLOW}(70^oC) = 0.4$ and $\mu_{THIGH}(70^oC) = 0.6$.

The input values of the CCLAM associated to the temperature are 0.4 and 0.6. The CCLAM associated to the temperature receives as input the values 0.4 and 0.6. The signal propagated from F_A to F_B is shown in the Table 18. In the cell corresponding to row G column H the returned result by $\Upsilon^C\left(R_T^G, m_{H,G}^C\right) = \min\left(R_T^G, m_{H,G}^C\right)$ appears. At the end of the row is the value provided by Ψ^C since this is applied on the values of this row.

The particular firing strengths of each rule due to each input value are unified to compute the global firing strength of the rules. The CCLAM that unifies the information receives as input the values present

Υ^C	TLOW	THIGH	Ψ^C
R_T^1	0.4	0	0.4
R_T^2	0.4	0	0.4
R_T^3	0	0.6	0.6
R_T^4	0	0.6	0.6

Table 18: Application of Υ^C and Ψ^C in the CCLAM associated to temperature.

in the layer F_B of the CCLAM's associated to voltage and temperature. The signal propagated from F_A to F_B is shown in the Table 19. In the cell corresponding to row G column H the returned result by $\Upsilon^C\left(R^G, m^C_{H,G}\right)$ appears. At the end of the row is the value provided by Ψ^C since this is applied on the values of this row.

	voltage				temperature				
Υ^C	R_V^1	R_V^2	R_V^3	R_V^4	R_T^1	R_T^2	R_T^3	R_T^4	Ψ^C
R_1	0.2	1	1	1	0.4	1	1	1	0.2
R_2	1	0.8	1	1	1	0.4	1	1	0.4
R_3	1	1	0.2	1	1	1	0.6	1	0.2
R_4	1	1	1	0.8	1	1	1	0.6	0.6

Table 19: Application of Υ^C and Ψ^C in the unifier CCLAM.

Υ^C	voltage	temperature	Ψ^C
y_1	0.5	0.7	1.2
y_2	2	0.7	2.7
y_3	0.5	3.5	4
y_4	5	7	12

Table 20: Application of Υ^C and Ψ^C in the unifier CCLAM.

Finally the weighted sum of the results obtained gives $9.32\mu A$ as the output of the whole system as shown in table 21.

value	*weight*	total
1.2	0.2	$0.24\mu A$
2.7	0.4	$1.08\mu A$
4	0.2	$0.8\mu A$
12	0.6	$7.2\mu A$
		total $9.32\mu A$

Table 21: Weighted sum of the results obtained.

6 CONCLUSIONS

- The correct choice of the functions which define the memory behavior allows CCLAM groupings to be composed which show a behavior in keeping with the needs of information storage and recovery.
- The Continuous Classifying Associative Memory CCLAM allows imprecise information expressed in linguistic terms to be correctly recovered.
- The storage of rules with CCLAM not only enables us to recover rules but also to obtain the appropriate consequent for any antecedent.
- The CCLAM allows specification of the functions which will control its operation and this enables any t-norm and t-conorm to be used for the application of the rules.
- The use of other associative memory models to store fuzzy rules is an inefficient solution due to the large quantity of necessary resources.

REFERENCES

Bailón, A. (2001). *Memorias Asociativas Difusas: Diseño e Implementación*. PhD thesis, Universidad de Granada.

Bailón, A., Delgado, M., and Fajardo, W. (1997). Clasificación de información con memorias asociativas. In *Actas de la VII Conferencia de la Asociación Española para la Inteligencia Artificial*.

Bailón, A., Delgado, M., and Fajardo, W. (2000). Clam: A new model of associative memory. *International Journal of Intelligent Systems*, 15:549–564.

Bailón, A., Delgado, M., and Fajardo, W. (2002). Continuous classifying associative memory. *International Journal of Intelligent Systems*, 17(4):391–407.

Mamdani, E. and Assilian, S. (1975). An experiment in linguistic synthesis with a fuzzy logic controller. *International Journal of Man-Machine Studies*, 7(1):1–13.

Sugeno, M. and Takagi, T. (1985). Fuzzy identification of systems and its application to modeling and control. *IEEE Transactions on Systems, Man, and Cybernetics*, 15(1):116–132.

Zadeh, L. (1979). A theory of approximate reasoning. *Machine Intelligence*, 9:149–194.

Zadeh, L. (1984). A theory of commonsense knowledge. In Skala, Termini, T., editor, *Aspects of vagueness*, pages 257–295. Reidel.

A CASE-BASED EXPERT SYSTEM FOR ESTIMATING THE COST OF REFURBISHING CONSTRUCTION BUILDINGS

Farhi Marir, Frank Wang and Karim Ouazzane
KMG Research Group, School of Informatics & Multimedi Technology, North London University, Holloway Road, UK
Email fmarir@unl.ac.uk, fwang@unl.ac.uk, Kouazzane@unl.ac.uk

Key words: Case-based Reasoning, Cost estimation and Building Refurbishment.

Abstract: CBRefurb is a case-based reasoning (CBR) system for the strategic cost estimation for building refurbishment. This domain is characterised by many uncertainties and variation. Its cost estimation involves large amount of interrelated factors whose impact is difficult to assess. This paper report on the problems faced by the building cost information Services (BCIS) databases and several rule-based expert systems to tackle this complex cost estimation problem and, the design and evaluation of CBRefurb system implemented using ReMind Shell. CBRefurb imitates the domain expert in its approach of breaking down the whole building work into smaller work (building items) by organising the refurbishment cases as a hierarchical structure composed of cases and subcases. The process of estimation imitates the expert by considering only these pieces of previous cases of similar situation (or context). For this purpose, CBRefurb defines some of the building and its component (or items) features as a global context and local context information used to classify cases and subcases into context cases and subcases, and to decompose the cost estimation problem into adaptable subproblems. This is followed by a two indexing schemes to suit the hierarchical structure of the case and the problem decomposition and to allow classification and retrieval of contextual cases. CBRefurb features consolidate the aim of the project that is allowing multiple retrieval of appropriate pieces of the refurbishment which are easier to adapt, reflecting the expert method of estimating cost for complex refurbishment work.

1 INTRODUCTION

Case-based reasoning (CBR) is a fresh reasoning paradigm for the design of expert systems in domains that may not be appropriate for other reasoning paradigms such as model-based reasoning [1]. As a result of this, and because of its resemblance to human reasoning, CBR has attracted increasing interest both from those experienced in developing expert systems and from novices [2, 3, 4]. This paper describes the design and the implementations of CBRefurb system for the strategic cost estimation of building refurbishment work using ReMind CBR shell.

Refurbishment is a work carried out on existing buildings in the attempt to improve and to update them to modern standards whilst retaining their current use. It represents a substantial part of the UK construction programme and is seen as an economic alternative to new build [5]. A recent investigation amongst the North West councils and contractors has shown the strategic importance of cost estimation for building refurbishment and the highly interrelated nature of the knowledge required to estimate efficiently this cost [6]. However, the design and development of several commercially available expert systems for the construction industry have shown the difficulties the knowledge engineer can meet during knowledge elicitation in such a complex domain [7]. Although the figures for each building repair can be produced using these expert systems or using Building Cost Information Service (BCIS) databases, we found that most of the experts use these sources to estimate costs of new build but never used them to estimate costs for building refurbishment work. Because the figures provided by these sources are calculated in the framework of new work rather than refurbishment work. Indeed, in new building work, the cost depends on quality, size and time. However, in refurbishment work, these factors are supplemented by many other features, or even outweighed, by major secondary (or broad-ranging) factors such as the safety of the structure and the effect of the repair of one building item on another. In the above systems, no considerations are given neither to the circumstance (or context) in which the work has taken places nor to the type and the size of the project in which the building or the item is repaired. Instead the repair cost is given on elemental cost basis as if each item or the element is repaired alone.

This paper presents CBRefurb as an alternative system using case-based reasoning (CBR). It estimates the strategic cost for refurbishing buildings by imitating the domain expert in its approach of breaking down the whole building work into smaller work (building items). This is by organising the refurbishment cases as a hierarchical structure composed of cases and subcases. Then it defines the contcept of context information to reflect the contextual reasoning of the expert who use only case of simailr context (or circumstances) to adapt previous solution. For this purpose, the building specification such as the state of the building, the type of work required and the size of the project as a *global contex.* Similarly the item state and the work required on that item as *local context.* CBRefurb use the concept of context to classify cases into *context cases* and *subacases*, and decompose the cost estimation *problem* into *adaptable subproblems.* In the same line, a convenient hierarchical indexing scheme to suit the hierarchical structure of the case and the decomposition of the problem is designed . In addition, this indexing scheme implements two interconnected schemes; *classification* and *retrieval* indexes. The classification indexes use *global* and *local context* features to classify cases and subcases into *context cases* and *subcases. This classification* reduces the retrieval search space within contextual cases instead of the whole case base. The retrieval indexes are used to select multiple cases and subcases among the context cases and subcases. These techniques implemented in CBRefurb allow multiple retrieval of pieces of case that can be adapted more easily.

To this end, section two presents the structural partitioning of building refurbishment cases and the classification of their features depending on their functionality's. Then the decomposition of the cost estimation problems presented. Section three is devoted to the two levels of indexing schemes. Section four describes the multiple case retrieval and the adaptation resulting from the decomposition of the cost estimation problem. The last section is devoted to the evaluation of the system and the contribution of CBRefurb to the CBR technology.

2 REPRESENTING AND REASONING WITH CASES

A building is a large complex artefact whose complete specification requires a high dimensional representational structure. Cost estimation involves finding and using the relevant information of a given job from a very large amount of information.. Moreover, some factors cannot be identified and their impact on the cost of refurbishment can neither be rigorously assessed nor predicted. It appears from this description that the building refurbishment case faces two major problems; the large number of factors involved in the estimation of the costs and the difficulty to quantify the effect of some of them on the costs.

2.1 Case Representation

Experience with monolithic case representation for real world large cases of a similar domain of construction has shown its limitations in accessing cases and in dealing with large number of cases [8]. To overcome these limitations and to allow efficient access and retrieval, several CBR systems have organised their cases into case-subcases hierarchies for different domains such as Clavier system for autoclave layout [9], Celia system for learning from expert problem solving [10] and PERSUADOR system for labour dispute [11]. We have been faced with a similar problem on how to represent this high dimensional real world case in ReMind environment. CBRefurb represents the refurbishment case as a flat structure combined with hierarchical subcases (Fig 1). Although this hierarchical organisation of cases is generally familiar, it goes beyond the normal ReMind framework. For practical reasons, each of the cases and subcases base is represented in a different case libraries. The link and the manipulation of these cases and their subcases is implemented using ReMind's *case field* and its C function library respectively.

Depending on the functionalities of the factors involved in the cost estimation, the main case contains, as shown in , essentially:

- The *Building Identification (bid)* identifies the characteristics of the building.
- the *Building Work Specification (bws)* describes the state and diagnosis of the building, a summary of the work required, and links to the item subcases involved in the refurbishment work.
- The Building Subjective Parameters (bsp) represents the factors whose impact on the cost

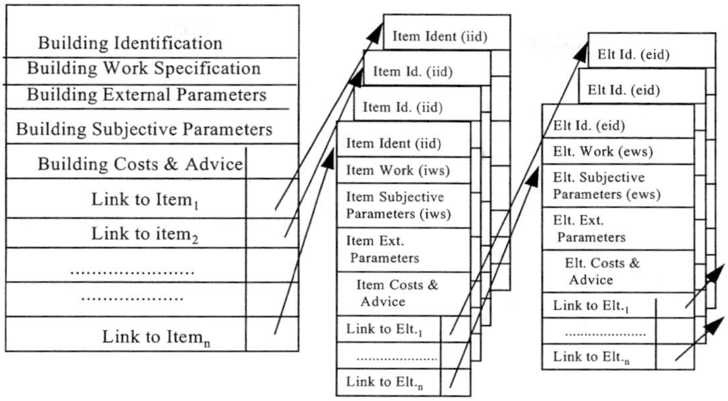

Figure 1: The hierarchical Structure of the Case.

is difficult to predict or quantify. This includes the state of the building, type of refurbishment project, site access, occupancy and other environmental parameters,

- The *Building External Parameters (bep)* represents factors like the region and the state of the market, which can be used as parameters for indexing and updating the prices, and
- the *Building Costs and Advice (bca)* is composed of the cost estimation that states the derived solution and advice to prevent potential problems.

Similar parameters are also present in each subcase that represent the work for each item of the building. This partitioning can go further into decomposing the building items themselves into subcases for different purposes such as defining shared elemental work between different items or the need for elemental cost estimation..

2.2 Context and Problem Decomposition

Even if the structural organisation resolves the problem of the high dimensionality of the cases, the impact of the interaction between the components of the building may prevent the decomposition of the cost estimation problem. In this situation, the hierarchical organisation of the case will have no benefit since the solution to the problem will require the retrieval and the process of *all* the items at the *same* time. As a result the adaptation will be more complex and difficult to implement due the uncertainty that characterise the broad-ranging (or secondary) factors whose impact on the costs is unpredictable. In practice the experts match the building items that need repair to previous items repairs which were in a similar situations (or context) and the overall cost can be estimated using the estimated cost of the items. This context information is given very high importance by the experts to the point that even very similar repairs are not considered if they took place in a different situation to the current one.

From the analysis of the refurbishment domain, the cost estimation problem is not a conflicting interaction of conjunctive goals that involve multi-agents who have different plans and goals as in PERSUADOR [11]. Instead, it is a single agent of high dimensional parameters some of which are difficult to assess given different circumstance (or context). The cost estimation problem does not require complex problem solving approach that use sequences of plans and subgoals [10,11,12] instead it is an equation whose solution will be the total amount that results from the addition of all items repair cost. The major problem however, is to define the context information in which the equation can be solved, since from one context to another the same equation may have different solutions. This is due to the impact on the costs of the wide-ranging parameters, which tend to be stable for a given context but changes when this context changes. We identified most of the wide-ranging factors whose impact on the costs is unpredictable and most importantly the factors that originate them and underline their importance. For instance, the impact of the safety factors on the costs depends in general on factors like the state and the type of the building, whether the occupants remain during refurbishing or not, the site access and the environment of the building. In CBRefurb these (subjective) parameters which are the source of the secondary or wide-ranging factors are used as context information. Context information is either *Global Context* if the subjective parameters concern the building or *Local Context* if they concern the building item. Global and internal or local context information are used in several work [9,10,13] for different purposes depending on the particularities of the domain and the type of the problem addressed which are different from one system to another. CBRefurb implements a practical solution to use the context information as a *similarity measure* to classify cases and subcases that share the same context information into *Context Cases* and *Subcases. This is to* allow the decomposition of the cost estimation problem into subproblems and to resolve the cost estimation equation. Using only context cases and subcases for any cost adaptation as the expert do, the impact in term of the cost of the secondary features on each item can be approximately defined in a boundary of figures. CBRefurb adaptation process implements a mechanism that uses these figures through its learning process to address more easily the problem of secondary factors and adapt them to new situations and save them in their appropriate case or subcase. To explain this the refurbishment cost estimation problem ($BuildingCosts_{bca}$) is represented in the following equation :

$$BuildCosts_{ica} \approx (Coeff_{bep} \oplus SubjFunc(bsp)) * \sum_{i=1}^{n} Item_i Costs_{ica} \oplus BuildCosts_{bid\,\&\,bws}$$

where :

- $Coeff_{bep}$: a cost index used to update the costs of each item to meet the building external parameters requirements e.g. region and speed of work,
- *SubjFunc(bsp)* : function whose value depends on the subjective features,
- $Item_i Costs$: represents the estimated costs of each works, and
- $BuildCosts_{bid\&bws}$: represents added costs resulting from the new regulations, contingencies and other environmental aspects.

Both $Coef_{bep}$ and $BuildCosts_{bid\&bws}$ can be provided by BCIS databases or calculated using cost estimation techniques used in construction. However, the *SubjFunc(bsp)* function is in fact equation subjective parameters that is not taken into account in BCIS databases and previous expert systems approach when calculating repair cost In contrast, CBRefurb takes into account it when adapting the cost at both case and subcase levels. As explained previously, using the context information and the context cases and subcases the boundaries [Minimum of *SubjFun(bsp)*, Maximum of *SubjFun(bsp)]* of the *SubjFunc(bsp)* will be *approximately* defined and an estimated value $SubjValue_{ctx}$ within this boundaries will be fixed and adapted to the new situation using previous similar experiences. Information on the boundaries and the importance of the subjective function for each secondary features will be saved in its appropriate case or subcase to reflect any changes as the domain evolve and to be used like any other parameter for future adaptation. The computation of the remaining $Item_i Costs$ expression that represent the costs for each item will follow a similar approach as for the $BuildingCost_{bca}$ equation. This means $Item_i Costs$ will in turn be calculated using a similar equation that represent the subproblem. Once all the items equation are resolved and estimated cost for each item is adapted then their results will be used to resolve and adapt the $BuildingCost_{bca}$ equation which represent the final cost estimation of the building refurbishment work. The resulting $BuildingCost_{bca}$ will be represented as:

$$AdaptBuild\ Costs_{CTX} \approx Coeff_{bep} * \sum_{i=1}^{n} Item_i Costs_{ica} \oplus SubjValue_{CTX} * \sum_{i=1}^{n} Item_i Costs_{ica} \oplus BuildCosts_{bid\,\&\,bws}.$$

Providing global and local context information does not mean that the uncertainty that characterise the refurbishment domain is taken away and the subproblems are completely independent. However, by representing separately indexed, linked subcases, each associated with its costs will facilitate flexible iterative cost estimation while retaining the coherency by the entire cases. A particular additional feature to CBRefurb is its use of global and local context information not only as a framework in which the decomposition of the cost estimation is possible but also as a *similarity measure* to differentiate and classify similar cases and subcases into *Context Cases* and *Subcases* at the learning phase of CBR i.e. the storage of the new solution, instead of its use at the retrieval phase. Such early classification of cases meets the expert requirements of using only context cases for adaptation and will reduce considerably the retrieval search space especially for large case base by directing it to context cases and subcases instead of the whole case base.

3 CASE INDEXING

In order for the mechanisms and data structure of case retrieval to be applicable to retrieving context cases and subcases, the indexing vocabulary for cases and subcases must be at an appropriate level of generality of the global and local context and to reflect the hierarchical structure of the cases. For this purpose, two main interconnected indexing schemes are provided in CBRefurb; the case indexing scheme and subcase indexing schemes (Fig.2). Each of the indexing scheme is composed of two type of indexes with different functionalities. *Classification indexes* represents the global and local context features of cases and their subcases, which represent the acquired knowledge in the domain. These indices are considered as difference-based indexing scheme by their main function of differentiating a case from another similar cases. However, these indexes are mainly used to classify and direct the retrieval to *Context Cases* and *Subcases*. This reflects the importance given to the context information in which the expert domain retrieve and adapt cases and also adds an advantage to CBRefurb by reducing the scope of the retrieval search space to classes of similar cases rather than the whole case-base. In CBRefurb, these classification indexes compose the static part of the inductive tree (or *static subtree*) built using ReMind Cluster Editor.

Retrieval indexes is concerned by the details of the refurbishment work. They specify the defect diagnosis, the type and the quality of the repair for both the building and the items. These indexes are also used to further push down classification of context cases and subcases into groups that share further details. Their importance can be changed as the refurbishment domain evolves either by using the inductive learning process if they are represented as an inductive tree or by assigning to them weights if they are represented as a vector. If the inductive process is used, they will be represented as second part of the inductive tree (or *dynamic subtree*) whose leaves contain pointers to the cases and the. In CBRefurb, manual and automated have been mixed to identify the features to be used as indices for the refurbishment cases and subcases.

The analysis of several specification documents

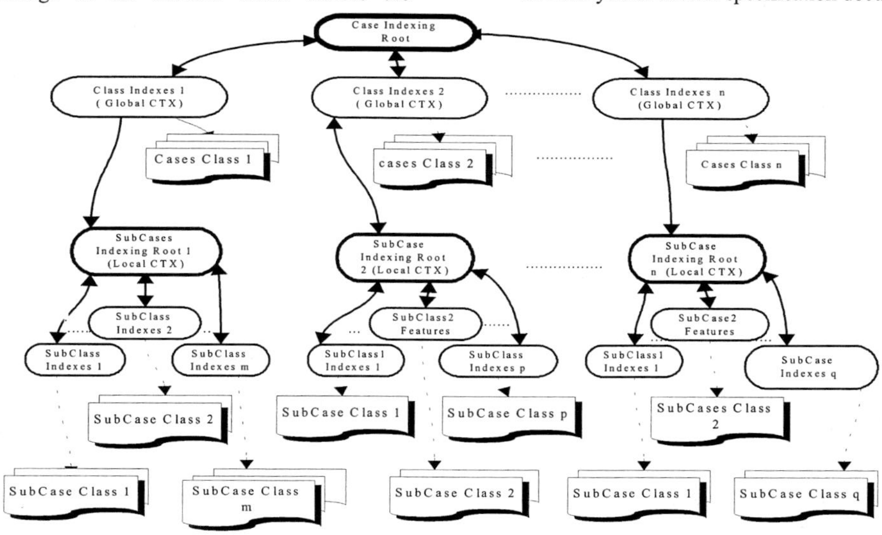

Figure 2: CBRefurb Indexing Scheme

for refurbishment work and discussion with expert has helped to identify those features that differentiate cases best [6,14]. It is similar to the *checklist-based* indexing implemented in MEDIATOR to index on type and function of disputed objects and relationship of disputants, and CHEF [12] to indexes on texture and taste. CBRefurb indexes on the circumstance of the project, the state of building, the extent of the damage and the type and quality of work required. Once the manual checklist is produced, further testing were performed on thirty real cases using ReMind's inductive learning methods [15] which has brought some adjustment to the predictions of the indexes of the checklist. This approach of combining manual and ReMind inductive learning methods for choosing the indices has shown interesting results in retrieving appropriate cases and subcases in CBRefurb system. This two-stage indexing schemes comes in line with the hierarchical case representation and the problem decomposition and consolidate the aim of the paper which is multiple retrieval of adaptable pieces of context cases and subcases. In addition, CBRefurb implements a mechanism that allows the user to make changes to the importance of the features to reflect his personal strategy of estimating cost.

4 CASE RETRIEVAL AND ADAPTATION

Pieces from multiple previous cases have been used to come up with a proposed contract in PERSUADOR [11], a diagnosis [10] and proposed layouts in Clavier [9]. Estimating the cost of refurbishment involve collating information from several old cases thus a strategy of *multiple-case-retrieval* is also used (Fig. 3). Our approach of finding multiple relevant cases during building refurbishment cost estimation problem solving is based on the fact that the global and local context information can serve as basis for recognising cases and their subcases that can be used to adapt and estimate the costs.

Given the context information of a problem, a retrieval algorithm, using the indices in the case-memory, should retrieve the most similar cases to the current problem or situation. The retrieval algorithm relies on the indices and the organisation of the memory to direct the search to potentially useful cases. The issue of choosing the *best* matching case has been addressed in several works [16,17,18]. It is apparent that cases are selected on the basis of their closeness of their specification similarities rather than their solution similarity [19]. CBRefurb gives consideration to both solution and specification similarities. Its retrieval mechanism guarantees retrieval of cases that are easier to adapt by giving explicit consideration to how cases can be adapted during the design of the representation and the indexing of the cases. Moreover, CBRefurb implements the strategy of multiple features and multiple case retrieval instead of a single *'best'* or *'most similar'* case as the basis for a solution (Fig 3.). This approach is facilitated by the hierarchical structure of the case, the different level of indexing schemes for the main case and its subcases, and the decomposition of the problem into subproblems that can be adapted iteratively. In this context, CBRefurb follows a two stage process for the retrieval of the main cases. A *filtering stage* which uses the static subtree (or global context) to identifies candidates from the main cases that are deemed to be contextually relevant to the target. A *selection stage* that uses further information existing at the main case level concerning the items the building and the items to repair, the *selection stage* walks through some branch of the dynamic tree to select among the context cases more useful cases to the target case. At this level, identification of relevant information on the selected context cases and their nearest cases of nearest branches of the dynamic tree are saved in an external data structure which can be used for backtracking and walking again to the top of the hierarchy. At this level a *global ball-park solution* to the cost estimation problem is generated and used as a framework for all adaptation process and refinement of the different subcases. The same approach using the filtering stage with its static subtree (local context) and the selection stage with further information the item and elements for each subcases base. The result will be *local ball-park solution* to the cost estimation problem which will also be used for adaptation process and plans for the refinement of elements that can be shared by different building items.

The adaptation process is also performed in two stages: local adaptation for subcases and global adaptation for the whole case. Both implements parameter adjustment and derivational mechanisms during the adaptation of the cases. First, the local adaptation is triggered to adapt subcases in the framework of global ballpark and local ballpark using pieces from different subcases. If a piece is matched, its cost is adapted mixing the refurbishment regulation rules, parameters adjustment for updating prices, altering region, altering quantities, such as speed of construction

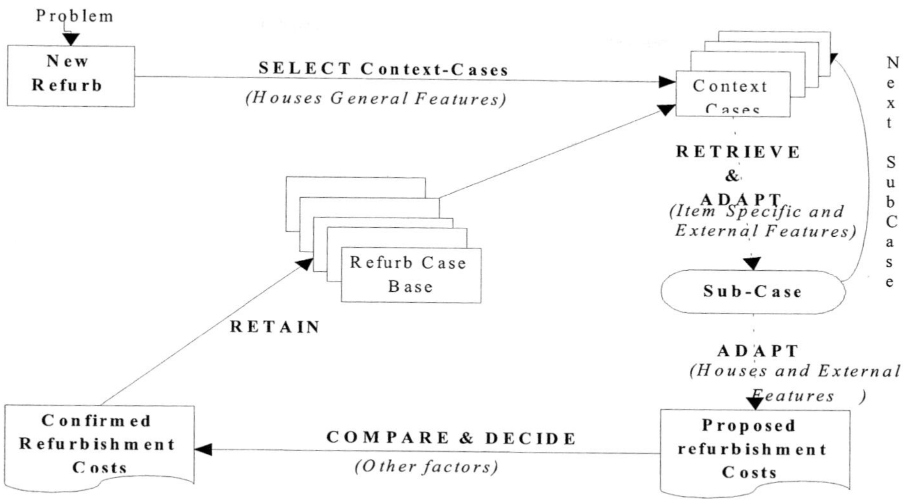

Figure 3: CBRefurb Reasoning Process

and urban location. If no similar pieces of cases exist, CBRefurb provides a mechanism which use the external data structured and perform backtracking up to the hierarchy to return to context cases and search for other pieces of context cases that match the remaining unmatched features. The derivational mechanism is used to estimate additional cost resulting from the impact of each of secondary factors by using their boundary of figures and information on how it was estimated in a that similar situation. In the event of no similar pieces match, the derivational mechanism estimates the cost using elemental costs estimation techniques and the user altering procurement and adapt the resulting costs to the target context. Once the local adaptation i.e. solution of each equation of the subproblem, the global adaptation will add all the subcases costs and the result will be similarly adapted for the whole case i.e. solution to the cost estimation problem equation.

5 EVALUATION OF CBREFURB

CBRefurb is being evaluated by experts in the domain of refurbishment, this feedback will serve to debug our approach of contextual retrieval and the adaptation. Several experts have been impressed by the systems which is in fact the automation of their approach of estimating refurbishment cost. CBRefurb can be seen as a real world intelligent database designed to give realistic refurbishment Costs. It can be used to respond to queries about the estimated cost of any size and type of repairs from large projects of building refurbishment to the building element repair. Moreover, CBRefurb can be used as a decision support tool for the managers while taking strategic decision to go for refurbishment or redevelopment of an important. In theory the technique should also be applicable to other estimating task that rely on prior experience.

The primary contribution to CBR field is the investigation of CBR for hard real-world domain and the application of ReMind to an interesting and challenging cost estimation for refurbishment. In addition CBRefurb contributes to CBR field by providing a "proof of concept" of CBR architecture for reasoning with multiple cases and addresses the important issue of improving the adaptation process. The major contribution of CBRefurb are the method of hierarchical cases and subcases that goes outside the normal ReMind framework and the Context Information concept whose benefit cut across all the stages of CBR reasoning. Context information is used for many purposes. It provides means for the design of a hierarchical indexing that fits with the case representation. It is used as a similarity measure to classify cases into context cases that reduce considerably the search space of the retrieval process and more importantly used as a framework to decompose the complex problem into adaptable subproblems.

REFERENCES

1. Schank, R. (1982). Dynamic memory: a theory of reminding and learning in computers and people. Cambridge University Press, Cambridge, UK
2. Kolodner, J.L. (1993). Case-Based Reasoning. Morgan Kaufmann.
3. Aamodt, A. & Plaza, E. (1994). Case-Based Reasoning: Foundational Issues, Methodological Variations, and System Approaches. *AI Communications*, 7(i): pp 39-59.
4. Watson, I. & Marir, F. 1994. Case-Based Reasoning: A Review. The Knowledge Engineering Review, Vol. 9, No. 4: pp.327-354
5. Douglas J.F. and Peter S.B. (1991). Cost Planning of Buildings (6th Edition). BSP Professional Books
6 Marir, F., & Watson, I.D. ,(1995a). CBRefurb : Case-Based Cost Estimation. Colloquium on Case Based Reasoning: Prospects for applications. Organised by Professional Group C4 (Artificial Intelligence), 7, March, 1995.
7. Watson, I.D., & Brandon, P.S. (1992). Strategic Maintenance Prediction: An Expert System for Facilities Managers. In Facilities Management: Research Direction, Proc. 2nd. IFMA International Symposium. (Ed. Barett P.).
8. Pearce, M., Ashok K.G., Kolodner, J.L., Zimring, C. & Billignton, R. (1992) Case-Based Design Support- A case study in Architectural Design.*IEEE Expert* Oct. 1992
9. Hennessy, D. et al.[1992]. Applying Case-Based Reasoning to autoclave Loading., IEEE Expert,.Vol 17, pp14-20,pp21-25.
10. Redmond, M. A. 1992. Learning by observing and understanding expert problem solving. *Georgia Institute of Technology, College of Computing Technical Report no. GIT-CC-92/43.* Atlanta
11. Sycara , K. [1987] . *Resolving Adversial Conflicts: An approach Integrating cases-Based Reasoning and Analytic Methods.* PhD thesis , School of Information and Computer Science, Georgia Institute of Technology.
12 Hammond, K.J. (1986). CHEF: A Model of Case-Based Planning. *In Proc. American Association for Artificial Intelligence, AAAI-86, August 1986.* Philadelphia, PA, US.
13. Barletta, R. & Mark, W.,(1988). Explanation-Based Indexing of Cases.In DARPA'88 Proceeding , see Kolodner J.L.,(Ed.) 1988.
14 Marir, F., & Watson, I.D. (1995b). Can CBR imitate human intelligence and are such systems easy to design and *maintain? A critique.* Proceedings of the First UK CBR Workshop, 12th January at the University of Salford. (Ed. Watson I.D., F. Marir & Perera S.)
15. Lebowitz, M., (1987). Experimental with incremental concept formation: UNIMEM. *Machine Learning, 2(ii): pp 103-38.*
16 Navichandra, D. (1991). Exploration and innovation in design:towards a computational model. Springer Verlag, New York. NY, US.
17 Maher, M.L. & Zhang, D.M. (1991). CADSYN: using case and decomposition knowledge for design synthesis. In *Artificial Intelligence in Design*, Gero, J.S. (ed.), Butterworth-Heinmann. Oxford. UK
18 Domeshek, E., (1993). A case study of case indexing: Designing index feature sets to suit task demands and support parallelism. In, Advances in connectionnist and neural computation theory, Vol.2: Analogical connections, eds. J. Barenden and K. Holyoak, Norwood, NJ. US.
19 Smyth, B., & Keane M.T., [1993]. Retyrieving Adaptable Knowledge in Case Retriieval. EWCBR-93, 1st Worksop on CBR, Vol2 , 1-5Nov. 93, Germany

PROOF RUNNING TWO STATE-OF-THE-ART PATTERN RECOGNITION TECHNIQUES IN THE FIELD OF DIRECT MARKETING

Stijn Viaene*, Bart Baesens, Guido Dedene & Jan Vanthienen
Department of Applied Economic Sciences, K.U.Leuven
Naamsestraat 69, B-3000 Leuven, Belgium
{stijn.viaene;bart.baesens;guido.dedene;jan.vanthienen}@econ.kuleuven.ac.be

Dirk Van den Poel
Department of Marketing, Ghent University
Hoveniersberg 24, B-9000 Ghent, Belgium
dirk.vandenpoel@rug.ac.be

Key words: Direct marketing, Customer scoring, Repeat purchase, Purchase incidence, RFM analysis, Multilayer perceptron (MLP), Bayesian learning, Evidence Framework, Least squares support vector machine (LS-SVM).

Abstract: In this paper, we synthesize the main findings of three repeat purchase modelling case studies using real-life direct marketing data. Historically, direct marketing — more recently, targeted web marketing — has been one of the most popular domains for the exploration of the feasibility and the viable use of novel business intelligence techniques. Many a data mining technique has been field tested in the direct marketing domain. This can be explained by the (relatively) low-cost availability of recency, frequency, monetary (RFM) and several other customer relationship data, the (relatively) well-developed understanding of the task and the domain, the clearly identifiable costs and benefits, and because the results can often be readily applied to obtain a high return on investment. The purchase incidence modelling cases reported on in this paper were in the first place undertaken to trial run state-of-the-art supervised Bayesian learning multilayer perceptron (MLP) and least squares support vector machine (LS-SVM) classifiers. For each of the cases, we also aimed at exploring the explanatory power (relevance) of the available RFM and other customer relationship related variable operationalizations for predicting purchase incidence in the context of direct marketing.

1 INTRODUCTION

Successful customer profiling is clearly of the utmost importance to business in this era of information and communication technology. Opportunities must be seized before the competition does. Therefore, optimal use of all available customer data should be strived for. Questions like *Which customers contribute most to profitability? Which new customers are worth approaching? (customer acquisition) Which customers are worth retaining? (customer retention) What are the principal drivers of customer satisfaction and loyalty? Which market segment provides the greatest possibility for cross-selling, bundling and up-selling? (customer efficiency)* are among the most profound issues driving current marketing research. Using data exploration and modelling techniques to effectively profile likely future customers proves essential for targeting the *right*, i.e. cost/benefit-wise interesting, customers.

Conventional business wisdom now holds that, typically, only a small percentage of the customer base accounts for the major part of the profits (Berry and Linoff, 2000; Cooper and Kaplan, 1991; Juran, 2001). This rationale was coined into the famous Pareto Principle (also known as the 20:80 rule), according to which 20% of the customers make up for 80% of the sales volume. The principle was named after economist Vilfredo Pareto (1848-1923). Dr. Juran formulated the Pareto Principle after expanding on the work of Pareto (Juran, 2001). Of course, the exact numbers are not all that important. For company A, the rule may actually be something like 30:60, whereas for company B, it may well be 25:75, or similar. It may even morph into the 20:225 rule suggested by Cooper and Kaplan in their 1991 Harvard Business Review Article (Cooper and Kaplan, 1991): "A 20 - 225 rule was actually operating: 20% of customers were generating 225% of profits. The middle 70% of customers were hovering around the break-even point, and 10% of customers were losing 125% of profits." The gist: try to appeal to and accordingly spend money on targeting only those customers that

*Stijn Viaene is currently holder of the KBC Insurance Research Chair at the Leuven Institute for Research on Information Systems (LIRIS), Department of Applied Economic Sciences, K.U.Leuven.

are really worth it. Nowadays, prospecting campaigns (database marketing) still often use very expensive advertising or other broadcast media. The idea underlying customer relationship management (CRM) applications (enabled by e.g. response modelling, campaign management, sales force automation, on-line analytical processing, data mining) is to help us identify and cost-effectively target only those customers belonging to the high revenue segment.

Customer scoring methods, that assign a score to each customer proportional to his/her intrinsic value or likelihood of (re-)purchase, underly prioritized target customer lists. Success of a campaign essentially relies on the quality of the target list (+ scoring technique) and on the effectiveness/efficiency of subsequent targeting of only the best customers. In the process of generating the target list, we may also hope to gain a better understanding of prospective and existing customers and discover the best marketing strategy. Predicted *lift* charts (or *cumulative gains charts*), listing the cumulative percentage of responders recovered in the high-end quantile of the model-score-ordered target list, and *receiver operating characteristic (ROC) curves* are standard and widely used tools for visualizing the relative performance of these customer scoring methods (Berry and Linoff, 2000; Piatetsky-Shapiro and Steingold, 2000; Provost and Fawcett, 2001).

For mail-order response modelling, several alternative problem formulations have been proposed in the literature based on the choice of the dependent variable. One of the most prominent is the purchase incidence problem formulation (Berry and Linoff, 2000; Bult, 1993; Nash, 1994; Van den Poel, 1999). Here, the main question is whether a customer will repurchase during the next mailing period, i.e. one tries to predict the purchase incidence within a next, fixed time interval (typically half a year) based on a given (historical) set of labelled training instances. The three sets of predictors most often used for this kind of response modelling are recency, frequency and monetary (RFM). RFM analysis has a long history and a good track record in the direct marketing industry (Bauer, 1988; Berry and Linoff, 2000; Cullinan, 1977; Kestnbaum, 1992; Van den Poel, 1999). The focus is on customer retention, i.e. repeat purchase, rather than on customer acquisition.

In this paper, we synthesize the main findings of three direct-mail purchase incidence modelling case studies using real-life direct marketing data obtained from a Belgian mail-order company. We report on the use of quite novel supervised (neural) learning techniques, i.c. Bayesian learning multilayer perceptron (MLP) classifiers based on MacKay's Evidence Framework (Bishop, 1995; MacKay, 1992) and least squares support vector machine (LS-SVM) classifiers (Suykens and Vandewalle, 1999; Suykens et al., 1999; Van Gestel et al., 2000), least squares variants of Vapnik's support vector machine (SVM) classifiers (Vapnik, 1998). The purchase incidence modelling case studies at hand presented the ideal occasion to trial run these state-of-the-art pattern recognition techniques on real-life direct marketing data. The work covered in this paper is the result of a close cooperation between the KBC Insurance Research Chair at K.U.Leuven (Belgium), the Department of Applied Economic Sciences at K.U.Leuven, the Department of Marketing at Ghent University (Belgium), and the SISTA (Signals, Identification, System Theory and Automation) research division of the Department of Electrical Engineering at K.U.Leuven (Belgium).

The paper is organized as follows. In what follows, a separate section is devoted to each of the three case studies. We retrospectively look at three case studies that were conducted sequentially in time. Each of the Sections 2-4 contains an extended abstract covering the essentials (i.e. the setting, the data, the experiment, the results and the conclusions) of the corresponding case study. Since this paper is intended as a synthesizing document, we cannot possibly go into all the details of the cases nor of the algorithms. In the text, we therefore consistently refer to more lengthy transcripts of the case studies and algorithm discussion for those seeking more detail. In Section 5, we sum up the discussion and formulate our main conclusions.

2 CASE STUDY 1

In this study, we tried to validate existing theory on and develop additional insight into mail-order repeat purchase behavior based on a meticulously collected data sample of 1,200 Belgian customer records (Van den Poel, 1999). For each customer, we had information on the past purchasing behavior at the order-line level, i.e. we knew when a customer purchased what quantity of a particular product at which price as part of what order. The input variables were measured for the period between July 1st 1993 and June 30th 1997. The goal was then to predict whether an existing customer would repurchase in the observation period between July 1st 1997 and December 31st 1997 using the information provided by the purchase behavior variables. Approximately 38% of the records represented actual buyers. The data set in this first study was limited to several alternative operationalizations of RFM predictor categories. This choice of predictors was mainly motivated by the fact that most previous research cites them as being most predictive and because they are internally available at very low cost (Bauer, 1988; Bult and Wansbeek, 1995; Van den Poel, 1999).

Traditional statistical techniques that have been widely used for response modelling purposes are logistic regression, linear and quadratic discriminant analysis. Their predetermined functional form and restrictive (often unfounded) model assumptions, however, may limit their modelling power (Bishop, 1995). This is especially true in situations where one is confronted with a lack of domain knowledge which prevents any valid argumentation to be made concerning an appropriate model selection bias on the basis of prior domain knowledge. MLPs have shown to be very promising supervised learning tools for modelling non-linear relationships; see e.g. (Chang et al., 1996; Desai et al., 1996; Lacher et al., 1995; Mobley et al., 2000; Piramuthu, 1999; Salchenberger et al., 1997; Sharda and Wilson, 1996). In this first case study, we opted for a (least squares) Bayesian learning implementation for MLPs (based on Mackay's Evidence Framework) as our baseline modelling technique (Bishop, 1995; MacKay, 1992).

Even though the modelling flexibility of MLPs makes them a very attractive and interesting alternative for pattern recognition purposes, unfortunately, many practical problems still remain when implementing MLPs, e.g. *How to choose the appropriate number of hidden neurons? What is the impact of the initial weight choice? How to set the weight decay parameter? How to avoid the network from fitting noise in the training data?* These issues are often dealt with in an ad-hoc way (Berry and Linoff, 2000). Nevertheless, they are crucial to the success of the MLP implementation. The Bayesian learning paradigm has been suggested as a way to deal with these problems during MLP training in a principled, i.e. Bayesian, rather than an ad-hoc fashion (Bishop, 1995; MacKay, 1992). Performance of the trained classifiers was measured in terms of mean percentage correctly classified (PCC) and mean area under the receiver operating characteristic curve (AUROC) for a 10-fold cross validation (10cv) experiment. AUROC results allowed us to assess the behavior of a classifier without regard to class distribution or error cost, so it effectively decouples classification performance from these factors (Egan, 1975; Swets and Pickett, 1982).

The case study also involved the detection and qualification of the most important RFM inputs for the purchase incidence setting at hand. As argued in (Van den Poel, 1999), this had never been thoroughly investigated, let alone in the context of connectionist modelling. Bass and Wind (Bass and Wind, 1995) cite the confidentiality of the data, resulting from the high business value of information in this area, as one of the major obstacles to the disclosure of this information for research purposes. A compact, yet highly accurate model may well come in very handy in (on-line) customer profiling systems. Furthermore, by reducing the number of inputs, both human understanding and computational performance can often be vastly enhanced. The input selection experiment we ran, was based on a step-wise, sensitivity-based[1] input pruning method designed to make use of the combined information from the 10cv set-up at each stage of the pruning process.

Table 1: Full Model & Reduced Model MLP classification performance for case study 1.

Results (10cv)	Full Model	Reduced Model
PCC Training	74.03%	73.30%
AUROC Training	78.14%	77.25%
PCC Test	71.33%	71.83%
AUROC Test	73.72%	74.68%
Number of Inputs	18	6

Results have been summarized in Table 1, covering the predictive performance of the MLP models, and Table 2, covering the order of input removal from the initial data set for the conducted input pruning experiment. The models trained on the initial data set with all available input variables are termed *Full Model*, whereas the models trained on the pruned input data are termed *Reduced Model*. For a good understanding of Table 2, variables starting with *Rec* are recency variables, with *Fr* are frequency variables, and with *Mon* are monetary variables. The last 6 inputs (underlined) were the ones retained in the reduced response model after input selection. The results indicate that elimination of redundant and/or irrelevant inputs from the initial data set (18 inputs) by means of the discussed input selection method allowed for a significant reduction of model complexity without degrading the predictive generalization ability. Furthermore, the empirical findings highlight the importance of a combined use of RFM variables for predicting repeat purchase behavior. Nevertheless, the frequency variables seem to play a dominant role. A model including only (the 4 most important) frequency variables still yielded satisfactory classification accuracy compared to the optimally reduced model. The interested reader is referred to the discussion in (Viaene et al., 2001a) for further details.

[1]In casu, the importance of an input was assessed by uniformly perturbing the input column to its mean value and assessing the impact of this operation on model performance.

Table 2: Order of input removal for the input pruning experiment in case study 1. Each input is qualified by its category with r, f, m standing for recency, frequency, monetary, respectively.

Pruning Steps					
1-6		7-12		13-18	
FrHistNoRetOrderlines	f	ln(MonMaxNoRet)	m	MonAvgNoRet	m
Recency	r	MonMaxNoRet	m	ln(Recency)	r
FrHistReturnsDiffOrders	f	MonHistNoRet	m	FrYearReturnsOrderlines	f
FrHistReturnsOrderlines	f	FrYearNoRetDiffOrders	f	FrYearReturnsDiffOrders	f
ln(MonHistNoRet)	m	ln(MonAvgNoRet)	m	FrYearNoRetOrderlines	f
MonYearNoRet	m	ln(MonYearNoRet)	m	FrHistNoRetDiffOrders	f

3 CASE STUDY 2

In this study, the binary — buyer vs. non-buyer — repeat purchase classification problem was tackled by using least squares support vector machine (LS-SVM) classifiers. LS-SVMs have only recently been introduced in the pattern recognition literature by Suykens et al. (Suykens and Vandewalle, 1999; Suykens et al., 1999). Excellent benchmark results have been reported in (Van Gestel et al., 2000). For this study, we obtained Belgian data on past customer purchasing behavior at the order-line level from the same mail-order company that provided the data for case study 1; this time, for a total sample size of 5,000 customers, of which approximatively 38% buyers. As for the previous study, we derived all the purchase behavior variables for each customer in the period between July 1st 1993 and June 30th 1997. Again, the goal was to predict whether an existing customer would repurchase in the observation period between July 1st 1997 and December 31st 1997.

The case study extends beyond the standard RFM modelling semantics in two ways: a) by including alternative operationalizations of the RFM variables, and b) by adding several other non-RFM customer relationship predictors.

Table 3: Full Model classification performance of RBF kernel LS-SVM vs. LS-SVM optimized using a linear kernel for case study 2.

Results (PCC) (Full Model)	LS-SVM RBF kernel	LS-SVM Linear kernel
Training (3,750 obs.)	77.54%	76.26%
Test (1,250 obs.)	74.48%	73.76%

Having constructed an LS-SVM classifier on all available predictors, we, just as in case study 1, engaged in an input selection experiment. A step-wise, sensitivity-based input pruning method, constructed as a wrapper (John et al., 1994) around the LS-SVM classifier, allowed for the elimination of several redundant and/or irrelevant inputs and resulted in a significant reduction of model complexity without degrading predictive performance compared to the model trained on the full input set. The results have been summarized in Tables 3 and 4, covering the predictive performance of the fitted LS-SVM models, and Table 5, covering the order of input removal from the initial (full) predictor set (25 inputs) for the conducted input pruning experiment. The last 9 inputs (underlined) were the ones retained in the reduced response model after input selection.

Table 4: Full Model & Reduced Model LS-SVM classification performance for case study 2.

Results (PCC)	Full Model	Reduced Model
Training (2,500 obs.)	77.36%	76.04%
Pruning (1,250 obs.)	76.72%	77.20%
Test (1,250 obs.)	73.92%	73.52%
Number of Inputs	25	9

The empirical findings highlighted the importance of frequency and monetary variables, while the recency variable category seemed to be of somewhat lesser importance to the case at hand. Results also pointed to the added value of considering non-RFM variables for improving customer scoring. More specifically, customer/company interaction, measured by indicators of information requests and complaints, and merchandize returns provided additional predictive power to purchase incidence modelling for database marketing. The interested reader is referred to the discussion in (Viaene et al., 2001b) for further details.

Table 5: Order of input removal for the input pruning experiment in case study 2. Each input is qualified by its category with r, f, m and o standing for recency, frequency, monetary and other CRM-related information, respectively.

Pruning Steps									
1-5		6-10		11-15		16-20		21-25	
RetPerc	o	ProdclaM	o	RecHistN	r	FrYearN	f	MonYearR	m
ln(MonHistN)	m	MonHistR	m	IncrHist	o	ln(MonHistR)	m	MonYearN	m
RecHistR	r	IncrYear	o	RecYearR	r	MonHistN	m	GenInfo	o
Ndays	o	ln(MonYearR)	m	RecYearN	r	GenCust	o	FrHistR	f
ProdclaT	o	ln(MonYearN)	m	FrHistN	f	RetMerch	o	FrYearR	f

4 CASE STUDY 3

In this study, we again made use of Bayesian learning MLPs for our response modelling assignment. This time, however, we disposed of a much larger data set (again obtained from our Belgian mail-order company) in terms of the number of data instances. We obtained a sample of 100,000 customers of European origin, of which approximatively 55% represented buyers (i.e. an approximately class-balanced data set). Here too, we started from order-line level customer data, derived all the necessary purchase behavior variables for each customer in the period between July 1st 1993 and June 30th 1997, and aimed at predicting whether an existing customer would repurchase in the observation period between July 1st 1997 and December 31st 1997.

Bayesian learning of the MLPs was implemented according to the Evidence Framework for classification presented by MacKay in (MacKay, 1992).[2] The predictive performance of response models (PCC and AUROC) based on fitting logistic regression, linear discriminant analysis, quadratic discriminant analysis and Bayesian learning MLPs was contrasted. Novel is the use of the Automatic Relevance Determination (ARD) scheme for predictor relevance assessment. ARD was readily integrated into MacKay's Evidence Framework for classification implementation of Bayesian learning (MacKay, 1994; Neal, 1998). This scheme essentially allowed us to open the neural network black box and have a look at its mechanics. ARD of input variables determines the relative importance of input variables to the trained MLP for predicting the outcome by simple inspection of the (optimized) input-dependent weight regularization parameters of the MLP objective function, i.e. regularized cross-entropy. We thus were capable of rank ordering the predictors according to their relative importance to the trained MLP. The ARD regularization scheme also proved to effectively counter overfitting to the training data. A further advantage of ARD, documented in the literature, is that it allows for the inclusion of a large number of *potentially relevant* input variables in the MLP model without damaging effects (MacKay, 1994; Neal, 1998).

The basic response models (*basic RFM experiment*) used operationalizations of the standard recency, frequency and monetary (RFM) predictor categories. In a second experiment (*extended RFM experiment*), the basic RFM response framework was enriched by the inclusion of other (non-RFM) customer profiling predictors. By means of experimental evaluation, we illustrated that, from a performance perspective (PCC and AUROC), Bayesian learning MLPs offer an interesting and viable alternative for purchase incidence modelling. The results have been summarized in Tables 6 and 7, covering the predictive performance of the constructed classifiers in terms of PCC and AUROC.

The ARD results advocated a combined use of all three RFM predictor categories for response modelling. Also, as illustrated by the second experiment, the inclusion of non-RFM variables proved to further augment the predictive power of the constructed classifiers. The ARD results mainly attributed this rise to the inclusion of customer/company interaction variables and to a variable measuring whether a customer used the credit facilities of the direct mail company. The main results of the ARD predictor importance assessment were summarized in Figures 1 and 2. These plots were constructed as follows. For each experiment (basic and extended), we created a matrix R with elements $R(i,j)$ indicating how many times input variable i was ranked at the jth position according to the ARD semantics (with the variable assigned

[2] There is a subtle difference between the implementation of Bayesian MLP learning used for case study 1 and the implementation used for case study 3: in case study 1, we used a regularized least squares objective function, whereas in case study 3, we made use of a regularized cross-entropy objective function, which theoretically is superior for classification purposes. In practice, i.c. tested for the case studies at hand, the difference in terms of predictive performance between both implementations proved to be negligible.

Table 6: Performance assessment (mean & standard deviation) over 10 runs of the algorithms, i.e. each time using a different bootstrap resample of the data (1/2 training;1/2 test), for the basic RFM experiment in case study 3.

	PCC		AUROC	
	Training	*Test*	*Training*	*Test*
logistic regression	70.3 ± 0.1	70.3 ± 0.2	77.5 ± 0.1	77.4 ± 0.2
linear discriminant analysis	68.9 ± 0.1	68.9 ± 0.2	76.0 ± 0.1	75.9 ± 0.2
quadratic discriminant analysis	63.6 ± 0.4	63.2 ± 0.4	74.4 ± 0.2	74.3 ± 0.2
MLP 2 hidden neurons	71.2 ± 0.1	71.2 ± 0.1	78.5 ± 0.1	78.4 ± 0.2
MLP 4 hidden neurons	71.3 ± 0.2	71.2 ± 0.1	78.8 ± 0.2	78.5 ± 0.2
MLP 6 hidden neurons	71.4 ± 0.2	71.3 ± 0.2	78.9 ± 0.2	78.6 ± 0.2
MLP 8 hidden neurons	71.4 ± 0.2	71.3 ± 0.2	78.9 ± 0.2	78.6 ± 0.2
MLP 10 hidden neurons	71.4 ± 0.2	71.3 ± 0.1	78.9 ± 0.2	78.6 ± 0.2
MLP 12 hidden neurons	71.4 ± 0.2	71.3 ± 0.1	78.9 ± 0.2	78.6 ± 0.2
MLP 14 hidden neurons	71.4 ± 0.2	71.3 ± 0.1	78.9 ± 0.2	78.6 ± 0.2
MLP ARD 6 hidden neurons	71.4 ± 0.2	71.2 ± 0.1	78.7 ± 0.2	78.5 ± 0.2

Table 7: Performance assessment (mean & standard deviation) over 10 runs of the algorithms, i.e. each time using a different bootstrap resample of the data (1/2 training;1/2 test), for the extended RFM experiment in case study 3.

	PCC		AUROC	
	Training	*Test*	*Training*	*Test*
logistic regression	71.4 ± 0.2	71.4 ± 0.2	78.7 ± 0.2	78.6 ± 0.2
linear discriminant analysis	69.7 ± 0.2	69.7 ± 0.2	76.9 ± 0.2	76.8 ± 0.2
quadratic discriminant analysis	65.0 ± 0.8	64.9 ± 0.7	73.3 ± 1.2	73.2 ± 1.2
MLP 2 hidden neurons	72.3 ± 0.3	72.2 ± 0.2	79.7 ± 0.2	79.5 ± 0.2
MLP 4 hidden neurons	72.5 ± 0.2	72.4 ± 0.2	80.0 ± 0.2	79.7 ± 0.2
MLP 6 hidden neurons	72.6 ± 0.3	72.3 ± 0.2	80.2 ± 0.2	79.7 ± 0.2
MLP 8 hidden neurons	72.8 ± 0.3	72.4 ± 0.2	80.4 ± 0.2	79.8 ± 0.2
MLP 10 hidden neurons	72.8 ± 0.3	72.4 ± 0.2	80.4 ± 0.2	79.8 ± 0.2
MLP 12 hidden neurons	72.8 ± 0.3	72.4 ± 0.2	80.4 ± 0.2	79.8 ± 0.2
MLP 14 hidden neurons	72.8 ± 0.3	72.4 ± 0.2	80.4 ± 0.2	79.8 ± 0.2
MLP ARD 8 hidden neurons	72.5 ± 0.3	72.4 ± 0.3	80.0 ± 0.3	79.7 ± 0.2

Figure 1: Basic RFM experiment (case study 3): Contour plot of matrix R, with elements $R(i,j)$ indicating how many times input variable i was ranked at the jth position according to the ARD semantics (with the variable assigned rank 1 being the most important) aggregated over 10 alternative runs of the algorithm, i.e. each time using a different bootstrap resample of the data (1/2 training;1/2 test).

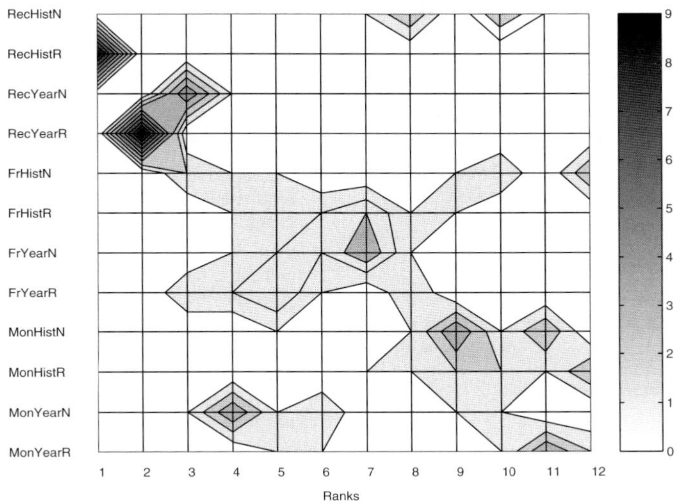

Figure 2: Extended RFM experiment (case study 3): Contour plot of matrix R, with elements $R(i,j)$ indicating how many times input variable i was ranked at the jth position according to the ARD semantics (with the variable assigned rank 1 being the most important) aggregated over 10 alternative runs of the algorithm, i.e. each time using a different bootstrap resample of the data (1/2 training;1/2 test).

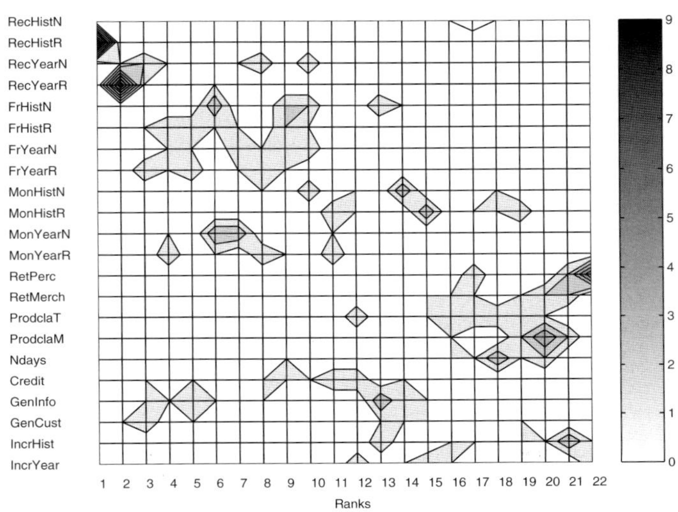

rank 1 being the most important) aggregated over 10 alternative runs of the algorithms, i.e. each time using a different bootstrap resample of the data (1/2 training;1/2 test). We visualized the matrix R in the form of the contour plots presented in Figure 1, for the basic RFM experiment, and in Figure 2, for the extended RFM experiment. Illustrative of the semantics of the plots is the dark zone in the contour plot for the basic experiment at the intersection of rank 1 and the RecHistR variable which clearly points towards that variable's importance. The interested reader is referred to the discussion in (Baesens et al., 2002) for further details. In summary, with this study, we contributed to the literature by providing experimental evidence that: a) Bayesian learning MLPs offer a viable alternative for purchase incidence modelling; b) a combined use of all three RFM predictor categories is advocated by the ARD method; c) the inclusion of non-RFM variables allows to significantly augment the predictive power of the constructed RFM classifiers; d) this rise is mainly attributed to the inclusion of customer/company interaction variables and a variable measuring whether a customer uses the credit facilities of the direct mailing company.

5 CONCLUSION

In this paper, we synthesized the main findings of three exploratory purchase incidence modelling cases using real-life Belgian direct marketing data. The synthesis constitutes a retrospective summary of three cases that were conducted sequentially in time. The cases in the first place allowed us to trial run and assess the predictive capabilities of Bayesian learning multilayer perceptron (MLP) and least squares support vector machine (LS-SVM) classifiers on available real-life mail-order data.

The cases provided us with the necessary evidence that both pattern recognition techniques offer an interesting and viable alternative to more traditional (statistical) techniques like linear and quadratic discriminant analysis and logistic regression. However, we should point out that, for all three the cases, the predictive abilities of a simple (regularized) logistic regression were only slightly inferior to those of the state-of-the-art machine learning algorithms in terms of PCC and AUROC. This definitely provides evidence to the thesis that the underlying functional relationship in the researched data sets is *close to* linear.[3] Nevertheless, as argumented and illustrated in (Baesens et al., 2002), the substantive relevance of response modelling comes from the fact that an increase in response of only one percentage point can result in substantial profit increases.

For each of the cases, we also aimed at exploring the explanatory power (relevance) of the available RFM and other CRM-related variable operationalizations for predicting purchase incidence in the context of mail-order direct marketing. When comparing the results of the case studies (i.e. based on three data sets with similar semantics obtained from the same anonymous Belgian mail-order company), we observe that they all highlight:

1. the importance of a combined use of all three RFM predictor categories for predicting mail-order repeat purchase behavior;
2. the performance gains by including non-RFM variables into the response models, e.g. variables characterizing customer/company interaction.

However, there is some disagreement between the cases on the relative importance of some of the RFM and non-RFM variables. These differences may be due to a.o. different data sets covering different customer populations, resulting in a.o. diverging class proportions (i.e., approximately 38% buyers in (Viaene et al., 2001a; Viaene et al., 2001b) compared to approximately 55% buyers in (Baesens et al., 2002)); the inclusion of different predictors and/or alternative transformations; the use of alternative classification techniques and input selection heuristics (e.g. *hard* step-wise, sensitivity-based pruning in (Viaene et al., 2001a; Viaene et al., 2001b) vs. *soft* input ranking in (Baesens et al., 2002)).

[3] Remarkably enough, this observation was also made for most of the UCI (http://www.ics.uci.edu/~mlearn/MLRepository.htm) classification data sets benchmarked in (Van Gestel et al., 2000).

ACKNOWLEDGEMENT

This work was sponsored by the KBC Insurance Research Chair, a pioneering co-operation between the Leuven Institute for Research on Information Systems (LIRIS), Department of Applied Economic Sciences, K.U.Leuven and KBC Bank & Insurance (http://www.kbc.be).

REFERENCES

Baesens, B., Viaene, S., Van den Poel, D., Vanthienen, J., and Dedene, G. (2002). Bayesian neural network learning for repeat purchase modelling in direct marketing. *European Journal of Operational Research*, 138(1):191–211.

Bass, F. and Wind, J. (1995). Introduction to the special issue: Empirical generalisations in marketing. *Marketing Science*, 14(3):G1–G6.

Bauer, A. (1988). A direct mail customer purchase model. *Journal of Direct Marketing*, 2(3):16–24.

Berry, M. and Linoff, G. (2000). *Mastering data mining: the art and science of customer relationship management*. John Wiley & Sons.

Bishop, C. (1995). *Neural networks for pattern recognition*. Oxford University Press.

Bult, J. (1993). *Target selection for direct marketing*. PhD thesis, Groningen University, Institute of Economic Research.

Bult, J. and Wansbeek, T. (1995). Optimal selection for direct mail. *Marketing Science*, 14(4):378–394.

Chang, L., Han, I., and Kwon, Y. (1996). Hybrid neural network models for bankruptcy predictions. *Decision Support Systems*, 18(1):63–72.

Cooper, R. and Kaplan, R. (1991). Profit priorities from ABC. *Harvard Business Review*, 69(3):130–135.

Cullinan, G. (1977). *Picking them by their batting averages' recency-frequency-monetary method of controlling circulation*. Manual release 2103. Direct Mail/Marketing Association. N.Y.

Desai, V., Crook, J., and Overstreet Jr., G. (1996). A comparison of neural networks and linear scoring models in the credit union environment. *European Journal of Operational Research*, 95(1):24–37.

Egan, J. (1975). *Signal detection theory and ROC analysis*. Series in Cognition and Perception. Academic Press.

John, G., Kohavi, R., and Pfleger, K. (1994). Irrelevant features and the subset selection problem. In *Eleventh International Conference on Machine Learning*, pages 121–129, New Brunswick.

Juran, J. (2001). The non-pareto principle; mea culpa. Juran Institute.

Kestnbaum, R. (1992). Quantitative database methods. In Nash, E., editor, *The Direct Marketing Handbook*, pages 588–597. McGraw Hill.

Lacher, R., Coats, P., Sharma Shanker, C., and Fant, L. (1995). A neural network for classifying the financial health of a firm. *European Journal of Operational Research*, 85(1):53–65.

MacKay, D. (1992). The evidence framework applied to classification networks. *Neural Computation*, 4(5):720–736.

MacKay, D. (1994). Bayesian non-linear modelling for the prediction competition. In *ASHRAE Transactions V.100, Pt.2*, Atlanta. ASHRAE.

Mobley, B., Schechter, E., Moore, W., McKee, P., and Eichner, J. (2000). Predictions of coronary artery stenosis by artificial neural network. *Artificial Intelligence in Medicine*, 18(3):187–203.

Nash, E. (1994). *Direct marketing: Strategy, planning, execution*. McGraw Hill, third edition.

Neal, R. (1998). Assessing relevance determination methods using Delve. In Bishop, C., editor, *Neural networks and machine learning*, pages 97–129. Springer.

Piatetsky-Shapiro, G. and Steingold, S. (2000). Measuring lift quality in database marketing. *SIGKDD Explorations*, 7(2):81–85.

Piramuthu, S. (1999). Financial credit-risk evaluation with neural and neurofuzzy systems. *European Journal of Operational Research*, 112(2):310–321.

Provost, F. and Fawcett, T. (2001). Robust classification for imprecise environments. *Machine Learning*, 42(3):203–231.

Salchenberger, L., Venta Enrique, R., and Venta Luz, A. (1997). Using neural networks to aid the diagnosis of breast implant rupture. *Computers and Operations Research*, 24(5):435–444.

Sharda, R. and Wilson, R. (1996). Neural network experiments in business failures prediction: A review of predictive performance issues. *International Journal of Computational Intelligence and Organizations*, 1(2):107–117.

Suykens, J., Lukas, L., Van Dooren, P., De Moor, B., and Vandewalle, J. (1999). Least squares support vector machine classifiers: A large scale algorithm. In *European Conference on Circuits Theory and Design*, Stresa.

Suykens, J. and Vandewalle, J. (1999). Least squares support vector machine classifiers. *Neural Processing Letters*, 9(3):293–300.

Swets, J. and Pickett, R. (1982). *Evaluation of diagnostic systems: Methods from signal detection theory*. Academic Press.

Van den Poel, D. (1999). *Response modeling for database marketing using binary classification*. PhD thesis, K.U.Leuven, Department of Applied Economic Sciences.

Van Gestel, T., Suykens, J., Baesens, B., Viaene, S., Vanthienen, J., Dedene, G., De Moor, B., and Vandewalle, J. (2000). Benchmarking least squares support vector machine classifiers. Technical Report 00-37, ESAT-SISTA, K.U.Leuven, Leuven.

Vapnik, V. (1998). *Statistical learning theory*. John Wiley & Sons.

Viaene, S., Baesens, B., Van den Poel, D., Dedene, G., and Vanthienen, J. (2001a). Wrapped input selection using multilayer perceptrons for repeat-purchase modeling in direct marketing. *International Journal of Intelligent Systems in Accounting, Finance and Management*, 10(2):115–126.

Viaene, S., Baesens, B., Van Gestel, T., Suykens, J., Van den Poel, D., Vanthienen, J., De Moor, B., and Dedene, G. (2001b). Knowledge discovery in a direct marketing case using least squares support vector machines. *International Journal of Intelligent Systems*, 16(9):1023–1036.

SIMPLE DECISION SUPPORT SYSTEM BASED ON FUZZY REPERTORY TABLE

J.J. Castro-Schez, L. Jimenez
Dpto Informatica, Escuela Superior de Informatica de Ciudad Real, Universidad de Castilla-La Mancha
Paseo de la Universidad, 4, 13071 Ciudad Real, Spain
{jjcastro,ljimenez}@inf-cr.uclm.es

J. Moreno
Dpto. Informatica, Escuela Universitaria de Ingenieria Industrial de Toledo, Universidad de Castilla-La Mancha
Avd. Carlos III, s/n, 45004 Toledo, Spain
jmgarcia@iti-to.uclm.es

L. Rodriguez
Dpto. Informatica, Escuela Universitaria Politecnica de Almaden, Universidad de Castilla-La Mancha
Plaza Manuel Meca, 1, 13400, Almaden, Ciudad Real, Spain
lrbenitez@pol-al.uclm.es

Key words: Fuzzy repertory table, repertory grid, decision support systems, Knowledge driven decision support systems.

Abstract: This paper shows how *fuzzy repertory table technique* (Castro et al., 2001) can be used as a simple decision support system for helping to a manager of a company when he is faced with a choice in which the options are clear (for instance, the choice of a suppliers from among all existing suppliers, or the choice of sell one product from among all existing posiblities). The manager must analyse each option making use of his knowledge, with the aim to highlight its characteristic qualities which are admirable in themselves or useful for our purpose and also its defective qualities. Next, the manager choices the more advantageous opcion according to this information. When the possible options are clear, the analysis implies make comparisons among the several options. Thus, the manager find out the characteristic and defective qualities associated to each option. With the suggested method in this paper, we identity the relevant information (characteristic and defective) associated to each option and recommend one option according to this information.

1 INTRODUCTION

Decision Support Systems (DSS) are being advocated, built and deployed in an increasing array of complex application domains. They are very useful when there are loads of information available for be processed by decision maker's intuition and the answer precision and optimality are of importance. According to *Druzdzel et al.* (Druzdzel and Flynn, 2000) *"DSS can aid human cognitive deficiencies by integrating various sources of information, providing intelligent access to relevant knowledge, and aiding the process of structuring decisions. They can also support choice among well-defined alternatives ... They can also employ artificial intelligence methods to address heuristically problems that are intractable by formal techniques"*. Thus, DSS can be defined as information systems developed for informing and supporting manager when he takes a decision.

A wide range of DSS have been developed, which vary in many ways. In the literature about this topic, we can find a number of frameworks for categorizing such systems (Alter, 1980; Holsapple and Whinston, 1996; Dhara and Stein, 1997; Power, 2001). In accordance with them, the principal DSS categories are data-oriented or data-driven, model-oriented or model-driven and intelligent or knowledge driven DSS. Data-driven DSS focus on data, they access and process large databases of structured data (some example are file drawer and management reporting systems, data warehousing and analysis systems). Model-driven DSS emphasize on access to and manipulation of a model (some examples includes systems that use accounting and financial models, representational models, and optimization models). Finally, Knowledge-driven DSS focus on the dominant knowledge base component (for instance, management expert systems). The Knowledge-driven DSS are systems based on expert systems technologies.

DSS are a research topic share for many disciplines, such as statistics, economics, information science, cognitive psychology, and artificial intelligence. In this paper, we combining ideas from cognitive psychology and artificial intelligence for develop a knowledge-driven DSS.

The developed DSS will be useful for helping to a decision-maker when he is faced with a choice in which the options are clear. The suggested method facilitates the identification of the significant characteristics associated to each option. The method adapts a technique from knowledge acquisition field where the fuzzy repertory table (FRT) approach has been used to identify input variables for machine learning algorithms (Castro et al., 2001) and to acquire domain knowledge for negotiations agents based on fuzzy constraints (Castro-Schez et al., 2001).

The fuzzy repertory grid is a technique that is based on the repertory grid technique which has already used as DSS (Boose, 1989). Nevertheless, this approach had some limitations that we resolve with the FRT.

The remainder of this paper is structured in the following manner. Section 2 justifies and describes our choice of the fuzzy repertory table as a tool useful for support decisions. Section 3 shows the fuzzy repertory table performance when it acts as a DSS. Finally, section 4 concludes and outlines the avenues of future research.

2 FUZZY REPERTORY TABLE, A METHOD FOR ACQUIRING SIGNIFICANT CHARACTERISTICS

We could apply many manual and automatic methodologies for identifying the significant characteristics associated to each option, some of them are card or concept sorting (McDonald et al., 1986; Schreiber et al., 2000), laddered grid (Schreiber et al., 2000),(Shadbolt and Burton, 1989), interviewing (Evans, 1988; Gammack and Young, 1985; Graessar and Gordon, 1991; Schreiber et al., 2000)... We suggest the fuzzy repertory table technique as a good method for do it. Next, we give some reasons that justify such decision:

Generic reasons

- It has a solid foundation in human psychological theory.
- It represents in a reliable way the repertoire of constructions (or attributes) that the individual use based in his personal experience in the field.
- It has demonstrated useful in eliciting and acquiring knowledge from people.
- It is easy to formalize or implement.
- The method is incremental.
- It is dynamic, because it makes instantaneous analysis on data just introduced.

Specific reasons

- It is intuitive and easy-to-use, decision-makers do not need be computer-trained.
- It is based on a interaction with the decision-maker, helping him to express his knowledge in a freely way.
- It is bases on intuitive human reasoning.
- It supports unaided human intuition,
- It allows provide insight into a decision.

2.1 Background

The FRT is based on the repertory grid technique (RG). The RG is a knowledge acquisition technique devised by clinical psychologist (Kelly, 1955). The principal concepts in RG are: *Elements*, that is, people, things, events or experiences which are related to the particular problem or purpose for using the grid and *Constructs*, that is, dimensions of similarity and differences among elements. The most basic form for a RG is a rectangular matrix with elements as columns and constructs as rows. Each row-column intersection into the grid contains a rating showing how a person applied a given construct to a particular element.

The interaction of the repertory grid with the user can be briefly described as follows (see Figure 1):

Step 1. Identify the set of elements.

Step 2. Repeat the following steps until all triad are done or user stops:

- **Step 2.1.** Identify three elements from the set, which are currently rated similarly on all constructs.
  1. Identify a way in which two are similar and the other different.
  2. Do a rating for all elements on the new construct scale.
- **Step 2.2.** Identify two constructs that are given similar rates for all the entities.
  1. Human user tries to find (and add) a new element, which breaks the similarity.
  2. Do the rating for this new element on all other constructs.
- **Step 2.3.** Go to Step 2.

Step 3. End.

Similarities may occur either for elements or constructs. Two or more elements will be similar if they have similar ratings on many constructs-dimensions. On the other hand, two or more constructs will be similar if they have same ordering of elements, they do not help in discriminating among the elements.

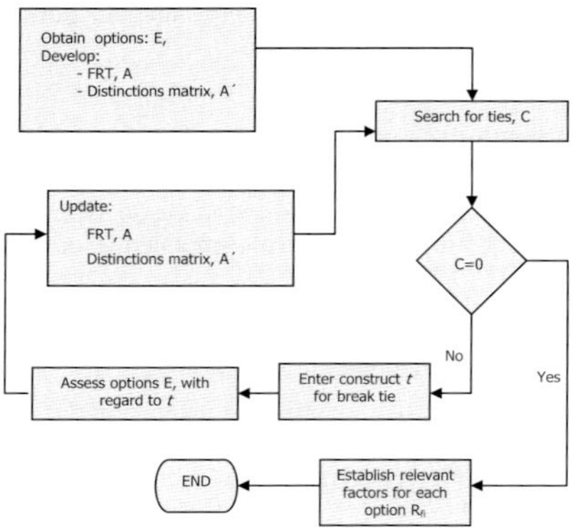

Figure 1: The operation of the RG Algorithm.

There are different distance measures for assess the similarity among elements. In any of these measures used, the lower the distance between two elements, the more similar the elements are deemed to be. Some measures used traditionally are *Euclidean, Manhattan* and *Hamming distances*.

2.2 FRT an useful improvement to RG technique

According to *Boose* (Boose, 1989), the RG interaction with the user can be useful for identifying relevant factors (attributes) associated to each option, and facilitate the decision-maker's work. However, it has some drawbacks, with respect to the types of knowledge that it can process, that hinder its capacity of be used as DSS.

Since that there is a reciprocal influence of the technique and the decision-maker, the obtained attributes plus its definition domains (rating used for each input variable) must be understood by the decision-maker. For facilitating it, we suggest that the decision-maker has license to express his knowledge as he usually expresses oneself. In order to achieve this, we have to improve the RG, because the available RG have the following limitations:

- *Classic* or *Kelly's repertory grid* (Kelly, 1955), which works with bipolar distinctions, does not allow represent attributes that take intermediate states between left and right distinctions poles.
- *Extended classic repertory grid*, which works with values chosen from a predefined rating scale, requires that decision-maker rate each element accurately, that is, he must make crisp distinctions. However, in the decision-maker's mind there is vagueness.
- *Bathia's approach* (Bhatia and Yao, 1993) treats vagueness allowing to decision-maker enter a range of ratings rather than a crisp value.
- *Gaines' approach* (Gaines and Shaw, 1980) makes use of the concept of fuzzy set for representing each construct pole. To assign a rate to construct is considered as give degree of belonging to the fuzzy set that defines each construct pole.
- *Ford's approach* (Ford et al., 1991) obtains uncertainty expressed as rules but it works with values chosen from a predefined rating scale.
- *Hwang's approach, the fuzzy table* (Hwang, 1995) allows introduce linguistic labels, this table adapts the grid for treating fuzzy logic expressed by means of linguistic values. This is very usual when decision-maker expresses his vague knowledge.

In this way, Hwang's fuzzy table is the most appropriate for describing and manipulating linguistic information, frequently used by the user. Nevertheless, a RG that only takes into consideration fuzzy values does not seem to be appropriate for our purpose of allowing to decision-maker expresses himself freely, because not everything in the user mind is vague. We need a technique that allows acquire vague and crisp values.

FRT suggested in (Castro et al., 2001) solves these limitations (see Figure 4). It allows represent all values (crisp and vague) that a decision-maker uses when he takes a decision and these are ordered-discrete or ordinal, unordered-discrete or nominal, boolean, ranking and continuous. All values are represented as fuzzy with a membership function, and the similarity between elements is assessed by means of a measurement that calculates the area existing between two fuzzy values (Castro et al., 2001; Castro-Schez et al., 2001).

In the process of development of FRT, a new data type is used, it is named *distinctions matrix*, A' (see Figure 5). The distinctions matrix is a bi-dimensional matrix with $n \times n$ cells, where n is the number of FRT elements. Each cell (i, j) contains information about which are the attributes that help to distinguish between i and j elements and the strength with which are distinguished. The strength with which a construct x distinguishes between elements i and j is named as *strength*(i, j, x) and it is calculated as *strength*$(i, j, x) = d_N(e_i, e_j, x)$, where d_N is the separability measurement suggested in (Castro et al., 2001). The distinctions matrix will be used for obtaining the relevant factors (attributes) associated to each option, R_{fi}.

3 FRT as a DSS

In this section, we show how FRT works when it is used as a DSS. The performance of a FRT (as a DSS) is the same to when it is used for acquiring knowledge (see Section 2.2). It is newness in the way in which it establishes relevant factors for each option from the distinctions matrix. Thus, the FRT after identifying a set of options, the decision-maker is asked to define some constructs, which characterise those options. For doing it, FRT searches similarities among the options and it presents three similar options to him with a request to state in what way are two alike and differ from the third. When he introduces a new construct he is asked to estimate its importance or priority at the moment of take a decision. In early phases of FRT development, we recommend higher priorities.

Once the options are distinguished in a clear manner, we are going to obtain the relevant factors associated to each option and recommend the best option according to the acquired knowledge, for doing it we use the following algorithm.

Algorithm

Input: The set of valid options for decision-maker, $|\mathcal{E}| = k$, FRT (named A) and its associated distinctions matrix (named A').

Output: An option that is recommended to the decision-maker and knowledge for justifying such recommendation.

Step 1. Derive two matrixes from FRT, one for holding the positive constructs and the other one with the negative constructs. We will name them *Pos* and *Neg*

Step 2. For $A' = \{Pos, Neg\}$

For $i = 1$ to k do

For $j = 1$ to k do

1. if $|A'[i,j]| = 1$ then introduce the construct C_x in its relevant factors (R^+_{fi} for Pos or R^-_{fi} for Neg).

2. if $|A'[i,j]| > 1$ then

2.1. Develop a set $\mathcal{C}$, such that $C_x \in \mathcal{C}$ *iff* $C_x \in A'[i,j]$ and $strength(i,j,x) = \max_y\{strength(i,j,y)\}$

2.2. if $|\mathcal{C}| = 1$ introduce the construct $C_x \in \mathcal{C}$ in its relevant factors (R^+_{fi} or R^-_{fi}).

2.3. if $|\mathcal{C}| > 1$

2.3.1. Develop a set $\mathcal{C}'$, such that $C_x \in \mathcal{C}'$ *iff* $C_x \in \mathcal{C}$ and C_x is the most priority construct.

2.3.2. if $|\mathcal{C}'| = 1$ introduce the construct $C_x \in \mathcal{C}'$ in its relevant factors (R^+_{fi} or R^-_{fi}).

2.3.3. if $|\mathcal{C}'| > 1$ introduce in its relevant factors (R^+_{fi} or R^-_{fi}), all constructs $C_x \in \mathcal{C}'$, such that $C_x \notin R_{fi}$ (R^+_{fi} or R^-_{fi}).

Step 3. Calculate the goodness attached to each option making use of (1) formula.

Step 4. Recommend the option with the highest goodness value (named e).

For $j = 1$ to k do Show $A[Neg[j,e],e]$

Step 5. End.

We firstly determine for each option what factors are near of construct value that is considered by the decision-maker as ideal value (positive constructs) and those that are far of that ideal value (negative constructs) (Step 1).

Next, we obtain for each option the set of its positive and negative relevant factors (Step 2), these will be those constructs and its values that distinguish this element from any other. When several constructs distinguish between two options, we choose the construct that distinguishes with highest strong. If there are several constructs that distinguish equally (with the same strong) we chose the one that is the most *priority*. When all options have the same priority, we choose that construct which has not yet been included in the set. If any has not been included, we introduce all of them.

Then we study these factors for recommending one option (Step 3). We calculate a measurement (1) over each option for comparing the options.

$$\mathit{Goodness}(O_i) = O_i^+ - O_i^-, \qquad (1)$$

where

$$O_i^+ = \sum_{\forall x \in R^+_{fi}} strength(Pos[x,i]) \times Prior(x) \quad (2)$$

$$O_i^- = \sum_{\forall x \in R^-_{fi}} strength(Neg[x,i]) \times Prior(x) \quad (3)$$

Prior(C_x) is a function that return the priority associated to C_x construct.

The recommended option will be that with the highest goodness value. For justifying this decision, we show the constructs belonging to the set of negative constructs that distinguish the option recommended from the remainder (Step 4).

4 A REAL EXAMPLE OF HOW PROPOSED DSS WORKS

We make use of an example taken from accommodation renting scenario for showing how the suggested method works for helping in making decision (renting accommodation can be a difficult and frustrating experience).

We want to develop a DSS for helping a student when he is searching an accommodation and an estate agency shows him several accommodations. He must choose among them.

In this scenario, options are available accommodations in the estate agency, that is,

$$\mathcal{E} = \{A_1, A_2, A_3, A_4, A_5, A_6\}.$$

We ask student to complete FRT session in which he describes and analyses the differences and similarities among these options. In Figures 4 and 5, we show the FRT and its associated distinctions matrix. We also show relevant information about acquired constructs in Table 1.

Next, we apply the algorithm suggested to them. We obtain the following information:

- *Pos* matrix (See Figure 2).
- *Neg* matrix (See Figure 3).
- Positive and Negative *relevant factors* (R^+_{fi} or R^-_{fi}), and *Goodness* of each option (See Figure 6).

	A_1	A_2	A_3	A_4	A_5	A_6
A_1	Nil	$C_5(1)$;	$C_6(1)$;	$C_3(1)$;$C_5(1)$;	$C_1(1)$;	$C_2(1)$;$C_6(1)$;
A_2		Nil	$C_6(1)$;	$C_3(0.67)$;	$C_1(1)$;	$C_2(1)$;$C_6(1)$;
A_3	$C_4(1)$;	$C_4(0.75)$;$C_5(1)$;	Nil	$C_3(1)$;$C_5(1)$;		$C_2(1)$;
A_4	$C_4(0.75)$;		$C_6(1)$;	Nil		$C_6(1)$;
A_5	$C_4(1)$;	$C_4(0.75)$;$C_5(1)$;	$C_6(1)$;	$C_5(1)$;	Nil	$C_6(1)$;
A_6		$C_5(1)$;		$C_3(1)$;$C_5(1)$;	$C_1(1)$;	Nil

Figure 2: Positive constructs matrix.

	A_1	A_2	A_3	A_4	A_5	A_6
A_1	Nil		$C_4(1)$;	$C_4(0.75)$;	$C_4(1)$;	
A_2	$C_5(1)$;	Nil	$C_4(0.75)$;$C_5(1)$;		$C_4(0.75)$;$C_5(1)$;	$C_5(1)$;
A_3	$C_6(1)$;	$C_6(1)$;	Nil	$C_6(1)$;	$C_6(1)$;	
A_4	$C_3(1)$;$C_5(1)$;	$C_3(0.67)$;	$C_3(1)$;$C_5(1)$;	Nil	$C_5(1)$;	$C_3(1)$;$C_5(1)$;
A_5	$C_1(1)$;	$C_1(1)$;			Nil	$C_1(1)$;
A_6	$C_2(1)$;$C_6(1)$;	$C_2(1)$;$C_6(1)$;	$C_2(1)$;	$C_6(1)$;	$C_6(1)$;	Nil

Figure 3: Negative constructs matrix.

According with information shown in Figure 6, we recommend the accommodation A_1(it is the option with the highest goodness value). The justification of such recommendation will be:

- A_1 has phone, A_2 has not it.
- A_1 has cooking facilities, A_3 has not it.
- A_1 condition is good and has phone, A_4 condition is bad and it has not phone.
- A_1 rental_rate is cheap, A_5 is Expensive.
- A_1 is near from University and has cooking facilities, A_6 is far from University and has not cooking facilities.

5 CONCLUSIONS

In this paper, we have develop a DSS for helping to a decision-maker when he is faced with a choice in which the options are clear. The method suggested makes use of ideas taken from psychology and knowledge acquisition fields. Firstly, we use the fuzzy repertory table for identifying relevant factors (attributes) associated to each option. Thus, we solve some limitations of others RG that have been apply as DSS. Then we apply an algorithm to recommend an option to the decision-maker and we also extract knowledge for justifying such recommendation.

REFERENCES

Alter, S. (1980). *Decision Support Systems: Current Practice and Continuing Challenge.* MA:Addison-Wesley, Reading, 1st edition.

Bhatia, S. and Yao, Q. (1993). A new approach to knowledge acquisition by repertory grids. In *Second International Conference on Information and Knowledge Management.* In B. Bhargava, et. Al. (eds.), CIKM 93, Washington, D.C. ACM Press, pp. 738-740.

Boose, J. (1989). Using repertory grid-centered knowledge acquisition tools for decision support. In *HICSS-22.* Vol III:211-221.

Castro, J., Castro-Schez, J., and Zurita, J. (2001). *Fuzzy repertory table, a method for acquiring knowledge about input variables to machine learning algorithms.* Submitted to IEEE Transactions on Fuzzy Systems.

Castro-Schez, J., Jennings, N., Luo, X., and Shadbolt, N. (2001). *Acquiring Domain Knowledge for Negotiating Agents: A case of Study.* Submitted to IEEE Transactions on Knowledge & Data Eng.

Dhara, V. and Stein, R. (1997). *Intelligent Decision Support Methods: The Science of Knowledge.* NJ:Pretince-Hall, Upper Saddle River, 1st edition.

Druzdzel, M. and Flynn, R. (2000). *Decision Support Systems.* Encyclopedia of Library and Information Science, Allen Kent (ed.), Marcel Dekker, Inc., New York, 1st edition.

Evans, J. (1988). *The knowledge elicitation problem: A psychological perspective.* Behavior and Information Technology, 1(2):111-130.

Ford, K., Petry, F., Adams-Webber, J., and Chang, P. (1991). *An approach to knowledge acquisition based on the structure of personal construct systems.* IEEE Trans. Knowl. Data Eng, 3(1):78-87.

Gaines, B. and Shaw, M. (1980). *New directions in the analysis and interactive elicitation of personal construct systems.* International Journal Man-Machine Studies, 13:81-116.

Gammack, J. and Young, R. (1985). *Psychological techniques for eliciting expert knowledge.* In M.Bramer, ed. Research and Development in Expert Systems, pages 105-112, London: Cambridge University Press, 1st edition.

Graessar, A. and Gordon, S. (1991). *Questions answering and the organization of the world knowledge.* In W. Kesesen, A. Ortony, and F. Craik (Eds.), Memories, thoughts, and emotions, Hillsdale, NJ:Earlbaum.

Holsapple, C. and Whinston, A. (1996). *Decision Support Systems: A Knowledge-based Approach.* MN:West Publishing Co., Minneapolis.

Hwang, G. (1995). *Knowledge Acquisition for Fuzzy Expert Systems.* Int. J. Intelligent Systems, 10:541-560.

Kelly, G. (1955). *The Psychology of Personal Constructs.* New York:Norton.

McDonald, J., Dearholt, D., Paap, K., and Schvanevedt, R. (1986). A formal interface design methodology based on user knowledge. In *CHI'86 Proceedings, pages 285-290.*

Power, D. (2001). Supporting decision-makers: A expanded framework. In *Informing Science Conference'01.* Krakov, Poland.

Schreiber, G., Akkermans, H., Anjewierden, A., Hoog, R., N.Shadbolt, de Velde, W. V., and Wielinga, B. (2000). *Knowledge Engineering and Management: The CommonKADS Methodology.* Massachusetts Institute of Technology Press, Cambridge, Massachusetts, 1st edition.

Shadbolt, N. and Burton, A. (1989). *The empirical study of knowledge elicitation techniques.* SIGART Newsletter, 108:15-18.

	A_1	A_2	A_3	A_4	A_5	A_6
Rental rate	Cheap a=100 b=100 c=250 d=300	Cheap a=100 b=100 c=250 d=300	Normal a=250 b=300 c=400 d=450	Normal a=250 b=300 c=400 d=450	Expensive a=400 b=450 c=600 d=600	Cheap a=100 b=100 c=250 d=300
Distance to work place	Near a=0 b=0 c=15 d=25	Near a=0 b=0 c=15 d=25	Near a=0 b=0 c=15 d=25	Normal a=15 b=25 c=30 d=35	Normal a=15 b=25 c=30 d=35	Far a=30 b=35 c=50 d=50
House condition	Good $a=b=c=d=1$	Normal good $a=b=c=d=2$	Good $a=b=c=d=1$	Bad $a=b=c=d=4$	Normal bad $a=b=c=d=3$	Good $a=b=c=d=1$
Lodging Type	Room in guest house $a=b=c=d=1$	Shared house $a=b=c=d=2$	Apartment $a=b=c=d=5$	Flat $a=b=c=d=4$	Apartment $a=b=c=d=5$	Hall $a=b=c=d=3$
Has phone	Yes $a=b=c=d=1$	No $a=b=c=d=0$	Yes $a=b=c=d=1$	No $a=b=c=d=0$	Yes $a=b=c=d=1$	Yes $a=b=c=d=1$
Has cooking facilities	Yes $a=b=c=d=1$	Yes $a=b=c=d=1$	No $a=b=c=d=0$	Yes $a=b=c=d=1$	Yes $a=b=c=d=1$	No $a=b=c=d=0$

Figure 4: Fuzzy repertory table obtained in accommodation renting scenario.

	A_1	A_2	A_3	A_4	A_5	A_6
A_1	Nil	$C_5(1)$;	$C_4(1)$;$C_6(1)$;	$C_3(1)$; $C_4(0.75)$; $C_5(1)$;	$C_1(1)$;$C_4(1)$;	$C_2(1)$;$C_6(1)$;
A_2	$C_5(1)$;	Nil	$C_4(0.75)$;$C_5(1)$; $C_6(1)$;	$C_3(0.67)$;	$C_1(1)$;$C_4(0.75)$; $C_5(1)$;	$C_2(1)$; $C_5(1)$;$C_6(1)$;
A_3	$C_4(1)$;$C_6(1)$;	$C_4(0.75)$;$C_5(1)$;$C_6(1)$;	Nil	$C_3(1)$;$C_5(1)$; $C_6(1)$;	$C_6(1)$;	$C_2(1)$;
A_4	$C_3(1)$;$C_4(0.75)$; $C_5(1)$;	$C_3(0.67)$;	$C_3(1)$;$C_5(1)$; $C_6(1)$;	Nil	$C_5(1)$;	$C_3(1)$;$C_5(1)$; $C_6(1)$;
A_5	$C_1(1)$;$C_4(1)$;	$C_1(1)$;$C_4(0.75)$; $C_5(1)$;	$C_6(1)$;	$C_5(1)$;	Nil	$C_1(1)$;$C_6(1)$;
A_6	$C_2(1)$;$C_6(1)$;	$C_2(1)$;$C_5(1)$;$C_6(1)$;	$C_2(1)$;	$C_3(1)$;$C_5(1)$; $C_6(1)$;	$C_1(1)$;$C_6(1)$;	Nil

Figure 5: Distinctions matrix associated to FRT shown in Figure 4, with $C_i(\alpha)$ being the construct i, and its meaning in the cell (x, y) is that i separates between x and y in a α degree, *strength(x,y,i)*=α.

Construct	O_i^+	O_i^-	R_{fi}^+	R_{fi}^-	*Goodness*
A_1	38.4	0.5	$C_1(1)$;$C_2(1)$;$C_3(1)$;$C_5(1)$;$C_6(1)$	$C_4(1)$	37.9
A_2	35.46	0.3	$C_1(1)$;$C_2(1)$;$C_3(0.67)$;$C_6(1)$	$C_5(1)$	35.16
A_3	18.1	0.1	$C_2(1)$;$C_3(1)$;$C_4(1)$;$C_5(1)$	$C_6(1)$	18
A_4	0.475	8.3	$C_4(0.75)$;$C_6(1)$	$C_3(1)$;$C_5(1)$;	-7.825
A_5	0.9	20	$C_4(1)$;$C_5(1)$;$C_6(1)$	$C_1(1)$;	-19.1
A_6	28.3	10.1	$C_1(1)$;$C_3(1)$;$C_5(1)$;	$C_2$1);$C_6(1)$	18.2

Figure 6: Obtained information with the suggested algorithm.

Variable	*Definition domain*	*Ideal Value*	*Priority*
Rental rate (£)	{Cheap(100, 100, 250, 300), Normal(250, 300, 400, 450), Expensive(400, 450, 600, 600)}	Cheap	20
Distance to work place (Minutes walk)	{Near(0, 0, 15, 25), Normal(15, 25, 30, 35), Far(30, 35, 50, 50)}	Near	10
House condition	{Bad(4, 4, 4, 4), Normal bad(3, 3, 3, 3), Normal good(2, 2, 2, 2), Good(1, 1, 1, 1)}	Good	8
Lodging type	{Room in guest house(1, 1, 1, 1) Shared house(2, 2, 2, 2) Hall(3, 3, 3, 3) Flat(4, 4, 4, 4) Apartment(5, 5, 5, 5)}	Apartment	0.5
Has phone	{Yes(1, 1, 1, 1) No(0, 0, 0, 0)}	Yes	0.3
Has cooking facilities	{Yes(1, 1, 1, 1) No(0, 0, 0, 0)}	Yes	0.1

Table 1: Information about constructs acquired during FRT interaction.

SUPPORTING THE OPTIMISATION OF DISTRIBUTED DATA MINING BY PREDICTING APPLICATION RUN TIMES

Shonali Krishnaswamy
School ofNetwork Computing, Monash University(Peninsula Campus)
McMahons Rd, Franskton, VIC 3199, Australia
Email: Shonali.Krishnaswamy@infotech.monash.edu.au

Seng Wai Loke
School of Computer Science and Information Technology
RMIT University, GPO Box 2476V, Melbourne, VIC 3001, Australia
Email: swloke@cs.rmit.edu.au

Arkady Zaslavsky
School of Computer Science and Software Engineering, Monash University,
900 Dandenong Rd, Caulfield East, VIC3145, Australia
Email: A.Zaslavsky@monash.edu.au

Key words: Distributed Data Mining, Optimisation, Predicting Application Run Times.

Abstract: There is an emerging interest in optimisation strategies for distributed data mining in order to improve response time. Optimisation techniques operate by first identifying factors that affect the performance in distributed data mining, computing/assigning a "cost" to those factors for alternate scenarios or strategies and then choosing a strategy that involves the least cost. In this paper we propose the use of application run time estimation as solution to estimating the cost of performing a data mining task in different distributed locations. *A priori* knowledge of the response time provides a sound basis for optimisation strategies, particularly if there are accurate techniques to obtain such knowledge. In this paper we present a novel rough sets based technique for predicting the run times of applications. We also present experimental validation of the prediction accuracy of this technique for estimating the run times of data mining tasks.

1 INTRODUCTION

Distributed data mining (DDM) is the process of performing data mining in distributed computing environments, where users, data, hardware and data mining software are geographically distributed. Distributed data mining emerged as an area of research interest to address the scalability bottlenecks of mining very large datasets and to deal with naturally distributed and heterogeneous databases (typically in organisations that are global). Research in distributed data mining can be divided into two broad categories: development of distributed data mining algorithms which focus on efficient techniques for knowledge integration and development of distributed data mining architectures which focus on the processes and technologies that support construction of software systems to perform distributed mining. The core concept of distributed data mining algorithms is that each local data set is mined individually and the results obtained are combined to produce a global model of the data. Several surveys of distributed data mining algorithms and knowledge integration techniques have been written including (Fu 2001). Some studies, such as (Kamath 2001), focus on parallel and distributed data mining algorithms, where, parallel implies parallelisation of sequential data mining algorithms.

There is an emerging focus on efficiency and optimisation of response time in distributed data mining (Parthasarathy and Subramonian 2001, Turinsky and Grossman 2000, Krishnaswamy *et al.* 2000a). This can be attributed to two reasons.

Firstly, DDM aims to improve the scalability of mining large data sets. Scalability in turn is intrinsically linked with better performance in terms of response times. Secondly, the emergence of several Internet-based data mining service providers is driving the need to improve the efficiency of the distributed data mining process (Krishnaswamy *et al.* 2002). Response time is an important Quality of Service (QoS) metric in web-based data mining services for both clients and service providers. The advantage for the clients is that it helps to impose QoS constraints on the service level agreements and the benefit for the service-providers is that it facilitates optimising resource utilisation and scheduling.

In general, the principle that governs the optimisation process is the need to reduce the time taken to perform a distributed data mining task by:

1. Identifying factors that affect the performance in distributed data mining (such as datasets, communication and processing)
2. Computing/assigning a "cost" (where cost has an inverse relationship with performance) to those factors for alternate scenarios or strategies
3. Choosing a strategy that involves the least cost and thereby optimises the performance

Thus, optimisation models in DDM attempt to reduce the response time by choosing strategies that facilitate faster communication and/or processing. A significant issue in the success of an optimisation model is the computation of the cost of different factors in the DDM process. The response time of a DDM task is broadly dependent on three factors:

1. *Communication:* The communication time is the time taken to transfer datasets or mobile agents carrying data mining software to remote datasets (depending the DDM model) and the time taken to transfer results from remote locations for integration.
2. *Data Mining.* This is the time taken to perform data mining on the distributed data sets and is a core factor irrespective of the DDM model.
3. *Knowledge Integration.* This is the time taken to integrate the results from the distributed datasets.

In this paper we focus on computing the cost of the data mining component of the DDM process. We propose *a priori* estimates of the run time of a data mining application as the basis for computing the cost of data mining. The knowledge regarding the time taken to execute a data mining task at different distributed locations can be an effective basis for optimisation of a DDM task. We have developed a novel rough sets algorithm to estimate application run times. We present the use of this algorithm to estimate the run times of data mining tasks to support cost computation and optimisation of the distributed mining process. We also present experimental evaluation of this technique to establish its estimation accuracy and validity.

The paper is organised as follows. In section 2 we review related work in the field of distributed data mining with a particular focus on optimisation techniques. Section 3 describes application run time techniques. In section 4 we present our rough sets based approach to estimate application run times. In section 5, we present experimental results of our technique to estimate the run times of data mining tasks. Finally, in section 6, we conclude by discussing the current status of our project and the future directions of this work.

2 RELATED WORK

Work on improving performance of DDM systems by using an optimal/cost-efficient strategy has been the focus of (Parthasarathy and Subramonian 2001) and (Turinky and Grossman 2000). IntelliMiner (Parthasarathy and Subramonian 2001) is a client-server distributed data mining system, which focuses on scheduling tasks between distributed processors by computing the cost of executing the task on a given server and then selecting the server with the minimum cost. The cost is computed based on the resources (i.e. number of data sets) needed to perform the task. For example, if a server A requires datasets X and Y and another server B already has dataset X and only requires Y, then the second server is preferred. Thus, the cost of performing a task on a server is the number of resources that it has to acquire in order to compute the given task. While this model takes into account the overhead of communication that is increased by having to transfer more datasets it ignores several other cost considerations in the DDM process such as processing cost and size of datasets.

In Turinky and Grossman (2000), the optimisation is motivated by the consideration that mining a dataset either locally or by moving the entire dataset into a different server is a naïve approach. They use a linear programming approach to partition datasets and allocate the partitions to different servers. The allocation is based on the cost of processing (which is assigned manually in terms dollars) and the cost of transferring data (which is also assigned manually in terms of dollars). The manual assignment of cost requires expert knowledge about different factors that affect the DDM process and quantification of their respective impact, which is a non-trivial task.

Thus the computation of the cost is an important question for any optimisation model. In the models discussed, the cost is either assigned manually or computed using a simple technique, which only takes into account the availability of datasets. In Krishnaswamy *et al.* (2000a) cost formulae for estimating the communication component of the distributed data mining process have been presented. However, to the best of our knowledge techniques for estimating the processing cost in the distributed data mining process has not been addressed. In this paper we present the *a priori* estimation of the response time for data mining tasks. The following sections of this paper present a technique for predicting the run times of data mining tasks and advocate the use of such an estimate to be the "cost" of mining at different distributed locations.

3 APPLICATION RUN TIME TECHNIQUES

Regardless of the optimisation strategy adopted for distributed data mining, there is a need to estimate the time taken to perform data mining at various distributed locations so as to be able to effectively determine the optimal/cost-efficient site. In this section, we present application run time estimation techniques as an approach to estimating *a priori* the time taken to perform data mining. We first present an overview of the general principles of application run time estimation and then introduce our novel rough sets based approach to estimating the run time of applications.

Application run time prediction algorithms including (Downey 1997, Gibbons 1997, Smith *et al.* 1999) operate on the principal that applications that have similar characteristics have similar run times. Thus, a history of applications that executed in the past along with their respective run times is maintained in order to estimate the task run time. Given an application for which the run time has to be predicted, the steps involved are:

1. Identify "similar" applications in the history.
2. Compute a statistical estimate (e.g. mean, linear regression) of the run times of the "similar" applications and use this as the predicted run time.

The fundamental problem is the definition of similarity. There can be diverse views on the criteria that make two applications similar. For instance, it is possible to say that two applications are similar because the same user on the same machine submitted them or that two applications are similar because they have the same application name and are required to operate on data of the same size. Thus, as discussed by (Smith *et al.* 1999), the basic question that needs to be addressed is the development of techniques that can effectively identify similar applications. Such techniques must be able to accurately choose the attributes of applications that best determine similarity. The obvious test for such techniques is the prediction accuracy of the estimates obtained by computing a statistical estimate of the run times of the applications identified as being similar. Thus, the closer the predicted run time is to the actual run time, the better is the prediction accuracy of the technique. Several statistical measures can be used for computing the prediction (using the run times of similar applications that executed in the past) including measures of central tendency. Studies by Smith *et al.* (1999) have shown that the mean performs very well as a predictor.

Early work in this area by Downey (1997) and Gibbons (1997) proposed the use of "similarity templates" of application characteristics to identify similar tasks in the history. A similarity template is a set of attributes that are used as the basis for comparing applications in order to determine if they are similar or not. Thus, for histories recorded from parallel computer workloads, Downey (1997) selected the queue name as the characteristic to determine similarity. Applications that were assigned to the same queue were deemed similar. In Gibbons (1997) several templates were used for the same history including: (user, application name, number of nodes and age) and (user, application name). Thus, in order to estimate the run time for a new task, the following steps are performed:

1. The template to be used is defined/selected
2. The history is partitioned into different categories where each category contains applications which have the same values for the attributes specified in the template. That is, if the template used is (user, application name), then tasks that had the same user and the same application name are placed into a distinct category.
3. The current task (whose run time has to be predicted) is matched against the different categories in the history to determine which set it belongs to.
4. The run time is predicted using the run times of the applications in the similar category.

This technique obviously has the limitation of requiring a sufficient history in order to function.

It was proposed by Smith *et al.* (1999) that manual selection of similarity templates had the following limitations:

- It is not always possible to identify the characteristics that best determine similarity
- It is not generic. Thus, while a particular set of characteristics may be appropriate for one domain, it is not always applicable to other domains.

They proposed automated definition and search for templates and used genetic algorithms and greedy search techniques. They were able to obtain improved prediction accuracy using these techniques. For a detailed description of the template identification and search algorithms readers are referred to Smith *et al.* (1999).

We have developed a rough sets based algorithm to address the problem of automatic selection of characteristics that best define similarity to estimate application run times. Rough sets provide an intuitively appropriate theory for identifying good "similarity templates" (or sets of characteristics on the basis of which applications can be compared for similarity). The following sections of the paper discuss the theoretical soundness of our rough sets based approach and present experimental results of this technique establishing its good prediction accuracy and low mean error.

4 SIMILARITY TEMPLATE SELECTION USING ROUGH SETS

Zdislaw Pawlak introduced the theory of Rough Sets as a mathematical tool to deal with uncertainty in data (Pawlak 1982). For a good overview of rough sets concepts, readers are referred to Komorowski *et al.* (1998).

4.1 Suitability of Rough sets for Similarity Template Selection

The primary objective of similarity templates is to identify a set of characteristics, on the basis of which applications can be compared. It is possible to attempt identical matching – that is if n characteristics are recorded in the history, two applications are defined as similar if they are identical with respect to all n properties. However, this limits the ability to find similar applications considerably since not all properties that are recorded are necessarily relevant in determining the run time. Such an approach could also lead to errors as applications which have important similarities might be considered dissimilar even if they differed in a characteristic that had little bearing on the run time. This has been the main reason for previous efforts by Downey (1997), Gibbons (1997) and Smith *et al.* (1999) to use subsets of the properties recorded in the history.

Rough sets theory provides us with a sound theoretical basis to determine the properties that define similarity. The history represents an information system (as shown in figure 1), where the objects are the previous applications whose run times (and other properties) been recorded. The attributes in the information system are the properties about the applications that have been recorded. The decision attribute is the application run time that has been recorded. The other properties that have been recorded constitute the condition attributes. This model of a history intuitively facilitates reasoning about the recorded properties so as to identify the dependency between the recorded attributes and the run time. Thus, it is possible to concretise similarity in terms of the condition attributes that are relevant/significant in determining the decision attribute (i.e. the run time). Thus, the set of attributes that have a strong dependency relation with the run time can form a good similarity template. The fact that rough sets operate entirely on the basis of the data that is available in the history and require no external additional information is of particular importance as the lack of such information (beyond common sense and intuition) was the bane of manual similarity template selection techniques.

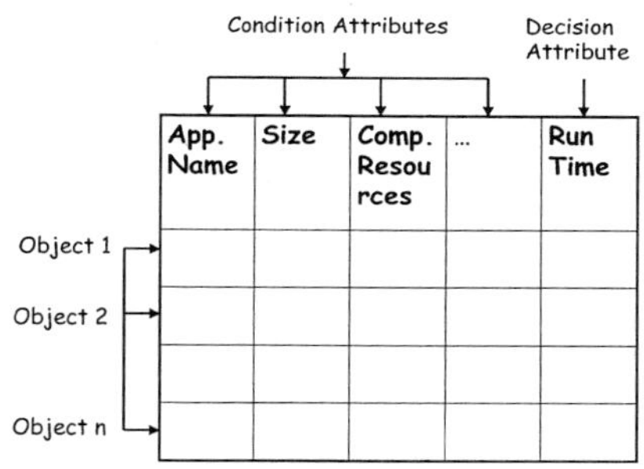

Figure 1: A Task History Modelled as a Rough Information System

Having cast the problem of application run time as a rough information system, we now examine the fundamental concepts that are applicable in determining the similarity template.

Degree of Dependency. It is evident that the problem of identifying a similarity template can be stated as identifying a set of condition attributes in the history that have a strong degree of dependency with the run time. This measure computes the extent of the dependency between a set of condition attributes and the decision attribute and therefore is an important aspect of using rough sets for identifying similarity templates.

Significance of Attributes. The similarity template should consist of a set of properties that are important for determining the run time. The significance of an attribute allows computing the extent to which an attribute affects the dependency between a set of condition attributes and a decision attribute.This measure allows quantification of the impact of individual attributes on the run time, which in turn results in identification and consequent elimination of attributes that do not impact on the run time and therefore should not be the basis for comparing applications for similarity.

Dispensability. This notion is also closely related to the concept of eliminating attributes that are superfluous or irrelevant from being considered in the criteria that define similarity.

Reduct. A reduct consists of the minimal set of condition attributes that have the same discerning power as the entire information system. All superfluous attributes are eliminated from a reduct. A similarity template should consist of the most important set of attributes that determine the run time without any superfluous attributes. In other words, the similarity template is equivalent to a reduct which has the most significant attributes included.

It is evident that rough sets theory has highly suitable and appropriate constructs for identifying the properties that best define similarity for estimating application run time estimation. A similarity template should have the following properties:

1. It must include attributes that have a significant impact on the run time.
2. It must eliminate attributes that have no impact of the run time.

This ensures that the criteria on which applications are compared for similarity have a significant bearing in terms of determining run time. As a consequence, applications that have the same characteristics with respect to these criteria will have similar run times.

4.2 Algorithm for Similarity Template Selection

Our technique for applying rough sets to identify similarity templates centres round the concept of a reduct. A reduct by definition is a set of condition attributes that are minimal (i.e. contain no superfluous attributes) and yet preserve the dependency relation between the condition and decision attributes by having the same classification power as the original set of condition attributes. As explained before, conceptually a reduct is equivalent to a similarity template in terms of comprising attributes that have the best ability to determine the run time and thereby are best suited to form the basis for determining similarity.

In computing a reduct for use as a similarity template in application run time estimation we require the reduct to consist of attributes that are "significant" with respect to the run time. For this purpose, we use a variation of the reduct generation algorithm proposed by Hu (1995), which was intended to produce reducts that included user specified attributes. The modified algorithm we use to compute the reduct for use as a similarity template is shown in figure 2. It computes reducts by iteratively adding the most significant attribute to the D-core (note: the *core* of a rough information system is the intersection of all reducts and the *D-core* is the core with respect to the set of decision attributes). An improvement we have included in the algorithm is the identification of any reduct of size |D-core + 1|. From our experiments we found that it is not unusual for the D-core to combine with a single attribute (typically the most significant attribute) to form a reduct. This iteration in Step 6, is computationally inexpensive as it involves only simple additions and no analysis. Thus, if a reduct of size |D-core + 1| exists, we find it without further computation. In the absence of such a reduct, the most significant attribute is added to the reduct and the dependency is computed as discussed. Then attributes (starting from the next most significant one) are iteratively added to the "new" reduct and the dependency between the new reduct and the decision attributes is re-computed. This process of re-computation of the dependency is expensive as it involves finding equivalence classes and the previous iteration we initiated was principally an attempt to avoid it. This process is repeated until the dependency between the reduct (which is constantly growing due to the addition of attributes) and the decision attributes is the same as the dependency between the condition attributes and the decision attributes. Thus, at the end of the iteration, the reduct is the set of attributes, which have some significance (or are useful in determining the decision attributes). However, at this stage the reduct might not be minimal – as it could contain attributes that may be redundant. Since minimality is a characteristic of reducts, it is necessary to eliminate superfluous attributes. The algorithm iteratively removes an attribute and checks whether the removal changes the dependency. A superfluous attribute will not affect the dependency and can be removed.

The computationally most expensive component of this algorithm is the need to determine equivalence classes several times since this is necessary to determine the degree to dependency (i.e. equivalence classes are the basis of the positive region which is used in calculating the degree of dependency). As an implementation enhancement we introduce the notion of an "incremental equivalence class". Typically, in Step 8 of the above algorithm, the dependency is computed as follows. Let REDUCT be the set of initial attributes. An attribute *a* is added to the reduct and equivalence classes are computed.

Let E1 be the set of equivalence classes for the objects in the information system with respect to the attributes {REDUCT,*a*}:

EQ(REDUCT,*a*) = E1 = $\{e_{11}, e_{12},\ldots,e_{1n}\}$

By the definition of equivalence class, the objects in any of the sets e_{1j} ($1\leq j \leq n$) are indiscernible with respect to the attribute set {REDUCT,*a*}.

Let E2 be the set of equivalence classes for the objects in the information system with respect to the attributes {REDUCT,*a*,*b*}:

EQ(REDUCT,*a*,*b*) = E2 = $\{e_{21}, e_{22},\ldots,e_{2n}\}$

By the definition of equivalence class, the objects in any of the sets e_{2j} ($1\leq j \leq n$) are indiscernible with respect to the attribute set {REDUCT,*a*,*b*}.

We can show that that for any equivalence class e_{2j} ($1\leq j \leq n$), given e_{1j} ($1\leq j \leq n$), it is sufficient to determine the equivalence classes for the objects with respect to the attribute *b* instead of the attribute set {REDUCT,*a*,*b*} as follows.

Let e_{1j} ($1\leq j \leq n$) = {1,2,3}

Thus, by definition, with respect to attributes {REDUCT,*a*} the objects labelled 1,2 and 3 are indiscernible. Now the attribute *b* is added and as required the equivalence classes have to be computed. However, since the objects 1,2 and 3 are known to be indiscernible with respect to {REDUCT,*a*}, the question of whether they are indiscernible with respect to {REDUCT,*a*,*b*} is determined solely by the values of the objects for the attribute *b*.

This incremental computation of equivalence classes is important in the above algorithm, where equivalence relations are computed several times by iteratively adding a single attribute. The following example illustrates the reduction in the number of comparisons that need to be performed by using incremental evaluation of equivalence classes. Consider a simple example:

Let *n* be the number of records = 200.

Let *M* be the total number of attributes = 10.

Let *m* be the number of D-core attributes = 3.

In order to find the significance of an attribute *a* in the above algorithm, we need to find the degree of dependency between the 3 D-core attributes and the decision attributes and then the degree of dependency between the 3 D-core attributes ∪ *a* and

```
1.  Let A={a1, a2,....,an}be the set of condition attributes and D be the set of decision attributes.
2.  Let C be the D-Core
3.  REDUCT = C
4.  A1 = A – REDUCT
5.  Compute the Significances of the Attributes (SGF) in A1 and sort them in ascending order
6.  For i = |A1| to 0
          K(REDUCT, D) = K(REDUCT, D) + SGF(ai)
          If K(REDUCT,D) = K(A,D)
                    REDUCT = REDUCT ∪ ai
                    Exit
          End If
          K(REDUCT, D) = K(REDUCT, D) - SGF(ai)
    End For
7.  K(REDUCT, D) = K(REDUCT, D) + SGF(a|A1|)
8.  While K(REDUCT,D) is not equal to K(A,D)
9.  Do
       REDUCT = REDUCT ∪ ai (where SGF(ai) is the highest of the attributes in A1)
       A1 = A1 - ai
       Compute the degree of dependency K(REDUCT,D)
10. End
11. |REDUCT| -> N
12. For i = 0 to N
       If ai is not in C (that is the original set of attributes of the REDUCT at the start and SGF(ai) is
       the least)
          Remove ai from REDUCT
       End If
       Compute degree of dependency K(REDUCT, D)
       If  K(REDUCT, D) not equal to K(A,D)
          REDUCT ∪ ai -> REDUCT
       End If
    End For
```

Figure 2: Rough Sets Algorithm for Identifying Similarity Templates the decision attributes. Let COMP(x) denote the number of comparisons to compute the equivalence class for an attribute set x.

Determining equivalence classes without the incremental approach:

COMP(D-core) = $m * n^2 = 3 * 200 * 200 = 120{,}000$

COMP(core + a) = $(m+1)\, n^2 = 4 * 200 * 200 = 160{,}000$

Total number of comparisons = 280,000

Determining equivalence classes using an incremental approach:

EQ(core) = $m * n^2 = 3 * 200 * 200 = 120{,}000$

EQ(core + a) = $n^2 = 200 * 200 = 40{,}000$

Total number of comparisons = 160,000

This is generally true for any attribute significance computation. However, this change can make quite a positive impact on the above algorithm – since attribute significances and degrees of dependencies have to be computed several times over. In the first stage, we need to compute the attribute significances of all attributes that are not in the core. Since we have 7 attributes, that becomes 7 * 160000. Using the incremental approach, we only need to make 7 * 40000 comparisons.

The next stage of the algorithm (Step 8), computes degrees of dependencies by adding attributes incrementally to the core (i.e core + a, core + a + b etc.). The incremental inclusion of attributes again makes it feasible to use the incrementally computed equivalence classes. Let us assume that the l attributes have to be added to the core to arrive at a reduct ($m < l < M$). The difference in the number of comparisons that have to be made are as follows:

Comparisons (without incremental evaluation):

$mn^2 + (m+1)n^2 + (m+2)n^2 + \ldots + ln^2$

⇨ $n^2 * ((l * (l + 1) / 2) - ((m-1) * (m) / 2))$

⇨ Since $((l * (l + 1) / 2) - ((m-1) * (m) / 2))$ will reduce to a squared expression (m^2)

⇨ $n^2 * m^2$

Comparisons (with incremental evaluation):

$mn^2 + ln^2$

⇨ $n^2 (m + l)$

⇨ Let $(m + l) = m$

⇨ $n^2 * m$

We have discussed how important it is to be able to compute the cost of processing for any distributed data mining optimisation model. We have presented our rough sets approach to application run time estimation techniques as a way of estimating the cost of processing as it allows prediction of the time taken to perform mining at a given location. Obviously, the success of such a technique is dependent on the prediction accuracy.

5 EXPERIMENTAL RESULTS

We now present the experimental results of our technique in estimating the run time of data mining tasks. For comparative experimental results of our algorithm and other application run time estimation techniques readers are referred to Krishnaswamy *et al.* (2002).

We compiled a history of data mining tasks by running several data mining algorithms on a network of distributed machines and recording information about the tasks and the environment. We executed several runs of data mining jobs by varying the parameters of the jobs such as the mining algorithm, the data sets, the sizes of the data sets and the machines on which the tasks were run. The algorithms used were from the WEKA package of data mining algorithms (Witten and Eibe1999). We generated several data sets of sizes varying from 1MB to 20MB. The data mining jobs were executed on three distributed machines with different physical configurations and operating systems. Two machines had Windows 2000 and one machine had Sun OS 5.8. One of the windows machines was a Pentium III with 833 Mhz processor and 512 MB memory, while the other was a Pentium II with 433 Mhz processor and 128 MB memory. The third machine was a Sun Sparc with 444 Mhz processor and 256 MB memory. The rational for building a history using a distributed network of nodes was twofold. Firstly we wanted to obtain a diverse history and test the prediction accuracy given a varied history. Secondly, it represents a realistic scenario for DDM, where a distributed network of servers would be used.

For each data mining job, the following information was recorded in the history: the algorithm, the file name, the file size, the operating system, the version of the operating system, the IP address of the local host on which the job was run, the processor speed, the memory, the start and end times of the job. Currently we record only static information about the machines, however we are currently implementing a feature to enable recording dynamic information such as memory usage and CPU usage. The history was used to conduct experiments using the process described in section 3. We used histories with 100 and 150 records and as before each experimental run consisted of 20 tests. The mean error we recorded was 0.34 minutes and the mean error as a percentage of the mean run time was 8.29. The mean error is less than a minute and the error as a percentage of the actual run times is also very low, which indicates that we obtained very good estimation accuracy for data mining tasks. This good performance accuracy is illustrated in figure 3, which presents the actual and estimated run times from one of our experimental runs.

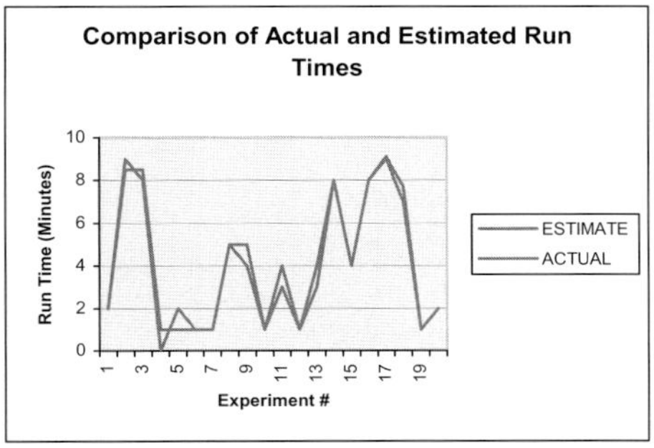

Figure 3: Actual Vs. Estimated Run Times

The reduct that our algorithm selected as a similarity template included the following attributes: algorithm, file name, file size and operating system. It must be noted that we used an automated data set generator to generate files of different sizes and the file names recorded included the full path.

6 CONCLUSIONS

This paper has focussed on computing the cost of the distributed data mining process by estimating the response time of the computational component - the run time of data mining tasks. Accurate costing is vital for optimisation of the DDM process and we address the need for good cost estimation techniques. We have proposed the use of application run time techniques to compute the cost of data mining tasks. We have developed a rough sets based application run estimation algorithm for predicting the run times of data mining tasks. We have experimentally validated the prediction accuracy of our rough sets algorithm, which is shown to have low mean errors and high accuracy. The cost estimation technique presented in this paper is generic and can be applied to any optimisation strategy.

ACKNOWLEDGEMENTS

The work reported in this paper has been funded in part by the Australian Co-operative Research Centre for Enterprise Distributed Systems and Technology.

REFERENCES

Downey,A,B., (1997), "Predicting Queue Times on Space-Sharing Parallel Computers", *Proc. of the 11th Intl. Parallel Processing Symposium (IPPS)*, Geneva, Switzerland, April.

Fu,Y., (2001), *"Distributed Data Mining: An Overview"*, in Newsletter of the IEEE Technical Committee on Distributed Processing, Spring 2001, pp.5-9.

Gibbons,R., (1997), "A Historical Application Profiler for Use by Parallel Schedulers", *Lecture Notes in Computer Science (LNCS)*, 1291, Springer-Verlag, pp.58-75.

Hu,X., (1995), "Knowledge Discovery in Databases: An Attribute-Oriented Rough sets Approach", PhD Thesis, University of Regina, Canada.

Kamath,C., (2001), *"The Role of Parallel and Distributed Processing in Data Mining"*, in Newsletter of the IEEE Technical Committee on Distributed Processing, Spring 2001, pp.10-15.

Komorowski,J., Pawlak,Z., Polkowski,L., and Skowron, A., (1998), "Rough sets: A Tutorial", in *Rough-Fuzzy Hybridization: A New Trend in Decision Making*, (eds) S.K.Pal and A.Skowron, Springer-Verlag, pp. 3-98.

Krishnaswamy,S., Loke,S,W., & Zaslavsky,A. (2000a). "Cost Models for Heterogeneous Distributed Data Mining", *Proc. of the Twelfth Intl. Conf. on Software Engineering and Knowledge Engineering (SEKE)*, pp.31-38.

Krishnaswamy,S., Zaslavsky,A., & Loke,S,W. (2000), "An Architecture to Support Distributed Data Mining Services in E-Commerce Environments", *Proc. of the Second Intl. Workshop on Advanced Issues in E-Commerce and Web-Based Information Systems(WECWIS)*, pp.238-246.

Krishnaswamy,S., Loke,S,W., & Zaslavsky,A, (2002), "Application Run Time Estimation: A Quality of Service Metric for Web-based Data Mining Services", *To Appear in ACM Symposium on Applied Computing (SAC 2002)*, Madrid, March.

Parthasarathy,S., and Subramonian,R., (2001), *"An Interactive Resource-Aware Framework for Distributed Data Mining"*, in Newsletter of the IEEE Technical Committee on Distributed Processing, Spring 2001, pp.24-32.

Pawlak,Z.,(1982), "Rough sets", *International Journal of Computer and Information Sciences*, Issue. 11, pp. 413-433.

Smith,W., Taylor,V., and Foster,I.,(1999), *"Using run-time predictions to estimate queue wait times and improve scheduler performance"*, *Lecture Notes in Computer Science (LNCS)*, 1659, Springer-Verlag, pp.202-229.

Turinsky,A., and Grossman,R., (2000), "A Framework for Findidng Distributed Data Mining Strategies that are Intermediate between centralized Strategies and In-place Strategies", Workshop on Distributed and Parallel Knowledge Discovery at KDD-2000, Boston, pp.1-7.

Witten,I,H., and Eibe,F., (1999), "Data Mining: Practical Machine Learning Tools and Techniques with Java Implementations", Morgan Kauffman.

PART 3

Information Systems Analysis and Specification

BUSINESS MODELLING WITH UML: DISTILLING DIRECTIONS FOR FUTURE RESEARCH

Sergio de Cesare, Mark Lycett
Department of Information Systems and Computing, Brunel University
Uxbridge, Middlesex, UB8 3PH
United Kingdom
{Sergio.deCesare, Mark.Lycett}@brunel.ac.uk

Dilip Patel
School of Computing, Information Systems and Mathematics, South Bank University
103 Borough Road
London SE1 0AA
United Kingdom
dilip@sbu.ac.uk

Key words: Business modelling, UML diagrams, Extensibility.

Abstract: The Unified Modelling Language (UML) was originally conceived as a general-purpose language capable of modelling any type of system and has been used in a wide range of domains. However, when modelling systems, the adoption of domain-specific languages can enable and enhance the clarity, readability and communicability amongst modellers of the same domain. The UML provides support for extending the language for defining domain-specific meta-elements. This paper approaches the UML from a business perspective and analyses its potential as a business modelling language. The analysis proceeds along two complementary paths: a critical study of UML diagrams and a description of UML extensibility mechanisms for the definition of a business profile.

1 INTRODUCTION

The Unified Modelling Language (UML) has emerged as a dominant software modelling language within the object-oriented development community (Kobryn 2000). Conceived as a general-purpose language for the modelling of software systems, the UML is defined as "a language for specifying, visualising, constructing, and documenting the artefacts of software systems, as well as for business modelling and other non software systems" (OMG, 2000). This definition is based on the assumption that the same underlying concepts and principles characterise all systems (software and non-software), regardless of the domain of applicability. Consequently, the UML has been applied to a wide range of domains from aerospace to e-commerce underlining its potential for modelling systems that are complex yet very different in nature. The generality of the language is strengthened by a drive for its standardisation. It is at present a de facto standard of the Object Management Group (OMG) who is currently proposing the UML specification for international standardisation by the International Organisation of Standardisation (ISO) (Kobryn 1999).

The assumption of general applicability undoubtedly holds true when having to describe systems whose behavioural patterns remain stable over a long period of time. It may be argued, however, that a standard modelling language alone is not sufficient as the nature and characteristics of the domains of applicability can be intensely different. Business domains, in particular, have a set of specific concepts and semantics, commonly applied by people operating within that domain. These concepts and the relationship amongst them form the basis of a common understanding people have of and within a domain. This shared understanding can aid in the identification of specialised metaconcepts, which UML recognises via the dual concepts of extensibility mechanisms and 'profiles'. Extensibility mechanisms are included in the language to allow modellers to specialise detail (i.e., adapt it to context) without having to modify the underlying modelling language. Profiles represent tailored sets of extensibility mechanisms that are applicable to particular application domains.

With the above in mind, this paper explores the following. Firstly, the extent to which the semantics and the notation of the UML adhere to the representation of the 'fundamental' generalised concepts of the business domain. Secondly, the extent to which extensibility mechanisms and profiles are sufficient, as stand, to specialise standard UML modelling elements to the needs of the business domain. To enable this exploration, the paper is structured as follows. Section 2 describes the complex adaptive nature of business organisations and the differences with other complex systems. Since business complexity mainly derives from an organisation's complex behaviour, section 3 presents an overview of business process modelling techniques, attempting to identify the basic concepts underpinning any business model. On the basis of these basic business concepts, Section 4 attempts to assess the suitability of UML diagrams for business modelling alongside their major limitations. Section 5 describes UML extensibility mechanisms and their application to the definition of business specific modelling concepts. The broad conclusion of the work is that the UML, as stands, is not ideally suited for business modelling and an agenda for further research is presented in Section 6.

2 BUSINESS COMPLEXITY

It is argued here that a case exists for investigating whether special modelling techniques and formalisations should be derived for business organisations. This is based on the observation that business organisations are complex systems that constantly need to adapt and change to internal and external factors in order to be competitive (Johansson, McHugh et al. 1993). Business organisations do not evolve in a stepwise fashion but are best thought of as 'emergent' entities whose features are products of continuous social negotiation and consensus building (Truex, Baskerville et al. 1999). Consequently, the specification, visualisation, construction, and documentation of business requirements is, at best, only going to produce a static picture of a dynamic situation (Lycett and Paul 1999). This is a unique feature of social systems as, in natural systems, the relationship between analyst and object is that of 'concept to thing', where only the analyst's knowledge may be subject to scrutiny (changing knowledge of unchanging thing). This situation is complicated in the social world where the object of investigation exists within a pre-interpreted reality. The relationship is that of 'concept to concept', where both the observer's knowledge *and* knowledge of the observed may be placed under scrutiny (changing knowledge of changing knowledge).

Other factors contribute to aggravate this modelling problem and help explain the internal factors that generate change in the organisation. Firstly, unacknowledged or unconscious motivation and tacit skills may limit stakeholders' understanding of themselves. Secondly, unintended consequences and unacknowledged conditions (or political factors) may limit the stakeholders and/or analysts understanding of the social world. These account for views expressed in the literature that 'users cannot know what they want' and 'cannot explain what they know' (see Ackoff 1967; Parnas and Clements 1986; Baskerville, Travis et al. 1992; Jones and Walsham 1992; Paul 1994). Thirdly, in a business, knowledge of problems is not/could not be concentrated in one sole person. Business processes are carried out within different organisational units and by different people. As a consequence some processes may become so complex as to not be describable appropriately by anyone in the organisation. In part, this relates to the extent that an organisational problem exists as an independent reality that can be modelled (Boland 1979; Checkland 1981). Lastly, some knowledge relevant to the problem situation may be difficult or impossible to express within the descriptive techniques available (Stage 1991); part reflecting a view that descriptions of systems that abstract away their complexity often abstract away their essence (Brooks 1987).

3 BUSINESS MODELLING

Business modelling can be defined as the abstraction of the elements of a business organisation and the relationships between them. In modelling terms, the UML makes a claim as an appropriate language and there is a nominal applicability of UML elements (likely specialised) and relationships. Most of the literature on business modelling is focussed on business *process* modelling, on the basis that the major complexities of organisations derive from behaviour. A business process can be defined as "a lateral or horizontal organisational form that encapsulates the interdependence of tasks, roles, people, departments and functions required to provide a customer with a product or a service" (Earl 1994, p.13). Business processes define the dynamics of business behaviour, act on entities or resources and are carried out by parties. A party can be a person or an organisational unit as defined by Fowler (1997).

Business process models can represent the organisation as it currently behaves (descriptive 'as-is') or as it could behave if changes in the business processes are required (prescriptive 'to-be'). Whilst the forms of model are complimentary, the prescriptive view is instrumental to strategies such as business process reengineering (BPR) and improvement (BPI). BPR is more radical in nature and tends to revolutionise present business processes (Hammer and Champy 1993), whereas the latter is more gradual in nature looking at improving the efficiency of business processes in an evolutionary fashion (Davenport 1993).

A plethora of techniques exists that have been applied to business process modelling, each technique focusing on a specific aspect or set of aspects of the business to model. Kettlinger et al. (1997), in a study on methodologies, techniques and tools for BPR, identify several techniques, most of which (e.g. flowcharting and data flow diagramming) derive from the software modelling domain. It should be noted that a few of the techniques listed are in reality methods, e.g. Socio-Tech System Design and Soft Systems Method, nonetheless these methods provide techniques for the representation of different views of the business.

In order to understand whether the UML can add positively to the above mix, an understanding of the essential elements needed for business modelling is required. Given that business organisations are social systems, the characteristics of a business therefore derive from those of a society. Homans (1950) identifies the elements related to the behaviour of social groups and then applies them within a business context. These elements are: concepts, activities, interactions and sentiments. The latter can definitely be related to the informal side of a business and its subsystems (e.g. information system) and Homans defines a mutual dependency between interaction and sentiment. Whilst it is beyond the scope of this paper to look into the informal aspects of an organisation and its influence on the formal system, it is useful to underline that only a few methods such as ETHICS (Mumford 1994) take 'sentiments' into account to a certain extent. In a broad sense, however, the mapping of the informal aspects to the formal aspects of an organisation still remains an open research issue.

The elements identified by Homans (concepts, activities and interactions) are implicitly also defined by the techniques considered by Kettlinger et al. (1997). Other elements also emerge. Ould (1995) identifies the following basic concepts in business process modelling: roles, actors, activities, interactions, process goals and entities. These concepts derive from STRIM, a modelling technique based on Role Activity Diagramming. The reason for considering these elements is directly connected to the definition of business process given earlier in this section. Actors interact through an interdependency of tasks and business processes achieve the goal of providing a customer with a product or service. These elements or concepts described by Ould (1995) will be taken into account to assess the suitability of UML diagrams to business modelling.

4 UML DIAGRAMS

The UML has a rich set of diagrams for the representation of both structural and behavioural aspects of a system. These diagrams are to various extents applicable during all phases of the system's lifecycle, from requirements specification to implementation. A total of nine diagrams are defined in the UML. This assortment of diagrams allows for the representation of multiple perspectives, especially for the representation of behaviour. Some diagrams, namely statechart and activity diagrams, are not derived from the object-oriented paradigm, thus giving rise to potential problems in mapping them to other diagrams of the system model (Berkem 1998).

Although business modelling and business process modelling are mentioned in different parts of the UML specification, the documentation (OMG 2000) lacks a valid argumentation as to how the individual diagrams can be applied in the context of business modelling. The UML diagrams are summarised for reference in Table 1. For each diagram its potential to model each of the basic business concepts is indicated. The business concepts considered in this section are those identified by Ould (1995).

The following subsections describe the potential of the UML diagrams for business modelling and present their main limitations in terms of their role in business modelling and problems related to the mapping between models and diagrams. Since implementation diagrams model software components and run-time processing they will not be discussed in this section.

Section	Diagram	Description	Business Modelling Potential					
			ROLES	ACTORS	ACTIVITIES	INTERACTIONS	PROCESS GOALS	ENTITIES
4.1	Use case	Models the functionality of the system as it is visible to external actors that stimulate this functionality.	●	●			●	
4.3	Class	Models the static part of a system in terms of classes, relationships amongst classes and their packaging.	●					●
	Object	Models the representation of instances of class models.	●					●
4.2	Collaboration	Models object interaction via message passing placing emphasis on the roles in the interaction and their links to each other.		●		●	●	●
	Sequence	Models object interaction via message passing placing emphasis on the sequence of interactions.		●		●	●	●
4.4	Statechart	Models the states and state transitions of an object of a given class.			●			●
	Activity	Models the flow of activities defined for any given procedure.			●		●	
	Component	Models the dependencies amongst software components.	Not considered					
	Deployment	Models the configuration of run-time processing elements and the software components, processes, and objects that live in them.	Not considered					

Table 1: UML diagrams and business modelling concepts.

4.1 Use Case Diagrams

Description: Use case diagrams model the functionality of a system, as it is visible to external actors that stimulate this functionality. Use cases have been introduced by Jacobson et al. (1992) and have proven to be an excellent tool for capturing high-level system requirements. Use cases capture the system as it is viewed from the outside and depict the interaction between the system and external actors. Actors lie outside of the system boundary. Shifting the boundary of the system can provide a useful mechanism for understanding how business functionality (behaviour) maps to the high-level functionality of the computer-based information system. Fig. 1 illustrates such an example.

Fig. 1 illustrates two use case diagrams. Fig. 1a represents functionality at a business level in which the boundary is placed around the entire business organisation. All functionality represented at this level is seen by actors standing outside the business and interacting with it, e.g. customers, suppliers, revenue service, etc. Two use cases are depicted in fig. 1a (*order products* and *deferred payments*). In fig. 1b the system boundary is taken to a lower level, that of the computer-based information system. In this specific instance, the actors lying beyond the system boundary and interacting with the system are workers of the organisation (sales clerk and finance clerk). The two use case diagrams can be mapped to one another to form an initial mapping between business and computer-based information system models. In this very simplified example:

Order products maps onto process order, process high value order and browse profile;

Deferred payment maps onto arrange deferred payment and browse profile.

The business metaconcepts that use cases are capable of modelling are actors and process goals. Actors are explicitly represented; process goals are represented by one or more use cases. A use case does not necessarily coincide with an entire business process; however, groups of use cases can map into one process to achieve a goal. In Fig. 1a the use cases *order products* and *deferred payment* may be mapped each to a corresponding business process, whereas in Fig. 1b one process can be mapped to the use cases *process order*, *process high value order* and *browse customer profile*. The other business

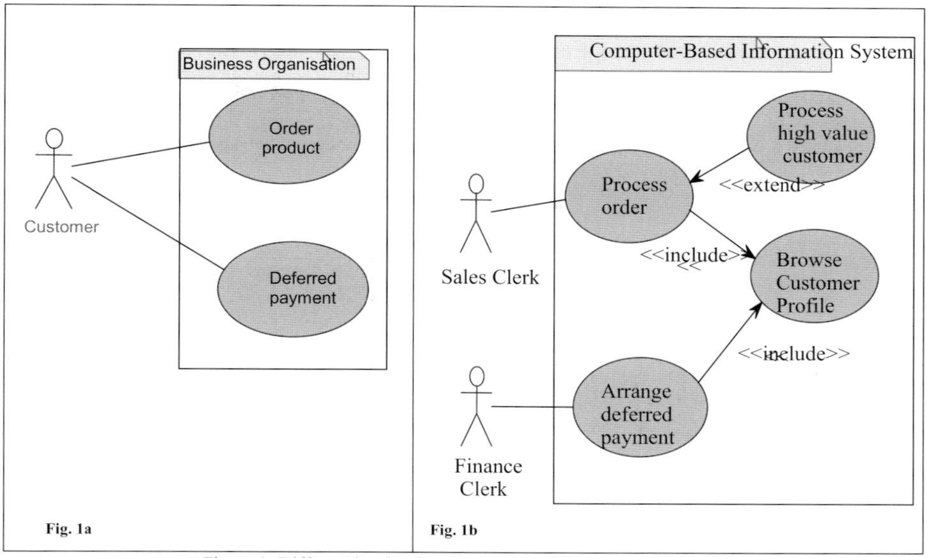

Figure 1: Different levels of representation with use case diagrams.

process can be mapped to the use cases arrange *deferred payment* and *browse customer profile.*

A role provides another business metconcept that can be represented in use case diagrams. Modellers often incur into some ambiguity between the concepts of actor and role. An actor plays a role when interacting with the system. For example, a company can play the role of a customer or a supplier whether it is buying or selling goods or services. Hence the representation of an actor implicitly states a role. Roles can also be modelled explicitly by generalising/specialising an actor. In Fig. 1b sales clerk and finance clerk can be modelled as specialisations of clerk.

Limitations: In the modelling of actors, process goals and roles, use cases *per se* do not present major limitations. Problems can however arise when mapping use case diagrams to other diagrams. Since a use case merely models high-level functionality as one or more actors perceive it, the internal activities performed within the organisation to achieve such functionality needs to be represented elsewhere, such as an activity diagram. As a consequence, integration and traceability amongst use case diagrams and other UML diagrams becomes an important issue (Berkem 1998). This matter will be discussed further in sections 4.2 and 4.4.

4.2 Interaction Diagrams

Description: Interaction diagrams can assume two forms: collaboration and sequence diagrams. In object-oriented modelling an interaction occurs between two objects when one object sends a message to another object. The sending object requests an operation and the receiving object is responsible for knowing how to carry out that operation and its execution. A set of interactions or collaboration is defined within an interaction diagram in order to 'realise' a use case. A collaboration diagram represents an interaction organised around the roles in the interaction and their links to each other. A sequence diagram represents the collaboration differently highlighting the temporal sequence of the interactions. Although collaboration and sequence diagrams are considered semantically equivalent, a sequence diagram provides better visual support for branching. This allows for a clearer representation of multiple scenarios of a use case on the same diagram, whereas the representation of branching in a collaboration diagram becomes less readable as the number of collaborating objects and scenarios grow.

In business process modelling with RAD techniques, interactions are normally defined between roles and not between objects. The meaning of interaction is slightly different than that assigned to the term in the UML and object-orientation in general. For instance, Ould (1995) explains business interactions through the following examples: a manager delegating a task to a subordinate, or the handing over of a report. In both examples interaction occurs between roles played by humans. In collaboration and sequence diagrams interactions can occur between objects or between actors and objects.

For example, a business process aimed at carrying out a design project can be defined by the following activities: a designer prepares an estimate, which is then sent to the project manger (Ould 1995). In a RAD the designer (role) prepares an estimate (activity) and the project manager (role) obtains the estimate from the designer (interaction), hence interaction between roles. In an interaction diagram the same example could be modelled as follows:

The designer (actor) sends a message to the 'estimate' object invoking the 'prepare estimate' operation (interaction between actor and object);

The 'estimate' object then sends the prepared estimate as a result back to the designer;

The 'estimate' object then sends a message to itself invoking the 'send to project manager' operation;

The 'estimate object' sends the estimate to the project manager (actor);

As a point of note, it is beyond the scope of this paper to delve into architectural issues related to the distinction between boundary, control and interface objects as described by Jacobson et al (1992). For this reason the estimate object described in the example is a hybrid of the above-mentioned types.

Although interactions are defined and modelled differently in RAD and UML, the end result is equivalent. In the previous example both in the RAD-based and UML-based textual descriptions, the overall result has been an interaction between the designer and the project manager. This is important at a business level because it emphasises the complementary roles of two different types of diagrams, in which the former is aimed at representing flow of activities, whereas the latter models flow of messages amongst objects.

Limitations: Besides interactions, collaboration and sequence diagrams have the potential of representing actors, process goals and entities. Since interaction diagrams generally map to realisations of use cases, the actors and process goals are the same as those defined in use case diagrams. Entities are defined as objects whose structural and behavioural properties are defined in class diagrams. A major limitation of interaction diagrams is their inability to link to other collaborations. This is fundamental when modelling complex business processes in which various levels of refinement may be necessary in order to manage the underlying complexity. For this purpose, the Objectory method (Jacobson, Christerson et al. 1992) defines the concept of probe, which can be used within a sequence diagram to insert additional behaviour defined in a use case.

4.3 Class and Object Diagrams

Description: Class and object diagrams are directly capable of representing business entities as objects. Objects are logically manipulated during business processes. The shared attributes and operations of objects are defined in classes. A class is a description of a set of objects sharing the same attributes, operations, relationships and semantics. Class diagrams also represent different types of relationships amongst classes. When two classes are associated to one another, the association can carry on both ends the name of roles played by the objects in the relationship. For example, in the case of a payment there is a relationship between a 'person' object and a 'payment' object. In this association the person making the payment plays the role of the payee.

Limitations: Given the static nature of classes/objects, these diagrams seem to be adequate for defining business entities; however, as section 5 will discuss, classes can be stereotyped (i.e. specialised at a metamodelling level) in order to enhance class modelling for business organisations.

4.4 State and Activity Diagrams

Description: Statechart diagrams, also known as state diagrams or state machines, model the sequence of states and state transitions that an object traverses during its lifetime. Although state diagrams have originally been defined for modelling real time systems (Harel 1987), they can be used to model workflows manipulating and/or transforming one object. State diagrams do not explicitly model any of the business metaconcepts defined in section 3, however when an object is in a given state, different types of activities can be performed. Whether a state diagram can represent a whole business process is debatable, since the complexity of business processes usually encompasses several objects. More appropriate for this type of modelling are activity diagrams.

The contribution of activity diagrams to business process modelling seems to be promising, but as yet the potential of activity diagrams has not been fully exploited in this area. Activity diagrams have been originally defined with the purpose of modelling the computation and flow of control of the algorithm of an operation. The UML specification defines an activity diagram in terms of state machines. An activity diagram is a variation of a state machine in which the states represent the performance of actions or subactivities (OMG 2000). Although correct, this definition may generate some confusion when trying to conceptually associate states/activities with objects. In a state diagram all the states are defined for objects of a specific class, in an activity diagram the action states do not necessarily (and generally do not) refer to actions performed by the same object.

Activity diagrams presently lie outside of the object-oriented philosophy. They are not semantically integrated with other diagrams, as are use case, interaction and class diagrams. The UML specification does not adequately define the relationship between the elements of activity/state diagrams and elements of other diagrams. This represents a general problem/pitfall of the current version of the UML, with implications of a more specialised nature when taking into account the business domain.

The main elements of an activity diagram are action states. UML 1.3 introduces subactivity states, which are basically invocations to other activity diagrams. A transition from one state to another is triggered by the termination of the action or subactivity. With the term activity the UML refers to the set of actions and transitions forming the entire activity diagram. An action state represents the execution of an atomic action, typically the invocation of an operation. An activity diagram, therefore, in a way reflects the contents of interaction diagrams. Whilst interaction diagrams represent objects passing messages, activity diagrams represent the operations of the messages being passed. In other words, in an activity diagram the emphasis is placed on the operations rather than the objects they belong to. Within the context of object-oriented business modelling, an action therefore generally maps onto an operation and a subactivity to a collaboration. In the light of this the link between activity and interaction diagrams becomes more apparent.

Limitations: Activity diagrams are therefore capable of representing business activities. The representation of business processes is also possible, however, as Berkem (1998) points out, business process modelling requires, amongst other things, the representation of past states of objects to allow for better decisions and design with an evolutionary pattern. Although referred specifically to activity diagrams, these comments could also be applied to use case and interaction diagrams. None of these diagrams are, as they stand, able to model past states of objects and evolutionary patterns. Such requirements can be modelled ad hoc within the system model (e.g. by defining a composite class modelling its present and past states), nonetheless the issue remains at a metamodelling level.

Roles can also be modelled in activity diagrams by partitioning the diagram in so-called swimlanes. The UML does not assign the term role to swimlanes. In the UML swimlanes are merely an arbitrary partitioning of elements with no semantics (Kleppe and Warmer 2000); hence the underlying roles can represent anything from an object to an organisational unit or functional area. There is no constraint imposing the nature of the role nor the consistency amongst the roles defined (e.g. all objects, all organisational units, etc.) This deficiency also restricts the application of the concept of responsibility to activity diagrams.

5 UML EXTENSIBILITY

Business systems form a proper domain, in which individuals communicate and interact by using a set of specialised concepts. The semantics of these concepts and the relationships amongst them are defined by the context of the business domain. Common concepts allow individuals to have a common understanding of the domain they operate in. This common understanding is generally referred to as 'ontology' and definition of ontological specialisations or domain specific semantics of a modelling language is an emerging issue amongst the UML community. UML 1.3 introduces profiles, which serve the purpose of defining extensions to the language. Profiles are containers for the three extension mechanisms that are currently legal within the UML: stereotypes, tagged values and constraints. These extensions are not mutually exclusive.

A stereotype is defined by specialising a pre-existing modelling element. For example, subsystem is an example of a stereotyped package. A subsystem, just like a package, groups logically related concepts. Modelling elements are the basic building blocks of a language, e.g. class, association, operation, attribute, etc. A stereotype is defined by a name and its semantics. The new semantics add to those of the specialised modelling element. Since stereotypes are specialisations of pre-existing modelling elements, the stereotyped element behaves like the element it derives from plus some additional behaviour defined by the new semantics. Stereotypes prevent a modelling language from becoming overly complex and represent the most sophisticated extension mechanism (Eriksson and Penker 1998). Expanding the above example a subsystem could represent an organisational unit of an enterprise or the monitoring subsystem of an environmental control system. The new semantics of the subsystem stereotype consists of representing elements, which together constitute a system part of a greater system being modelled.

Constraints restrict the semantics or usage of modelling elements and represent rules that restrict the semantics of one or more modelling elements. The new semantics is represented in the model simply by specifying conditions that must be held true. For example, in a university only final year students have a supervisor for their project. Hence the association between student and academic staff representing this association can be restricted to final year students {year = final year}. Tagged values qualify a modelling element with pairs of name-value information. For example, software components can be labeled with tagged values representing the author and the version: {Author = John Smith}, {Version = 1.3}.

An initial attempt in extending the UML has been made in version 1.1. UML 1.1 integrates within its complete documentation the *UML Extension for Business Modelling* document. However, as the document emphasises, the extension merely serves the purpose of registering the document. The current version of the UML has not completed these extensions either. The documentation only provides a list of thirteen stereotypes; neither tagged values nor constraints are defined. Table 2 lists the thirteen business stereotypes.

Apart from a few of the stereotypes in Table 2 (e.g. work unit and worker), most of them only vaguely resemble business-oriented concepts. They are instead more oriented toward UML itself, i.e. based on UML modelling elements such as use cases. In fact use case models, systems and packages are quite general and applicable throughout all types of systems. The same can be said of object models and systems.

Metamodel Class	Stereotype Name
Model	Use case model
Package	Use case system
Package	Use case package
Model	Object model
Subsystem	Object system
Subsystem	Organisation unit
Subsystem	Work unit
Class	Worker
Class	Case worker
Class	Internal worker
Class	Entity
Collaboration	Use case realisation
Association	Subscribes

Table 2: UML defined business stereotypes.

Whilst extension mechanisms themselves work quite well, the UML extension does not specify how the business stereotypes have been derived, nor does it seem complete. The UML business profile cannot be considered a formal attempt to define 'the set' of business concepts; however although the *UML Extension for Business Modelling* lacks in the definition of a set of recurrent business modelling elements, this documentation can be used as a starting point. In this direction Capozza et al. (1999) propose various business stereotypes categorised into seven groups (business i/o, persons, space-related concepts, time-related concepts, logical aggregates, functional concepts and other general concepts). Eriksson and Penker (2000) propose another set of business extensions to the UML. The future work of the OMG will most likely also be orientated toward the expansion of the extension for business modelling and this provides a major direction for future research.

6 CONCLUSION

The UML is a general-purpose modelling language potentially capable of modelling any type of system. For specific domains, however, it may be useful to work with specialised modelling concepts reflecting recurrent semantics of the domain. The business domain is one such example. Business complexity is augmented due especially to the uncontrollable and unpredictable nature of change and evolution of business requirements. This paper has presented a critical analysis of the UML in the context of business modelling. The analysis has focussed on two main problem areas: suitability of UML diagrams to model business organisations and the use of the UML for abstracting high-level business-specific concepts. In both areas the UML currently presents deficiencies and research is not fully developed.

The main limitations of UML diagrams to business modelling can be directly or indirectly related to the use and/or semantics of activity diagrams and can be summarised in the following points:

Business process modelling with the UML has not been adequately achieved. Although activity diagrams provide potential support for this purpose, they are not semantically integrated with other dynamic modelling diagrams (use case and interaction diagrams).

The representation of roles is an important part of an activity-based representation of a business process. Roles can be represented in activity diagrams by partitions or swimlanes, however the semantics of partitions are not defined in the UML.

UML diagrams provide no mechanism for the representation of past states of objects or for that of evolutionary patterns.

Inability of sequence diagrams to refer to or invoke other collaborations via mechanisms such as probes.

Business organisations continually change and adapt with inevitable consequences on business requirements and models. These continuous modifications produce ripple effects throughout the business model(s) and model diagrams. A change in one diagram conceptually relates to one or more elements of other diagrams. Hence a change in one part of the model maps semantically to other parts and such semantic relationships need to be formally defined within the specification of the modelling language in order to map the effects of a change throughout the model. For this reason, semantic consistency throughout UML diagrams and modelling elements is vital to business modelling.

Further research is necessary in order to understand what elements of the business need to be modelled. Significant effort should be focussed on identifying other business concepts besides those considered in this paper (roles, actors, activities, interactions, process goals and entities). Examples of such concepts are business services, rules (Rouvellou, Degenaro et al. 2000) and events (Snoeck, Poelmans et al. 2000). Future research should also be directed toward the definition of a UML profile for the business domain. Besides providing a set of business-specific metaconcepts, a specialised profile could enhance the semantics of those UML modelling elements that are limited in the way they currently represent business concepts. This could also lead to a better integration of UML diagrams within a business model. A further step in the evolution of the UML is its use as an ontology language (Cranefield and Purvis 1999). Research in the area of UML profiling could provide a better understanding of how and to what extent UML extension mechanisms and elements can be applied to defining ontologies.

REFERENCES

Ackoff, R. (1967). "Management Misinformation Systems." Management Science 14(4): 147-156.

Baskerville, R., J. Travis, et al. (1992). Systems without Method: The Impact of New Technologies on Information Systems Development Projects. The Impact of Computer Supported Technologies on Information Systems Development. K. Kendall, J. DeGross and K. Lyytinen. Amsterdam, Elsevier Science Publishers, B.V., North Holland Press: 195-213.

Berkem, B. (1998). Formalizing a bridge from the UML's Activity Diagram to Use Cases. Workshop On the Usage of the UML - OOPSLA '98, Vancouver.

Boland, R. J. (1979). "Control, Causality and Information System Requirements." Accounting, Organisations and Society 4: 239-275.

Brooks, F. P. (1987). "No Silver Bullet: Essence and Accidents of Software Engineering." IEEE Computer 20(4): 10-19.

Capozza, F., S. deCesare, et al. (1999). Modelling Extensions for the Business Domain. 12th International Conference on Software and Systems Engineering and their Applications, Paris, France.

Checkland, P. (1981). Systems Thinking, Systems Practice. Chichester, John Wiley and Sons.

Cranefield, S. and M. Purvis (1999). UML as an Ontology Modelling Language. IJCAI-99 Workshop on Intelligent Information Integration.

Davenport, T. H. (1993). Process Innovation. Reengineering Work through Information Technology, Harvard Business School Press.

Earl, M. J. (1994). "The New and Old of Business Process Redesign." Journal of Strategic Information Systems 3(1): 5-22.

Eriksson, H. E. and M. Penker (1998). UML Toolkit, John Wiley & Sons.

Fowler, M. (1997). Analysis Patterns, Addison-Wesley.

Hammer, M. and C. Champy (1993). Reengineering the Corporation: A Manifesto for Business Revolution. New York, Harper Business.

Harel, D. (1987). "State charts: A Visual Formalism for Complex Systems." Science of Computer Programming 8: 231 - 274.

Homans, G. C. (1950). The Human Group. New York, Harcourt, Brace.

Jacobson, I., M. Christerson, et al. (1992). Object-Oriented Software Engineering: A Use Case Driven Approach, Addison-Wesley. ACM Press.

Johansson, H. J., P. McHugh, et al. (1993). Business Process Reengineering, BreakPoint Strategies for Market Dominance, John Wiley& Sons.

Jones, M. and G. Walsham (1992). The Limits of the Knowable: Organisational and Design Knowledge in Systems Development. The Impact of Computer Supported Technologies on Information Systems Development. K. Kendall, J. DeGross and K. Lyytinen. Amsterdam, Elsevier Science Publishers: 195-213.

Kettlinger, W. J., J. T. C. Teng, et al. (1997). "Business Process Change: A Study of Methodologies, Techniques, abd Tools." MIS Quarterly 21(1): 55-80.

Kleppe, A. and J. Warmer (2000). Making UML Activity Diagrams Object-Oriented. Technology of Object-

Oriented Languages and Systems (TOOLS 33), St. Malo, France, IEEE Conference Proceedings.
Kobryn, C. (1999). "UML 2001: A Standardization Odyssey." ACM Communications 42(10).
Kobryn, C. and T. Weigert (2000). "OMG UML 2.0 RFPs." ftp://ftp.omg.org/pub/docs/ad/00-09-05.pdf.
Lycett, M. and R. J. Paul (1999). "Information Systems Development: A Perspective on the Challenge of Evolutionary Complexity." European Journal of Information Systems 8(2): 127-135.
Mumford, E. (1994). "New Treatment or Old Remedies: Is Business Process Reengineering Really Socio-Technical Design?" Journal of Strategic Information Systems 3(4): 313-326.
OMG (2000). OMG Unified Modeling Language Specification: http://www.rational.com/media/uml/post.pdf.
Ould, M. (1995). Business Process: Modelling and Analysis for Re-engineering and Improving, Wiley.
Parnas, D. L. and P. Clements (1986). "A Rational Design Process: How and Why to Fake It." IEEE Transactions on Software Engineering 12(2): 251-257.
Paul, R. J. (1994). "Why Users Cannot 'Get What They Want'." International Journal of Manufacturing Systems Design 1(4): 389-394.
Eriksson, H. E. and M. Penker (2000). Business Modeling With UML: Business Patterns at Work, John Wiley & Sons.
Rouvellou, I., L. Degenaro, et al. (2000). Extending Business Objects with Business Rules. Technology of Object-Oriented Languages and Systems (TOOLS 33), St. Malo, France, IEEE Conference Proceedings.
Snoeck, M., S. Poelmans, et al. (2000). An Architecture for Bridging OO and Business Process Modelling. Technology of Object-Oriented Languages and Systems (TOOLS 33), St. Malo, France, IEEE Conference Proceedings.
Stage, J. (1991). The Use of Descriptions in the Analysis and Design of Information Systems. Collaborative Work, Social Communications and Information Systems. P. Kerola, R. Lee, K. Lyytinen and R. Stamper. Amsterdam, Elsevier Science Publications: 237-260.
Truex, D. P., R. Baskerville, et al. (1999). "Growing Systems in Emergent Organisations." Communications of the ACM 42(8): 117-123.
Winograd, T. and F. Flores (1986). Understanding Computers and Cognition. Norwood NJ, Ablex.

UPDATING DATA IN GIS: HOW TO MAINTAIN DATABASE CONSISTENCY?

H. Kadri-Dahmani
IGN-LIPN
2,4 Avenue Pasteur, 94164 S.Mandé Cedex
Email: hakima.kadri-dahmani@ign.fr

A. Osmani
LIPN-CNRS 7030
99, avenue J.-B. Clément, 93430 Villetaneuse
Email: ao@lipn.univ-paris13.fr

Key words: GIS, Versioning, incremental updating, GIS database consistency.

Abstract: Preserving the consistency of a geographical database requires the development of tools for integrating or removing data and making several versions of any geographical objects coexist without altering neither the global consistency, nor the informational power of the database. To construct such tool, two problems must be solved: how to organize the data for efficient updating and how to maintain the database consistency during and after the integration of updates. The latter may be automated in the form of an Integration Module. One of its main tasks is to detect conflicts which perturb the consistency of the database during the update integration. This paper describes the Integration Module we have designed and its role in the general updating process we propose for GIS.

1 INTRODUCTION

Updating is an essential step in any GIS life cycle. If data are not regularly updated the results and decisions deduced from spatial analysis are unreliable. However, this is a very difficult task to achieve. Due to the temporal property of the natural (a dry river) or non natural (a road change) phenomena they represent, data require regular if not continuous updating. Data suppliers eg.the national mapping agencies, have to update their basic databases regularly and to update also all the products derived from these databases (e.g. cartography dedicated products, other databases with different scales or possibly previous versions of user databases). While these databases were usually conceived without taking the temporal property of spatial information into account, today suppliers must propose solutions to a variety of issues: How to minimize the cost of the updating operation? How to formalize the different updating operations to reduce interactive work (Ray96)? How to integrate the updating in the derived products (UOM98) (HH99)? Or even what is the best delivery mode for the updating information (Far91)(Faa91)(VA95)(BH98)(BvCP97) (BR00)? and how to preserve the consistency of the database when modifications have to be integrated and propagated? Some papers dealing with the updating problem in GIS propose solutions which are inspired by classical (not geographical) database concepts (CM95). Others rely on their practical experience and constraints such as research at the NMAs [1].

In our work, we treat the question concerning the preservation of database consistency during and after the integration of the updates. Some appropriate approaches have been proposed during the last years. Many of them use GIS conceived without consideration for the notion of data evolution. Ours is the inverse approach: our focus is on how to interprete and support the consideration of the data evolution at the time of the GIS conception. The main motivations for this work are:

(i) update integration is an important part of the global updating problem (KD01a) and has been kept hidden in the other proposals;

(ii)updating integration in geographical databases deals with the modification of all the objects nominally or mediately concerned by the updating. This relies on retrieval of different relationships between objects. These relationships are often implicit (i.e. not explicitly stored in the database) and have to be retrieved on the fly;

(iii) several kinds of conflicts may emerge when an update is integrated into a database. In most of

[1] NMA : National Mapping Agencies.

the current approaches, these conflicts can not be removed without human intervention.

In this paper we describe how our so-called Integration Module can be used to detect possible conflicts when updating is integrated into a database. Our objective is to maintain the consistency of this database. Section 2 reviews the data model used by our system. Section 3 introduces the overall architecture and the individual components of the system. In section 4 we describe the integration process, and then the Integration Module in UML modelling. Finally, section 5 assesses the contribution of our system to the general requirement of geographical information updating.

1.1 Related Work

In recent years, some work has been done on updating data in GIS. Although these work was able to give excellent solutions of several precise points, they could or did not deal with the totality of the maintenance of GIS problem for different reasons: the vastness of the problem itself, the fact that they were generally motivated by an objective of production or that they were limited by the tools which they used and so on. It would probably be useful to consider these works and draft a taxonomy or classification of the different methods of updating. We have identified 3 major domains in the updating problem(KD01a) (KD01b): (i)how to integrate updating in databases, (ii)how to exchange updating information and (iii) how to diffuse updating informations from a database to another database. How recent studies relate to these three categories may be reviewed as follows:

(i) Update integration in a geographical database requires the identification of all the entities of the database directly or indirectly concerned by the evolution. More precisely, this task consists in retriev different relationships between objects and analysing the semantics of the entities stored in the database. The relationships are often implicit (i.e. not explicitly stored in the database) and have to be retrieved on the fly. Several work propose various methods to establish these relations such as the method of matching proposed in (Bad99) and (Bon98) or the mechanisms of history in (Spe99). In (UOM98) the matching process depends on the abstraction rules.

(ii) Many other studies deal with the update exchange. In his paper (BH98), Beyen summarises the different approaches of this point of interest since 1991 especially, the question "how can the updates be supplied?". Some answers propose to deliver the whole updated database (Faa91), others (Far91) propose to supply change-only information. The first solution implies that the destination database has to be completely replaced by the delivered one. This can entail loss of information in the destination database (the user's database for example). Indeed, the user may have added, into the database, data relative to his application. These own data will be lost when he replaces completely the database.
The second solution needs having the change-only information and sometimes, it involves to extract them from the source database (the producer's database for instance) and then, to integrate them into the destination one (the user's database for instance). It implies that only the modified objects, between two states of the database are delivered. In 1998, Beyen proposes an approach which implies that the modified objects are automatically derived by the comparison of the data supplier's new database state with the users old database state, and they are automatically integrated into the user's database (BH98). This approach is very advantageous because it allows to pass on only the data which should be updated, without affecting the other data. However, it supposes the existence,of an identification system, and this is not always acquired in the GIS.

(iii) Diffusing an update consists in deducing update from an initial database (or a database source), and integrating them in other different database. This can be done between a database and a derived product or between two independently surveyed databases. Many kinds of conflicts exist between different databases, for example different models, schemas, classes and data structures. With spatial information there are extra conflicts, for example different geometries (polygons Vs polylines), different segmentations (road Vs road segments) and different aggregations (houses Vs building blocks). One of the interesting studies which focus on update diffusion is reported in (Kil95). Kilpelainen's work addresses the issue of maintaining multiple representations in geoagraphic database. It defines an approach that uses operations of generalization to update a geographical database from an other geographical database at a higher scale. This approach is called incremental generalization. Incremental generalization requires that the problem can be divided into "modules". Kilpelainen (1995) defines a module as a geodata entity that can be processed independently from its surroundings. Generalization is then performed only for the modules influenced by the updates. This updating method supposes the knowledge and the automation of the generalization process then it can only be performed in this specific case of multi-scale databases. Another problem is how to find the border line for a module: identification of modules is a crucial point but it is far from being easy to implement.

An other interesting approach is defined in (UOM98). It addresses the propagation of updates between two independently surveyed databases. The idea is to establish a knowledge base which contains a set of "Abstraction rules" and to "synchronize" both databases according to this knowledge base, then to establish the relations between the objects of the two databases to find corresponding objects. Finally, using these correspondencies, to integrate the updates in the second database. This approach emphasises the relevance of defining a strategy to perform a consistent and complete propagation of updates between databases at different scales. However full scale update propagation depends on the knowledge of the abstraction rules of the data. Databases providers should express their abstraction rules in a shared vocabulary.

In the two previous studies, the updates are assumed to be clearly identified, which is far from being a general case. In (BL99) a mechanism dedicated to the update diffusion is proposed, in which updates are not identified: a process for automatic retrieval of updates between two databases is included. The approach defined in (BL99) seems more generic but has been implemented and validated only on databases produced by the IGN and more precisely, just between a database and its derived product (even if a part on interactive work is involved in the derivation process).

The different studies previously mentioned have a common point: they use geographical information systems constructed on a models which don't take the notion of evolution into account. This observation urges us to see the problem of update at the level of the representation of the data. We think that the reorganisation of the geographical data view on updates can be a first step towards a generic solution of this problem.

1.2 Example

The following example (figure 1 and 2) is extract from the BDTOPO, a 1:25000 topographic database with 1-meter resolution produced by the IGN France. It will be used throughout this paper to illustrate how our update integration system works. A road that was not there before (figure 1) has been constructed (figure 2). We must add an object "ROAD" to represent the construction of the new entity road but we must also divide the "WOOD" object into two "WOOD" objects to reflect the splitting of the real wood entity by the real road entity.

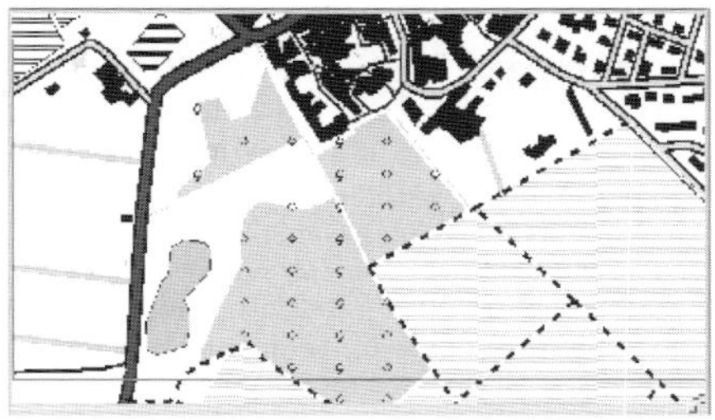

Figure 1: Database before updating.

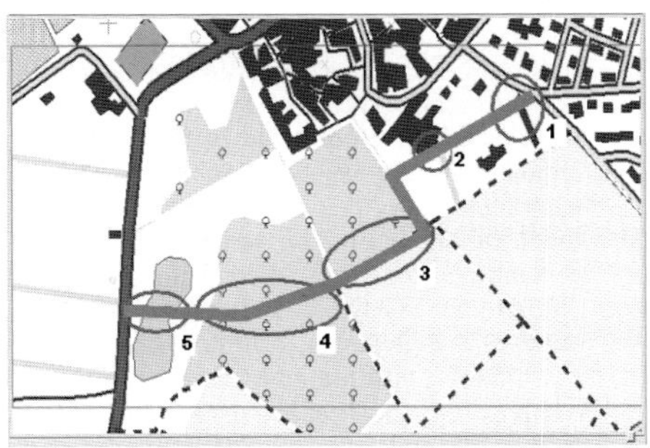

Figure 2: Database after raw updating.

Figure 2 shows that the addition of the "ROAD" object in the database generates five conflicts which can disrupt the consistency of the database if not corrected. For instance, conflict **(1)** lies in the road passing over the building.

2 MODEL

Preserving the consistency of a geographical database requires the development of tools for integrating updates without altering neither the global consistency, nor the meaning power of the database. To construct one such a tool, two problems must be solved: how to organize the data for efficient updating and how to maintain the database consistency during and after the updating integration. The data organization is made meant not only for the data stored in the database but also for those to be integrated: it is necessary to structure the update information compatibly with the database structure, so that they can be integrated easily. We think that a good approach to facilitate the integration requires that we separate explicitly, in the database, the representation of data from that of the relations between data (in classical geographical approaches, relations are extracted from data). This approach has as the following model:

$$\xi = (D, R, M, C)$$

where:

1. **D**=$\{o_1, ..o_n\}$ is a set of the geographical "objects" stored in the database. We consider three types of objects:
   - basic objects: They represent the geometry of the different objects we handle. We consider three primitives : points, lines and surfaces.
   - simple objects: We consider as simple object each elementary geographical object. They are made of one geometric primitive and a set of semantic information. For example, an object "ROAD_SECTION" is a simple object which is made of one geometric primitive (line) and a set of semantics informations (*name, length...etc).*
   - *complex objects: They are defined by a set or sequence of simple objects and/or complex objects. For instance, a "ROAD" is a complex object composed of a sequence of "ROAD_SECTION" simple objects;*
2. **R**= $\{R_{(o_i,o_j)}, ...\}$ denotes a set of relationships defined between objects. According to the nature of the knowledge they are meant to support, we distinguish four main types:
   - Topological relationships. They translate the notion of the sharing of geometry which can exist between two objects, such as the adjacency, the inclusion, etc.Example: When a section of a road is bordered by a row of trees, the two objects "ROAD_SECTION" and "TREE_ROW" share the same geometry[2].
   - Composition relationships. They are involved in the creation of complex objects. For instance, an object "ROAD" is composed of several "ROAD_SECTION" objects.
   - Correspondence relationships. This kind of relationships is used in the context of multirepresentation. They give the correspondence between objects in different representations. For instance, that complex object "TOWN" at a large scale representation corresponds to that point object "TOWN" at the small scale representation.
   - The Dependency relationships. This relationships are used to calculate attribute values of an object if these values depend on an attribute value of another object. For instance, the value of the attribute "LENGTH" of the object "ROAD" depends on the "LENGTH" attribute values of all its components (the objects "SECTION_ROAD").
3. **M** represents the evolutions to be integrated in the database. M represents the sequence of updating operations and the set of objects affected by these operations.
   $M = \{D_M, (oper_1(D_{m_1}), ..., oper_k(D_{m_k}))\}$ such that:

   D is a set of objects.

   D' is a subset of D. It contains the element of D witch are directly affected by updating operations.

   $D"$ is a set of new elements created by the updating operations.

   $D_M = D' \cup D"(D' \subset D, D" = \{o_{n+1}, ..., o_{n+j}\}(D" \cap D = \emptyset))$

   $D_{m_1}, D_{m_2}, ...$ and D_{m_k} are subsets of D_M.

   $oper_i(D_{m_i}),\ i \in \{1, ..., k\}$ is an updating operation. We consider, in our work, two kinds of operations:
   - Canonical operations: creation, deletion and semantic modification.
   - Composed operations. Each composed operation is obtained by the application of a sequence of canonical operations. For instance, the fusion operation can be decomposed into a sequence of $(destruction, destruction, creation)$.

   $(oper_1(D_{m_1}), ..., oper_k(D_{m_k}))$ is a sequence of updating operations.

[2] In the specification of IGN BDTopo.

4. **C** represents a sequence of constraints that allow on the one hand to identify conflicts and on the other hand to decide how to solve them. We consider two types of constraints:
   - Thematic constraints: these are constraints defined in the classical databases, they include semantic constraints on data types, key uniqueness and so on.
   - Spatial constraints: constraints belonging to the geometry of objects.

3 SYSTEM ARCHITECTURE

The basic architecture of the system we propose is depicted in Figure 3 which shows the components of this system. The adapter allows to see as if every application uses the same format of the evolution data as defined in our system. This module exports the update data of the various applications in the Lambda format, whereas the Integration Module allows to integrate the evolution data into the database while maintaining its consistency. One of the main tasks of the latter is to detect the conflicts which can disturb this consistency and to make decision with regard to these conflicts.
We can see in Figure 3 how the different components interact during the integration. First of all, the system receives an external set of evolution from an application. These evolutions are expressed in the application format. If this format is the one that we propose in our work(see Section 2), then the evolutions are directly passed on to the Integration Module. On the other hand, if the format is different (for example, the evolutions in the IGN are expressed in XML format) then the set of evolution is passed to the Adapter. This last one, converts it in the Lambda format which can be understood by our Integration Module and recovers as well the identifiers as the operation parameters which it needs for the maintenance of the order in which the update information arriveds. It needs also to keep the dependences between the different operations. When the Integration Module received the set of evolutions, it has to execute the different updating operations included in this set. This execution must be free from conflicts otherwise the Integration Module has to detect them and to take decision with regards to these conflicts. To detect the conflicts, it uses the Reasoning module which, basing itself on the constraints database and the algorithms of consistence preservation, decides of the manner of modifications integration on the data of the database.
Although this architecture seems intuitive, its originality is found in three levels:

- How data are represented;
- how data evolution are represented;
- and what the features offered by the various modules are.

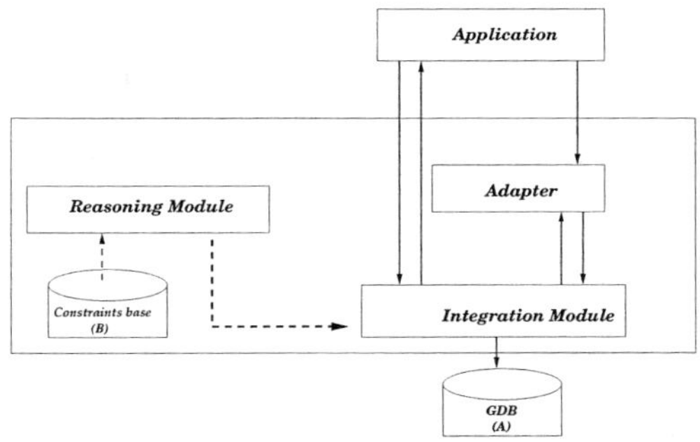

Figure 3: System Architecture

4 UPDATES INTEGRATION PROCESSING

The Integration Module allows integrating the updates from the Adapter, conveyed by the set of evolution, inhe database. This means the execution of all the updating operations included in the set. The resulting must be free from conflicts.

4.1 What kind of conflicts are considered?

We call **conflict** any violation of any of the constraints defined in the model. We distinguish two kinds of conflicts:

- **Error:** An error is a constraint violation which stop totally the progress of the process. Example: Destruction of an object which does not exist.
- **Warning:** A warning is a constraint violation tolerated by the process. Example: A warning is generated when a road crosses a lake. It's necessary to have a bridge [2].

4.2 How are the entry data structured

The Integration Module receives a sequence of canonical operations which he should execute. this sequence is defined as follow:

$$M' = \{op_1(O_1), ..., op_k(O_k)\}$$

where:

M' is a sequence of updating operations;

$O_i \in D_M$ and O_i is a simple object;

op_i is a canonical operation.

This sequence is atomic then, it can be validated only if all the operations which it contains are executed with success. It would mean that no conflicts had been detected during the execution. Nevertheless, a sequence can be validated by the intervention of a human operator even if during its execution, a *warning* is detected. If the detected conflict is an *Error* then the execution of the sequence is cancelled. During the execution of the sequence, the database is in a temporary state. State changes only if the sequence is validated. Figure 4 shows the changes of state during the execution of a sequence of operations.

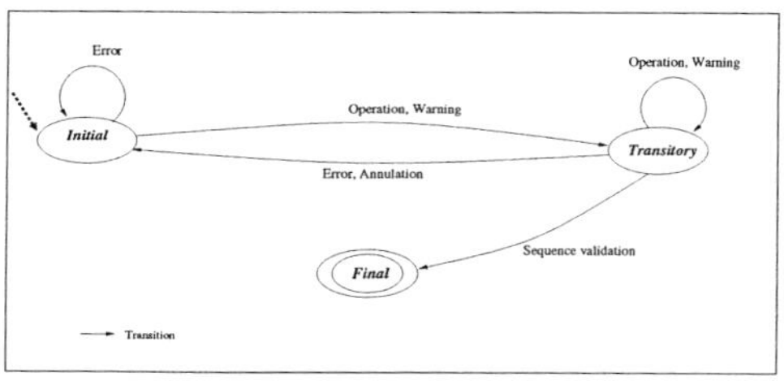

Figure 4: States of the database regarding to the integration process described by a finite state machine.

To explain the updates integration process, two aims diagram from an UML modelling of this process are given. Figure 5 shows the class diagram of the module and Figure 6 illustrates the diagram of the cases of use of the module.

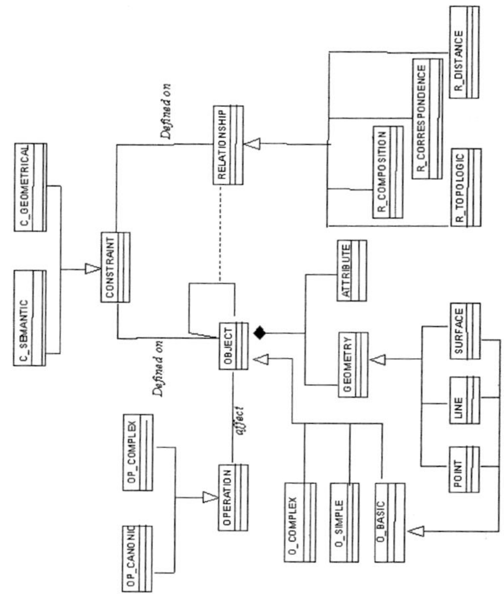

Figure 5: Diagramme des classes

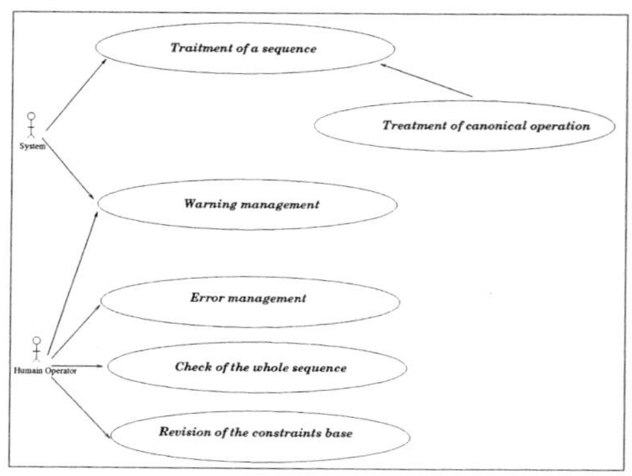

Figure 6: use cases diagram of the updating process.

5 CONCLUSION

Updating problem in GIS is a vast problem which can be divided into several precise sub-problems. We tried in this paper to explain briefly these various points and give some works which handle each of these points.

We showed, consequently, that the point to which we are interested, "the maintenance of the database consistency during and after the update integration" is an important part of the global problem but which is generally hidden in other proposals.

We presented in this paper, how we tackle this point. We propose an approach based on the fact that the notion of evolution is taken into account concurrently with the conception of the GIS and not afterward. So, we show how we organize data for efficient updating. In this organisation, we separate explicitly, in the database, data representation of that of the relation between data.

REFERENCES

T. Badard. On the automatic retrieval of updates in geographic databases based on geographic data matching tools. In *Proceedings/Actes, 19th International Cartographic Conference, 11th General Assembly of ICA, Ottawa*, 1999.

J. Beyen and J. Henrion. Updating topographic databases with arc info ; client-fitted creation of change-only information. 32(part4), 1998.

T. Badard and C. Lemri. Propagating updates between geographic databases with different scales. 1999.

L. Bonani. Etablissement de liens de corrlation dans un but de mise jour des bases de donnes gographiques. Master's thesis, Univerit Paris XI Dauphine, Laboratoire COGIT, IGN-SR, septembre 1998.

T. Badard and D. Richard. Using xml for the exchange of updating information between geographical information systems. In *RGISRUK 2000, York, UK*, Avril 2000.

Y. Bedard, Y. van Chestein, and G. Poupart. Actualistion des donnes rfrence spatiale. Technical report, Centre de recherche en gomatique, universit Laval, Quebec, Canada, 1997.

C. Claramunt and M. Mainguenaud. Spatial view: A dynamic and flexible vision of gis database. In *Proceedings of the DEXA International Conference and Workshop on Database and Expert System Applications, Revell, N. and Min Tjoa, A. eds, Omnipress, London, UK*, pages 483–493, 1995.

Ch. Faad. Updating the french topographic database. In *Updating digital data by photogrametric methods, ISPRS and OEEP joint workshop, Oxford*, 1991.

J. Farrow. Ordonnance survey revision problems and solutions. In *Updating digital data by photogrametric methods, ISPRS and OEEP joint workshop, Oxford*, 1991.

L Harrie and A. Hellistrom. A case study of propagating updates between cartographic data sets. In *Proceedings/Actes, 19th International Cartographic Conference, 11th General Assembly of ICA, Ottawa*, 1999.

H Kadri-Dahmani. Updating in GIS: Towards a more generic approach. In *Proceedings/Actes, 20th International Cartographic Conference, Beijing, China*, August 6-10 2001.

H Kadri-Dahmani. Vers une approche de modlisation des bases de donnes gographiques pour une intgration cohrente des mises jour. In *A apparaitre dans le Bulletin d'Information de l'IGN*, pages num. 72, pp., 2001.

T. Kilpelainen. Upating multiple representation geodata bases by incremental generalisation. *Geo-Informations-System, Jahhrgang 8, Heft 4, Wichmann*, pages 13–18, 1995.

L. Raynal. Some elements for modelling updates in topographic databases. In *in Proceedings of GIS/LIS'96, Annual Exposition and Conference. Denver, Colorado, USA.*, novembre 1996.

L. Spery. PhD thesis, 1999.

H. Uitermark, N. Oosterom, Mars, and M. Molenaar. Propagating updates corresponding objects in a multi-source environnement. In *in Proceedings of 8th International Symposium on SSpatial Data Handling.*, pages pp. 202–213, 1998.

P. Van Asperen. Updating top10 vector. In *Revision of digital topographic databases, CERCOWG IX workshop, Emmen*, 1995.

ANALYSIS OF THE RELATION BETWEEN THE PRESCRIPTIVE AND DESCRIPTIVE APPROACHES OF THE INFORMATION SYSTEM PLANNING

Jorge Luis Nicolas Audy
Computer Science School , Pontifical Catholic University of Rio Grande do Sul, Av. Ipiranga, 6681, CEP:90.619.900, Porto Alegre, Brazil
E-mail: audy@inf.pucrs.br

Key words: Information Systems Planning, Information Systems Strategic Planning, Prescriptive and Descriptive Model, Organizational Learning.

Abstract: The information system planning area presents today several challenges to managers and researchers. This has happened because modern information technologies are quickly changing the way they affect and impact the company's competition. In this context, the Information Systems Strategic Planning (ISSP) becomes a critical issue on the area of information system management. For years, ISSP models have been oriented towards a prescriptive approach. New approaches for ISSP, in a descriptive line, may contribute to the search of solutions for current challenges. This article's goal is to analyze the relations between descriptive and prescriptive approaches on ISSP elaboration, looking for an explanatory model regarding the implementation of the plan created. The study is based on a qualitative research, and cases studies the main research method. As a contribution, it develops an analysis of cases studies results and presents the proposed model.

1 INTRODUCTION

Traditionally, the ISSP methodologies have been oriented towards a prescriptive approach, focusing its attentions on traditional information systems and administrative support. New approaches, in a descriptive line, may contribute on searching for tools to help the information management process in organizations and to study the problem of creating implementable strategy in Information Systems (IS) areas. We understand as implementable the development plans that can be executed in the organization for which the plan was developed, respecting its characteristics and particularities.

Among many different research areas on descriptive lines, learning becomes a new and critical concept on IS development strategies. The basic idea is concentrated on the subject presented by Senge (1990), focusing on the creation of a shared view concerning how to use the new technology. When there is a genuine and common view in the organization, people learn, not because they are manipulated towards the learning, but because they want to, and because this behavior, which is turned towards learning, is part of the human nature. However, there is a large gap in models and methodologies concerning the transposition of individual or small group views or shared visions (Raponen, 1998).

This study reviews the descriptive models, which goes beyond the existent prescriptive models technical basis. This article's goal is to analyze the relation between descriptive and prescriptive approaches on ISSP elaboration, looking for an explaining model regarding the implementability of the plan created. Doing this, the intention is to confirm the descriptive approach relevance, using Organizational Learning (OL) techniques, in ISSP process, and then, stimulate more studies and researches related to the usage efficiency of the descriptive approach in ISSP subject.

Next, in section 2 presents the theoretical basis, involving the main concepts of the study areas: information systems planning and organizational learning. In section 3, the research method. Section 4 describes the case studies results. Section 5 presents and develops the proposed explaining model. Finally, section 6 brings the final considerations about results and potential contributions.

2 THEORETICAL FOUNDATION

2.1 Strategic Planning: From The Prescriptive View To The Strategic Formulation.

With the development of the studies on strategy, the strategic planning had great improvement, reaching its high point in Porter and Mintzberg during the 80's. In the 90's, the strategic planning view was somewhat frayed; however, in the late 90's, the issue became once again strongly researched and studied under the perspective of new contributions originated from different areas of knowledge, such as organizational learning and decisory process.

Mintzberg (1995) develops a study classifying different strategic planning schools in three categories: prescriptive, descriptive and configurationally. The prescriptive school represents the analytical and mathematics planning tradition, visualizing the strategic process as a conceptual project and of formal planning. The planning process begins with an internal analysis (organizational) and external (environmental), from which the strategic alternatives are developed. The choice of the best strategy and implementation is the final outcome of the planning process.

The descriptive school visualizes the planning process as a learning process, considering the mental aspects related to the decisory process and the values and lines of thoughts of the decision makers. In this path, transitory and unexpected aspects, of political basis or not, must be used for learning and action, directly affecting the strategies. In this school, the basic principles that surround the OL area may be clearly identified through authors as Argyns, Senge and De Geus.

The configurational school deepens in the prescriptive school line, based on the manager and expert's knowledge and experience. This knowledge is transformed (formalized) and used for manipulating management issues.

2.2 Information Systems Strategic Planning (ISSP)

Information System Strategic Planning is the process of identifying an application portfolio that is based on computers to support the organization business plan and to aid the concretization of the organizational objectives. Several authors (Lederer and Sethi, 1992; Gottschalk and Lederer, 1997; Reponen, 1998) examine the strategic planning nature in the Information Systems area. This way, studies are developed aiming to assess if the IS strategy must be applied separately or if it is a continuous process in which new ideas emerge throughout the operations. These authors' starting point is the descriptive school (Mintzberg, 1995), in which the strategy formulation is seen as a learning process.

Next, it is identified the main prescription and approaches for ISSP planning. These prescriptions and approaches will be used as analysis element of lived deeply experiences and the developed study cases.

2.2.1 ISSP Prescriptions

Two decades of intense research have produced a large number of prescriptions, methods and guidelines to be applied in the IS planning. Such prescriptions help IS planners on designing an efficient IS planning process.

In this research, summaries provided by other researchers (Galliers, 1987; Boyton and Zmud, 1987; Henderson and Sifonis, 1998; Lederer and Sethi, 1996) pointing out the studies brought out by Salmela (1996) were used. It was assumed that these summaries, better focused on the prescriptions identification, include the essence of the knowledge created in these researches, in terms of IS planning.

The prescriptions were divided in six categories: objectives, resources, analysis, process, result and evaluation. These categories were derived from the ISSP model brought out by King (1988). The model prescribes an operational approach for an IS strategic planning process in an organization. It describes an IS planning system that is directed by three types of inputs, which create outcomes (outputs). These models were tested in a large number of empirical studies (Prenkumar and King, 1991, 1992, 1994).

All the identified prescription will be numbered to ease later reference when analyzing the lived deeply experiences and developed case studies. At total, 40 prescriptions were identified, numbered from P1 to P40. The IS planning objectives (Chart

1) are the purpose for which the planning is developed. In this manner, the objective prescriptions define which objectives the ISP must have.

P1	The planning scope must be kept manageable.
P2	The planning objectives must incorporate all the relevant aspects of the organizational performance.
P3	The IS planning objectives must stimulate creativity, as well as command.
P4	The planning objectives validation must be appraised through multiple models and external criteria.
P5	The planning objectives must reflect the high-level administrators expectations.

Chart 1: Objectives Prescriptions

The resource prescriptions (Chart 2) define the required resources. They also define the key-person or the groups that must participate on the planning process.

P6	The process must involve non-technical personnel, as well as experts on information systems.
P7	The information systems planning process must involve people from different levels in the organization.
P8	The members of the planning team must be chosen based on their skills and preferably their availabilities.
P9	To keep the process going on, the key-people must be kept on the planning process from its beginning to end.
P10	High-level executives must act as sponsors to provide a propitious environment and assure implementation without any problems.

Chart 2: Resources Prescriptions

The analysis prescriptions (Chart 3) define which information inputs are necessary in a planning process. In this manner, they define the analysis content that must be done.

P11	IS plans and strategies must be based on business plans and strategies.
P12	The IS planning must analyze external tendencies.
P13	IS planning must involve inter-organizational political analysis to understand the relative influence kept by key-collisions of an organization.
P14	IS planning must analyze current investments on IS in the organization.
P15	The IS planning must evaluate resources and abilities on IS basis and other areas of the organization.
P16	The IS planning must analyze the opportunities created through information technology advances.
P17	The IS planning must use multiple perspectives while deriving IS decisions from the analysis results.
P18	The IS planning must analyze risks and suppositions related with the existent and planned application folder

Chart 3: Analysis Prescriptions

The process prescriptions (Chart 4) helps the planning process organization. They define how interactions within the planning team must be organized, as well as the interactions among the team and other work groups on the organization.

P19	There must be a strong connection between the business planning process and the information systems planning process.
P20	The connection between business planning strategies and information system planning must be seen as an interactive process.
P21	The IS planning must not overlook important organizational and environmental events.
P22	The IS planning must allow a continuous review, from the moment in which business objectives are interim by nature.
P23	To encourage a continuous, even intermittent planning process, an informal network of planning requirements needs to be settled or fed.
P24	The IS planning must create a commitment and totally support the planning process.
P25	The IS planning process must allow a broad opportunity to discuss and debate different viewpoints, aiming to reach a consensus throughout the process.
P26	Key-collisions must be regularly identified to accumulate contributions and support the plan.

Chart 4: Process Prescriptions

Results prescriptions (Chart 5) define the items that must be included in the resultant plan. In addition, they define organizational results required to assure successful implementation.

P27	The IS plan must define a portfolio and a priority diagram for projects in the IS area.
P28	The planning must lead to applications identifications with competitive potential.
P29	Organizational implications of the IS plan implementation must be included in it.
P30	Plans must assure that implementation efforts must be coordinated on a short-term basis, but must be integrated on a broader term.
P31	Plans must be formulated in such way that the implications on the information systems from derived nuances in circumstances/strategies may be easily identified in the plan.
P32	The IS planning process must lead to a continuously improved comprehension by the potential management of the information systems.
P33	The IS planning must increase IS personnel consistence regarding the organizational objectives.
P34	The IS planning must create shared hypothesis or at least clarify and maybe reduce the existent conflicts between inaccurate or incorrect hypothesis.
P35	The IS planning must create a common language for high-level manager, IS management and user management.
P36	The IS planning must assure organizational support for decision and a strong commitment regarding the required resources.

Chart 5: Result Prescriptions

Finally, evaluation prescriptions (Chart 6) define the criteria to be used in an IS planning process evaluation.

P37	The planning process must incorporate a monitoring and diagnostic system for its own evaluation and continuous improvement.
P38	The IS planning process must be evaluated according to the planning prescriptions and standards usually accepted.
P39	The IS planning process must be evaluated in terms of specific objectives that have been defined.
P40	The planning process must be evaluated in terms of interests, complaints and objectives of different groups in the organization.

Chart 6: Evalution Prescriptions

The process prescriptions may be seen as completing other prescriptions. Objectives establishment, crew selection, analysis conduction, results and evaluations formulation requires a process to be achieved. In this study, all prescriptions related to the planning process are listed as process prescriptions. The other prescription categories (objectives, resources, analysis, results and evaluation) refer only to the planning content. The distinction between process and content reflects the way prescriptions have been suggested in literature. The prescriptions normally refer to planning as a whole, while the content prescriptions refer to a specific task.

2.2.2 ISSP Approaches

Studying the approaches used for the IS planning, researchers have found that there are significant differences between the IS planning processes used in many companies. Four elements are essential in discussions of the planning approaches (Salmela, 1996): range of analysis (Mclean and Soden, 1997), process formalism (Pyburn, 1993, place where the decision is taken (Guimarães and McKeen, 1989) and scope of the planning process (Earl, 1993).

Next, the identified approaches are presented in order to describe the variations between each of them. These variations will later be used to characterize the differences between traditional approaches and the approach suggested in this study, utilizing OL and PD contributions. Chart 7 synthesizes the main elements of each identified approach.

TYPOLOGY	ELEMENT	MAIN AUTHOR	VARIANTS
A	Range of Analysis	McLean and Soden, 1997	Rational / Intuitive
B	Formalism	Pyburn, 1993	Predefined / Flexible
C	Decision	Guimarães and McKeen, 1989	Centralized / Decentralized
D	Scope	Earl, 1993	Organization level / Project level

Chart 7: ISSP approaches elements.

2.4 Organizational Learning.

Organizational Learning is the process in which the value basis and organization knowledge changes, taking it to a skills increase on solving problems and on the organization's action capability front the environment demands. (Probst and Buschel, 1997). The OL has been identified as an important element on solving organization problems, especially those related to strong competitive pressures of the market and to the changes of technological basis.

The usage of creative techniques (Altier, 1999, Couger, 1996, Kao, 1997) and the dynamic non-linear thought perform an important role on the creation of a learning environment. In the last years, the OL has captured manager and researchers' attention (Argyris, 1993; Senge, 1990). This focus on learning points out the cognitive approaches relevance, in which individuals beliefs and insights are seen as critical in the organizational efficiency. Recently, a few researches are developing studies to understand how can OL be used in IS planning (Ang et al, 1997, Baets, 1998, Reponen, 1998).

3 RESEARCH METHODS

This research is characterized as an exploratory study and the methods used are case studies and lived deeply experience. The study case method is adopted as proposed by Yin (1994), and the lived experience characterized as a case study in which the research is reporting and living the case (Benbasat et al, 1987; Janissek, 2000), that is, living the process, with greater involvement than the conventional study case. Two lived experiences were described and a study case was developed.

The usage and definition protocols for the lived experience and study case development and to formalization, which are based on a consistent theoretical observation, had as objective uniform and systemize the analysis and observation task, increasing the study's reliability.

The analysis unit of the lived experience, as well as the case study, were ISSP projects developed in organization of the service sector. What has justified the organization's choice was the organization's importance (great importance), the adoption of a formal process and ISSP documentation, the existence a IS subject structured on a directive level in the organization.

The Data analysis technique used was the content analysis. Associated to the content analysis the documental analyses were used, to understand the information provided by the people interviewed, and the lexical analysis. The usage of several methods and information sources made possible the triangulation of the collected data, to extend the description, explanation and comprehension of the study object the most.

4 CASE STUDY RESULTS

The strategic planning model used in the organizations has presented the following phases: diagnostic (or evaluation), formulation (or strategy definitions) and implementation (Boar, 1993). The conduction methodology planning process was: (a) in the diagnostic phase there was the presentation of the points to be analyzed, definition of the interview techniques and document analysis, definition of the data collecting instruments, of the data crossing to identify the critical points and diagnostic report structure; (b) in the formulation phase there was a presentation of the critical points, the definition of the meeting techniques for solutions formulation and construction, and at last, the final structure of the strategic plan; and (c) in the implementation phase there was the presentation of the continuous review methodology, definition of the control indicators and results feedback at the end of the planning period, enabling to obtain improvements for the next period.

4.1 Lived Experience 1: State's Office

The studied organization is an agency of the direct management of one of the State Governments of Brazil, in a State's office. The organization presents an organizational structure composed by the secretary's cabinet and direct assessors - legal, planning and social communication; public income department (management, police stations and collection stations), in direction level; department of public expenses, in direction level; department of the accounting department and general auditorship of the hip accounts of the State, in direction level. Besides the assessorships, three supervisions report directly to the secretary cabinet: information systems, general management, and organizational development and quality.

Trying to synthesize an evaluation, it is present next the planning prescriptions identification that was observed and the ones that were not observed in the analyzed process (Chart 8), according to the theoretical basis presented in section 2.2.1.

Situation	Group	ISSP Prescriptions
Observed	1 – objectives	4
	2 – resources	6 9
	3 – analysis	11 12 16
	4 – process	19
	5 – results	27 28
	6 – evaluation	40
Not observed	1 – objectives	1 2 3 5
	2 – resources	7 8 10
	3 – analysis	13 14 15 17 18
	4 – process	20 21 22 23 24 25 26
	5 – results	29 30 31 32 33 34 35 36
	6 – evaluation	37 38 39

Chart 8: Observed and not observed prescriptions in lived experience 1.

Regarding the ISSP approaches utilized, the following variable analysis behavior is identified (Chart 9), according to the theoretical basis presented in section 2.2.2.

Variable	Evaluation
Scope	Ample
Range	Rational
Formalism	Strict
Decision	Decentralized
Conclusion	Traditional (synoptic)

Chart 9: Variable related to the lived deeply Experience 1 approach.

4.2. Lived Experience 2: University

The organization studied, at that time, one of the three greatest private universities of the country in student number, with more than 24 thousand enrolled students, in undergraduate and graduate courses, more than 2.000 professors and employees. The University Hospital (HU) had more than 6.000 employees, divided in technical (doctors, nurses, nutritionists etc.) and the administrative area. The University is entailed to a sponsor entity of confessional basis.

The organization presents an organizational structure with five pro-rectories, an advanced campus direction (located in other city of the same state) and several assistants in rectory level.

Trying to synthesize this evaluation, the planning prescription identification observed or not observed in the analyzed process is presented next (Chart 10).

Situation	Group	ISSP Prescriptions
Observed	1 – objectives	4
	2 – resources	6 8 9
	3 – analysis	11 12 14 16
	4 – process	21 26
	5 – results	27 30 31 33 34 36
	6 – evaluation	39
Not Observed	1 – objectives	1 2 3 5
	2 – resources	7 10
	3 – analysis	13 15 17 18
	4 – process	19 20 22 23 24 25
	5 – results	28 29 32 35
	6 – evaluation	37 38 40

Chart 10: Observed and not observed prescriptions in lived experience 2

In relation to the ISSP approaches utilized, the following variable analysis behavior is identified.

Variable	Evaluation
Scope	Ample
Range	Rational
Formalism	Strict
Decision	Centralized
Conclusion	Traditional (synoptic)

Chart 11: Variable Related to the lived deeply experience 2 approach

4.3. Case Study Results

After the lived experience development, the study case allowed the analysis of the OL techniques usage and PD approaches in an ISSP process. This way, it has tried to track the ISSP process in one organization that has been using these techniques and approaches efficiently and has evaluate the variable's behavior and defined constructor in research models.

The case study was developed in a Medical Center (UMC) filiated to a great North American university, being the greatest medical center in its sphere of activity. It is also the greatest employer of the region, with 6.200 employees. It owns two hospitals, considering that the major one has 473 beths and several research centers, it attends over 20.600 patients annually, managing an annual budget of $375 millions of dollars.

Trying to relate to results obtained in this study, the planning prescriptions identification that were observed or not observed in the process analyzed are presented next (Chart 12).

Situation	Group	ISSP Prescription
Observed	1 – objectives	1 2 3 4 5
	2 – resources	6 7 8 9 10
	3 – analysis	11 12 13 14 15 16 17
	4 – process	19 20 24 25
	5 – results	27 28 29 30 31 33 34 35 36
	6 – evaluation	39 40
Not observed	1 – objectives	-
	2 – resources	-
	3 – analysis	18
	4 – process	21 22 23 26
	5 – results	32
	6 – evaluation	37 38

Chart 12: Observed and not observed prescriptions in UMC case

In relation to the utilized ISSP approaches, the following behavior of the variable analyzed is identified.

Variable	Evaluation
Scope	Incremental
Including	Intermediate
Formalism	Intermediate
Decision	Descentralized
Conclusion	Incremental

Chart 13: Variable related to the approach in the UMC case

It is important to note that the incremental approach identified by the research team matches the project participants' view that evaluated this way and the project leaders that explained the search for this type of approach.

5 RESULT ANALYSIS: RELATION BETWEEN PRESCRIPTIVE AND DESCRIPTIVE MODELS

One of these challenges concerns understanding the reason that has allowed the case study (of prescriptive basis) to present results with relation to the adherence to the ISSP prescription better than the lived experience (of descriptive basis, Chart 14). This challenge has led to an intellectual exercise aiming to understand this apparent paradox. In this chapter, before presenting the proposed model, an analysis is developed and a model, which explains the result, is proposed. For such way, an analysis of epistemological basis, relating both the prescriptive planning (rational) and descriptive models is made.

When analyzing the behavior of the ISSP prescriptions in the studies developed in this research, it is possible to identify that the used incremental approach in the case study in the UMC has contributed for the observation of a significantly bigger number of prescriptions of the ISSP theory (Chart 14).

Group of Prescription	Liv. Exp. 1	% on total	Liv. Exp. 2	% on total	UMC case	% on total
1 – objectives	1	20%	1	20%	5	100%
2 – resources	2	40%	3	60%	5	100%
3 – analysis	3	37,5 %	4	50%	7	87,5 %
4 – process	1	12,5 %	2	25%	4	50%
5 – results	2	20%	6	60%	9	90%
6 – evaluation	1	25%	1	25%	2	50%
TOTALS	**10**	**25%**	**17**	**42,5%**	**32**	**80%**

Chart 14: Matching between ISSP prescriptions identified in the study

These results lead to an apparent paradox, since the prescriptions are clearly identified as a rational and deterministic view. However, analyzing more carefully, we will notice that the greater commitment and involvement of the users with the planning process ends up making a great part of the prescriptions searched by the theory possible. The information indicates that, for this study case, the incremental approach in an OL context strongly stimulates the involvement and commitment, setting positive effects in relation to the users' perception and process participants, influencing directly the implementation phase. Consequently, even using the typical evaluation criteria of the prescriptive planning school, the descriptive approach (incremental) observed in the case study obtains more satisfactory results.

Deepening this analysis and trying to relate it to the OL and PD theory studied, the model presented in Figure 1 can be inferred. When developing this model, the objective is to relate prescriptive approach, typical of the rational line, and the descriptive approach, typical of the OL subject.

The rational model (upper circle) works with the idea that there is and it is possible to always find the best solution (that is, the truth about the fact being studied). In fact, the rational model stubbornly pursues this truth (objective) and, for that, it uses the so call scientific or rational methods and experiments. These methods are typical of the operational research approach (OR) that has developed itself under the perspective of the prescriptive school. Using these methods, when finding the truth, this school prescribes procedures. From the point of view of the conduction process, a group of people (normally reduced) or even one person conducts the entire process. From the implementation of the decision taking point of view (or the generated plan), the rational model believes in the idea that the implementation will occur simply because the truth, indicated in the plan or the decision, is determinant by itself. Following these prescriptions, the truth found through rational methods would be implemented (lower circle).

The descriptive model (circle to the left), where several contributions in the OL area are found, pursues the participation of the personnel in the decision process. When working with learning, implicitly the OL and the incremental approach pursue participation. In one hand, this participation generates commitment, which will ease the

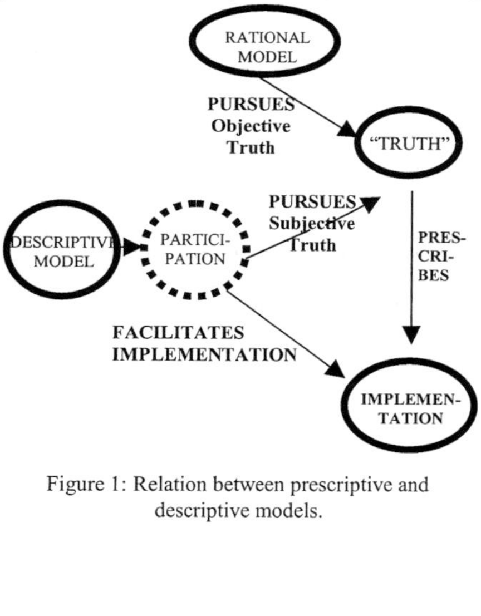

Figure 1: Relation between prescriptive and descriptive models.

implementation process; on the other hand it contributes to obtaining the truth (subjective) too, only obtained through major participation and personal involvement.

It is interesting to notice that the research on OL does not deal with the issue this way, as it does not presenting the ideal solution (that wouldn't exist). Thus, the truth (objective) to be search wouldn't exist. However, as shown in the model above, it ends up obtaining this truth (subjective), or something very close to it (the possible in that socio-political content). From this model, it is possible to say, if this truth really exists, that it will get close to it. And if the truth does not exist, something else better or possible in that context (objective truth) will be found.

The objective is to show that the "truth" does exist, although it is not objective (and, according to the rational model, seen and accepted for everybody after its discovery). As the descriptive model, this truth is subjective, it depends on people's involvement to be achieved, that is, the subjective truth is built continuously, being constantly modified. According to the proposed model, in this search for the truth, what is different is the method used in the rational school and in the descriptive school. And it is related to the different worldviews of the classic rational and prescriptive models. While the rational models pursue and sees an objective truth, in the absolute way, believing that the truth is static and the search preferably using few experts, the prescriptive model pursues and sees a subjective truth, in the relative way, believing that the truth is dynamic and can be incremented and the search as result of the participative process.

Ending this cycle, the proposed model aims to explain the *why* of the results found in relation to the ISSP prescriptions. That is, what has significantly varied the way to do things. And, when working aiming to increase participation, potentialized the commitment and results in the implementation phase. This way, it makes sense that a larger number of prescriptions had been observed in the case study (descriptive model).

6 CONCLUSION

The results obtained suggest that a different scientific referential can be characterized to study and execute the planning process in the IS subject. This means to start from a more positive and prescriptive view towards a more interpretative view, based on action science, following the descriptive planning school line of thought.

Argyris (1993) points out that the action science can be the starting point to develop an interactive learning process aiming strategy generation. And this means that the responsible for the planning process, as well as the researchers, must assemble with the participants from the different areas of the organization in a collaborative process that stimulates the critics in relation to the social practice's processes and problems in a learning context. The main characteristic of this project must be that it shall be designed specifically to stimulate the learning.

Throughout the years, the researches in the field of ISSP have generated certain knowledge in this area. The major part of this knowledge is concentrated in studies of the prescriptive like and classical rational and it is represented by many articles. The results obtained, and considering all the limitations that are typical of this kind of research, suggest clearly the relevance o the use of descriptive approaches in the ISSP context. This gives empirical support to the many studies that have explored the convergences of ISSP and OL.

REFERENCES

ALTIER, W. *Effective processes for problem solving e decision making*. New York, Oxford Press, 1999.

ANG, K., THONG, J e YAP, C. IT implementation through the lens of OL: a case study of insuror. *Proceedings of ICIS*, Atlanta, 1997.

ARGYRIS, C. *On organizational learning*. Oxford, Blackwell, 1993.

BAETS, W. *Organizational Learning and Knowledge Technologies in a dynamic environment*. Dordrecht, The Netherlands, Kluwer Academics Publishers, 1998.

BENBASAT, I., GOLDSTEIN, D. e MEAD, M. The case reserch strategy in studies of information system. *MIS Quarterly 11(3)*, 1987.

BOAR, B. *The Art of Strategic Planning for Information Technology*. New York, John Wiley and Sons, 1993.

BOYNTON, A. e ZMUD, R. Information Technology planning in the 90's: direction for practice and research. *MIS Quarterly* 11(1), 1987.

COUGER, J. *Creativity and inovation in IS organizations*. Danver, MA, Boyd and Fraser Publishing, 1996.

GALLIERS, R. Information systems planning in the UK and Australia: a comparation of current practice. In: *Oxford Surveys of IT* (4), 1987.

GUIMARAES, T. e McKEEN, J. The process of selecting information systems projects. *DataBase Management* 20(2), 1989.

HENDERSON, J. e SIFONIS, J. The value of strategic IS planning: understanding consistency, validity and IS markets. *MIS Quarterly*, June 1988.

JANNISSEK, R. *A influência da internet em negócios empresariais: identificação e caracterização de elementos para análise de sites*. Dissertação de mestrado, PPGA, EA, UFRGS, 2000.

KAO, J. Jammimg. Rio de Janeiro, Campus, 1997.

KING, W.R. How effective is your IS planning?. *Long Range Planning* (21:2), 1988.

LEDERER, A. e SETHI, V. Root causes of strategic information system planning implementation problems. *Jornal of MIS* 9(1), 1992.

LEDERER, A. e SETHI, V. Key prescriptions for strategic information system planning. *Journal of MIS* 13(1), 1996.

McLEAN, E. e SODEN, J. *Strategic planning for MIS*. John Willey and Sons, 1977.

MINTZBERG, H. Crafting Strategy. In: Harvard Bussiness Review Paperback. Boston, *Harvard Business Review*, 1995.

PRENKUMAR, G. e KING, W.R. Assessing strategic information system planning. *Long Range Planning* (24:4), 1991, pp41-58.

PRENKUMAR, G. e KING, W.R. An empirical assessment of IS planning and the role f IS in organizations. *Journal of MIS* (9:2), 1992.

PRENKUMAR , G. e KING, W.R. Organizational characteristics and information system planning: an empirical study. *Information System Research* 5(2), 1994.

PROBST, G. e BUCHEL, B. *Organizational learning*. London, Prentice Hall, 1997.

PYBURN, P. Linking the MIS plan with corporate strategy: na exploratory study. *MIS Quarterly* 7(2), 1993.

REPONEN, T. The Role of Learning in Information System Planning and Implementation. In: GALLIERS, H. e BAETS, R. *Information Technology and Organizational Transformation*. Chichester, England, John Wiley and Sons, 1998.

SALMELA, H. *The requirements of ISP in a turbulent environment*. Ph.D. Dissertation. Turku School of economics and business administration. Sarja, 1996.

SENGE, P. M. *A Quinta Disciplina*. São Paulo, Best Seller, 1990.

YIN,R. *Case study research: design and methods*. London, Sage, 1994.

DESIGNING BUSINESS PROCESSES AND COMMUNICATION STRUCTURES FOR E-BUSINESS USING ONTOLOGY-BASED ENTERPRISE MODELS WITH MATHEMATICAL MODELS

Henry M. Kim
Schulich School of Business, York University, Toronto, Ontario M3J 1P3
Email:hkim@schulich.yorku.ca

K. Donald Tham
Department of Mechanical, Aerospace and Industrial Engineering, Ryerson University, Toronto, Ontario M5B 2K3
Email:dtham@acs.ryerson.ca

Key words: Ontologies, business process, communication structures, e-business, enterprise modeling.

Abstract: Organizations are apprehensive about developing e-business systems because the endeavor is novel. If e-business is considered as the conduct of business using the Internet—a network of networks—then e-business systems design can be represented as a network design problem. This paper outlines an approach for analysis and design of business process and communications structure networks for e-business. Network design alternatives are generated by applying best practices and design principles to business requirements, using ontology-based enterprise models. Alternatives then are modeled mathematically for analysis and comparison. Domains relevant for e-business systems design are described, formally and systematically, using this approach. These formal descriptions are general axioms, used to logically and mathematically infer prescriptions for specific design problems. These descriptions and prescriptions are sharable and re-usable. The mathematical models are developed using known algorithms, heuristics, and formulae. Therefore, fidelity of prescriptions based on these models can be objectively justified. Due to these characteristics, models developed using this technique are especially useful for developing novel e-business systems. An example application of this technique is presented, and research questions addressed using the approach are discussed.

1 INTRODUCTION

Many organizations are apprehensive about developing e-business systems because the endeavor is novel. A useful definition of e-business is "the conduct of business on the Internet, not only buying and selling but also servicing customers and collaborating with business partners" (Whatis.com, 1999). Organizations use physical, informational, and social networks for buying, selling, servicing, and collaborating. These networks are used to support business processes and as infrastructure for communications. If the Internet is considered a "network of networks," then the design of e-business systems can be conceptualized and modeled in part as the design of business processes and communication structure networks. This abstraction decomposes a task not well understood (designing e-business systems) to tractable sub-tasks of modeling:- (1) business processes and communication structure networks, and (2) how the Internet and other information technologies affect characteristics of such networks. Not only are these models invaluable in designing a *specific* system, they can be re-used, thus making *general* e-business systems design a less unknown task.

Business processes and communication structures are general, tangible facets of the organization, and hence can be represented using a (computational) *enterprise model*[1], "a computational representation of the structure, activities, processes, information, resources, people, behavior, goals, and constraints of

[1] Henceforth, the term, enterprise model, will refer to computational enterprise models.

a business, government, or other enterprise" (Fox & Grüninger, 1998) . Though seemingly less tangible, organizational knowledge about how information technologies—especially the Internet—can be leveraged for novel business processes and communication structures' design can also be modeled in an enterprise model as information, goals, and constraints. Enterprise models are data models that represent enterprise facets in a data modeling language as entities, relationships, attributes, and axioms. Mathematical models can be used to state functional relationships of enterprise facets using mathematics. Math models for analyzing networks are especially useful for modeling business processes and communication structures.

Whether they are represented using a data modeling language or mathematics, or another type of language, the following are desirable properties of models of business processes and communication structures for e-business:-

1. *Descriptive*: The models should describe business processes and communication structures.
2. *Prescriptive*: The models should apply knowledge about developing e-business business processes and communication structures to the descriptions so as to prescribe to developing good designs
3. *Sharable* and *re-usable*: Since the endeavor for which the models are developed is novel, it is important that it be sharable and capable of re-use, both within and among organizations.
4. *Formal*. To effectively use computers to enable prescription, and sharing and re-use, the models should be represented in a formal language with limited syntax and semantics that minimizes interpretation ambiguity. These representations then can be encoded so that computers can automatically apply prescriptions and intended meanings of the model builder when the model is shared or re-used by others.

2 ONTOLOGY-BASED ENTERPRISE MODELING

Using ontologies, Kim (1999) and Tham (1999) develop enterprise models for quality management and cost management respectively with the four desirable properties. An *ontology* is a data model that "consists of a representational vocabulary with precise definitions of the meanings of the terms of this vocabulary plus a set of formal axioms that constrain interpretation and well-formed use of these terms" (Campbell & Shapiro, 1995). Vocabulary, definitions, and axioms that describe the enterprise are formally represented using ontologies, and prescriptions for achieving goals are formally defined using these ontologies' representations in models by Kim and Tham. Kim describes enterprise quality and prescribes to ISO 9000 compliance. Tham describes enterprise activity-based costing (ABC), and prescribes to strategic cost management. Parts of these models can be shared and re-used by others with minimized interpretation ambiguity because they are modeled formally. Therefore, an ontology is an explicit representation of shared understanding (Gruber, 1993).

An example use of ontologies for business process or communication structure design is presented by Atefi (1997), who represents Hammer and Champy's (1994) business process re-engineering principles as formal axioms of an ontology. These axioms are applied to different business scenarios to offer prescriptions. Alternatively, Buzacott (1996) models these principles mathematically. He models networks of business processes that are consistent with each principle, and then analyzes networks' performance using queuing models. There are merits to both modeling approaches. Business processes can be formally and systematically described using ontologies; and since there are numerous, well-known mathematical models for network analysis, prescriptions resulting from analyzing these models can be objectively justified. Next, a discussion about the four desirable properties of business processes and communication structure models for e-business is presented so as to rationalize an approach that combines ontology-based enterprise modeling and mathematical modeling.

3 ONTOLOGY-BASED ENTERPRISE MODELS AND MATHEMATICAL MODELS

To enable ontology sharing and re-use, key assumptions, vocabulary, and business rules about enterprise facets must be stated, organized, and formally defined and constrained. Thus, ontologies should be richly descriptive so that what is often implicitly held is explicitly represented. Ontologies by design are constructed from existing ontologies. For example, Kim's and Tham's ontologies for quality management and strategic cost management respectively are developed using ontologies of activity, state, causality, time, resource, and organizational structure that describe fundamental concepts about an enterprise. These are collectively called the TOVE Core Ontologies (Grüninger &

Fox, 1995). However, ontological engineering is still a new endeavor, and sharable libraries of ontologies are not extensively available as, say, math libraries. Unless representations from robust sharable ontologies can be used, developing richly descriptive ontologies is time consuming. It entails anticipating unintended interpretations of terms in the vocabulary or improper applications of business rules, and mitigating them. Moreover, expressiveness of descriptive ontologies bound problem solving capabilities of prescriptive ontologies constructed from them. The more expressive the descriptive ontologies, the more likely are insights from using the prescriptive ontologies.

There are numerous libraries of algorithms, heuristics and formulae, and research supporting them. So, formal mathematical models whose analyses yield prescriptive insights can be constructed from existing libraries with much less work than using ontology-based models. When evaluating a math model, only the fidelity—accuracy, appropriateness of assumptions, etc—of its development to the point at which it is expressed using libraries may need to be evaluated, not the libraries themselves. Since shared ontologies are not supported by similar volume of research, the fidelity of the representations of shared ontologies may be questioned, as well as those representations built from them. It is often possible to prove, analytically or by simulation, that one mathematical model performs better than a similar one as per some concrete, quantitative criteria. However, it is difficult to categorically state that a definition of a business process represented in a given descriptive ontology is better than a similar ontology's definition, or that Hammer and Champy's BPR principles represented in a given prescriptive ontology is better than Davenport's (1993) business process insights represented in another ontology.

Mathematical models are more re-usable and prescriptive than ontology-based models. Extensively available libraries can be re-used, thus shortening model development time. Fidelity of mathematical prescriptive models can be objectively justified. Often however, math models can be re-used and offer prescriptions only if there is an interpreter who understands the mathematics. As well, assumptions and analysis of the domain used to develop the models are informally documented in natural language, and hence, subject to interpretation ambiguity inherent in natural language use. Even these descriptions are sometimes sparsely documented, and much knowledge is "lost" after model construction. Therefore, mathematical models are not richly descriptive. Say that the following subtle distinction is made:

- Re-use: Using parts of existing models to develop new ones, the builder of the existing model plays some role in new development.
- Sharing: Using parts of existing models as intended by the builder of the model, the model builder does not play an active role in its use.

Then because they are cryptic and not descriptive, math models are often not sharable, though re-usable.

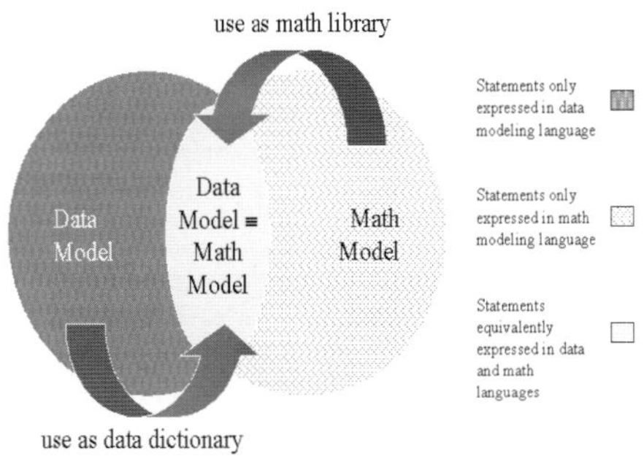

Figure 1: Relationship between Data and Mathematical Models.

Often data models are useful simply as descriptive abstractions of entities, relationships, and attributes. Formal models further commit to supporting automatic inference of implicit descriptions. Mathematical models formally represent functional relationships that govern behavior of systems. Formal data models can be used to infer implicit relationships between entities and their attributes, and when they access mathematical expressions, they can be used to further infer functional relationships. Used this way, mathematical models serve as libraries for a formal data model. When mathematical models access formal data model expressions, the assumptions and principles that math models use, which may otherwise be implicit or informally stated, are explicitly stated using a data model. This explicitness provides meanings and constraints of terms used in the math model so as to ensure their proper use for clarification and validity testing. Formal data models serve as data dictionaries for a mathematical model. There are some expressions in either language types that are logically equivalent, namely first-order mathematical expressions—i.e. those of the form $f(x)$, not $f(g(x))$—can be equivalently expressed in First-Order Logic. These expressions are important because they are used to translate between ontology-based models and mathematical models.

Next, a formal modeling approach that combines

the descriptiveness and sharability of ontology-based models with the prescriptive capability and re-usability of math models is detailed.

4 COMBINED ONTOLOGY-BASED ENTERPRISE AND MATHEMATICAL MODELING APPROACH

Below, different models developed using this approach are presented along with their uses.

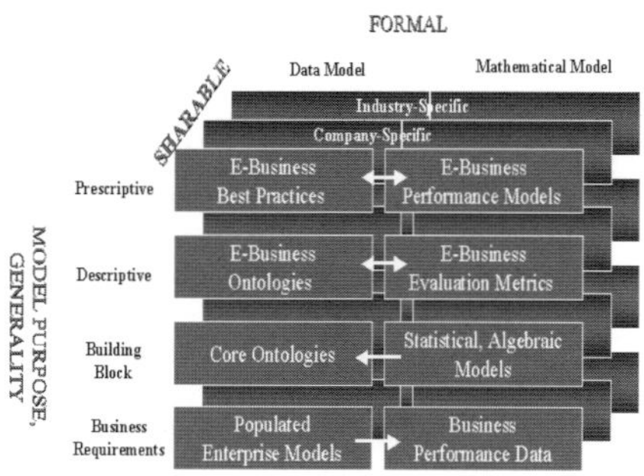

Figure 2:Using Enterprise Models of E-Business Best Practices and Evaluation Metrics

There are two types of formal models, data and mathematical. These models can be characterized by the degree to which they can be shared and re-used - general, industry-specific, or company-specific. Models can also be characterized by their purpose, which also defines their generality using this approach. Prescriptive models are developed using descriptive ones, which in turn are developed using building block models. Business facts and requirements are represented as data instances of a populated (instantiated) enterprise model or raw numbers comprising business performance data.

Building block models provide general form with which business facts and requirements are represented. For example, **activity(A)** is a Core Ontology term. The fact, `lathing using equipment #1` is an activity, can be represented as an instance **activity(**lathing1**)**—i.e. the variable **A** is bound to the constant lathing1—in the populated enterprise model. Say that the `average duration of the activity is 5 minutes`. This can be represented as an instantiation of the term **activity_duration(A,Tp)** as **activity_duration(**lathing1,5**)**. The arrows in the diagram denote that one model uses translated representations from the other. The mathematical model of business performance data translates **activity_duration(**lathing1,5**)**, and represents it as $s_{lathe1}=5$. Next, example uses of such representations in the modeling approach is presented.

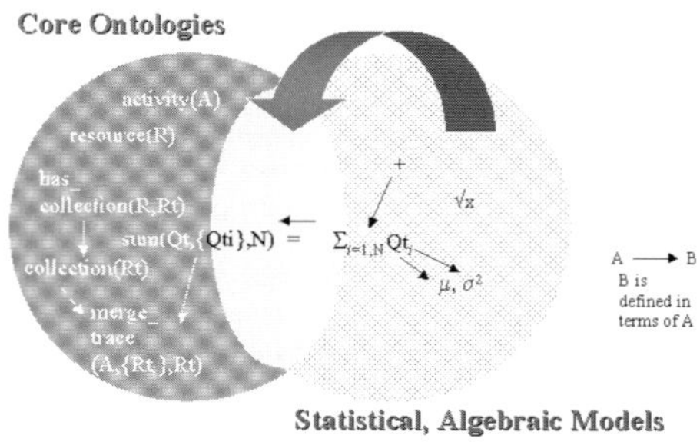

Figure 3: Relationship between Data and Mathematical Models at the Building Block Level

A building block math model comprises elementary terms like **Σ**, which is used as a math library term in defining the ontology term **sum(Qt,{Qti},N)**. This term is used in turn to define **merge_trace(A,{Rti},Rt)** in First-Order Logic (Kim, 1999):

Term-1. $Qt=\Sigma_{i=1,N}\, Qt_i$

Defn-1. sum({Qti},N,Qt)

$\forall N \forall Qt\ \{\forall i\ Qt=\Sigma_{i=1,N}\, Qt_i \equiv \forall(Qt_1,Qt_2,,Qt_N)$ sum($\{Qt_1,Qt_2,,Qt_N\}$,N,Qt)}.

A *merge trace* relationship exists between one merged *collection* (e.g. batch or lot) and the *collections* from which it is comprised, if there is an activity which produces one *collection* of quantity Qup, which is the sum of the quantities $Quc_1,Quc_2,,Quc_N$ of the *collections* that are consumed for the activity, and all the produced and consumed *collections* are all of the same resource type[2]:

Defn-2.merge_trace(A,{Rti},Rt)

$\forall A \forall s \forall Rt \exists(Rt_1,,,Rt_n)\exists R \exists St \exists Quc \exists s_o$
[*holds*(***merge_trace(A,{Rt₁,Rt₂,,Rtₙ},Rt)***,s) ≡
holds(primitive_activity(A),s) ∧
holds(produce(St,A),s) ∧ *holds*(produces(St,Rt),s) ∧
holds(has_collection(R,Rt),s)
∧ *holds*(amount_produced(Rt,Qup),s) ∧ $\neg\exists St_o \neg\exists Rt_o$
{ *holds*(produces(St_o,Rt_o),s_o) ⊃ $Rt \neq Rt_o$ }
∧ $\exists(St_1,,,St_n)\exists(Quc_1,,,Quc_n)$ { (∪i=1,,n

[2] The First-Order Logic definition for *merge trace* merely illustrates the form of ontology representations, and full description of terms with which the definition is composed is beyond the scope of this paper. The reader is referred to [3 for fuller descriptions.

(*holds*(consume(St_i,A),s_o)
$\wedge$ *holds*(consumes(St_i,Rt_i),s_o) $\wedge$
holds(has_collection(R,Rt_i),s_o)
$\wedge$ *holds*(amount_committed(St_i,Rt_i,Quc_i),s_o)) $\wedge$ $s_o<s$
) $\wedge$ sum({Quc_1,Quc_2,,Quc_N},N,Qup) }].

Say that *average response time* is represented in an e-business evaluation metric math model. It is defined using terms like Σ from building block math models. Say that term **measured_attribute(At)** from the e-business ontologies is instantiated as **measured_attribute(**average_response_time**)**.

The following are representations about *measured attribute*:

Term-2.has_unit_of_measurement(At,U)

Cons-13. All measured attributes must have a unit of measurement

$\forall$At$\forall$U$\forall$s$\exists$Rt [*holds*(collection(Rt),s) $\wedge$
holds(has_attribute(Rt,At),s) $\wedge$
holds(measured_attribute(At),s) $\wedge$
$\exists$A$\exists$Un
holds(unit_of_measurement(Rt,Un,U,A),s)
$\supset$
holds(***has_unit_of_measurement(At,U)***,s
].

These representations then are used to constrain proper use of *average response time.* Namely, the ontology provides a data dictionary function of stipulating that there must be a unit of measurement associated with *average response time.*

Another metric, *service quality*, may be defined as a function of the *average response time* in the math model:

Term-3. servQ(Tp) = *f*(average_response_time$_{Tp}$).

Then the term *measurement point* can be expressed in the ontology as follows for *service quality* as a measured attribute. Used this way, **servQ(Tp)** is used as a math library term for the ontology definition:

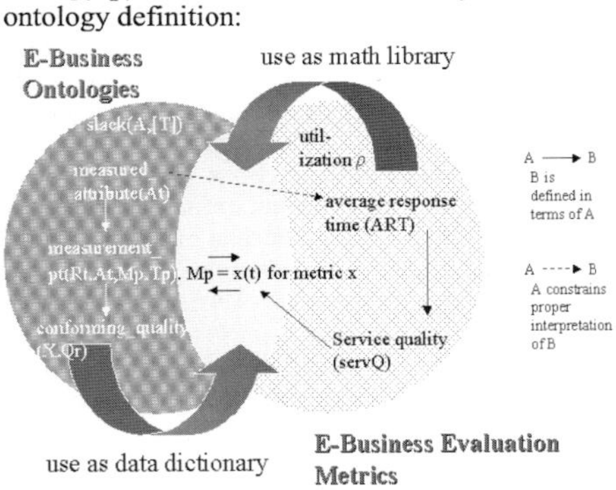

Figure 4: Relationship Between Data and Mathematical Models at the Descriptive Modeling Level

Defn-3. measurement_pt(Rt,At,Mp,Tp), where **At=**servQ

$\forall$Rt$\forall$Mp$\forall$Tp$\forall$s$\exists$T[
holds(measured_attribute(servQ),s) $\wedge$
holds(has_attribute(Rt,servQ),s) $\wedge$ *holds*(has_attribute_value(Rt, servQ,Mp),s)
$\wedge$ Mp=servQ(Tp) $\wedge$ $\exists$A (
holds(collection(Rt),s)
$\wedge$ *holds*(use_res_collection(A,Rt),s)
$\wedge$ *holds*(primitive_measure(A),s) $\wedge$
occurs$_T$(activity_duration(A,T))) $\wedge$
has_point(T,Tp) } $\supset$
holds(**measurement_pt(*Rt*,**servQ,***Mp,Tp***)
,s)]

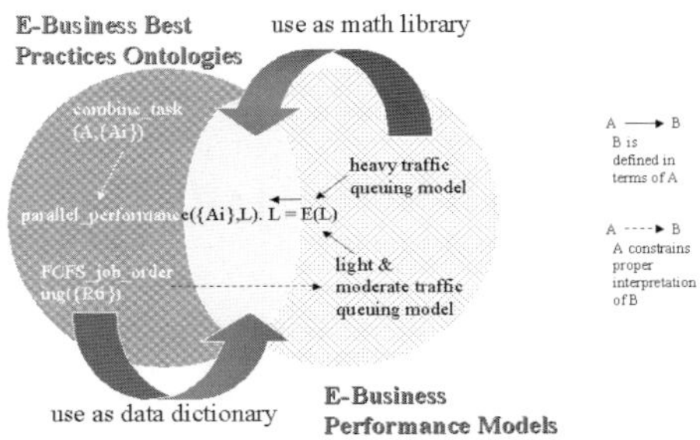

Figure 5: Relationship Between Data and Mathematical Models at the Prescriptive Modeling Level

Measurement point in turn is used to define an ontology term called *conforming quality*.

Buzacott (1996) uses heavy traffic, and light & moderate G/G/I queuing models to calculate average queue length **E(L)** to mathematically analyze Hammer & Champy's re-engineering principle - 'several tasks are combined into one'. These models can be included in the e-business performance math models. An assumption of the light & moderate queuing model is first-come-first-serve (FCFS) sequencing of jobs. An e-business best practices ontology term **FCFS_job_ordering({Ati})** can be used to describe the sequencing heuristic. As well, **E(L)** can be used as a math library term to define an ontology term called:
parallel_performance({Ai},L), which represents a prescription for re-sequencing activities {Ai} to perform in parallel to lower average queue length L. A term that represents a prescription to validly combine tasks, **combine_task(A,{Ai})**, is also used to define parallel performance.

Figure 6 shows how model representations are defined in terms of representations from more general model, e.g., prescriptive models defined from descriptive ones.

[3] Cons denotes a constraint.

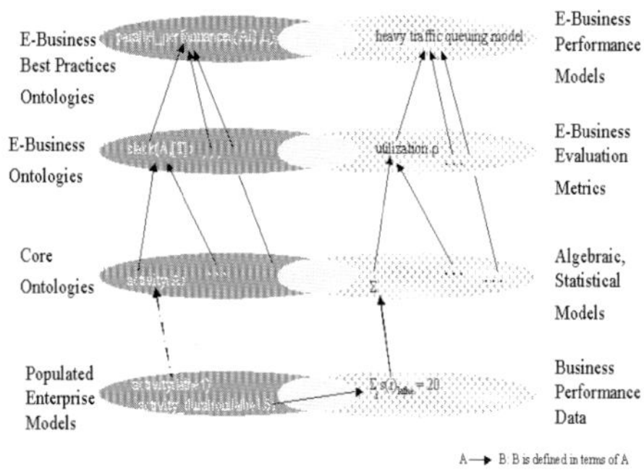

Figure 6: Relationship between Modeling Levels

5 CONCLUDING REMARKS AND FUTURE WORK

There is a need to use models to analyze and design e-business systems. By conceptualizing and modeling e-business systems as business process and communication structure networks, existing research in modeling network performance can be applied to address this novel research area. It is desirable that these e-business models be descriptive, prescriptive, formal, sharable and re-usable. Ontology-based enterprise models are descriptive, formal, and sharable. Mathematical models are formal, and more prescriptive and re-usable. By using an approach in which business processes and communications structures for e-business are modeled using both model types, all desirable properties can be brought to bear in model use. In this approach, business facts and requirements are represented as populated enterprise models (data modeling) and business performance data (math modeling). Core ontological representations provide schema for representing populated enterprise models, and statistical and algebraic models provide general form for representing business performance data. These are building block models, which in turn are used to develop descriptive models: E-business ontology representations formally define enterprise facets relevant for e-business using terms from the Core Ontologies; and e-business evaluation metrics are mathematically defined using statistical and algebraic models. E-business best practices' ontologies and mathematical e-business performance models can be used to prescribe better e-business systems' designs, and are formally defined using descriptive models. By designing e-business systems with models developed using this approach, prescriptions are:-

1) Objectively justified with mathematical rigor, as well as richly described.
2) Shared with minimized risk of unintended or improper interpretation of the prescriptions.
3) Re-used for developing additional e-business systems.

Ultimately by using these models, designers of e-business systems have a more rational basis for making their design choices, thus making their endeavor a less unknown task.

The example illustrated in this paper demonstrates promise for application of this modeling approach to address specific e-business systems' design problems. The following are such problems, for which there already exist ontology or math modeling research upon which to build:-

(a) Business process best practices and principles for e-business. Works by Atefi (1997) and Buzacott (1996) represent and analyze Hammer and Champy's (1994) principles. These works provide a starting point. However, they precede popular adoption of the Internet and WWW, and do not explicitly consider Internet technologies. To develop ontologies and math models for e-business process design, these works need to be augmented with current works in "e-process", e.g. (Keen & McDonald, 2000). Outputs of this research are business processes, and Internet best practices' models; as well as representations, defined using these models, comprising e-business process best practices' models.

(b)Web site design. When a web site provides information, there is a communication structure network of links between its pages, as well as links to other sites. When it supports transactions, there is an underlying business process network associated with its pages. Palmer and Griffin (1998) provide principles for web site design from a marketing perspective based on a site's information intensity and transactional (selling) functions. There are also numerous works stating design principles from a usability perspective, e.g.Fuccella (1997). Such works provide qualitative principles that can be represented using ontologies. Buzacott's (2000) queuing models of service system structure can be applied to design web sites that support business processes such as selling and customer support. Albert et. al. (1999) apply the 'Small Worlds Effect'—graph theory based analysis of the structure of social networks (Watts & Strogatz, 1998) —to estimate that any given web page is reachable from another via an average of 19 hyperlinks. These models can be applied to analyze web sites with extensive underlying communication structures, such as portals and search engines, and intranets of large corporations. Outputs of this research are ontologies whose representations describe web sites and evaluation metrics with which to evaluate the sites, as well as qualitative prescriptions for web site design and math models to analyze web site performance as per the evaluation metrics.

REFERENCES

Albert, R., Jeong, H., and Barabási, A.-L., 1999. Diameter of the World-Wide Web, *Nature*, 401, pp. 130-1.

Atefi, Katy, 1997. Formal models of business process reengineering for design and design validation, *M.A.Sc. Thesis*, Department of Mechanical and Industrial Engineering, University of Toronto., Toronto, Ontario, CANADA, M5S 3G9.

Buzacott. J.A., 1996. Commonalities in Reengineered Business Processes: Models and Issues. *Management Science,* Vol. 42, pp. 768-782.

Buzacott, J.A., 2000. Service System Structure, *International Journal of Production Economics*, Vol. 68, No. 1, pp. 15-27.

Campbell, A. E. and Shapiro, S. C., 1995. Ontological Mediation: An Overview", *Proceedings of the IJCAI Workshop on Basic Ontological Issues in Knowledge Sharing*, Menlo Park CA: AAAI Press.

Davenport, T.H., 1993. *Process Innovation*, Harvard Business School Press, Boston, MA.

Fox, Mark S. and Grüninger, Michael, 1998. Enterprise Modeling, *AI Magazine*, AAAI Press, Fall 1998, pp. 109-121.

Fuccella, Jeanette, 1997. Using User Centered Design Methods to Create and Design Usable Web Sites, *ACM SIGDOC 97*, Snowbird, Utah, pp. 69-77.

Gruber, Thomas R., 1993. Towards Principles for the Design of Ontologies Used for Knowledge Sharing, In *International Workshop on Formal Ontology*, N. Guarino & R. Poli, (Eds.), Padova, Italy.

Grüninger, M., and Fox, M.S., 1995. Methodology for the Design and Evaluation of Ontologies, *Workshop on Basic Ontological Issues in Knowledge Sharing*, IJCAI-95, Montreal.

Hammer M. and Champy J., 1994. *Reengineering the Corporation: A Manifesto for Business Revolution*, Harper Business.

Keen, P. and McDonald J., 2000. *e-Process Edge: Creating Customer Value and Business Wealth in the Internet Era*, McGraw-Hill Computing.

Kim, Henry M., 1999. Representing and Reasoning about Quality using Enterprise Models, *Ph.D. Thesis*, Department of Mechanical and Industrial Engineering, University of Toronto, Toronto, Ontario, CANADA, M5S 3G9.

Palmer J.W. and Griffith D.A., 1998. An Emerging Model of Web Site Design for Marketing, *Communications of the ACM*, Vol. 41, No. 3, March, pp. 45-51.

Tham, K. Donald, 1999. Representing and Reasoning about Costs using Enterprise Models and ABC, *Ph.D. Thesis*, Department of Mechanical and Industrial Engineering, University of Toronto, Toronto, Ontario, CANADA, M5S 3G9.

Watts, D.J. and Strogatz, S.H., 1998. Collective Dynamics of "Small World" Networks", *Nature*, 393, pp. 440-2.

Whatis.com, 1999. All Categories: Internet: Internet Technology Terms: e-business, [Online], *Available: http://www.whatis.com*, October 13.

ONTOLOGIES SUPPORTING BUSINESS PROCESS RE-ENGINEERING

Alexandra Galatescu, Taisia Greceanu
National Institute for R&D in Informatics, Averescu Avenue 8-10, 71316 Bucharest 1, ROMANIA, E-mail:{agal, gresta}@std.ici.ro}

Key words: business process re-engineering, upper-level ontology, BPR/ domain/ communication ontology.

Abstract: The paper motivates the ontologies for the automation of a Business Process Re-engineering (BPR) methodology (in particular, for the continuous and incremental improvement of the business processes using TQM - Total Quality Management). It describes and exemplifies an upper-level ontology with linguistic features and its application to three particular ontologies: BPR, domain and communication ontology. The main benefits from ontologies for BPR are: (1) they facilitate the (virtual) team work by providing a common vocabulary and understanding, (2) the ontological axioms support the organization and formalization of the BPR specific knowledge, as well as the inferences upon it, (3) an upper-level ontology helps for the integration of BPR and domain specific information and knowledge.

1 INTRODUCTION

Business Process Re-engineering (BPR), as rethinking and redesign of the business processes, means lately the analysis and redesign of the team-based workflows and processes within and between organizations ((Grover, 1995), (Malhotra, 1998) etc). Any metodology for BPR should take into account the virtual organization and the continuous evolution of the enterprise processes.

The process evolution (and also of the information and knowledge resources and infrastructure) can be kept under control by the continuous and incremental improvement of these processes, from both organizational and technological viewpoints and using a less radical BPR methodology. For instance, a metodology relying on Total Quality Management (TQM) (e.g. (MIT, 1996), (DON, 1996)). TQM is the inspiration source for tools like: Pathmaker (Skymark, 2000), Memory Jogger (GOALQPC, 1999), Solutions-PROSPER, PRO-QMS (DSS Infotech, 2000) etc.

BPR can be considered a precursor of the knowledge management in enterprises from historical, organizational and technological perspectives (Davenport, 1998) and the ontologies contribute to this kind of management.

As a 'specification of a conceptualization' (Gruber, 1993), an *ontology* is, practically, 'a vocabulary used to describe a certain reality, plus a set of explicit assumptions regarding the intended meaning of the vocabulary words' (Guarino, 1998). In an ontology, the relations between words (concepts) allow inference for the information interpretation and for the derivation of new information/ knowledge. The explicit *axioms* allow the approximation of the term meaning, the validation of its specification, the representation of the relationships between terms etc. As ontology *representation language,* the most important are: KIF (Knowledge Interchange Format), OntoLingua, OKBC (Object Knowledge Base Connectivity) Model, OIL (Ontology Interchange Language), RDF (Resource Description Framework), etc.

For BPR automation, the ontologies are motivated by several requirements:

- the need for the organization and formalization of the BPR specific knowledge;
- the need for the virtual and team-based management of the enterprise, relying on a common vocabulary and understanding of the concepts exchanged by the team members;
- the need for combining and inferring on BPR and domain specific knowledge simultaneously;
- the need for organizing and inferring on both objects and processes simultaneously.

Previous applications of the ontologies to business process management already exist. For example, in (Grover et al., 1995), as common language, IDEF5 ontology is proposed to describe "the ontological enterprise". In (Hawryszkiewycz, 1999), an enterprise ontology is used, relying on a common terminology and on generalized terms referring to roles, artifacts, interactions between people, norms to create teams, collaborative services etc. In (Uschlod et al., 1998), an enterprise ontology is proposed, as a collection of terms and definitions relevant to business processes. In (Schlenoff et al., 1998), a PSL (Process Specification Language) two-tiered ontology is proposed for the manufacturing integration. In (Scacchi et al., 1999) an ontology for business processes is described, together with its formal representation in Loom. And so on

This paper sketches a possible solution to satisfy the above requirements using an upper-level ontology with linguistic features for representing and integrating knowledge on BPR and domain specific objects and processes. This ontology is also intended for ideas acquisition from the members of BPR team, in a stylized format of natural language (NL). It is supposed to eliminate the NL ambiguities and, at the same time, to be close to the free expression of ideas during the BPR brainstorming sessions. The implementation of the ontologies presented in the next sections is under development.

Section 2 presents the basic ontological terms and axioms (sentences) in the upper-level ontology proposed for ontology integration (BPR, domain and communication ontology) and for ideas expression. Section 3 exemplifies the vocabularies and axioms in the three ontologies. Section 4 suggests the logic behind some of the ontological axioms.

2 AN UPPER-LEVEL ONTOLOGY WITH LINGUISTIC FEATURES

Natural language helps with its *universality*, its *morphological and syntactic stability* and, implicitly, with its *integration ability*. The linguistic ontologies are preceded by *lexical ontologies*, e.g. WordNet (Miller, 1995) and FrameNet (Baker et al., 1998, etc), that mainly emphasize the relations inside the lexical categories, without concern about the composition and correlation of the sentences (and, implicitly, of the ideas). Instead, the ontology proposed here basically approaches the last aspects.

Object and Process Integration by Linguistic Means. Object and process conceptual integration by linguistic means has been first proposed in the *functional grammar* (FG) that, later, has inspired *COLOR_X* (Static Object Model and Event model) ((Burg et al., 1995), (Riet et al., 1998)). COLOR-X is the most important domain-independent implementation today of FG. However, the event model proposed in COLOR-X cannot represent complex ideas about processes, because it is merely a trace of events. As support for linguistic ontologies, the *conceptual graphs* (Sowa, 2000)) might also be used, unfortunately only for data-centric situations, where the object behaviour and the processes are not important as a representation goal. But, these graphs are the inspiration source for the upper-level ontology proposed in this section.

Using the proposed upper-level ontology, both objects and processes can be defined and described by simple, compound and complex ontological sentences, using a uniform representation.

Ontology Integration using an Upper-level Ontology. The three ontologies (BPR, domain, communication ontology), briefly described in Sect. 3, have *different vocabularies* and *different axiomatizations*. But, their axiomatizations must be correlated in the automatic reasoning. So, they need the *same conceptual representation* means. Two *alternative solutions* seem to be appropriate for the integration of the three ontologies:

- by an upper-level ontology, able to represent both objects and processes in the domain and BPR ontologies, the communicative acts in the communication ontology, as well as the correlations between them;
- by a translation and correlation algorithm between the concepts and rules in the three ontologies.

But, the disadvantage of the algorithm is that it is mostly encoded. Also, the ontology integration is better achieved in the conception phase of the ontology-based system. Hence, the first alternative is a better solution.

In the following, the basic vocabulary and axioms of the upper-level ontology will be outlined.

Basic Vocabulary. The basic vocabulary of the ontology is composed of (see examples in Sect. 3):

- active objects (direct participants in activities), standing for nouns in NL;
- object attributes, standing for adjectives in NL;
- activities/operations, standing for verbs in NL;

- activity attributes, standing for adverbs in NL;
- object and activity determiners/ modifiers/ substitutes, standing for the noun/ verb determiners/ modifiers/ substitutes in NL.

Ontological Sentences as Axioms. The axioms are here ontological simple/ compound/ complex sentences build as follows:

- the ontological simple sentence unifies the objects involved in the activity description and execution, together with their syntactic roles;
- the ontological compound/ complex sentences correlate the activities (and implicitly the simple sentences that describe them) by intersentential relations.

The semantic relationships between objects or between activities are also represented by ontological simple sentences that describe generic operators (synonymy, antonymy, hypernymy, etc).

Object or activity dynamic qualification is represented by generic qualification operators.

The ontological simple, compound and complex sentences are briefly described below. Section 3 exemplifies them for BPR, domain and communication ontologies.

Ontological Simple Sentence. This sentence was conceived as a simplified and technical view on the NL simple sentence. It is a *star conceptual graph* (Sowa, 2000)), where the *nodes* are objects or activities (operations) and the *links* are: (1) roles, standing for 'object-operation' links or for 'active object--attributive object' links, and (2) intersentential links among operations.

In its linear form, the *star graph* that represents the ontological simple sentence is:

```
(OPERATION)
 AGNT   ∀[AGENT]
 PTNT   ∃/∃?[Object_Type₁:C/D{}]
 RCPT   ∃/∃?[Object_Type₂:C/D{}]
 <preposition role> ∃/∃?[Object_Type₃]
 <adverb role>  ∃/∃?[Object_Type₄]
```

where:

- OPERATION stands for the Predicate, i.e. a definition/ functional/ dependence/ event/ interrogation operation;
- AGNT stands for the role of the Subject(s) in the active voice; PTNT is the role of the Direct Object(s), i.e. the object upon which OPERATION acts; RCPT is the role of the Indirect Object(s), i.e. the recipient of the results of OPERATION;
- 'preposition role' is the role of the Prepositional Object(s); 'adverb role' is the role of the adverbial modifier(s) (i.e. *operation modifier*);
- universal quantifier ∀ replaces the indefinite pronouns 'any', 'all', 'every', 'each' in NL; the two existential quantifiers: ∃, meaning *compulsory existence* ('must exist') and ∃?, meaning *optional existence* ('may exist'), replace the definite or indefinite articles in NL;
- C/ D{} suggest the collective/ distributive plural.

Preposition and adverb roles are abstracted by acronyms like: RSLT (result of activity), INST (instrument to achieve the activity), LOC (location of activity), SRC (source of activity), DEST (destination of activity), PART (part of an object/ operation meaning a whole), TIME (point in time when the activity begins), DUR (duration of the activity), EVNT (object-like event that stimulates the activity execution), CAUS (activity's cause), GOAL (activity's goal), COND (activity's pre/post-condition) and so on (including *domain specific roles*, see examples in Sect. 3). Each acronym has a preposition, conjunction or adverb as *linguistic synonyms*, e.g. 'by' for AGNT, 'upon' for PTNT, 'for/ to' for RCPT, 'into' for RSLT, 'with' for INST, 'from' for SRC, 'at/ in/ on' for LOC, 'to' for DEST, 'since' for TIME, 'when' for EVNT, etc.

The main *advantages* from these generic roles are: (1) they allow the domain independent description and processing of the objects and operations, because the code can use these roles only instead of domain specific types of objects; (2) with their intrinsic and disjunctive semantics, they eliminate the ambiguities in NL, facilitating the (semi)automatic comparison of the ideas.

The *object determiners* are: type, quantifier, plural, cardinality. The a*ctivity (operation) determiners* are the direct, indirect and prepositional objects that describe the operation.

Ontological Compound and Complex Sentence. By *intersentential relation*, we mean a generic relation between two or more activities, each activity being described by one or more ontological simple sentences. These relations correlate the respective simple sentences into compound or complex sentences. As in NL, the *compound sentence* joins independent simple sentences and the *complex sentence* is composed of *dependent* (subordinated) *sentences* correlated to a *main sentence.*

Examples of intersentential relations for *ontological compound sentences* are AND, GROUP, REPEAT, OR, RESULT, CAUSE, BUT, NOT.

In a *complex sentence*, the activities are correlated by subordinating relations abstracted by: IF-THEN-ELSE, DSCR (description), TIME (a certain point in time when a time condition becomes true), GOAL, EVENT, DO, WHILE, subordinating CAUSE or RESULT, MUST, THEN, CASE, SPEC (specialization), BEFORE, AFTER, etc.

3 BPR, DOMAIN AND COMMUNICATION ONTOLOGIES

3.1 BPR Ontology

BPR ontology describes the BPR specific terms and methodology (e.g. concepts for the implementation of the methodology steps, for TQM statistical diagram creation/ modification/ description/ interpretation, etc). BPR ontology is *predefined* and should be *logically correlated with the domain ontology* (e.g. the correlation between certain results in the statistical analyses and the steps in the BPR methodology).

BPR Vocabulary. The BPR vocabulary contains terms in two basic categories: BPR objects and BPR (atomic or complex) activities. The BPR process and its steps are seen as complex activities.

Examples of *BPR specific objects* upon which the BPR (by TQM) process acts are : Domain Process, Improvement Objective, Quality Characteristic, Team, Member, TQM Diagram (e.g. FlowChart, Pareto, Cause-Effect Diagram, Histogram, Control Diagram, Affinity diagram, etc), Root Cause, Specification Limit, Inspection Sheet, Idea etc.

Examples of BPR specific activities are:

- complex activities like (1) the steps of the BPR methodology: Select the process to improve, Organize the team, Define the ontology, Define the AS-IS process, Simplify the process diagram, Verify the process stability, Verify the process improvement capability, Identify root causes, Develop a collection plan, Collect data etc; (2) subordinate activities like Brainstorming, Multivoting, Diagram comparison, Ideas comparison etc.
- atomic activities as Team or Member definition, Chart creation, Chart interpretation, Ideas acquisition, Report creation etc.

BPR Axioms. They are predefined ontological simple or complex sentences.

Ontological simple sentences aim at:

1. *BPR object definition*, by attributive objects or other active objects. For example, the object MEMBER is defined by the sentence:

```
(Object IDENTIFICATION)  - generic operator
   RCPT   ∀[Member]
   NAME   ∃[Member_Name]        - attributive object
   LOC    ∃[Department]         - active object
   CHRC   ∃[Specialization].....
```

2. *BPR object description*, also by attributive or active objects, dynamically associated to the objects during the BPR process. An example is:

```
(Object QUALIFICATION)    - generic operator
   RCPT  ∀[Member]
   GOAL  ∃[Responsability:D{}]
```

3. *BPR operation definition*, using operation internal determiners like in the following example for BRAINSTORMING operation:

```
(Operation IDENTIFICATION)    -generic operator
   RCPT     ∀(BRAINSTORMING)
   ONTO     ∃[Ontology: BPR]
   TYPACT   ∃[ActivityType:subprocess]
   INST     ∃?[ComplexSentence]
```

4. *BPR operation description*, with attributive or active objects that determine the operation. For example, BRAINSTORMING is described by:

```
(BRAINSTORMING)
   AGNT  ∃[Member:C{}]
   DSCR  ∃[Rules]
   TIME  ∃[DateTime]
   DUR   ∃[Period]
   SUBJ  ∃[Subject]
   INST  ∃?[Questionnaire]
   CHRC  ∃?[SpecificIndications:C{}]
   RSLT  ∃[IdeasList:C{}]....
```

5. *Semantic relationships between BPR objects*, similar to the relationships provided in WordNet (*noun* meronymy/holonymy, hyponymy/ hypernymy, synonymy, antonymy, homonymy). Examples of holonymy and hyponymy are:

```
(Object_HOLONYMY)           - generic operator
   DEST    ∀[FlowChart]          - whole object
   PART1   ∃[StartPoint]         - component object
   PART2   ∃[Activity:C{}]
   PART3   ∃[DecisionPoint:C{}]...

(Object_HYPONYMY)  - generic operator
   RCPT ∀[TeamLeader]       - subtype
   PTNT ∃[Member]           - supertype
   INST ∃[RESTR:Member.GOAL= 'Leadership']
```

```
(Mediator_PARTICIPATION)                    -Guide for human mediator participation in brainstorming session
MUST   (Member SELECTION)
MUST   (Instructions TRANSMISSION)         EVENT (MINFORM)    - (MINFORM) is the mediator's
MUST   (Subject TRANSMISSION)              EVENT (MINFORM)      communicative act and subtype of
MAY    (Questionnaire TRANSMISSION)        EVENT (MINFORM)      (INFORM) operation in the
MAY    (PrelimDocumument TRANSMISSION)     EVENT (MINFORM)      communication ontology
MAY REPEAT (Additional_toolEXECUTION)
MAY    (Diagram CREATION)
MUST   (Ideas COLLECTION)      EVENT (Ideas STORING)
MAY    (Multivot)
MUST   (Ideas COMPARISON)      EVENT (Ideas INTEGRATION)
MUST   (IdeasList TRANSMISSION)         EVENT (MINFORM)
MAY    (AffinityDiagram CREATION)
CASE   (FinalIdeasList TRANSMISSION)   EVENT (MINFORM)
       (FinalDiagram TRANSMISSION)     EVENT (MINFORM)
```

6. *Semantic relationships between BPR operations*, similar to the relationships provided in WordNet (*verb* meronymy/ holonymy, hyponymy/ hypernymy, synonymy, antonymy, homonymy and also troponymy and entailment). An example of operation entailment (implication) is:

```
(Operation_ENTAILMENT)        - generic operator
  RCPT ∀(Diagram INTERPRETATION) -entailed
  PTNT ∃(Diagram CREATION) -entailing oper.
```

Ontological complex sentences are used to describe the scenarios for BPR methodology, for its steps and for the complex/ compound BPR operations. For each kind of user (member or mediator) and for each BPR step, the BPR ontology contains a scenario like an ontological complex or compound sentence. Below are exemplified few steps from the scenario for automating the mediator's participation in a brainstorming session. Each operation is described by ontological simple sentences and executed according to the logic of the intersentential relations (see Sect. 4).

3.2 Domain Ontology

Domain ontology ascribes the meaning to the terms exchanged between the members of the team regarding the target domain (manufacturing, transportantion, healthcare etc). In (DON, 1996), the manual brainstorming relies on 'operational definitions' of the domain specific concepts. For the brainstorming automation, these definitions compose the domain ontology and must be *dynamically created* by the BPR team.

An example of process to improve in the healthcare domain (described in (SKYMARK, 2000)) is 'Medication administration' and a possible improvement objective can be 'Reducing medication errors'. We will exemplify some terms in the vocabulary and some of the domain specific axioms needed for this process and represented using the upper-level ontology described in Sect. 2.

Domain Vocabulary. The domain vocabulary consists of necessary active objects, atomic operations, complex operations, all defined and described by domain specific axioms.

For the medication administration process, examples of active objects are: Patient, Hospital, Physician, Nurse, Medicament, Error, Pharmacy, Hospital_Ward, Dose etc. Examples of operations are: Med ORDER, Order TRANSCRIPTION, Pharmacy CHECK, Med REORDER, Med PICK, Cart LOAD, Med ADMINISTRATION etc.

Domain Axioms. Each object and each operation referred to in a process, as well as the inter-object and inter-operation semantic relationships, can be defined and described by ontological simple sentences. These sentences force the members of the BPR team to select only the most important and relevant elements of the target process and to deeper analyze them, better then they would have done using pure NL.

For example, 'Patient' object is defined by:

```
(Object IDENTIFICATION)    - generic operator
  RCPT   ∀[Patient]
  NAME   ∃[PersonName]
  DATE   ∃[BirthDate]
  LOC    ∃[Address]
  CHRC   ∃[Sex]  .....
```

and can be dynamically described by a qualification operator with one or several attributes associated to the object 'Patient':

```
(Object_QUALIFICATION)      - generic operator
   RCPT   ∀[Patient]
   POSS   ∃[Medicament]
   STAT1  ∃[HealthState]
  STAT2 ∃[Investigation_Result:C{}] .....
```

In order to match different vocabularies (e.g. a scientific and a popular one) used during brainstorming sessions, one may find necessary to explicitly represent synonymy relationships like:

(Object SYNONYMY)	(Operation SYNONYMY)
PTNT1 ∃[Medicament]	PTNT1 ∃[Med_ORDER]
PTNT2 ∃[Drug]	PTNT2 ∃[Med_PRESCRIBE]
PTNT3 ∃[Med]	

Each atomic/ complex operation can be described by a simple/ complex ontological sentence. For instance, the atomic operations Med ORDER and Order TRANSCRIPTION can be described by the sentences:

(Med ORDER)	(Order TRANSCRIPTION)
RCPT ∀[Patient]	PTNT ∀[Med:D{}]
AGNT ∃[Physician]	AGNT ∃[Nurse]
PTNT ∃[Med:C{}]	RCPT ∃[Pharmacy] ...
QTY ∃[Med_Dose]	

The process to improve can be described in a flow scenario (similar to a flowchart) represented as a complex ontological sentence like:

```
MUST (Med ORDER)
MUST (Order TRANSCRIPTION)
MUST (Pharmacy CHECK)
IF(Pharmacy CHECK.Result='Available')
   THEN (Med PICK)
      MAY (Tray FILL)
      MAY (Cart LOAD)
      MUST (ToNurse SEND)
      MUST (Med ADMINISTRATION)
   ELSE (Med REORDER)
```

Expressing Domain specific Ideas. An example of idea issued from a brainstorming session for the process above is "Doc prescribes med which conflicts with other med; pharm must substitute". This idea can be represented by the following complex sentence:

```
MUST (Med PRESCRIBE)
   CAUSE  (Med CONFLICT)
          EVENT  (Med SUBSTITUTE)
```

where (Med PRESCRIBE) is synonymous with (Med ORDER), hence is described by the same sentence (see above) and the other two operations are described by the following simple sentences:

(Med CONFLICT)	(Med SUBSTITUTE)
PTNT1 ∃[Med:C{}]	SRC ∃[Med]
PTNT2 ∃[Med:C{}]	DEST ∃[Med]

The idea "Physician prescribes incorrect dose" is represented by the sentence for Med ORDER (synonymous with Med PRESCRIBE) where the object 'Med_Dose' is dynamically qualified by:

```
(Object_QUALIFICATION)
   RCPT   ∃[Med_Dose]
   CHRC   ∃[Attribute:incorrect]
```

From the conceptual viewpoint, the user can express any idea using simple, compound and complex ontological sentences, possibly by dynamically adding roles or intersentential relationships, in addition to the predefined ones. The user should be guided first to create and then to use the domain ontology, in order to structure his ideas. Apparently, the expression of ideas using this ontology seems restrictive and difficult and depends on the attractiveness and simplicity of the automatic guidance tools. But, this solution makes possible the ideas grouping and comparison according to the semantics and logic of the domain independent roles and relations. Using the graphical, Web-oriented interfaces, the attractiveness of the ontology representation and processing may be substantially improved.

3.3 Communication Ontology

Communication ontology describes the communication acts (at least 'query', 'reply' and 'inform') and the protocols between the team members. It facilitates the dialog and should be correlated with the domain and BPR ontologies.

Communication Vocabulary. It is composed of:

- the basic communication acts QUERY, REPLY, INFORM, as atomic operations;
- the active and attributive objects that describe the communication acts;
- the semantic relationships between the communication acts (e.g. subtyping MINFORM from INFORM) or between the communication specific objects they refer to.

Communication Axioms. These axioms are ontological simple sentences that define or describe the communication acts and the communication specific objects they refer to.

In the scenario in Sect. 3.1 for the mediator's participation in the brainstorming, one may see that the BPR specific operations are correlated, for message transmission, with the communicative act INFORM. This operation can described by an ontological simple sentence like:

```
(INFORM)                              - communicative act
AGNT ∃[Member]
RCPT ∃[Member:D{}]
PTNT ∃[Subject:D{}]
TYPE ∃[InformType:{knowledge, belief,
        intention, desire,  criticism}]
RSLT1 ∃?[Message]
RSLT2 ∃?[Document]
RSLT3 ∃?[Diagram]
RSLT4 ∃?[QuestionnaireModel]
RSLT5 ∃?[Ideas_List] ...
```

Sometimes, the information might not be always reliable or might be only a critical comment. In this case, the attribute InformType can differentiate the type of information.

Similarly, one can describe the communicative act QUERY, by a sentence like.

```
(QUERY)                          - communicative act
AGNT   ∃[Member]
RCPT   ∃[Member:D{}]
PTNT   ∃[Subject:D{}]
TYPE   ∃[QueryType: define_object,
     modify_object, define_operation,...}]
GOAL   ∃?[QueryGoal]
DSCR   ∃?[QueryContent]
STAT   ∃[QueryState:with/ without reply]
RSLT   ∃?[Reply:D{}]
```

MINFORM is a subtype of INFORM operation as the following sentence suggests:

```
(Operation_HYPONYMY)   - generic operator
  RCPT ∀(MINFORM)       - subtype
  PTNT ∃(INFORM)            - supertype
  INST ∃[RESTR:INFORM.AGNT = 'Mediator']
```

where 'Mediator' is a subtype of the object 'Member' in BPR ontology.

4 LOGIC OF THE UPPER-LEVEL ONTOLOGY

The axioms in the upper-level ontology proposed in Sect. 2 have a logical background useful for their interpretation and for further inferences upon them (see details in (Galatescu, 2001)).

Logic of the Ontological Simple Sentence. The basic logic of the upper-level ontology relies on the logic of the ontological simple sentence:

```
(OPERATION)
   role_1       ∀[Object_1 ]
   role_2       ∃[Object_2] ......
    role_p       ∃?[Object_p]
```

Its uniform formalization and logical interpretation can be expressed by a first order logic formula, where the operation is defined/ described by a λ-expression with $(x_{i1},\ldots,x_{ik})$ (input/ output parameters) as bound variables and $(x_{i1},\ldots,x_{ik}) \subset (x_1,\ldots,x_p)$:

$$\text{OPERATION} = \lambda(x_{i1},\ldots,x_{ik})\,(x_{j1},\ldots,x_{j(p\text{-}k)})\,(\forall x_1)\,(\text{Object}_1(x_1) \wedge \text{role}_1\,(x_1)) \supset (\exists x_2)\ldots(\exists x_p)\,(\text{Object}_2(x_2) \wedge \text{role}_2(x_2) \wedge \ldots \wedge (\text{Object}_p(x_p) \vee \text{NULL}) \wedge (\text{role}_p(x_p) \vee \text{NULL})) \wedge \text{OPERATION}(x_1,\ldots,x_p)$$

where NULL helps for the representation of the quantifier ∃?.

Logic of the Generic Operators. A particular type of ontological sentences are the sentences around the generic operators. For example, 'Object IDENTIFICATION' for object definition. The definition of an object 'x' can be expressed in predicate calculus by a λ-expression, where 'x' is a bound variable:

```
Defined_Object = (λx)(x_1,…,x_n)
(∀x)(Defined_Object(x)∧ RCPT(x)) ⊃
(∃x_1)…(∃x_n)(Object_1(x_1)∧ role_1(x_1)∧/∨ …
∧/∨(Object_n(x_n)∨ NULL)∧(role_n(x_n)∨ NULL))∧
Object IDENTIFICATION(x,x_1,…,x_n)
```

The generic operator for object dynamic qualification:

```
(Object QUALIFICATION)
  PTNT  active_object_type
  ROLE  attributive_object_type
```

has the logical interpretation:

```
(∃a)(attributive_object_type(a)) ⊃
(∃o)(active_object_type(o))(PTNT(o)∧
ROLE(a))∧ Object QUALIFICATION(o,a)
```

where any *attributive object* 'a' necessarily qualifies an *active object* 'o' (that directly participates in an operation). However, the attributive object can become active object in other circumstances.

Logic of the Intersentential Relationships. Each intersentential relationship may be associated with a *constraining inference rule*, with the last activated operation as *premise* and with the conjunction or disjunction of the operations proposed for the process continuation, as *conclusion.* For example, MAY, EVENT, CASE used in the examples above have the following logical interpretation:

PO MAY Oi_1, ..., Oi_n

$(\forall x)((PO(x) \supset (Oi_1(x) \vee NULL)) \wedge ... \wedge (PO(x) \supset (Oi_n(x) \vee NULL)))$

EO EVNT / CAUSE O

$(\forall x)((\exists e) EVNT(e) \supset O(x))$, where $EVNT(e) = (\lambda e)\ \lambda\text{-definition}(EO)[e]$. 'e' is a particular event/ cause and 'λ-definition (EO)' is the λ-expansion of the event/ cause operation EO.

PO (CASE ∧ condition_value) Oi_1 ...,Oi_n

$(\forall x)((PO(x) \wedge \text{condition value}_1) \supset Oi_1(x) \vee (PO(x) \wedge \text{condition value}_2) \supset Oi_2(x) \vee ... \vee (PO(x) \wedge \text{condition value}_n) \supset Oi_n(x))$

where 1) x is an individual of an output object type in the premise operation, transferred to its child operations, 2) $\supset$ means the compulsory activation of the implied operations, 3) $\wedge$ means the conjunction of the operations or rules, 4) $\vee$ means the (exclusive or not) disjunction of operations or rules, 5) NULL is a null (ineffective) operation.

5 CONCLUSIONS

The paper has motivated and exemplified the ontologies for BPR automation. It also has outlined the basic elements of an upper-level ontology with linguistic features proposed as communication infrastructure between the members of the BPR team. This ontology stylizes the morphology and syntax of NL and the semantics of its vocabulary borrows from NL semantics.

The need for an upper-level ontology with linguistic features is justified by: (1) the lack of general ontologies that uniformly represent objects and processes, (2) the need for ontology integration, (3) the need for representing, mediating and inferencing upon ideas expressed in a format closer to a free expression.

The ontologies relying on the proposed upper-level ontology can be stored, retrieved and managed using relational DBMSs, as in our current implementation.

REFERENCES

Baker C., Filmore C., 1998. Berkeley FrameNet Project. *Computer Science Inst.*, USA

Burg, J. and Van De Riet, R, 1995. COLOR-X. Linguistically based Event Modeling: A General Approach to Dynamic Modeling. In *Proc. of Conf. on Advanced Information System Eng. (CAISE'95)*, Springer-Verlag

Davenport T.H., Prusak L., 1998. Working Knowledge: How Organizations Manage What They Know. Harvard Business School Press, Boston, MA

DON (Department Of Navy), 1996. *Handbook for Basic Process Improvement*, Dept. of Navy, USA

DSS Infotech, 2000. *Solutions Prosper– Software for Implementation of Continual & Break-through Improvement* (demo), *DSS Infotech Pvt. Ltd*, India

DSS Infotech. 2000. *PROQMS– Process Quality Management System* (demo), DSS Infotech , India

Galatescu A. A Unifyng Translation of Natural Language Patterns To Object and Process Modeling. In vol. *Information Modeling in the New Millenium*, Idea Group Publ., 2001

GOALQPC, 1999. *Memory Jogger Software*, GOAL/QPC, USA, http://www.goalqpc.com

Grover V., Kettinger W., 1995. *Business Process Change – Re-engineering Concepts, Methods and Technologies*, Idea Group Publishing

Gruber T., 1993. Toward Principles for Design of Ontologies Used for Knowledge Sharing. In *Formal Ontology in Conceptual Analysis and Knowledge Representation*, Kluwer Academic Publ.

Guarino N. (Ed), 1998. Formal Ontology and Information Systems, IOS Press

Hawryszkiewycz I. (1999). Supporting Teams in Virtual Organizations. In *Proc. of Conf. on Database and Expert Systems Applications*, Italy

Malhotra Y, 1998. Business Processs Redesign: An Overview. In *IEEE Engineering Management Review*, 26(3),

Miller G., 1995 WordNet: A Lexical Database for English. In *Comm. of ACM* 38(11)

MIT, 1996. TQM Toolkit, http://web.mit.edu/tqm

Riet R., Burg H., Dehne F., 1998. Linguistic Instruments in Information Systems Design. In *Formal Ontology and Information Systems*, IOS Press

Scacchi W., Valente A., 1999. Developing a Knowledege Web for Business Process Redesign. *http://www1.ics.uci.edu/~wscacchi/Papers/KnowledgeWeb*

Schlenoff C., Ivester R., Knutilla A. (1998). A robust process ontology for manufacturing systems integration. *CommerceNet ECO Framework*

SKYMARK, 2000. The PathMaker 2.5 Software, *http://www.skymark.com/pathmaker/*

Sowa JF, 2000. *Knowledge Representation – Logical, Philosophical and Computational Foundation*, Brooks Cole Publishing Co., Pacific Grove, CA

Uschold M., King M., Moralee S., Zorgios Y. (1998). The Enterprise Ontology. *Knowledge Engineering Review*, 13

SEQUENCE CONSTRAINTS IN BUSINESS MODELLING AND BUSINESS PROCESS MODELLING

Monique Snoeck
Managment Information Systems group
Department of Applied Economic Sciences, Katholieke Universitieit Leuven
Naamsestraat 69, 3000 Leuven, Belgium
email: monique.snoeck@econ.kuleuven.ac.be

Key words: Object Oriented Analysis, Domain Modelling, Business Process Modelling.

Abstract: Separation of concerns is one of the main principles for achieving maintainability and adaptability of software systems. In particular, when analysing business rules it is important to separate business process aspects from essential business rules. Current object-oriented analysis methods offer little support for this. In this paper we explore the problem of sequence constraints on business events. Some of these constraints are the result of the way the business is organised whereas other are essential for the business. In addition we investigate how to ensure the compatibility between business rules and business processes.

1 INTRODUCTION

One of the main drivers for Business Modelling is the very large step of formalisation that must be taken when developing information system support for business activities. The gap between perceived business reality and what can be represented in a computerised way is usually wider and deeper than initially thought. Business modelling is a way to bridge that gap and at the same time it helps constructing a better understanding of what the business really is like (Lindström 1999).

People involved in business modelling ought to be specialists in the business rather than specialist in some sophisticated modelling method. As a consequence, business modelling will benefit from modelling methods that offer a number of simple modelling techniques, whereby each technique concentrates on only a few aspects of the problem. Each of those modelling techniques allows to build a partial model of the business that involves only one or two dimensions. The full picture is obtained by considering all the models together. In this kind of approach it is important to ensure that all aspects are covered and to ensure that different models do not contradict each other.

Usually, at least three dimensions are identified for a full coverage of the business: *Intentions*, *Concepts* and *Ways of working/Organisation* (Nellborn 1999), (Nilsson 1999). The intentional dimension describes the strategic dimension in terms of e.g. goals, critical success factors, strengths and weaknesses. It answers the question of *Why* things are done in the business. The *Concepts* dimension describes the "vocabulary" of the domain, mainly in terms of business entities, relationships between business entities, and, in the case of object-oriented modelling, in terms of behaviour of entities. Simply said, it answers the *What* question. Finally, the Ways of working describes the organisational dimension in terms of actors, activities and workflow. It describes the *How* of a business. This paper concentrates on the relation between the latter two dimensions.

In business modelling the modelling of the organisational dimension is called business process modelling. The modelling of the concepts is called business domain modelling. Both domains have largely evolved independently, and not much research can be found in which business process modelling principles have been linked to domain modelling or vice-versa (Nilsson 1999), (Snoeck 2000). In domain modelling, the primary emphasis is on the specification of a structural model of business object types and associations between these object types, whereas the business process part is largely neglected or supposed to be given. Especially when object-oriented analysis and design methods are used for domain modelling (e.g. (Booch 1995), (Rational), (Coleman 1994), (Cook 1994),

(D'Souza 1999), (Fowler 1997), (Snoeck 1999), business process modelling is still treated in a fairly limited way (Snoeck 2000). Similarly, in business process modelling, the domain model is often neglected or supposed to be given. When the complementary aspects are ignored, the danger exists that these aspects are not properly separated in the specifications. For example, in current OOA practice, the danger exists that business process aspects are modelled as part of the behaviour of domain classes. Separation of concerns is however one of the main principles to ensure adaptability and flexibility of information system. This principle dictates to keep process aspects separated from the domain model. In order to achieve this, it should be clearly defined how the business process model links to the domain model in order to be able to compose the full picture of a business. Exactly this link is missing in many domain modelling and business process modelling approaches. MERODE is an object-oriented enterprise modelling method (Snoeck 1999), (Snoeck 1998). A particular feature of this approach is that it explicitly identifies business events and that these are treated as individual concepts at the same level of importance as enterprise object types. This allows to more adequately model the dynamic aspects of a business than with classical object-oriented analysis and design methods. In (Snoeck 2000) it has been argued that the business event concept of MERODE can serve as a hinge to link process aspects to the behavioural aspects of business domain object types. A similar idea is found in MALDIV 0. At the conceptual level, the business process model is defined as a layer on top of the domain model. Business processes are defined in terms of a.o. activities that invoke the business events defined in the domain model (see Figure 1).

This way of working leads to a layered architecture for information systems (Snoeck 2000). The layers are organised in such a way that the lowest layer contains the most stable elements. Subsequent layers contain elements that are more often subject to change. The objects in an upper layer interact with objects of the same layer or of lower layers to deliver the desired functionality. They are unaware of objects in upper layers. In this way, propagation of change is limited from lower layers towards upper layers.

Both the business process layer and the domain layer allow to define sequencing of business events. In the domain layer this is done directly by defining state charts for domain objects. In the business process layer this is done indirectly by defining sequences of tasks. The first question that we address is : where do we put a particular sequence constraint on business events ? In the domain layer or in the business process layer ?

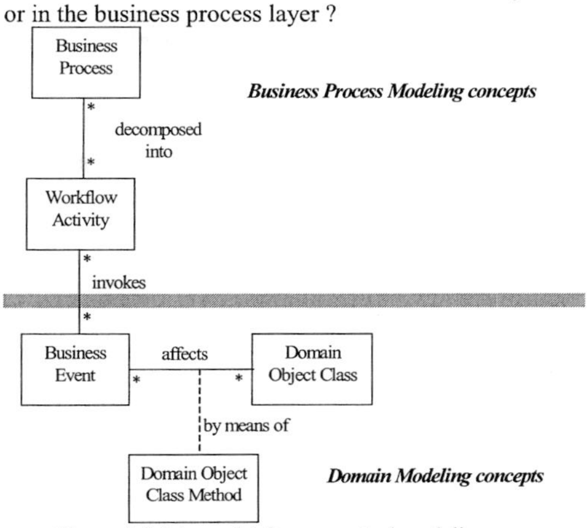

Figure 1. Meta-model for conceptual modeling

The rule that is given in MERODE is that sequences that arise from a particular way of working should be put in the workflow layer, whereas sequences that are inherent to the business should be put in the domain layer. The underlying idea is that the essential business domain rules are more stable than the organisational aspects and hence should be put in the inner layer of the system.

The second question to address is how to ensure that the sequences defined in the business process layer do not contradict the sequences defined in the domain layer. Since the business processes are defined on top of the domain layer, they cannot violate rules that are defined in that layer. Indeed, every time a business process task invokes a business event, this event is validated by the domain model. If the event violates a sequence constraint defined by one of the involved domain objects the event is rejected. Hence, only rules that should never be violated can be put in the domain layer.

Usually, all kinds of statements about the business are called "business rules". In the context of this paper, we need to discern between different types of business rules. Therefore, in the remainder of the paper we will make a difference between business *rules* and business *policies*. Business *rules* are rules that always hold, that should never be broken. Business *policies* are rules that hold in general, but that can be broken occasionally, in exceptional situations for example. The working hypothesis in this paper is that sequences that emerge from business rules should (mostly) be put in the domain layer, whereas sequences that emerge from business policies should always be put in the business process layer. In addition one has to ensure that event sequences from the business process layer and business event sequences defined in the domain layer do not contradict each other.

The remainder of the paper is organised as follows. The next section describes a case-study. First a domain model is elaborated. We then illustrate the problem of event sequencing and the problem of contradicting event sequences by looking at the business process model. The third section then formalises when a business process model is consistent with a domain model from the point of view of sequence constraints on event types.

2 CASE STUDY

2.1 Domain Model

A company sells product that must be installed at the Customer's site. The domain model defines the concepts of product, sales order, order line, customer. A simple class diagram is given in Figure 2.

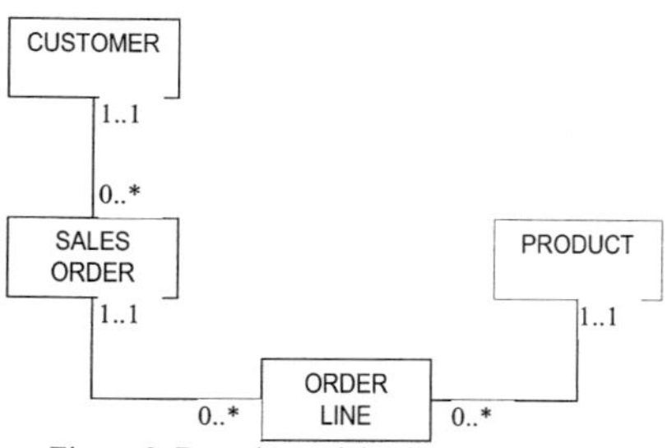

Figure 2: Domain model, Class diagram

In the domain model we also identify business event types. These are real-world event types that affect and change the state of enterprise objects. Let us assume that each enterprise object type has a business event type for creating, modifying, and terminating objects of that type. The business event types are listed in the Object Event Table below (Figure 3). In this Object-Event Table (OET for short) we mark which type of event affects which object type and in what way: C = creation, M = modification, E = End. A detailed discussion of the rules governing the construction of this OET is beyond the scope of this paper, but can be found in (Snoeck 1998), (Snoeck 1999). We merely note here that each marked entry identifies a possible place for information gathering. If for example, we wish to keep track of how many times a product is ordered, it makes sense to mark the entries PRODUCT/*cr_order_line*. Similarly, if within the class CUSTOMER we wish to keep track of the total number of orders placed by this customer (e.g. to identify "golden" customers, or to specify some discounting rules), we need to mark the entry CUSTOMER/*cr_order*. At implementation time, methods that are empty because no relevant business rule was identified, can be removed to increase efficiency.

	customer	sales order	product	order line
cr_customer	C			
mod_customer	M			
end_customer	E			
cr_sales_order	M	C		
mod_sales_order	M	M		
end_sales_order	M	E		
cr_product			C	
mod_product			M	
end_product			E	
cr_order_line	M	M	M	C
mod_order_line	M	M	M	M
end_order_line	M	M	M	E

Figure 3: Domain Model, Object-Event Table

To complete the behavioural aspects object lifecycles must be specified. In the library for example, a copy should be returned before it can be borrowed again. With each class we will thus associate a lifecycle expression. The default lifecycle is that objects are first created (a choice between the C-entries), then modified an arbitrary number of times (an iteration of a choice between the M-entries) and finally come to an end (choice between the E-entries). In most object-oriented methods such lifecycles are represented using state charts. The default life cycle for sales order is represented as state chart in Figure 4.

The lifecycle expression of a domain class should contain all events for which an entry has been marked in the corresponding column of the OET. In addition, the lifecycle expression should respect the type of the entries: events marked with a 'C' should appear as creating events, events marked with an 'M' should appear as modifying event types and events marked with an 'E' should terminate the life of the object[1].

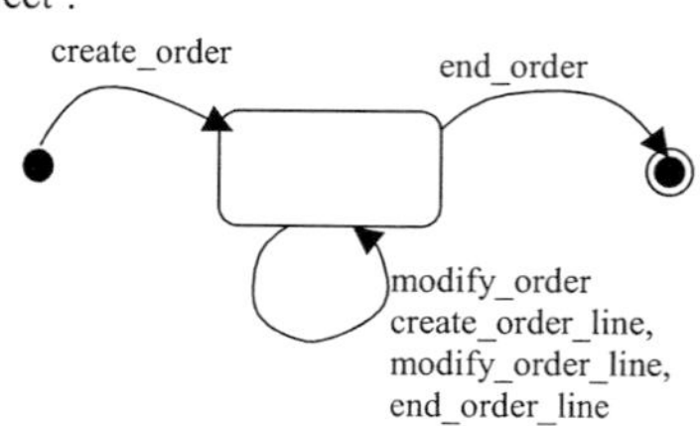

Figure 4: State chart for default life cycle of sales order.

[1] Additional rules that guarantuee consistency between the object-relationship schema, the object-event table and the lifecycle expressions can be found in (Snoeck 1998), (Snoeck 1999).

2.2 The business process model

Analysis of the business processes allows to discover more relevant business event type and sequence constraints between event types. As an example, let us consider the business process for creating a sales order (represented in Figure 5):

A sales person has a lead, visits the customer, consults technical people for the optimal choice of products, reaches an agreement on what the customer wants to buy, registers the sales order, prints it and has it signed by the customer. The Sales Order is then passed on to Customer Operations. They register the sales order in their planning and install the products at the customers site. At the end of the installation process, the custome, signs for the acceptation of the products and from then on the billing of the installed services is started.

By analysing each task, additional business events are discovered. In terms of enterprise modelling, the following additional business events are required for a sales order:

- to register the signature of the customer: *customer_sign*
- to plan the sales order: *operations_accept*
- to register the successful installation: *customer_accept*

The sequence constraints that emerge from this business process description are the following:

- A sales order is first signed, then accepted by Customer Operations.
- After the *operations_accept* event, installation will proceed and eventually the customer will accept the installation.
- It is assumed that once a sales order has been signed, it cannot be modified any more: it is a contract with a customer and you cannot change the terms of a contract after it has been signed.

(For the sake of simplicity we assume that orders never are cancelled).

The state chart representation for the event types of sales order is given in Figure 6. Notice how sales order implies sequence constraints between its own event types and those acquired from order line: event types from order line are only allowed to occur as long as the sales order is in the state "modifiable/unsigned".

In the case of complex configurations, the technical background of sales people is not always sufficient to ensure that the products on the sales order meet all technical requirements. The possibility that a change of the sales order will be required during the installation process is real, although it occurs only in a minority of cases. The state machine given above however enforces that a signed sales order cannot be modified any more. For this reason, the sales order must be reviewed by Customer Operations *prior* to the registration and signature of the order by the Customer. This alternative business process for complex sales orders puts the *operations_accept* event before the *customer_sign* event .

As a result, the analysis of two scenarios results in two conflicting state machines for sales order. Hence, some of the sequence constraints should not be put in the domain model, but rather in the business process model. In this case-study, the sequence constraints between modifying events and signature of the sales order are an example of a business *rule*: these sequence constraints should never be violated. Once a sales order has been signed, it cannot be modified any more without having it re-signed by the customer (which amounts to creating a new sales order and have this new sales order signed). The sequence constraints between customer_sign and operations_accept are however to be formulated as a business *policy*. For efficiency purposes, it is the policy of the business to have a sales order signed before passing it to customer operations. However, in complex situations (the notion of "complex" can at its turn be defined by a number of rules & policies), the sales person must check the sales order with customer operations prior to the signature by the customer.

In order to allow different scenarios in the business process layer, the domain layer must leave sufficient degrees of freedom. In this particular case, the behaviour definition of sales order must not enforce sequence constraints between customer_sign and operations_accept. The resulting state chart is given in Figure 7.

3 FORMALISATION

3.1 Definitions

The concept of sequence constraints has been formalised in MERODE by means of process algebra (Snoeck 1999), (Dedene 1995). In this section we formalise the notion of sequence constraints as defined in the business process model. We first review the basic definitions of the process algebra.

A business model is a tuple $<\mathcal{M}, A, \leftarrow>$, whereby $\mathcal{M}$ is a set of object types P, A is a universe of business event types and $\leftarrow$ is an existence dependency relationship that is a partial ordering relationship on the object types in $\mathcal{M}$. An object type P is a pair $<\alpha,e>$ where α is a subset of A. α is called the alphabet of P and defines the set of business

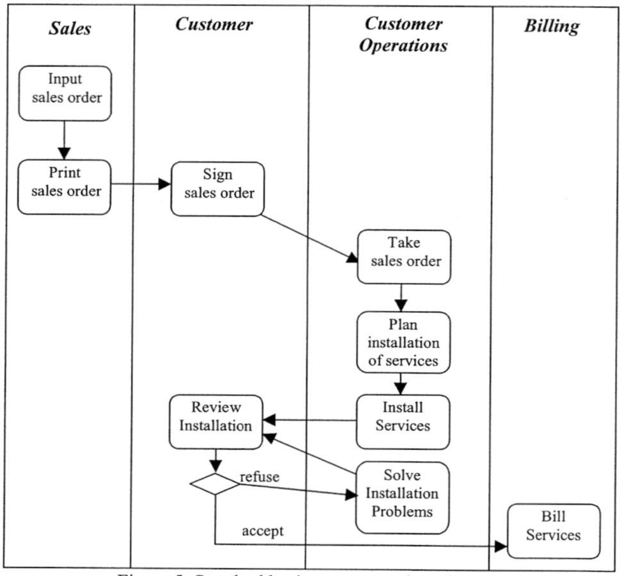

Figure 5: Standard business process for sales

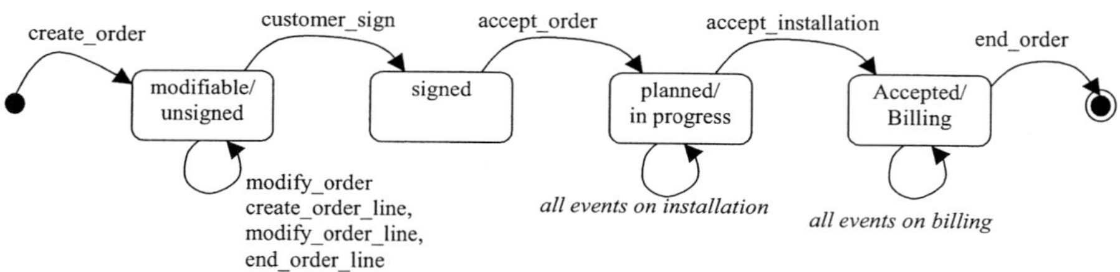

Figure 6: State chart for Sales Order (standard business process)

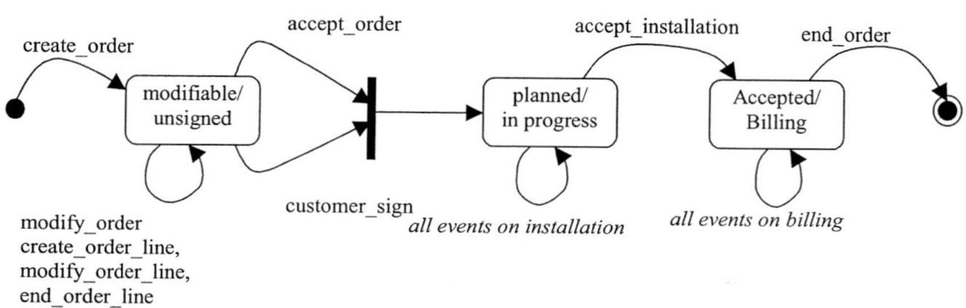

Figure 7: State chart for sales order that allows for the two business processes.

event types objects of P are involved in. e is a regular expression over α that defines the sequence constraints imposed by P on the business event types in α. The regular expression e can be build using the operators +, ., * and ||.

Let A be the universe of business event types. R(A) is the set of regular expressions over A.

$e \in R(A) \Leftrightarrow e = 1$ or $\exists a \in A : e = a$ or $\exists e', e'' \in R(A) : [e = e' + e''$ or $e = e'.e''$ or $e = e' \| e''$ or $e = (e')^*]$

whereby 1 is the do-nothing event, + stands for choice, . stands for sequence, || stands for parallel composition and * stands for iteration.

Every regular expression defines a set of scenarios over A. A scenario is a sequence of event types from A where ^ acts as the concatenation operator and 1 as the empty scenario. A* is the set of all scenarios over A and is defined by

$1 \in A^*$,
$\forall a \in A: a \in A^*$
let $s, t \in A^*$: then $s \hat{} t \in A^*$

Scenarios can be projected on a set of event types as follows. Let $B \subseteq A$ then

$1 \backslash B = 1$
$\forall a \in A: [a \backslash B = a \Leftrightarrow a \in B$ and $a \backslash B = 1 \Leftrightarrow a \notin B]$
$\forall r, s \in A^*: (r \hat{} s)\backslash B = r\backslash B \hat{} s\backslash B$

For a regular expression, we can determine the set of event types that appear in this regular expression by means of a function φ:

$\varphi(1) = \emptyset$, $\varphi(a) = \{a\}$,
$\varphi(e+e') = \varphi(e.e') = \varphi(e \| e') = \varphi(e) \cup \varphi(e')$.

The *language*, that is, the set of scenarios, defined by a regular expression is defined as follows:

$L(1) = 1$, $L(a) = a$, $L(e + e') = L(e) \cup L(e')$
$L(e.e') = \{s \hat{} t \mid s \in L(e) \text{ and } t \in L(e')\}$
$L(e^*) = \{1\} \cup L(e) \cup L(e.e). \cup L(e.e.e) \cup L(e.e.e.e) \cup ...$
$L(e \| e') = \{s \in A^* \mid s\backslash\varphi(e) \in L(e) \text{ and } s\backslash\varphi(e') \in L(e')\}$

The execution of a task implies the triggering of business events. A a result, a task can be defined as a regular expression over the set of business event types. In its turn, a Business Process is defined as a regular expression over the set of task types. As result, a business process is itself a regular expression over the business event types. Each business process defines a set of scenarios of business event types in the same way as an enterprise object type defines a set of scenarios (its language).

The business events triggered by the business process layer will only be accepted provided they satisfy all constraints defined by the domain model. As a result, in order to be consistent with the domain layer, each of the scenarios defined by a business process must be accepted by the domain layer. Comparing scenarios of events generated by a business process with the behaviour definitions of object types is however not straightforward since the life cycle of one object can be spread across different tasks and even across different business processes. If we consider for example the task of modifying an order from the point of view of a single order line, this task will generate either a single *cr_order_line* event, a single *mod_order_line* event or a single *end_order_line* event. Usually, a task will move a domain object one step further in the life cycle. In addition, a single task can treat several domain objects of a certain type. The "modify order" task can manipulate several order lines at once. Hence, if we analyse the *types* of events that are generated by this task, we see that this task generates scenarios with *cr_order_line, mod_order_line* and *end_order_line* events in a random order. As a result, the analysis of business event type scenarios generated by tasks and business processes must be done by looking at the events that affect a single object occurrence and not by looking at the types of the events only.

The next definitions define the instance view on objects and events[1].

An instance $\mathcal{O}$ of $\mathcal{M}$ is a set of object instances of the types defined in $\mathcal{M}$. Each object belongs to exactly one class or enterprise object type. This is expressed by the classification function type (.) and its inverse function oids(.) that returns all the objects of a given type

type(.): $\mathcal{O} \rightarrow \mathcal{M}$: $o \rightarrow$ type(o)
oids(.): $\mathcal{M} \rightarrow \mathcal{O}$: $P \rightarrow$ oids(P) such that $\forall$ P,Q $\in \mathcal{M}$: $P \neq Q \Rightarrow$ oids(P) $\cap$ oids(Q) $= \emptyset$

In addition:

$\mathcal{M}$ is a model of $\mathcal{O}$
$\Leftrightarrow \mathcal{O}$ is an instance of $\mathcal{M}$
$\Leftrightarrow \forall o \in \mathcal{O}$: type(o) $\in \mathcal{M}$

Occurrences of event types are defined in a similar way. Let T be the universe of events of types in A. Each event in T has a type and a list of participating objects, called the olist:

type(.): $T \rightarrow A$: $t \rightarrow$ type(t)

[1] In this paper only a part of the definitions is given. The full set of definitions can be found in (Dedene 1995).

$olist(.): T \rightarrow 2^{O}: t \rightarrow oids(t)$

Events can be ordered according to the time at which they occur. In analogy with scenarios, a stream of event is a sequence of events whereby the events of the stream are in increasing time order . T* is the set of all streams over T.

$\&$ is the empty stream, $\& \in T^*$

$\forall t \in T: t \in T^*$

$\forall s \in T^*, t \in T: (t^\wedge s)_0 = t$

$\forall s \in T^*, t \in T,\ t < s_0 : , t^\wedge s \in T^*$

The type of a stream is the scenario obtained by taking the type of all events in the stream:

$type(\&)=1, type(r^\wedge s) = type(r)^\wedge type(s)$

The projection of a stream on an object o is defined as follows. Let $o \in O$, then

$\&\backslash o = \&$

$\forall t \in T: [t\backslash o = t \Leftrightarrow o \in olist(t)]$ and $[t\backslash o = \& \Leftrightarrow o \notin olist(t)]$

$\forall r, s \in T^*: (r^\wedge s)\backslash o = (r\backslash o)^\wedge(s\backslash o)$

Finally, as each business process covers only a part of the life cycle of an object type, we must define when a stream of events is "compatible" (denoted by the symbol '≈') with a life cycle definition of an object type. A stream of events is compatible with the lifecycle definition of an object type if the type of the stream is a substring of a valid scenario for that object type. Let $\omega \in T^*$, $e \in R(A)$,then

$$type(\omega) \approx e \Leftrightarrow \exists\, r, s \in A^*: r^\wedge type(\omega)^\wedge s \in L(e)$$

This definition allows to formally define when a business process model is consistent with a domain model. Let $\mathcal{B}$ be a business process model. Each business process in $\mathcal{B}$ can be considered as a regular expression over the universe of event types. That is: $\forall \beta \in \mathcal{B}: \beta \in R(A)$. A business process model $\mathcal{B}$ is consistent (≈) with a domain model $\mathcal{M}$ if and only if for each business processes in $\mathcal{B}$ there exists at least one stream that is consistent with all instances of $\mathcal{M}$. Formally:

$\mathcal{B} \approx \mathcal{M} \Leftrightarrow \forall \beta \in \mathcal{B} : \exists\, \omega \in L(\beta) : \forall\, O$ instance of $\mathcal{M}$: $\forall o \in O$: $type(\omega\backslash o) \approx type(o)$

3.2 Applying this to the case study

The business process of Figure 5 can be defined as the following regular expression on tasks:

β = **input_sales_order**. print_sales_order.
sign_sales_order.take_sales_order
plan_installation_of_services.install_services
.(review_installation$_{\textbf{refuse}}$
.solve_installation_problems)*
.review_installation$_{\textbf{accept}}$ .bill_services.

The tasks in boldface generate event types where one of the domain object types from the domain model is involved in. Each of these tasks can at its turn be defined as a regular expression on business event types:

input_sales_order = *cr_sales_order*
.(mod_sales_order + cr_order_line +
*mod_order_line + end_order_line)**

sign_sales_order = *customer_sign*

take_sales_order = *operations_accept*

review_installation$_{\textbf{accept}}$ = *customer_accept*)

As a result, the business process can be defined as regular expression on the set of business event types:

β = *cr_sales_order*
.(mod_sales_order + cr_order_line +
*mod_order_line + end_order_line)**
.customer_sign . operations_accept
.customer_accept

Each instance of this business process concerns only a single sales order. Hence:

$\forall \omega \in L(\beta), \forall o \in oids(\text{SALES ORDER}): type(\omega\backslash o) = \beta$

In addition, this business process is compatible with sales order since it is enough to add an *end_sales_order* event type to each scenario from β to obtain a valid scenario of SALES_ORDER:

$\forall \omega \in L(\beta)$:

$\omega^\wedge end\_sales\_order \in L(\text{SALES ORDER})$

$\Rightarrow \beta \approx \text{SALES ORDER}$

The projection of the business process β on the alphabet of an order line is:

β\ ORDER LINE = *(cr_order_line + mod_order_line*
*+ end_order_line)**

In the business process β, several order lines are entered for one sales order. If we take the stream of events generated by this business process for a single order line, we have the same expression. This expression is compatible with the life cycle of

ORDER LINE, since some of the streams will be valid for ORDER LINE.

Projection of β on the alphabets of customer and product gives the empty scenario, which is always compatible with any object type.

4 CONCLUSIONS

By means of a case-study we have illustrated the problem of imposing sequence constraints on business events. As a general rule, business policies, (these are rules that hold in general but can be broken at some occasions) should be modelled as part of the workflow layer. The domain layer should only contain business rules that can never be broken. When deciding whether something is a business rule or a business policy, one must keep in mind that business processes must be flexible in order to adapt easily to a changing business environment. In order to allow for flexibility at the workflow level, the domain model should leave sufficient degrees of freedom.

Although the formal definitions given above define when a business process model is consistent with a domain model, it is not obvious how to check this in practice. In particular, the projection of a stream on a single object cannot be done in an automated way since a conceptual model typically only defines events and objects at the type level. This is a limitation of the proposed formalisation.

Usually, workflows are modelled with Petri-nets. Also the activity diagrams of UML (Rational), (Booch 1995) are an example of a Petri-Net like diagramming technique. The expressive power of Petri-Nets is larger than the expressive power of regular expressions and finite state machines. Their ability to model interleaving and the ability to model individual tasks as tokens makes Petri-net a more attractive theory for the formalisation of business process theory. Further research should investigate whether Petri-Net theory offers the possibility of a practical and automated consistency checking algorithm. We expect that when tokens are used to represent individual objects, automated consistency checking with the domain model must be possible.

REFERENCES

(Booch 1995) Booch, G., Rumbaugh, J., Jacobson, I., *The unified modeling language user guide*, Addison Wesley, 1999

(Coleman 1994) Coleman, D. et al, Object-oriented development: The FUSION method, Prentice Hall, 1994

(Cook 1994) Cook, S., Daniels, J., Designing object systems: object-oriented modeling with Syntropy, Prentice Hall, 1994

(Dedene 1995) Dedene G., Snoeck M., Formal deadlock elimination in an object oriented conceptual schema, Data and Knowledge Engineering, Vol. 15, 1995, 1-30.

(D'Souza 1999) D'Souza, D.F., Wills, A. C. Wills, Objects, Components and Frameworks with UML, The Catalysis Approach, Addison-Wesley, 1999, 785 pp..

(Fowler 1997) Fowler, M., Analysis Patterns, Reusable Object Models, Addison Wesley Longman, 1997.

(Lindström 1999) Lindström, Claes-Göran, Lessons Learned from Applying Business Modelling: Exploring Opportunities and Avoiding Pitfalls, in Nilsson, Anders.G., Tolis, Christopher, Nellborn, Christer, (eds.), Perspectives on Business Modelling, Understanding and Changing Organisations, Springer-Verlag Berlin-Heidelberg, 1999, pp.151-164.

(Nellborn 1999), Christer, Business and Systems Development: Opportunities for an Integrated Way of Working, in Nilsson, Anders.G., Tolis, Christopher, Nellborn, Christer, (eds.), Perspectives on Business Modelling, Understanding and Changing Organisations, Springer-Verlag Berlin-Heidelberg, 1999, pp.197-213.

(Nilsson 1999) Nilsson, Anders G., The Business Developer's Toolbox: Chains and Alliances between Established Methods, in Nilsson, Anders.G., Tolis, Christopher, Nellborn, Christer, (eds.), Perspectives on Business Modelling, Understanding and Changing Organisations, Springer-Verlag Berlin-Heidelberg, 1999, pp. 217-241.

(Rational) Rational Software Corporation, The Unified Modelling Language, http://www.rational.com/

(Snoeck 1998) Snoeck M.., Dedene G. Existence Dependency: The key to semantic integrity between structural and behavioral aspects of object types, IEEE Transactions on Software Engineering , Vol. 24, No. 24, April 1998, pp.233-251

(Snoeck 1999) Snoeck M., Dedene G., Verhelst M; Depuydt A.M., Object-oriented Enterprise Modeling with MERODE, Leuven University Press, 1999

(Snoeck 2000) Snoeck M., Poelmans S. Dedene G., A Layered Software Specification Architecture, in A. H. F. Laendler, S. W. Liddle, V.C. Storey, Conceptual Modeling -ER2000, 19th International Conference on Conceptual Modeling, Salt Lake City, UTAH, USA, Oktober 2000, Lecture Notes In Computer Science 1920, Springer, pp.454-469

ANALYSING COMMUNICATION IN THE CONTEXT OF A SOFTWARE PRODUCTION ORGANISATION

M. Cecilia C. Baranauskas
Institute of Computing, State University of Campinas, Unicamp, Cx Postal 6176 13083970 Campinas, SP, Brazil
Visiting Fellow at the Department of Computer Science, University of Reading, UK
Email: cecilia@ic.unicamp.br

Juliana P. Salles
Computer Science Department,Federal University of Minas Gerais, UFMG, Belo Horizonte, MG, Brazil
Email: jusalles@dcc.ufmg.br

Kecheng Liu
Department of Computer Science, University of Reading, Whiteknights, Reading RG6 6AY, UK
Email: k.liu@reading.ac.uk

Key words: Communication, Organisational Semiotics, Design Process, Design Quality, Human-Computer Interaction.

Abstract: While quality has been widely stressed in literature as a goal of the software design methodologies, quality as a result of the interaction among the actors involved in the design and development processes has not received the same attention. This work aims to investigate the software production process by addressing the communication among work groups in the organisation. Our focus is on understanding the communication process that takes place among the groups, considering that the computational artefact emerges as a result of the communicational acts issued between people with different roles in the process. We base our understanding of communication in semiotic foundations, to propose a framework for analysing communication in the whole process of system design and development. The design process of a real organisation that produces commercial software illustrates our main ideas.

1 INTRODUCTION

Organisational issues involved in software development and use have long been the focus of the Information Systems (IS) field. Nevertheless, some approaches in the Human-Computer Interaction (HCI) field also have concerns about organisational aspects influencing the design and use of computational systems. HCI and information systems development has evolved from different backgrounds and focus to a common end: to achieve high quality in software usage [3]. Quality has been widely stressed in literature as a goal of the software design methodologies, and it has been grounded in the Software Engineering tradition, focusing on optimising technical quality in the product and in the process. For the HCI community, quality has been understood as how well applications fit the needs of individual users. We argue that both perspectives should be considered in order to achieve a global view of quality in the whole design and development process. This work aims to investigate the soft-ware production process by addressing quality in the communication that takes place among the different work groups involved in a software production organisation, including several categories of users.

A comprehensive and integrated understanding of the connections among design, development, and evaluation activities are necessary at all levels of the software de-sign process. Understanding and integrating the whole process requires an under-standing of how different groups in the organisation acquire and communicate their views. As pointed out by some authors [5], [6] this seems to be true in any large sys-tem (e.g. a new automobile design). Participatory [9] and Contextual Design [2] pro-pose several techniques as communication mechanisms in order to bring a design team to a shared understanding of the customer. While we recognise the efforts of some methodologies for a shared understanding of the subject of design, we argue that a global view of the communication among the different groups in the organisation is important to inspect quality in the process and in the product, as a consequence.

The study of the signs used in communication and the rules operating upon them and upon their user forms the core of the study of communication. Thus, there is no communication without a system of signs. Semiotics as a discipline concerns the analysis of signs or the study of the functioning of sign systems. Organisational Semiotics (OS) is one of the branches of Semiotics particularly related to business and organisations [8]. As Liu [13, p.19] points out, the study in OS is based on the fundamental observation that all organised behaviour is effected through the communication and interpretation of signs by people, individually or in groups. The aim of OS studies is to find new and insightful ways of analysing, describing and explaining structure and behaviour of organisations, including their inner workings, and the inter-actions with the environment and with one another.

Our focus in this work is on understanding the communication process that takes place among groups in a software design organisation, in order to inform about the main production process. A meta-model, proposed in previous work [12], organises an analysis space that is extended based on OS foundations towards a framework to inspect quality in communication.

The paper is organised as follows: Section 2 presents the theoretical foundations for the work: the semiotic approach to modelling an organisation, and the concept of communication. Section 3 discusses the software design process as a matter of communication and presents the fractal model of communication. Section 4 outlines a framework for inspecting quality of communication based on the OS foundations and on the fractal model of communication, and discusses results of applying it to a real organisation. Section 5 concludes.

2 THE THEORETICAL FOUNDATIONS

2.1 The Semiotic Approach to Modelling an Organisation

According to the OS approach, an organisation can be seen as an information system where agents employ signs to perform purposeful and co-ordinated actions. An organisation can be characterised by a structure of three layers: the informal, the formal and the technical, which Stamper [15] names "the organisational onion". The whole organisation is regarded as an informal information system in which its culture – values, beliefs, habits and pattern of behaviour of each individual member plays an important role. It is in this layer that meanings are established, intentions are under-stood, beliefs are formed, commitments are made and responsibilities are negotiated through discussion and physical actions. Inside the informal layer there is the formal information system layer, where literate culture dominates through rules that specify how the work should be done and how the tasks should be performed. In this layer, form and rule replace meaning and intention. As far as the tasks are mechanistic and repetitive the rules and procedures can help to achieve efficiency. However, the vision of people being used only to transmit and process sign-tokens is certainly problematic. As people lose understanding of the meanings of the signs they process they lose the global context and cannot anymore evaluate their actions or relate it to the other agents actions to know whether they are doing what was supposed to be done. The third layer concerns the technical system that is placed inside the formal layer to automate part of the formal system. It presupposes well-defined work processes, clearly understood human responsibility for the jobs and explicitly specified rules for operations. However, as far as the introduction of a technical system in an organisation is intended not just to automate work but to support work practices, a clear under-standing of the whole process, as well as flexibility to change as the organisation changes is needed. In summary, the three layers have a strong connection and a representation suitable to adapt and adjust to the global view of the organisation is needed for modelling it. To go deeper in the understanding of this whole structure, the communication among the groups involved in the organisation should be carried out.

A traditional method for organisational analysis is the hierarchical diagram showing the different positions and reporting relationships. This type of representation does not help us to understand neither what an organisation does nor how it does it. The organisational semiotics approach helps us to focus on the organisational functions rather than just the structure, providing morphology of the tasks and functions of an organisation. Three areas of organisational functions and its consequent types of tasks and of associated norms are defined: the substantive, the message passing, and the control areas. Functions in the substantive area are concerned with and directly contribute to the organisation main objective. Functions in the message passing area are related to the information people must have about the relevant facts about the work, to co-ordinate the temporal and spatial use of resources from the substantive area. Functions in the control area aim to reinforce the substantive and message passing areas through tasks that include monitoring and evaluation of substantive and message passing actions. Each area can be further sub-divided in the same way until the level of detail is sufficient to the analysis required. A balance of the three areas should be observed in a healthy organisation. As Liu [8] points out, an "unhealthy" or badly designed organisation will consume a great part of its energy with message-passing and control subsystems.

According to the semiotic approach we are considering, a sound modelling must cover the issues in semantic, pragmatic and social levels. To clarify the semantic problems and represent a social organisation clearly is the most critical and difficult task [8]. It is important to know how people are involved and co-ordinate their tasks and duties. This means more then knowing how they implement a plan or conduct their particular jobs, we are interested in knowing the communicational actions that take place among people in each position of the organisation. For this purpose we need to focus attention of analysis on several levels of the communication among the groups involved in the production organisation. This means identifying communicative agents, messages, channels, and their substantive, communicative and controls actions. An analysis of the communication, taken in a broad sense, among the agents could inform about the "health" of the organisation.

To understand communication in the organisational process, we must first form a coherent understanding of what communication itself involves. Several models for communication have been presented and discussed by thinkers from diverse philosophical schools. In the next section we will examine some of them in order to highlight the essential aspects of the concept.

2.2 Communication Models

There are two main schools in the study of communication, with different standpoints and associated models. The first one, which Fiske [4] names the "process school", sees communication as the transmission of messages. It is concerned with how senders and receivers encode and decode and how the transmitters use channels and media of communication, with efficiency and accuracy. This school sees communication as a process by which one person affects the behaviour or state of mind of another. If the effect on the receiver is different from the intended by the sender, it is considered a failure in communication and the causes of it are searched in the stages of the process. This school has its foundation on the Shannon and Weaver's Mathematical Theory of Communication [14]. Grounded in the Theory of Information as a system of mathematical basis to study the problems of transmitting messages through physical channels, it is therefore a technique of communication engineering in which they identify source, encoder, channel, noise, decoder and receiver of information.

This mathematical theory first arose in telegraphy and telephony, being developed for the purpose of measuring the information content of telecommunication signals. It concerned only the signals themselves, as transmitted along wires or broadcasted, and is abstracted from all questions of "meaning". As a theory, it lies at the syntactic level of sign theory and is abstracted from semantic and pragmatic levels.

Other models developed with other concerns were derived from this very influent model. Westley and MacLehan [16] proposed a model for mass communication that reflects the various interactions among the entities (sender, receiver and channel), involved in the communication, including the receiver-sender, receiver-channel and channel-sender directions. To understand the linguistic process of verbal communication, Jakobson [7] proposed a model in which he identifies 6 factors that constitute every verbal communication act: addresser, addressee, context, message, contact, and code.

The second school sees communication as the production and exchange of meaning [4]. The main method of study in this school is Semiotics. This school is concerned with how messages, or texts, interact with people in order to produce meanings. It does not consider misunderstanding to be necessarily evidence of communication failure, as they may result from the cultural differences between the parts involved in communication. Searle, as described in [8], studied the roles of language usage in communication and defined an illocutionary act as a basic, meaningful unit of human communication. The fundamental aspect of this model is that, during conversation, the hearer receives that communication unity and interprets the meaning based on his own perspective, which can be different from the meaning intended by the sender. It is interesting to notice that the sender himself is a hearer while utters an expression and this cause also on him a perlocutionary effect. This model illustrates how the agents involved in communication alternate roles as sender and receiver of messages.

Our understanding of communication in this work is in line with the school of Semiotics. To understand the computer as media, and the way it can shape communication, we need to go deeper in situating the concept in the process of software construction.

3 THE SOFTWARE DESIGN PROCESS AS A MATTER OF COMMUNICATION

Design has been understood as a technical term referring to a particular step in the software production in which the lines of code are put together according to some software development methodology. In this work, as used by some influential authors in the area of HCI [17],[11],[13], the English language usage is adopted for the term, meaning the invention and organisation of any structure. Therefore, we adopt here a broad understanding of design referring to the software design as a process embracing all the intertwined activities related to the creation and development of a computational artifact: the design of the look and feel, the functionality definition, the codification etc.

According to semiotic approaches in HCI, the software interface can be understood as a message sent from designers to users using the computer as channel [1], [10]. In this work, we argue that to understand the dimensions involved in the construction of the interface as message, it is important to develop a better understanding about the dialogue that occurs among the many parties involved in the design activity. Besides designer-user communication, the other groups are also engaged in some type of communication through different channels: designers talk to marketing people, customer support mediates between developers and users, external consultants help both users' and developers' organisations, etc. The use of different channels is related to the needs of the communicational acts: the nature of information desired, the projects' contexts, the audience language, etc. The focus of this work is in the communication among the several groups involved in the design and development of computational artefacts. The dialogue between designers and users is just one aspect of this communication.

3.1 The Fractal Model of Communication

We argue that in order to design the interface as a message, not only designers and users, but also the remaining actors must engage in a process of negotiation, which we understand as a conversational process. In this conversation, many communication acts occur, many messages are exchanged using different channels. Furthermore, in designing the artefact, the designer establishes a conversation with the design medium, in the sense explained by Schon [13]. This level of communication is also part of the process and thus should be considered.

A fractal model of communication proposed in our previous work [12] captures the structure of the communication process involved in the whole process of software design. It stresses the fact that, in order to design the primary message (the interface), other fractionated messages must carefully be designed and appropriate channels must be chosen to convey them. Figure 1 illustrates the main concepts of the fractal model of communication.

In this diagram, nodes represent the agents in communication (A and A') and the channels (C and C') used by them. The links are bi-directional, which means that the agents share (both send and receive) messages. Nodes C' represent the fractal nature of communication. Different foci of the design process can be highlighted: the de-signer-user communication (A-A') using the interface as message, in a first level, as the interface is the unity-message conveyed by the computer (which is the first channel). The designer-artefact communication, in the sense discussed by Schon (A-C), and the user-computer communication (C-A') are represented in a second level of the fractal, having C' as channels.

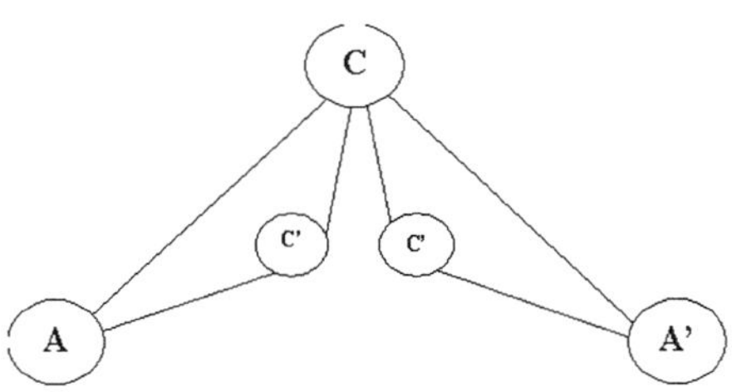

Figure 1: The fractal model of Communication

An inner level could be opened for analysis, showing a third level of the fractal structure, as illustrated by Figure 2. Usability engineers, for example, communicate with users using a usability test as channel. In designing the test, usability engineers communicate with the emergent artefact (the test) through a checklist as channel, for example.

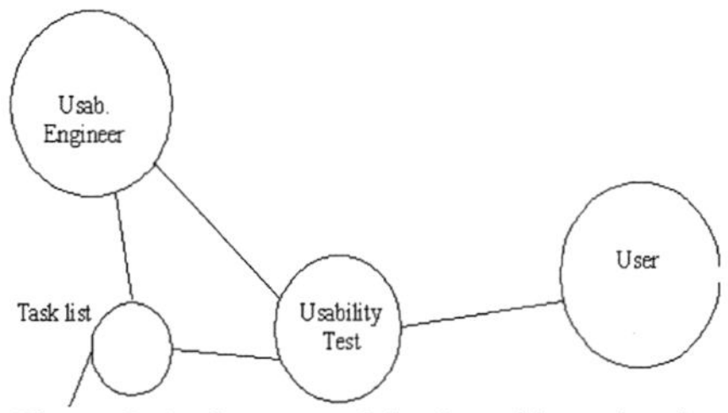

Figure 2: An instance of the fractal inner level

In this model, the interface is understood as a unity-message that reflects what was grasped through the fractionated messages. So, the interface as a unity-message is directly affected by the choice of channels and messages used to compose the fractionated messages during the design process. This means that, in designing the software interface, or the unity message, many fractionated messages are being ex-changed. Each one of those messages is also being designed and should be carefully designed to make the designer-user communication through the unity-message smoother. As both senders and receivers in this communication process, designers and users change turns and co-operate on the development of the interface.

4 TOWARDS A FRAMEWORK TO INSPECT QUALITY IN ORGANISATIONAL COMMUNICATION

As we have already seen in the previous sections, from the OS standpoint, an "organisation" is seen as an information system where agents employ signs for communication towards the performance of purposeful and co-ordinated actions. We need now to focus attention of analysis in the several interconnected levels of communication among the groups involved in the work. Different levels of the Fractal Model of Communication can be represented to grasp communication in the different layers (informal, formal and technical) and to show the connections between the nested layers. Furthermore the morphology of functions can also be identified in order to evaluate the balance among substantive, message passing and control functions of the agents.

Understanding the relationships among the several groups involved in a production organisation, and how they articulate actions towards the main objective involves understanding how they communicate with each other in the organisational structure. The quality of communication as a whole depends on the quality of communication between agents in each level of the fractal structure, which should consider the substantive, message passing and control actions.

4.1 Modelling Communication in a Product Development Cycle: an Example

To exemplify the main ideas proposed for the framework, a major software design company, here given the pseudonym "ORG" will be considered. This organisation employs leading professionals in all areas involved with the creation of commercial applications also called off-the-shelf software. The main groups identified as agents of the communication process are marketing people, program managers, designers, usability engineers, developers, testers, and support people. Customers, market, beta-users and users are four types of external agents called "users": customers are people who have already bought the product and receive the service of the support team for problems with the product. Market represents the people who are identified by the marketing as a potential client. Users are the subjects recruited by the usability team to participate in the usability tests. Beta-users are people already using the beta version of the product. Actually, these four categories of people are potential end-users for the product.

Typically the life cycle of the ORG products has three phases: planning, development and stabilisation phases. During the planning phase, communication between the marketing and the program manager is established to produce the vision document. This artefact defines a set of goals that drive the product development. These agents also produce a high level specification for the product with a preliminary list of features to be present in the final product. The product life cycle at ORG is oriented by this vision document and by the high level specification. During the development phase, communication between program managers and developers takes place and the functional specification evolves as a result of this conversation. Developers have an important role in the choice of the features to be implemented. Subsets of this functionality are defined and milestones are stated for their release. Each set of features liberation involves intensive communication between developers and testers. While developers write code based on functional specification, the later test it for bugs. It is also in this phase that the interface is designed and tested for usability problems. After the last liberation, modifications in the main interface components (menus, dialogue boxes, etc.) are not allowed anymore. During the stabilisation phase, the software product is extensively tested at ORG and outside, with Beta-version clients. Testers and developers establish communication with Beta-version clients during this phase. When high severity bugs are not found, the product is liberated to manufacturing.

The different agents also establish conversation with the emergent artefact, using channels related to their function in the organisation. For example, there is a conversation between usability engineers and the emergent interface, using inspection methods as channels; developers establish a conversation with the code they are creating, through the tools they use (compilers, debugging tools, etc.). Figure 3 illustrates the Fractal Model of Communication applied to the product development cycle of this particular organisation. An overview of the communication among the groups is shown in a simplified way, with two levels of the fractal structure.

Marketers have their tasks and responsibilities in the informal layer, as they are in charge of ensuring a product meets the need for which people will buy it. They have a message passing function as they act as channel between people who would buy the product and the program manager. Their substantive functions are concerned with marketing research. Their substantive actions consist of identifying what kind of customer makes up the market. Their substantive objects of action are questionnaires, feature list, list of customer needs, requirement list, wish list, and so on. Besides dealing with issues related to the market, they are engaged in product planning activities, with the product manager. Despite their substantive actions being concerned to the informal layer, they focus on demographics rather than on users' work practice. No control functions are associated to them.

Program managers are people who make a bridge from the informal layer to the formal layer. Their primary function is control, as they are in charge of the whole project, and have as primary responsibility to ensure the promised features are being finished on time and with acceptable quality. The object of action in the control area is the project schedule. Their substantive functions are to specify what the overall product (for example a computational application) must offer, and to manage the project. Their substantive actions involve defining the vision document (sharing it with marketers), and defining the functional specifications (sharing it with developers). Their substantive objects of action include the vision documents and the functional specification. They have a function of message passing as they act as channel between marketers and developers. Furthermore, they act as channel between all the other agents, excluding the four categories of users.

Developers (programming engineers) have their tasks and responsibilities in the technical layer with focus on technology and on what makes a clean program code. They are receivers of marketers message through message passing mechanisms of the program manager, as they get directions from the marketing, through the program manager, who specifies what the overall system must offer. Their primary function is substantive, related to the implementation of system functions. Their substantive action is codifying and their substantive objects of action are the functional specification and the program code. Their control functions are carried by as a consequence of their communication with

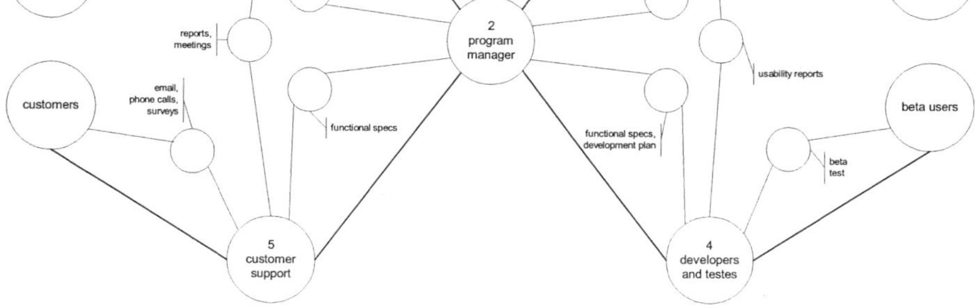

Figure 3: Meta-model for the product development cycle at ORG.

testers, who test code and report bugs.

Usability engineers are the people whose main actions are in the informal layer as they have the direct observation of the problems experienced by users interacting with the application. Their primary function is control, as they function as quality control agents for product design to assure usability to it. Their substantive function is quality control of the usability of the product. Their substantive actions are related to designing and applying usability tests. Their substantive objects of actions are basically usability tests and usability reports. At ORG designers are people in charge of the product interface design. They should lay a bridge between the informal and formal layers. Their function is primarily substantive and their substantive actions involve designing the interface. Thus their substantive object of action is the product inter-face. Their control functions are conducted as a consequence of communication with the usability engineers. Together, designers and usability engineers have message passing functions as they act as channel between users and developers, and between users and the program manager.

Customer supporters are people who make the bridge from the technical to the in-formal layer. Their substantive function is concerned to responding to problems en-countered by clients in using the application. Their substantive actions involve emailing, phoning or sending a survey to the clients. Substantive objects are questions from and answers to the clients.

The four categories of agents representing users are in the social layer and their functions in the organisation are mostly concerned with the control area as they feed message passing mechanisms of usability engineers, testers and customer support groups.

4.2 Discussion

The instantiation of the framework presented tells us that the process is marketing-oriented, which is consistent with the economic and cultural contexts of ORG. This is reflected in the development driven by the functionality. The program manager acts as a channel between the marketing and all the other groups (developers, testers, de-signers and usability engineers). His object of conversation with developers and testers is the functional specification (substantive area), communicating the intended functions for the product and the priorities to implement them (control area). From the developer perspective, this is an efficient message as both program managers and developers share the specification document as one of their substantive objects. However, designers and usability engineers need more elements to understand how the functions should be arranged and structured in the product as a whole, determining the user experience. There is a lack in the message passing function between the program manager and the designers/usability group concerning the vision document, which should be part of the substantive actions of the latter. Designers and usability engineers' vision should be considered especially in the planning phase of the cycle.

The understanding about the user has different meanings to different agents of the process. The meta-model shows us different "users" communicating to different agents: some users participate in the usability tests, communicating to the usability engineers; customers are the people who marketing is targeted to; clients are users in communication with the support group; beta-test participants are users communicating to testers. Nevertheless, the identification of the "user" is only in the substantive actions of the marketing group as it is the only agent involved in knowing (who are) the prospective users. Other agents in the process demand understanding about the users: designers, for example, should know for whom they are designing. Marketers use a specific substantive function (market research) to get a demographic description of the prospective users. However, the substantive objects of action of the marketing group do not necessarily fit interests of the designers group. New substantive actions could be introduced for the agents in communication with users to convey a more complete view of the user and to accommodate specific necessities of substantive functions of designers and usability engineers.

The substantive object of action of the customer support group and of the testers group would be powerful additional objects to identify (what are) the usability problems, as these agents have direct access to problems pointed out by users. However, in the first case, an expansion in the substantive area of the usability group would be necessary to include new substantive objects of action. In the second case, new messages should be designed in the beta-test to address also usability issues. Using data from beta-tests and from the support group records would mean the utilisation of al-ready existent substantive objects of action. Data collected through these channels could be used as input in the design of usability tests to answer how the problems occur. Thus, the whole set of messages would be complemented more effectively.

Certain channels, despite being present, do not establish a psychological connection between two groups. In analysing a channel, it is important to adequate the messages to the audience. One group needs ways to communicate that they are tailored to the concerns and work style of the other group. This means that they must share substantive objects of action. The program manager acts as a channel between the marketing and designers/usability engineers using the functional specification document. While developers and marketers share substantive objects of action - developers think in functions as units of implementation consistently with marketing objectives, designers need a much broader view that is not communicated by the specification document- designers and marketers do not share the same substantive objects of action. Also, the communication between usability engineers and developers through the usability re-port and email does not seem adequate to the developers whose substantive objects of action are much more technically focused. As a consequence the message from us-ability group does not reach the developer.

Results of a first analysis on the meta-model using the proposed framework point to the necessity of new channels and messages, as well as more shared substantive areas among some agents to enhance communication among key elements of the process. The dynamic enabled by improving quality in communication could lead to a more integrated design and development process and potentially a better product.

5 CONCLUSION

In this work we presented our understanding of design as a communication process and proposed a framework based on Organisational Semiotics to model communication in a software design organisation. The framework captures the sharing of substantive areas that should occur among the different agents of communication, as senders and receivers in this communication process, and the aspects of control and message passing among the agents. It also stresses the fact that, in order to design the final product, several messages should be carefully designed and appropriate channels must be chosen to convey them.

Summarising, the Fractal Communication Model organises an analysis space in which foundations from Organisational Semiotics can be used for modelling communication among agents in the organisation. This view of the organisational context of software development allows to search for continuous improvement in the process and potentially to develop more usable and useful software.

Acknowlegdements: We gratefully acknowledge the Brazilian agency CNPq (Conselho Nacional de Desenvolvimento Científico e Tecnológico) for partial financial support.

REFERENCES

Andersen, P. B.,1997. *A Theory of Computer Semiotics*. Cambridge University Press, Cambridge.

Beyer, H. B., Holtzblatt, K., 1998. *Contextual Design: Defining Customer-Centered Systems*. Morgan Kaufmann Publishers.

Ehn, P., Lowgren, J., 1997. Design for Quality-in-use: Human-Computer Interaction meets Information Systems Development. In: Helander et al (eds.) *Handbook of Human-Computer Interaction*, Elsevier Science.

Fisk, J., 1990. *Introduction to Communication Studies*. Routledge, London.

Grudin, J., Markus, M.L., 1997. Organizational Issues in Development and Implementation of Interactive Systems. In: Helander et al (eds.) *Handbook of Human-Computer Interaction*. Elsevier Science.

Hix, D., Hartson, H.R., 1993. *Developing user interfaces: ensuring usability through product and process*. John Wiley and Sons, New York .

Jakobson, R., 1960. Closing Statement: Linguistics and Poetics. In: Sebeok, A. (ed.): *Style in Language*. The MIT Press, Cambridge, Mass.

Liu, K., 2000. *Semiotics in Information Systems Engineering*, Cambridge University Press.

Muller, M., 1997. Participatory Practices in the Software Lifecycle. In: Helander et al (eds.) *Handbook of Human-Computer Interaction*. Elsevier Science, New York.

Nadin, M., 1998. Interface Design and Evaluation – Semiotic Implications. In: Hartson, H. R and Hix, D, (eds.): *Advances in Human-Computer Interaction*. v. 2. Ablex Publishing Corporation.

Norman, D.A., 1998. The Invisible Computer, The MIT Press, Cambridge, Massachusetts.

Salles, J.P., Baranauskas, M.C.C., Bigonha, R.S., 2000. A Communication Model for the Interface Design Process. *Workshop on Semiotic Approaches to User Interface Design*, CHI2000.

Schön, D., Bennet, J., 1996. Reflective Conversation with Materials. In: Winograd, T, (ed.), *Bringing Design to Software* ACM Press.

Shannon, C. L., Weaver, W., 1949.*The Mathematical Theory of Communication*, Urbana, Univ. of Illinois Press.

Stamper, R. K., 1973. *Information in Business and Administrative Systems*. John Wiley and Sons, New York.

Westley B. H., MacLehan, M. S., 1972. Un modelo conceptual para la investigacíon en comunicaciones. In Smith G, (ed.): *Comunicacíon y cultura* Nueva Visión, Buenos Aires (1972)

Winograd, T. (ed.), 1996. *Bringing Design to Software*, ACM Press.

A FUNCTIONAL SIZE MEASUREMENT METHOD FOR EVENT-BASED OBJECT-ORIENTED ENTERPRISE MODELS

Geert Poels
VLEKHO Business School, Koningsstraat 336, 1030 Brussel, Belgium
Email: gpoels@vlekho.wenk.be

Key words: Metrics, software sizing, function points, object-orientation, layered architectures, events, enterprise models.

Abstract: The effective management of IS-related processes requires measuring the functional size of information systems. Functional size measurement is usually performed using the Function Points Analysis method. Earlier attempts to apply Function Point counting rules to object-oriented systems met with serious problems because the implicit model of functional user requirements in Function Points Analysis is hard to reconcile with the object-oriented paradigm. The emergence of a new generation of functional size measurement methods has changed this picture. The main implementation of this generation, COSMIC Full Function Points, explicitly defines a generic model of functional user requirements onto which artifacts belonging to any IS specification or engineering methodology can be mapped. In this paper we present specific COSMIC-FFP mapping rules for methodologies that take an event-based approach to information system engineering. In particular we show that the event-oriented nature of the COSMIC-FFP measurement rules provides for a natural mapping of concepts. To illustrate the mapping rules we use MERODE, a formal event-based object-oriented methodology for systems development in information processing intensive domains. The mapping rules presented are confined to the enterprise layer in a MERODE IS architecture.

1 INTRODUCTION

To effectively manage the process of IS specification, development, and implementation, it is necessary to know the functional size of the required information system.

According to the ISO standard for functional size measurement, the functional size of an information system is captured by the user's perspective on the functional IS requirements (ISO, 1998). This perspective relates to the subset of user requirements that focus on what the system must do to fulfill the user's information needs, without considering how this will be accomplished. The functional user requirements therefore exclude all technical, quality, and performance requirements. Moreover, functional size measurement must be independent of the technical IS development and implementation decisions that are taken during the IS lifecycle, providing an 'objective' basis of comparison and assuring the timeliness of the size measurement.

Functional size measurement has traditionally been performed using Function Points Analysis (FPA) (Albrecht et al., 1983), a method for data-rich and information processing intensive systems that identifies transaction functions and logical data files based on the requirements specifications. These base functional components are subsequently quantified using a fixed schema of weights that reflects the amount of data stored in a file or manipulated by a function.

The FPA view of functional size reflects contemporary IS engineering methodology and practices based on structured principles and functional decomposition. This function-oriented view is not compatible with modern approaches towards the development of enterprise information systems that use object-oriented (OO) specifications and layered IS architectures.

In OO information systems, data and the procedures operating on these data are encapsulated in a same unit of software called the object. There is no natural mapping between the concept of object and the FPA notion of function. Dismembering object classes into data (i.e. files) and procedures (i.e. transaction functions) is an option, but poses a granularity problem. The scope of the average FPA function in non-OO software is a magnitude of order larger than the scope of a typical class method.

Another problem with FPA is that its implicit model of the system to be sized does not accommodate the concept of layered architecture, which is used to distinguish different kinds of IS components based on the type of functionality they offer to the user. The method does therefore not consider the exchange of data between system layers, positioned at different levels of functional abstraction. As a consequence, it is hard to apply the FPA measurement rules to a layer that does not directly exchange data with the system's users.

These and other problems have motivated a group of experts, called the COmmon Software Measurement International Consortium (COSMIC), to work on the principles of a next generation of functional size measurement methods. The main result of this work is COSMIC Full Function Points (Abran et al., 2001).

The COSMIC-FFP functional size measurement method proposes measurement rules for an abstract model of functional user requirements. This model is based on a base functional component typology that no longer requires data to be separated from the procedures operating on these data. Moreover, the model incorporates the notion of layers in requirements specifications.

The independence of specific IS development methodologies realized by COSMIC-FFP is due to the abstractness of its underlying model. The cost of this generality is the absence of detailed measurement rules for specific requirements specification artifacts. There is currently a need for mapping the constructs used by current IS development methodologies to COSMIC-FFP concepts.

In this paper we provide a set of rules to apply COSMIC-FFP to a specific class of OO methodologies for developing enterprise information systems, i.e. the event-based approach. Event-based methodologies have in common that they assume object behavior to be triggered by the occurrence of real-world or system events, for which explicit modeling constructs are offered. We show that the presence of 'triggering events' in COSMIC-FFP provides for a natural mapping of concepts. To substantiate and exemplify this mapping we use MERODE (Snoeck et al., 1999), a formal event-based, and (partly) UML notation based, methodology that is used in the business administration domain. The scope of the mapping presented in this paper is limited to the enterprise model, i.e. the layer in a MERODE system architecture that captures the essential business requirements that the system must fulfill.

This paper is organized as follows. In section 2 we review the main principles of event-based OO enterprise modeling and illustrate these principles using MERODE. In section 3 we briefly describe the COSMIC-FFP method. Sections 4 and 5 present specific COSMIC-FFP rules for MERODE event-based OO enterprise models, respectively focusing on model mapping rules and function point counting rules. Finally, section 6 discusses related work and section 7 presents conclusions.

2 EVENT-BASED OBJECT-ORIENTED ENTERPRISE MODELING

MERODE prescribes a layered IS architecture that partitions an object model following the principle of model-driven development. According to this principle, different kinds of system specifications are distinguished based on their expected change rates. The enterprise model contains the set of specifications that stem from essential business requirements, reflecting the relevant domain knowledge for running a business. The functionality model consists of the specifications that originate from the work organization (i.e. the input services) and the end user's or organization's information needs (i.e. the output services). Finally, the user interface model specifies the facilities to trigger, interrupt, and resume the execution of the input and output services. The most stable specifications are those of the enterprise model, as they meet requirements that are also valid in the absence of an information system. The most volatile specifications are in the user interface model, which captures workflow, presentation, and dialogue aspects.

Each type of specifications gives rise to a number of object classes, which are organized in layers. The innermost layer contains the enterprise object classes; the middle layer the function object classes; the outermost layer the user interface classes. Objects are only allowed to use the services of objects in the same or a more inner layer. That way, classes are prevented to depend upon less stable classes, ensuring a strict control on the propagation of changes and hence a flexible and stable architecture.

In this paper we are concerned with the functional size measurement of enterprise models. MERODE enterprise models consist of three interrelated sub-models, presenting different views of the same business reality. The first sub-model is a class diagram (for which UML notation can be used) containing a set of object type specifications that are classified according to two mechanisms: existence dependency[1] and generalization-

[1] The principle of existence dependency is the most distinctive feature of MERODE. For more information on this topic we refer to (Snoeck et al., 1999).

specialization. The second sub-model is an object-event table specifying which (type of) enterprise objects are involved in which (type of) real-world events. According to this formalism, objects interact when they are involved in the same event. Within the enterprise model, object communication is therefore modeled using the event broadcasting mechanism instead of direct message passing between enterprise objects. The third sub-model is a collection of object life cycle models (formalized by Finite State Machines), expressing the sequence constraints that hold for the participation of enterprise objects in real-world events.

In order to apply functional size measurement we assume that there exists a unified and detailed view of these three sub-models, consisting of a set of object class specifications. Each of these specifications contains an object class name, the object class attributes, and the object class methods. Methods have a specification, consisting of the method signature (including parameters) and the method preconditions, and an implementation consisting of the method body. Each time an enterprise object participates in a real-world event, a method is triggered that may modify the value of the object's attributes. Within class specifications, inherit clauses are used to specify inheritance relationships between object classes as indicated by the generalization-specialization relationships in the class diagram. Existence dependency relationships are specified by means of the abstraction mechanism (i.e. attributes are declared of an object class data type). Sequence constraints and other business constraints are specified within the method preconditions.

3 EVENT-BASED FUNCTIONAL SIZE MEASUREMENT

The COSMIC-FFP method can be applied to a system as a whole, or to any layer within a system that is obtained by an architectural decomposition based on a functional view. Once the scope of measurement is established and the system or layer boundaries are defined, the COSMIC-FFP method proceeds through two stages: a mapping phase and a measurement phase.

3.1 The Mapping Phase

During the mapping phase functional processes and data groups are identified within the system or system layer that must be sized. These are the only two types of constructs that are used within the system model assumed by COSMIC-FFP.

A functional process is seen as a unique set of data exchanges across the boundaries of the system (or system layer), that implement a cohesive and logically indivisible set of functional user requirements. For any system or system layer, two boundaries are considered: a front-end boundary and a back-end boundary. The front-end boundary separates the system or system layer from its user, which in case of a layer can be another system layer. The back-end boundary separates the system or system layer from data storage, which in case of a layer can be realized through invoking the services of another system layer. Data exchanges across system or layer boundaries can take four forms: entry, exit, read, and write. Fig. 1 illustrates these four types of data exchange for the software component of an information system. In the front-end direction data is exchanged with the user across the I/O boundary. In the back-end direction data is exchanged with the storage devices.

As a practical guideline to delimit a cohesive and logically indivisible set of functional user requirements, the COSMIC-FFP measurement manual states that a functional process is triggered by an event occurring outside the system or layer boundary and is complete when it has executed all that is required to be done in response to the triggering event.

Apart from functional processes, all data groups referenced by these functional processes need to be identified. A data group is defined as a distinct, non-empty, non-ordered, and non-redundant set of data attributes, where each included data attribute describes a complementary aspect of the same object of interest.

3.2 The Measurement Phase

Within each functional process, all COSMIC-FFP sub-processes are identified. In the current version of COSMIC-FFP, these sub-processes are exactly the same as the data exchanges occurring during the execution of a functional process. There are four COSMIC-FFP sub-process types:

1. An ENTRY (E) is a movement of one or more data attributes found in one data group from the user's side of the boundary to the inside of the boundary.
2. An EXIT (X) is a movement of one or more data attributes found in one data group from inside the boundary to the user side of the boundary.
3. A READ (R) is a movement of one or more data attributes found in one data group from storage

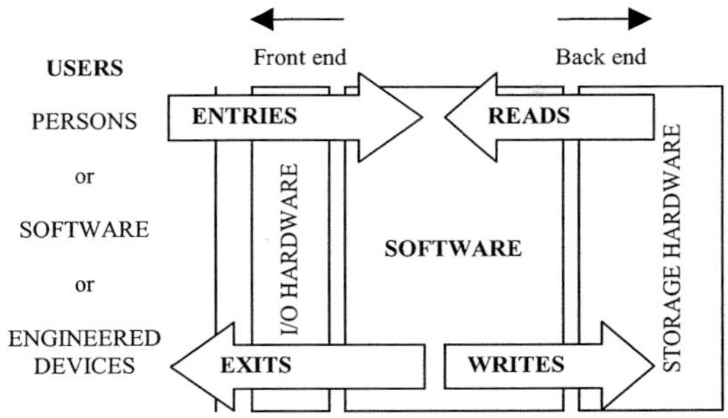

Figure 1: Generic exchange of data through software from a functional perspective

to the functional process to which the read sub-process belongs.

4. A WRITE (W) is a movement of one or more data attributes found in one data group from the functional process to which the write sub-process belongs to storage.

The COSMIC-FFP sub-process types are the base functional component types used by the COSMIC-FFP method. They determine the particular point of view of functional size taken by this method.

The function point counting procedure of COSMIC-FFP is trivial once sub-processes are identified. Each instance of a sub-process type found in the functional processes has a functional size equal to 1 Cfsu (Cosmic functional size unit), which is the measurement standard used by COSMIC-FFP. The sum of these values is the functional size of the system or system layer to be sized. Given the choice of measurement standard, this sum is equal to the count of sub-processes (or data exchanges).

4 FUNCTIONAL SIZE MEASUREMENT MAPPING RULES

The COSMIC-FFP mapping phase can be subdivided in two sub-phases. The first sub-phase results in an instance of the COSMIC-FFP context model, where the scope of the functional size measurement exercise is determined by identifying system layers and boundaries. The second sub-phase constructs an instance of the abstract COSMIC-FFP model that determines the functional structure (i.e. functional processes and data groups) of the system or system layer within the scope of functional size measurement.

4.1 COSMIC-FFP Context Model for MERODE Enterprise Models

According to the COSMIC-FFP measurement manual, the identification of system layers is facilitated by the use of a layered IS architecture on condition that it provides a functional view of the various system components. The MERODE architecture provides such a view, as it distinguishes between business functionality, information system functionality, and user interface functionality. The manual further stipulates that if a specific architectural paradigm is used, then an equivalence should be established between specific architectural objects and the concept of layers in COSMIC-FFP. The principle of model-driven development allows distinguishing three such layers in the COSMIC-FFP context model for MERODE: the enterprise layer, the functionality layer, and the user interface layer.

The boundaries between these three layers are clearly defined in MERODE (Fig. 2). The user interface classes use the services of the function object classes, which in turn use the services of the enterprise object classes. Therefore, the user interface layer is a client to the functionality layer, which is in turn a client to the enterprise layer. The user interface layer has a front-end boundary with the user, via some intermediate layers outside the scope of MERODE (e.g. I/O devices, device drivers, OS, GUI). The enterprise layer has a back-end boundary with storage devices, again via a number of subordinate layers like DBMS, OS, and device drivers.

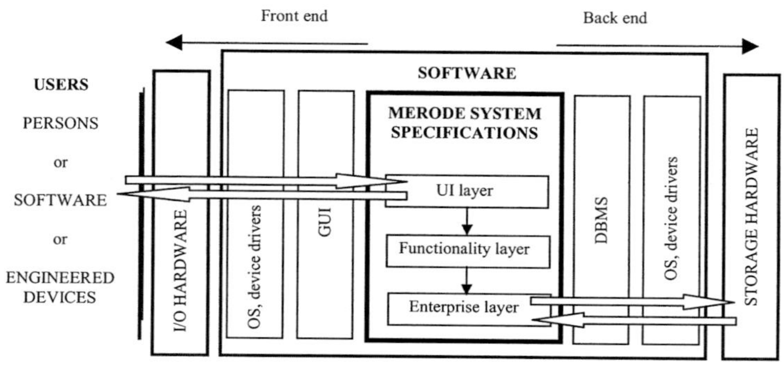

Figure 2: COSMIC-FFP context model for MERODE

As this paper is only concerned with functional size measurement for MERODE enterprise models, we limit the scope of functional size measurement to the enterprise layer of the software application. It should be understood that the enterprise object classes specify only a subset of the functional user requirements. Though it seems that these business requirements do not directly deliver information system functionality (i.e. information products) to the system users, which is the aspect of size considered by COSMIC-FFP, they do represent part of the user practices and procedures that the system must perform to fulfill the user's needs. We therefore consider the business functionality specified in the enterprise object classes as part of the functionality delivered by the system to the users (via the functionality and user interface layers). The functional size of the enterprise layer contributes to the functional size of the entire system. As opposed to other functional size measurement methods, COSMIC-FFP allows measuring the functional size of separate layers.

Fig. 3 details the COSMIC-FFP context model for MERODE by focusing on the data exchanges across the boundaries of the enterprise layer.

In the front-end direction, function objects communicate with enterprise objects by means of messages and status inspections. When an event occurs in the real world, a function object sends an event message to all enterprise objects involved. For each of these enterprise objects an event method is triggered by the event message. If this method has parameters, then the event message carries the required data. With this type of object communication, there is no exchange of data from the enterprise layer to the functionality layer, as event methods have no return type. Status inspections[2] allow function objects to inspect the value of enterprise object attributes. Hence, they carry data from the enterprise layer to the functionality layer.

In the back-end direction, it is assumed that the services of a DBMS are used to store and retrieve the enterprise object state vectors, which contain the object attribute values.

4.2 Abstract COSMIC-FFP Model for MERODE Enterprise Models

The abstract COSMIC-FFP model contains all elements of the functional user requirements within the scope of the context model (in our case limited to the enterprise layer), that are considered as relevant for a COSMIC-FFP functional size measurement exercise.

The definition of a functional process in the measurement manual leads to an unambiguous interpretation of this concept in the context of MERODE enterprise models. This definition states that "A functional process is a unique set of data movements [...] implementing a cohesive and logically indivisible set of [functional user requirements]. It is triggered directly, or indirectly via an 'actor', by an Event (-type) and is complete when it has executed all that is required to be done in response to the triggering Event (-type)" (Abran et al., 2001, p. 26). Furthermore, this triggering event must occur outside the boundary of the measured system or system layer.

[2] Status inspections can be implemented by sending messages to trigger 'accessor' methods, having return types. Such methods are however not specified in MERODE enterprise classes, as they are considered an implementation issue.

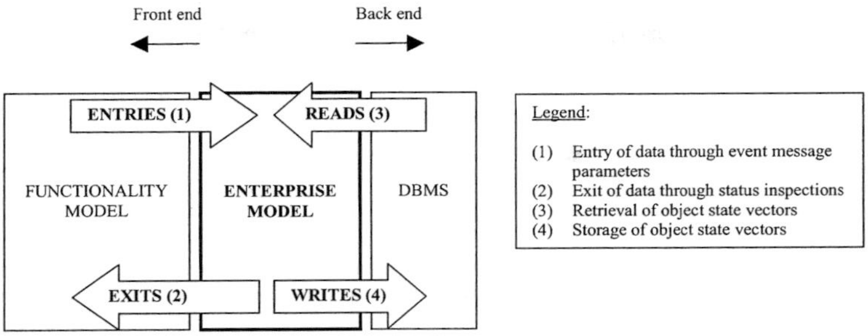

Figure 3: detailed COSMIC-FFP context model for MERODE enterprise models

In case of MERODE enterprise models, business functionality is triggered by events occurring in the real world. Input function objects qualify as actors that transmit real-world events to the enterprise model via event messages. These messages trigger a set of event methods, leading to the execution of the corresponding method bodies. Adhering to the above definition, a MERODE enterprise model functional process can therefore be defined as the collection of data exchanges that are contained within the set of event methods triggered by a real-world event (type). This definition is operationalized as Mapping Rule 1.

Mapping Rule 1: For each event type in the object-event table, identify a functional process. Include in this functional process all event methods specified in the enterprise object classes, occurrences of which are involved in occurrences of the event type.

According to their definition (cf. section 3.1) data groups in COSMIC-FFP correspond to the sets of attributes in the enterprise object classes.

Mapping Rule 2: For each object type in the object-event table, identify a data group. This data group is the set of attributes found in the enterprise object class that specifies the data, functionality, and behavior of the object type.

5 FUNCTIONAL SIZE MEASUREMENT COUNTING RULES

A COSMIC-FFP sub-process is defined as "a data [exchange] occurring during the execution of a functional process" (Abran et al., 2001, p. 34). Data exchange sub-processes move data contained in exactly one data group. The data is moved across the boundary of the system or system layer.

The following kinds of data exchange occur during the execution of a MERODE enterprise model functional process:

1. The functional process is triggered by event messages, which may carry data from the functionality layer to the enterprise layer.
2. During the execution of the functional process, the values of enterprise object attributes are updated and stored in the enterprise object state vectors.
3. During the execution of the functional process, values of enterprise object attributes may be retrieved from the enterprise object state vectors.

The first type of data exchange relates to entry sub-processes in COSMIC-FFP. Data is moved from the functionality layer's side of the boundary to the side of the enterprise layer. As each ENTRY moves data from only one data group, the triggering of a functional process by a real-world event may result in the execution of more than one entry sub-process. Each event method that is triggered may require parameters referring to the enterprise object attributes. Hence, the potential number of entry sub-processes is equal to the number of object types involved in the event type. This reasoning is formalized in Counting Rule 1.

Counting Rule 1: For each functional process, an ENTRY functional sub-process is counted for each of the event methods it includes, on condition that the method signature has at least one parameter.

The second type of data exchange relates to write sub-processes. Each time that the execution of an event method body involves initializing or modifying the value of at least one enterprise object attribute, a WRITE occurs. Conceptually, the data is moved from the enterprise layer's side of the boundary to the DBMS side. As during the execution of a functional process more than one event method can be triggered and all these triggered methods relate to different data groups (i.e. enterprise objects), more than one write sub-process may be identified.

Counting Rule 2: For each functional process, a WRITE functional sub-process is counted for each of the event methods it includes, on condition that the method body updates the value of at least one enterprise object attribute.

The third type of data exchange relates to read sub-processes. The processing within an event method body may require a READ to supply the value of one or more enterprise object attributes. Even before a method body is executed, it might be necessary to get the value of enterprise object attributes when checking method preconditions. This access to the enterprise object attributes can conceptually be described as a movement of data from the DBMS side of the boundary to the enterprise layer's side. Again, more than one read sub-process can be involved in the execution of a MERODE enterprise model functional process.

Counting Rule 3: For each functional process, a READ functional sub-process is counted for each of the event methods it includes, on condition that the method body or preconditions retrieve the value of at least one enterprise object attribute.

There is no equivalent to the COSMIC-FFP EXIT functional sub-process in MERODE enterprise models. Although, conceptually, status inspections bring data lying inside the enterprise layer within reach of the functionality layer (cf. Fig. 3), these data movements are not within the realm of the MERODE enterprise model functional processes. Exit data exchanges are part of the MERODE functionality model functional processes, which implement information system functionality required by users. As such they are not documented in the MERODE enterprise model.

To summarize, the functional size of a MERODE enterprise model is equal to the number of ENTRY, WRITE, and READ sub-processes in its functional processes.

6 RELATED WORK

To 'solve' the OO-FPA mapping problem, many FPA variants have been proposed (Rains, 1991; Whitmire, 1993; Thomson et al., 1994; Hastings, 1995; Zhao et al., 1995; Sneed, 1996; Caldiera et al., 1998; Fetcke et al., 1998; Uemura et al., 1999; Pastor et al., 2001; Ram et al., 2001). None of these proposals has succeeded in becoming a widely accepted functional size measurement method for OO systems.

The feasibility of mapping OO concepts onto the abstract COSMIC-FFP functional user requirements model is evidenced by recent work in the field (Bévo et al., 1999; Jenner, 2001; Diab et al., 2001).

Both Bévo et al. (1999) and Jenner (2001) provide a mapping for UML-based specifications. Bévo et al. map constructs used in class diagrams and use case diagrams onto the abstract COSMIC-FFP model. The use case diagram is used to identify the system (i.e. the collection of use cases modeled), its boundary (i.e. the system boundary specified in the use case diagram), and its users (i.e. the actors in the use case diagram). An equivalence to the layer concept in COSMIC-FFP is not established. Bévo et al. further contend that UML classes correspond to COSMIC-FFP data groups and that use cases correspond to COSMIC-FFP functional processes. A scenario, i.e. a specific sequence of actions illustrating a use case instance, is considered as a sequence of COSMIC-FFP sub-processes.

As shown by Jenner, Bévo et al. confuse in their examples the concept of scenario with that of detailed use case. They provide for a same system specification widely ranging size 'estimates', depending on the level of detail in the use case diagram. As argued by Jenner, the fact that a system specification may look very different according to who produces it (i.e. according to the level of granularity with which use cases are described), suggests that a mapping of use cases onto COSMIC-FFP functional processes may not be appropriate. As an alternative, Jenner proposes to look at the sequence diagram for each use case and regard each use case as a sequence of COSMIC-FFP functional processes. Each functional process is triggered by something done or requested by an actor, as documented in the sequence diagram. According to Jenner, sequence diagrams are specified at a level of detail, where the granularity problem observed when specifying use case diagrams, does not occur. Jenner further uses the concept of "swimlanes" in UML sequence diagrams to establish an equivalence with the layer concept in COSMIC-FFP.

The different interpretations of functional processes in UML by Bévo et al. and Jenner stem from the fact that the concept of a 'triggering event' is not explicitly present in UML. Diab et al. (2001) provide a mapping for ROOM (Real-time Object-Oriented Modeling) specifications, which correspond more closely to the event-based approach to system specification described in this paper. Diab et al. identify functional processes based on the transitions in statechart specifications.

These transitions are triggered by messages, which can be considered as external events. The interpretation of COSMIC-FFP sub-processes is largely the same as in this paper. It must be noted, however, that ROOM specifications are not organized using layered architecture principles. The application of functional size measurement to a specific layer within the IS architecture distinguishes our work from (Diab et al., 2001).

7 CONCLUSIONS

This paper presented five rules to map the constructs and artifacts used in MERODE enterprise modeling onto the concepts, definitions, principles, and rules of the COSMIC-FFP method. COSMIC-FFP is the principal implementation of a new generation of functional size measurement methods, which is meant to improve the first generation of Function Points based methods (i.e. FPA and variants).

The main distinguishing feature of COSMIC-FFP is the explicit definition of a generic, abstract model of the functional user requirements, onto which the operational artifacts of the IS development methodology that is adopted, are mapped before measurement takes place. It is this feature that makes a functional size measurement method not only independent of technology and implementation choices, as with FPA, but above all really free from the development methodology. The paradigm clash between OO methodologies and first generation Function Points based methods is therefore not observed when mapping the OO specifications in a MERODE enterprise model onto the abstract COSMIC-FFP functional user requirements model.

Two other features of COSMIC-FFP provide for a natural mapping of concepts. First, the notion of layers in COSMIC-FFP allows determining the scope of functional size measurement in the context of a layered system (or software) architecture, and thus helps conceiving specific functional size measurement procedures for the enterprise layer in the MERODE IS architecture.

Second, the focus on external events as process triggers in both COSMIC-FFP and MERODE, helps determining the appropriate level of granularity of the mapping rules. It is especially this event-orientation in COSMIC-FFP that goes well with the event-driven nature of MERODE and the event-based approach to requirements specification in general.

In our future work we will investigate the applicability of Early & Quick COSMIC-FFP (Meli et al., 2000; Santillo, 2001), a functional size measurement method currently being developed for functional user requirements at a higher level of abstraction than usually assumed in COSMIC-FFP. This would allow measuring the functional size of a MERODE enterprise model using partial, early available, information, such as an object-event table. One such high-level functional size measure, the Level of Object-Event Interaction (LOEI), which is basically a count of the object type - event type interactions in the object-event table, has recently been proposed (Poels et al., 2001). We will investigate whether the LOEI measure complies with the Early & Quick COSMIC-FFP method.

REFERENCES

Abran, A., Desharnais, J.-M., Oligny, S., St-Pierre, D., Symons, C. (2001). COSMIC-FFP Measurement Manual, Version 2.1. The Common Software Measurement International Consortium

Albrecht, A.J., Gaffney, J. (1983). Software function, source lines of code and development effort prediction. IEEE Transactions on Software Engineering 9(6) 639-648

Bévo, V., Lévesque, G., Abran, A. (1999). Application de la méthode FFP à partir d'une spécification selon la notation UML: compte rendu des premiers essais d'application et questions. Proceedings of the 9th International Workshop on Software Measurement, Lac Supérieur, Canada, 230-242

Caldiera, G., Antoniol, G., Fiutem, R., Lokan, C. (1998). Definition and Experimental Evaluation of Function Points for Object-Oriented Systems. Proceedings of the 5th International Symposium on Software Metrics, Bethesda, Maryland, USA, 167-178

Diab, H., Frappier, M., St-Denis, R. (2001). A Formal Definition of COSMIC-FFP for Automated Measurement of ROOM Specifications. Proceedings of the 4th European Conference on Software Measurement and ICT Control, Heidelberg, 185-196

Fetcke, T., Abran, A., Nguyen, H. (1998). Function point analysis for the OO-Jacobson method: a mapping approach. Proceedings of the 1st European Software Measurement Conference, Antwerp, 395-410

Hastings, T. (1995). Adapting Function Points to contemporary software systems: A review of proposals. Research report, Department of Software Development, Monash University, Australia

ISO (1998). ISO/IEC 14143-1998 - Software Engineering - Software Measurement - Definition of Functional Size Measurement. The International Organization for Standardization

Jenner, S.M. (2001). COSMIC-FFP 2.0 and UML: Estimation of the Size of a System Specified in UML - Problems of Granularity. Proceedings of the 4th European Conference on Software Measurement and ICT Control, Heidelberg, 173-184

Meli, R., Abran, A., Ho, V.T., Oligny, S. (2000). On the Applicability of COSMIC-FFP for Measuring Software

Throughout its Life Cycle. Proceedings of the 11th European Software Control and Metrics Conference, Munich

Pastor, O., Abrahao, S.M., Molina, J.C., Torres, I. (2001). A FPA-like Measure for Object-Oriented Systems from Conceptual Models. Proceedings of the 11th International Workshop on Software Measurement, Montréal

Poels, G., Dedene, G. (2001). Measuring event-based object-oriented conceptual models. L'Objet: Software, Databases, Networks 7(4) 497-514

Rains, E. (1991). Function Points in an ADA Object-Oriented Design. OOPS Messenger 2(4) 23-25

Ram, D.J., Raju, S.V.G.K. (2001). Estimating Relative Size when Alternative Designs Exist. Proceedings of the 5th International ECOOP Workshop on Quantitative Approaches in Object-Oriented Software Engineering, Budapest, 35-44

Santillo, S. (2001). Early & Quick COSMIC-FFP Analysis Using Analytic Hierarchy Process. Proceedings of the 10th International Workshop on Software Measurement, Berlin, 2000. Lecture Notes in Computer Science, Vol. 2006, Springer-Verlag, Berlin, 147-160

Sneed, H. (1996). Estimating the Development Costs of Object-Oriented Software. Proceedings of the 7th European Software Control and Metrics Conference, Wilmslow, UK, 135-152

Snoeck, M., Dedene, G., Verhelst, M., Depuydt, A.-M. (1999). Object-Oriented Enterprise Modelling with MERODE. Leuven University Press

Thomson, N., Johnson, R., Macleod, R., Miller, G., Hansen, T. (1994). Project Estimation Using an Adaptation of Function Points and Use Cases for OO Projects. Proceedings of the OOPSLA'94 Workshop on Pragmatic and Theoretical Directions in Object-Oriented Software Metrics

Uemura, T., Kusumoto, S., Inoue, K. (1999). Function Point Measurement Tool for UML Design Specifications. Proceedings of the 6th International Symposium on Software Metrics, Boca Raton, Florida, USA, 62-69

Whitmire, S.A. (1993). Applying Function Points to Object Oriented Software Models. In: Software Engineering Productivity Handbook. McGraw-Hill, New York, 229-244

Zhao, H., Stockman, T. (1995). Software Sizing for OO software development - Object Function Point Analysis. Proceedings of the 2nd GSE International Conference on Information Technology and Management, Berlin

CONCEPTUAL ARCHITECTURE FOR THE ASSESSMENT AND IMPROVEMENT OF SOFTWARE MAINTENANCE

Félix García, Francisco Ruiz, Mario Piattini, Macario Polo
Alarcos Research Group, Escuela Superior de Informática, Universidad de Castilla-La Mancha, Paseo de la Universidad, 4, 13071, Ciudad Real (España)
Email: (fgarcia|fruiz|mpiattini|mpolo)@inf-cr.uclm.es

Key words: Software Process Assessment, Software Process Improvement, Maintenance Software, MOF, XMI.

Abstract: The management of software processes is a complex activity due to the great number of different aspects to be considered. For this reason it is useful to establish a conceptual architecture which includes all the aspects necessary to be able to manage this complexity. The fundamental element in all conceptual architecture is constituted by meta-data, which, organized in different levels of modeling, can be used to manage effectively the complexity of the software processes and especially the maintenance process (Pigosky, 1996). In this study we present a conceptual architecture of 4 levels to represent and manage the assessment and improvement of software process by means of the definition of the appropriate models and meta-models. This architecture is based on the standard MOF (Meta object Facility) proposed by the Object Management Group (OMG,2000). In particular this architecture includes all the necessary aspects for carrying out the assessment and improvement of the Software Maintenance Process (SMP) and allows us to represent the different data and meta-data used in its management by means of the modeling of concepts at different levels of abstraction: meta-models of generic processing, models of software processes, concrete software processes (in our case, that of the assessment of other processes) and instances of carrying out a specific process. As a support to this architecture we present MANTIS- Metamod, a tool for the modeling of software processes based on the concepts discussed previously. MANTIS- Metamod is a component of MANTIS, an integral environment for the management of the SMP, including its assessment and improvement.

1 INTRODUCTION

Until recently software construction was performed like an artistic task where success in projects depended principally on the "art" of the developers and not on projects being developed with an engineering arose, the principal objective of which is to obtain quality software products. A fundamental element which affects the quality of the products is the way of developing and maintaining them, that is to say the processes involved both in the development and the maintenance of the software. According to ISO 12207 norm, a process is a set of interrelated activities which transform inputs into outputs (ISO/IEC, 1995). A process defines who is doing what, when, and how to obtain a specific objective. Software processes are inherently complex. They involve many people, each with individual responsibilities and skills , and they produce or modify an ample range of elements (Becker & Webby, 1999).

Current efforts in the investigation of software processes focus fundamentally on their assessment and improvement. Software process assessment can be defined as the set of activities to evaluate the given process. The assessment aims to inspire the confidence that the product will be of the quality desired. With such an aim in mind, different standards have been proposed, such as CMM (SEI, 1995), BOOTSTRAP (BOOTSTRAP, 1993), SPICE, IEEE 730 (IEEE, 1998), etc, which provide a framework for the assessment of the quality of software processes. SPICE stands out especially among these initiatives, having formed the basis of ISO 15504 (ISO/IEC, 1998a).

In order to be able to apply plans for improvement in the software processes of an organization it is essential to carry out beforehand an assessment process of their quality. The improvement of software processes is based on guaranteeing certain results from the process, and as such it is necessary, in the process of assessment, to take effective measures of certain indicators associated with the processes.

Given the importance of improvement and hence of the assessment of the quality of software processes, it is important to be able to treat all the concepts involved in these processes in an integrated way. To do so it is useful to establish a conceptual architecture with encapsulation layers which can be specified, designed and constructed independently. To achieve integration, different levels of abstraction must be defined, and hence it is useful to make use of the ideas put forward in the different standards concerning meta-modeling and the exchange of meta-data, among which the MOF (OMG, 2000) and XMI (OMG, 1999) stand out.

In this study we present a conceptual architecture of 4 levels, based on the standard MOF, for the effective quality assessment and improvement of software processes. This architecture is being used in MANTIS, an integral environment for the management of the software maintenance process . The elements considered at each level of abstraction are based on widely accepted proposals which will be discussed in the following sections.

The structure of the study is as follows: first we give a general description of the conceptual architecture proposed. In the next section we describe each of the levels and their mappings in detail. In section 4, we present a tool which automates the management of meta-data at different levels of abstraction, and finally, in section 5, we present conclusions and plans for future studies.

2 DESCRIPTION OF THE CONCEPTUAL ARCHITECTURE

The current study is within the framework of MANTIS (Ruiz et al. 2001) which attempts the definition and construction of an environment for the integral management of the SMP. MANTIS defines the way in which the SMP is organized, managed, measured and supported.

For the management of the SMP, MANTIS integrates, amongst other aspects, people (with certain skills and who carry out certain roles in the project), techniques (or methodologies) employed by the people, tools (which help them to meet the standards) and activities (in which teams participate, and which help them to meet significant mile-stones).

To achieve integration, 4 conceptual models are defined in MANTIS, based on the standard MOF (Meta Object Facility) for object oriented meta-modeling (OMG, 2000) proposed by the Object Management Group. MOF is a model for specifying, constructing, managing, exchanging and integrating meta-data in software systems allowing a flexible integration of systems. MOF describes an abstract modeling language in line with the core of the UML (OMG, 1999a). Table 1 shows the 4 levels of the architecture MOF and its adaptation to MANTIS.

Level	MOF	MANTIS
M3	MOF-model (Meta-Metamodel)	*MOF-model*
M2	Meta-model	Generic SMP metamodel
M1	Model	Process Software Assessment concrete models
M0	Data	Instances of Software Process Assessment (real-world concrete Software assessment projects)

Table 1: Conceptual levels in MOF & MANTIS

At level M0 are the results of the application of an assessment process to a maintenance project. That is to say, at this level there would be the results of a process from which it would be possible to establish its strong and weak points. The data handled at this level are instances of the concepts defined at level M1. The specific model used at level M1 is based on a specific model for assessment following ISO 15504, which will be discussed in more detail in the sections below. Level M2 corresponds to a generic meta-model of software processes. In this meta-model all the elements common to any type of process are defined. In our case, this meta-model must include abstract concepts from which it will be possible to derive the concepts handled in the assessment model. For example the generic concept "*Activity*" used in M2, would be instanced in the concepts "*Define the input of the Assessment*" or "*Perform the Assessment Process*" of level 1, which at level MO will correspond to the application of such activities in a specific organization, on a specific project.

At the final conceptual level of MANTIS, M3, the generic meta-data of software processes is represented in the form of model-MOF. A model-MOF is basically formed from two types of objects:

MOF-classes and MOF-associations (these are the main objects for us, although others do exist: packages for re-use, data-types etc.) Hence, all the concepts represented at level M2 are now considered as models of MOF-classes or MOF-associations. For example, "*Activity*", "*Actor*" or "*Attribute*" will be instances of the MOF class; and "*Activity uses Resources*" or "*Artefact_is_input_of_Activity*" are instances of MOF-association. For the effective representation of the meta-data which make up this conceptual architecture and above all to ensure their portability between tools in a Software Engineering Environment (SEI), which is what we are interested in MANTIS, we use XMI (XML Meta-data Interchange) (OMG, 1999b), a language based on XML (eXtensible Markup Language).

3 LEVELS AND MAPPINGS

3.1 M2 level: Generic Software Process Metamodel

At level M2 of conceptual architecture the generic meta-model of software processes is represented, from which concrete models of processes can be instanced. The meta-model of this level is based on the proposal of the IESE (Institut Experimentelles Software Engineering) (Becker, & Webby, 1999) which represents a generic schema for the modeling of software processes, in which a fundamental aspect of these processes is presented: the measurement. The main aspects to be taken into account when modeling processes are:

- how things are done,
- who does them and
- what is produced, used or modified during the activity.

In figure 1 the basic components which should be included in any model of processes are shown in more detail. As can be seen from figure 1,within the schema which represents the generic meta-model of software processes, three subschemas stand out:

- Software Process Modelling subschema,
- Measurement subschema,
- Human Resources subschema

3.1.1 Software Process Modeling subschema

This subschema is made up from the necessary constructors to define models of software processes. Every model of processes is made up of a set of activities, which in their return can include other activities. An activity is an abstraction of "how things are done". An activity is a step in a process which may contain anything from activities of software development or maintenance to project management or quality assessment activities. The superclass *entity* represents an abstraction of an element of a model of processes. The subclasses of entity are: *project*, *activity*, *artefact*, *resource*, *agent*. The same entity could be involved in more than one project.. Among the other classes which stand out in the meta-model are: the class *agent*, which is an abstract class that describes the human agent who does one or more activities; the class *resource*, which describes entities necessary for carrying out the project; and the class *artefact* which is an abstraction of the products which are modified, used or produced in a project. Another significant of this subschema is that using it we can represent the relationship between entities. The interrelationships between entities of the process are modeled using the class *relationship*. It is equivalent to association MOF, but with the difference that they can have a degree greater than 2 (ternaries, etc.) and that this class *relationship* models relations between instances of entities and not between instances of class MOF (the level of abstraction is different).

3.1.2 Measurement subschema

A fundamental element when modeling software processes is to be able to define a set of metrics which will then allow us to check how things are being done. For the software engineering to be considered as such, it is essential to be able to measure what is done. Therefore, we must include in the Generic SMP Meta-model the possibility of defining indicators when modeling processes. These indicators must allow us to check the quality of these processes in order to be able to apply improvement plans.

For this reason, in figure 1 we can clearly distinguish the subschema of the measurement which includes the aspects related to the measurement of processes. As seen in the subschema of the measurement, each element or the model can have certain attributes associated with it. Examples of attributes are: the duration of an activity, the number of derived errors, process indicators, (properties of a process). Each attribute can have a possible value or set of values associated with it, and in addition the calculation of the value of an attribute can be based on certain expressions. The same expression can be associated with various attributes. This subschema serves as an effective complement to the generic meta-model of software processes it makes possible the application at an inferior level of specific models of processes such as assessment and improvement.

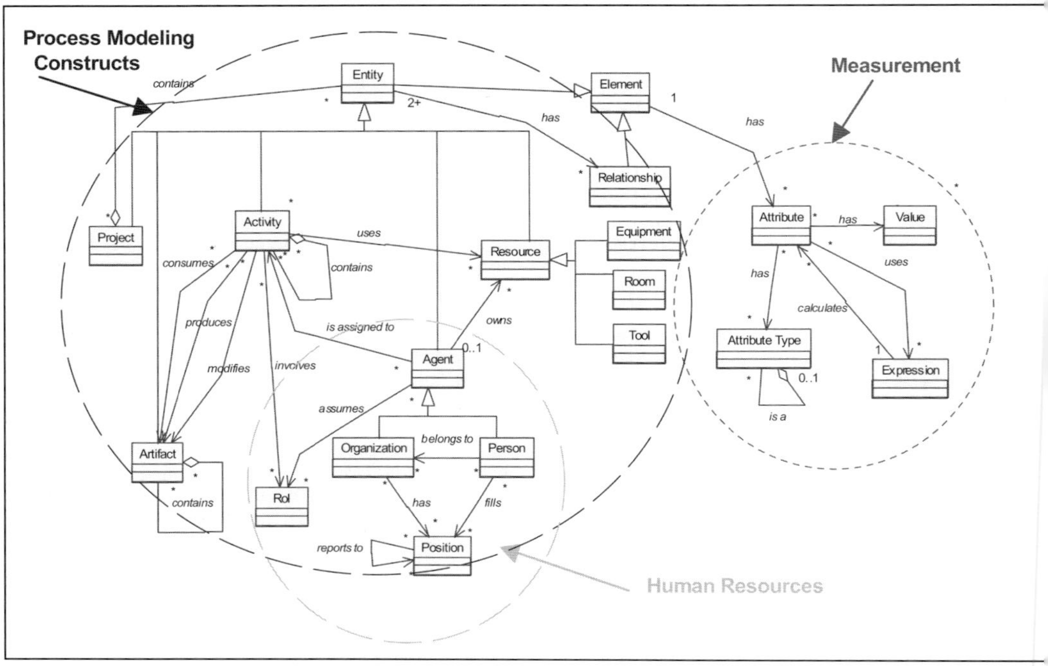

Figure 1: Generic Metamodel of software processes

3.1.3 Human Resources subschema

This subschema is outstanding in the meta-model since human resources are the key element for performing successfully software processes. With this schema we can model in detail who is performing the activities. In this subschema the following classes stand out:

Role: this is an abstraction of some abilities and necessary conditions to perform an activity. Each activity is associated with certain roles in the project and these roles can only be assumed by human resources.

Organization: this describes the context from the administrative point of view in which the software process occurs. Examples of organization are the software development team, the testing team or a software development company.

Person: this is an individual human agent, for example a programmer or a software engineer. A person can belong to several organizations such as in the case of a programmer who takes part in the development team and the testing team in the project. Besides, all people have a position in an organization, for instance the manager's position in the testing team.

Position: this describes a post in an organization. A person can perform several positions and a position can be performed by several people.

3.2 M1 Level: Software Process Assessment Model

The process model to consider in this level is based on the assessment model proposed in part 5 of ISO 15504 standard based on the first proposal of the SPICE project. SPICE is a major international initiative to support the development of an International Standard for Software Process Assessment. The main goal of this project, to develop a working draft for a standard for software process assessment and their documents have been carried through the international standardization process and have been published as ISO/IEC TR 15504. This norm defines a two dimensional reference model for describing processes through assessment of process attributes structured into capability levels (ISO/IEC, 1998b). The process dimension in which the measurable aims which each process should attain and its functional character are identified, and the ability dimension which is based on assessing and attributes the group associated with each process to determine its ability which is necessary for its management and its improvement.

ISO 15504 provides the guidance to perform a software assessment process and a method for continually improving processes. In M1 Level we focus on the guidance that ISO provides with regard to the assessment process. The main activities that ISO identifies to assess a software process are the following:

Planning, Collecting data, Validating Data, Process Rating and Reporting. As a consequence of performing these activities, certain products are created (as shown in the software processes generic meta-model) amongst which the report stands out that shows the assessment result of a process (process profile).

In table 2 the correspondences are shown between the elements of software processes metamodel (constructors of process models) and the main elements of the assessment process defined in ISO 15504- part 3.

The basic concepts of all assessment processes are shown in brief in table 2. The assessment process implies:

- Defining process input
- Performing the process. This means performing the planning, collecting and validating the necessary data, assigning the process rating (levels that identify the process ability according to SPICE defined levels)
- Creating the appropriate reports and,
- Recording the relevant output

Assessment process output is formed by the process profile. In this artefact all data related to the assessment of a specific process are recorded.

With this model, the tools used in the lower level to perform specific assessment processes could exchange their data efficiently. These data can even be useful for improvement plans. The elements of this model could be formed into two groups:

Assessment Input Information, describes the purpose of the assessment, its range and its limitations.

Assessment Output Information, describes the structure of assessment processes shown in SPICE. It includes a process profiles group and ratings of ability levels for each process.

In figure 2 you can see the UML diagram corresponding to the structure of an assessment process output according to ISO 15504. As it can be observed, all necessary elements to record a software assessment process based on ISO 15504 standard are shown in the assessment results model. The key element of assessment process output is the *Process Profile* element that includes information about who performs the assessment process, strong and weak points of the process to assess, the level of process ability and especially the results of process indicators defined in SPICE (PA 1.1, PA 2.2, etc) and the ratings that have to be fulfilled by these indicators. The output of the assessment, in the form of a process profile, shows the adequacy ratings of the generic practices of the process, but it does not show why a particular practice was assigned a particular rating. Indicators help to identify what is present or missing from a process or work product and provide guidance to the assessor when assigning a rating of adequacy to a practice. The information provides an '*indication*' of the extent to which a practice supports the purpose of the process. The

M2 Classes		M2 instances (M1 Classes)
A	Activity	*Defining the assessment input* Perform the assessment process Planning Collect Data Validate Data Process Rating Reporting Record the assessment output
Art	Artifact	Process to Assess Process Profile
A contains A	Activity contains Activity	Perform the assessment process contains Planning Perform the assessment process contains Collect Data Perform the assessment process contains Validate Data Perform the assessment process contains Process Rating, *Perform the assessment process contains Reporting*
A consumes Art	Activity consumes Artifact	*Perform the assessment process consumes Process to Assess*
A produces Art	Activity produces Artifact	*Perform the assessment process produces Process Profile*

Table 2: Mapping between Generic SMP and Assessment Model

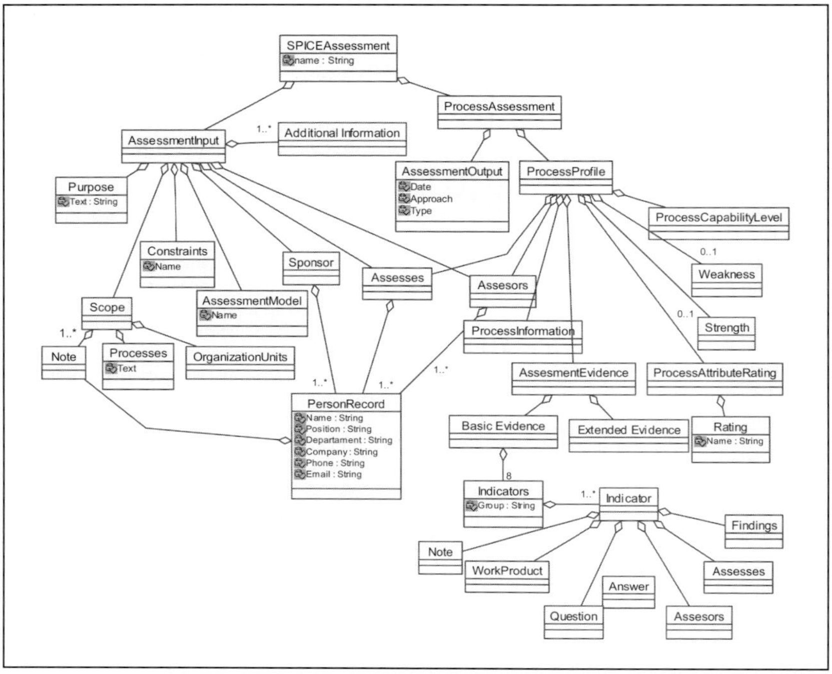

Figure 2: Structure of the SPICE assessment output

detailed information collected during the assessment about the presence or absence of specific indicators provides the valuable input into analysis and process improvement planning.

3.3 M0 Level: Concrete Data

At this level, there are the concepts related to the application of a specific assessment process following the guidelines of its assessment model defined in the higher level (M1). An example of this level is the following: '*Planning of the assessment process of the software maintenance process carried out in the Company Example S.A*'. Besides, it includes all data shown (according to the pattern indicated in the process profile) during the assessment process to control how the maintenance process is carried out in this company. These data correspond with the indicators defined in the higher level. For example if '*Maintenibility*' is defined as an attribute of process, this attribute will have a specific value in this level.

4 WORKING WITH ALL THE CONCEPTUAL LEVELS

With the aim of carrying out an effective management of metadata in the different abstraction levels, using an intuitive and easy form of working with the correspondences among different levels and to represent these meta-data in an open way for their exchange, MANTIS-METAMOD (Garcia et al, 2001) has been developed. The aim of MANTIS-METAMOD is to manage the meta-models definition (level 2 MOF) and models (level 1 MOF) and to represent them in an open way.

The following figure 3 shows how MANTIS-METAMOD displays the correspondence between the generic metamodel of software processes and the process assessment model appearing in the previous section.

To represent in an open way metadata, MANTIS-METAMOD uses a manager of a repository of metadata stored according to XMI Standard (OMG, 1999b). With the use of XMI it is possible the information about models and metamodels can be exchanged among tools that use

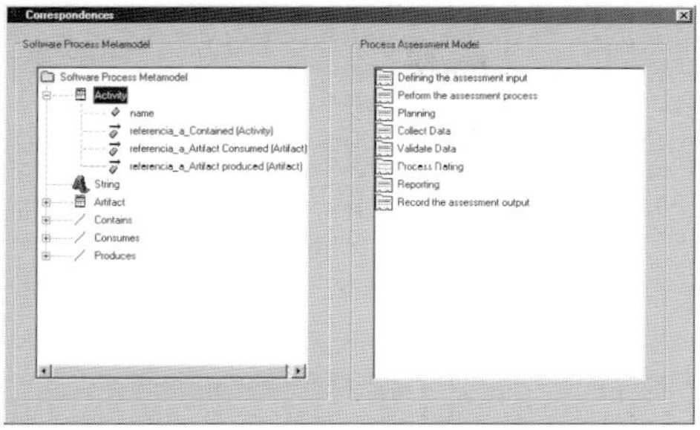

Figure 3: View of MANTIS-Metamod

this open format. This increases to a great extent the ability of integration with other tools and environments. With MANTIS-METAMOD has been possible:

- to represent the conceptual architecture mentioned before and
- to store it in a consistent way. It can be easily updated for changes in the process generic metamodel or in the assessment model.

The figure 4 is a scheme of the tool based on its storage layer and which sums up the previously mentioned concepts.

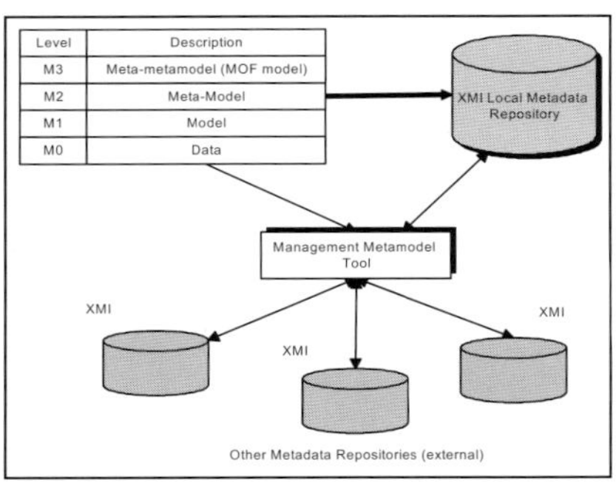

Figure 4: Mantis-METAMOD storage layer

5 CONCLUSIONS

In this work a conceptual architecture based on MOF standard for the effective management of the software assessment process has been shown. In this architecture the assessment model based on ISO 15504 has been integrated according to generic metamodel builders of software processes defined by IESE. This architecture has been used in the MANTIS environment to apply assessment concepts and process improvements to software maintenance.

The performance of a good assessment process is an essential aspect to apply improvement plans in the software processes of an organization. Therefore, the effective management of the assessment process is fundamental for its success when it is put it into practice. With the generic model of software processes defined in level 2 of MOF rank it is possible to define any model of software processes. Therefore several assessment models of software processes could be defined in which elements of previous versions are being refined, obtaining in each version a more effective assessment model. All these models can be processed in an integrated and consistent way since their elements are examples of the concepts defined in the generic meta-model of level 2. For an automatic management of models and meta-models according to these architecture, the tool MANTIS-METAMOD has been developed. With this tool, the models and meta-models defined in the form of XMI documents can be exported or imported. This makes possible the collaboration of MANTIS with any other meta-modeling tool based on MOF, permitting the sharing of different defined models and meta-models.

6 FUTURE AND RELATED WORKS

Very recently has been published the OMG SPEM (Software Process Engineering Metamodel Specification) (OMG, 2001). This document is an OMG Final adopted specification whose FTF recommendation and report will be published in July, 1, 2002. SPEM is based on the definition of the minimal set of process modeling elements necessary to describe any software development process. In general, all software process metamodel should include the three basic elements exposed in this paper: modeling constructs, human resources and measurement. In SPEM this elements are included and it would be very useful considering it as our generic software process metamodel (level 2) when this specification will become a standard.

Other work to take into account is the study of the possibility of using UML profiles in order to define the metamodels used in level 2. For example, SPEM is defined both as a metamodel (as the metamodel used in this work to model software processes) and as a UML profile.

Beside among our future studies is important to emphasize the need for:

- The implementation in MANTIS-METAMOD of the correspondence among the levels M1-M10 managing the relationship between the elements of the processes model defined in M1 and its performance in level M0.

- Refining and improving the assessment model of software processing through the definition, testing and validation of a group of software process metrics.
- Integrating in conceptual architecture in level M1 an improvement model of the software maintenance process based on ISO 15504 which uses the results of the assessment process to improve the ability of an organization for maintenance when they carry out their processes (Niessink, 2000).
- Creation of tools in level M0 to collect and to manage automatically the performance of an assessment process and software processes improvement in an organization (Park & Kyung, 2001). For instance, using DTD's proposal of these authors to represent as XML documents the results of the assessment.

ACKNOWLEDGEMENTS

This work has been undertaken in collaboration with the company Atos ODS subsidized by the MANTIS project. MANTIS has been partially supported by the European Union and CICYT-Spain(1FD97-1608TIC).

REFERENCES

Becker-K., U., and Webby, R., A (1999): Comprehensive Schema Integrating Software Process Modeling and Software Measurement, Fraunhofer Institute, IESE report Nº 047.99/E., v. 1.2, 1999.

BOOTSTRAP (1993): BOOTSTRAP: Europe's Assessment Method, in: David Card (Ed.), IEEE Software, pp. 93-95, July 1993.

García, F. , Márquez, L., Ruiz, F., Piattini, M., Polo, M (2001): A Tool for the Management of the Software Maintenance Process. Multiconference on Circuits, Systems, Computers and Communications (CSCW). July 2001.

IEEE (1998): IEEE 730. Standard for Software Quality Assurance Plans.

ISO/IEC (1998a): ISO IEC 15504 TR2:1998, part 2: A reference model for processes and process capability, ISO/IEC JTC1/SC7, 1998

ISO/IEC (1998b): ISO IEC 15504 TR2:1998, part 4: Guide to conducting assessment, ISO/IEC JTC1/SC7, 1998

Niessink, F. (2000): Perspectives on Improving Software Maintenance. PhD Thesis, Vrije Universiteit, Netherland. In http://www.opencontent.org/openpub/, 2000.

OMG (1999a): UML Unified Modeling Language, v 1.3, Jun-1999.

OMG (1999b): XML Metadata Interchange (XMI), v. 1.1, Oct-1999.

OMG (2000): Meta Object Facility (MOF) Specification, v. 1.3 RTF, Mar-2000. In http://www.omg.org.

OMG (2001): Software Process Engineering Metamodel Specification, December-2001. In http://www.omg.org.

Pigosky (1996): Practical Software Maintenance. Best Practices for Managing your Investment. Ed. John Wiley & Sons, USA 1996.

Park, J.; Kyung Wan, L. (2001); A XML-Based Approach to Software Process Improvement over the Internet.

SEI (1995): The Capability Maturity Model: Guidelines for Improving the Software Process,1995. In http://www.sei.cmu.edu/cmm/cmm.html

W3C (2000): Extensible Markup Language (XML) 1.0 (second edition), oct-2000. In http://www.w3.org

A TOOL FOR ASSESSING THE CONSISTENCY OF WEBSITES*

Sibylle Steinau, Oscar Díaz, Juan J. Rodríguez and Felipe Ibáñez
The EKIN group
Apdo 649 – 20080 San Sebastián (Spain)
steinau_sibylle_44@yahoo.co.uk
{jipdigao,jibrojij,jipibanf}@si.ehu.es

Key words: Usability Testing, XML, Consistency, Web Development.

Abstract: Usability is becoming an increasingly important design factor for web sites. However time and budget contstraints for web projects prevents the hiring of usability professionals to conduct tests that are costly and time consuming to perform. A number of automatic usability assessment tools have been developed most of which offer reports on a per-page basis. However, they fail to provide inter-page assessments to test, for example the consistency of the site. Consistency refers to the extent to which a set of pages share a common layout. This work presents *CAT*, a Consistency Analysis Tool that, besides providing static, page-based usability measures, strives to assess the consistency of a website using Java and XSLT. The tool is based on a consistency model which is updated every time a page has been processed. Consistency testing involves collating the page with this model, reporting mismatches with the consistency attributes and adapting the model as new features are encountered for the first time.

1 INTRODUCTION

Usability is becoming an increasingly important design factor for websites. This is partly due to the high competition between websites. Indeed, the usability of a website not only determines the success of the company but also of its products. In a physical environment customers are unable to assess the usability of a product until after they have already bought it. However in the Internet users experience the usability of a website before they see the product and before they have bought it. Furthermore most users are impatient and strive for instant gratification of their needs and requirements. If they find a website difficult to use or cannot find what they are looking for, they will not take the time to solve the problem as they can easily switch to the competitor's website (Nielsen, 2000).

However, a lot of the smaller companies often do not have usability professionals to assist them in their web-design and many companies are not even aware of the importance of usability for the success of their website and potentially their company. Additionally many websites are developed under time constraints and on a very tight budget. This prevents the hiring of usability professionals to conduct tests that are costly and time consuming to perform particularly for iterative design(Scholtz et al., 1998).

Based on this observation distinct automatic usability assessment tools have been developed (e.g. (Chi et al., 2000), (Oskoboiny, 2001), (WebCriteria, 1999), (Team, 2000)). Most of these tools only offer reports on a per-page basis however, some important usability guidelines imply inter-page assessment. This paper focuses on consistency as a main usability measure. Consistency assesses to which extent a set of pages share a common layout (e.g. fonts, background-color etc.). Although, the use of Cascading Style Sheets (CSS) can promote consistency some aspects can only be enforced by strict adherence to the site's conventions. However, often no mechanism is in place to enforce these conventions.

This paper presents *CAT* a Consistency Analysis Tool that besides providing static, page-based usability measures, strives to assess the consistency of a set of pages that form a website. It is based on an adaptive consistency model that allows to "instantiate" the

*This paper is a revision of the MSc thesis written by S. Steinau for the University of Manchester. This research was partially supported by the Secretaría de Estado de Política Científica y Tecnológica of the Spanish Government under contract TIC 1999-1048-C02-02.

predicates (i.e. the values used for the consistency assessment) as the pages are processed.

CAT is based on Java and XSLT and the latest version of the tool can be found at http://www.atarix.org/cat/.

The remaining part of this document is structured as follows: Usability guidelines and the consistency model are discussed in section 2, *CAT*'s architecture is described in section 3, section 4 describes a *CAT* sample evaluation, related work and the tool itself are discussed in section 5 followed by the conclusion and future work in section 6.

2 USABILITY GUIDELINES

The impact of usability on websites is much higher than on traditional software. For e-commerce sites the website itself is the company and therefore, the user interface becomes the marketing materials, the store front and interior, the sales staff and the post sales support. Consequently, a user interface with a bad usability design can jeopardize the success of the whole company (Nielsen, 2000). In fact the actual design of a website in terms of usability and especially download times can have a serious impact on users' perception of the overall quality of the company's services (Bhatti et al., 2000).

When interacting with any system people develop their own theories (*mental models*) in order to understand the casual behaviour of the system. The ease with which users are able to form a correct model is influenced by a number of factors including consistency, which relates to a likeness in behaviour that has arisen from similar situations previously experienced (Dix et al., 1992).

This work focuses on the following web-usability categories.

Consistency. Consistency is one of the most important usability characteristics. In a user interface consistency implies that the same action and commands always have the same effect (Nielsen, 1993). For example each site should contain a consistent style and layout for images, fonts, colours and functionalities. This helps users to establish a pattern of the site structure and has a substantial impact on learning time, performance speed, error rates and user satisfaction. Thus consistency increases the likelihood that users look at and revisit the site as it facilitates fast and easy access to the services they require. Additionally providing a common "look and feel" for a site helps to unify all web pages together. This is important for establishing a professional look because users trust professionalism (Brannon and Sellati, 2000). The *CAT* consistency model is described in more detail in section 2.1.

Accessibility. Accessibility refers to the ease with which users can access the web-content. It is affected by users' physical abilities and differences in hardware and software platforms. The former refers to any kind of disability that makes it difficult for a person to use traditional computer input and output devices. In the United States alone this affects approximately 30 million people (Nielsen, 2000), predominantly those with vision, hearing, dexterity and short-term memory problems. Furthermore the average age of the population in many countries is increasing, causing a general increase in users with physical deficits as a result of aging. Therefore few organizations and especially e-commerce businesses can afford to deliberately miss the market sector of physically impaired users (Brewer, 2000). A possible way of enhancing the accessibility of a web-page is by using HTML *alt* attributes for all non-textual elements to provide an alternative presentation to those who cannot view these elements (Chisholm et al., 1999).

Form Use. Forms are a popular way to collect information from website users. However form usability, especially for e-commerce sites, can have serious business implications because badly designed forms discourage users and often lead to incorrectly submitted information which is dissatisfying for the user as well as for the site administrator (Nielsen, 2000). For example, to ensure that all text fields are correctly identified by screen readers for visually impaired users, the HTML *label* element should be used because it is implicitly associated with exactly one text field (IBM, 2001).

Performance. According to (Nielsen, 2000) "fast response times are the most important design criterion for web pages" (Nielsen, 2000, p.42). Slow download times have been shown to have a negative effect on the users' perception of the company because they tend to blame the company's lack of resources rather than their network connection or their server for the delay. Furthermore users associate poor performance with poor security measures (Bhatti et al., 2000). Research has shown that system response times of less than one second are necessary to enable users to navigate freely through a website. Therefore websites should be designed to minimize download times by keeping page sizes to a minimum (no more than 2KB) and graphics and multimedia effects should only be used if they enhance the user's understanding of the information presented. Providing *height* and *width* attributes for all images and tables can also reduce down-load times because the browser does not have to recalculate these measurements (Nielsen, 2000).

Navigation. One of the main problems of the WWW (World Wide Web) is that users can easily become disoriented (*lost in hyperspace*) because there are no restrictions on how to move through the information space (Mukherjea and Yoshinori, 1997). It is therefore essential to provide users with navigation support because if they are unable to locate the information they are looking for they will leave the site. The fundamental information that every navigation interface should prove is: the current location, which locations have already been visited and which locations can be visited from the current position. Usability studies have shown that users prefer navigational interfaces that are similar to those of other sites. Standardization (e.g. standard link colours) saves users the time and effort to learn a new interfaces when visiting a site for the first time because they are able to rely on their existing mental models (Nielsen, 2000).

Readability. Readability refers to the ease with which users are able to read the information presented on the page. Usability studies have shown that most web-users scan new web pages for main content indicators e.g. headlines and bullet points before they decide to read the page. Furthermore it has been demonstrated that users take 25% longer to read information on a computer screen compared to reading it from a hard copy. Consequently, web pages should be designed for optimal scanability by breaking long texts into paragraphs with separate headings and by using bullet points where possible. For optimal legibility all text should be presented in high contrast with a maximum line length of 8cm as this corresponds to a comfortable eye span for most readers (Nielsen, 2000),(Lynch and Horton, 2001).

For a complete list of all usability guidelines evaluated by the tool, please refer to the *CAT* online version[1].

2.1 Consistency Model

CAT is based on a consistency model that is specified by a number of values specified for presentation features. The consistency features measured by the tool include: colour (background and font), font-size and typography. Furthermore all sites should provide a standard navigation menu(Brannon and Sellati, 2000). Therefore a website can be said to be consistent if the same values for most of the above features have been used throughout the site. It is permissible to introduce some inconsistencies, e.g. background-colours, to distinguish between different areas of the site however these variations should be limited to one or two features (Cook, 1997).

Unless the designer has provided some consistency values, the model is initialized by measuring the values of the above described consistency features on the home page. For illustrative purposes, table 1 shows some examples of consistency guidelines that are tested by the tool. These values are stored in memory. When the next page is assessed, by selecting a link from the home page, the model measures consistency by performing boolean comparisons between the consistency values of the previous page and the current page. The more boolean comparisons are true, the higher the consistency of the design.

3 CAT'S ARCHITECTURE

CAT is built from five main components: an interface, an HTML2XHTML converter, a consistency model manager and a tester. The former is a set of JSP pages that provide the interface to access the other components. The converter transforms an HTML document into an XHTML document[2]. The consistency model manager records the parameters needed to assess the consistency. Finally, the tester is an XSLT file that contains XSLT patterns for each of the usability recommendations that have been described in the previous section.

The processes presented in figure 1 are:

1. *CAT* begins by prompting the user to provide the URL of the home-page of the site to be assessed. The tester retrieves this page and converts it to an XHTML page with the help of the converter.

2. This XHTML document is sent to the consistence model manager. This component generates the XSLT patterns that assess the consistency. These patterns are generated dynamically from the current state of the model each time a page is assessed.

3.The XHTML document and the new XSLT patterns that assess the consistency of the page are sent to the tester. The tester updates the XSLT document that performs the usability test with the new patterns. The updated document is used to transform the XHTML document to obtain a reporting XML document.

4. The XHTML document is processed in order to extract the available links from the page.

5. The result document is presented to the user together with a list of links available in the current page (back to point 1).

The usability tester is the core component of *CAT*. The guidelines that are checked by the tool are grouped into six categories (consistency, accessibility, form usability, performance, readability and navigation). Each guideline is realized as a template that contains patterns to select the required target nodes that determine the usability of the document. For illustrative purposes, the following template checks whether all images and graphics contain *alt* attributes:

<xsl:value-of select="count(//
[extra:toLower(local-name())='img' and
not(./@*[extra:toLower(local-name())='alt'])])"/>*

[1]The CAT online version can be accessed via http://www.atarix.org/cat/.

[2]This class uses the JTidy library (see: http://sourceforge.net/projects/jtidy/ for further details).

Table 1: Consistency guidelines and values evaluated by *CAT*.

Features that should be kept constant	**HTML check**
Font sizes (Brannon and Sellati, 2000)	The tool memorises and compares the different values that have been specified for the *font* node *size* and *point-size* attributes, the *style* node *font* attributes and the *style-font* attributes.
Font colours (Brannon and Sellati, 2000)	The tool memorises and compares the different values that have been specified for the *font* node *color* attributes, the *style*-node *color* attributes and the *style-color* attributes.
Font faces (Brannon and Sellati, 2000)	The tool memorises and compares the different values that have been specified for the *font* node *font* attributes, the *style* node *font-family* attributes and the *style-font-family* attributes.
Background Colour (Brannon and Sellati, 2000)	Depending on how the background has been specified, the tool memorises and compares either the *bgcolor* or the *background* attribute value of the *body* node or the *background* value of the *style* node.
Structural Links (Nielsen, 2000)	The tool memorises and compares the different *href* attribute values of those *a* nodes that have such an attribute and whose parent node does not have text or only contains '\&nsp;'

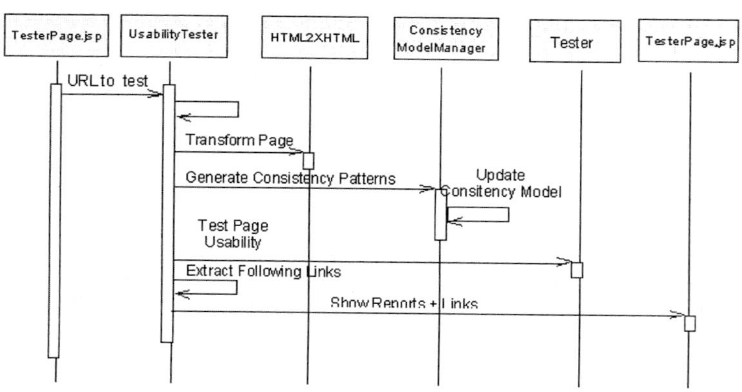

Figure 1: Interaction diagram that illustrates the common usage pattern.

XPath processes target nodes case sensitively however HTML tags are case insensitive. To overcome the problem of having to define each possible spelling of the target node in the pattern, the stylesheet transforms every source document node into lower cases before applying the XPath notation. Therefore the above pattern proceeds by selecting all nodes below the root node, denoted by a '//*', and passing them to the *toLower* function to convert the nodes into lower cases. Only those nodes which produce an *img* output are selected.

The next part of the pattern checks whether the current node, the *img* node, does not have an *alt* attribute by selecting all attributes of the current node, denoted by a './@*', checking whether the lower case name of the attribute is *alt* and negating this part of the pattern, denoted by a *not*. Finally the XSLT *count* function is used to count the number of selected nodes. The remaining patterns of the XSLT stylesheet proceed in a similar fashion.

4 *CAT* SAMPLE EVALUATION

The University of Manchester website has been used to illustrate how usability, in particular consistency of web pages is evaluated by *CAT*[3]. The tool starts by evaluating the usability of the home page. Because it is the first page to be evaluated, the consistency of the page cannot be assessed as the tool is unable to compare the current page values to any previous values.

However, the tool is able to assess inter-page usability. For example, the accessibility of the page is impaired because eight images do not have *alt* attributes and seven of the *alt* attribute texts provided are shorter than 2 or longer than 10 words. Furthermore, the page contains scripting language without an alternative presentation making it impossible to view this part of the page in a browser that does not support scripting language.

Concerning form usability, two guideline violation have been found because the page contains a form without a submit and a reset button. However, closer inspection of the page shows that this form is in fact the 'Fast Finder' pull down menu and therefore, does not require a submit or reset button. Currently, the tool is unable to differentiate between different kinds of forms. The performance, i.e. the loading time, of the page could also be improved by including height and width specifications for all page elements (e.g. tables and images) as they have been omitted for 7 elements.

[3]The University of Manchester website can be found at: http://www.man.ac.uk/.

Furthermore, the tool records three readability guideline violations. The first violation concerns the use of a horizontal line which turns out to be very short and therefore does not impair the readability of the page. The second readability guideline violation concerns the specification of the main layout table and the header, both of which have been specified wider than 500 pixels. Consequently, users with smaller screens are unable to view the home page without having to scroll sideways. Although, *CAT*'s assessment result indicates too many structural links on the page (26 instead of the preferred 5-7 links), these violation can be dismissed because home pages should display a higher number of links than its sub-pages to provide more initial navigation options.

The next page to be evaluated is the *Undergraduate Courses* sub- home page which can be reached by selecting the 'http://www.man.ac.uk/study/ugrad/' link from the home page. This time consistency can be evaluated and the results show that the font-sizes, -faces and -colours of the current page differ from those of the home page. The same applies to the navigation menu. The only feature that has been kept constant is the background colour which has the default colour white. Consequently, the consistency of the current page compared to the home page is very low. The evaluation results for the other usability categories are similar to those recorded for the home page. The only major difference is the percentage of links contained in the current page as it is only 10% compared to 27% recorded for the home page. The former is well within the recommended maximum of 20% link text for sub-pages and indicates that this page has far more content than the home page, which is indeed the case.

The consistency of the *Student Life* page, which can be reached by selecting the *life1.html* link from the *Undergraduate Courses* page, is far higher than has been recorded on the previous page. For example, the font-sizes and -colours and the background-color are all the same as in the previous page. On the other hand, the font-face has not been kept consistent, because the previous page contained a paragraph written in italics. Furthermore, the navigation menu has been altered by adding 5 structural links.

Overall, the above example shows that *CAT* is a reliable tool for evaluating the usability, particularly the consistency of web pages. Although, occasionally the guideline violations registered by the tool do not affect the usability of the particular page e.g. the omission of the reset and submit button for the *Fast Finder* pull-down menu. Furthermore, *CAT* is currently unable to differentiate between the weighting of the different consistency values. For example, whether the change of font-faces between the *Undergraduate Courses* and the *Student Life* page only affects a paragraph, which was in fact the case, or the whole text. Additionally, the URLs of the links available on the current page, that are displayed together with the evaluation results, are often meaningless and it would be more user friendly to display the link descriptions instead. However, these shortcomings will be addressed in future versions of *CAT*.

5 RELATED WORK AND DISCUSSION

The majority of automatic evaluation methods concentrate on the statistical analysis or visualization of usage patters in server logs (e.g. (Chi et al., 2000)). Such evaluations consist largely of traffic-based analysis (e.g. pages-per-visitor or visitors-per-page) and time-based analysis (e.g. click paths and page-view durations) which need to be interpreted by an evaluator to identify usability problems. However these methods are problematic because web-server logs provide only incomplete traces of user behaviour (e.g. do not capture use of back button) and timing estimates might be incorrect because of network delays (Ivory et al., 2001).

Another approach is WebCriteria's Site Profile which evaluates websites by simulating a user's information-seeking behaviour within a model of an implemented site. The tool assumes an idealized user model which navigates through the website following an explicit, pre-specified path and measures usability metrics such as page load and optimal navigation times (WebCriteria, 1999). However the approach is unable to account for the effect of various web page attributes, e.g. the amount of text presented on each page or the layout of the links (Ivory et al., 2001).

The fullest automation support according to Ivory et al. is provided for guideline review inspection methods (Ivory et al., 2000). Such methods automatically detect and report violations of usability guidelines and try to suggest ways of correction. Other methods compare quantitative web page measures (e.g. number of links or graphics) to predefined thresholds (Ivory et al., 2001).

An example is the *Web Static Analyzer Tool (SAT)* which checks the static HTML code of a website according to a number of pre-defined usability guidelines, e.g. whether all graphics contain *alt* tags or whether each page contains at least one link. Currently the tool is only able to evaluate individual HTML pages but not a whole site. However plans exist to extend the tool to inspect an entire site in order to identify potential problems in the interaction between pages (Team, 2000).

The W3C (The World Wide Web Consortium) have developed their own HTML Validation Service which assesses HTML and XHTML documents for conformance to their recommendations and other standards. They also offer a *CSS Validation Service* and an *XML Schema Validator* for checking cascading style sheets and XML schemas for conformance to their recommendations. The tools are able to check documents by a given URL or by uploading files and provide feedback for all guideline violations found in the document. However like the *WebSAT* the tools are currently only able to check individual pages or documents (Oskoboiny, 2001).

Most of the above tools measure usability in a per-page basis. By contrast, *CAT* strives to measure consistency among distinct page belonging to the same web site.

The problem with automatic guideline review inspection tools such as *CAT* is that they are only able to assess usability aspects that are inherent in the HTML syntax and that can be tested automatically. Other guidelines for example the ease with which users understand instructions and error messages or how well users can navigate around the site are not evaluated (Nielsen, 2000). These aspects of usability are very difficult to assess automatically because they involve complex cognitive, social and cultural processes that determine the interpretation of textual, visual, audio messages, the selection of relevant information and learning (Brajnik, 2000).

The question is, how effective is *CAT*, i.e. how well do the usability problems highlighted by the tool determine the overall usability of the site? Brajnik pointed out that the lack of a standard evaluation methodology to determine the effectiveness of assessment tools prevents the evaluation and comparison of the quality of the different tools currently available. However the definition of such a standard methodology depends on clearly defined models of usability which so far have not been developed (Brajnik, 2000).

Therefore, the only method currently available for evaluating the effectiveness of automatic assessment tools is by comparing the usability problems found by the tool with the results of usability inspection methods and user testing. A high degree of overlap between the findings of the tool and the traditional evaluation methods would indicate that the tool is at least to some extent effective. However, a low degree of overlap would not necessary mean that the tool is ineffective as it could be possible that the usability problems found by the tool are different from those found by the manual usability tests. In fact, usability findings for the same interface can vary considerably between different evaluators even if the same evaluation techniques are used. For example, Molich et al. found only 1% overlap for results among different usability testing teams that evaluated the same user interface. Because of these difficulties effectiveness testing has not been included in the current study (Molich et al., 1999).

Ivory et al. criticized automatic usability assessment tools that are based on usability guidelines(Ivory et al., 2001). The reason is that designers often have difficulties implementing such guidelines especially if the guidelines conflict with each other (Ivory et al., 2001). Ivory et al. assume that this is caused by the lack of agreement among designers about which guidelines are correct (Ivory et al., 2001). Their study showed that page-level metrics (e.g. number of words, colours, fonts and graphics per page) can to 85% predict if a site will be highly rated by judges and users. However the results also showed that the importance of certain usability metrics e.g. the composition, layout and overall characteristics differ among large and small website as well as among different categories such as education, community and finance. Therefore, Ivory et al. concluded that there are several ways of developing well-designed and highly usable websites. Furthermore, the quality of the design is determined by a combination of different usability metrics depending on the nature of the site (Ivory et al., 2001).

6 CONCLUSION

To the best of our knowledge no usability assessment tool currently available is able to measure inter-page consistency of websites. However, as Nielsen (Nielsen, 1993, p.90) pointed out, "consistency is one of the most important usability characteristics". Those features of a site that are noticed first by website users is not the title but the overall layout of the design elements of the page. Consistency not only aids users to navigate around the site but also increases their confidence in the information presented because they associated a unified design with professionalism (Brannon and Sellati, 2000). Furthermore, increasing the consistency of intranet sites can enhance productivity. For instance it has been estimated that the redesign of Sun's intranet site could save each employee as much as 5mins per week which amounts in an overall saving of $10 million dollars per year through avoiding lost productivity (Lynch and Horton, 2001). Future extensions of the tool might include consistency testing for a set of pages. I.e. the current page is evaluated against consistency patters derived from a group of pages rather than only the previous page. To reduce the time and effort needed to perform maintenance activities the tool could be extended to indicate the location of usability violations in the syntax and suggest possible ways of correction.

REFERENCES

Bhatti, N., Bouch, A., and Kuchinsky, A. (2000). Integrating User-Perceived Quality into Web Server Design at http://www.w3.org/w9edrom/92/92.html.

Brajnik, G. (Austin, 2000). Automatic Web Usability Evaluation: What Needs to be Done? at http://www.tri.sbc.com/hfweb/brajnik/hfweb-brajnik.html. In *Proceedings of the 6th Conference on Human Factors and the Web.*

Brannon, D. and Sellati, A. (2000). Design Consistency, Website Development and Administration at http://slis-two.lis.fsu.edu/ consist/introduction.html.

Brewer, J. (2000). Overview of the Web Accessibility Initiative at http://www.w3.org/talks/wai-intro/slide1-0.html.

Chi, E., Pirolli, P., and Pitkow, J. (2000). The Scent of a Site: A System for Analyzing and Predicting Information Scent, Usage, and Usability of a Web Site. In *Proceedings of the ACM CH'00 Conference on Human Factors in Computing Systems.*

Chisholm, W., Vanderheiden, G., and Jacobs, I. (1999). Web Content Accessibility Guidelines 1.0, W3C Recommendation 5-may-1999 at http://www.w3.org/tr/wai-webcontent/.

Cook, J. (1997). The Sev Guide to Web Design: Consistency at http://www.sev.com.au/webzone/design/ consistency.asp.

Dix, A., Finlay, J., Abowd, G., and Beale, R. (1992). *Human-Computer-Interaction.* Prentice Hall International (UK) Limited.

IBM (2001). IBM Web Accessibility Checklist - Version 3.0 2001 at http://www-3.ibm.com/able/accessweb.html.

Ivory, M., Rashmi, R., and Hearst, M. (2000). Preliminary Findings on Quantitative Measures for Distinguishing Highly Rated Information-Centric Web Pages. In *Proceedings of the 6th Conference on Human Factors and the Web*, Austin.

Ivory, M., Sinha, R., and Hearst, M. (2001). Empirically Validated Web Page Design Metrics. In *CHI 2001, ACM Conference on Human Factors in Computing Systems, CHI Letters 3(1).*

Lynch, P. and Horton, S. (2001). Web Style Guide: Basic Design Principles for Creating Web Sites at http://info.med.yale.edu/caim/manual/ contents.html.

Molich, R., Thomsen, A., Karyukina, B., Schmidt, L., Ede, M., van Oel, W., and Arcuri, M. (1999). Comparative Evaluation of Usability Tests. In *Proceedings of the Conference on Human Factors in Computing Systems*, pages 83–86, Pittsburg. ACM Press.

Mukherjea, S. and Yoshinori, H. (1997). Focus+Context Views of World-Wide Web Nodes. In M. Bernstein, L. C. and Østerbye, K., editors, *Hypertext 97, The Eigth ACM Conference on Hypertext, University of Southampton, UK*, pages 187–196. Association for Computing Machinery (ACM).

Nielsen, J. (1993). *Usability Engineering*. Academic Press.

Nielsen, J. (2000). *Designing Web Usability: The Practice of Simplicity*. New Riders Publishing.

Oskoboiny, G. (2001). W3C HTML Validation Service at http://validator.w3.org/.

Scholtz, J., Laskowski, S., and Downey, L. (1998). Developing Usability Tools and Techniques for Designing and Testing Web Sites. In *Proceedings of the 4th Conference on Human Factors and the Web*.

Team, W. D. (2000). NIST WebMetrics Project, Web Static Analyzer Tool (SAT) at http://zing.ncsl.nist.gov/ webmet/.

WebCriteria (1999). Max, and the Objective Measurement of Web Sites at http://www.webcriteria.com.

PART 4

Internet Computing and Electronic Commerce

AN AUTOMATED APPROACH TO QUALITY-AWARE WEB APPLICATIONS

Antonio Ruiz, Rafael Corchuelo, and Amador Durán *
Escuela Técnica Superior de Ingeniería Informática. Universidad de Sevilla
Avda. de la Reina Mercedes, s/n. Sevilla E-41012. Spain
Email: {aruiz, corchu, amador}@lsi.us.es

Key words: Web applications, optimality, conformance, constraints, automatic reasoning.

Abstract: Multi–Organisational Web–Based Systems (MOWS) are becoming very popular in the Internet world. It would be desirable for such systems to be quality–aware, and this feature turns the problem of selecting the web services of which they are composed into a complex task. The main reason is that the catalog of available services that meet a set of functional requirements may be quite large, and it is subject to unexpected changes due to the inherent volatility of the Internet. Thus, such systems need an infrastructure able to select the best services at run time so that they can deliver their functionality at the best possible quality level. In this article, we present a proposal that aims at being the core of a run–time system able to support the construction of quality–aware MOWS.

1 INTRODUCTION

The incredible successfulness of the Internet world has paved the way for a sub–industry devoted to developing and running web services (Microsoft, 2001; Sun, 2001; UDDI, 2000), which some authors tend to describe as the core of the next–generation Internet. Built on the standard integration fabric of XML and widely–accepted Internet protocols, web services bring programmers a new way to develop advanced applications that can integrate any group of services on the Internet into a single solution to which we refer to as a Multi–Organisational Web–based System (MOWS) (Orfali et al., 1996; Booch et al., 1999; Corchuelo et al., 2001; Corchuelo and Ruiz, 2002).

The reason why many gurus forecast such a change from site–centric applications to web-service–based ones is the recent bankrupt of dotcoms. They have not fallen through because of a lack of customers, but because of a lack of plans to make profit on them. In the near future, profit will be as important as ever, but the model will change from one based on competition to one based on collaboration (Sessions, 2001). The success of the overall collaboration will define the success of each of the individual units. In e–commerce, for instance, collaboration means selling through partner relationships, which amounts to sharing profits, and, thus, forces companies to scrutinise their profit model at every step of the collaboration.

In this context, quality parameters such as time to failures, time to repair, performance or bandwidth usage are fundamental and very frequently bias customers against using a MOWS that does not live up to the hype, even though it is fully functional. Therefore, it is desirable for such systems to be quality–aware so that they can select the web services on which they rely according to a number of user–defined quality requirements that maximise end users' satisfaction. Such a selection is not easy at all because the Internet changes with every passing minute and the set of available web services is increasing steadily. This argues for an infrastructure able to select the best services at run time so that MOWS can deliver their functionality at the highest possible quality level.

In this article, we present such an infrastructure. It is based on formal quality documents by means of which software engineers can state what quality requirements their web services can meet or must meet in order to be candidates to be integrated into a MOWS. Otherwise, it would be impossible to ask for liabilities if something fails (Corchuelo et al., 2001; Ruiz et al., 2001). Our proposal is *product–oriented*

*The work reported in this article was partially funded by the Spanish Interministerial Commission on Science and Technology under grant TIC 2000-1106-C02-01 (GEOZOCO Project).

(Chung et al., 2000), and the state–of–the–art proposal in this category is QML (Frolund and Koistinen, 1998). Its most important drawback is that its expressiveness is very limited. For instance, it is not possible to constraint several parameters simultaneously. Thus, a constraint of the form "the average time to failures plus its variance must be smaller than 70 seconds" cannot be written in QML. Neither is it possible to define requirements that state several constraints on the same parameter. For instance, it is not possible to constraint the cost per connection of a web service between $10 and $20. In our opinion, this limited expressiveness makes the language not appropriate in general. Furthermore, extending it so that such constraints can be incorporated is not easy at all because its semantics rely on the syntactic form of the constraints. Our proposal also relies on using constraints, but it does not limit their expressiveness syntactically. Furthermore, we offer an elaborate infrastructure that relies on web services that makes it appealing to be used in the context of MOWS, whereas the goal of QML is to deal with classical components off the shelf, and its supporting infrastructure cannot be easily adapted to the Internet world.

The rest of the article is organised as follows: Section 2 goes into details about conformance and optimality; Section 3 shows how these problems can be interpreted as constraint satisfaction problems; Section 4 describes the infrastructure we need to implement these ideas; finally, Section 5 presents our conclusions and some future research directions.

2 CONFORMANCE AND OPTIMALITY

In order to maximise profit, MOWS must be designed as open systems with some automatic reasoning capabilities. The goal is that they should be able to reconfigure themselves and use new service providers if they are more adequate according to their ratio quality/price.

However, if we want to achieve a good rate of return, we first need to tackle two important problems: conformance and optimality. We introduce and motivate them by means of a simple, but realistic problem. Consider, for instance, that someone is interested in setting up a web portal specialised in films, so that it offers a potentially infinite catalog of films and the same functionality as a domestic video player. In order to achieve such a goal, the portal should sub–contract three kinds of web services, at least: a service for streaming videos on the Internet, a service for managing catalogs and keeping them up–to–date, and a service for managing virtual shops. This way, the portal really becomes a service that integrates other

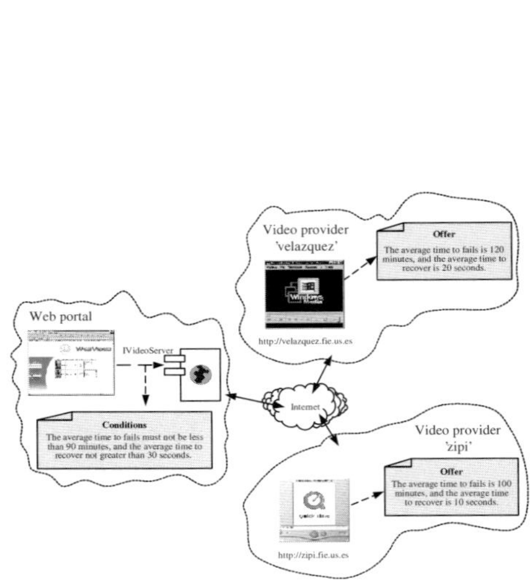

Figure 1: A fragment of the architecture of a web video portal.

low–level services that are provided by other organisations. (The reader may find a functional prototype at `http://zipi.lsi.us.es/WebVideo`.)

Figure 1 shows a fragment of the component view corresponding to this portal. The interface `IVideoServer` abstracts the operations a component able to deliver video on demand needs to have if we want to incorporate it into the system. This component may change according to factors such as the requirements of the clients, the price, the quality they offer, and so forth. This component is stereotyped with a world icon, which means that it is fetched from the Internet, and connected by means of a dotted arrow, which means that it is not selected and bound at compile time, but at run time. The note associated with interface `IVideoServer` states the set of quality requirements that a web service must fulfill so that it can be used by the portal. Hereafter, we refer to this document as the *conditions*. In this case, it states that the average time to fails must not be less than 90 minutes, and ii) the average time to recover from failures must not be greater than 30 seconds.

Figure 1 shows two providers that use *Microsoft Windows Media Server* and *Apple Quick Time Server* to deliver video on demand, respectively. Each provider describes its services using a document to which we refer to as the *offer*. If we read both offers, we can easily check that both providers satisfy the quality requirements needed to be subcontracted by the portal, that is, they both are *conformant*.

When several providers are conformant to a given set of conditions, one might select amongst them arbitrarily. However, customers usually have preferences: for instance, there are clients who want the average time between failures be the highest possible, whereas others may be happy with more frequent failures as long as they are repaired very quickly. Thus, a MOWS is optimum when it is composed of a set of services whose quality parameters maximise the utility from a client's perspective (Corchuelo et al., 2001). Utility may be expressed in different ways, but we use linear weighted functions over the set of quality parameters under consideration because it is a common, expressive technique, and it is simple enough to be implemented efficiently. A weight can be either negative, which implies its associated quality parameter should have a value as small as possible, nought, which implies the associated quality parameter does not really matter, and positive, in which case the corresponding parameter should be as high as possible.

The reader might argue that checking conformance and optimality is quite a simple problem, and that the administrator of the portal might do it manually. However, there are several concerns that argue for an automatic solution to this problem:

- If the number of quality requirements is high, this check might consume too much time and be an error prone task. Furthermore, the inherent ambiguity of Spanish, English or other natural languages might introduce inadvisable interpretation problems.
- The time used to check for quality requirements should be as small as possible, chiefly if there are human clients waiting for a connection to be set up so that they can use a given service.
- The quality level a provider may offer is usually subject to unexpected changes due to the inherent volatility of the Internet world. Thus, it is necessary to check for conformance and optimality even in the case of well–known providers, which increases the number of checks to be carried out

Therefore, it is needed an automatic solution to these problems. In this paper, we present an architecture whose goal is to provide MOWS with an infrastructure so that they can be composed at run time and be both conformant and optimal.

3 INTERPRETATION AS A CSP

In this section, we introduce the foundations of our proposal. It consists of interpreting the set of conditions and offers with which we are dealing as if it was a constraint satisfaction problem, or CSP for short. Such a problem consists of a set if variables defined over a set of domains that contain the the values they may take, and a set of constraints on the values they may have in a given context.

This way, if we re-write both conditions and offers as constraints, they can be analysed using standard tools and techniques, and we avoid misinterpretations due to the inherent ambiguity of natural languages (Hentenryck and et al., 1996; Marriot and Stuckey, 1998; Freuder and Wallace, 2000).

3.1 Conformance

To interpret conformance as a CSP, we first need to express both offers and conditions by means of mathematical constraints on the quality parameters with which we are dealing (in this case, the quality parameters correspond to the set of variables of the CSP).

In general, modelling in this context is quite a simple, intuitive task in most cases. For instance, if we define the real variable TTF as the average time to failures and the real variable TTR as the average tome to recover from failures, then the conditions associated with the web portal that we presented in Figure 1 may be re–formulated as follows:

$$TTF \geq 90 \wedge TTR \leq 30 \qquad (1)$$

Therefore, if we want to check if the offer of the provider that uses *Windows Media Server* conforms to these conditions, what we have to do is to check if the set of values described by the constraint $TTF = 120 \wedge TTR = 20$ (its solution space) satisfies the constraint $TTF \geq 90 \wedge TTR \leq 30$. Roughly speaking, we have to find if the solution space of the first constraint is a subset of the solution space of the second one. That is, any value the provider can assign to the quality parameters under consideration can satisfy the client; otherwise, some values would not satisfy it and the provider would not be chosen.

From a mathematical point of view, determining if the solution space of constraint c_1 is a subset of the solution space of c_2 amounts to determining if the implication constraint $c_1 \rightarrow c_2$ is satisfiable or not, i.e., its solution space is not empty (Marriot and Stuckey, 1998). To check it, we have to solve the following problem:

$$c_1 \rightarrow c_2 \Leftrightarrow sat(c_1 \wedge \neg c_2) = false \qquad (2)$$

where sat is a function that we identify with the constraint solver we are using. It can be applied on a constraint c and returns one of the following results: $true$, if c is satisfiable, $false$ if it is not satisfiable, and $\perp$ if the constraint solver cannot determine if c is satisfiable or not.

Notice, that we have not limited the kind of constraints we can use so as to offer a great deal of expressiveness; however, there are not general solvers able to deal with any constraint. Thus, if $sat(c) = \perp$, we assume that the service under consideration is not conformant. We might be wrong, but if our constraint solver cannot solve the corresponding constraints, then our decision will not lead to a non–conformant system. Anyway, most problems we have tackled do only require linear constraints that can be solved using the well–known SIMPLEX method (Borgwardt, 1987; Klabjan et al., 2000). Thus, our decision does not reduce the applicability of our proposal substantially.

3.2 Optimality

Given that we associate weights with each quality parameter in an attempt to model user's preferences, we can model the problem of optimality as an optimisation problem in which our goal is to find the service that maximises the following utility function:

$$\mathcal{U}(a_1, \ldots, a_n) = \sum_{i=1}^{n} w_i N_i(a_i) \tag{3}$$

Here, each a_i denotes a quality parameter, each w_i its associated weight, and each N_i its associated user–defined normalisation function ($i = 1, 2, \ldots, n$). We need normalisation functions that map each parameter into a real number that ranges from 0 to 1 because each parameter measures a different quality factor and adding or scaling them directly would not make sense.

In general, a provider may offer a service at a quality level that cannot be characterised by means of an equality. For instance, a provider might state $TTF \geq 100 \wedge TTF \leq 120$ to indicate that its average time to failures ranges from 100 to 120 seconds. This is the reason why we need to carry out a fringe analyse in order to find the values that characterise the fringe limit a parameter may take in a given provider. This analysis amounts to solving the following optimisation problem:

$$\begin{array}{ll} \max & \mathcal{U}(a_1, \ldots, a_n) \\ \text{st} & C_S \end{array} \tag{4}$$

where C_S denotes the set of constraints associated with the offer of provider S. As mentioned previously, the constraint solver we are using might not be able to solve this problem. In such cases, we do not take that service into account as a candidate to be the optimum.

4 COMPUTER SUPPORT

In this section, we present the framework that constitutes the computer support we need to put our ideas into practice. It consists of some linguistic support and a run–time system.

```
catalog Reliability {
    TTF: real {TTF >= 0};
    TTR: real {TTR >= 0};
}
```

a) A catalog of quality parameters

```
using Reliability;
conditions for IVideoServer {
    TTF >= 90;
    TTR <= 30;
}
preferences {
    TTR = -30;
    TTF = 90;
}
```

b) Conditions

```
// Service that uses Windows Media Server
using Reliability;
offer for IVideoServer {
    TTF = 120;
    TTR = 20;
}

// Service that uses Apple QuickTime Server
using Reliability;
offer for IVideoServer {
    TTF = 100;
    TTR = 10;
}
```

c) Offers

Figure 2: Specification of parameters, conditions and offers in QRL.

4.1 Linguistic support

Mathematical constraints allow to express conformance and optimality problems straightforwardly. However, they lack a standardised syntax to express the domains of the variables and the implied constraints on them, for instance. This is the reason why we have designed a simple language called *Quality Requirements Language*, or QRL for short, that allows to express these details and others that we describe later.

Figure 2 shows an example in which we formalise the conditions, the offers, and the parameters involved in our web portal example. Section (a) presents a simple catalog of quality parameters related to realiability; section (b) shows the conditions associated with the portal, which include both the weights the user assigns to each parameter and the constraints he or she imposes on them; section (c) shows the documents that describe the offers that both providers present to their clients. QRL is thus quite a simple language because it does only provide some linguistic support that normalises the way we declare quality parameters and the constraints on them.

4.2 Run–time support

Figure 3 shows an overview of the architecture of the run–time system we have designed. Its structure is highly modular in order to facilitate future modifications and reuse of its components. Furthermore, the architecture is fully distributed because most of the components run on different platforms and can be configured and operated independently from the rest.

Some components are stereotyped as web services so that their functionality can be accessed from any application on the Internet. The others are local to each organisation participating in a MOWS.

Next Generation UDDI (NUDDI): The Universal Description, Discovery and Integration (UDDI) project is a sweeping industry initiative (UDDI, 2000). The project creates a platform–independent, open framework for describing services, and discovering web services as well as an operational registry that is available today. UDDI is the first truly cross–industry effort driven by all major platform and software providers, as well as marketplace operators and e–business leaders. Unfortunately, UDDI does not support quality contracts. Our proposal consists of creating a Next Generation UDDI with quality information, so that it can act as a universal repository of quality–enabled web services.

Certification authorities (CA): This authorities are responsible for testing web services and issuing certificates only to those that implement correctly the interfaces they expose. CA play a prominent role in our architecture because a system in an open world would not use a third–party web service unless a CA certificates it works properly and can meet the quality offers it exposes.

Quality trader: This component is responsible for searching for web services that meet the requirements of a system. If necessary, it can negotiate if no web service satisfying those requirements is found. Obviously, this component relies on NUDDI for discovering components and on CA for searching certified web services.

Local repository and trader: Having an NUDDI service on the web and quality traders allow systems to discover new web services on demand, which makes them extremely open and reliable. However, it is not a good idea to try to have access to these services on demand because they may become a serious bottleneck of the system. In order to increase performance, the idea is to have local web service repositories and quality traders that work locally on them in order to increase efficiency. Thus, NUDDI or a web quality trader should only be a last resort if no web service can be found locally. It is also important to point out that local repositories do not store web services themselves, but only URL references by means of which they can be reached at run time.

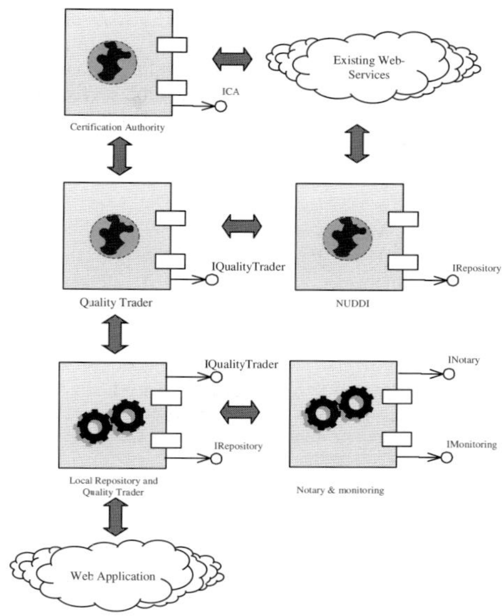

Figure 3: Architecture of our run–time system.

Auditors: Auditors are responsible for monitoring web services so that a system using them can check if they really implement the quality they claim in their offer.

5 CONCLUSIONS

In this article, we have presented a novel application of mathematical constraints to the problem of searching for the set of web services that best fulfill a number of quality requirements. Our proposal improves the state of the art because it allows for unrestricted constraints, and the infrastructure we have developed is appropriate to be used in the Internet because it relies on web services.

In the future, we are going to work on incorporating

negotiation capabilities into QRL, and also temporal features so that we can state the values certain quality parameters may take depending on the day of the week, the month or the hour. We think that this feature may be quite novel because we are not aware of any proposal that takes temporal properties into account.

REFERENCES

Booch, G., Rumbaugh, J., and Jacobson, I. (1999). *The Unified Modeling Language User Guide*. Addison–Wesley.

Borgwardt, K. (1987). *The simplex method*. Springer–Verlag.

Chung, L., Nixon, B., Yu, E., and Mylopoulos, J. (2000). *Non–Functional Requirements in Software Engineering*. Kluwer Academic Publishers.

Corchuelo, R. and Ruiz, A. (2002). *Advances in Business Solutions*. Catedral.

Corchuelo, R., Ruiz, A., Mühlbacher, J., and García-Consuegra, J. (2001). Object-oriented business solutions. In *Chapter 18 of ECOOP'2001 Workshop Reader, LNCS n^o (to appear)*. Springer-Verlag.

Freuder, E. and Wallace, M. (2000). Science and substance: A challenge to software engineers. *Constraints IEEE Intelligent Systems*.

Frolund, S. and Koistinen, J. (1998). Quality–of–service specification in distributed object systems. *Distributed Systems Engineering Journal*, 5(4).

Hentenryck, P. and et al., S. (1996). Strategic directions in constraint programming. *ACM Computing Surveys*, 28(4).

Klabjan, D., Johnson, E., and Nemhauser, G. (2000). A parallel primal–dual simplex algorithm. *Operations Research Letters*, 27(2):47–55.

Marriot, K. and Stuckey, P. (1998). *Programming with Constraints: An Introduction*. The MIT Press.

Microsoft (2001). Building ASP.NET web services. Available at the MSDN web site.

Orfali, R., Harkey, D., and Edwards, J. (1996). *The Essential Distributed Objects Survival Guide*. John Wiley and Sons.

Ruiz, A., Corchuelo, R., Duran, A., and Toro, M. (2001). Automated support for quality requirements in web-services-based systems. In *Proc. of the 8th IEEE Workshop on Future Trends of Distributed Computing Systems (FTDCS'2001)*, Bologna, Italy. IEEE Press.

Sessions, R. (2001). Java 2 enterprise edition (J2EE) versus the .NET platform — two visions for ebusiness. Technical report, ObjectWatch, Inc.

Sun (2001). Open, smart web services. Available at Sun's web site.

UDDI (2000). Uddi technical white paper. Available at UDDI's web site.

INTERNET TECHNOLOGY AS A BUSINESS TOOL
A test of its effectiviness

Sebastián Bruque
Departament of Business Administration, Accounting and Sociology. University of Jaen. E.U.P. Linares; 23700 Linares, Spain
Email: sbruque@ujaen.es

Key words: TCP/IP; Internet; competitive advantage; profitability, Resource Based View.

Abstract: Since the beginnings of the computing era people have suggested that the implementation of Information Technology (IT) would have a positive effect on firm performance. Indicators like productivity, profitability and market share could be improved by these tools. Among these technologies, firms can now use TCP/IP or Internet technologies for strategic purposes but, until now, their real effects have been unclear. In this work we try to provide some evidence about the impact of the Internet on competitive advantage in a Spanish Industry. Also, we give some insights that can help to understand the role of the Internet as a competitive weapon in modern firms.

1 INTRODUCTION

Since the beginnings of the computing era (Kaufman, 1966) people have suggested that the implementation of this type of computing technologies would have a series of positive effects (McLean and Soden, 1977; McFarlan, 1984; Porter and Millar, 1985; Parsons, 1983; Cash and Konsynski, 1985). These authors claim that IT can play a role as a strategic tool: by affecting the conditions in which products are supplied and produced, the market structure itself or economies of production. From the strategic point of view, IT could affect every one of Porter's competitive strategies (1980), whether cost leadership, differentiation or specialisation in a market niche.

Restricting the analysis to the impact on the organization of TCP/IP technologies – Internet – it is surprising that there are so few papers looking at how these types of technologies influence the competitive position of companies. Most of the work on this question forms part of a large number of general information publications that extol the net profit gains obtained by those firms actively involved in the so-called virtual economy. From the point of view of the literature on Strategic Management, certain authors stress the potential advantages of the virtual market, or *marketspace* against the traditional market, or marketplace (Rayport and Sviokla, 1995). Venkatraman (2000) confirms that executives are now aware of the potential and possibilities of the Internet as a strategic element, although normally this potential is not well exploited. However very few studies exist that look at the level of real presence of these advantages and with what intensity they can be converted into economic profitability, market share or improved client perception of the organization.

2 INFORMATION TECHNOLOGIES AND COMPETITIVE ADVANTAGE

The first line of study which we shall mention began with various studies that started at the end of the eighties and the beginning of the nineties. These drew attention to the zero, or even negative productivity increases of the work factor of those American firms that used information technology intensively (Solow, 1987). This perception, which clashed with the techno-enthusiasm that was dominant in the eighties (Parsons, 1983; McFarlan, 1984), was evident in two authors with differing approaches (Strassmann, 1990 and Brynjolfsson, 1993), who affirmed that the decrease in productivity of the work factor coincided with the od in which the companies invested enormous sums in equipment and computing systems (Strassmann, 1997, p. 1).

From this moment various works appeared involving the same researcher (Hitt and Brynjolfsson, 1995, 1996; Brynjolfsson and Hitt, 1996; Brynjolfsson, Hitt and Yang, 2000; Brynjolfsson and Hitt, 2001) in which one can see a sustained evolution towards positions which are more optimistic about the impact of IT. In this line, in the publications of 1996 (Brynjolfsson and Hitt, 1996; Hitt and Brynjolfsson, 1996), the researchers admitted that investment in IT were associated with an increase in the productivity of workers who work with information, and additionally they claim that investment in computing generates greater levels of productivity than any other type of investment, despite the short life-span of this type of tool (Brynjolfsson and Hitt, 1996, p. 49-50). However the authors maintain that the results obtained do not imply that investing in IT guarantees net productivity gains, but that other factors may influence the relation. Another of the fundamental discoveries of this period is that there is no relation between growth in market share or business profit and investment in IT. They even found slightly negative correlation coefficients between both variable pairs (Hitt and Brynjolfsson, 1996, p. 130).

However in more recent work (Brynjolfsson, Hitt and Yang, 2000; Brynjolfsson and Hitt, 2001) the researchers have found evidence of a relation between investment in IT and an improvement in global business performance, and not only productivity of work factor. Taking as a global result indicator Tobin's Q ratio, based on the firm's value in the stock market, they concluded that those firms which invested more in IT in the period 1987-1994 achieved superior results. What is more, this correlation was stronger when the organization, along with the investment in IT, underwent a structural re-organization involving interdisciplinary workgroups, increase in independent decision-making and support for employee training.

This positive view of the competitive impact of IT has, nevertheless, failed to convince many authors in this field. Strassmann (1990; 1997; 1998; 1999), for example, has not found evidence of a relation between IT investment – in which we can include technologies based on TCP/IP – and an increase in either productivity or company results (McCune, 1998). What is more, the results achieved by Brynjolfsson are based on the evolution of share values of companies using IT heavily. The values of these firms have sharply appreciated in the past decade, while there has been a sudden and dramatic downturn at the end of this period (Fernández, 2001, p. 9). Under these circumstances, it is unclear if they would have achieved similar results in a different financial climate.

Looking at it methodologically there are other difficult points. Among them we might suggest the exclusive use of aggregate level analysis focussed on big companies – public corporations – (Brynjolfsson, Hitt and Yang, 2000)- which may underestimate those aspects which affect the IT-company result binomial, and which are only revealed in studies focussing on the organization. What the mechanisms are by which an increase in technological investment might influence the competitive position of the organization, is not clear. Nor is it clear what role other internal or external variables might play in this relation. Finally the investigation needs to be extended to different economic areas and types of organization distinct from American firms.

At the same time as the first work of Brynjolfsson another theoretical current was developed which has tried to explain the impact on organizations of IT. We are referring to the approach known as hypothesis of strategic necessity, term that was introduced by Clemons and Kimbrough (1986) and later developed by Clemons and Row (1991). These researchers indicate that a large part of the progress achieved by companies thanks to the introduction of IT is quickly neutralised by their competitors. The mechanism of introduction of the technology, the creation of temporary advantages that follows and then the immediate neutralisation, is due to the fact that this type of technology spreads quickly amongst the competitors, according to the authors, and that these competitors expect to obtain the same positive effect, at least, as the pioneer did. From this point of view, IT is a necessary but not sufficient element: without the technology it is not possible to begin competing, but it is not sufficient to achieve superior results that are sustained through time.

More recently, during the second half of the nineties, the discussion on the correlation between information technology and company results has seen a new development regarding strategic development. Specifically, the paradigm that sees an organization as a reflection of its internal resources, or Resource Based View of the Firm (RBV) (Wernelfelt, 1984; Barney, 1991; 1995; 1996), provides, indirectly, the basis by which we can explain the effect of IT on the results of organizations (Ullmann and Voss, 2000), and more specifically, on competitive advantage (Bharadwaj, 2000; Amit and Zott, 2001).

3 TCP/IP TECHNOLOGIES AND COMPETETIVE ADVANTAGE

In this section we consider whether "Internet" technology in its current form can be an element that generates sustainable competitive advantage, and how such advantage might be achieved. To do this, we shall take Internet to mean that international computing network with facilities that companies can use for the interchange of information internally and for communicating externally with other organizations (Águila and Padilla, 1999, p. 65). The Internet offers various useful tools for business communication, among which we might stress electronic mail, the World Wide Web, newsgroups, remote access, file transfer, text-based and voiced-based chat (Águila, 2000, p. 32). In the current work we shall consider only those forms of communication based on the Web, e-mails and file transfer, those having, in fact, the most impact on activity in the Spanish firm (Escobar, 1999; Águila, 2000).

Once we have limited our field of analysis, we shall try to answer the question of whether Internet technologies can be considered a strategic resource for the companies that implement them. If this is the case those companies that use these technologies more intensely could achieve a more favourable competitive position, which, like the other strategic resources, would lead to positive profit differentials or increased market share (Mehra, 1996; Miller and Shamsie, 1996; Powell, 1996; Lee and Miller, 1999; etc.).

According to the approach of the company based on its resources, not every technical element, economic or human, is liable to bring competitive advantage. From the RBV perspective a strategic or key resource must have a number of minimum characteristics for it to be not only able to generate income, but to maintain this income over time (Wernelfelt, 1984; Barney, 1986). To obey these conditions, business resources susceptible to becoming strategic resources, such as IT in this case, must obey certain conditions, which we shall analyse below.

The **first condition** suggested by the theory resides in the effective capacity to provide value (Barney, 1995; 1996) by which, firstly, **a strategic resource must be a valuable element** (Prahalad and Hamel, 1990). Value refers to the level to which the resource is able to take advantage of opportunities, or fights against the threats emerging from the competitive environment (Barney, 1991, p. 111). It is definitely recognized that a resource generates value, or competitive advantage, if and only if, it reduces the costs of the organization, or it increases its income compared to the situation when the company lacks such a resource (Barney, 1996, p. 147).

It is not enough, however, for a firm to possess a resource that generates value for it to be able to achieve improvements in its competitive position. If this critical resource were available to any rival it would be unlikely to lead to competitive advantage, because all the organizations with access to the valuable resource would be comparable to the opposition. There is therefore a **second condition** concerning the **scarcity of the element** that is susceptible to generate improvements in the competitive position (Grant, 1996). This condition has also been given the name heterogeneous diffusion of the resource (Peteraf, 1993) or relative scarcity (Barney, 1995).

If all or a large number of firms had access to the income-generating element this would only give rise to competitive parity (Mata, Fuerst and Barney, 1995). On the other hand scarce and valuable resources will give rise to a temporary competitive advantage at least. For example, as Powell and Dent-Micallef (1997) point out, the growth in use of scanners in firms of the retail distribution industry in the US lead to improvements in the competitive position of those firms that used them first. These advantages were however neutralised subsequently by rival organizations which implemented the same equipment, re-establishing competitive parity.

There are different ways that a heterogeneous distribution of a key resource can be maintained between competing firms. Most authors consider that a **third condition** applies: that this unequal **diffusion is sustained** whenever rivals cannot replicate the valuable resources or substitute them for equivalent ones, or that in doing so, they suffer significant disadvantages.

The **fourth and last condition** needed for a strategic resource to bring sustainable improvement in the position of an organization, is for it to be **complementary with other elements or resources in the organization** (Barney, 1996). In this way, the complementary nature of the critical resource would reside in complementary or synergic effects, which would explain more-than-proportional improvements in the competitive position when the resources act jointly, as against when they act separately.

4 INTERNET TECHNOLOGIES, THEORETICAL BACKGROUND AND HYPOTHESIS

Once we have established the theoretical basis, we might consider if information technologies in general and Internet technologies in particular can be elements that generate sustainable competitive advantage. Following the argument above, the first requirement that IT as a key resource must have is a capacity for generating income, or for improving the competitive position of organizations, so that it can be considered a valuable resource. As we have already said, there is no agreement on this point among researchers: there are studies which show positive effects owing to the technology (Brynjolfsson, Hitt and Yang, 2000), but there are others that fail to find this (Strassmann, 1997). Until now, neither are there conclusive studies showing that firms which use Internet technologies intensively achieve better results than firms which do not.

Even in the case that IT really is a source of economic income generation, it would still have to satisfy the requirements of scarcity and difficulty of imitation or substitution (Barney, 1996). The rapid diffusion of technologies based on TCP/IP in recent years (Baquia, 2001) prompts us to infer that these elements are more and more within the reach of all organizations. That means that in the best of cases first mover advantage might be achieved by those organizations that pioneer the installation and development of the new technologies, and that therefore temporary competitive advantage might be achieved.

However it is difficult for this temporary competitive advantage to be sustained if there are no barriers to the mobility, substitution or duplication of the resource. In the case of the Internet, considering that this is the universal media par excellence, these barriers to mobility or imitation don't appear to exist. On the contrary, the basic tools like the World Wide Web, e-mail, news groups and their derived utilities, have spread widely among firms of all kinds.

What, then, are those elements that might make tools based on TCP/IP a source of sustainable competitive advantage? It is possible to suggest answers to this question following certain studies that show that such advantages can be achieved when IT acts in conjunction with other resources of the organization. Mata, Fuerst and Barney (1995) indicate that IT becomes a really effective weapon when it is managed proactively. Additionally Ross, Beath and Goodhue (1996) mention, among others, certain human factors as acting as catalysers of the competitive capacity of IT. For example, those firms that have a creative technical team who have good teamwork skills, will be able to exploit the advantages that these types of technologies may offer, and with greater chance of success.

Similarly, Powell and Dent-Micallef (1997) identify certain human and management elements which show association relations with the beneficial effects of IT. In this way they affirm that those firms with less internal conflict, better managerial support for the development of technological tools, and better organizational flexibility, achieve better results if they, additionally, use IT intensively. Finally Bharadwaj (2000) concludes that those organizations with a recognized capacity for innovation and technological management achieve better business results than their rivals.

We should remember, however, that even if the above studies provide solid results, they refer to the effects of IT in general and not the Internet tool in particular. In the next section we shall try to provide more empirical evidence which shows how this type of tool might influence the competitive position of the firm.

In the theoretical framework discussed above, consisting of the Resource Based View, and by the hypothesis of strategic necessity, we can propose the following hypothesis defining the connection between Internet technologies and sustainable competitive advantage.

Hypothesis H1: The intensive use of Internet technologies is not associated with the presence of sustainable competitive advantage.

4.1 Analysis of data and results

In the aim of testing the above hypothesis we have applied different quantitative analyses to a population of companies from one single industry of activity (Rouse and Daellenbach, 1999). For the investigation we have chosen as industry the group of pharmaceutical distribution firms that operate in 10 provinces in the south of Spain. The reasons for this choice lie in the highly technological nature of these firms, providing a suitable framework for studying the behaviour and inter-relations which affect the technological element in the organization.

The geographical area chosen comprises all the provinces of the Andalucia region (southern Spain), and, additionally, the two provinces of Ciudad Real and Murcia (two provinces bordering Andalucia). These two provinces have been included because of the strong similarities that there are in this industry between them and Andalucia. Thus the firms that operate in these two provinces are, in general, the same as those that operate in Andalucia.

The territory being studied had a population in 2000 of 8,834,000 inhabitants, which is 22% of the total population of Spain. Final pharmaceutical consumption in this area in 1998 reached a value of 320,134 million pesetas – 1,384.2 million euros – which represents 22.4% of total pharmaceutical consumption in Spain[1]. In the region a total of 16 firms operated in the pharmaceutical distribution industry in 2000, among which were four of the biggest five in the national market.

Two types of measure have been used. The first was to measure the presence of Internet technologies in the organizations forming part of the study. The second is an estimate of the competitive position of the various companies. The respective positions of the companies in Internet – INTi – during the period 1998/2000 were ascertained by interviewing at less two managers and employees of each organization at the company's physical headquarters. The information was obtained by using *Likert*-type scales of 5 degrees to identify the level of introduction of the technologies in the companies. Five variables were used to measure the presence of Internet technologies: (1) existence of Corporate website with root URL; (2) supplying technical and/or professional information from the website; (3) possible access to the firm's Intranet via the corporate website; (4) e-commerce of non-medical products and (5) existence of e-mail and file transfer among the departments in the company. The number of companies looked at in this analysis is 16, the totality of the population in the industry for this region.

As a measure of the competitive position of the organizations – Ic – we use the sum of two variables. The first variable refers to the increase in marketshare achieved by the organization during the period 1994/1998 ($C_{i94/98}$). Its calculation is based on gross sales income of the firms of the industry and has been obtained from various secondary sources: Fomento de la Producción (1997, 1998, 1999a, 1999b and 2000) and the database of the Subdirección General de Asistencia y Prestación Farmacéutica of the Spanish Ministry of Health. The second variable (Vi) has been obtained by measuring the perception that customers expressed to have about the level of quality of service provided by the distribution company. In order to measure this perception, a postal questionnaire was sent to 1,060 pharmaceutical clients resident in the area under study. After sending the questionnaires, 231 valid replies were received (21.86%) which is a rate of reply comparable to that of other similar studies (Hall, 1992; Powell, 1992; Powell and Dent-Micallef 1997). The combined index of competitive position was obtained by adding the variables $C_{i94/98}$ and Vi, once standardized, while the level of use of Internet technologies for each organization was measured using the arithmetic mean of the scores obtained in each of the five scales of analysis.

The scores in each of the variables by the companies that are being analysed appear in Table 1. As table 1 shows the majority of organizations use some form of TCP/IP technology. Among the most widespread of the technologies: e-mail, file transfer and existence of corporative website with root URL, the latter present and fully implemented in 9 organizations, which represents 56% of the population. The fact that practically all the organizations have ruled out e-commerce is striking. This can be justified in view of the important legal and corporate obstacles that limit the expansion possibilities of e-commerce – B2C – for pharmaceutical products. The other variables have intermediate levels of presence in the companies, with some companies not using any TCP/IP technology – as is the case of Company 1 – while others have a high level of technology – Company 10.

Table 1: INTERNET TECHNOLOGY PRESENT

Comp.	TI1	TI2	TI3	TI4	TI5	INTi
1	0	0	0	0	0	0
2	.50	.5	.50	0	4	1.10
3	5	4	4	0	4	3.40
4	0	0	0	0	3	.60
5	5	5	5	0	5	4
6	5	1.5	2	.50	5	2.80
7	1	1	1	1	3.25	1.45
8	5	0	5	0	5	3
9	4.5	2	4.50	0	4.50	3.10
10	5	4.33	5	2.33	4.66	4.26
11	4	4.50	4.50	0	5	3.60
12	4	4	3.50	2.50	5	3.80
13	5	3	0	0	5	2.60
14	1	1	1	0	3	1.20
15	1	1	1	0	1	.80
16	1	1	1	0	1	.80
Mean	2.93	2.05	2.37	.39	3.65	2.28

Note: T11: Website with root URL; T12: System of technical or professional information via the website; T13: Access to Intranet via the corporate website; T14: e-commerce of non-medical products; T15: e-mail and file transfer; INTi: Mean presence of Internet Technology.

In order to test Hypothesis H1 we have calculated the Spearman correlation coefficients, which measure the level of association which exists between the technological variables and the index of competitive position achieved by the companies (Ic). The Spearman parameter (Visauta, 1998) has been chosen as measure because the variables which easure technological presence (maximum test values Kolmogorov Smirnov Z = 0.405, p = 0.997) fail the normality condition. The results of the correlation analysis are shown in Table 2. At first sight it is possible to see a certain level of association between some Internet technologies and the competitive position of the firm. The connection that T11 and T12 respectively have with competitive position is especially strong. However, considering the mean presence of technology (INTi) the coefficient of association is sufficiently weak for us to say that there can be no strong relation between both variables.

It is however necessary to look at the results in Table 2 with some care. Firstly, it is important to take into account the influence that variables outside the model might have. After a previous study on the different variables liable to influence competitive position (Bruque, 2001), we identified various factors, normally industrial in character, which we shall propose as control variables: (1) size of organization; (2) strategic orientation regarding territorial expansion; (3) legal status of the company and (4) regional differences in pharmaceutical consumption.

Of these, the size[i] is the variable that has been found to explain best the differences in competitive position between companies. For this reason we calculated a partial correlation[ii] of the associations between the technological variables and competitive position, in which organization size has been introduced as a modulating variable. The results of this modification are shown in Table 3. From this we can see that there is absolutely no relation between the presence of Internet technologies and competitive advantage, company size assumed constant, from which the claim made in Hypothesis H1 is demonstrated.

5 DISCUSSION AND FINAL REMARKS

The above analyses allow us to advance a number of interesting conclusions that throw light on the influence of Internet technologies on the competitive position of organizations. The initial positive effects that connect these variables are diluted when some control factors are introduced, these factors being related to competitive advantage. The moderating effect of the size of the organization is especially strong: this converts the variables of Internet technology and competitive position into two independent variables. The weakness of the link between use of the Internet and success of the organization allows us to affirm that, up to now, we can see no cause-effect relation whatsoever between use of Internet and improvements perceptible for the client that are liable to change the competitive dynamic of the industry.

These results do not provide support to the abundant professional literature which finds a net positive effect of the Internet on the position of the company (Porter and Millar, 1985; Parsons, 1983; Cash and Konsynski, 1985). Nor do they entirely support the latest work of Brynjolfsson, Hitt and Yang (2000), work that claims IT is able to improve business results on its own. There is a certain agreement between our results and those found by supporters of the productivity paradox (term used in is strictest sense) (Brynjolfsson, 1993), and with some reflections from the techno-sceptical works of Strassmann (1990, 1997).

At the present time, there is a line of investigation that is attempting to clarify under which circumstances the Internet technologies become value-generating resources (Powell and Dent-Micallef, 1997). One explanation is the possible existence of complementarities between some human or management intangible factors and IT. However the question remains as to whether these factors are identical for the case of Internet technologies, and whether they have a similar positive influence as the other computing, robotic or telecommunications tools. Another explanation differentiates value creation and value appropriation, in the sense that firms can not appropriate the generated value by Internet technologies in the form of economic returns or improved competitive position (Amit and Zott, 2001). We shall try to throw more light on these questions in later studies

Table 2
CORRELATION MATRIX TECHNOLOGICAL PRESENCE AND COMPETITIVE POSITION

	Ic	**TI1**	**TI2**	**TI3**	**TI4**	**TI5**	**INTi**
Ic	---						
TI1	**.485**	---					
TI2	**.555**	.646	---				
TI3	.189	.698	.588	---			
TI4	.330	.210	.285	.226	---		
TI5	.347	.768	.593	.577	.294	---	
INTi	.393	.787	.842	.848	.418	.783	---

Note: It is not useful to calculate the signification index because the data comes from the whole population (there is no sample error).

REFERENCES

ÁGUILA OBRA, A.R. (2000): Comercio electrónico y estrategia empresarial, Ra-Ma, Madrid.

ÁGUILA OBRA, A.R. and PADILLA MELÉNDEZ, A. (1999): "Los modelos de negocio basados en las redes interorganizacionales", Proceedings of the XIII National Congress and IX Spanish-French Congress of the European Association of Business Management, AEDEM, pp. 65-74.

AMIT, R. and ZOTT, C. (2001): "Value creation in e-business", *Strategic Management Journal,* Vol. 22, pp. 493-520.

ARTHUR, W.B. (1989): "Competing technologies, increasing returns, and lock-in by historical events", *Economic Journal,* Vol. 99, pp. 116-131.

BAQUÍA (2001): "El business to business en España y las oportunidades sectoriales", *http://www.baquia.com/com/20010214/bre00022.html,* 25th 2001.

BARNEY, J. (1986): "Organizational culture: Can it be a source of competitive advantage?", *Academy of Management Review,* Vol. 11, pp. 656-665.

BARNEY, J. (1991): "Firm resources and sustained competitive advantage", *Journal of Management,* Vol. 17, Nº 1, pp. 99-120.

BARNEY, J. (1995): "Looking inside for competitive advantage", *Academy of Management Executive,* Vol. 9, Nº 4, pp. 49-61.

BARNEY, J. (1996): Gaining and sustaining competitive advantage, Addison-Wesley, Reading.

BHARADWAJ, A.S. (2000): "A resource-based perspective on information technology capability and firm performance", *Management Information Systems Quarterly,* Vol. 24, Nº 1, pp. 169-198.

BRUQUE CÁMARA, S. (2001): "Tecnologías de la Información, recursos coadyuvantes y ventaja competitiva. Especial referencia al sector de distribución farmacéutica en España", Forthcoming, Universidad de Jaén.

BRYNJOLFSSON, E. (1993): "The productivity paradox of Information Technology", *Communications of the ACM,* Vol. 26, Nº 12, pp. 67-77.

BRYNJOLFSSON, E. and HITT, L. (1996): "The customer counts", *InformationWeek,* Nº 596, pp. 48-53.

BRYNJOLFSSON, E.; HITT, L. and YANG, S. (2000): "Intangible assets: How the interaction of computers and organizational structure affects stock market valuations", Mass. Institute of Technology Working Paper, *http://ecommerce.mit.edu/erik/index.html,* 30th November 2000.

BRYNJOLFSSON, E. and HITT, L. (2001): "Beyond computation: Information technology, organizational transformation and business performance", *Unpublished,* MIT, Cambridge, Ma.

CASH, J.R. and KONSYNSKI, B.R. (1985): "Information Systems redraw competitive boundaries", *Harvard Business Review,* Vol. 63, Nº 2, pp. 134-142.

CLEMONS, E.K. and KIMBROUGH, S.O. (1986): "Information systems, telecommunications, and their effects on industrial organization", *Proceedings of the Seventh International Conference on Information Systems,* San Diego, December 1986, pp. 99-108.

CLEMONS, E.K. and ROW, M.C. (1991): "Sustaining IT advantage: the role of structural differences", *Management Information Systems Quarterly,* September, pp. 275-292.

CRUZ, J. (1996): "La política de telecomunicaciones. Distintos enfoques: EE.UU., Gran Bretaña y la Unión Europea", *Boletín del Círculo de Empresarios,* Nº 61, pp. 57-75.

DIERICKX, I. and COOL, K. (1989): "Asset stock accumulation and sustainability of competitive advantage", *Management Science,* Vol. 35, Nº 12, December, pp. 1504-1511.

ESCOBAR ESPINAR, M. (1999): *El comercio electrónico, perspectiva presente y futura en España,* Escuela de Organización Industrial, EOI, Madrid.

FERNÁNDEZ DE LIS, P. (2001): "La lección amarga de Teknoland", El Pais, Business section, p. 7, 25th February 2001.

FOMENTO DE LA PRODUCCIÓN (1997): *España 30.000,* Fomento de la Producción, Barcelona

FOMENTO DE LA PRODUCCIÓN (1998): *España 30.000,* Fomento de la Producción, Barcelona.

FOMENTO DE LA PRODUCCIÓN (1999a): *España 30.000,* Fomento de la Producción, Barcelona.

FOMENTO DE LA PRODUCCIÓN (1999b): *Las 2.000 mayores empresas españolas,* Fomento de la Producción, Barcelona.

FOMENTO DE LA PRODUCCIÓN (2000): *España 30.000,* Fomento de la Producción, Barcelona.

GRANT, R.M. (1996): "Prospering in dynamically-competitive environments: organizational capability as knowledge integration", *Organization Science,* Vol. 7, Nº 4, pp. 375-387.

HALL, R. (1992): "The intangible analysis of strategic resources", *Strategic Management Journal,* Vol. 13, pp. 135-144.

HITT, L. and BRYNJOLFSSON, E. (1995): "Productivity without profit?: Three measures of I.T. value", *Sloan School of Management,* Working Paper.

HITT, L. and BRYNJOLFSSON, E. (1996): "Productivity, business profitability, and consumer surplus: three different measures of information technology value", *Management Information Systems Quarterly,* Vol. 20, Nº 2, pp. 121-143.

KAUFMAN, F. (1966): "Data systems that cross company boundaries", *Harvard Business Review,* January-February, pp. 141-145.

LEE, J. and MILLER, D. (1999): "People Matter: commitment to employees, strategy and performance in Korean firms", *Strategic Management Journal,* Vol. 20, pp. 579-593.

LIEBERMAN, M.B. and MONTGOMERY, D.B. (1988): "First mover advantages", *Strategic Management Journal,* Vol. 9, pp. 41-58.

MARTÍNEZ, F. (1996): "Cooperativa de Farmacéuticos de España: Cofares", *Revesco, Revista de Estudios Cooperativos,* Nº 62, pp. 127-176.

MATA, F.J., FUERST, W.L. and BARNEY, J.B. (1995): "Information technology and sustained competitive advantage: A resource based analysis", *Management Information Systems Quarterly,* December, pp. 487-505.

McCUNE, J. (1998): "The productivity paradox", *HR Focus,* Vol. 75, Nº 4, pp. 1-4.

McFARLAN, W. (1984): "Information technology changes the way you compete", *Harvard Business Review,* Vol. 62, Nº 3.

McLEAN, E.R. and SODEN, J.V. (1977): *Strategic Planning for Management Information Systems,* John Wiley & Sons, N. York.

MEHRA, A. (1996): "Resource and market based determinants of performance in the U.S. Banking industry", *Strategic Management Journal,* Vol. 17, pp. 307-322.

MILLER, D. and SHAMSIE, J. (1996): "The resource based view of the firm in two environments: The Hollywood film studios from 1936 to 1965", *Academy of Management Journal,* Vol. 39, Nº. 3, pp. 519-543.

PARSONS, G.L. (1983): "Information Technology: A new competitive weapon", *Sloan Management Review,* Fall, pp. 3-14.

PORTER, M. E. (1980): Competitive strategy: techniques for analyzing industries and competitors, Free Press, New York.

PORTER, M. E. and MILLAR, V.E. (1985): "How information gives you competitive advantage", *Harvard Business Review,* Vol. 64, Nº 4, pp. 149-160.

PORTER, M. E.and MILLAR, V.E. (1986): "Cómo obtener ventajas competitivas por medio de la información", *Harvard Deusto Business Review,* 1st Trimester, pp. 4-20.

POWELL, T.C. (1992): "Strategic alignment as competitive advantage", *Strategic Management Journal,* Vol. 13, Nº 7, pp. 551-558.

POWELL, T.C. (1996): "How much does industry matter?, An alternative empirical test", *Strategic Management Journal,* Vol. 17, pp. 323-334.

POWELL, T.C. and DENT-MICALLEF, A. (1997): "Information technology as competitive advantage: the role of human, business and technology resources", *Strategic Management Journal,* Vol. 18, Nº 5, pp. 375-405.

PRAHALAD, C.K. and HAMEL, G. (1990): "The core competences of the corporation", *Harvard Business Review,* May-June, pp. 79-91.

RAYPORT, J.F. and SVIOKLA, J.J. (1995): "Exploiting the Virtual Value Chain", *Harvard Business Review,* November-December, pp. 75-85.

RICARDO, D. (1817): Principles of political economy and taxation, Murray, London.

ROSS, J.W.; BEATH, C. M. and GOODHUE, D.L. (1996): "Develop long-term competitiveness through IT assets", *Sloan Management Review,* Fall, pp. 31-42.

ROUSE, M.J. and DAELLENBACH, U.S. (1999): "Rethinking research methods for the resource-based perspective: isolating sources of sustainable competitive advantage", *Strategic Management Journal,* Vol. 20, pp. 487-494.

SOLOW, R. M. 1987. We'd better watch out, New York Times Book Review, 12nd July, p. 36.

STRASSMANN, P.A. (1990): *The business value of computers,* Information Economic Press, New Canaan.

STRASSMANN, P.A. (1997): "Facts and fantasies about productivity",: *http://www.strassmann.com/pubs/fnf/factnfantasy.shtml,* 10th March 2000.

STRASSMANN, P.A. (1998): "Of men and machines: Productivity declines", *Forbes,* 11st June.

STRASSMANN, P.A. (1999): "Numbers indicate that firms overspend on information management", *InfoWorld,* 22nd March.

TEECE, D.J.; PISANO, G. and SHUEN, A. (1997): "Dynamic capabilities and strategic management", *Strategic Management Journal,* Vol. 18, Nº 7, pp. 509-533.

ULLMANN, K.D. and VOSS, C. A. (2000): "Bridges and motorways. Exploring the strategic impact of using SAP R/3 in manufacturing businesses", *Proceedings of the I World Congress on Production and Operations Management, POM 2000,* Sevilla.

VENKATRAMAN, N. (1994): "IT enabled business transformation: from automation to business scope redefinition", *Sloan Management Review,* Winter, pp. 73-87.

VISAUTA VINACUA, B. (1998): *Análisis estadístico con SPSS para Windows,* Mc-Graw Hill, Madrid.

WERNELFELT, B. (1984): "A resource based view of the firm", *Strategic Management Journal,* Vol. 5, pp. 171-180.

TOWARDS EXTENDED PRICE MODELS IN XML STANDARDS FOR ELECTRONIC PRODUCT CATALOGS

Oliver Kelkar
Competence Center Electronic Business, Fraunhofer IAO, Nobelstr. 12c, 70569 Stuttgart, Germany
Email: oliver.kelkar@iao.fhg.de

Joerg Leukel, Volker Schmitz
Department of Information Systems, University of Essen, Universitaetsstr. 9, 45117 Essen, Germany
Email: joerg.leukel@uni-essen.de, volker.schmitz@uni-essen.de

Key words: XML Standards, E-Catalog, E-Procurement, B2B, Price Model.

Abstract: The extending interorganizational electronic business (business-to-business) means system to system communication between business partners without any manual interaction. This has led to the development of new standards for the exchange of electronic product catalogs (e-catalogs), which are the starting point for business-to-business trading. E-catalogs contain various information about products, essential are price information. Prices are used for buying decisions and following order transactions. While simple price models are often sufficient for the description of indirect goods (e.g. office supplies), other goods and lines of business make higher demands. In this paper we examine what price information is contained in commercial XML standards for the exchange of product catalog data. For that purpose we bring the different implicit price models of the examined catalog standards together and provide a generalized model.

1 INTRODUCTION

Given the rapid growth and success of web-based procurement systems, e-catalogs gain an outstanding importance. Both in buy-side systems, the so-called e-procurement systems, and on B2B markets, e-catalogs are the foundation for buying decisions and the release of order transactions (Baron/Shaw/Bailey, 2001). E-catalogs are exchanged between companies. The catalog-supplying company delivers the catalog as an electronic document to the catalog-receiving company, which imports the catalog data into a procurement application (target system).

In catalogs the supplier transmits the product prices. The applicable catalog standards provide more or less powerful structures for the representation of prices. In other words, each catalog standard contains an implicit price model. The capacity of these models is very different; in particular no standard is complete, meaning that it is not possible to represent all real world price models in an e-catalog using one of the available standards.

The process of constructing a general price model for a XML catalog standard should take in mind the spectrum of pricing and pricing strategies. Therefore this paper is structured as follows: First we will describe pricing, as it is used in business-relationships and determine the requirements on our model. The second step is a closer look at the use of catalog data in e-business to obtain further requirements. The main task is the examination of price models of six commercial catalog standards. We will check how the selected standards meet the requirements. Finally we will present a price model, which integrates all relevant aspects and can serve to improve commercial standards.

2 PRICING IN MARKETING

Our basis for the construction of price models is the spectrum of pricing strategies and tactics, which can be used in business relationships between suppliers and buyers. The price of a product is not limited to a direct quotation, which consists of the amount, currency and tax, but it is the result of a system of price components and rules. We define a price as the value agreed upon by the buyer and the supplier in an exchange; it is one of the four controllable variables of the marketing mix: product, promotion, price and place (Nagle/Holden, 1995).

The aim of many pricing strategies is to sell equal or similar products to different customers paying different prices. Differential pricing tries to gain higher profits in imperfect markets. For this to be effective the market must be divisible and the different segments must have different levels of demand. In general we can assume seven types of pricing:

a) Individual Pricing
b) Product Form Pricing
c) Quantity Pricing
d) Bundled Pricing
e) Customer Segment Pricing
f) Geographical Pricing
g) Promotional Pricing

Individual Pricing says that the price is dependent on the buyer or customer. Especially the price is the result of an individual negotiation and fixed in a bilateral agreement; the price is customer-specific. To express this in an e-catalog, we need price types indicating, how to read a given price. Common price types are gross list price, net list price and net customer price. Additionally, buyer and supplier can define own price types (e.g. a net wholesale price with express delivery), hence it should be possible to use user-defined types in catalog documents.

An essential instrument for individual prices is granting discounts. A discount is a reduction of the price offered by a supplier to a buyer. In most cases a discount relates to an otherwise valid list price. Simple price models allow the declaration of only one discount. The effect is that two discounts must be transformed into one. For example:

- price $100
- regular discount 5%: new price $95
- special discount 10%: final price: $95 x 0,9 = $85.5
- transform: ($100-$85.5) / $100 = 14.5%

Offering slightly different variants of the same basic product with different prices is a case of *Product Form Pricing*. It is closely related to Product Differentiation, a strategy that attempts (through design, packaging, positioning, etc.) to make a clear distinction between products serving the same or different market segments. Product Form Pricing means, that one or more characteristics of the basic product are varied, so that the offered product itself is varied. Hence it follows that we need complex product models to represent these variations in an e-catalog. One component of those complex product models is the price calculation, so the price model. Due to this close relationship we look at Product Form Pricing as a question of extended price models.

The dependence of a price on the quantity being ordered is subject of *Quantity Pricing*. Its central instrument is the quantity discount, which is often defined through a quantity scale. A quantity scale defines for each non-overlapping quantity interval a product price, which is decreasing with higher quantity. The economic reasons are decreasing marginal costs for the supplier and at the same time decreasing marginal utility for the buyer. We can distinguish two types of quantity scales: is the relevant price applied to the whole order quantity or do we apply a different price for each reached interval; e.g. the first twenty pieces: $5, the next twenty $4,50.

Bundling is a technique used by suppliers that consists of packaging goods or services and selling them as a single package. The price of the package is less than the sum of the included product prices. The effect of *Bundled Pricing* can be very different: either a set of rules and related discounts determines the price or the price is independent from the single prices.

A close relation exists between Individual Pricing and *Customer Segment Pricing*. Latter sets the price in dependence on the membership of the buyer to a specific segment of customers (e.g. industry, wholesale trade, retail trade, consumers). The price is not individual and not fixed in a bilateral agreement.

Geographical Pricing varies the price dependent on the place of delivery. Though this does not include costs for transportation and shipping, but it refers to other, geographic specific aspects, which often deal with separated, national markets. Coming back to e-catalogs, we should be able to determine prices for one or a set of territories (e.g. countries). Close to this determination is a respective currency tag.

A firm can set different prices for limited periods with the instrument of *Promotional Pricing*. Special promotional efforts are one reason for this. Seasonal issues, which lead to alternating prices over time (e.g. raw materials) or restricted availability of products (e.g. collections of clothing), are another reason. The conclusion for e-catalogs is that it must be possible to express none-overlapping periods of validity and specify the type or promotional reason for the period.

3 PRODUCT CATALOGS IN E-PROCUREMENT

The theoretical concepts of pricing must be adjusted to the specific requirements of electronic procurement and enriched with further aspects. For that purpose we will point out some characteristics of e-procurement in B2B.

The main motivation of e-procurement is the reduction of process costs through speeding up and reorganizing procurement process on the basis of a convenient and fast data exchange. This leads to the extension of markets to a global level and enables in short time the interaction between large numbers of market participants with low entry costs (Gebauer/ Beam/Segev, 1997). Electronic B2B communication needs, beside a technical infrastructure, a common language or at least accepted standards on the level of business data and documents.

Current examinations see many problems and obstacles for the lasting success of e-business solutions, especially of market places. Catalog management is considered as one critical success factor (Aberdeen Group, 2001). It comprehends all tasks of creating, handling and exchanging electronic catalog data. Many companies are still not able to deliver e-catalogs in appropriate form and quality.

Both in buyer-side systems (e-procurement systems), and on B2B markets, e-catalogs are the foundation for buying decisions and the release of order transactions. They serve as marketing instruments for the presentation of products as well as substitutes for offers, and must meet the requirements of professional buyers as well as ordinary employees. Next we will outline the application fields of e-catalogs in different business models.

Public web shops are the first type of B2B applications. They offer non-personalized product information and list prices. The access is not restricted. In addition, customer web shops offer customer-specific prices and sometimes customer-specific products. The access is limited and personalized. The use of multiple currencies and country-specific product variants and availability is necessary if the customers come from different countries.

The intermediary between suppliers and buyers in a marketplace builds customer-specific catalogs (or views on catalogs) and manages a multi-vendor master catalog (Ginsburg/Gebauer/Segev, 1999). Open accessible markets often demand supplier catalogs with graduated prices, multi-language product descriptions, country-specific currencies and even country-specific products. Closed markets moreover demand customer-specific prices, product assortments and products.

Table 1 shows the mentioned business models and their requirements as they relate to prices and products.

	multi-language	**multi-territory**	**multi-prices**	**event-prices**	**customer prices**	**customer products**	**territory products**	**customer features**	**customer assort-ments**
public web shop (sell-side)	+	+	-	+	+	-	+	-	-
customer web shop (sell-side)	+	+	++	+	++	++	+	++	++
public marketplace (intermediary)	+	+	-	+	++	-	+	-	-
customer marketplace (intermediary)	++	++	++	+	++	++	++	++	++
e-procurement system (buy-side)	+	+	-	+	++	++	++	++	++

++ = common requirement, + = possible requirement, - = no requirement

Table 1: Requirements of Business Models

The provision of catalog data for the named requirements and application needs a uniformed or standardized model. The use of catalog data makes high demands on the model relating to universal validity, flexibility and clearness (van Blommestein/ Boekhoudt, 2001).

Catalog-oriented e-procurement has its roots in direct purchasing systems, these are Intranet applications which allow any employee to order needed goods of indirect demand without the participation of a purchasing department (Granada Research, 1999). Many catalog standards are tailored to indirect goods, which are not the subject of production processes. Thus the representation of direct goods and complex products is not possible. Particularly the standard price models are not sufficient to model all pricing strategies and tactics of suppliers. For example: product variants, dynamic prices and multi-staged discount systems.

The stated situation is one reason why direct or complex products are seldom integrated in e-procurement systems or catalog-oriented markets. Subsequently we notice that software companies and market places develop their own systems and modify or expand catalog standards to solve the problems. This must be seen critically as new proprietary systems are created.

Besides meta information (e.g. provider, recipient, format), a catalog document contains two areas of data: master data and transaction data. The master data consists of information about the products and this information does not change over time (or very seldom), therefore it has to be updated not very often (e.g. product number, classification, features). In contrast to this, transaction data shows a higher updating frequency. Prices, availability and delivery times are transaction data.

For the exchange of catalog data some commercial standards offer transaction types:

- complete catalog (master and transaction data)
- update of one or more products (master and
- transaction data)
- update of the prices of one or more products
- (transaction data)

The update of transaction data can be done in an asynchronous or synchronous way. For example, an electronic price list is an asynchronous update transaction, while an online query for prices or availabilities is a synchronous transaction.

4 PRICE MODELS IN XML CATALOG STANDARDS

Being aware of the pricing instruments and the general conditions of catalog-based e-procurement now we can analyze existing price models in commercial XML standards. Object of the analysis are *structures* representing price information. This is a main difference to the marketing view on pricing, which emphasizes the *economic reasons and motivations* for a specific price instrument (Klein/Loebbecke, 1999).

Starting points for answering the question, which price information is modeled in catalog standards, are the specifications, documentations and (if available) the data models. The analysis covered 20 XML standards in all. Due to limited space we will concentrate on six selected standards. The selection contains the most important standards being used in B2B e-commerce:

- cXML and xCBL: two standards developed by major e-business software companies (Ariba, 2001; CommerceOne, 2001)
- BMEcat: successful standard in Germany and Europe (Schmitz/Kelkar/Pastoors, 2001)
- EAN.UCC: standard by EAN (EAN International, 2001)
- OAGIS: documents will be integrated into ebXML (Open Applications Group, 2001)
- RosettaNet: horizontal standard (RosettaNet, 2001)

Table 2 shows basic information about the selected standards.

The result of our empirical analysis is a general price model, which will be presented as an XML Schema (W3C, 2001). During the following description of the price model and its components we state the names of the relevant data elements in angular brackets, e.g. *(Price)* as the root element.

4.1 Structure of Price Models

In Section 2 we have described the instruments of pricing, though we can not assume that neither these instruments are fully integrated in product catalogs nor that they are represented in an one-to-one relation. Rather catalog standards introduce a couple of concepts that are necessary to reduce the complexity of a price model:

(1) Concept of Levels: Assuming that a price model consists of components, which together describe the product price, we can identify three business levels for price components: Product, Transaction, Contract.

Standard	cXML	xCBL	BMEcat	EAN.UCC	OAGIS	RosettaNet
Version	1.2.007	3.5	1.2	1.0	7.2.1	1.0
	November 2001	November 2001	March 2001	July 2001	November 2001	June 2000
Organization	Ariba, Inc.	CommerceOne, Inc.	eBSC	EAN	Open Applications Group	RosettaNet
Line of Business	independent	independent	independent	independent	independent	IT & Electronic Components
Origin	USA	USA	Germany	International	International	International
URL	www.cxml.org	www.xcbl.org	www.bmecat.org	www.uc-council.org	www.openapplications.org	www.rosettanet.org

Table 2: Selected XML Catalog Standards

Product catalogs represent the level Product, all price components are assigned to products of the catalog. In contrast to this, the components on the level Transaction describe factors, which are determined by the order transaction, e.g. costs for packing and transportation of all products of one specific order. The level Contract comprises definitions, which are fixed in a bilateral agreement. A contract aggregates timely or functionally related transactions. For example, at the end of a period the supplier gives an allowance on a previously defined order volume. In most cases product catalogs reference to one or more contracts; the contract itself is not specified through a contract model.

(2) Concept of Dependence: The price of a product is dependent on many factors (e.g. customer, territory). To describe a price we must set the values of these determining factors, so we determine the validity of the price. The set of factors leads to an even model.

(3) Concept of Allowances and Charges: All components of a price model, which result in a reduction or addition to a basic price, can be united to a model of allowances and charges. By way of explanation it is sufficient to specify the type or reason for the allowance or charge.

4.2 Product Prices and their Determining Factors

The real product price is dependent on many factors: order unit, place of delivery, customer, price type, contract, (time) interval and currency. Each of these factors is independent from the others and can be used without any overlapping to specify an actual price. The theoretically number of prices for one product is calculable through the combination of values of all factors. Many catalog standards make restrictions by allowing only one value per definition (e.g. all prices are net list prices), or the supplier must set default-values for all products of the catalog document (e.g. the currency of all prices is Euro). The complexity of a price model is reduced through these two measures.

Afterwards we explain relevant factors:

(1) Order Unit: The most evident factor of a price is the order quantity and order unit. Though equal basic products with different order units can be seen as separate products also.

(2) Territory: Prices are due to Geographical Pricing often dependent on the place of delivery. Therefore, a supplier is able to set different prices for each territory. Often logistic costs, taxes and duties are included, so these price components must not be declared explicit. (*DeliveryRegion*)

(3) Customer: Individual Pricing is characteristic for B2B relations; it leads to customer-specific prices. In multi-buyer catalogs it is necessary to transfer, besides the customer-independent core data, for each customer individual prices. (*Customer*)

(4) Price Type: Price types serve to express short and clear statements about the price. In many cases, the trade level of the buyer and the handling of turnover taxes are stated (gross or net prices). Information about special promotions (restricted by time and/or region) is also a matter of price types. As far as that goes price types are a component for implementing Individual, Geographical and Promotional Pricing. (*PriceType*)

(5) Interval: In general prices are valid for a limited period of time. Hence it is evident to differentiate prices to their interval of validity (Promotional Pricing). If no interval is transferred in an e-catalog, then the price is valid until a new price is transferred. (*ValidityTimePeriod*)

(6) Contract: A skeleton or project agreement defines often all price components, which can be fixed in advance. In this case the complexity of price factors in e-catalogs is very small. The catalog supplier has to give a reference to the agreement (Individual Pricing). (*Agreements*)

(7) Currency: Each price is to be expressed in a currency. For internationally used e-catalogs it is important to assign at the same time prices in different currencies. The currency results from Geographical Pricing. (*Currency*)

For example most of the mentioned factors are implemented in the BMEcat standard (Hümpel/Schmitz, 2000). The data element ARTICLE_PRICE_DETAILS can be used multiple with disjunctive intervals. The key values for ARTICLE_PRICE are currency

(PRICE_CURRENCY), lower bound of a quantity scale (LOWER_BOUND), a set of territories (TERRITORY) and the attribute price type, which is not shown in figure 1.

Besides the factors we must take in mind that the price quotation itself can show a varied complexity (*ProductPrice*). In principle we can differentiate three complexity levels:

- Price quotation through an amount and an optional multiplier, e.g. $5 per 1,000 pieces (*SimpleAmount*)
- The price is linear dependent on one or many product features, which will be instantiated through a real order transaction, e.g. 5 piece of cable each with a length of 6 meters. (*ParametrizedAmount*)
- The price is dependent on any parameters and it will be calculated through a formula at the time of order. Examples for these parameters are market prices, delivery terms, delivery range and delivery time. (*AmountFormula*)

In a special case, the price is not expressed in the catalog document, but it must be requested from the supplier at the moment of order (*PriceRequest*).

4.3 Product Bundling

As described above Bundled Pricing means packaging goods or services and selling them as a single item. The price of the package is less than the sum of the included product prices. In e-catalog we can look at product bundles as separate products with a price being independent from the single prices. To sum it up, all types of pricing can be applied to a bundle as well. (*SetPrice*)

4.4 Allowances and Charges

Allowances and charges are a powerful instrument for pricing. Analogous to this, the complexity of necessary models must be seen: it ranges from simple multipliers to high complex relations. (*AllowOrCharge*)

The calculation of allowances and charges happens on a basis (*BaseType*), which identifies how allowances and charges (*AllowOrChargeValue*) flow into the price calculation. There are four different methods, which all are realizing both allowances and charges:

- relative, percent: the allowance or charge is multiplied with the product price using a factor (e.g. 10% discount per product, factor is 0.9) (*PercentageFactor*)
- relative, amount: the allowance or charge is added to the product price with a fixed value (e.g. $10 for shipping). (*MonetaryAmount*)
- absolute: the product price is replaced by the allowance or charge. This can be combined with rules. Minimum or maximum rules are often used, e.g. use the lower amount of the product price and the allowance. (*MonetaryAmount*)
- natural: the number of delivered products is higher than the number ordered, but only the ordered products are charged (e.g. rebate in kind). (*AdditionalOrderUnits*)

To reveal why an allowance or charge is applied, we need a characterization (*AllowOrChargeType*) optionally combined with a description (*AllowOrChargeDescription*). The first aspect is whether it is a volume-based or a functional allowance (or charge). In case of the volume-based kind, the allowance begins to take effect if a certain volume limit is crossed (*PriceBracket*). These volume limits are either quantitative (e.g. quantity scale, (*UpperBoundAmount*)) or in terms of value (e.g. allowance at the end of a settlement period, (*UpperBoundQuantity*)). Both allowances are instruments of Quantity Pricing. The functional allowances relate to performance-oriented criterions, these criterions are described through textual remarks or special codes (e.g. packaging flat rates, duties or cash discounts (Product Form Pricing).

The relative amount allowances can be modeled in another way: often separate products are inserted instead of charges. Theses products describe the

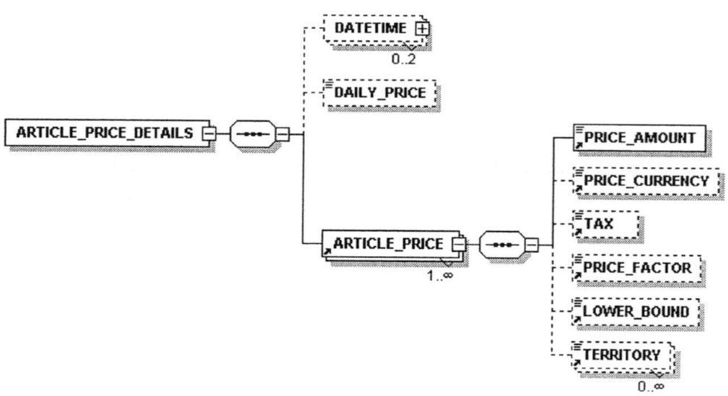

Figure 1: Price Factors in XML Standard BMEcat

charge and appear as additional positions in the invoice. To use this alternative in e-catalogs, we need relations between products, which are similar to configurable products. Though product configuration is a not subject of this paper.

The kind of calculation of allowances and charges determines how and when the amount is credited to the buyer (*SettlementType*). This is according to the Concept of Levels. An allowance can be credited for all products of a transaction or at the end of a contract period.

The order of calculation of allowances and charges plays an important part *(SequenceNumber)*. A multistage system of discounts needs a defined order of calculation. On each stage of this system two or more discounts "of equal rights" can exists at the same time. In this case, the discounts have to be added before they can be applied.

Another question is how to document the allowances in an e-catalog. An answer is to give the final price and name the applied discounts (e.g. \$95 including 5% senior discount). The alternative is to name the list price and all discounts without giving the final price (e.g. \$100, 5% discount, 8% special discount, plus 16% tax).

4.5 Taxes

Taxes are a special form of charges, which must be - due to their legal importance - expressed separately. According to country and line of business it is necessary to describe more than one tax. (*Tax*)

5 COMPARISON & SYNTHESIS OF PRICE MODELS

To compare the price models of the selected standard, we show in table 3 the six determining factors. A plus ("+") indicates that the corresponding factor can be set multiple for each product. For example, in BMEcat the prices of a product are valid for different territories and intervals, in different types and currencies, but all prices relate to the same customer (no multi-buyer catalogs).

	Territory	**Customer**	**Price Types**	**Interval**	**Contract**	**Currency**
cXML	-	-	-	-	-	-
xCBL	-	+	+	+	-	+
BMEcat	+	-	+	+	-	+
EAN UCC	-	-	-	+	-	-
OAGIS	-	+	+	-	-	-
RosettaNet	-	-	-	-	-	-

Table 3: Determining Parameters in XML Catalog Standards

	Basis				**Cal-cula-tion Order**	**Types**	**Scale**		**Kind of Calculation**
	relative, percent	**relative, amount**	**absolute**	**natu-ral**			**Quantity**	**Value**	
cXML	-	-	-	-	-	-	-	-	-
xCBL	-	-	-	-	-	-	-	-	-
BMEcat	+	-	-	-	-	-	+	-	-
EAN UCC	+	+	+	-	+	+	+	+	+
OAGIS	-	-	-	-	-	+	+	+	-
RosettaNet	-	-	-	-	-	-	+	+	-

Table 4: Allowances and Charge in XML Catalog Standards

The model components that specify allowances and charges are summarized in table 4.

On the basis of the model components, which were identified from the standards and structured above, we can develop a general model. The model in figure 2 uses the data element names that we have introduced before. To keep clearness, some simplifications are made. For example, elements that can appear more than once are not represented with an own container ("ListOf...").

The model shows only the level of product prices. It is possible to model the levels Contract and Transaction quite similar.

Further we have simplified the issues of price formulas (not handled in detail in this paper) and product bundling. All determining factors are modeled as mandatory elements; the reason is their meaning as key values. As explained in Section 3, an alternative would be to set default values for some or all factors in the catalog header. In this case, the data elements for factors are optional.

Figure 2: Derived Price Model

6 CONCLUSION

In this paper we have discussed the problem of modeling price information in e-catalogs and suggested a general price model for XML catalog standards, which is the result of a theoretical (pricing strategy) and empirical analysis (commercial standards).

We found out that the spectrum of real world price models is covered in a limited way by available standards. Speaking of the suppliers and buyers, it is necessary to represent more complex price models in catalog documents. For example, the industrial trade uses multi-staged discount systems along the trade levels. As long as this is not covered, we see a major obstacle for the fast success of e-business applications. On the other hand it is necessary to reduce the complexity of price models to be able to develop, deploy and handle a generalized model.

The developed model is the result of an empirical analysis catalog standards published at the time of the survey. As a general model it is in a position to represent all issues that are modeled by the available standards. The question of its general validity cannot be answered finally, since it is possible that in practice or theory price-relevant circumstances exist, which were considered so far by no standard. However, two modeling concepts increase the scope of validity considerably: On the one hand the Concept of Dependence and on the other hand the Concept of Allowances and Charages. If additional price determing factors are needed, then the Concept of Dependence can be extended by these easily. Besides price modeling, the representation of complex goods is another unsolved problem. This underlines our conviction that further research and standardization must be done to come to universal and accepted business documents.

REFERENCES

Aberdeen Group, 2001. *Content Integration: e-Catalog Aggregation for Buyers and Asset Control for Suppliers*, An Executive White Paper, Boston.

Ariba, 2001: *cXML*, Version 1.2.007. Online: http://xml.cxml.org/current/cXML.zip.

Baron, J. P. / Shaw, M. J. / Bailey, A. D., 2000. Web-based E-catalog systems in B2B Procurement. In *Communications of the ACM (CACM)*, Vol. 43 (2000), No. 5, p. 93-100.

CommerceOne, 2001: *XML Common Business Library (xCBL)*, version 3.5. Online: http://www.xcbl.org/xcbl35/xcbl35.html.

van Blommestein, F. / Boekhoudt, P., 2001. *Electronic Procurement of Technical Materials,* Project Report, Telematica Instituut, Netherlands.

EAN International, 2001: *EAN.UCC Business Message Standards*, Version 1.0, 2001. Online: http://www.uc-council.org.

Gebauer, J. / Beam, C. / Segev, A., 1997. *Impact of the Internet on Procurement,* Research Report 97-WP-1024, Haas School of Business, University of Berkeley.

Ginsburg, M. / Gebauer, J. / Segev, A., 1999. Multi-Vendor Electronic Catalogs to Support Procurement: Current Practice and Future Directions. In *12th International Bled Electronic Commerce Conference*, Bled, Slovenia.

Granada Research, 1999. *E-Catalog 99: Business-To-Business Electronic Catalog,* Technology Report, El Granada.

Hümpel, C. / Schmitz, V., 2001: BMEcat - an XML standard for electronic product data interchange. In: *Proceeding of the 1st German Conference XML 2000*, Heidelberg, Germany, p. 1-11.

Klein, S. / Loebbecke, C.: Signaling and Segmentation on Electronic Markets: Innovative Pricing Strategies for Improved Resource Allocation. In: *Proceedings of the 6th Research Symposium on Emerging Electronic Markets*, Muenster, Germany, p. 127-142.

Nagle, T. T. / Holden, R. K., 1995. *The Strategy and Tactics of Pricing: A Guide to Profitable Decision Making*, Prentice Hall, 2nd Edition.

Open Applications Group, 2001: *Open Applications Group Integration Specification*, Release 7.2.1. Online: http://www.openapplications.org.

RosettaNet, 2001: *PIP2A1: Distribute New Product Information*, Release 1.0. Online: http://www.rosettanet.org.

Schmitz, V. / Kelkar, O. / Pastoors, T., 2001: *Specification BMEcat,* Version 1.2. Online: http://www.bmecat.org.

A SEMI-UNIVERSAL E-COMMERCE AGENT
Domain-dependant information gathering

Aleksander Pivk, Matjaz Gams
Jozef Stefan Institute, Jamova 39, 1000 Ljubljana, Slovenia
Email: aleksander.pivk@ijs.si, matjaz.gams@ijs.si

Key words: Intelligent agent, Comparison shopping, Information extraction, Inductive learning, Wrapper.

Abstract: A universal e-commerce agent should provide commerce functions through the Internet by accessing arbitrary e-commerce sites and on this basis offer intelligent information services on its own. Our system ShinA (SHoppINg Assistant) is a semi-automatic e-commerce agent. It can enter an arbitrary e-commerce site by observing a human user performing the first query. By understanding key concepts of the first query, ShinA performs following queries by other users. In a consequence, a user enters ShinA by asking for a particular item, and ShinA provides all relevant e-commerce options from various providers. The major advantage of ShinA is a semi-automatic creation of a wrapper around a particular e-commerce site demanding minimal human interaction/corrections. ShinA is a successor of the EMA (EMployment Agent) prototype, which performs similar functions in job queries over the Internet.

1 INTRODUCTION

The explosive growth of the Internet has resulted in an overload of online information and services. There are millions of heterogeneous Internet sites offering various services thus making the Internet uncomprehendable for any single user conducting a non-trivial task. Therefore, serviceability of the Internet to a large degree depends on the amount of automated uniform user-friendly services, systems and tools [Levy, 2000; Pazienza, 1997].

Internet services offer several advantages over the classical ones thus already changing the way companies, customers and users perform their everyday activities. But the Internet introduces several disadvantages as well. In particular, the Internet is poorly structured, and disorganized [Lewis, 1999]. The negative side within the Internet success can be observed when gathering information. One of the first approaches, dealing with information overload, was to build a search engine. Typically, a user enters a couple of key words, and search engines find relevant sites over many different and heterogeneous Web sites.

This simple approach has several drawbacks. A shopper using search engines must visit innumerable e-commerce sites to check for a specific item. A shopper therefore manually visits various e-commerce sites, and further browses and/or searches for the particular product of interest [Balabanovic et al., 1995]. Furthermore, there is no single site that caters to all shopping needs, which increases the (user) search time for each new product category. It additionally involves getting acquainted to new interfaces, slowing down the user browsing and hindering impulse shopping. Also, this approach favors largest vendors (due to name-branding), which in turn reduces the effectiveness of the market. To further complicate matters, a customer soon becomes unaware of changes in pricing, availability, etc. unless he/she revisits the sites very frequently.

A universal tool extracting only information about a specific product would be much more helpful [Cowie et al., 1996]. But this task is a difficult one as the type, amount, and organization of the information provided on e-commerce sites differs from company to company. There have been several approaches in this direction with various benefits.

A rather simple approach is to provide alert services when a price changes. Several e-commerce sites already allow shoppers to sign up to receive price alerts that notify a shopper when the price of a product changes or falls below a specified amount. Some of the services require lengthy surveys to be filled out, while at the same time most provide little to no personalization. A further drawback of this approach is the weakening of user privacy that it implies [Jakobsson, 1998].

Another approach involves voluntary ratings and reviews of vendors and products by users, and the compilation of such information [Jakobsson et al., 1998; Pivk, 2001]. As in the previous approach, such recommendation systems are likely to reduce the size of the marketplace and to introduce bias, as it is difficult to obtain a sufficient number of ratings for every existing vendor, and to control the reliability of the sources.

As early as 1995, shopping agents [Maes, 1994; Maes et al., 1999] (also referred to as comparison shopping agents) were proposed as one of the most advanced solutions to find a product under the best terms (where price was the most important feature early on) among different e-commerce sites [Dastani et al., 1999.]. A shopping agent queries multiple sites on behalf of a shopper to gather pricing and other information on products and services. Most of these comparison-shopping agents [Greenwald et al., 1999] however present a marketplace that is biased in favor of those e-commerce sites that collaborate with the shopping agent. In addition to the biased marketplace, a shopper has only a limited number of e-commerce sites to choose from and often the participating sites do not offer the best prices. Typically, e-commerce sites that are included into agent's repertoire follow specific protocols or include hand-coded wrappers to transform data into agent-readable forms [Hammer, 1997; Muslea et al., 1998].

In this paper we present our new approach based on several years of experience with a semi-uniform intelligent agent [Levy et al., 2000] for employment task. Our principal goal is to improve the accessibility and expand the benefits of e-commerce shopping to consumers. We propose a new type of a shopping agent that extends the above approaches by providing automatic uniformity, user autonomy and privacy.

Uniformity refers to the ability of a shopping agent to automatically enter various e-commerce sites and adapt to the type, amount, and organization of the information provided by various companies. Since this property demands human-level intelligence, the task is beyond current computer systems. In reality, we accept limited uniformity, i.e. *semi-uniformity*.

Autonomy refers to the idea that a shopping agent can provide the best possible service by remaining as independent as possible from both customers and vendors. Autonomy from vendors implies that the service is to remain unbiased by performing wide searches (as opposed to only searching the databases of a few "preferred" vendors). This can be achieved by progress in making interfaces more uniform, and by improved methods for interpreting potential hits. Autonomy from the customer means that users can be relieved from the tedious task of searching for information and of needing to adjust to different e-commerce sites.

Our research addresses the *privacy* of the shopper by concealing the identity and behavior of the user. However, we note that the privacy provided is conditional, and should be selectively revoked if abuse is suspected. The aspects of our proposed agent provide for an unbiased marketplace where the user benefits in many respects.

2 EMA

EMA (EMployment Agent) is an intelligent employment agent providing employment information in a way similar to human employment agents [Gams, 2001]. An Internet-based intelligent employment agent should perform like a human agent providing basic information about available jobs and available workers, and try to match these two databases as efficiently as possible (Figure 1).

Employment is not a typical e-commerce domain; however, there are many similarities. Internet systems in both domains offer information about desired objects, which differ in properties, benefits and costs. Users browse through a large number of potential candidates and compare several similar possibilities to finally choose specific objects. In addition, employment objects - jobs and available users - are among most valuable human resources.

Unemployment is one of major problems in developed countries although trends differ in various states. Even after September 11th events, the unemployment rate in Europe is roughly twice higher than in the U.S. thus presenting one of the major national and international problems. Users typically want to get a job - any job, a good job, better than a current one. In this way, a typical task of the agent is to find relevant information about a specific job offer (analogy – a specific e-commerce item) from various information sources. Situation in Slovenia is similar to that in Europe. With 2.000.000 inhabitants there are around 100.000 unemployed workers and 100.000 new job offers each year.

EMA is a "classical" agent providing user-friendly information on demand or when it notices relevant information. EMA can store search patterns, perform search on its own or following direct commands, it can send online replies or offline emails regarding vacant jobs or available workers. EMA can store and observe interesting WEB sites chosen by users, and match available jobs and workers.

EMA is a big software system especially for our R&D group of intelligent systems at the Jozef Stefan Institute. EMA consists of several modules and submodules, written in different programming languages and running on different platforms and operating systems. The system is a 30K lines program written mainly in C, partly in other languages and by Internet programming tools. Together with text and data it occupies 30 MB on a disk.

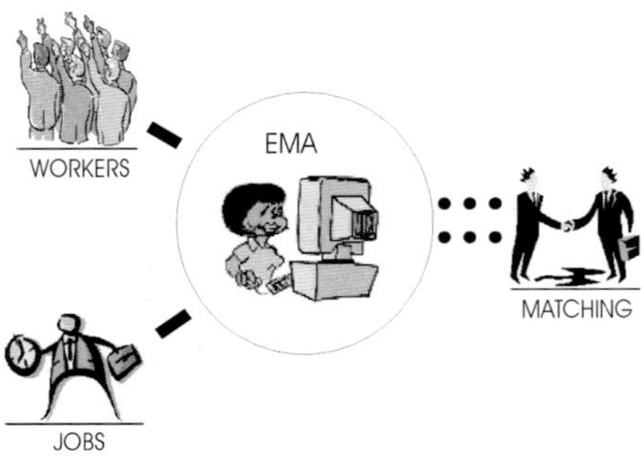

Figure 1: The basic task of the EMA Internet-based intelligent employment agent is to provide employment information as human agents do.

Several modules of the EMA system represented a novel research at that time in Slovenia, including language and translation capabilities such as Slovenian text-to-speech interface, some semantics like ontologies about profession definitions or ability to access an arbitrary employment site and perform connections on its own.

Language functions.

A common input to EMA is a partially constrained Slovenian text. In bulletin boards, the language is a matter of choice, but titles and information are either in Slovene or in English. Consequently, majority of text is either Slovene or English, with a couple of exceptions. No censorship is performed regarding language or specific details as long as input if dedicated to the desired employment task and inside minimal decency requirements.

The system is capable of translating Slovene text into English. The translation is based on a dictionary consisting of up to four words observed before in the employment data. New combinations are in the worst case translated as direct word-by-word translation and stored for further overview by humans. Stored combinations are sorted by frequency and translated by humans if reasonable. In addition, the translation system looks into the morphology dictionary to capture different forms of the same words. Finally, a spell-checker module corrects spelling errors. The translation is currently not yet at the level performed by systems translating between larger European languages; however, it is sufficiently good to enable understanding since the syntax is quite limited. The Internet site of the EMA system is presented in Figure 2

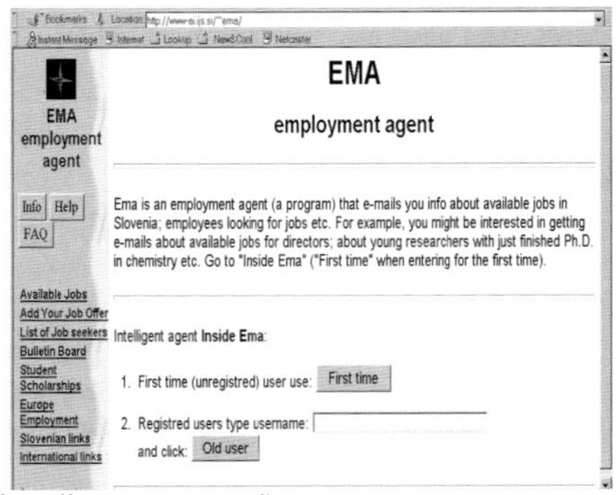

(http://www.ess.gov.si).

Figure 2: Home site of the intelligent employment agent

Semantics.

EMA performs some of its advanced functions based on ontologies. In this way, EMA understands the basic employment tasks. One of the most common employment tasks (besides basic queries) is to find some relation between different job descriptions and jobs definitions. The former also represents the basic concept of all employment tasks. E.g., from a basic search query consisting of applicant's properties and desires, one should extract relevant job offers. Or, from a job definition one should look for available workers. With machine and statistical text-learning methods we [Bezek et al., 2001; Freitag, 1998; Mladenic, 1999] have designed ontologies, i.e. meta-knowledge about job definitions from interesting words.

Semi-uniformity.

During the first years of the EMA system, several competing Internet-based employment sites were designed. Since EMA was a national employment site sponsored by Employment Services of Slovenia (ESS), an idea emerged to represent also the information from other employment sites. Instead of handwriting wrappers around each particular employment site, we have designed an algorithm that semi-automatically [Ashish et al., 1997, Kusmerick et al., 1997] attaches to other employment sites and then automatically gathers information from those particular sites. Although the algorithm published in [Gams, 2001] was never fully implemented, we have designed two slightly modified modules of this kind and implemented them in EMA. Another version was independently designed by a student group (JobProvider) on the basis of lectures of the second author at Faculty of economics. All versions were functional for a particular time thus showing that the idea is sound. On the basis of these experiences we have decided to design another system, the ShinA system, for e-commerce tasks [Pivk et al., 2000].

The EMA agent was and still is among most successful applications of intelligent agents in Slovenia and in Central Europe. In the first year of its implementation, our country was the third in Europe to offer national employment information through the Internet. At that time, we were the first country in the world to provide over 90% of all nationally available jobs on the Internet. On the other hand, in absolute terms there are employment systems in big countries or employment systems connected to major Internet information providers such as Yahoo or AltaVista that provide orders of magnitude bigger amounts of employment information.

EMA was among the most often visited serious sites in Slovenia. At its best, there were over 200.000 visits monthly which represents one tenth of the whole population. Most of the visitors were driven by unemployment and partially by ambition to find better job.

3 SHINA

A shopping assistant is a mediator system that automatically collects the product description from a number of online stores on a user's behalf. ShinA is based on the EMA employment-agent system, but performs a slightly different task of a shopping assistant. Moreover, ShinA is reprogrammed from a scratch using only experiences and some algorithms of EMA. ShinA's essential ability of semi-automatic gathering information from various sites replaces hand-coding of systems called wrappers [Yang et al., 2000].

3.1 Wrapper

There is a classical solution when dealing with heterogeneous information sources (in our case e-commerce sites), where each source has a unique way of providing information to the user, without considering a priori any program or agent to analyze it. In such environment, an agent may be able to integrate information from those sources, if only there existed a communicator-translator, generally referred to as wrapper, to produce translation rule for each store.

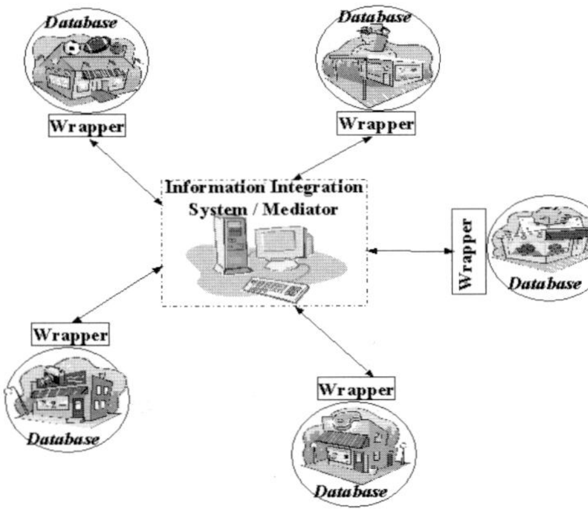

Figure 3: An information integration system classically uses wrappers.

Formally, a wrapper is a program or a rule that understands information provided by a specific source and translates it into a regular form that can be further reused. A wrapper is an essential component of a mediator system (see Figure 3), which accepts queries from users, translates each one into the appropriate query for the individual source, fetches the relevant pages from that source, extract the requested information from the retrieved pages and returns the result to the user. Essentially, the wrappers make the Web sources look like databases that can be queried through the mediator's query language.

Wrappers can be either hand-coded or created automatically by software agents [Muslea, 1999]. Hand-coding wrappers is a tedious and time-consuming task.

In addition, a comparison shopper with these manually written wrappers is not scalable because new stores will not be automatically integrated. Automatic construction of wrappers by agents for online stores is a challenging issue mainly because the Web pages written in HTML are not agent-friendly [Liu et al., 2000]. Fortunately, online stores are mostly semi-structured [Atzeni et al., 1997], and we can extract some of the page's meaningful parts without the help of semantics-based modules.

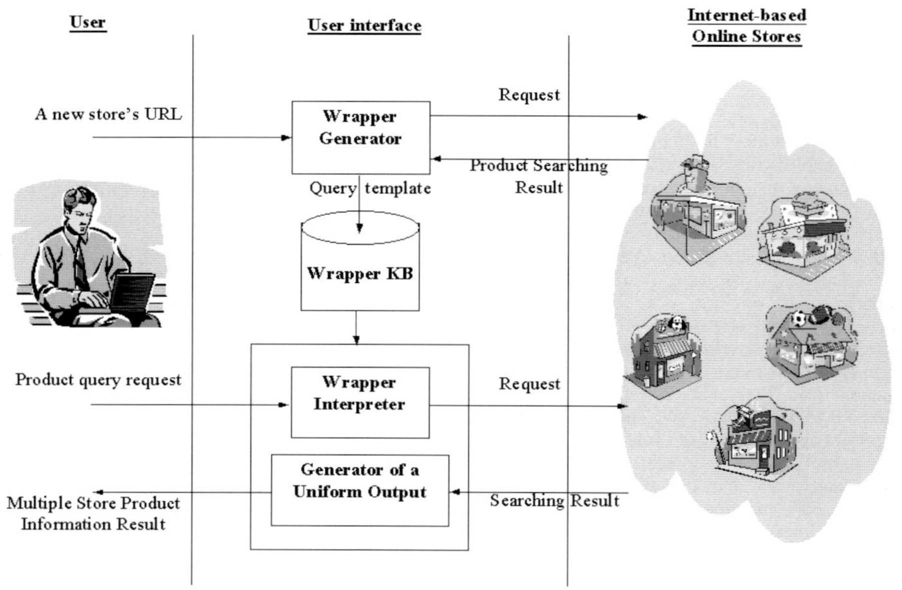

Figure 4: An overall architecture of ShinA

Another difficulty of automatic wrapper-generation comes from the heterogeneity of scores in a sense that different stores employ different mechanisms of manipulating customer queries and different styles of displaying product information.

3.2 System Architecture

A comparison shopper must be able to perform the following tasks:

Since e-commerce sites have various input mechanisms, the comparison shopper must locate the position of a query form, and must be able to intelligible parse at least the most relevant parts of the query. ShinA does both by observing a user and his/hers communication with the e-commerce site. A user presents a new store's URL and performs a query for a particular item. It suffices to generate a query template. In this way, ShinA generates an appropriate query template for each online store. Secondly, a comparison shopper must extract only the product information from the resulting page, ignoring redundant and unnecessary fragments. Thirdly, it must be able to delineate a product description and recognize the attributes of a product such as the price, the manufacturer, the size, etc. Finally, it must represent information from various sites in various formats in a user-friendly uniform way to a user.

Figure 4 shows the architecture of our ShinA comparison shopping agent that we propose to fulfill these requirements. The wrapper generator is the main learning module that constructs one dedicated wrapper for each particular store. During the process, the wrapper generator learns two things. Firstly, it recognizes a store's query scheme and secondly, it learns how to extract a store's content. The wrapper interpreter is a module that executes generated wrappers to get the current product information. This module forms several actual queries by combining each store's query template with the keywords that the user actually typed in, and sends them to the corresponding shopping sites. The search results from the stores are then collected and fed to the uniform output generator module. The uniform output generator integrates search results from several stores and generates a uniform output.

3.3 Learning Algorithm

In this paper, learning is defined as the task of building a rule from a single or a set of resulting pages. This rule is used to learn the format of product description from successful searches in a new shopping site. We adopt an inductive learning mechanism. Here, the examples correspond to the pages of a search result and the concept to be learned corresponds to the extraction rule [Yang et al., 2001].

Each page contains one or more product descriptions that matched the query. A product description is composed of sequence of attributes of the product. For example, a music store displays search results in which the attributes of a product include the CD title, the artist name, the price, etc.

The wrapper-learning module has to find the starting and ending position of the list of product descriptions in the entire result page, and to recognize the pattern of a product description. To do this, our method is divided into three phases. In the first phase, the HTML source of the page is broken into three parts. The first and last part represents redundant and irrelevant fragments of the page (header, advertisement, script) that must be ignored. The useful (middle) part must be extracted, and consists of a set of attributes that describe the product. In the next phase, the algorithm recognizes each HTML line by examining HTML tags (delimiters) and categorizes it, accordingly. In the last phase, where a page is expressed by a sequence of categories, the algorithm finds a repeating pattern in the sequence. The most frequent pattern becomes the representative product description.

3.4 Implementation

ShinA's Web interface is shown in Figure 5. Unlike EMA, ShinA is quite a dedicated system without modules for translation, speech, and huge amount of local data. However, the core task of parsing and understanding heterogeneous sites is more difficult in e-commerce than in employment, because of higher diversity in e-commerce.

The ShinA system has been implemented on a Windows 2000 operating system, running Apache HTTP Server, version 1.3.20. As developing tools, JDK 1.3.1 and Jakarta Tomcat 3.2 were used. System is written from scratch in Java programming language, using servlet/JSP technology and approximately consists of 10K lines of code. Tomcat is a servlet container that is used in the official Reference Implementation for the Java Server and JavaServer Pages technologies. Both Apache Server and Tomcat are developed in an open and participatory environment and are therefore freely available.

System is temporarily publicly unavailable due to final testing and fine-tuning, but can be obtained for academic purposes only.

4 RELATED WORK

BargainFinder [Krulwich, 1995] and Jango [Jango] are first-stage comparison shoppers. They specify functions that agents must have in order to be applied to Electronic Commerce. Both systems employ the manual rule extraction method.

Figure 5: ShinA's main interface

ShopBot [Doorenbos et al., 1997], like our system, suggests an automatic rule extraction technique by analyzing and learning the shopping sites. In order to integrate specific product information, Shopbot first removes irrelevant information such as advertisements by using inductive learning mechanism and then extracts necessary product information. Shopbot, however, uses several strong biases about the structure of HTML and the display format of product search results to learn. Therefore, Shopbot is unable to learn a shopping mall that does not conform to these strong biases. By contrast, the only bias of our method is that the result of a product search should be displayed in a semi-structured way, that is, each product description unit has the same output format (which conforms to almost all shopping malls). We expect our method to function more robustly than Shopbot. The thesis can be verified by empirical tests - the success rate of correct wrapper constructions. These tests are to be performed in future months.

PersonaLogic [PL] is a comparison shopping system that compares not the shopping malls but the products itself.

Kasbah [Kasbah], AuctionBot [AB], and Tete-a-Tete [TT] are negotiable mediators with which the user can buy and sell products based on negotiation strategies between agents in the virtual marketplace. They do not enter e-commerce sites in an automatic or semi-automatic way similar to the idea presented here.

To our knowledge, today's commercial comparison shoppers, including MySimon [MS], PriceWatch [PW], and BottomDollar [BD] all employ the manual rule extraction methods, and consequently suffer from the lack of scalability to new stores and format-changed stores.

5 CONCLUSION

We have proposed a customized comparison shopping agent ShinA. It successfully constructs correct wrappers for "normal" e-stores without assuming many structural constraints.

ShinA contains a quick, simple and robust inductive learning algorithm that automatically generates wrappers. Since we do not exploit specific e-store domain knowledge, but rely on a uniform e-commerce patterns, the learning algorithm can be simple, domain independent and uniform.

There are also some limitations in our current system. Firstly, we have assumed that users give a proper URL and path for the test query. Secondly, each product description must contain the price attribute. We think that this is not a severe restriction since most stores that produce semi-structured product information contains the price attribute. Thirdly, we only extract the price information from a product description that may contain several other attributes. Lastly, the system relies heavily on HTML. If a shopping site provides information exclusively by embedding it in graphics or using Java, ShinA will be unable to handle the site.

This technique can also be applied to other information integration systems for heterogeneous information sources.

ACKNOWLEDGEMENTS

Financial support was provided by an international project INCO-Copernicus 960154, Cooperative Research in Information Infrastructure, CRII, by the Ministry of education, science and sports in Slovenia, and by ESS. We would like to thank the CEO of the Employment Service of Slovenia, Mr. J. Glazer.

REFERENCES

Ashish, N., and Knoblock, C., 1997. Semi-Automatic Wrapper Generation for Internet Information Sources. In *Proceedings of Second IFCIS Conference on Cooperative Inforamtion Systems (CoopIS).*

Atzeni, P., Mecca, G., and Merialdo, P., 1997. Semi-structured and Structured Data in the Web: Going Back ad Forth. *ACM SIGMOD Workshop on Management of Semistructured Data*, pp.1-9.

AuctionBot. http://auction.eecs.umich.edu/

Balabanovic, M., and Shoham, Y., 1995. Learning Information Retrieval Agents: Experiments with Automated Web Browsing. In *Proc. of the AAAI Spring Symp. on Information Gathering from Heterogeneous, Distributed Environments.*

Bezek, A., Gams, M., 2001. An agent that understands job description. *Informatica (Ljubljana)*, 25(1), pp.99-105.

BottomDollar. http://www.bottomdollar.com/

Cowie, J., and Lehnert, W., 1996. Information Extraction. *Comm. of the ACM, 39(1)*, pp.80-101.

Dastani, M., Jacobs, N., Jonker, Catholyn, M., and Truer, J., 1999. Modelling User Preferences and Mediating Agents in Electronic Commerce. In *Proc. of the Agent-Mediated Electronic Commerce (AMEC) SIG-Meeting of AGENTLINK.*

Doorenbos, R., Etzioni, O., and Weld, D., 1997. A Scalable Comparison-Shopping Agent for the World Wide Web. In *Proceedings of the First International Conference on Autonomous Agents*, pp.39-48.

Freitag, D., 1998. Information Extraction from HTML: Application of a General Machine Learning Approach. In *Proceedings of the 15th National Conference on Artificial Intelligence (AAAI-98).*

Gams, M., 2001. A Uniform Internet-Communicative Agent, *Electronic Commerce Research, 1*, Kluwer Academic Publishers, pp.69-84.

Greenwald, A.R., and Kephart, J.O., 1999. Shopbots and pricebots. In *Proceedings of the 16th International Joint Conference on Artificial Intelligence*, pp.506-511.

Hammer, J., Garcia-Molina, H., Nestorov, S., Yerneni, R., Breunig, M., Vassalos, V., 1997. Template-based wrappers in the TSIMMIS system. In *Proceedings of the ACM SIGMOD International Conference on Management of Data*, pp.532-535.

Jakobsson, M., Yung, M., 1998. On assurance structures for WWW commerce. In *Financial Cryptography '98.*

Jango. http://www.jango.com/

Kasbah. http://kasbah.media.mit.edu/

Krulwich, B., 1995. Bargain Finder agent prototype. *Technical Report*, Anderson Consulting. http://bf.cstar.ac.com/bf/

Kusmerick, N., Weld, D.S., and Doorenbas, R., 1997. Wrapper Induction for Information Extraction. In *International Joint Conference on Artificial Intelligence*, pp.729-735.

Levy, A.Y., and Weld, D.S., 2000. Intelligent Internet Systems. *Artificial Intelligence, 118*, pp.1-14.

Liu, L., Pu, C., Han, W., 2000. XWRAP: An XML-enabled Wrapper Construction System for Web Information Sources. In *Proceedings of the Sixteenth International Conference on Data Engineering*, pp. 611-621.

Lewis, T., 1999. Microsoft Rising : ... and Other Tales of Silicon Valley, ACM.

Maes, P., 1994. Agents that reduce work and information overload. *Comm. of the ACM, 37(7)*, pp.31-40.

Maes, P., Guttman, R., and Moukas, A., 1999. Agents that buy and sell. *Comm. of the ACM, 42(3)*, pp.81-91.

Mladenic, D., 1999. Text-learning and related intelligent agents. *IEEE EXPERT, Special Issue on Applications of Intelligent Inforamtion Retrieval.*

Muslea, I., Minton, S., and Knoblock, C., 1998. Wrapper Induction of Semistructured, Web-based Information Sources. In *Proceedings of the Conference on Automatic Learning and Discovery.*

Muslea, I., Minton, S., and Knoblock, C., 1999. A Hierarchical Approach to Wrapper Induction. In *Proceedings of the Third International Conference on Autonomous Agents*, pp.190-197.

MySimon. http://www.mysimon.com/

Pazienza, M.T., (ed.), 1997. Information Extraction, Springer.

PersonaLogic. http://www.personalogic.com/

Pivk, A., 2001. Item-based Collaborative Filtering Algorithms, In *Proc. of the Fourth International Conference on Information Society*, pp. 65-68.

Pivk, A., Gams, A., 2000. E-Commerce Intelligent Agents, In *Proceedings of ICTEC'00*, pp.418-429.

PriceWatch. http://www.pricewatch.com/

Tete-a-Tete. http://ecommerce.media.mit.edu/tete-a-tete/

Yang, J., Seo, H., and Choi, J., 2001. MORPHEUS: A Customized Comparison Shopping Agent. In *Proceedings of the 5th International Conference on Autonomous Agents (Agents-2001)*, pp. 63-64.

Yang, J., Lee, E., and Choi, J. 2000. A Shopping Agent that Automatically Constructs Wrappers for Semi-Structured Online Vendors. *Lecture Notes in Computer Science, Vol. 1983*, pp.368-373.

E-COMMERCE BUSINESS PRACTICES IN THE EU

Hamid Jahankhani, Solomon A. Alexis
University of East London,East London Business School, Longbride Road, Dagenham, Essex RM8 2AS
Email: hamid.jahankhani@uel.ac.uk, solomonalexis@hotmail.com

Key words: ADR, Consumers and e-commerce, Compliance Plan, e-commerce, Electronic Online Dispute Resolution, e-economy, Electronic Payment, e-money, EU, Internet Regulation, Law and Internet, Risks, Regulation of e-commerce.

Abstract: This paper describes and evaluates the e-commerce issues addressed by the EU legislative framework (Directives), examines the extent of their influence on e-commerce business practices and the factors that drive e-commerce in the EU.
The countdown has started for the implementation and compliance of the various EU initiatives and although opinion is divided over the regulation merits, the issues of privacy, consumer protection and progress will continue to be in the limelight. Various consumer groups have argued that the EU initiatives provide greater protection for online shoppers, while the critics claim that they halt and hinder the growth of the e-economy in Europe by making it complex and risky for smaller firms to trade online.
Although, many European on-line businesses are aware of the EU Directives relating to e-commerce, they have not put into place plans to act in accordance with them.
Today there are no less than fifteen different initiatives and although the Directives pose problems for businesses that operate in the Euro-zone, there is an intense effort to minimise the perceive disadvantages that they can cause.
What the EU has done for e-commerce in the last decade has not been done anywhere else in the world.

1 INTRODUCTION

There is an intense interest in the Internet's potential to contribute to various sociological and economic phenomena, primarily from European Internet enthusiasts. Foremost among these ideas is that the Internet and in particular e-commerce will contribute to, or even be primarily responsible for, a new era of participatory democracy and a revitalisation of the public sphere.

Accenture, has prepared an in-depth and detailed report on e-commerce in the global sphere entitled "e-Europe: Connecting the dots?" Accenture's main argument is that "*European business leaders have embraced e-commerce so strongly that a majority now thinks that Europe has the potential to become the hub of a global economy.*"(Accenture 2001), which makes their work influential among Internet enthusiasts and policy makers.

Accenture and other IT business-consulting firms like Arthur Andersen, Ernst & Young, and PriceWaterhouseCoopers, have promoted the view that e-commerce in the EU is a lucrative business. This notion has been solidified after the correction of the global stock market that saw share prices brought more in-line with other share options.

Both Accenture's and Baker & McKenzie's (2001) work are chosen as a starting point, because it taps into several important issues that have great influence on e-commerce in the European Union. The Accenture publication is punctuated with the latest statistical data on e-commerce within the EU, which was carried out by surveys and experiments. It also highlights a number of case studies within which one can base a proper research document. The Baker & McKenzie publication takes on a more generic view to doing e-commerce in Europe.

The EU is a relatively late starter in adopting e-commerce but recent surveys have shown that by 2003 the EU will surpass the US in the overall value of electronic trading (Forrester Research Inc 2001). The EU is also seen as a "perfect springboard" for truly globalise trading. This is because it has a variety of cultures, languages, country specific laws and different attitudes to the new technology.

The focus here is on the B2C sector of e-commerce, because this is the primary area of concern for the EU Directives.

One of the rationale for undertaking this research is that; European on-line organisations are either unaware of the EU Directives or they are not complying with them. The aim of research is to briefly describe and evaluate the e-commerce issues addressed by the legislative framework (Directives) and to develop a compliance plan.

2 THE ECONOMIC DIMENSION OF E-COMMERCE IN THE EU

The Internet is one of the most regulated areas of society. In the EU there are at least fifteen Directives, proposals and recommendations to try to regulate e-commerce. The impact is significant, although such regulations seem to have been introduced in a piece meal fashion. The EU has attempted to assert regulatory control of online issues and it is hoped that as each country incorporates the various EU legislative packages into local law, the opportunity will be taken to abolish outdated provisions and set forth an e-commerce-friendly approach throughout Europe.

If the viability of the European Union lies in electronic commerce, then there needs to be a shake-up of the rule of law and how it affects the proliferation of the forever-changing new technology. Trading online – via the Internet is a logical extension to traditional business practices, modules and concepts. The Internet has enabled and in some instances given new meaning to commerce. The prefix 'e' is now being attached to practically all business concepts; e- business, e-branding, e-marketing, e-commerce to name a few. To sustain and for many countries to revitalise national economies and attain a competitive advantage with our neighbours on the other side of the Atlantic, the EU has to "*shake off the clubby industrial model for a more open, dynamic system*," according to Donlon (2000). In effect, he argues, a more failure tolerant culture is need. It is imperative to note here, that this new technology – the Internet, has achieved its notoriety due to the fact that it is a free and open forum, a land where no one man is king or ruler, a land without national boundaries and or national or international law. In the early days of its development, the Internet was often considered a space free of rules, thereby helping the electronic marketplace to develop rapidly. In the meantime, national and international bodies like the EU, the OECD and the UN have attempted to apply traditional rules - or to create new rules thereby, to some extent threatening the Internet's economic potential.

On 8th December 1999, the European Commission announced an initiative called "e-Europe – An Information Society for All" (Accenture 2001). The key objectives of e-Europe are; to create a digitally literate Europe; to bring every citizen, home, school and every business online supported by an entrepreneurial culture to finance and develop new ideas; to ensure that the whole process is socially inclusive, builds customer loyalty and strengthens social cohesion.

The commission proposed ten priority areas to achieve these objectives. The ambitious targets were to be achieved through joint action by the commission, the member states, industry and the citizens of Europe. The ten areas of action were:

1. Bringing European youth into the digital age.
2. Cheaper Internet access.
3. Accelerating e-commerce.
4. Fast Internet for researchers and students.
5. Secure networks and Smart cards.
6. Risk capital for high-tech small and medium sized enterprises (SMEs).
7. E-Participation for disabled people.
8. Healthcare online.
9. Intelligent transport.
10. Government online.

E-commerce is rapidly becoming embedded in European business. In a reversal of the wait-and-see attitude of the past, European businesses are being driven to invest in e-commerce because of intense competition, advances in technology, the political landscape and other socio-economic issues

3 GLOBALISATION VS. LOCALISATION

The e-commerce environment in which organisations operate has come about as a result (to a large extent) of globalisation. There is an increasing interdependence of markets and industries, which has lead to the globalisation of the world economy. Blurred market boundaries, resulting in the changing barriers to entry have changed the internal and external structure of markets, as is seen in the EU. These factors have, further resulted in the need for mergers, alliances and acquisitions on a scale not seen before.

The Internet has also created a more dynamic supply chain for businesses. Business processes are now more modularised and the trend is to achieve a better vendor/consumer relationship. The Internet has allowed businesses to reach customers and suppliers in new areas. This global reach has also opened up the possibility for organisations to sell more of their products across all of the goods lifecycle. For example raw material, finished goods, second hand goods and even scrap can now be sold.

Despite this obvious trend in the world economies (that of globalisation) there is a flip side to the coin. It is called localisation. Baker & McKenzie (2001) in an extensive report identified four main reasons why organisations localise their web sites:

- To organise their market appearance and be accessible to buyers under a local top level domain name. For example; _.uk, _.de, _.fr, _.it and so on.
- To communicate with buyers/consumers in their local language.
- To meet the requirement of the local market.
- To meet the requirements of local laws and regulations.

Fifty per cent of Western European executives identify a national or regional language and culture website, a local presence, local fulfilment capability and the ability to launch across countries as important success factors.

Research work (Forrester, 2001), has shown that US web sites draw a lot of traffic, but very little trade from overseas. Most make no attempt to localise the contents of their web site and international fulfilment is poor, this is mostly due to the homogeneous nature of the US environment. On the other hand Europe's environment of distinct natural characteristics and laws is much more like the rest of the world. Europe's dot-coms are able to succeed in fighting their way through cultural, tax and regulatory obstacles, using their local knowledge to become long-term players. Having viewed both sides of the coin, one may now be tempted to ask the question "Which way do businesses go?" The answer is both, a little bit here and a little bit there. It is what business analysts call *"glocalisation"* meaning act global, but think local. With this, businesses would benefit from the best of both worlds.

4 THE LEGAL REGIME IN THE EU AND THEIR IMPACT ON E-COMMERCE BUSINESS PRACTICES

Directives are the most common forms of European legislation. They are essentially instructions to the Member States to introduce laws in their own parliament. In general they indicate the goals to be achieved not the manner of achieving them. In most cases it is left to the national parliaments to interpret the Directives and bring about the necessary mechanism for implementing them in their own countries. On average, Member States have a two-year transition period to translate a Directive into national law. There are also other initiatives such as proposals and recommendations, which are a little more relaxed in nature.

Back in 1998 the Committee (A European initiative in electronic commerce"` 98/C 180/03) opined in a communiqué that the aim of the initiative was to *"to encourage the vigorous growth of electronic commerce in Europe."* It would do this by providing a coherent policy framework for future action and by establishing a common European position to achieve consensus in international negotiations. The Committee recognised that the characteristics of European businesses were different, when compared to the rest of the world and that there was huge diversity in the social and economic arenas. But, it can be seen that the European Union Commissioners intention is to regulate a highly unregulated arena and at the same time give confidence to both consumers and businesses that e-commerce venture had come of age.

Overall, the EU initiatives are a welcome not just for their content but also for the philosophy, which appears to underpin them. In the last few years the EU has done quite a lot when it comes to enhancing e-commerce. Having waited and watched what the US and others have done, the EU has awoken.

The EU is keen to formulate directives, policies and frameworks to promote e-commerce. The EU believes that Internet commerce will offer significant opportunities for Europe, with estimated revenues to increase to $US1.5 trillion by 2003. E-commerce is expected to have considerable impact on the structure and operations of the labour market, which will subsequently trigger a need for training and education for the new skills required. Faced with intense, global competition in a border-less digital environment, the EU hopes to ensure that these new jobs are created and maintained in the European Single Market (EITO, 1997).

Many people especially lawyers/solicitors and organisations have lambasted the many initiatives, claiming that they impede e-commerce development and deployment within Europe.

There has been significant progress on both the specific e-commerce issues and on the setting up of a broader context in which e-commerce can flourish. But despite these efforts, Accenture (2001) claims that there are four issues that continue to pose problems for Europe. They are:

Balancing public protection with promotion of e-commerce, whereas consumers demand protection there is repeated furore when legislation like RIP (EU site 2001) is introduced. The favour seems to be in co-regulation rather than the top-down approach.

Regulation of competition, governments have a fine balance to achieve as the new economy tends towards concentration. Governments prefer a competitive market place.

A business friendly environment, on issues like freedom of speech, taxation and employment, the mass of different laws impose significant costs and managerial overheads on businesses operating within the Euro-zone.

European social model, today Europe is built on cohesion and stability, the environment of risk-taking and rapid decision-making (which the Internet provides) tends to threaten this social model.

In an article published in the International Review of Law (Murray August 1999) the authors argue that the "*Internet is one of the most regulated areas of society...*" The EU has at least 15 such directives to try to regulate e-commerce. The impact is significant, although such regulations seem to have been introduced in a piece meal fashion.

Here, we examine some of the major Directives and its impact on e-commerce business practices.

5 E-SIGNATURE DIRECTIVE

In the case of the directive on e-signatures, this Directive has been sanctioned in several EU countries, much to the delight of the financial services sector (in particular banks). They had lobbied hard for its introduction. For e-commerce what this means is that there is now a fresh way of doing business from the perspectives of both the customer and the business. Customers and business expectations for web-enabled transactions can now be initiated, thus enabling a more streamlined business process.

6 THE DISTANCE SELLING DIRECTIVE AND THE DISTANCE CONTRACTS DIRECTIVE

The EU directive on distance selling that came into force recently also has implications for businesses. Whereas it seeks to protect consumers, Andy McCure (November 2000) thinks that it *"will put etailers at risk"*. Accordingly, the most costly aspect of law is that if a customer cancels a contract, the business will have to refund the money before the product is sent back to the company. McCue's article quotes a solicitor as saying *"... they will have to chase consumers through the courts. When you are talking about potentially low cost goods, it isn't economically viable."* This in itself is quite significant as recent figures indicate that a typical purchase on the net cost under £50.

Another key issue that always crop up is redress. In the event of a dispute, which country has jurisdiction? Pachl (1999(1)) in an intervention on the ISF suggested to the BEUC that the consumers go to the court in their own country. Any other solution, namely that the consumer has to go to the courts in the country where the business is established is pointless. She argues that the new economy makes the consumer a target for businesses. As selling is increasingly profiled-based on consumers' previous purchasing patterns.

Therefore the distinction between an active and passive consumer must be considered and the same for an active and passive web site. Also, there must be a distinction between the types of web sites used by businesses in promoting their business.

This issue of jurisdiction is one that has been written about in many quarters. Lorna Gillies (2001) recently considered this in a detailed JILT commentary Therein, she asserts that the provisions will have implications for states outside of the EU.

However, the traditional methods of tracking down the place of business might create difficulties. This is particularly true where organisations have their physical place of business outside of the EU because of tax reasons, for example in the Bahamas. Diedrich (2000) in another article published in JILT, explores the attempts to regulate e-commerce. Using a typical case example, he highlights the impact to e-commerce business practices. Let us look at this scenario:

A consumer domicile in Germany ordered an item via the Internet from a company with its place of business in the USA. Payment is done via credit card in advance for US$200. The delivered item turns out to be the wrong one (not the one ordered). The US company refuses to an exchange and also to reimburse the buyer. The standard contract on the company's web site provided a 7-day period for inspecting the item upon delivery and for reporting any sort of discrepancy immediately. The buyer in Germany, however, was on holiday for 2 weeks and had not read the relevant provision.

The article reports that such a case could be solved by using the buyer contractual right to be reimbursed by his credit card company thereby shifting the risk of performance to the seller. The impact here is that such goodwill if seen to be fraudulent the credit card companies will not meet such conditions in the future. Many Internet transactions are international as in the example above. Many times the consumer may not even be aware of this as the web site is presented in his local language. Given such uncertainties of conflicts of laws and the high cost of starting legal proceeding (especially outside one's own country), the consumer will only become aware of this when problems with the contract are experienced.

The issue of ADR's is also another grey area. In practice, an ombudsman (whether physical or on-line) has to base their decision on some law. Is it the consumer country law or the business country law? This question of redress is still being debated in many quarters and at many different levels. Hornle (2001) discusses many of these issues in a "work in progress" article published in the Journal of Information, Law & Technology.

The Distance Selling Directive also makes provisions for certain information to be given to the consumer before the conclusion of the contract in a "clear and comprehensive manner in any way appropriate to the means of distance communication used". There is issue with the presentation of such information. Experience has shown that the way information is presented and accessible is crucial to ensure consumer protection. Sidkin and Elliot (2001) writing in the E-commerce Law & Policy newsletter mentions some anomalies of this directive. Although the directive in Schedule 1 lists email and tele shopping as "means of distance communication", it does not mention the web! Another anomaly is the absence of WAP – Wireless Application Protocol in the Schedules. Via WAP one can purchase/trade via Internet. The regulations require that a host of information be presented to the consumer prior to the purchase. Although it is easy to do this via a web site, it is not so easy over the small screen of a mobile phone. A third anomaly is that the regulation does not define auctions (auctions are a common e-commerce business model) and it is still unclear whether a reverse auction is subject to the Directive. Lastly, consumers are given the opportunity through the right of withdrawal, where they can terminate a contract within a specified period of time. The Directive defines "working days" to mean all days other than Saturdays, Sundays and public holidays. A supplier and consumer for that matter will need to take account of different public holidays in each Euro-zone member state.

For consumers contracting on-line there is an issue with regards to this directive. Businesses worldwide have to consider the benefits and risks of conducting business on-line with consumers who are based in Europe because they will have to comply with all applicable laws concerning jurisdiction in each EU state.

7 DATA PROTECTION DIRECTIVE

This Directive has also been the most discussed piece of legislation pertaining to the Internet and e-commerce since it was mooted a few years ago. Consumers, businesses and other interest groups throughout Europe lobbied their respective parliaments to ensure that their national interpretation was not more restrictive than the directive envisaged. Some of the main areas of concern to the DP directive were and to some extent still are:

- The definition of processing has been widened to include everything from the collection to the destruction of personal data.
- Explicit consent must be attained prior to the processing of personal data.
- The consumer has the right to be informed before personal data is disclosed for the first time to third parties or used on their behalf for the purposes of direct marketing.
- Security and privacy of personal data has to be ensured.
- The Directive restricts the transfer of personal data to a country or territory outside the European Economic Area unless that country or territory ensured an adequate level of protection for the rights and freedoms of consumers in relation to the processing of personal data.

Achieving explicit consent for the processing of personal data prior to collection has been implemented by many in the form of a check box on the web page prior to requesting the consumer to input his/her personal information. Others have used a click through button on the web page that the user has to click <OK> to prior to being asked to input personal data.

On the issue of being informed before personal data is disclosed for the first time to third parties or used on their behalf for the purposes of direct marketing what some web-sites have done is to given consumers the option to opt-out (less have gone for the opt-in route). This has been implemented with the use of a check box on the web page. This provision arguable makes it more difficult to sell or swap mailing lists, as informing every member of any lengthy mailing list would be a huge undertaking.

For many people security and privacy ranks amongst their biggest concern as it relates to e-commerce. Whereas the Directive says that security and privacy of personal data has to be ensured, for businesses this also means that outsourcing e-commerce projects carry with it certain legal obligations. Businesses now have to ensure that their third party employees are adequately entitled to process personal data. In fact, the Directive requires that written contracts be entered into between parties must include sufficient guarantees in respect of the technical and organisational security measures that are taken to protect the data.

Shaun O'Shea (August 2000) examined the consequences of the Directive for e-commerce. He states "The Data Protection Directive applies to information collected by e-commerce businesses on the Internet, just as it does to information gathered by any other method." The question of cross border transfers was one of the hotter issues discussed during the latter part 1998 and throughout 1999. Due to the inherent nature of the Internet this criteria would be difficult, if not impossible to police. The EU and the US held numerous high-level meetings to ensure that personal data could be transferred across the Atlantic.

8 E-COMMERCE DIRECTIVE

The EU Directive on e-commerce has provisions on information requirements on the identity of service providers and on commercial communications (advertising, direct marketing etc.). The issue here is with the presentation of such information. Experience has shown that the way information is presented and accessible is crucial to ensure consumer protection. If information is spread over several web sites and it cannot be easily printed, or are in different structures (formats) then it will not be receptive. (Pachl 1999(1)) addressed this issue in her intervention on the ISF, which was delivered in Helsinki. Therein she advises that technological solutions on presentation should be developed to ensure that the information is easy to find and easy to access. Meaning that it should only be one click away. A sign/logo/hyperlink should be on every page, which would ensure access to that information. It was also suggested that terms and conditions of the contract should be presented in a user-friendly manner.

Pachl (1999(2)) in another intervention by the European Consumers Organisation delivered to the European Parliament makes the point that commercial communications is targeted at specific markets and specific groups of consumers. Thus, if suppliers decide to offer their products/services on a web site, it seems only reasonable that they should be prepared to pay for that advantage by respecting the legislation of the markets, which their advertising is seeking to influence. For example, if a vendor wants to get at the French market and sets up a website in French, why should that organisation not be obliged to respect the rules of the French marketing Act? The Directive as it stands does not force a vendor to comply with national legislation relating to the targeted market once the vendor complies with legislation in his own market.

9 COPYRIGHT DIRECTIVE

The material that is carried, stored, forwarded or delivered by on-line intermediaries (for example ISP's) can infringe the rights of another. Julia-Barcelo (1999) sites two types of liabilities for ISP's in this regard: 1. Strict Liability – this is where the ISP will be held responsible whenever a right is violated. That is, whenever material (that is considered to infringe or is illegal) is carried, stored, forwarded or delivered using their facilities, whether they know (or have reason to know) about it and can control it or not. 2. With-fault liability – this is where an on-line intermediary intentionally or negligently violate the rights of others.

Because monitoring is technically difficult to monitor and expensive especially for small organisation measures must be put in place to ensure that copyright rights are not infringed. Two recent court cases; the first case was between Godfrey –v– Demon Internet Ltd; here Godfrey claimed that his rights were infringed when unsavoury remarks were posted on a Demon's newsgroups and the second was when Demon won an injunction which prevented publishing the names of the two infant killers- in the UK highlights the problems associated with on-line intermediaries.

10 COMPLIANCE PLAN - A PROPOSED STRATEGY FOR DEVELOPING AND OR ENHANCING WEBSITE IN THE EU

Successful compliance requires establishing standardised, uniform, and consistent policies and procedures, co-ordinating them across all e-commerce functions and communicating them to all affected personnel and departments. Without a plan, it is highly unlikely that European-wide compliance can be maintained. Thus, in order to begin addressing the enormous business, social, operational and legal issues confronting businesses by virtue of the development of e-commerce laws in Europe, companies need to have a defined "battle plan". However, before presenting compliance plan we present the mechanisms that European CEOs have put in place to assist in successfully pursuing e-commerce opportunities.

It is clear that businesses in Europe are taking measures to pursue e-commerce opportunities. Nearly three-quarters have an e-commerce strategy and more than half will have a training plan and cost-benefit analysis. However, in the climate that they operate, it is imperative that compliance with local and regional laws be a major part of that strategy as failure can be potentially costly, embarrassing and will diminish customer trust.

According to successive research documents, the reasons why organisations are not complying with the legislative framework are as follows:

- Management have not identified the relevant factors.
- There are unclear procedures.
- There are considerable contradictory interpretations of the regulations in Europe.
- The industry is unaware of the applicability of the regulations.
- There is a lack of audit, which leads to insufficient checks.

It is therefore envisaged that a comprehensive, well-integrated and clearly articulated plan would play a large role in improving compliance.

Therefore, developing a formal e-commerce Compliance Plan is vital to all e-commerce ventures. It will be the organisation's road map to successful compliance. It will define exactly how the organisation will integrate regulations and requirement into the existing organisational structure and processes. The plan will define responsibility and accountability so customers and vendors will know whom to turn to for answers. The plan (Policies and Procedures) will provide guidance to all affected personnel to ensure they know what is required of them and how they are expected to do it. The plan will minimise capital expenditure and operating costs while achieving full compliance with applicable laws and requirements.

In the European Union, the Directives that affect e-commerce require extensive changes to be made by organisations that wish to trade electronically. The aforementioned Directives are now EU-wide controlled and there are severe civil penalties for violations.

From a managerial perspective the following is the basic summarised structure for setting up a relevant procedure. Management must:

1. Recognise the e-commerce regulatory framework within the European Union.
2. Establish a senior role/post to oversee and progress a programme of compliance, which, inter alia informs all of the new laws/Directives and their practical consequences.
3. Audit/analyse all e-commerce websites.
4. Amend terms and conditions on the particular aspects as per the Directives.
5. Establish appropriate security mechanisms.

11 CONCLUSIONS

What is it that businesses can do to achieve a balance as the e-commerce regulatory framework unfolds? So far, they have not done a great job at making the case for the economic, operational and marketing benefits that accrue to consumers through the legitimate collection and use of personal data. Nor have they allayed the concerns of consumers with regards to security. Until these occur, it will be difficult to explain the costs and disadvantages that businesses will incur as e-commerce laws increase.

The EU is not afraid of technology, their approach is very different from that of the US. The pragmatic approach of waiting for proven, reliable solutions is opposite to that of the early adopters.

Although, many European on-line businesses are aware of the EU Directives relating to e-commerce, they have not put into place plans to act in accordance with them. This may be consequence of the huge number of Directives and the fact that many of them are yet to take full effect in all member states.

Also, in the European Union member states, e-commerce has contributed to the social and economic development of the region. This is evident from the tremendous support that the EU Commission has and continues to place on the Internet and e-commerce. Initiatives such as *e-Europe* prove that the technocrats and policy makers are embarking on a smooth transition from the off-line brick and mortar to on-line ventures.

E-commerce is being seen as a mechanism for revitalising the public sphere in the EU. It's geographic-less nature, common laws, protection for consumers aids this transition. This is particularly important for SMEs who see their bigger competitors as simply competitors and not "big sharks".

REFERENCES

Accenture 2001, "E-Europe: Connecting the dots?" Cited August 2001, URL: http://www.accenture.com

Baker & McKenzie 2001, "Doing E-commerce in Europe" cited August 2001, URL: http://www.bakerinfo.com/BakerNet/default.htm

Diedrich, F (October 2000); "A Law of the Internet? Attempts to Regulate Electronic Commerce"; JILT (Journal of Information, Law and Technology), cited September 2001, URL: http://elj.warwick.ac.uk/jilt/00-3/diedrich.html

The European Parliament, Committee of the Regions on the 'Communication from the Commission to the Council, the European Parliament, the Economic and Social Committee and the Committee of the Regions on "A European initiative in electronic commerce"' (98/C 180/03).

EITO – ActivMedia, ROMTEC in European Information Technology Observatory, 1997.

Forrester Research (2001), cited August 2001, URL: http://www. Forrester.com

Gillies, L (February 2001); "A Review of the New Jurisdiction Rules for Electronic Consumer Contracts Within the European Union"; JILT (Journal of Information, Law and Technology), cited August 2001, URL: http://elj.warwick.ac.uk/jilt/01-1/gillies.html

Hörnle, J (July 2001) "Disputes Solved in Cyberspace and the Rule of Law"; JILT (Journal of Information, Law and Technology) cited July 2001, URL: http://elj.warwick.ac.uk/jilt/01-2/hornle.html

Julia-Barcelo, R (October 1999) "Liability for on-line Intermediaries: A European Perspective"; ECLIP (Electronic Commerce Legal Issues Platform).

Murray A, D (August 1999) *"Regulating e-commerce: Formal transactions in the digital age"*, International Review of Law, Computers & Technology, Abingdon.

McCue A, (November 27, 2000*), "EU rules 'will put etailers at risk'"*, Computing, VNU Publications.

O'Shea S, (August 2000*) "Data Protection in an e-commerce era"*, Accountancy Ireland, Dublin.

Pachl, U (1999(1)) "The consumer in the electronic marketplace – the role of regulation and the role of technology", Bureau European de Unions de Consommateurs (BEUC) – BEUC/291/99 cited August 2001, URL: http://www.beuc.org/public/papers/pa1999/291up99e.pdf

Pachl Ursula (1999(2)), "E-commerce and the consumers interest – legal aspects of e-commerce and the consequences for SME's", Bureau European de Unions de Consommateurs (BEUC) – BEUC/064/99. Source; http://www.beuc.org/public/papers/pa1999/064up99.pdf

RIP – Regulation on Investigatory Powers, to enable state interception and monitoring of private Internet communication, cited September 2001, URL: http://www.eu.int/tempcom/echelon/pdf/prechelon_en.pdf

Sidkin, S, Elliott, J (May 2001), "Distance Selling – coming to terms with the new regime." E-Commerce Law and Policy, 3, 5.

AUTOMATIC VERIFICATION OF SECURITY IN PAYMENT PROTOCOLS FOR ELECTRONIC COMMERCE

M. Panti, L. Spalazzi, S. Tacconi, S. Valenti
Istituto di Informatica, University of Ancona
Via Brecce Bianche, Ancona, Italy
{panti,spalazzi,tacconi,valenti}@inform.unian.it

Key words: payment protocols, electronic commerce, security requirements, model checking, automatic verification, protocol attacks.

Abstract: In order to make secure transactions over computer networks, various cryptographic protocols have been proposed but, because of subtleties involved in their design, many of them have been shown to have flaws, even a long time after their publication. For this reason, several automatic verification methods for analyzing these protocols have been devised. The aim of this paper is to present a methodology for verifying security requirements of electronic payment protocols by means of NuSMV, a symbolic model checker. Our work principally focus on formal representation of security requirements. Indeed, we propose an extension of the correspondence property, so far used only for authentication, to other requirements as confidentiality and integrity. These are the basic security requirements of payment protocols for electronic commerce. We illustrate as case study a variant of the SET protocol proposed by Lu & Smolka. This variant has been formally verified by Ly & Smolka and considered secure. Conversely, we have discovered two attacks that allow a dishonest user to purchase a good debiting the amount to another user.

1 INTRODUCTION

In the last years, the diffusion of computer networks has received an enormous development. These systems provide a growing number of different services (for instance e-commerce services) each needy of peculiar security requirements. In order to satisfy such requirements, various cryptographic protocols have been proposed. A cryptographic protocol is a protocol that exploits cryptographic primitives in order to satisfy one or more security requirements. Among various kinds of security protocols, the spread of electronic commerce makes very attractive those devoted to protection of on-line payments. The most popular payment protocol is the Secure Electronic Transaction (SET in short), a protocol jointly developed by Visa and Mastercard (Mastercard and Visa, 1997) to guarantee secure transactions over open networks. Unfortunately, the definition of a cryptographic protocol involves many subtleties that often lead designers into error. For this reason many protocols have been shown to have flaws, even a long time after their publication. To avoid these subtle misconceptions, several automatic verification methods for analyzing cryptographic protocols have been devised. Model checking has been proved to be very useful for this purpose. Model checking is a general-purpose, automatic technique for verifying finite-state concurrent systems. Indeed, given the model of the system to analyze, a model checker simulates all its possible behaviors in order to verify whether a requirement is satisfied. When a requirement is not satisfied, a counter-example is produced. In applying this approach to the verification of cryptographic protocols, security requirements (properties) are expressed by a propositional temporal logic, and protocols are modelled as state-transition systems. In this context, the counter-examples can be used for discovering possible attacks on protocols. This is possible only when the model of the environment includes the presence of a dishonest entity having the control of network where protocols run. The aim of this paper is to present a methodology for analyzing cryptographic protocols by means of NuSMV (Cimatti et al., 1999), a symbolic model checker. The most innovative feature of our methodology is constituted by formal representation of security requirements. Indeed, we propose an extension of the correspondence property, so far used only for authentication, to other requirements as secrecy and integrity. Notice that, these are the basic security requirements of payment protocols for electronic commerce. We illustrate the feasibility of our approach using as case study a simplified variant of SET proposed by Lu and Smolka (Lu and Smolka, 1999). This variant has been analysed by the same authors and considered secure. Conversely, we have discovered two attacks that allow a dishonest entity to purchase a good debiting the amount to another user. The rest of paper is organised as follows. In Section 2 we sketch a brief description of the Lu-Smolka protocol. At this point, we describe how we have employed the model checking to verify the security of this protocol. For this purpose, we first describe the model of protocol in Section 3, then we illustrate the formalization of security requirements in section 4. In Section 5, we discuss the attacks that we have found and their effects. In Section 6 we compare our work with those dealing with automatic verification of SET and of its variants. Final remarks are drawn in Section 7.

2 THE LU-SMOLKA VARIANT OF THE SET PROTOCOL

SET is a suite comprising seventeen subprotocols, each devoted to make secure a specific phase of a commercial transaction. The Lu-Smolka variant of this protocol, depicted in Figure 1 both graphically and formally, is a simplified version of the subprotocols involved in the payment phase only. Therefore, it is assumed that such a variant is invoked during a web-based commercial transaction. This means that a client (the cardholder) selects the goods/services that it wishes to purchase/request, the shipping address, the billing address (if any) and after that uses the protocol to perform the on-line payment. In Figure 1, C denotes the cardholder, M the merchant, and P the payment gateway. $\{m\}_{K_x}$ expresses a message m encrypted with the public key of X, whereas $S_x\{m\}$ is a message m signed by X. $TIDR$ denotes a record with initialisation data for the protocol. TID represents the unique identifier of the transaction, it can be considered as a nonce. PA is the amount that the cardholder is supposed to pay, PY is the amount that the cardholder is willing to pay, and AA is the amount of charge that the merchant requests for authorization. CA and MA are the identifiers of cardholder's account and merchant's account, respectively. Finally, Tr denotes the answer of the gateway that can be either an authorization or a negation of authorization.

Intuitively, the protocol works as follows. In step (1), C sends to M the request for a unique transaction identifier. M assigns the TID to the transaction, signs it, and returns it to C in step (2). At this point, in step (3), C sends to M the Ordering Information (OI), i.e., TID and PA, and the Payment Instruction (PI), i.e., TID,PY,CA. PY may be lower than PA if the cardholder tries to deceive the merchant. Moreover, the PI is destined to the payment gateway, while OI is destined to merchant. In step (4), M decrypts OI, checks if it is correct, then encrypts a new OI (OI' composed by TID,AA,MA) with the payment gateway's public key. Finally, M sends to P, in a single message, an authorization and capture request. Notice that AA might be higher than PY. In step (5), P authorizes C's payment card, checks for consistency between OI' and PI, performs appropriate account operations, and returns the transaction result Tr to M. In step (6), M reads the response and forwards the message to C.

3 MODEL OF THE PROTOCOL

Our approach is based upon model checking, an automatic technique for verifying finite state concurrent systems. In the temporal logic model checking, the concurrent system is modelled as a state transition diagram.The NuSMV model checker, following the above approach, adopts a structured input language to describe the model of system. In this context, the model of protocol describes all the issues related to the behavior of the honest and the dishonest entities belonging to the system where the protocol runs. The model of protocol has a modular structure. Each module is associated to an entity of the system and describes its behavior. As showed in the overall view, depicted in Figure 2, the model consists on honest entities, i.e., the client C, the merchant M, the payment gateway P, and a dishonest entity I.

3.1 Honest Entities

The model of protocol is composed by several variables and processes. First of all, we have the communication channel, a set of variables which are shared among all the entities. In particular, we treat protocol messages flowing in the channel as records having a specific field for each message component. For each honest entity C,M and P, we have a set of processes. Each process of any entity corresponds to an instance of the entity involved in a particular execution of the protocol. Moreover, all the processes work asynchronously and concurrently. The concurrency is simulated by means of a non-deterministic interleaving of process running. Each process that constitutes an entity is a very simple automaton. The most important variable involved in these processes, named *state*, is initialised at *idle*. When the automaton of an honest entity sends a message h, the variable is set to $send_h$, when it receives a message k, the variable is set to $receive_k$, finally when the protocol session

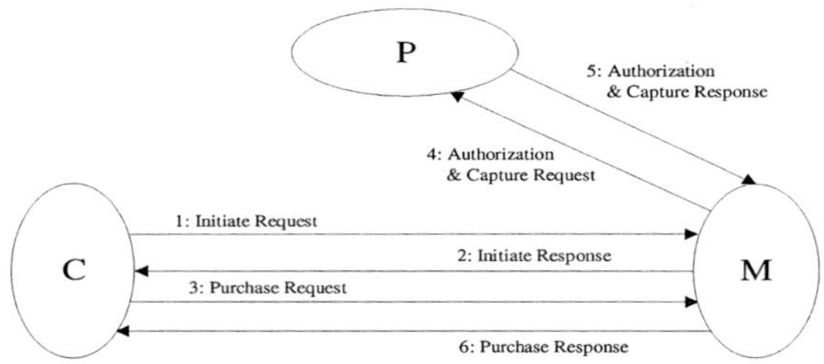

$$
\begin{array}{lll}
(1)\ C \rightarrow M & : & \textit{Initiate Request} \\
 & & TIDR \\
(2)\ M \rightarrow C & : & \textit{Initiate Response} \\
 & & S_m\{TID\} \\
(3)\ C \rightarrow M & : & \textit{Purchase Request} \\
 & & S_c\{TID\}, \{TID, PA\}_{K_m}, S_c\{\{TID, PY, CA\}_{K_p}\} \\
(4)\ M \rightarrow P & : & \textit{Authorization \& Capture Request} \\
 & & S_c\{\{TID, PY, CA\}_{K_p}\}, S_m\{TID\}, \{TID, AA, MA\}_{K_p} \\
(5)\ P \rightarrow M & : & \textit{Authorization \& Capture Response} \\
 & & S_p\{TID, Tr\} \\
(6)\ M \rightarrow C & : & \textit{Purchase Response} \\
 & & S_p\{TID, Tr\}
\end{array}
$$

Figure 1: The Lu-Smolka variant of SET

ends successfully, the value is *terminated*. Each entity has also a set of counters that are used to specify the security properties, as discussed in section 4. Such variables are the following:

- $X.begin(role, Y)$, $X.end(role, Y)$ counts the number of protocol executions that the entity X has begun/ended with the entity Y acting as specified in $role \in \{init, resp\}$, with $X, Y \in \{C, M, P\}$ and $init/resp$ standing for initiator/responder. We allow a multi-role behavior for C and M among different protocol executions. For this reason, C can be a responder and M can be an initiator. Conversely, the role of P is forced to be only a responder.
- $X.send(Y, term)$, $X.recv(Y, term)$ counts how many times the entity X has sent/received the sensible information specified in $term$ to/from entity Y. The counter $X.recv(Y, term)$ is incremented only if X is able to extract $term$ from the received message. There are different kinds of terms, each defined over a set of possible values. In the model exists a pair of counters for each possible value of each kind of term.

As a consequence of finiteness of model checking approach, the value of each counter can range from 0 to the maximum number of protocol executions admitted in the model. For the same reason, each term ranges inside a finite set of values.

3.2 Dishonest Entity

Modelling the dishonest entity requires identification of relevant assumptions that allow to capture its possible behaviors. A dishonest entity is usually assumed to be as powerful as possible, in order to verify the protocol in the possible worst situation where it can be executed. Therefore, we assume that a dishonest entity has a complete control of the communication channel. In other words, it must be able:

- to *eavesdrop* each message sent over the channel;
- to *remove* a message sent to another principal;
- to *generate* new protocol messages;
- to *store* in the *memory* messages eavesdropped;
- to *send* messages to other principals.

The dishonest entity must be able to generate messages built out of messages previously sent over the channel by honest entities. As a consequence, the model of the dishonest entity must be provided with a memory to store eavesdropped messages sent during the current or previous sessions of the protocol. In the general case, a dishonest entity must be able to build new messages starting from the readable components of the messages eavesdropped or from components belonging to its initial knowledge about the protocol. The model of the dishonest entity is made

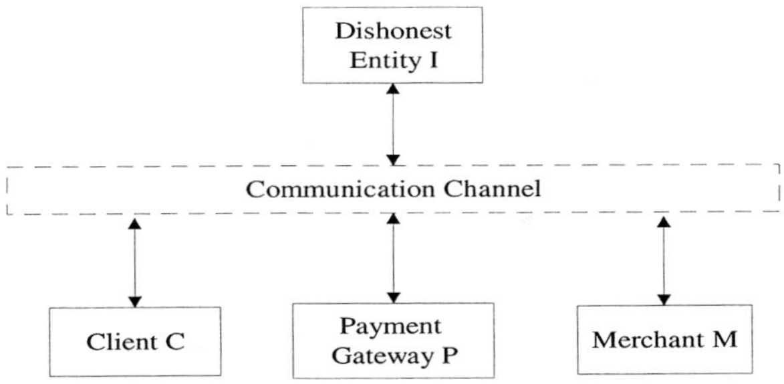

Figure 2: The overall view of the model

according to the above assumption. The most important variables involved are the following:

- *state* ranges over the possible actions that the dishonest entity can perform and whose value in each state represents the action it has chosen. According to dishonest entity's abilities previously enumerated, *state* admits the following values: *eavesdrop, remove, generate, store, send.*
- *memory* represents the memory of the dishonest entity and is an array whose elements range over the messages of the protocol. The dishonest entity stores eavesdropped messages in this array. The size of the array basically depends on the number of messages of the protocol and the maximum number of distinct sessions allowed in the model.

At any step, the dishonest entity non deterministically chooses an action between all the possible actions, for this reason *state* can non deterministically take any of its values. The automaton of dishonest entity performs the current action specified by the value of *state* and changes all the other local variables accordingly. Finally, in order to formalize security requirements, the model of the dishonest entity is also provided with counters similar to those of honest principals.

4 SECURITY REQUIREMENTS

There are several requirements that a security protocol needs to satisfy. In the analysis of Lu and Smolka protocol, we have focused our attention on: *authentication*, i.e. the parties convince each other of their identities, *confidentiality*, i.e. nobody but the authorized parties must know a term, and *integrity*, i.e. assurance that a term has not been altered by an unauthorized entity. These properties express the security goals of the original version of SET and thus those of the Lu and Smolka variant as well. In order to formalize the above requirements, we propose to adopt the so called *correspondence property*. This property has been introduced for authentication (Woo and Lam, 1993). An attempt to generalize correspondence can be found in (Marrero et al., 1997), but the authors still apply this property to authentication only. In the following section we will show it can encompass confidentiality and integrity too.

4.1 Generalization of Correspondence Property

In its most general formulation, the *correspondence property* states that the relation between an *event* E and an *event* F must be a one to one mapping. Usually, it must be taken into account multiple sessions of the same protocol to verify security. Indeed, many attacks occur in the presence of multiple sessions only. In such a situation, we may have several events of type E and F, and thus we need to count them. Therefore, the correspondence property can be reformulated (Marrero et al., 1997) as follows:

> If the event E occurs n times, then the event F must have occurred at least n times.

In $NuSMV$, system requirements are formalized in the propositional temporal logic CTL (Computational Tree Logic) (Emerson, 1990). When we represent the generalized correspondence property in CTL, we use the counters (one for each event) introduced in the model. Therefore, the correspondence property can be formalized by means of the following general schema:

$$AG(X.counter_F >= Y.counter_E) \qquad (1)$$

$X.counter_E$ and $Y.counter_F$ denote counters related to entities X and Y. These meta-variables must be instantiated to appropriate counters, depending on the property to formalize. AG is a CTL operator (it is an abbreviation for *Always Globally*. Informally speaking, $AG\ p$ means that the propositional formula p must be true in every possible state of the system.

4.2 Authentication

In the original formulation for authentication, the correspondence property states that when an entity finishes its part of the protocol, the other entity must have taken part in the protocol execution. In other words, if an entity X ends n protocol executions with Y as responder (initiator), then in the past the entity Y must have started at least n protocol executions with X as initiator (responder). The above property asserts that Y must prove its identity to X. In the case of mutual authentication protocol, there exists a similar property for representing X that must prove its identity to Y. A violation of this property means that an entity ends a session (i.e., it accepts the authentication of the other entity) that the other entity has not started, i.e., the dishonest entity must have impersonated an entity. In order to formalize in CTL the authentication property according to the above schema, we use some of the counters that we have introduced in the model. Thus, the authentication property is represented by the following CTL specification:

$$AG(X.begin(init, Y) >= Y.end(resp, X)) \quad (2)$$

$$AG(X.begin(resp, Y) >= Y.end(init, X)) \quad (3)$$

4.3 Confidentiality

The extension of correspondence property to other requirements is quite natural. Intuitively, confidentiality means that a term must not be known by unauthorized entities. In other words, it is required that the dishonest entity never receives or deduces this term. From another point of view, a dishonest entity can receive only the terms intended for it. Therefore, this entity can not obtain $term$ from an entity X more times than this term has been expressly sent to it. Thus, we can write the following specification:

$$AG(X.send(I, term) >= I.recv(X, term)) \quad (4)$$

Obviously, this formula assumes that the dishonest entity can be a legitimate member of the system. Notice that when I does not take part to a certain protocol execution, nobody sends confidential terms to it, thus $X.send(I, term)$ is always equal to 0. As a consequence, in this case the specification requires that $I.recv(X, term)$ must be 0. Nevertheless, the above conditions are necessary but non sufficient. Indeed, a dishonest entity, even if does not know a confidential term, can trick an entity Y into thinking that it has received a secret $term$ from the entity X, whereas in fact X has never sent $term$ to Y. In order to cover this situation, the following specification must be added:

$$AG(X.send(Y, term) >= Y.recv(X, term)) \quad (5)$$

Informally speaking, the above expression means that if an entity X receives n times a term from Y, then in the past the entity Y must have expressly sent at least n times this term to X. Notice that, if this term must be fresh, the maximum value admitted for these counters is 1.

4.4 Integrity

Integrity is the assurance that an information has not been altered by unauthorized entity. In the model, when X sends a term to Y, it increases the counter $X.send(Y, term)$ associated to this specific term. Similarly, the intended recipient Y, after the receipt of this term, increases the counter $Y.recv(X, term)$. If an alteration of this term is occurred on the network during its transit, the associated counter of the recipient does not increase, but increases the counter $Y.recv(X, term')$, with $term \neq term'$. As a consequence, specification (5) is not satisfied. Indeed, this specification, only necessary for confidentiality, assures also integrity. This is congruent, since typically, for a confidential term it is also required integrity. Conversely, integrity may be required without confidentiality (for example, when a term is only signed). For this reason, we employ the specification (5) (in conjunction with (4)) to express integrity of a confidential term, whereas we adopt only the specification (5) for integrity of terms transmitted in clear.

5 ATTACKS ON THE PROTOCOL

The above model and requirements have been submitted to $NuSMV$. From the verification arises that the expected security requirements do not hold. In order to justify this outcome, the model checker has generated a counter-example showing how a dishonest entity can compromise an execution of the protocol. In the attack traces, when the dishonest entity intercepts a message m in transit from X to Y, preventing from its receipt, we write $X \to I(Y) \ : \ m$. When the dishonest entity sends a message m to Y, impersonating X, we write $I(X) \to Y \ : \ m$. The first attack proceeds as reported in Figure 3. The dishonest entity I acts as merchant in α with C while in session β it impersonates the client C towards another merchant M. As a consequence of the above attack on a commercial transaction, a dishonest buyer I succeeds into debiting to another buyer C a purchase that C in fact has never performed. Moreover, if the good is delivered by means of the network system, as the content of a web-page, or I has altered the shipping address in the (often insecure) phase before the invocation of the protocol, I is able to obtain that good without paying it. From the point of view of requirements, this attack violates the requirements of authentication and secrecy. Indeed, it is a counter-

$(\alpha.1)\ C \rightarrow I\ :\ TIDR$
$(\beta.1)\ I(C) \rightarrow M\ :\ TIDR$
$(\beta.2)\ M \rightarrow I(C)\ :\ S_m\{TID\}$
$(\alpha.2)\ I \rightarrow C\ :\ S_i\{TID\}$
$(\alpha.3)\ C \rightarrow I\ :\ S_c\{TID\}, \{TID, PA\}_{K_i}, S_c\{\{TID, PY, CA\}_{K_p}\}$
$(\beta.3)\ I(C) \rightarrow M\ :\ S_c\{TID\}, \{TID, PA\}_{K_m}, S_c\{\{TID, PY, CA\}_{K_p}\}$
$(\beta.4)\ M \rightarrow P\ :\ S_c\{\{TID, PY, CA\}_{K_p}\}, S_m\{TID\}, \{TID, AA, MA\}_{K_p}$
$(\beta.5)\ P \rightarrow M\ :\ S_p\{TID, Tr\}$
$(\beta.6)\ M \rightarrow I(C)\ :\ S_p\{TID, Tr\}$

Figure 3: The first attack on the protocol

example of the following instances of specifications (2) and (5):

$$AG(C.begin(init, M) >= M.end(resp, C))$$

$$AG(C.send(M, PA) >= M.recv(C, PA))$$

The second attack, reported in Figure 4, is similar to the previous one, but now the dishonest entity acts as buyer in session β. As a consequence, also this attack allows I to perform a purchase from M, debiting the payment to an unaware buyer C. This attack violates only the requirement of authentication. Indeed, it is a counter-example of the following instance of specification (3):

$$AG(M.begin(resp, C) >= C.end(init, M))$$

The first attack is possible because who receives the message of step (3) is not able to deduce the identity of the intended receiver. This problem exists also in the original version of SET and has also implications on the non-repudiation requirement (Van Herreweghen, 2000). However, in the original protocol, the presence of the identifier of merchant in the Payment Instruction allows the gateway P to deduce the real identity of intended merchant and thus to avoid the above fraud. The second attack occurs when M does not check the second signature of the message received in step (3), but it simply forwards it to P. Notice that, the original protocol does not require such a control. Indeed, the signature is inside the encryption with the gateway's public key. However, also in this case, in the original protocol the gateway is able to detect the fraud in step (4).

6 RELATED WORK

The literature about formal verification of cryptographic protocols is very wide. Many papers concern on verification of authentication and key exchange protocols. Among these, the work that has mostly influenced our approach to the formalization of security requirements is (Woo and Lam, 1993). In that paper, the correspondence property is used to formalize the authentication requirement for the classical authentication protocols. Conversely, in our work we have generalized the correspondence property to capture also secrecy and integrity requirements. Moreover, we have extended the domain applicability, applying this property to electronic payment protocols. In literature there exists various attempts aimed to extend the formal verification methods previously devised for authentication protocols to electronic payment protocols. We restrict our brief survey on papers dealing with the analysis of the SET protocol. With the paper of Lu and Smolka (Lu and Smolka, 1999) we share the same variant of SET. The aim of their work is to verify their protocol with FDR, a model checker based on the CSP language. The result of their verification is that their variant of SET is secure. On the contrary, we have discovered two attacks on such a protocol. In (Meadows and Syverson, 1998), it is proposed the use of *NRL Protocol Analyzer* to verify SET. In this work, specifications are expressed with a temporal language, named $NPATRL$, but the authors leave the complete analysis of the protocol to future work. Another work concerning the analysis of SET is (Bella et al., 2000). In this paper, the authors show how they have analyzed the first subprotocol of SET, named *Cardholder Registration*, by means of the theorem prover *Isabelle*. From their verification many ambiguities and contradictions on the protocol specification arise. In our work, we have focused on a different phase, i.e., the payment phase. The work (Van Herreweghen, 2000) proposes a methodology based on a language expressing the claims that the participants to a protocol execution must be able to prove. From this analysis some problems about non-repudiation requirement emerge. In particular, the fact that SET does not provide a secure receipt of payment to the cardholder. In (Kessler and Neumann, 1998), the authors propose an authentication logic that extends the $AUTLOG$ logic of belief in order to model accountability in electronic payment protocols. This logic is also applied to verify SET. The result is that SET is secure. Finally, in (Bolignano, 1997), it is described a verification methodology that allows to analyze a payment protocol by means of modal logic proofs. The authors use as case-study C-SET, a different variant of SET.

$$
\begin{array}{l}
(\alpha.1)\ C \rightarrow I(M) : TIDR \\
\quad (\beta.1)\ I \rightarrow M : TIDR \\
\quad (\beta.2)\ M \rightarrow I : S_m\{TID\} \\
(\alpha.2)\ I(M) \rightarrow C : S_m\{TID\} \\
(\alpha.3)\ C \rightarrow I(M) : S_c\{TID\}, \{TID, PA\}_{K_m}, S_c\{\{TID, PY, CA\}_{K_p}\} \\
\quad (\beta.3)\ I \rightarrow M : S_i\{TID\}, \{TID, PA\}_{K_m}, S_c\{\{TID, PY, CA\}_{K_p}\} \\
\quad (\beta.4)\ M \rightarrow P : S_c\{\{TID, PY, CA\}_{K_p}\}, S_m\{TID\}, \{TID, AA, MA\}_{K_p} \\
\quad (\beta.5)\ P \rightarrow M : S_p\{TID, Tr\} \\
\quad (\beta.6)\ M \rightarrow I : S_p\{TID, Tr\}
\end{array}
$$

Figure 4: The second attack on the protocol

7 CONCLUSION

We have proposed a methodology for verifying security requirements of electronic payment protocols by means of model checking. Our approach is based on the extension of correspondence property, so far used only for authentication, to other requirements, as confidentiality and integrity. We have illustrated as case study a variant of SET proposed by Lu and Smolka. Even if this protocol was considered secure, we have discovered two attacks that allow a dishonest user to purchase a good debiting the amount to another user.

Acknowledgments

The authors wish to thank Lorenzo Baldini, Loic Jay, Johann Dimarti, and Luca Roganti for their help in verifying the Lu and Smolka variant of the SET protocol.

REFERENCES

Bella, G., Massacci, F., Paulson, L., and Tramontano, P. (2000). Formal Verication of Cardholder Registration in SET. In *Proceedings of* 6th *European Symposium on Research in Computer Security (ESORICS)*.

Bolignano, D. (1997). Towards the Formal Verification of Electronic Commerce Protocols. In *Proceedings of* 10th *Computer Security Foundations Workshop*, pages 133–146.

Cimatti, A., Clarke, E., Giunchiglia, F., and Roveri, M. (1999). NuSMV: A New Symbolic Model Verifier. In *Proceedings of* 11th *Conference on Computer-Aided Verification*, number 1633 in Lecture Notes in Computer Science, pages 495–499. Springer.

Emerson, A. (1990). *Handbook of Teoretical Computer Science*, volume 2. Elsevier.

Kessler, V. and Neumann, H. (1998). A Sound Logic for Analysing Electronic Commerce Protocol. In *Proceedings of* 5th *European Symposium on Research in Computer Security (ESORICS)*.

Lu, S. and Smolka, S. (1999). Model Checking the Secure Electronic Transaction (SET) Protocol. In *Proceedings of* 7th *International Symposium on Modeling, Analysis and Simulation of Computer and Telecommunication Systems*, pages 358–365.

Marrero, W., Clarke, E., and Jha, S. (1997). Model Checking for Security Protocols. In *Proceedings of the DIMACS Workshop on Design and Formal Verification of Security Protocols*.

Mastercard and Visa (1997). *SET Secure Electronic Transaction Specification*. Mastercard & Visa. Available at http://www.setco.org.

Meadows, C. and Syverson, P. (1998). A Formal Specification of Requirements for Payment Transactions in the SET Protocol. In *Proceedings of the* 2nd *Financial Cryptography*.

Van Herreweghen, E. (2000). Non-repudiation in SET: Open Issues. In *Proceedings of the* 4th *Conference on Financial Cryptography*.

Woo, T. and Lam, S. (1993). A Semantic Model for Authentication Protocols. In *Proceedings of IEEE Computer Society Symposium on Research in Security and Privacy*, volume 25, pages 178–194.

STAGED IMPLEMENTATION OF E-BUSINESS NETWORKS THROUGH ERP:

A Case Study of Siemens (1998-2001)

Colin G. Ash, Janice M. Burn
Edith Cowan University, Pearson Street, Perth, Australia
Email: c.ash@ecu.edu.au, j.burn@ecu.edu.au

Key words: e-Business Implementations, ERP, Business Networks, Siemens.

Abstract: Internet technologies offer an ERP based organisation the opportunity to build interactive relationships with its business partners. The Siemens case of e-Business evolution is viewed in terms of buy-side and sell-side solutions and services that inter-relate. e-Business solutions were seen to evolve in six stages with increasing business value and network complexity; from infrastructure to e-marketplaces. By viewing the Siemens case as a staged implementation, it may easily be evaluated in terms of the attributes of the "virtual organizing" model.

1 INTRODUCTION

Numerous papers have been written about e-business and how this concept will change the way companies do business, characterised by rapid exchange of information within a virtual network of customers and suppliers working together to create value-added processes (Ticoll et al, 1998; El Sawy et al, 1999; Jansen et al, 1999; Burn and Barnett, 2000). However, little information is available on how organisations successfully integrate e-Business projects with ongoing ERP implementations or already productive ERP systems (Hesterbrink, 1999, Holland and Light, 1999). As more and more established organisations realise that they need to form alliances with their customers, partners and suppliers over the Internet, e-business integration with ERP systems becomes a critical implementation issue (Gable, 1998, Markus and Tanis, 2000).

Although these technologies have distinctly different functions, integrated they offer a sound infrastructure for doing e-business. (Venkatraman and Henderson, 1998). Here e-business means 'making the key business processes of an organisation available over the Internet' (Boey, 1999). In general, it is about "electronic interactions" between organisations. Although simple, this definition nevertheless incorporates some subtle but key points about e-business applications with ERP systems.

Less than three years ago, the ERP paradigm was largely confined within the walls of the traditional business enterprise. The Internet serves to extend the original value proposition of ERP, by breaking down organisational barriers. Now those boundaries have become almost obsolete. In the future, the structure of such organisations will be more like the web (Larsen, 2000). Internet technologies offer an ERP based organisation the opportunity to build interactive relationships with its business partners, by improved efficiencies and extended reach, at a very low cost (Hesterbrink 1999). An ERP implementation has a defined lifecycle, typically 12-24 months depending on the scope and other parameters (Blain, 1999). After the initial implementation, upgrade and functional enhancement projects follow in irregular intervals. e-Business implementations need to be significantly faster than initial ERP implementations (Hesterbrink, 1999). An e-business implementation is from the outset aimed at integrating business processes with external business partners and is built on and supported by the ERP foundation. The main focus of the implementation will therefore be the integration of cross-company value chains using e-business tools (Kalakota, 1999). The problem, however, is how can businesses best effect these transitions?

According to Forrester Research (2000), industry projections expect the dollar value in online transactions in the B2B and B2C sectors to be $6.3 billion and $0.4 billion, by 2004. This implies the ratio of B2B: B2C will have increased to 14:1. This has significant implications for traditional business with respect to future cost reductions and IT investment (ROI) in the B2B sector of the economy. Table 1 shows the worldwide estimates for the dollar value of B2B and B2C transactions (Forrester Research, 2000). Specifically the last column shows the ratio of B2B:B2C as a coarse measure of their relative value to business. B2B is already greater than eleven (11) times the dollar value of B2c transactions for year 2000.

Table 1: Comparison of $values for B2B and B2C

Yr 2000	million $	B2B	million $	B2C	B2B : B2C
North America	468.79	77.6%	40.48	75.9%	**11.58**
Asia & Pacific	49.89	8.3%	3.81	7.1%	**13.09**
Western Europe	78.82	13.1%	8.54	16.0%	**9.23**
Latin America	3.32	0.5%	0.25	0.5%	**13.09**
Africa / Mid-East	2.00	0.3%	0.15	0.3%	**13.09**
Eastern Europe	0.90	0.1%	0.07	0.1%	**13.09**
Total	**603.72**	**100%**	**53.31**	**100%**	**11.32**

Given the growth in B2B this study focused on this sector but included in this definition all inter-business transactions. This includes Buy and Sell applications with business partners as shown in Figure 1.We refer to these two concepts as $B2B^S$ (supplier chain) and $B2B^C$ (customer chain).

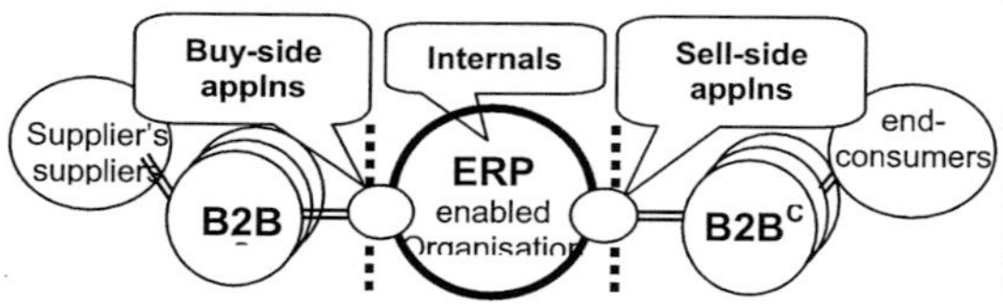

Figure1: B2B Model of a Single ERP enabled Organisation for doing e-Business

This model was used as a general guide to assess the e-business implementation patterns of ERP enabled organisations. The study took place over a three year period and covered over 20 organisations worldwide with at least two face-to-face interviews with each organisation over the three year period supported by document analysis, telephone calls, e-mails and web searches. The summary results of these studies are available elsewhere but all cases showed that a staged pattern of change was the preferred transition route to e-business through ERP. In this paper we illustrate this stage pattern using the case of Siemens Corporation.

2 CASE BACKGROUND

Siemens is a global powerhouse in electrical engineering and electronics, with its headquarters in Germany. Established in 1842, Siemens is a global player in over 190 countries and the fourth largest electrical and electronics manufacturing company in the world. In 1999 the annual turnover was 68 billion euros with R&D expenditure of 5.6 billion euros (Siemens, 2000).

Siemens has major business segments in; Energy, Healthcare, Information and Communication, Industry, Components, Transportation, Household, and Lighting (Figure 2). The Information and Communications business segment consists of three groups: Information and Communication Networks (59,000 employees, $13 billion in sales), Information and Communication Products (33,000 employees, $11 billion in sales) and Siemens Business Services (21,000 employees, $4 billion in sales). The Communication Devices Division (within the ICP group) is the world's leading provider of digital phones (Siemens, 1999b).

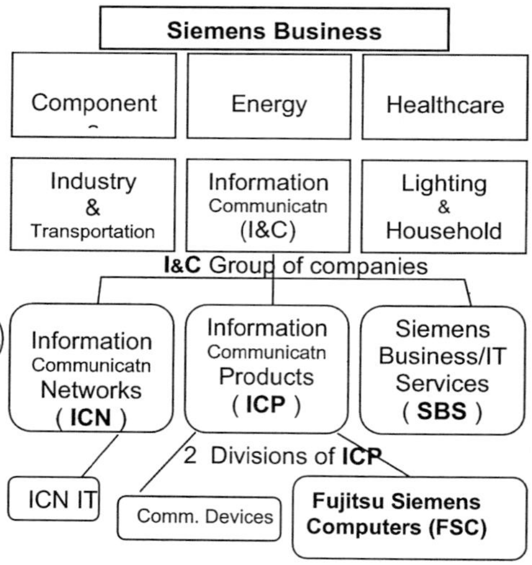

Figure 2: Part of Siemens' Organisational Structure

The ICP product group is positioned in the strategic growth fields of information and communication technology and offers the entire product range of IT and communications from a single source: from PCs, notebooks, servers and mainframes all the way to digital products and corded, cordless and mobile phones. The strategy for the mobile phone business is to expand its global market share while SBS complement the portfolio with an emphasis on value-added services. Fujitsu Siemens Computers (FSC) was formed through a joint venture between Fujitsu and Siemens and commenced operations on Oct. 1, 1999. The company is jointly owned and has its headquarters in Amsterdam. From extensive European manufacturing facilities, customer-focused companies in 25 European countries and more than 9,000 experienced employees, FSC aims to be the No. 1 computer company in its home market (Europe) by the end of year 2001 (Siemens, 1999b).

3 STAGED IMPLEMENTATION

3.1 In the Beginning – the e-Business Platform (1995-1999)

Siemens ICN IB, a subsidiary of Siemens AG, has of roughly 1,400 employees, with annual revenues of DEM 3.5 billion, and is represented in 160 countries across the globe. The company is a strategic partner for network providers and companies operating in the market for IP network solutions. Siemens ICN IB went live with the R/3 System in 1995, and implemented SAP ITS as an Internet platform together with Siemens Mail and Siemens' Online Business System in mid-1998 (Siemens, 1999b).

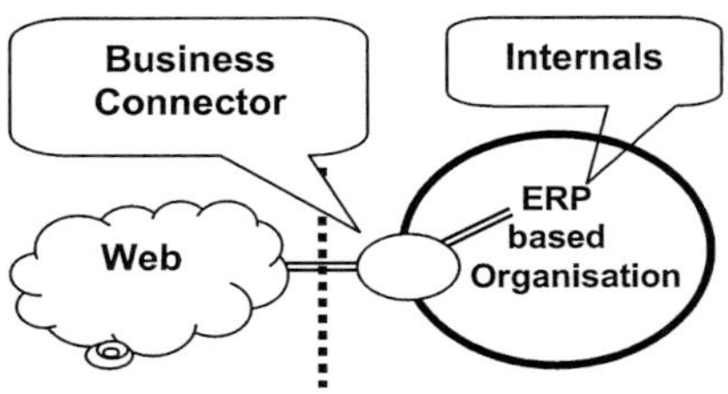

Figure 3: B2B Infrastructure Based on ERP

As a move to an e-business platform the SAP Business Connector (BC) was implemented in June 1999 as the backbone of the multi-tier strategy and replaced the existing ITS installation. The Siemens subsidiary can now embed R/3 process logic and data transparently in its customers' or suppliers' ERP or Internet catalogue systems – without having to access a common base. Interaction is guaranteed by using BC templates that visualize data and control user actions. SAP's Business Connector now promotes data exchange between ERP systems on the Web using XML as the business language. The solution is more agile and cost-effective than the company's previous (1997/8) data connection. SAP software is now Web-enabled. From SAP R/3 to Advanced Planner and Optimiser, SAP Business Information Warehouse to SAP Business-to-Business Procurement (Siemens, 1999b).

The multi-tier strategy gives rise to two requirements that are covered by the Business Connector:

a) exchanging company, master, and transaction data with external systems (both R/3 and non-R/3 systems),
b) presenting data or process logic in the context of external systems (process sharing).

At this time, an inhouse e-business development was having impact in the Computer Systems division (FSC) of the company (Siemens, 1999c).

3.2 Stage 2 - Storefronts at Siemens (1997-1999)

The SAP-based **Order and Request System** (ORS) was developed by Siemens Business Services (SBS), and has been used at FSC since 1998 on the most diverse SAP R/3 systems all over Europe (Siemens, 1999c).

ORS was created primarily to optimise processes between FSC and its partners. In July 1997 SBS in Germany were commissioned to develop an Internet connection for its three SAP R/3 retailing systems. An "inside-out" approach to implementation was adopted using the SAP Internet Transaction Server. The over-riding goal of Siemens Computers was to implement an international reference solution in Germany with a view to multi-language development (Siemens, 1999c).

The first group of functions related to *Order Tracking* was released in March 1998. This was followed in July 1998 by *News Channel* functionality, the active provision of information to users by means of order and delivery notifications. Since October 1998 it has been possible to display *original R/3 order documents* online in PDF format. *Online Ordering* was then introduced in December 1998 and additional configuration tools were incorporated online at the client end. The final touch was added to the classical shop in the first quarter of 1999 by the release of customer specific *Premium Pages* (Siemens, 1999d).

The Order and Request System (ORS) provides Fujitsu Siemens Computers with a simple way of presenting its configurable products for sale via the Internet. The online connection optimises ordering time and simultaneously minimises the number of incorrect orders. All sales executives and partners are able to place orders online at any time and track their progress or request current information on the orders and delivery dates. A news channel is provided to enable customers and partners to obtain information automatically on their orders. The range of products can be presented in a hierarchical form in shops which serve a particular clientele. To simplify ordering *premium pages* address specific customers and show products and configurations frequently ordered by those customers. This demonstrates a move towards the intelligent web site as in virtual organizing (VOing). A tiered access concept ensures that confidential information is visible only to authorised users. Access and data are protected by means of authentication and encryption.

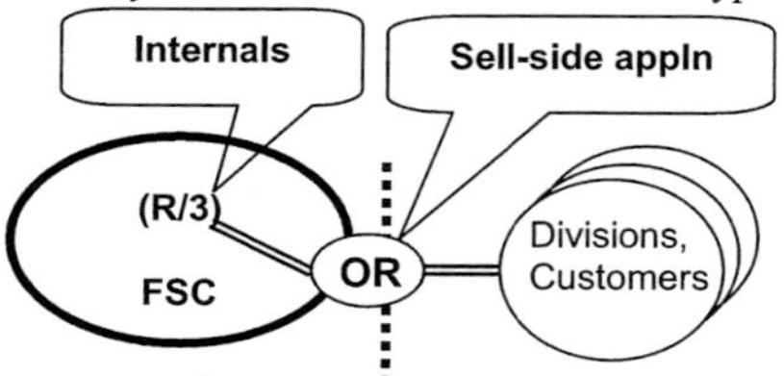

Figure 4: B2B^C as an e-Store for Corporate Customers

Developed and manufactured in Europe for European customers, the product portfolio benefits from the technologies and worldwide sourcing networks of the parent companies.

In addition FSC demonstrates the connecting into the customer's value chain.

3.3 Stage Three - Global Engineer-ing Network (1999-2000)

Given its geographic expanse, Siemens decided to create national accounting service centres in countries where it had a significant presence. It also created cross-border accounting centres to support its smaller offices with cost cuts of 30%. This involved personnel issues of training, motivating and transitioning of accounts from a head-quarters style accounting approach to a service model where "accounting people are no longer overhead producers, but quality producers" at a measurable price (Hoffman, 2000). By mid 1999, Siemens had moved towards a global engineering network (GEN) development. "GEN's overall goal is to make structured information and knowledge easily accessible in all business processes" (Timmers, 1999: 95). As a concept GEN not only enables faster access to information, but also leads to better management of information. Customers can search for specific components, design or services. Data can be pulled together to build up a complete project involving multiple partners (Timmers, 1999).

Table 2: Assessment of Siemens Attributes for Global Engineering Network

Key Assets:	Key Weakness:
• Strong presence in Germany and in many other countries. • Strong information technology base. • Near to information of GEN-like system	• Relatively strong national orientation. • Management commitment not clear. • Relatively new electronic commerce

[Source: Timmers, 1999: p.96]

Table 2 shows Timmer's (1999) assessment of Siemens as a company with mixed capabilities for success within developments of the GEN concept. In addition, the core of the GEN concept is a collaborative design and engineering platform. As such, it is of an infrastructural nature and likely to be most effective if it is used throughout an industrial sector or business segment to "be number one or nothing" By June 2000, the company's increasing experience with electronic commerce had lead to two strategic innovations of sell-side and buy-side of e-SCM; e-Mall and e-GateCentre (Siemens, 2000).

3.4 Stage Four – The e-Mall (2000)

The Siemens' e-Mall is an Internet marketplace for Siemens' companies to sell their products and services to business customers. The system architecture has the capability to connect/interact with a range of *Buyer* companies SAP R/3 and R/2 systems, and other ERP systems.

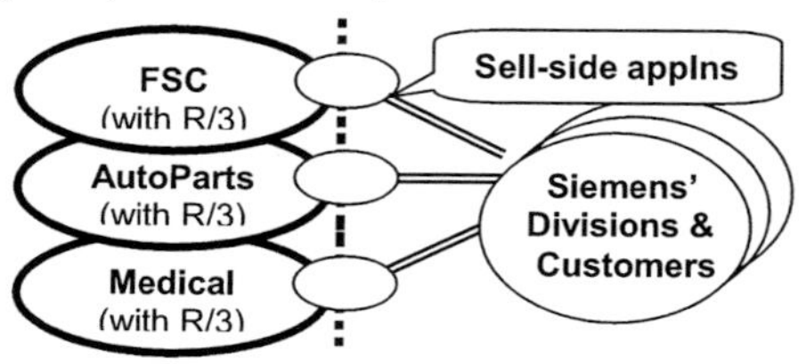

Figure 5: e-Mall as a Group of Companies with e-Storefronts for Customers

The intended benefits of e-Mall flow from the streamlining of sell-side business processes:

a) Siemens group specific product presentation;
b) Integration of Group's materials systems;
c) "One face" to the customer;
d) Sales presence round the clock and world-wide

By June 2000, the company's e-Mall had progressed to version 2 with three companies - ICP, A & D, Medical (Siemens, 2000).

a) Siemens Computer Supplies (MRO) using Order and Request System (ORS)
b) Siemens Insurance Mall /MedShop
c) Seimens Auto-Parts Distribution

The lessons learned were two fold:

a) The use of a common platform (SAP-based) needs the agreement of all functionality.
b) The internal and external marketing of the facility is essential to initialize and develop customer base.

In the near future the next step was determined to be the evolution to Siemens Corporate Portal for B2B procurement of supplies.

3.5 Stage Five – Corporate Portal (2000 - 2001)

In 2000 Siemens introduced "Gatecentre" as an Internet marketplace for 520 Siemens' companies to purchase their products and services from business suppliers. The worldwide presence of the Siemens purchasing network supports global sourcing and corporate-wide combined requirements. The intended benefits of Gatecentre flow from the streamlining of buy-side business or procurement processes into a single corporate solution. Gatecentre featured; individualised offers, up-to-date cross group Siemens' offerings, and convenient ordering at any time and anywhere (Siemens, 2000).

The B2B[S] model in Figure 6, used the SAP B2B Procurement application to link supplier' catalogues with the individual Siemens Companies' R/3, through a common gateway.

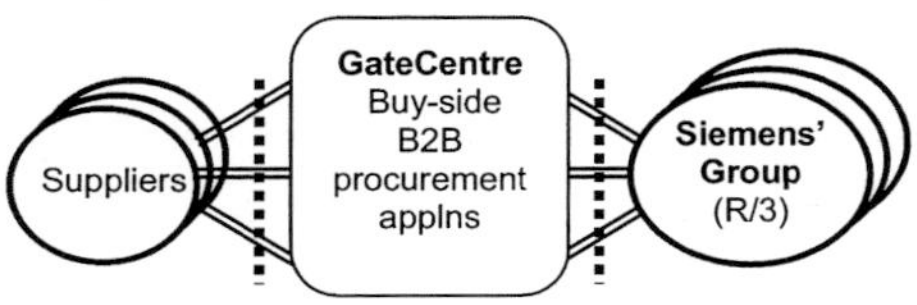

Figure 6: B2B[S] Model of e-Procurement from Supplier Catalogues to Siemens Group

The potential for procurement was defined by the company focus on cost-reduction. This was assessed in terms of procurement marketing and procurement logistics:

a) Procurement Marketing – strategic cost-reduction through global sourcing, market transparency and supplier management and demand bundling.
b) Procurement Logistics – operative cost-reduction through standard procurement processes and optimisation of time, costs, and quality.

By June 2000, the company's Gatecentre had progressed to the capability for answering the challenges of procurement landscape. An independent market analysis confirmed that this corporate Portal would eventually lead to a complete supply chain management (SCM) (Gartner Group, 2000).

3.6 The Final Stage (2000 -)

In May 2000 the company's fragmented e-business landscape in the regions and groups produced a corporate initiative and access to the Internet for all employees. For e-business at Siemens to be successful would require transforming a fragmented web presence to a company-wide approach. Here the change process is to be driven by the "e-community" and the "Centre of e-Excellence" (Siemens, 2001).

The Centre of e-Excellence is committed to collaborate internally and externally and promote; a constitution of the e-community competencies, and corporate e-services, and promote lead projects and accelerator programs using controlling scorecards.

The specific tasks include:

a) e-learning by HR training, in regions from SBS groups.e-technology by corporate R&D.
c) Marketplace sell by regions and groups.
d) Marketplace buy by corporate procurement and logistics.
e) e-Logistics by corporate logistics.

Two cross-regional and cross-divisional e-business related projects, are currently running in the Mid-Southern Europe (MSE) mandated by the MSE-board. e-MSE and e-Utilities are the two lead projects to define the marketplace development process for Siemens in general. A definition of regional customer-clusters for private marketplaces (including e-readiness evaluation and e-business organization) is creating "cross-border and cross-divisional optimization of business competencies, with one face to our customers".

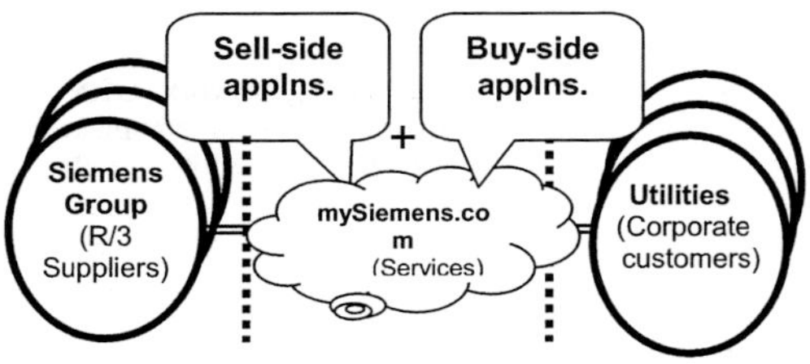

Figure 7: B2B Model of a Private e-Marketplace

3.7 Private e-Marketplace

Figure 7 illustrates the Web development of **mySiemens.com** as cross-divisional Siemens private electronic marketplace for utilities companies. The project e-Utilities was initiated by utility companies in Austria who wanted to have a shared communication platform with Siemens. By May 2001 the first e-Utilities project had begun in the MSE (Mid South Europe, 17 countries) region. France has also committed to participate in this marketplace and other countries are preparing to join. The goal was to offer customers a personalized marketplace in their own language and corresponding to their needs. They are offered news and information about Siemens products, services, and e-business solutions.

The private e-marketplace will be a collaboration hub to let participants exchange information and discuss offers and projects while also acting as a discussion forum and a calendar to arrange appointments. In addition the concept includes e-learning and travel management. It will also be possible to select and order products, solutions and services. Plans additionally foresee the inclusion of partners and local services. The Siemens internal R/3-based business rules remain unchanged (Siemens, 2001).

4 SUMMARY OF THE SIEMENS CASE AS VIRTUAL ORGANISING

Siemens is about the transition of a large German based conglomerate through a change in attitude towards doing business online. Siemens' corporate wide e-business strategy is presented as a new customer focus through speed, innovation, and optimisation of business competencies.

Venkatraman and Henderson, (1998) have defined their e-business model for the learning organisation that promotes harmony over three dimensions; customer/market interaction, asset configuration, and knowledge leverage, supported by a strong information technology platform. They see this as the virtual organising model for the 21st Century and as such a management strategy in itself. Figure 8 gives a view of an organisation using an Enterprise Resource Planning (ERP) system such as SAP, as an integrated system to support the management of knowledge across the three e-business dimensions of the organisation.

Siemens within its various divisions (INC and FSC) can be used to illustrate a staged implementation progressing across all three development levels of VOing.

Stages of Implementation

In the Siemens case, the e-Business evolution is presented in six stages with increasing business value and complexity, from e-business infrastructure to private e-marketplaces:

1. Infrastructure ➔ 2. e-Stores ➔ 3. e-Communities ➔ 4. e-Malls ➔ 5. Portals ➔ 6. e-Marketplaces.

Current research by Ash and Burn (2000) suggests the VOing model is particularly useful for examining the elements of e-business strategy. Table 3 summarises key parts of the Siemens case that match each element of VOing. The six stages of the case are shown collectively to demonstrate all the elements of VOing. In doing so the case study

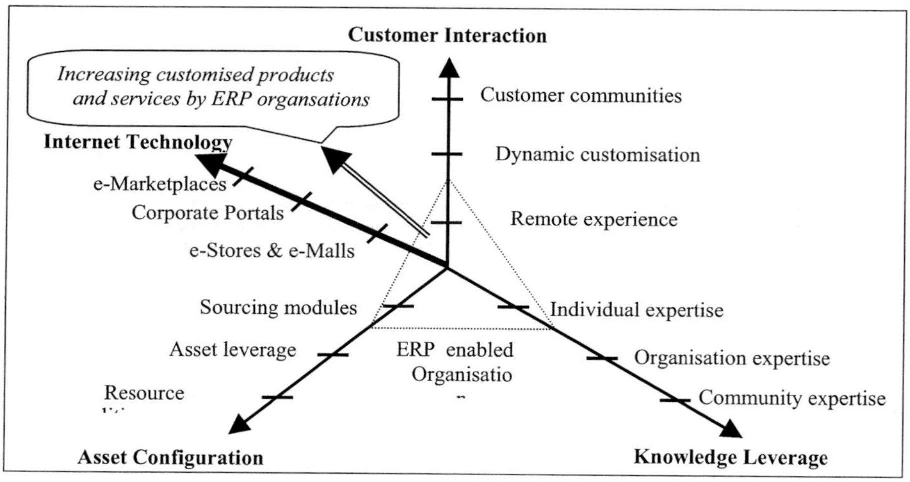

Figure 8: e-Business with ERP for Virtual Organising

Table 3: Virtual Organising Development Levels for Siemens

	Developmental Levels		
VOing Dimensions	**Level 1**	**Level 2**	**Level 3**
1.Customer Interaction	Remote experience of Products/Services	Dynamic Customisation	Customer Communities
Case(Stage)	FSC(2)	FSC(2), GEN(3)	eMall(4), eUtilities(6)
2. Asset Configuration	Sourcing Modules	Process Interdependence	Resource Coalitions
Case(Stage)	GateCentre(5)	GateCentre(5)	GateCentre(5), eUtilities(6)
3. Knowledge leverage	Work-unit Expertise	Corporate Asset	Professional and Community Expertise
Case(Stage)	INC(1)	INC(1), GEN(3), eUtilities(6)	eCommunity(6) eUtilities(6)
Business Focus	**Task-units**	**Organisation**	**Inter-organisation**
Outcomes and Performance Gains	Improved operating efficiency (ROI)	Virtual and economic value added (EVA)	Sustained innovation and growth (MVA)

makes some contribution to better understanding the theory within the model.

5 CONCLUSIONS

The Siemens case is about an innovative "sell-side" system was developed initially to optimise processes between Siemens Computer Systems (FSC) and its partners. To achieve the benefits for business customers, Siemens then move from a fragmented group of companies, towards a global engineering network (GEN) concept. Next the company's Gatecentre needed to progress to a capability for answering the challenges of the procurement landscape. By collaboration and the optimisation of business competencies, Siemens' divisions are now building a cross divisional/cross regional private e-marketplace. At this final stage the change process is driven by the "e-community" and managed through "Centre of e-Excellence".

By viewing the Siemens case as a staged implementation, it can easily be evaluated in terms of the attributes of model of virtual organising (VOing). Siemens exhibits development in each of the dimensions of the VOing model but in a different order. This model (Table 3) helps to focus on two related issues. The company was able to leverage the latent resources of networking its R/3 systems and as well as the worldwide presence of the Siemens purchasing network.

Finally, for e-business at Siemens to be successful would require transforming a fragmented web presence to a company-wide approach. If successful, Siemens will become Germany's first digit economy conglomerate through a massive e-business push to conduct 50% of sales online. It will have evolved in six stages with increasing business value and complexity, from an initial ERP based infrastructure loosely connected, to strategic set of private e-marketplaces.

REFERENCES

Blain, J. (1999) *Special Edition: Using SAP R/3 (2nd/3rd Edition).* ASAP World Consultancy, Que Corporation. Chapter 23 : 502-527

Boey, P. Grasso, M. Sabatino, G. Sayeed, I. (1999). Architecting e-Business Solutions. Vol II No 7 www.cutter.com/consortium/freestuff/dcar9907.html

Burn, J. M. Barnett, M. L. (2000) Emerging Virtual Models for Global e-commerce - world wide retailing in the e-grocery business. Special Millennium Issue of Journal of Global Information Technology Management, Vol 3, No. 1, 18-32.

EL Sawy, O. A., Malhotra, A., Gosain, S. AND Young, K. M. (1999) IT-Intensive Value Innovation in the Electronic Economy: Insights from Marshall Industries. MIS Quarterly, Vol 23, No 3, 305-335.

Forrester Research (2000). In Proceedings of BLED 20001 e-Commerce Conference, Bled, Slovenia

Gable, G. G. (1998) Large Packaged Software: a neglected technology? Editorial Journal of Global Information Management, 6(3), pp 3-4.

Hesterbrink, C. (1999). e-Business and ERP: Bringing two Paradigms together. PriceWaterhouse Coopers, September, 1999. http://www.pwc.au/

Holland, C. P. and Light, B. (1999). Generic Information Systems Design Strategies. Americas Conference on Information Systems, Milwaukee, August.

Jansen, W., Steenbakkers, W. AND Jagers, H. Electronic Commerce and Virtual Organisations. Special Issue of eJov (Vol. 1, No. 1) pp 54-68.

Kalakota, R. Robinson, M. (1999) *e-Business: Roadmap for Success* Addison-Wesley Longman, USA

Larsen, C. (2000). Fusing of e-Business and ERP. SAP America. http://www.sap.com/

Markus, M. L. C., and Tanis, C (2000). Multi-site ERP Implementations, Communications of the ACM 43(40, pp 42-46.
Siemens, (1999a) "Service and Solution Offerings: Electronic Commerce with SAP R/3", Apr '99, Siemens Business Services GmbH & Co. http://www.siemens.de/sap/
Siemens, (1999b) "Simplified Communication" *sapinfo.net/_: Focus E-Commerce /September1999*, Magazine of SAP Group, pp.34-37 (on ICN Siemens]
Siemens, (1999c) "Success Story Linking SAP R/3 and the Internet" Nov'99, Siemens Business Services GmbH & Co. http://www.siemens.de/sap/
Siemens, (1999d) "SAP Online Selling: Siemens special solution for your SAP link to the Internet" Nov'99, Siemens Business Services GmbH & Co. http://www.siemens.de/sap/
Siemens, (1999e) "Electronic Business Services: E-commerce Capability Profile" v4.doc, Nov '99, Siemens Business Services UK.
Siemens, (2000) "e-Business Services from SBS" May '00, Slides by Wilson, M, Business Development Manager, Siemens Business Services, London UK
Siemens, (2001) "Siemens e-Business Program", presentation by Freist, G. at International Conference in e-Commerce BLED, Slovenia, 24-26 June 2001
Ticoll, D., Lowry, A. and Kalakota, R. (1998) Joined at the Bit, in *Blueprint to the Digital Economy creating wealth in the era of e-business* Don Tapscott, Alex Lowy and David Ticoll, McGraw-Hill
Timmers, P. (1999) *Electronic Commerce: strategies and models for business-to-business trading,* John Wiley & Sons, UK, pp.95, 96* & 103 (on Siemens)
Venkatraman, N. Henderson, J.C. (1998) Real Strategies for Virtual Organising, *Sloan Management Review*, Fall '98; 33-48

AUTHOR INDEX